The Law of Cybercrimes and Their Investigations

The Law of Cybercrimes and Their Investigations

George Curtis

CRC Press
Taylor & Francis Group
Boca Raton   London   New York

CRC Press is an imprint of the
Taylor & Francis Group, an **informa** business

CRC Press
Taylor & Francis Group
6000 Broken Sound Parkway NW, Suite 300
Boca Raton, FL 33487-2742

Version Date: 20110804

International Standard Book Number: 978-1-4398-5831-8 (Hardback)

Library of Congress Cataloging-in-Publication Data

Curtis, George E., 1942-
    The law of cybercrimes and their investigations / George Curtis.
       p. cm.
    Includes bibliographical references and index.
    ISBN 978-1-4398-5831-8 (hardback)
    1. Computer crimes--United States. 2. Computer crimes--Investigation--United States. I. Title.

KF9350.C87 2011
345.73'0268--dc22
                                             2011005128

Visit the Taylor & Francis Web site at
http://www.taylorandfrancis.com

and the CRC Press Web site at
http://www.crcpress.com

Table of Contents

Section I

CYBERCRIMES AGAINST THE DIGITAL INFRASTRUCTURE AND COMPUTER SYSTEMS

Section II
CYBERCRIMES AGAINST INDIVIDUALS

3   Crimes against Morality   37

4   Crimes Threatening or Resulting in Physical or Mental Harm   81

Section III

CRIMES AGAINST INFORMATION ASSETS, AND DATA PRIVACY

Section IV

INVESTIGATION AND ENFORCEMENT OF CYBERCRIMES

Introduction: The Nature and Scope of Cybercrime

What Is Cybercrime?

A cybercrime is any conduct that involves the use of a computer or other digital device in the commission of a crime.

Cybercrime is a compound word, meaning that it consists of two distinct words, *cyber* and *crime*. Thus, it is perfectly proper to spell the subject of our focus as *cybercrime*, not *cyber crime*.[1]

Cyber, when used in conjunction with *crime*, modifies or restricts the application of crime. The meaning of *cyber* can be drawn from two sources: the compound word *cyberspace* and the dictionary definition of *cyber*. The term *cyberspace* was first used by William Gibson in his book *Neuromancer*, which was published in 1985. It commonly is known to refer to the electronic medium of computer networks where online communication takes place. I refer to cyberspace as the space that encompasses digital devices capable of communication with each other.

Merriam-Webster's Online Dictionary defines cyber as "of, relating to, or involving computers or computer networks (as the Internet) <the cyber marketplace>."[2] Thus, cybercrime can be defined as unlawful conduct involving the use of a computer or other digital device in the commission of a crime. For purposes of this text, cybercrimes include crimes committed:

1. By the use of a computer, digital, or electronic device as the instrumentality of the crime
2. Upon a computer, digital, or electronic device, in which case the device is the victim or target of the crime
3. By the use of a computer, digital, or electronic device for the storage of evidence of a crime

The federal laws that prohibit online child pornography provide a good illustration of the application of those three categories of cybercrime. Federal child pornography laws prohibit the distribution, receipt, and possession of child pornography (see 18 USC §§ 2252, 2252A). Clearly, distributing and receiving child pornography involves the use of a computer or digital device as the instrumentality of a crime. Distributors also are utilizing peer-to-peer networks to store child pornography on a person's computer for acquisition by others, many times without the knowledge of person whose computer is used to store the images. In that circumstance, the computer used for storage is both a victim and a device used for storage. Finally, the person who downloads pornographic images can store those images on someone else's computer, which would then be the category 3 type of cybercrime.

Cybercrime Distinguished from Computer Crime, Digital Crime, High-Tech Crime

There is considerable disagreement among scholars and professionals concerning the meaning or scope of the term *cybercrime*. I have utilized a rather broad definition similar to that stated a few years ago by Donn Parker: a "crime in which the perpetrator uses special knowledge of cyberspace."[3]

Notice that my definition does not require a "special knowledge of cyberspace." Parker distinguishes between cybercrime and computer crime by defining computer crime as a "crime in which the perpetrator uses special knowledge about computer technology."[4] I agree with Parker that there is a difference between computer crime and cybercrime. There are those who would, however, disagree. For example, the current edition of *Black's Law Dictionary* defines cybercrime as a "computer crime."[5]

I disagree, however, that cybercrime necessarily involves a "special knowledge of cyberspace." The mere fact that evidence relevant to a crime is stored in a computer or peripheral device also amounts to a crime. As discussed previously, a common example is the storage of images of pornography or child pornography on the hard drive of a person other than the individual who downloaded the images from various locations on the Internet. The storage of those images constitutes the crime commonly referred to as criminal possession of obscene materials or child pornography. Other examples include the unlawful downloading of copyrighted material to a digital device or the recording of illicit transactions on a spreadsheet application. Thus, the storage of digital evidence, by itself, may be a crime.

Our final potential term, *digital crime*, is the subject of an entire text,[6] which refers to digital crime as computer-related crime, or cybercrime.[7] Reading the text, however, one quickly realizes that digital crime and cybercrime, as I have defined it, are the same.

Trends Related to Cybercrime

Numerous studies are conducted each year related to cybercrime. The Computer Security Institute conducts an annual survey of computer crime and security. The survey[8] is currently released in the fall of each year. It reveals several important statistics concerning cybercrime that should be reviewed, particularly for analysis of trends.

The Internet Crime Complaint Center (IC3), a joint operation of the FBI and the National White Collar Crime Center, issues an annual report of Internet crime complaints that are filed with the IC3. The annual report is available at the I3C's website.[9]

The Federal Trade Commission publishes an annual report of complaints filed with that agency concerning identity theft and consumer fraud. The national results are available at the FTC's Consumer Sentinel site. The Consumer Sentinel site is accessible by law enforcement agencies who desire information concerning reported instances of identity theft. The annual report is, however, publicly available at the Sentinel site.[10]

Surveys and reports also are published from an international perspective. The Australian Computer Emergency Response Team (AusCERT) publishes an annual survey,[11] as does the Australian Government[12] and the auditing firms of Ernst and Young[13] and Deloitte Touche.[14]

About This Book

This book is divided into four parts. Part I, which consists of Chapters 1 and 2, focuses on the use of computers and other digital devices to commit traditional computer crimes (Chapter 1) and what is popularly referred to as information warfare and cyberterrorism (Chapter 2).

Part II, "Cybercrimes against Individuals," consists of Chapters 3 to 5. Chapter 3 considers cybercrimes that implicate morality—obscenity, child pornography, sexual predator conduct, and online gambling. Chapter 4 discusses cyberstalking, cyberharassment, cyberbullying, and other types of unlawful expression. Chapter 5 covers online frauds and other online crimes that do not fit neatly into any other category, including auction fraud, Ponzi and pyramid schemes, access device fraud, identity theft and fraud, securities fraud, bank fraud, money laundering, and electronic fund transfer fraud. Part III, "Crimes against Information Assets, and Data Privacy," consists of Chapters 6 and 7. Chapter 6 considers identity theft and data privacy crimes, including violations of the Fair Credit Reporting Act (FCRA), the Gramm-Leach-Bliley Act (GLBA), and the Health Insurance Portability and Accountability Act (HIPAA). Chapter 7 covers other online crimes against data, including economic espionage and intellectual property crimes.

Part IV, "Investigation and Enforcement of Cybercrimes," consists of Chapters 8 through 14. Chapter 8 provides an introduction to general principles applicable to searches and seizures. Chapter 9 discusses laws that apply to the search and seizure of computers, other digital devices, and peripherals. Chapter 10 focuses on those laws governing eavesdropping and the use of wiretaps in connection with electronic communications. Chapter 11 considers the law regulating access to stored communications. Chapter 12 covers the law applicable to other investigatory devices, such as pen registers, trap and trace devices, and global positioning system devices. Chapter 13 considers laws and rules governing the admission of digital evidence and provides an overview of criminal procedure. Chapter 14 discusses international laws and procedures for the investigation of cybercrimes and gathering of evidence beyond the borders of the prosecuting jurisdiction.

Each numbered chapter includes three additional features: key words and phrases, review problems, and weblinks. Key words and phrases identify topics or items you should be familiar with after reading the chapter and before reading the next chapter. You should be able to define or describe each of those items. Review problems have been included to enable the student to determine how much has been learned from the material or for a quick review of the chapter at a later time, perhaps for a quiz or an exam. Weblinks are provided to identify websites that provide additional information concerning the material covered in the chapter or information that can serve as a starting point for a research paper. You may notice missing sections. That was intentional. The statutes and cases were edited.

I hope you enjoy your experience as a student of cybercrime law and investigation.

Endnotes

1. See Garner, Bryan A. (ed.). (2009). *Black's Law Dictionary* (deluxe 9th ed.). St. Paul, MN: West Publishing, p. 443.
2. Merriam-Webster Online Dictionary. http://www.merriam-webster.com/dictionary/cyber (retrieved October 22, 2010).
3. Parker, Donn. (1998). *Fighting Computer Crime: A New Framework for Protecting Information.* New York: John Wiley & Sons, p. 72.
4. Id.
5. Garner, op. cit., n. i.
6. See Taylor, Robert W., et al. (2006). *Digital Crime and Digital Terrorism.* Upper Saddle River, NJ: Prentice Hall.
7. Id., at 4–5.
8. The 2009 survey can be obtained online at www.gocsi.com.
9. The 2009 IC3 report can be accessed at www.ic3.gov/media/annualreport/2009_IC3Report.pdf.
10. The Sentinel site is www.ftc.gov/sentinel/reports.shtml.
11. Available at www.auscert.org.au.
12. The 2008 Pacific Islands survey is at www.esecurity.net.au/PICCSS08_survey.pdf.
13. www.ey.com/Publication/vwLUAssets/Global_Information_Security_Survey_2009/$FILE/EY_Global_Information_Security_Survey_2009.pdf.
14. The 2009 survey is available at www.deloitte.com/assets/Dcom-Shared Assets/Documents/us_fsi_GlobalSecuritySurvey_0209.pdf.

About the Author

George E. Curtis is professor of criminal justice at Utica College, Utica, NY. He previously held the positions of dean of the School of Business and Justice Studies and executive director of the Economic Crime Institute of Utica College.

Curtis received a Bachelor of Arts degree from Syracuse University in 1964, and a Juris Doctor degree from Brooklyn Law School in 1967. He is an attorney admitted to the Bar of the State of New York. Curtis served as a confidential law clerk in the New York court system for more than 26 years and currently practices law limited to appellate work. He is a former president of his local bar association and a former delegate to the New York State Bar Association's House of Delegates.

Curtis currently teaches undergraduate and graduate law-related courses in economic crime and cybercrime. He is a Certified Fraud Specialist and a member of the Association of Certified Fraud Specialists, its Board of Regents, and its national faculty. He also is member of the Association of Certified Fraud Examiners and a life member of its Upstate New York Chapter, and the Criminal Justice Educators Association of New York State.

Cybercrimes against the Digital Infrastructure and Computer Systems

I

Crimes Involving the Use of Computers

1

Introduction

The history of criminal law dates back to biblical times. By comparison, the history of laws pertaining specifically to computer crime dates back slightly more than three decades. The U.S. government enacted its first computer crime statute, the Counterfeit Access Device and Computer Fraud and Abuse Law, in 1984. Every state has now enacted computer crime legislation, the first in time being Arizona and Florida in 1978, and the last, Vermont in 1999.[1]

In common law countries like the United States, legislatures and courts have defined and refined criminal laws over centuries. Over that time span, a significant body of legal literature facilitated research, advocacy, and judicial decision making concerning crimes. However, in the case of computer crime, and more generally cybercrime, the law has experienced difficulty in keeping pace with advances in technology. As a result, courts often attempt to resolve issues relating to cybercrime by drawing some analogy to traditional crime. For example, in seeking to resolve search and seizure issues, the files on computer hard drives have been likened to files in cabinets or closed containers.[2]

There is no settled jurisprudence concerning computer crimes, on either the substantive or procedural side. Federal, state, and local governments regulate computer crime in different ways. The consideration of computer crime law begins with a discussion of the development and interpretation of federal computer crime law, and a consideration of other statutes that can be applied to certain conduct involving computers and other digital devices. This chapter then moves to a discussion of state laws. Because they reflect different approaches to computer crime, New York and California laws have been selected for discussion and analysis.

Federal Laws Governing Computer Crimes—Historical Development

Prior to 1984, crimes involving computers were prosecuted in federal courts under existing provisions of the federal criminal code dealing with other crimes, typically wire fraud (18 USC § 1343). The first federal statute specifically addressing computer crime was the Counterfeit Access and Computer Fraud Act of 1984 (Pub. L. 98-473). That initial enactment, which first appeared in the U.S. Code at 18 USC § 1030, prohibited three types of conduct:

1. Accessing without authorization a computer and obtaining classified national defense or foreign relations information with the intent to believe that such information will be used to harm the United States or to benefit a foreign nation
2. Accessing without or in excess of authorization a computer to obtain information in the financial record of a financial institution or in the consumer file of a consumer reporting agency

3. Accessing without or in excess of authorization a government computer or computer used for or on behalf of the government to use, modify, or destroy data in such computer or to prevent authorized use of such computer

Because that act was very limited in its scope, it was virtually unused by federal prosecutors.[3]

The original version was revised substantially two years later by enactment of the Computer Fraud and Abuse Act of 1986 (Pub. L. 99-474). To address the concerns of limited application, Congress added three more types of conduct constituting computer crime, including the use of a computer in the commission of a fraud, and defined a "federal interest computer" to include not only computers used by or for the government or financial institutions, but also a computer "which is one of two or more computers used in committing the offense, not all of which are located in the same state" (Pub. L. 99-474, § 2(g)(4)).

Congress enacted minor revisions to Section 1030 in 1988, 1989, and 1990. Subdivision (a)(5) of the section was revised in 1994 to address a concern raised in *United States v. Morris* (*infra* at page 8) concerning an ambiguity in the statutory language.

The next major revision occurred in 1996 with enactment of the National Information Infrastructure Protection Act. That act added a seventh category of criminal conduct: the attempt to extort money or property by threatening to cause damage to a computer. The act also replaced the term *federal interest computer* with the term *protected computer* and amended the definition to include computers "used in interstate or foreign commerce or communication" (Pub. L. 104-294, § 201 (4)(a)(iii)). That change was designed to broaden significantly the application of the statute beyond attacks and fraudulent conduct targeted at government and financial institution computers. The effect of that change is discussed in greater detail later in the chapter.

Section 1030 was revised again in 2001 by the Uniting and Strengthening America by Providing Appropriate Tools Required to Intercept and Obstruct Terrorism Act (USA PATRIOT Act, Pub. L. 107-56). In addition to sentencing revisions, the act revised subdivision (a)(5) to set forth three levels of causing damage to protected computers based on the level of *mens rea* and defined the term *damage* to include, in addition to monetary loss, physical injury, a threat to public health or welfare, or damage affecting a computer system used by a government entity for the administration of justice, national defense or national security; revised subdivision (a)(7) to broaden the designation of victims to include "any person"; revised the calculation of "damage" and "loss" to include the costs of responding to an offense and restoring the system to its preincident status, as well as any lost revenue or other consequential damages resulting from an interruption of service; and added language to the definition of a "protected computer" to make certain that such computer included a computer in a foreign country that affects interstate or foreign commerce or communication of the United States. The Homeland Security Act of 2002 (Pub. L. 107-273) effected minor revisions, mainly to sentencing provisions of Section 1030.

Most recently, in 2008 Congress amended Section 1030 (Pub. L. 110-326, §§ 203, 204[a], 205–208) to expand criminal liability for extortion (subdivision (a)(7)), add a separate conspiracy provision (subdivision (b)), and add a provision for the criminal forfeiture of any real or personal property used in the commission of a violation of Section 1030 or that is derived from the proceeds of a violation of that section (subdivisions (i) and (j)).

Federal Laws Governing Computer Crime—18 USC § 1030

The current federal computer crime law appears in the United States Code at 18 USC § 1030. Subdivision (a) of the statute, which is also commonly referred to as the Computer Fraud and Abuse Act (CFAA), sets forth seven categories of criminal conduct, as follows:

(1) knowingly accessing a computer without, or in excess of, authorization and obtaining classified federal information, with intent or reason to believe such information shall be used to the injury of the United States or to the advantage of a foreign nation, **and** willfully communicating, delivering, transmitting, or causing to be communicated, delivered, or transmitted the classified federal information to any person not entitled to receive it, **or** willfully retaining that information and failing to deliver it to the officer or employee of the United States entitled to receive it;

(2) intentionally accessing a computer without, or in excess of, authorization and obtaining information in a financial record of a financial institution, the issuer of a credit card or consumer reporting agency; the information from any department or agency of the United States; or information from an protected computer;

(3) intentionally accessing a government computer without authorization and affecting the government's operation of the computer;

(4) knowingly and with intent to defraud, accessing a protected computer without or in excess of authorization and furthering the intended fraud by obtaining anything of value, unless the object of the fraud and the thing obtained consists only of the use of the computer and the value of such use does not exceed $5,000 in any 1-year period;

(5) knowingly causing the transmission of a program, information, code or command and thereby intentionally causing damage to a protected computer; or intentionally accessing a protected computer without authorization and recklessly causing damage; or intentionally accessing a protected computer without authorization and causing damage;

(6) knowingly and with intent to defraud, trafficking in any password or similar information through which a computer may be accessed without authorization if such trafficking affects interstate or foreign commerce or such computer is used by or for the United States government;

(7) with intent to extort from any person, firm, institution, etc., any money or other thing of value, transmitting in interstate or foreign commerce any communication containing any threat to cause damage to a protected computer.

Subdivision (b) of that section also imposes criminal liability upon anyone who "conspires to commit or attempts to commit" any of the above offenses.

Section 1030 defines a *computer* as

an electronic, magnetic, optical, electrochemical, or other high speed data processing device performing logical, arithmetic, or storage functions, and includes any data storage facility or communications facility directly related to or operating in conjunction with such device, but such term does not include an automated typewriter or typesetter, a portable hand held calculator, or other similar device.

That section also defines a *protected computer* as follows:

a computer—

(A) exclusively for the use of a financial institution or the United States Government, or, in the case of a computer not exclusively for such use, used by or for a financial institution or the United States Government and the conduct constituting the offense affects that use by or for the financial institution or the Government; or

(B) which is used in interstate or foreign commerce or communication, including a computer located outside the United States that is used in a manner that affects interstate or foreign commerce or communication of the United States.

The phrase "exceeds authorized access" means "to access a computer with authorization and to use such access to obtain or alter information in the computer that the accessor is not entitled so to obtain or alter" (18 USC § 1030 (e)(6)). Section 1030 also confers upon the U.S. Secret Service the authority to investigate computer crimes and exempts from its coverage any lawfully authorized investigative, protective, or intelligence activity of a law enforcement agency of the United States, a state, or political subdivision of a state, meaning that those law enforcement agencies cannot be held liable for a violation of Section 1030.

Case Applications

Although it would seem that one should be able to determine what is, or is not, a computer under Section 1030, the following case illustrates that the issue is not always that clear. In *United States v. Mitra*, the court was asked to decide two important issues: whether a police radio system constituted a computer within the meaning of Section 1030, and does the mere fact that a computer has access to the Internet provide a sufficient jurisdictional basis for Congress to regulate the conduct?

United States v. Mitra

405 F.3D 492 (2005)

U.S. COURT OF APPEALS, SEVENTH CIRCUIT

Madison, Wisconsin, uses a computer-based radio system for police, fire, ambulance, and other emergency communications. The system, Smartnet II by Motorola, spreads traffic across 20 frequencies. One frequency is designated for the control channel, which is used by the mobile or base radio unit to initiate a conversation. The computer hardware and software assigns the conversation to an open channel, and the system can link multiple roaming units to that conversation. This process is known as a trunking system, which enables 20 channels to support hundreds of users. Interference with the control channel, however, will render communication impossible; each remote unit will show the message "no system."

Beginning in January 2003, mobile units experienced occasional "no signal" conditions. On Halloween, the no-system condition spread citywide because a powerful signal affected all of the city's communication towers and prevented the computer from receiving data on the control channel, preventing the system from distributing communication traffic to the other 19 channels. The city was unable to coordinate public safety efforts that day. On November 11, 2003, the attacker changed tactics, and instead of blocking use of the system, he sent signals directing the Smartnet base station to keep channels open, and at the end of each communication the attacker appended a sound, such as a woman's sexual moan.

The city identified the source of the intruding signals and arrested defendant Rajib Mitra, a graduate student at the University of Wisconsin who held a BS degree in computer science. After trial, a jury convicted Mitra of two counts of intentional interference with computer-related systems in violation of 18 USC § 1030 (a)(5). On appeal the defendant contended that his conduct did not violate § 1030, and that if it did, the statute exceeds Congress's commerce power.

EASTERBROOK, Circuit Judge.

The prosecutor's theory is that Smartnet II is a "computer" because it contains a chip that performs high speed processing in response to signals received on the control channel, and as a whole is a "communications facility directly related to or operating in conjunction" with that computer chip. It is a "protected computer" because it is used in "interstate ... communication"; the frequencies it uses have been allocated by the Federal Communications Commission for police, fire, and other public-health services. Mitra's transmissions on Halloween included "information" that was received by the Smartnet. Data that Mitra sent interfered with the way the computer allocated communications to the other 19 channels and stopped the flow of information among public-safety officers. This led to "damage" by causing a "no system" condition citywide, impairing the "availability of ... a system, or information" and creating "a threat to public health or safety" by knocking out police, fire, and emergency communications. See §1030(a)(5)(A)(i), (B)(iv). The extraneous sounds tacked onto conversations on November 11 also are "information" sent to the "protected computer," and produce "damage" because they impair the "integrity" of the official communications. This time subsection §1030(a)(5)(B)(v) is what makes the meddling a crime, because Mitra hacked into a governmental safety-related communications system.

Mitra concedes that he is guilty if the statute is parsed as we have done. But he submits that Congress could not have intended the statute to work this way. Mitra did not invade a bank's system to steal financial information, or erase data on an ex-employer's system, see *United States v. Lloyd*, 269 F.3d 228 (3d Cir. 2001), or plaster a corporation's web site with obscenities that drove away customers, or unleash a worm that slowed and crashed computers across the world, see *United States v. Morris*, 928 F.2d 504 (2d Cir. 1991), or break into military computers to scramble a flight of interceptors to meet a nonexistent threat, or plant covert programs in computers so that they would send spam without the owners' knowledge. All he did was gum up a radio system. Surely that cannot be a federal crime, Mitra insists, even if the radio system contains a computer. Every cell phone and cell tower is a "computer" under this statute's definition; so is every iPod, every wireless base station in the corner coffee shop, and many another gadget. Reading §1030 to cover all of these, and police radio too, would give the statute wide coverage, which by Mitra's lights means that Congress cannot have contemplated such breadth.

Trunking communications systems came to market after 1984, when the first version of §1030 was enacted, and none of the many amendments to this statute directly addresses them. But although legislators may not know about trunking communications systems, they *do* know that complexity is endemic in the modern world and that each passing year sees new developments. That's why they write general statutes rather than enacting a list of particular forbidden acts.

Section 1030 is general. Exclusions show just *how* general. Subsection (e)(1) carves out automatic typewriters, typesetters, and handheld calculators; this shows that other devices with embedded processors and software are covered. As more devices come to have built-in intelligence, the effective scope of the statute grows. This might prompt Congress to amend the statute but does not authorize the judiciary to give the existing version less coverage than its language portends. What protects people who accidentally erase songs on an iPod, trip over (and thus disable) a wireless base station, or rear-end a car and set off a computerized airbag, is not judicial creativity but the requirements of the statute itself: the damage must be intentional, it must be substantial (at least $5,000 or bodily injury or danger to public safety), and the computer must operate in interstate or foreign commerce.

Let us turn, then, to the commerce requirement. The system operated on spectrum licensed by the FCC. It met the statutory definition because the interference affected "communication." Mitra observes that his interference did not affect any radio system on the other side of a state line, yet this is true of many cell-phone calls, all of which are part of interstate commerce because the electromagnetic spectrum is securely within the federal regulatory domain. Congress may regulate all channels of interstate commerce; the spectrum is one of them. Mitra's apparatus was more powerful than the Huygens probe that recently returned pictures and other data from Saturn's moon Titan. Anyway, the statute does not ask whether the person who caused the damage acted in interstate commerce; it protects computers (and computerized communication systems) used in such commerce, no matter how the harm is inflicted. Once the *computer* is used in interstate commerce, Congress has the power to protect it from a local hammer blow, or from a local data packet that sends it haywire. (Indeed, Mitra concedes that he could have been prosecuted, consistent with the Constitution, for broadcasting an unauthorized signal.) Section 1030 is within the national power as applied to computer-based channel-switching communications systems.

The following decision involves the first prosecution under the federal computer crime statute. In *United States v. Morris* (928 F.2d 504 (1991)), the Court of Appeals considered when a defendant accesses a computer without or in excess of authorization and whether the government is required to establish that the defendant intended to cause damage under subparagraph (5) of Section 1030 (a). Because the latter issue has been resolved by an amendment to the statute, the edited version below only discusses the issue of access.

United States v. Morris

928 F.2D 504 (1991)

U.S. COURT OF APPEALS, SECOND CIRCUIT

In the fall of 1988, Robert Tappan Morris, a graduate student in Cornell's computer science PhD program, was given an account with Cornell's Computer Science Division. This authorized Morris to use computers at Cornell. In October 1988, Morris began work on a computer program later known as INTERNET "worm" or "virus." The goal of this program was to demonstrate the inadequacies of security measures on existing computer networks by exploiting security defects that Morris discovered. The tactic he selected was the release of a worm into network computers, and Morris designed the program to spread across a national network of computers. On November 2, 1988, Morris released the worm from a computer at MIT, which was used to disguise the fact that the worm came from Morris at Cornell. The program was designed to spread the INTERNET worm widely and quickly through the network without drawing attention to itself. It was designed to occupy little computer operation, thereby not interfering with normal computer use, and it also was made difficult to detect so other programmers could not "kill" it. Morris soon discovered that the worm was replicating and reinfecting computers at a much faster rate than anticipated. Many machines throughout the country either crashed or became "catatonic." Upon realizing what had happened, Morris met with a friend at Harvard and a message was sent from Harvard over the computer network, instructing programmers how to kill the worm and prevent reinfection. Because the worm had clogged the network, the message did not get through until it was too late. Computers were affected at numerous installations, including leading universities, military sites, and medical research facilities. The estimated cost of dealing with the worm at each installation ranged from $200 to more than $53,000.

Morris was charged in the U.S. District Court, Northern District of New York, with intentionally accessing a federal interest computer without authorization. After a jury trial, he was convicted of violating 18 USC § 1030 (a)(5)(A).

JON O. NEWMAN, Circuit Judge:

This appeal presents two narrow issues of statutory construction concerning a provision Congress recently adopted to strengthen protection against computer crimes. Section 2(d) of the Computer Fraud and Abuse Act of 1986, 18 U.S.C. §1030(a)(5)(A) (1988), punishes anyone who intentionally accesses without authorization a category of computers known as "[f]ederal interest computers" and damages or prevents authorized use of information in such computers, causing loss of $1,000 or more. The issues raised are (1) whether the Government must prove not only that the defendant intended to prevent authorized use of the computer's information and thereby cause loss; and (2) what satisfies the statutory requirement of "access without authorization."

We conclude that section 1030(a)(5)(A) does not require the Government to demonstrate that the defendant intentionally prevented authorized use and thereby caused loss. We also find that there was sufficient evidence for the jury to conclude that Morris acted "without authorization" within the meaning of section 1030(a)(5)(A). We therefore affirm.

    II. The unauthorized access requirement in section 1030(a)(5)(A)

      Section 1030(a)(5)(A) penalizes the conduct of an individual who "intentionally accesses a Federal interest computer without authorization." Morris contends that his conduct constituted, at most, "exceeding authorized access" rather than the "unauthorized access" that the subsection punishes. Morris argues that there was insufficient evidence to convict him of "unauthorized access," and that even if the evidence sufficed, he was entitled to have the jury instructed on his "theory of defense."

      Morris was authorized to use computers at Cornell, Harvard, and Berkeley, all of which were on INTERNET. As a result, Morris was authorized to communicate with other computers on the network to send electronic mail (SEND MAIL), and to find out certain information about the users of other computers (finger demon). The question is whether Morris' transmission of his worm constituted exceeding authorized access or accessing without authorization.

The Senate Report stated that section 1030(a)(5)(A), like the new section 1030(a)(3), would "be aimed at 'outsiders,' those lacking authorization to access any Federal interest computer." Senate Report at 10, U.S. Code, Cong. & Admin. News at 2488. But the Report also stated, in concluding its discussion on the scope of section 1030(a)(3), that it applies "where the offender is completely outside the Government, ... or where the offender's act of trespass is inter-departmental in nature." Id. at 8, U.S. Code, Cong. & Admin. News at 2486.

Morris relies on the first quoted portion to argue that his actions can be characterized only as exceeding authorized access, since he had authorized access to a federal interest computer. However, the second quoted portion reveals that Congress was not drawing a bright line between those who have some access to any federal interest computer and those who have none. Congress contemplated that individuals with access to some federal interest computers would be subject to liability under the computer fraud provisions for gaining unauthorized access to other federal interest computers.

Moreover, the jury verdict need not be upheld solely on Morris' use of SEND MAIL and finger demon. As the District Court noted, in denying Morris' motion for acquittal,

> Although the evidence may have shown that defendant's initial insertion of the worm simply exceeded his authorized access, the evidence also demonstrated that the worm was designed to spread to other computers at which he had no account and no authority, express or implied, to unleash the worm program. Moreover, there was also evidence that the worm was designed to gain access to computers at which he had no account by guessing their passwords. Accordingly, the evidence did support the jury's conclusion that defendant accessed without authority as opposed to merely exceeding the scope of his authority.

Morris endeavors to bolster his sufficiency argument by contending that his conduct was not punishable under subsection (a)(5) but was punishable under subsection (a)(3). That concession belies the validity of his claim that he only exceeded authorization rather than made unauthorized access. Neither subsection (a)(3) nor (a)(5) punishes conduct that exceeds authorization. Both punish a person who "accesses" "without authorization" certain computers. If Morris violated subsection (a)(3), as he concedes, then his conduct in inserting the worm into the INTERNET must have constituted "unauthorized access" under subsection (a)(5) to the computers of the federal departments the worm reached, for example, those of NASA and military bases.

To extricate himself from the consequence of conceding that he made "unauthorized access" within the meaning of subsection (a)(3), Morris subtly shifts his argument and contends that he is not within the reach of subsection (a)(5) at all. He argues that subsection (a)(5) covers only those who, unlike himself, lack access to any federal interest computer. Congress understandably thought that the group most likely to damage federal interest computers would be those who lack authorization to use any of them. But it surely did not mean to insulate from liability the person authorized to use computers at the State Department who causes damage to computers at the Defense Department. Congress created the misdemeanor offense of subsection (a)(3) to punish intentional trespasses into computers for which one lacks authorized access; it added the felony offense of subsection (a)(5) to punish such a trespasser who also causes damage or loss in excess of $1,000, not only to computers of the United States but to any computer within the definition of federal interest computers. With both provisions, Congress was punishing those, like Morris, who, with access to some computers that enable them to communicate on a network linking other computers, gain access to other computers to which they lack authorization and either trespass, in violation of subsection (a)(3), or cause damage or loss of $1,000 or more, in violation of subsection (a)(5).

Although *Morris* was the first published decision involving Section 1030, it set the stage for subsequent applications of factual scenarios involving access to a computer or computer system. The important part of the analysis is that "access" is not limited to a perpetrator's physical touching of the computer. In *Morris*, the court determined that the defendant accessed computers without authorization because the malware code he used accessed distant computers and systems through the Internet.

New York's Computer Crime Law

New York first addressed the subject of computer crime in 1986 by its enactment of article 156 of the penal law. That legislation created five distinct crimes:

1. Penal Law § 156.05. Unauthorized use of a computer. Knowingly using or causing to use a computer or computer service without authorization when the computer being used is equipped or programmed with a device or coding system designed to prevent such unauthorized use.
2. Penal Law § 156.10. Computer trespass. Knowingly using or causing to use a computer or computer service without authorization with intent to commit or attempt to commit a felony or by knowingly gaining access to computer material.
3. Penal Law § 156.20. Computer tampering in the fourth degree. Using or causing to be used a computer or computer service without any right to do so and intentionally altering or destroying computer data or a computer program of another person.
   Penal Law § 156.25. Computer tampering in the third degree. Using or causing to be used a computer or computer service without any right to do so and intentionally altering or destroying computer data or a computer program of another person
   (a) with intent to commit or attempt to commit a felony; or
   (b) having been previously convicted of a crime in violation of article 156 or subdivision (10) or section 165.15 of the Penal Law; or
   (c) with intent to alter or destroy computer material; or
   (d) with intent to alter or destroy computer data or a computer program in an amount exceeding $1,000.

Penal Law § 156.26. Computer tampering in the second degree. Using or causing to be used a computer or computer service without any right to do so and intentionally altering or destroying computer data or a computer program of another person, causing damages in an aggregate amount exceeding $3,000.

Penal Law § 156.27. Computer tampering in the first degree. Same conduct as second degree tampering, except that aggregate damages must exceed $50,000.

4. Penal Law § 156.30. Unlawful duplication of computer related material. Copying, reproducing or duplicating in any manner computer data or a computer program, thereby intentionally and wrongfully depriving or appropriating from the owner an economic value or benefit in excess of $2,500 or with intent to commit or attempt to commit or to further the commission of a felony.

5. Penal Law § 156.35. Criminal possession of computer related material. Knowingly possessing any copy, reproduction or duplication of computer data or a computer program copied, reproduced or duplicated in violation of section 156.30 with intent to benefit himself or a person other than the owner.

Section 156.00 of the penal law separately defines *computer, computer program, computer data, computer service,* and *computer material.* An examination of these definitions indicates that the legislature intended a broad scope of coverage. Also, Section 156.50 provides defenses to certain computer crimes.

In the following case, a New York trial court was required to interpret the meaning and application of several sections of New York's computer crime law:

People v. Angeles

180 MISC. 2D 146 (1999)

CRIMINAL COURT OF THE CITY OF NEW YORK

OPINION BY Gabriel W. Gorenstein, J.

The defendant is charged with unauthorized use of a computer (Penal Law § 156.05), attempted criminal possession of computer related material (Penal Law §§ 110.00, 156.35), attempted unlawful duplication of computer related material (Penal Law §§ 110.00, 156.30 [1]) and criminal possession of stolen property in the fifth degree (Penal Law § 165.40). The information filed in this case alleges in substance that the defendant sold a computer list of Empire Car Service customers to an individual in exchange for United States currency. In addition, the information charges that: "(i) defendant did not have permission or authority to possess [the] list of customers; (ii) [the] list of customers could only be accessed and printed through [Empire Car Service's] computer system; (iii) defendant did not have permission or authority to access or print through said computer system; and (iv) the value of [the] list of customers exceeds two thousand five hundred dollars." The defendant moves to dismiss the information in its entirety. As set forth below, the defendant's motion is granted in part and denied in part.

A. Unauthorized Use of a Computer
Defendant argues that because the information does not allege that the computer he used had a "device or coding system," the information is jurisdictionally defective for failing to "establish … every element of the offense charged and the defendant's commission thereof" as required by CPL 100.40 (1)(c).

The People, in their motion papers opposing defendant's motion, fail even to address this argument.

The information is clear in alleging that the list obtained by the defendant came from the Empire Car Service's computer system and that he had no authority to obtain access to that computer system. The statute, however, on its face does not make criminal the mere use or accessing of a computer system without permission or authority. The Legislature has imposed the additional requirement that the computer be "equipped or programmed with any device or coding system, a function of which is to prevent the unauthorized use of [the] computer or computer system." (Penal Law § 156.05) The legislative history of the statute makes clear that this requirement was included on the ground that "[s]uch protective devices provide the first line of defense against unauthorized intrusion into a computer system." (See, Mem of Attorney-General in support of L 1986, ch 514, 1986 NY Legis Ann, at 233) The Legislature thus put computer owners on notice that in order to receive the protection of the criminal statute, they must equip their computers with some kind of protection mechanism, such as a password requirement or a lock.

The information in this case makes no allegations whatsoever regarding the existence of a device or coding system to prevent the unauthorized use of Empire Car Service's computer. This case thus stands in contrast to People v Johnson (148 Misc 2d 103 [Crim Ct, NY County 1990]), where the court found that the facts pleaded "reasonably, albeit circumstantially, suggest the existence of such a device or coding system." In the present case, to assume the existence of such a system would be pure conjecture. The mere allegation that an individual has obtained access to a computer without the owner's authority is insufficient to plead a violation of Penal Law § 156.05.

This count of the information is therefore dismissed.

B. Attempted Unlawful Duplication of Computer Related Material and Attempted Criminal Possession of Computer Related Material

Penal Law § 156.35 prohibits the possession of "any copy, reproduction or duplicate of any computer data ... which was copied, reproduced or duplicated in violation of [Penal Law § 156.30], with intent to benefit himself or a person other than an owner thereof." Defendant argues that these counts must be dismissed because the information fails to allege with more specificity that the list involved constitutes "computer data." The information, however, alleges that the list "could only be accessed and printed through [Empire Car Service's] computer system." The statute itself defines "computer data" to include any information that is "processed, or ha[s] been processed in a computer." (Penal Law § 156.00 [3].) Given the broad definition of computer data set forth in the statute, the information's allegations of this element are sufficient.

The defendant also argues that there are insufficient allegations that the defendant has "copie[d], reproduce[d] or duplicate[d]" the data. These are expansive terms. To "reproduce," for example, can mean "to present again" or "to make a representation (as an image or copy) of." (Webster's New Collegiate Dictionary 982 [1976].) Inasmuch as the information asserts that the defendant printed specific data through the computer system, this is sufficient to satisfy the requirement that the defendant "reproduced" the data at issue.

Finally, the defendant argues that he cannot be charged both with the crime of attempted criminal possession of computer related material (Penal Law §§ 110.00, 156.35) and attempted unlawful duplication of computer related material (Penal Law §§ 110.00, 156.30). He argues that it is "illogical" to charge that the computer list at issue was at the same time both a computer list that was improperly possessed and also a "copy, reproduction or duplicate" of the very same computer list. Yet this is exactly the way the statutory provisions have been written. In Penal Law § 156.30, the Legislature made the act of improperly copying, reproducing, or duplicating computer data a crime (provided there is a wrongful deprivation of property or intent to commit a felony). In Penal Law § 156.35, the Legislature made criminal the possession of the same data (where there is an intent to benefit the defendant or a person other than the owner of the data). The Legislature could properly distinguish these two crimes inasmuch as an individual is capable of causing computer data to be copied without ultimately possessing the data. Such an individual is chargeable under Penal Law § 156.30. If an individual ultimately takes possession of this copied data—regardless of whether the individual was the one who copied it unlawfully—the taking possession would constitute a separately chargeable crime as long as the remaining requirements of Section 156.35 are met. These two statutes thus address two different acts that are capable of being committed by the same individual.

For these reasons, the motion to dismiss these counts is denied.

C. Criminal Possession of Stolen Property

Defendant moves to dismiss the count of the information charging criminal possession of stolen property in the fifth degree on the ground that the information does not sufficiently allege that the customer list constitutes "stolen property" under Penal Law § 165.40. The information, however, alleges that the defendant wrongfully took the computer list from its owner without consent. The motion to dismiss this count is therefore denied.

What does it mean to "alter" a computer program? If an individual follows the command prompts in a computer program, has he altered the program? Consider the following:

People v. Versaggi

---

83 N.Y.2D 123 (1994)

NEW YORK COURT OF APPEALS

The telephone system at Eastman Kodak Corporation in Rochester is operated by two SL-100 computers. One computer is located at Kodak's State Street office, and the other at the Kodak Park Complex. On November 10, 1986, about 2,560 of the lines at the complex were shut down, and use of another 1,920 lines was impaired for about an hour and a half before company employees could restore service. As a result, a substantial number of employees were unable to receive calls or call 911 or other emergency services, if necessary. On November 19, 1986, a second interruption occurred, shutting down all service at the State Street offices for four minutes. All outside telephone calls from the company's customers and offices worldwide were disconnected.

The defendant was employed by Kodak as a computer technician, and he was responsible for maintaining and repairing several telephone systems, but not the SL-100s. Because his job often required him to work from home, Kodak provided the defendant with home computer equipment and a company telephone line that allowed him to connect with the Kodak systems. The defendant was also given an "accelerator," a security device that allowed him to access the Kodak systems.

At the defendant's trial, a Kodak telecommunications employee testified that a user had accessed the SL-100 system on November 10, 1986, and had issued commands that caused the computer at the complex to shut down. After an hour and a half and using some 40 commands, technicians were able to restore phone service. That same employee testified that a computer printout showed that, on November 19, 1986, a user accessed Kodak's electronic mail and then the SL-100 computer at the State Street Office. The user issued commands forcing two parallel processing units out of synchronization, and then issued commands that shut the entire system down. The supervisor of the telecommunications department testified that to discontinue service on the SL-100 computer, the user had to confront a list of 14 questions, asking him if he wished to continue with destructive commands, questions such as "Do you want to go ahead? Respond yes or no"; "Do you want to kill the program? Respond yes or no." In each case, the defendant answered yes. There was no evidence of physical damage to Kodak's computer programs; the defendant did not delete or add to the programs that ran the SL-100 computers. Instead, he selected and activated various options as they were presented by the programs.

The defendant was found guilty in Rochester City Court of two counts of computer tampering in the second degree (Penal Law § 156.20), determining that he intentionally altered two computer programs. The county court affirmed the conviction.

SIMONS, J.

Defendant contends that he is not guilty of altering the programs because he did not change them; he merely activated existing instructions which commanded the computers to shut down. The People maintain that defendant is guilty because he changed the instructions being received by the computers and thereby prevented the computers from performing their intended functions. We agree and therefore affirm the judgment of conviction.

In 1986, the New York State Legislature made significant changes to the Penal Law in an effort to control what a Task Force of the American Bar Association had described as the "frightening spectre" of increased computer crime in our society. A program bill submitted by the Attorney General sought to provide a "comprehensive statutory scheme" to allow for effective law enforcement in the area (Mem or Atty Gen, Bill Jacket, L 1986, ch 514, a p 32). The breadth of the changes manifests the Legislature's intent to address the full range of computer abuses.

The crime of computer tampering involves the use of a computer or computer service as the instrumentality of a crime (see, Donnino, Practice Commentary, p 177). The defendant uses the computer to sabotage its intended operation in some way. The American Bar Association's Task Force on Computer Crime found in its survey that such tampering was the most prevalent means of computer abuse.

Interpretation begins with the language of the statute. The Legislature did not define "alter," however, and thus the Court must give the word its ordinary meaning (Pizza Hut v Human Rights Bd., 51 NY2d 506, 511). As commonly understood, "alter" means to change or modify. For an alteration to occur, the identity of the thing need not be destroyed, nor need an entirely new thing be substituted. It is sufficient if some of the "elements or ingredients or details" are changed (Black's Law Dictionary [4th Edition, West Pub.]). Significantly, the Legislature attached expansive language to the verb it used in section 156.20, stating that the crime consisted of altering a computer program "in any manner."

The purpose of Kodak's computers was to provide telephone service and, absent instructions to the contrary, that is exactly what they did. By implementing the application programs, a set of coded instructions were executed by the computers which directed them to perform a computer operation. Those directions clearly came within the statutory definition of an "ordered set of instructions" which, when executed, directed a computer "to perform one or more computer operations." Thus those instructions constituted a "computer program."

Defendant encountered the application programs when he entered the SL-100 systems. By disconnecting them and commanding the computers to shut down, he altered the programs in some manner. Whether defendant used existing instructions to direct the phone system off-line or input new instructions accomplishing the same thing is legally irrelevant. He made the system "different in some particular characteristic without changing [it] to something else" (see, Webster's [Third International Dictionary (Unabridged)]). His conduct differed only in degree from shutting down the system by executing a command to add or delete program material. In either event, the result would be the same. The intended purpose of the computer program is sabotaged. Defendant's conduct constituted tampering within the intendment of the statute because it altered the computer programs at Kodak's State Street office and Kodak Park Complex by interrupting the telephone service to those two facilities.

Accordingly, the order of County Court should be affirmed.

California's Computer Crime Law

California Penal Code § 502. Computer crimes

(a) It is the intent of the Legislature in enacting this section to expand the degree of protection afforded to individuals, businesses, and governmental agencies from tampering, interference, damage, and unauthorized access to lawfully created computer data and computer systems. The Legislature finds and declares that the proliferation of computer technology has resulted in a concomitant proliferation of computer crime and other forms of unauthorized access to computers, computer systems, and computer data.

The Legislature further finds and declares that protection of the integrity of all types and forms of lawfully created computers, computer systems, and computer data is vital to the protection of the privacy of individuals as well as to the well-being of financial institutions, business concerns, governmental agencies, and others within this state that lawfully utilize those computers, computer systems, and data.

(b) For the purposes of this section, the following terms have the following meanings:

  (1) "Access" means to gain entry to, instruct, or communicate with the logical, arithmetical, or memory function resources of a computer, computer system, or computer network.

  (2) "Computer network" means any system that provides communications between one or more computer systems and input/output devices including, but not limited to, display terminals and printers connected by telecommunication facilities.

(3) "Computer program or software" means a set of instructions or statements, and related data, that when executed in actual or modified form, cause a computer, computer system, or computer network to perform specified functions.

(4) "Computer services" includes, but is not limited to, computer time, data processing, or storage functions, or other uses of a computer, computer system, or computer network.

(5) "Computer system" means a device or collection of devices, including support devices and excluding calculators that are not programmable and capable of being used in conjunction with external files, one or more of which contain computer programs, electronic instructions, input data, and output data, that performs functions including, but not limited to, logic, arithmetic, data storage and retrieval, communication, and control.

(6) "Data" means a representation of information, knowledge, facts, concepts, computer software, computer programs or instructions. Data may be in any form, in storage media, or as stored in the memory of the computer or in transit or presented on a display device.

(7) "Supporting documentation" includes, but is not limited to, all information, in any form, pertaining to the design, construction, classification, implementation, use, or modification of a computer, computer system, computer network, computer program, or computer software, which information is not generally available to the public and is necessary for the operation of a computer, computer system, computer network, computer program, or computer software.

(8) "Injury" means any alteration, deletion, damage, or destruction of a computer system, computer network, computer program, or data caused by the access, or the denial of access to legitimate users of a computer system, network, or program.

(9) "Victim expenditure" means any expenditure reasonably and necessarily incurred by the owner or lessee to verify that a computer system, computer network, computer program, or data was or was not altered, deleted, damaged, or destroyed by the access.

(10) "Computer contaminant" means any set of computer instructions that are designed to modify, damage, destroy, record, or transmit information within a computer, computer system, or computer network without the intent or permission of the owner of the information. They include, but are not limited to, a group of computer instructions commonly called viruses or worms, that are self-replicating or self-propagating and are designed to contaminate other computer programs or computer data, consume computer resources, modify, destroy, record, or transmit data, or in some other fashion usurp the normal operation of the computer, computer system, or computer network.

(11) "Internet domain name" means a globally unique, hierarchical reference to an Internet host or service, assigned through centralized Internet naming authorities, comprising a series of character strings separated by periods, with the rightmost character string specifying the top of the hierarchy.

(c) Except as provided in subdivision (h), any person who commits any of the following acts is guilty of a public offense:

(1) Knowingly accesses and without permission alters, damages, deletes, destroys, or otherwise uses any data, computer, computer system, or computer network in order to either (A) devise or execute any scheme or artifice to defraud, deceive, or extort, or (B) wrongfully control or obtain money, property, or data.

(2) Knowingly accesses and without permission takes, copies, or makes use of any data from a computer, computer system, or computer network, or takes or copies any

supporting documentation, whether existing or residing internal or external to a computer, computer system, or computer network.

(3) Knowingly and without permission uses or causes to be used computer services.

(4) Knowingly accesses and without permission adds, alters, damages, deletes, or destroys any data, computer software, or computer programs which reside or exist internal or external to a computer, computer system, or computer network.

(5) Knowingly and without permission disrupts or causes the disruption of computer services or denies or causes the denial of computer services to an authorized user of a computer, computer system, or computer network.

(6) Knowingly and without permission provides or assists in providing a means of accessing a computer, computer system, or computer network in violation of this section.

(7) Knowingly and without permission accesses or causes to be accessed any computer, computer system, or computer network.

(8) Knowingly introduces any computer contaminant into any computer, computer system, or computer network.

(9) Knowingly and without permission uses the Internet domain name of another individual, corporation, or entity in connection with the sending of one or more electronic mail messages, and thereby damages or causes damage to a computer, computer system, or computer network.

(e) (1) In addition to any other civil remedy available, the owner or lessee of the computer, computer system, computer network, computer program, or data who suffers damage or loss by reason of a violation of any of the provisions of subdivision (c) may bring a civil action against the violator for compensatory damages and injunctive relief or other equitable relief. Compensatory damages shall include any expenditure reasonably and necessarily incurred by the owner or lessee to verify that a computer system, computer network, computer program, or data was or was not altered, damaged, or deleted by the access. For the purposes of actions authorized by this subdivision, the conduct of an unemancipated minor shall be imputed to the parent or legal guardian having control or custody of the minor, pursuant to the provisions of Section 1714.1 of the Civil Code.

(2) In any action brought pursuant to this subdivision the court may award reasonable attorney's fees.

(3) A community college, state university, or academic institution accredited in this state is required to include computer-related crimes as a specific violation of college or university student conduct policies and regulations that may subject a student to disciplinary sanctions up to and including dismissal from the academic institution. This paragraph shall not apply to the University of California unless the Board of Regents adopts a resolution to that effect.

(4) In any action brought pursuant to this subdivision for a willful violation of the provisions of subdivision (c), where it is proved by clear and convincing evidence that a defendant has been guilty of oppression, fraud, or malice as defined in subdivision (c) of Section 3294 of the Civil Code, the court may additionally award punitive or exemplary damages.

(5) No action may be brought pursuant to this subdivision unless it is initiated within three years of the date of the act complained of, or the date of the discovery of the damage, whichever is later.

(f) This section shall not be construed to preclude the applicability of any other provision of the criminal law of this state which applies or may apply to any transaction, nor shall it make illegal any employee labor relations activities that are within the scope and protection of state or federal labor laws.

(g) Any computer, computer system, computer network, or any software or data, owned by the defendant, that is used during the commission of any public offense described in subdivision (c) or any computer, owned by the defendant, which is used as a repository for the storage of software or data illegally obtained in violation of subdivision (c) shall be subject to forfeiture, as specified in Section 502.01.

(h) (1) Subdivision (c) does not apply to punish any acts which are committed by a person within the scope of his or her lawful employment. For purposes of this section, a person acts within the scope of his or her employment when he or she performs acts which are reasonably necessary to the performance of his or her work assignment.

(2) Paragraph (3) of subdivision (c) does not apply to penalize any acts committed by a person acting outside of his or her lawful employment, provided that the employee's activities do not cause an injury, as defined in paragraph (8) of subdivision (b), to the employer or another, or provided that the value of supplies or computer services, as defined in paragraph (4) of subdivision (b), which are used does not exceed an accumulated total of one hundred dollars ($100).

The following case considers whether an individual who uses a computer to which the public has access can nevertheless unlawfully access a computer system on that public computer in violation of the California statute.

People v. Lawton

48 CAL. APP. 4TH SUPP. 11; 56 CAL. RPTR. 2D 521 (1996)

APPELLATE DEPT., SUPERIOR COURT OF CALIFORNIA, VENTURA COUNTY

OPINION BY O'Neill, J.

We affirm a conviction for unauthorized access to a computer system, and hold that such an offense can be committed by use of a public access terminal to bypass security and penetrate levels of software not open to the public.

Jeffrey Lawton (Appellant) was charged with three computer-related crimes, as defined in Penal Code section 502. Appellant was convicted of violating Penal Code section 502, subdivision (c)(7), which forbids unauthorized access to "any computer, computer system, or computer network." Probation was granted, and this appeal followed.

The Ventura County Library Services Agency utilizes a mainframe computer with over 200 terminals, a number of which are located in the Camarillo Public Library. Terminals are available for use by library patrons for the sole purpose of accessing the computerized catalog of books. Other portions of the software, containing such information as patrons' names, addresses, phone numbers and driver's license numbers, are closed to the public by a security system that includes employee passwords.

At three different times on May 11, 1994, Appellant was seen by a Camarillo library employee, Ms. Delgado, at or near three different public computer terminals. During the first encounter, Ms. Delgado noticed that terminal No. 1 was "off-line," displaying scrambled letters and numbers not part of the software accessible to the public. Fifteen minutes later she noticed Appellant at terminal No. 1. When she asked Appellant to move aside he entered a series of keystrokes including the word "abort." The display then came back "on-line" in the public data area.

After this incident Appellant moved toward the magazine room, where terminal No. 2 is located. Ms. Delgado did not see Appellant enter, but she did see him in the magazine room five minutes later. Her supervisor, Ms. Bell, saw Appellant at terminal No. 2. Thirty minutes after the problem with terminal No. 1, Mrs. Delgado noted that terminal No. 2 was running a "prime number" check, displaying a scrolling column of six- to seven-digit numbers. Ms. Delgado and Ms. Bell were unable to bring terminal No. 2 back on-line, and the problem was referred to the automation department.

Later the same day Ms. Delgado saw Appellant sit down at terminal No. 3 in the same library. She approached and watched as Appellant "knocked" the terminal off-line from the public access software level. She told Appellant what he was doing was illegal. He apologized and brought the terminal back on-line by a series of keystrokes.

The computer system's self-monitoring program recorded numerous unusual commands from at least three Camarillo library terminals on the date in question. They reveal that someone accessed both the operating system (UNIX) and the "Universe," or database, level. A number of specific commands were entered, such as the prime number check, a command designed to slow down the computer by tying up processing power, and "DUA," which results in a display of user passwords entered by others trying to log on to the system. Ms. Everson, the Ventura County information systems support analyst assigned to the library system, analyzed the record of unusual commands. She concluded that someone on that date was seeking passwords and other information in an attempt to gain more access to the system. She also noted that two different commands were entered with potential to purge data from the system. The weekly system check immediately after the date in question revealed some missing temporary data files, an event unique in her six years of managing the system. She attributed the deletions to the unusual commands entered at the Camarillo library on May 11, 1994. Specifically, the commands which could have purged data were "RM" (standing for "Remove") and "Clean. Account." She believes the latter command caused the deletions.

Experts called by each side debated the merits of the library computer system's security and the significance of the various unusual commands recorded by the self-monitoring program. The defense expert concluded that someone with surface knowledge of the UNIX system could have accidentally penetrated to the lower levels of the software due to a bug in the library's software. He conceded that temporary data may have been deleted as a result of the "Clean. Account" command, and that, unless that command was selected from a menu, it would not have been entered as the result of random keystrokes.

The prosecution expert found the security "perfectly adequate" for a library system. The "Remove" command is a powerful one, capable of erasing almost anything. It was entered but probably not executed, since "nothing important" had been deleted. The temporary files that were deleted covered the time period March 30 to May 11. This erasure was consistent with execution of the "Clean. Account" command by someone trying to "cover their tracks."

Appellant, an unemployed aerospace software engineer, told the sheriff's deputy who investigated that he did go "way beyond the application" by utilizing an invalid code and a "little trap door." He stated that his motivation was "partly out of curiosity" and also to learn about the UNIX system to "help my career."

The only issue pursued on appeal is the contention that the evidence at trial was insufficient as a matter of law, because one who uses a computer terminal with permission cannot as a matter of law violate Penal Code section 502, subdivision (c)(7). The People contend that permissible use of hardware to access impermissible levels of software is a violation of that section.

Penal Code section 502 was amended in 1987 to expand the protection of "the integrity of all types and forms of lawfully created computers, computer systems, and computer data," which the Legislature found "vital ... to the well-being of ... governmental agencies, and others within this state." (Pen. Code, § 502, subd. (a).) Subdivision (c) of the statute is a laundry list of illegal activity ranging from use of a computer to defraud or extort, to infecting a computer with a virus. As mentioned earlier, subdivision (c)(7) covers one who "knowingly and without permission accesses or causes to be accessed any computer, computer system, or computer network."

Subdivision (b) of Penal Code section 502 defines various terms used therein, not including the single word "computer." Subdivision (b)(5) defines "computer system" as "... a device or collection of devices, including support devices ..., one or more of which contain computer programs, electronic instructions, input data, and output data, that performs functions including, but not limited to, logic, arithmetic, data storage and retrieval, communication, and control." Subdivision (b)(2) defines "computer network" as "... any system which provides communications between one or more computer systems and input/output devices including, but not limited to, display terminals and printers connected by telecommunication facilities."

To paraphrase the statute, a "computer system" is a functioning combination of hardware and software. A "computer network" is the hardware and software which links one or more systems with each other and/or with terminals and printers.

In other words, we read both "computer system" and "computer network" as consisting of hardware and software.

Accordingly, we reject Appellant's contention that subdivision (c)(7) of Penal Code section 502 covers only unauthorized access of hardware. Such an interpretation would not only clash with the statutory language quoted above, but with the overall statutory intent to comprehensively protect the integrity of private, commercial, and governmental computer systems and data. (See Pen. Code, § 502, subd. (a).)

A review of the various provisions of Penal Code section 502, subdivision (c) reveals that adopting Appellant's argument would carve a giant loophole in the statute not intended by its drafters. Public access computer terminals are increasingly common in the offices of many governmental bodies and agencies, from courthouses to tax assessors. We believe subdivision (c)(7) was designed to criminalize unauthorized access to the software and data in such systems, even where none of the other illegal activities listed in subdivision (c) have occurred.

To the extent that "mere browsing" in this fashion may cause little or no harm, the statute appropriately sets modest penalties for unaggravated behavior which violates Penal Code section 502, subdivision (c)(7). (See Pen. Code, § 502, subd. (d)(3).)

We affirm the conviction and order granting probation.

The following case considers the access issue under rather unusual facts:

People v. Gentry

234 CAL. APP. 3D 131; 285 CAL. RPTR. 591 (1991)
COURT OF APPEAL OF CALIFORNIA, FOURTH APPELLATE DISTRICT

OPINION BY Sills, J.

In this modern computer age, creative entrepreneurs are carving out large fortunes by providing new and unique services to the untrained public. Lelas Charles Gentry was just such an entrepreneur, advertising his services in the field of credit history improvement to individuals who found themselves floundering in a financial morass. Unfortunately, rather than throwing them a lifeline, he merely offered them a rope and anchor.

Facts

Gentry was convicted based on the transcript of a preliminary hearing received into evidence without objection. At that preliminary hearing, three witnesses, each representing a different credit reporting company (TRW, CBI and Trans Union), testified about the nature of their businesses and the security measures taken to restrict access to their computer database of credit files. Each testified Gentry was not authorized "to access" their files. They explained that an inquiry about a person who had no prior listing with their subscribing companies would result in the creation of a "file" for that person. They also identified certain documents, products of their respective "data banks," which resulted from just such an inquiry about two names, "Dolores Manchester" and "Diane Wolfe."

Gloria D. Manchester testified she contacted Gentry in 1987 to assist her with improving her credit rating and gave him her Social Security number. She wanted a business loan but her credit history was "very negative." She was not sure what, if anything, could be done, but she did want to ascertain whether something could be done to improve her credit rating. She had heard Gentry speak at a business club luncheon on improving credit records and decided to contact him. Gentry took her to lunch where he told her he could "clean up" her credit report. She did not understand the process and he did not explain it. He simply told her he had many different ways to improve her credit rating. She paid him about $1,000.

At their next meeting, Gentry gave her some credit applications and detailed instructions on how to apply for certain credit opportunities. He told her, in essence, to commit fraud: to state she had been married to a recently deceased man; to say her name was Dolores G. Manchester instead of Gloria D. Manchester; and to assert a Social Security number that differed from her own by one digit. He also instructed her to tell the Department of Motor Vehicles that she had lost her driver's license, and wanted a replacement in her "correct" name of Dolores G. Manchester.

Along with the credit applications, he gave her some documents which he said were new, clean credit reports from Trans Union, CBI and TRW under the name "Dolores Manchester." Each report reflected no credit history and made no reference to the bankruptcy and collection problems listed on her true credit report.

Manchester was quite upset by these instructions and refused to comply with them. She had never given Gentry permission to enter information into these data bureaus and particularly not false information. She put the whole package in a drawer and never used it, even though she had paid him a fee of nearly $1,000.

As Manchester was brooding over the materials in her drawer, a "sting" operation was in progress to net the unwary Gentry. Detective Stockwell of the Anaheim Police Department contacted Diane Terry, the consumer relations manager of Trans Union. She agreed to participate in a computer access investigation. Diane Terry became Diane Wolfe. Her role, after creating a fictitious file in the Trans Union credit data bank on Diane T. Wolfe, was to telephone "National Credit Service" which advertised itself as a service for people with credit problems. She represented herself to be Diane Wolfe and spoke with Gentry who assured her he could clear up her credit record and create a new credit file for her. When she asked how he would do this, he told her he would create a new identity for her and asked for $24 to obtain copies of her TRW and CBI credit reports.

She eventually met with Gentry at his home in Anaheim Hills where he told her it would cost $1,000 to create a new credit file: $500 up front, and the balance later. She asked him to meet with her "boyfriend" who would take care of the details. She later introduced him to Detective Stockwell who masqueraded as her boyfriend, Richard Stearns.

Stockwell, as Stearns, asked Gentry what he would do to assist his "girlfriend" if she paid him the $1,000. Gentry told him he could create a new identity for her by making her appear to be her "twin" after which she could apply for credit under the new identity. He emphasized she would have to fill out the credit applications herself but he would provide the information. He also gave Stockwell a credit report on Diane Wolfe from Trans Union.

Diane Terry then checked the Trans Union files and discovered someone had inquired about Diane T. Wolfe and also about Dolores Manchester. Terry later testified Gentry was not authorized to gain access to Trans Union files. No one besides Terry, Stockwell and Gentry were aware of the name Diane T. Wolfe. The net had dropped on Gentry.

Besides the sting operation, a proverbial "snitch" was also involved. Upon this stage entered Marlon Steverson, a novice in the field of fraudulent schemes. Steverson met with George Panteras of Marathon Financial Services in March 1988. Steverson had known Panteras for about five years and hoped Panteras could help him obtain a loan of several thousand dollars. He could not qualify for it himself because of his poor credit background. Panteras told Steverson to get a new identity, preferably from a recently deceased person with "A-1" credit. He told him Gentry could procure a new driver's license and social security card for him for about $1,200. After obtaining this new identification, Steverson could apply for loans and credit cards. Panteras's fee would be 50 percent of the large loan. He suggested Steverson "milk" his new credit identity for as much as possible. Steverson then returned to Panteras's office where he met Gentry. Gentry took his picture. But, alas, before our bumbling "con-man" could return for these documents, he was arrested while helping another cohort cash a forged check in a scam unrelated to the facts of this case. Prudently, he experienced a twinge of conscience and decided to work with the police. He returned to Panteras's office in the company of an undercover officer. Panteras gave him a new driver's license, Social Security card and check guarantee card in the name of Peter J. Hixon. When they left, Steverson gave them to the undercover officer.

On January 29, 1988, Detective Stockwell searched Gentry's home pursuant to a warrant. He found a computer terminal, files and credit reports under the name of Diane Wolfe and a driver's license under the name of Leo W. Sailer bearing a photograph of Gentry. An obituary for Sailer was also found, taped to a credit report for the same person. Gentry was no longer in business.

Discussion

Gentry was convicted of "intentionally [gaining access to a] ... computer system ... for the purpose of (1) devising or executing [a] scheme or artifice to defraud ... or (2) obtaining ... services with false or fraudulent intent, ..." (Pen. Code, § 502, subd. (b).) Gentry contends the prosecution failed to prove any intention on his part to defraud. Relying on federal statutes and cases interpreting federal mail fraud, he argues he cannot be convicted in state court on a different definition of fraud. The argument hardly merits comment.

Relying on Civil Code sections 1572, 1709, and 1710, CALJIC No. 15.26 defines "intent to defraud" as "an intent to deceive another person for the purpose of gaining some material advantage over that person or to induce that person to part with property or to alter that person's position to [his] [her] [its] injury or risk, and to accomplish that purpose by some false statement, false representation of fact, wrongful concealment or suppression of truth, or by any other artifice or act designed to deceive." Here, Gentry gained access to the confidential files of TRW, CBI, and Trans Union without their permission or knowledge. Upon gaining access, he deliberately entered false information, such as the false names and numbers, which he knew would result in the subscribers to these companies' services extending credit to individuals they would otherwise refuse. Gentry's scheme was exactly the kind of manipulation of computer data files the statute was designed to prohibit.

Gentry also complains the statute requires evidence he obtained money or services as a result of gaining access to these computer systems by false pretense. He contends the evidence proved only that he gained access to the system without permission, not by a false pretense. The record contradicts him. The Trans Union documents on Diane Wolfe were altered by a subscriber service company by the name of Data Rentals. Although Gentry was not employed by Data Rentals, he gave a copy of this report to "Stearns." He could only have obtained it by misrepresenting himself as someone working for Data Rentals when accessing the Trans Union network. This was sufficient to show he obtained credit information under false pretenses.

Key Words and Phrases

Access

Computer Fraud and Abuse Act

Distributed denial of service

Extortion

Internet

Protected computer

Trespass

Worm

Review Problems

1. What does accessing a computer mean? Michigan defined a computer crime as intentionally gaining access to or causing access to be made to a computer, computer system, or computer network for the purpose of devising or executing a scheme or artifice with intent to defraud or for the purpose of obtaining money, property, or a service by means of a false or fraudulent pretense, representation, or promise. The law further provides that "access means to approach, instruct, communicate with, store data in, retrieve data from, or otherwise use the resources of, a computer, computer system, or computer network." Carolyn Jemison was employed by the Michigan Department of Social Services as an assistance payment worker. While so employed, Jemison opened two files, one in the fictitious name of Brenda Spencer and the other in the fictitious name of Edward Kinchlow. For a six-year period, the Department of Social Services paid a total of $63,220.50 in aid to dependent children in the name of Spencer and a total of $3,652 in food stamps in the name of Kinchlow. Jemison's sister, Jacqueline Patterson, posed as Spencer and cashed the assistance checks that were issued to Spencer. Also, with Spencer named as the representative of Kinchlow, Patterson received the food stamps issued in the name of Kinchlow. The files opened by Spencer eventually were fed into the department's computer. Jemison did not personally operate the computer. Instead, she delivered the documentation she created to her supervisor, who in turn gave the paperwork to a computer operator who fed the information into the department's computer network. Once in the computer, checks and food stamps were caused to be issued on a regular basis. Did Jemison "access or cause access" within the meaning of the Michigan statute? See *People v. Jemison*, 187 Mich. App. 90; 466 N.W.2d 378 (1991) for the court's answer.

2. In *Versaggi*, the New York Court of Appeals determined that the defendant "altered" the program because he made it perform in a manner that was not intended. However, is that really true? The final series of C prompts asked him if he wanted to shut down the phones. Why would that question be there if shutting down the phone system wasn't an intended alternative? Also, if one considers the plain meaning of the statute, by exercising commands permitted by the program, did the defendant really alter the program?

3. What are the differences between the federal statute and the New York and California laws? Are they real differences or simply differences in language?

Weblinks

www.cybercrime.gov

This is the website of the Computer Crime and Intellectual Property Section (CCIPS) of the U.S. Department of Justice. This site is an excellent resource for information on cybercrimes and their enforcement.

www.crime-research.org/articles/

This page, at the website of the Computer Crime Research Center, contains numerous links to articles on a variety of cybercrimes.

www.cert.org/certcc.html

   This is the webpage of CERT/CC (formerly, the Computer Emergency Response Team Coordination Center) at Carnegie Mellon University. This site has valuable resources on different types of computer crime and is a primary source for information on cybercrime.

www.findlaw.com/01topics/10cyberspace/computercrimes/index.html

   This page at the website of findlaw.com contains links to helpful resources on computer crime.

Endnotes

1. See, for a reference to each state's statute and the year of enactment, McCurdy, Jessica L. (Spring 2010). "Computer Crimes." 47 *Am. Crim. L. Rev.* 287, fn. 365.
2. See, for example, *United States v. Carey*, 172 F.3d 1268, 1272–1277 (10th Cir. 1999). In that case, the court discussed, but rejected, the government's argument that the court draw an analogy between folders and files on a computer hard drive and folders and files in a filing cabinet.
3. Andreano, Frank A. (Fall 1999). "The Evolution of Federal Computer Crime Policy: The Ad Hoc Approach to an Ever-Changing Problem." 27 *Am. J. Crim. Law* 81, 85–86.

Information Warfare and Cyberterrorism

2

What Is Information Warfare?

Just as there is little consensus about the meaning of *cybercrime*, there are differing views of the meaning of *information warfare*. Several definitions are considered here.

Brown Commission

In 1994, after several incidences of intelligence compromises, including the Aldrich Ames case, Congress created the Commission on the Roles and Capabilities of the U.S. Intelligence Community, which is more commonly known as the Aspin-Brown Commission or the Brown Commission (Congressman Lee Aspin served as the initial chair of the commission but died before the commission completed its work). In 1996, the commission submitted its report to Congress. (The report is available at www.gpoaccess.gov/int/index.html.) That report (at p. 27) defines information warfare as follows:

> "Information warfare" refers to activities undertaken by governments, groups, or individuals to gain electronic access to information systems in other countries either for the purpose of obtaining the data in such systems, manipulating or fabricating the data, or perhaps even bringing the systems down, as well as activities undertaken to protect against such activities.

The Brown Commission further commented (at p. 27):

U.S. intelligence agencies have been involved in aspects of information warfare, both offensive and defensive, for many years. New impetus has recently been given to these roles, however, by the explosion in information systems and information systems technology.

Government and public communications, transportation, financial, energy, and other industrial systems have become critically dependent on a complex set of interconnected automated information and control systems. Many of these systems are potentially vulnerable to computer-based disruption, manipulation, or corruption by hostile individuals, groups, or countries.

A number of witnesses pointed to the lack of an effective governmental structure to coordinate efforts to protect computer networks in the public and private sector from electronic attack. While several such efforts are underway, many believe they are not fully coordinated and do not sufficiently involve the private sector. While these concerns may be justified, the scope of the actions required to deal with the problem, especially the protection of computer networks in the private sector, would necessarily exceed the roles and capabilities of U.S. intelligence agencies.

Collecting information about "information warfare" threats posed by other countries or by non-governmental groups to U.S. systems is, however, a legitimate mission for the Intelligence Community. Indeed, it is a mission that has grown and will become increasingly important. It also is a mission which the Commission believes requires better definition.

While a great deal of activity is apparent, it does not appear well coordinated or responsive to an overall strategy.

Brian C. Lewis

Writing further based on the Brown Commission's report, Lewis defined *information warfare* as follows:

> Information warfare is the application of destructive force on a large scale against information assets and systems, against the computers and networks that support the four critical infrastructures (the power grid, communications, financial, and transportation). (http://www.fas.org/irp/eprint/snyder/infowarfare.htm)

Although Lewis does not exclude businesses and individuals as perpetrators of information warfare, the focus of his report is on infrastructure attacks.

Martin C. Libicki

Martin Libicki, a senior policy analyst for the Rand Corporation, has authored numerous articles on information warfare and has testified before Congress on various topics involving intelligence and information warfare. In 1995, Libicki authored a paper entitled "What Is Information Warfare?" (The complete paper, in PDF form, can be retrieved from www.dtic.mil/cgi-bin/GetTRDoc?AD=ADA367662&Location=U2&doc=GetTRDoc.pdf.) In that paper, Libicki set forth and defined six forms of information warfare:

> Information warfare, as a separate technique of waging war, does not exist. There are, instead, several distinct forms of information warfare, each laying claim to the larger concept. Seven forms of information warfare—conflicts that involve the protection, manipulation, degradation, and denial of information—can be distinguished: (i) command-and-control warfare (which strikes against the enemy's head and neck), (ii) intelligence-based warfare (which consists of the design, protection, and denial of systems that seek sufficient knowledge to dominate the battlespace), (iii) electronic warfare (radio-electronic or cryptographic techniques), (iv) psychological warfare (in which information is used to change the minds of friends, neutrals, and foes), (v) "hacker" warfare (in which computer systems are attacked), (vi) economic information warfare (blocking information or channelling it to pursue economic dominance), and (vii) cyberwarfare (a grab bag of futuristic scenarios).[1]

The important aspect of Libicki's definition is to parse from the definition those forms that apply to electronic information warfare. A full reading of his paper will help you do that.

Another interesting point is that, in categorizing those who have views on the likelihood of a significant cyber attack against the United States, Libicki would be classified as a naysayer. He has publicly questioned whether any such attack could be waged successfully in the near future.[2]

Dorothy Denning

Dorothy Denning is a leading scholar in the wide area of computer security. She currently is a professor in the Department of Defense Analysis at the Naval Postgraduate

School. Notably, Dr. Denning has authored *Information Warfare and Security* and coedited *Internet Beseiged: Countering Cyberspace Scofflaws*. Although we cannot spend enough time solely on the topic of information warfare to thoroughly enjoy Denning's text, one should read her article entitled "Activism, Hacktivism, and Cyberterrorism: The Internet as a Tool for Influencing Foreign Policy," which can be electronically accessed at www.iwar.org.uk/cyberterror/resources/denning.htm.[3] That brings us to the next question, and section.

What Is Cyberterrorism?

In her paper, Dr. Denning defines her three topics as follows:

> The paper is organized around three broad classes of activity: activism, hacktivism, and cyberterrorism. The first category, activism, refers to normal, non-disruptive use of the Internet in support of an agenda or cause. Operations in this area includes browsing the Web for information, constructing Web sites and posting materials on them, transmitting electronic publications and letters through e-mail, and using the Net to discuss issues, form coalitions, and plan and coordinate activities. The second category, hacktivism, refers to the marriage of hacking and activism. It covers operations that use hacking techniques against a target's Internet site with the intent of disrupting normal operations but not causing serious damage. Examples are Web sit-ins and virtual blockades, automated e-mail bombs, Web hacks, computer break-ins, and computer viruses and worms. The final category, cyberterrorism, refers to the convergence of cyberspace and terrorism. It covers politically motivated hacking operations intended to cause grave harm such as loss of life or severe economic damage. An example would be penetrating an air traffic control system and causing two planes to collide. There is a general progression toward greater damage and disruption from the first to the third category, although that does not imply an increase of political effectiveness. An electronic petition with a million signatures may influence policy more than an attack that disrupts emergency 911 services.[4]

In Denning's definition of *cyberterrorism*, is there any difference between cyberterrorism and information warfare? And better yet, is there any difference between cyberterrorism and cybercrime? Most scholars conclude that differences exist between all three. For example, Denning's definition of *cyberterrorism* is limited to politically motivated acts of terrorism that utilize hacking operations. That definition appears restricted to offensive attacks. Information warfare, by nearly all definitions, involves offensive and defensive tactics. Also, information warfare may be, but is not necessarily, politically motivated.

The differences between cyberterrorism and cybercrime also become obvious. Cyberterrorism includes conduct that is politically motivated, but most cybercrimes do not include that motivation (see www.crime-research.org/library/Cyber-terrorism.htm).

Laws Regulating Information Warfare and Cyberterrorism

Are there laws that impose criminal penalties for information warfare and cyberterrorism? Depending upon your definition, the answer clearly is yes.

Federal Laws

18 USC § 2332b: Acts of Terrorism Transcending National Boundaries

Among other acts, this section makes it a crime to engage in conduct "transcending national boundaries" by the use of any facility of interstate or foreign commerce in furtherance of the offense that

> creates a substantial risk of serious bodily injury to any other person by destroying or damaging any structure, conveyance, or other real or personal property within the United States or by attempting or conspiring to destroy or damage any structure, conveyance, or other real or personal property within the United States; in violation of the laws of any State, or the United States.

The primary thrust of this statute is to impose criminal penalties for acts of violence. The issue is whether, because cyber attacks can create a substantial risk of death or serious bodily injury, this section would impose criminal sanctions upon those who engage in cyberterrorism. Because the legislation is so recent, we have no published court decisions on the point.

Under this section, the government is not required to prove that the defendant had knowledge of any required jurisdictional predicate. Also, the statute expressly states that there is extraterritorial jurisdiction, and that the term "conduct transcending national boundaries" means conduct occurring outside of the United States in addition to the conduct occurring in the United States.

18 USC § 1030: Fraud and Related Activity in Connection with Computers

(a) Whoever—

(1) having knowingly accessed a computer without authorization or exceeding authorized access, and by means of such conduct having obtained information that has been determined by the United States Government pursuant to an Executive order or statute to require protection against unauthorized disclosure for reasons of national defense or foreign relations, or any restricted data, as defined in paragraph y.[(y)] of section 11 of the Atomic Energy Act of 1954 [42 USCS § 2014(y)], with reason to believe that such information so obtained could be used to the injury of the United States, or to the advantage of any foreign nation willfully communicates, delivers, transmits, or causes to be communicated, delivered, or transmitted, or attempts to communicate, deliver, transmit or cause to be communicated, delivered, or transmitted the same to any person not entitled to receive it, or willfully retains the same and fails to deliver it to the officer or employee of the United States entitled to receive it.

The conduct prohibited by this section resembles conduct that has been described as information warfare. For example, the conduct of penetrating a governmental computer system and removing data neatly fits into the Brown Commission's definition of information warfare. Likewise, a violation of this section would constitute an example of Libicki's hacker warfare.

Acts of espionage committed through the use of a computer or other digital media also could fit squarely within the Brown Commission's definition of information warfare. Section 1837 also makes it clear that economic espionage against the U.S. government, as described in the section below, may be committed by conduct occurring in a foreign country, provided that some act in furtherance of the espionage occurs within the United States.

18 USC § 1831: Economic Espionage

(a) **In general.** — Whoever, intending or knowing that the offense will benefit any foreign government, foreign instrumentality, or foreign agent, knowingly—

  (1) steals, or without authorization appropriates, takes, carries away, or conceals, or by fraud, artifice, or deception obtains a trade secret;

  (2) without authorization copies, duplicates, sketches, draws, photographs, downloads, uploads, alters, destroys, photocopies, replicates, transmits, delivers, sends, mails, communicates, or conveys a trade secret;

  (3) receives, buys, or possesses a trade secret, knowing the same to have been stolen or appropriated, obtained, or converted without authorization;

  (4) attempts to commit any offense described in any of paragraphs (1) through (3); or

  (5) conspires with one or more other persons to commit any offense described in any of paragraphs (1) through (3), and one or more of such persons do any act to effect the object of the conspiracy, shall, except as provided in subsection (b), be fined not more than $500,000 or imprisoned not more than 15 years, or both.

(b) **Organizations.** — Any organization that commits any offense described in subsection (a) shall be fined not more than $10,000,000.

State Laws

In the post-9/11 world, many states have enacted antiterrorism legislation. Many of the terrorist crimes are patterned after the federal statute. The New York crime of "soliciting or providing support for an act of terrorism" is a good example.

New York Penal Law § 490.10 provides:

> **§ 490.10. Soliciting or providing support for an act of terrorism in the second degree**
> A person commits soliciting or providing support for an act of terrorism in the second degree when, with intent that material support or resources will be used, in whole or in part, to plan, prepare, carry out or aid in either an act of terrorism or the concealment of, or an escape from, an act of terrorism, he or she raises, solicits, collects or provides material support or resources.
>
> Soliciting or providing support for an act of terrorism in the second degree is a class D felony.

Section 490.05 defines an act of terrorism as follows:

"Act of terrorism":

(a) for purposes of this article means an act or acts constituting a specified offense as defined in subdivision three of this section for which a person may be convicted in the criminal courts of this state pursuant to article twenty of the criminal procedure law, or an act or acts constituting an offense in any other jurisdiction within or outside the territorial boundaries of the United States which contains all of the essential elements of a specified offense, that is intended to:

  (i) intimidate or coerce a civilian population;
  (ii) influence the policy of a unit of government by intimidation or coercion; or
  (iii) affect the conduct of a unit of government by murder, assassination or kidnap-
       ping; or
(b) for purposes of subparagraph (xiii) of paragraph (a) of subdivision one of section 125.27
    of this chapter means activities that involve a violent act or acts dangerous to human
    life that are in violation of the criminal laws of this state and are intended to:
      (i) intimidate or coerce a civilian population;
      (ii) influence the policy of a unit of government by intimidation or coercion; or
      (iii) affect the conduct of a unit of government by murder, assassination or kidnapping.

And in particular in relationship to cybercrime, a "specified offense" is defined by the statute as

> a class A felony offense other than an offense as defined in article two hundred twenty, a vio-
> lent felony offense as defined in section 70.02, manslaughter in the second degree as defined
> in section 125.15, criminal tampering in the first degree as defined in section 145.20, identity
> theft in the second degree as defined in section 190.79, identity theft in the first degree as
> defined in section 190.80, unlawful possession of personal identification information in the
> second degree as defined in section 190.82, unlawful possession of personal identification
> information in the first degree as defined in section 190.83, money laundering in support of
> terrorism in the fourth degree as defined in section 470.21, money laundering in support
> of terrorism in the third degree as defined in section 470.22, money laundering in sup-
> port of terrorism in the second degree as defined in section 470.23, money laundering in
> support of terrorism in the first degree as defined in section 470.24 of this chapter, and
> includes an attempt or conspiracy to commit any such offense.

Key Words or Phrases

Activism	Hacker warfare
Command and control warfare	Hacktivism
Cyberterrorism	Information warfare
Cyberwarfare	Infrastructure
Economic espionage	Intelligence-based warfare
Economic information warfare	Psychological warfare
Electronic warfare	Terrorism

Review Problems

The United States charged that between March 2001 and March 2002, a resident of
England, Gary McKinnon, accessed without authorization computers belonging to the
U.S. Army, Navy, Air Force, Department of Defense, and NASA. The federal indictment charged that McKinnon scanned computers in the .mil network and accessed and
obtained administrative privileges on numerous computers. McKinnon then "installed
a remote administration tool, a number of hacker tools, copied password files and other
files, deleted a number of user accounts and deleted critical system files. Once inside a
network, McKinnon would then use the hacked computer to find additional military
and NASA victims. Ultimately, McKinnon caused a network in the Washington D.C.
area to shut down, resulting in the total loss of Internet access and e-mail service to

approximately 2000 users for three days. The estimated loss to the various military organizations, NASA and the private businesses is approximately $900,000" (http://www.cybercrime.gov/mckinnonIndict.htm).

1. Consider whether this conduct constitutes information warfare by (a) the Brown Commission, (b) Brian Lewis, or (c) Martin Libicki.
2. Based on Denning's descriptions, consider whether McKinnon would be (a) an activist, (b) a hacktivist, or (c) a cyberterrorist.
3. McKinnon is charged with violating the Computer Fraud and Abuse Act. What subdivision did McKinnon violate and why?

Weblinks

www.fas.org/irp/wwwinfo.html
> This page of the Federation of American Scientists contains numerous links and references to materials on information warfare and information security.

www.iwar.org.uk
> This is a private site in Great Britain that contains numerous links to other sites containing information on cybersecurity, cyberterrorism, and computer and information security.

www.dhs.gov/files/programs/critical-infrastructure.shtm
> This page at the Department of Homeland Security website focuses on protection of the information infrastructure.

www.infosyssec.net/index.html
> This site of the Information Systems Security Professionals contains an abundance of links to research materials on information warfare and cyberwar.

http://www.counterterrorismtraining.gov/pubs/02.html
> This site is maintained by the Bureau of Justice Affairs to provide information on counterterrorism for members of law enforcement. There are several publications on the subject of cyberterrorism and cybersecurity.

Endnotes

1. Libicki, Martin C. (1995). *What Is Information Warfare?* Washington, DC: U.S. Government Printing Office, p. x.
2. See www.cnn.com/US/9607/16/cyber.terrorism/.
3. The article has also been published in Arquilla, J., and Ronfeldt, D. (eds.). (2001). *Networks and Netwars: The Future of Terror, Crime, and Militancy.* Santa Monica, CA: RAND, chap. 8, pp. 239 et seq.
4. Ibid., p. 241.

Cybercrimes against Individuals

II

Crimes against Morality

3

Introduction

Online obscenity and child pornography have attracted considerable legislative attention over the past two decades. There is good reason; the downloading of pornography continues to be the leading type of improper use of business networks. As an example, Robert Johnson, the CEO of Bowne & Co. and former publisher of *Newsday*, a Long Island, New York, newspaper, and former member of the New York State Board of Regents, pleaded guilty in August 2006 for possession of child pornography that he downloaded by using the company network at Bowne & Co. The United States also indicted Johnson for obstruction of justice, charging that he attempted to remove the evidence of pornography from the hard drive of the company's desktop computer.[1]

Another reason is that federal and state prosecutions for the distribution, downloading, and possession of pornography (both adult and child) constitute the most prevalent of cybercrime prosecutions, and the numbers of such prosecutions continue to rise each year.[2]

In addition to online pornography, this chapter also discusses the effort of federal and state governments to bar online gambling.

Obscenity Crimes

Before exploring the laws that apply to online obscenity and child pornography, it is necessary to provide some constitutional law background and to distinguish between the two types of crimes. Both obscenity and child pornography involve a variety of expressive conduct. The First Amendment to the U.S. Constitution prohibits Congress (and the Fourteenth Amendment prohibits states) from enacting laws that regulate freedom of expression. As a result, the U.S. Supreme Court has decided numerous cases involving obscenity and child pornography.

With respect to obscenity, the three most important Supreme Court decisions are *Roth v. United States* (354 U.S. 476 (1957)), *A Book Named "John Cleland's Memoirs of a Woman of Pleasure" [Memoirs] v. Attorney General of the Commonwealth of Massachusetts* (383 U.S. 413 (1966)), and *Miller v. California* (383 U.S. 413 (1966)) and *Miller v. California* (413 U.S. 15 (1973)). In *Roth*, the court determined that obscene material or performances are not protected by the First Amendment and may be the subject of criminal legislation and prosecution. The *Roth* court adopted the test for obscenity as "whether to the average person, applying contemporary community standards, the dominant theme of the material taken as a whole appeals to prurient interest" (*Roth v. United States, supra,* at 489). In *Memoirs*, the court nine years later restated the *Roth* obscenity test to require that the government prove three criteria to establish obscenity: that "(a) the dominant theme of the material taken as a whole appeals to a prurient interest in sex; (b) the material is patently offensive because it affronts contemporary community standards relating to the description or representation of sexual matters; and (c) the material is utterly without redeeming social value" (*Memoirs v. Attorney General of the Commonwealth of Massachusetts*, 383 U.S., at 418). And then, in *Miller* the court further refined the three-prong test. The *Miller* test, which remains the current method for determining whether material or performances are obscene, rejected the third prong of the test announced in *Memoirs* and revised the obscenity test to require the government to establish that the material or conduct is obscene by proving: (a) whether the average person, applying contemporary community standards would find that the work, taken as a whole, appeals to the prurient interest ...; (b) whether the work depicts or describes, in a patently offensive way, sexual conduct specifically defined by the applicable state law; and (c) whether the work, taken as a whole, lacks serious literary, artistic, political, or scientific value" (*Miller v. California, supra*, at 24).

Congress also may impose criminal sanctions for the distribution, presentation, and receipt of possession of materials and productions that, although not obscene, may be harmful to minors. In *New York v. Ferber* (458 U.S. 747 (1982)), the U.S. Supreme Court upheld the constitutionality of a New York statute that criminalized the use of a child in a sexual performance, which was defined as "any performance or part thereof which includes sexual conduct by a child less than sixteen years of age" (N.Y. Penal Law § 263.00 (1)). The court recognized that, because of the greater vulnerability of children, "states are entitled to greater leeway in the regulation of pornographic depictions of children" (*New York v. Ferber, supra*, at 756), and that the test for child pornography differs from the obscenity test in that the government need not prove that the material appeals to a prurient interest, or that the sexual conduct be portrayed in a patently offensive way, or that the material be considered as a whole (Id., at 764–765).

Crimes related to obscenity are set forth in the criminal code at 18 USC §§ 1460 through 1470. Those statutes do not include a definition of obscenity. Instead, the definition of obscenity and whether certain conduct satisfies that definition are matters left to court interpretation. Although most obscenity crimes were created prior to development of the Internet, those crimes most relevant to the cyber world appear in Sections 1462, 1465, 1466, 1466A, 1467 (forfeiture and protective orders), and 1470.

18 USC § 1462

Section 1462 was created in 1948 and has been amended several times since then, most recently in 1996. Section 1462 prohibits three types of conduct:

1. the *importation* into the U.S.; or
2. the *use* of any express company, interstate carrier, or interactive computer service for the *transportation* in interstate or foreign commerce; or
3. *taking or receiving* from such company, carrier, or service with respect to the materials described below:

   (a)   any obscene, lewd, lascivious, or filthy book, pamphlet, picture, motion-picture film, paper, letter, writing, print, or other matter of indecent character; or

   (b)   any obscene, lewd, lascivious, or filthy phonograph recording, electrical transcription, or other article or thing capable of producing sound; or

(c)   any drug, medicine, article, or thing designed, adapted, or intended for producing abortion, or for any indecent or immoral use; or any written or printed card, letter, circular, book, pamphlet, advertisement, or notice of any kind giving information, directly or indirectly, where, how, or of whom, or by what means any of such mentioned articles, matters, or things may be obtained or made.

18 USC § 1465

Section 1465 was first enacted in 1955 and was last amended in 2006. It prohibits:

(1) knowingly
(2) producing with intent to transport, distribute or transmit, or
(3) transporting or traveling in, or using
(4) a facility or means of interstate or foreign commerce or an interactive computer service in or affecting such commerce
(5) "for the purpose of sale or distribution of any obscene, lewd, lascivious, or filthy book, pamphlet, picture, film, paper, letter, writing, print, silhouette, drawing, figure, image, cast, phonograph recording, electrical transcription or other article capable of producing sound or any other matter of indecent or immoral character."

For purposes of Section 1465, the transportation of two or more copies, or a combined total of five or more publications or articles, creates a rebuttable presumption that the publications or articles were intended for sale or distribution.

18 USC § 1466

Section 1466, which became law in 1988, prohibits engaging in the business of selling or transferring obscene matter by anyone

who knowingly receives or possesses with intent to distribute any obscene book, magazine, picture, paper, film, videotape, or phonograph or other audio recording, which has been shipped or transported in interstate or foreign commerce.

18 USC § 1466A

Section 1466A was added to this part of the federal criminal code by the Protect Act of 2003 (Pub. L. 108-21), in part, to remedy the Supreme Court's determination (see *Ashcroft v. Free Speech Coalition*, 535 U.S. 234 (2002)) that the provision (18 USC § 2256 (8)) of the Child Pornography Prevention Act of 1996 that defined virtual images, i.e., images that did not depict an actual minor but appeared to be those of a minor, be unconstitutional. By placing this provision with other obscenity provisions, the conduct must amount to what historically has been considered child pornography *and* obscenity as defined by the courts. This statutory enactment prohibits:

(1) knowingly
(2) producing, distributing, receiving, or possessing
(3) with intent to distribute

(4) a visual depiction of any kind that
    a. depicts a minor engaging in sexually explicit conduct *and* is obscene; *or*
    b. depicts an image that is, *or appears to be*, of a minor engaging in graphic bestiality, sadistic or masochistic abuse, or sexual intercourse, including genital-genital, oral-genital, anal-genital, or oral-anal, whether between persons of the same or opposite sex, *and* lacks serious literary, artistic, political, or scientific value, or attempts or conspires to do so

(5) under any of the following circumstances:

    (1) any communication involved in or made in furtherance of the offense is communicated or transported by the mail, or in interstate or foreign commerce by any means, including by computer, or any means or instrumentality of interstate or foreign commerce is otherwise used in committing or in furtherance of the commission of the offense;

    (2) any communication involved in or made in furtherance of the offense contemplates the transmission or transportation of a visual depiction by the mail, or in interstate or foreign commerce by any means, including by computer;

    (3) any person travels or is transported in interstate or foreign commerce in the course of the commission or in furtherance of the commission of the offense;

    (4) any visual depiction involved in the offense has been mailed, or has been shipped or transported in interstate or foreign commerce by any means, including by computer, or was produced using materials that have been mailed, or that have been shipped or transported in interstate or foreign commerce by any means, including by computer; or

    (5) the offense is committed in the special maritime and territorial jurisdiction of the United States or in any territory or possession of the United States.

    (f) Definitions. For purposes of this section—

        (1) the term "visual depiction" includes undeveloped film and videotape, and data stored on a computer disk or by electronic means which is capable of conversion into a visual image, and also includes any photograph, film, video, picture, digital image or picture, computer image or picture, or computer generated image or picture, whether made or produced by electronic, mechanical, or other means;

        (2) the term "sexually explicit conduct" has the meaning given the term in section 2256(2)(A) or 2256(2)(B) [18 USCS § 2256(2)(A) or 2256(2)(B)]; and

        (3) the term "graphic," when used with respect to a depiction of sexually explicit conduct, means that a viewer can observe any part of the genitals or pubic area of any depicted person or animal during any part of the time that the sexually explicit conduct is being depicted.

18 USC § 1470

This statute, which was enacted in 1993, prohibits the transfer of obscene material to children under the age of 16. It provides:

> Whoever, using the mail or any facility or means of interstate or foreign commerce, knowingly transfers obscene matter to another individual who has not attained the age of 16 years, knowing that such other individual has not attained the age of 16 years, or attempts to do so, shall be fined under this title, imprisoned not more than 10 years, or both.

Case Law Pertaining to Online Obscenity Crimes

One of the first issues to be raised in a prosecution for online distribution of obscenity concerns the issue of "contemporary community standards." For example, when a resident of Tennessee accesses an electronic bulletin board on the Internet that is hosted in California and downloads material from that bulletin board, whose community standards apply—those of the community in Tennessee or California? The following case considers that issue.

United States v. Thomas

74 F.3D 701 (1996)

U.S. Court of Appeals, Sixth Circuit

NANCY G. EDMUNDS, District Judge.

Defendants Robert and Carleen Thomas appeal their convictions and sentences for violating 18 U.S.C. §§ 1462 and 1465, federal obscenity laws, in connection with their operation of an electronic bulletin board. For the following reasons, we AFFIRM Robert and Carleen Thomas' convictions and sentences.

I.

Robert Thomas and his wife Carleen Thomas began operating the Amateur Action Computer Bulletin Board System ("AABBS") from their home in Milpitas, California in February 1991. The AABBS was a computer bulletin board system that operated by using telephones, modems, and personal computers. Its features included e-mail, chat lines, public messages, and files that members could access, transfer, and download to their own computers and printers.

Information loaded onto the bulletin board was first converted into binary code, i.e., 0's and 1's, through the use of a scanning device. After purchasing sexually-explicit magazines from public adult book stores in California, Defendant Robert Thomas used an electronic device called a scanner to convert pictures from the magazines into computer files called Graphic Interchange Format files or "GIF" files. The AABBS contained approximately 14,000 GIF files. Mr. Thomas also purchased, sold, and delivered sexually-explicit videotapes to AABBS members. Customers ordered the tapes by sending Robert Thomas an e-mail message, and Thomas typically delivered them by use of the United Parcel Service ("U.P.S.").

Persons calling the AABBS without a password could view the introductory screens of the system which contained brief, sexually-explicit descriptions of the GIF files and adult videotapes that were offered for sale. Access to the GIF files, however, was limited to members who were given a password after they paid a membership fee and submitted a signed application form that Defendant Robert Thomas reviewed. The application form requested the applicant's age, address, and telephone number and required a signature.

Members accessed the GIF files by using a telephone, modem and personal computer. A modem located in the Defendants' home answered the calls. After they established membership by typing in a password, members could then select, retrieve, and instantly transport GIF files to their own computer. A caller could then view the GIF file on his computer screen and print the image out using his printer. The GIF files contained the AABBS name and access telephone number; many also had "Distribute Freely" printed on the image itself.

In July 1993, a United States Postal Inspector, Agent David Dirmeyer ("Dirmeyer"), received a complaint regarding the AABBS from an individual who resided in the Western District of Tennessee. Dirmeyer dialed the AABBS' telephone number. As a non-member, he viewed a screen that read "Welcome to AABBS, the Nastiest Place On Earth," and was able to select various "menus" and read graphic descriptions of the GIF files and videotapes that were offered for sale.

Subsequently, Dirmeyer used an assumed name and sent in $55 along with an exe-cuted application form to the AABBS. Defendant Robert Thomas called Dirmeyer at his undercover telephone number in Memphis, Tennessee, acknowledged receipt of his application, and authorized him to log-on with his personal password. Thereafter, Dirmeyer dialed the AABBS's telephone number, logged-on and, using his computer/modem in Memphis, downloaded the GIF files listed in counts 2–7 of the Defendants' indictments. These GIF files depicted images of bestiality, oral sex, incest, sado-mas-ochistic abuse, and sex scenes involving urination. Dirmeyer also ordered six sexu-ally-explicit videotapes from the AABBS and received them via U.P.S. at a Memphis, Tennessee address. Dirmeyer also had several e-mail and chat-mode conversations with Defendant Robert Thomas.

On January 10, 1994, a search warrant was issued by a U.S. Magistrate Judge for the Northern District of California. The AABBS' location was subsequently searched, and the Defendants' computer system was seized.

II.

A.

Defendants' challenge to their convictions rests on two basic premises: 1) Section 1465 does not apply to intangible objects like the computer GIF files at issue here, and 2) Congress did not intend to regulate computer transmissions such as those involved here because 18 U.S.C. § 1465 does not expressly prohibit such conduct.

In support of their first premise, Defendants cite a Tenth Circuit dial-a-porn deci-sion which holds that 18 U.S.C. §§ 1462 and 1465 prohibit the interstate transportation of tangible objects; not intangible articles like pre-recorded telephone messages. See *United States v. Carlin Commun., Inc.*, 815 F.2d 1367, 1371 (10th Cir. 1987). Defendants claim *Carlin* is controlling because transmission of the GIF files at issue involved an intangible string of 0's and 1's which became viewable images only after they were decoded by an AABBS member's computer.

We disagree.

The subject matter in *Carlin*—telephonic communication of pre-recorded sexually suggestive comments or proposals—is inherently different from the obscene computer-generated materials that were electronically transmitted from California to Tennessee in this case. Defendants erroneously conclude that the GIF files are intangible, and thus outside the scope of § 1465, by focusing solely on the manner and form in which the computer-generated images are transmitted from one destination to another.

Defendants focus on the means by which the GIF files were transferred rather than the fact that the transmissions began with computer-generated images in California and ended with the same computer-generated images in Tennessee. The manner in which the images moved does not affect their ability to be viewed on a computer screen in Tennessee or their ability to be printed out in hard copy in that distant location.

The record does not support Defendants' argument that they had no knowledge, intent or expectation that members of their AABBS would download and print the images contained in their GIF files. They ran a business that advertised and promised its members the availability and transportation of the sexually-explicit GIF files they selected. In light of the overwhelming evidence produced at trial, it is spurious for Defendants to claim now that they did not intend to sell, disseminate, or share the obscene GIF files they advertised on the AABBS with members outside their home and in other states.

Defendants' second premise, that Congress did not intend to regulate computer transmissions because the statute does not expressly prohibit such conduct, is faulty as well. [W]e conclude that Defendants' conduct here falls within the plain language of Section 1465. Moreover, our interpretation of Section 1465 is consistent with Congress' intent to legislate comprehensively the interstate distribution of obscene materials.

C.

Defendants further argue that their convictions violate their First Amendment rights to freedom of speech.

1. Defendants' Right to Possess the GIF Files in their Home

Defendants rely on *Stanley v. Georgia*, 394 U.S. 557, 22 L. Ed. 2d 542, 89 S. Ct. 1243 (1969), and argue they have a constitutionally protected right to possess obscene materials in the privacy of their home. They insist that the GIF files containing sexually-explicit material never left their home. Defendants' reliance on *Stanley* is misplaced.

Defendants went beyond merely possessing obscene GIF files in their home. They ran a business that advertised and promised its members the availability and transportation of the sexually-explicit GIF files they selected. In light of the overwhelming evidence produced at trial, it is spurious for Defendants to claim now that they did not intend to sell, disseminate, or share the obscene GIF files they advertised on the AABBS with members outside their home and in other states.

2. The Community Standards to be Applied When Determining Whether the GIF Files Are Obscene

In *Miller v. California*, 413 U.S. 15, 37 L. Ed. 2d 419, 93 S. Ct. 2607 (1973), the Supreme Court set out a three-prong test for obscenity. It inquired whether (1) "'the average person applying contemporary community standards' would find that the work, taken as a whole appeals to the prurient interest"; (2) it "depicts or describes, in a patently offensive way, sexual conduct specifically defined by applicable state law"; and (3) "the work, taken as a whole, lacks serious literary, artistic, political, or scientific value." *Id.* at 24.

Under the first prong of the *Miller* obscenity test, the jury is to apply "contemporary community standards." Defendants acknowledge the general principle that, in cases involving interstate transportation of obscene material, juries are properly instructed to apply the community standards of the geographic area where the materials are sent. Nonetheless, Defendants assert that this principle does not apply here for the same reasons they claim venue was improper. As demonstrated above, this argument cannot withstand scrutiny. The computer-generated images were electronically transferred from Defendants' home in California to the Western District of Tennessee. Accordingly, the community standards of that judicial district were properly applied in this case.

Issues regarding which community's standards are to be applied are tied to those involving venue. It is well-established that:

> venue for federal obscenity prosecutions lies "in any district from, through, or into which" the allegedly obscene material moves, according to 18 U.S.C. § 3237. This may result in prosecutions of persons in a community to which they have sent materials which is obscene under that community's standards though the community from which it is sent would tolerate the same material.

United States v. Peraino, 645 F.2d 548, 551 (6th Cir. 1981).

3. The Implications of Computer Technology on the Definition of "Community"

Defendants and *Amicus Curiae* appearing on their behalf argue that the computer technology used here requires a new definition of community, i.e., one that is based on the broad-ranging connections among people in cyberspace rather than the geographic locale of the federal judicial district of the criminal trial. Without a more flexible definition, they argue, there will be an impermissible chill on protected speech because BBS operators cannot select who gets the materials they make available on their bulletin boards. Therefore, they contend, BBS operators like Defendants will be forced to censor their materials so as not to run afoul of the standards of the community with the most restrictive standards.

Defendants' First Amendment issue, however, is not implicated by the facts of this case. This is not a situation where the bulletin board operator had no knowledge or control over the jurisdictions where materials were distributed for downloading or printing. Access to the Defendants' AABBS was limited. Membership was necessary and applications were submitted and screened before passwords were issued and materials were distributed. Thus, Defendants had in place methods to limit user access in jurisdictions where the risk of a finding of obscenity was greater than that in California. They knew they had a member in Memphis; the member's address and local phone number were provided on his application form. If Defendants did not wish to subject themselves to liability in jurisdictions with less tolerant standards for determining obscenity, they could have refused to give passwords to members in those districts, thus precluding the risk of liability.

Thus, under the facts of this case, there is no need for this court to adopt a new definition of "community" for use in obscenity prosecutions involving electronic bulletin boards. This court's decision is guided by one of the cardinal rules governing the federal courts, i.e., never reach constitutional questions not squarely presented by the facts of a case. *Brockett v. Spokane Arcades, Inc.*, 472 U.S. 491, 502, 86 L. Ed. 2d 394, 105 S. Ct. 2794 (1985).

In the following case, the court considered whether 18 USC § 1462, as applied to electronic transmissions, was overly broad and whether the transmission or downloading over the Internet satisfied the interstate commerce requirement:

United States v. Reilly

2003 U.S. DIST. LEXIS 6005 (2003)

U.S. District Ct., Southern District of New York

ROBERT P. PATTERSON, JR., U.S.D.J.

Based on the First Amendment of the Constitution of the United States and *Stanley v. Georgia*, 394 U.S. 557, 22 L. Ed. 2d 542, 89 S. Ct. 1243 (1969), Defendant, Brian Reilly ("Reilly"), moves to dismiss Counts Six through Ten of the Superseding Indictment on the ground that "the statute as charged, 18 U.S.C. § 1462, insofar as it prohibits individuals from privately reviewing or downloading obscene material from the Internet, is unconstitutionally overbroad." For the following reasons, the Defendant's motion is denied.

BACKGROUND

An evidentiary hearing was held on April 8, 2002 and established that Defendant is an employee of the Bureau of Labor and Statistics ("BLS") of the United States Department of Labor ("DOL"). An agent of the DOL ascertained that between approximately January 9, 2001 and March 13, 2001, the Defendant's government Internet account had been used on multiple occasions to access Web sites displaying what appeared to be images of nude and partially-nude children, images of children displaying their genitals and images of adults engaging in sexual acts. The agent also ascertained that the Defendant's computer accessed these materials from within the BLS office, and generally after working hours.

In the early evening of March 13, 2001, federal agents observed the Defendant seated at his desk in front of his computer, and noted that the Defendant's computer screen contained a small window that indicated that material had just been downloaded from the Internet and a 3½-inch computer diskette lying on the desk next to Defendant's computer. An agent also observed that the Defendant had been downloading material from a Web site entitled, "http://worldlolitas.net/nude." Another diskette was found inside the government computer. The Defendant was detained for an interview and the computer and diskettes were seized.

Subsequent analysis of the diskette found inside the computer and the diskette that was on the desk revealed images that are the subject of Counts Six through Ten of the Superseding Indictment. The Defendant is not charged with distributing or displaying the offending materials to other persons.

DISCUSSION

The Defendant argues that the obscenity statute, 18 U.S.C. § 1462, under which he is charged in Counts Six through Ten of the Superseding Indictment, is unconstitutionally overbroad, because it prohibits and chills a substantial amount of protected speech, namely, the private possession of obscene matter, a right recognized in *Stanley v. Georgia* as protected by the First Amendment.

The Scope of the "Right to Receive" under *Stanley v. Georgia*

In *Stanley v. Georgia*, the Supreme Court held that the First and Fourteenth Amendments prohibit making mere private possession of obscene material a crime. The Court, while recognizing that the states retain broad power to regulate obscenity, held that that power does not extend to mere possession by the individual in the privacy of his own home. In reaching this holding, the opinion of the Court made the following statements: "it is now well established that the Constitution protects the right to receive information and ideas. 'This freedom (of speech and press) ... necessarily protects the right to receive....'"

Subsequent to *Stanley v. Georgia*, however, the Supreme Court in interpreting statutes regulating obscenity has limited the "right to receive," relying principally on extensions of its earlier decision in *Roth v. United States*, 354 U.S. 476, 1 L. Ed. 2d 1498, 77 S. Ct. 1304 (1957). In *Roth*, the Court held that 18 U.S.C. § 1461, the statute prohibiting the use of the mails for distribution of obscene materials was constitutional. The Court stated that obscenity "is not within the area of constitutionally protected speech or press."

Congress, in enacting the predecessor to 18 U.S.C. § 1462, intended to prevent channels of interstate commerce from being used to disseminate any matter that, in its essential nature, communicated obscene, lewd, lascivious, or filthy ideas. The 1996 Amendment to Section 1462, adding terms "or interactive computer service" and "receives," were intended to be "clarifying in nature." "Interactive Computer Service" merely added to the list of prohibited methods for transporting obscene matter in interstate commerce.

Using an Interactive Computer Service for carriage does involve the use of interstate commerce. At oral argument, the parties agreed that the nature of the Internet essentially requires the user to click a link, in order to command the electronic transportation of code from a remote server, to review a copy of a requested image. Moreover, there is case law holding that use of the Internet by interactive computer service involves interstate commerce. See e.g., *United States v. Carroll*, 105 F.3d 740, 742 (1st Cir. 1997) ("transmission of photographs by means of the Internet is tantamount to moving photographs across state lines and thus constitutes transportation in interstate commerce"); *United States v. Runyan*, 290 F.3d 223 (5th Cir. 2002) (finding interstate commerce element in 18 U.S.C. § 2252A established when Government linked specific images to the Internet); *United States v. Thomas*, 74 F.3d 701, 706-09 (6th Cir. 1996) (finding interstate commerce element in 18 U.S.C. § 1465 satisfied where pornographic material sent via the Internet).

As the plain words of 18 U.S.C. § 1462 equate an "interactive computer service" to "any express company or any other common carrier" it is clear that the use of the Internet by an interactive computer service can not be distinguished from the line of Supreme Court cases related to the knowing transportation and receipt of obscene material that has traveled in interstate commerce. Accordingly, Congress did not prohibit the individual's right under *Stanley v. Georgia* to receive obscene material, rather, it limited receiving obscene material by certain means of transportation or "modes of distribution," to use Mr. Justice Harlan's phrase.

ii. The Overbreadth Challenge

The Defendant's motion papers do not demonstrate that Section 1462 is unconstitutionally overbroad. The Defendant argues that privately downloading material freely available on the Internet should be considered the fundamental equivalent to reviewing material in one's private library. The Defendant maintains that a person who simply views or downloads material already freely available on the Internet has done nothing to offend the sensibilities of others or risk exposure to juveniles and is distinguishable from someone who causes such material to enter the stream of commerce. The Defendant argues that in light of the advent of the Internet and the new world of cyberspace, this Court should reexamine the distinction between constitutionally permitted and forbidden regulation of obscene material and engage in "new line drawing."

These assertions do not enunciate how 18 U.S.C. § 1462 is overbroad as pertaining to other persons affected by the amended statute. An overbreadth challenge allows a First Amendment litigant to "challenge a statute not because [his] own rights of free expression are violated, but because of a judicial prediction or assumption that the statute's very existence may cause others not before the court to refrain from constitutionally protected speech or expression," *Broadrick v. Oklahoma*, 413 U.S. 601, 612, 37 L. Ed. 2d 830, 93 S. Ct. 2908 (1973). The Defendant, however, has not demonstrated how any individual, even in the privacy of his or her own home downloading images of obscenity from the Internet, would be in a different position than his own and should have a constitutional protection for the interstate transportation of obscene material via an interactive computer service.

Here, the statute does not abridge the freedom to engage in any "protected speech" nor is it susceptible to the application of "protected expression." It has long been established that "obscenity" is not "protected" by the First Amendment. *Miller v. California*, 413 U.S. 15, 20-21, 37 L. Ed. 2d 419, 93 S. Ct. 2607 (1973) (citing *Roth v. United States*, 354 U.S. 476 at 484-485, 1 L. Ed. 2d 1498, 77 S. Ct. 1304). Any "obscene matter" is subject to the three-pronged *Miller* test which requires the Government to prove that the work, taken as a whole, appeals to the prurient interest, is patently offensive in light of community standards, and lacks serious literary, artistic, political, or scientific value. *Ashcroft v. Free Speech Coalition*, 535 U.S. 234, 122 S. Ct. 1389 at 1399, 152 L. Ed. 2d 403.

18 U.S.C. § 1462 is not unconstitutionally overbroad as it does not infringe on "protected speech." Nor does the statute offend the privacy right articulated in *Stanley v. Georgia*, as it is the act of electronic transportation and receipt, and not the private possession of obscene material in one's home, which the statute proscribes. Mr. Reilly's motion to dismiss the counts charging him with the violation of 18 U.S.C. § 1462 is denied.

Child Pornography Legislation

Legislative History

In the adult world, we usually use the terms *obscenity* and *pornography* interchangeably. That's okay when dealing with adults, but not when we consider child pornography. As noted by the statutory definitions that appear below, child pornography is not the same as obscenity, and by virtue of the Supreme Court decision in *Ferber v. New York* (458 U.S. 747 [1982]), it doesn't have to be the same.

In the past decade, Congress has actively sought to regulate the transmission and communication of child pornography through cyberspace. The following list includes the major legislative efforts over this period:

Communication Decency Act (CDA) of 1996
Child Pornography Prevention Act (CPPA) of 1996
Child Online Protection Act (COPA) of 1998
Protection of Children from Sexual Predators Act of 1998
Children's Online Privacy Protection Act (COPPA) of 1998
Children's Internet Protection Act (CIPA) of 2000
Can-Spam Act of 2003
Protect Act of 2003
Adam Walsh Child Protection and Safety Act of 2006

Current Child Pornography Laws

Child pornography is defined by federal law, 18 USC § 2256 (8), as follows:

any visual depiction, including any photograph, film, video, picture, or computer or computer-generated image or picture, whether made or produced by electronic, mechanical, or other means, of sexually explicit conduct, where—

(A) the production of such visual depiction involves the use of a minor engaging in sexually explicit conduct;
(B) such visual depiction is a digital image, computer image, or computer-generated image that is, or is indistinguishable from, that of a minor engaging in sexually explicit conduct; or
(C) such visual depiction has been created, adapted, or modified to appear that an identifiable minor is engaging in sexually explicit conduct.

A *minor* is defined in subdivision (1) of that section as any person under the age of 18.
Again, it is important to emphasize that obscenity and child pornography are defined differently. Child pornography involves the visual depiction of sexually explicit conduct, which is defined by 18 USC § 2256 (2) as follows:

"sexually explicit conduct" means—

(i) graphic sexual intercourse, including genital-genital, oral-genital, anal-genital, or oral-anal, whether between persons of the same or opposite sex, or lascivious simulated sexual intercourse where the genitals, breast, or pubic area of any person is exhibited;
(ii) graphic or lascivious simulated;
    (I) bestiality;
    (II) masturbation; or
    (III) sadistic or masochistic abuse; or
(iii) graphic or simulated lascivious exhibition of the genitals or pubic area of any person.

Under that definition, a visual depiction of a nude child does not constitute child pornography. So the typical photograph of a baby taking its first bath in the sink or bathtub is not child pornography. To constitute child pornography, the depiction must amount to a "lascivious exhibition" of the genital or pubic area. By comparison, however, the depiction of a minor engaged in sexually explicit conduct could constitute child pornography, but not obscenity. To constitute obscenity, the depiction must satisfy the three-prong test enunciated in the *Miller v. California* (*supra*) decision.

In *Ashcroft v. the Free Speech Coalition* (below), the Supreme Court concluded that § 2256 (8) was unconstitutional insofar as it sought to impose criminal liability for the distribution of, or use for marketing purposes of, virtual images, i.e., images of adults appearing to look like minors.

Ashcroft v. the Free Speech Coalition

535 U.S. 234 (2002)

U.S. Supreme Court

JUSTICE KENNEDY delivered the opinion of the Court.

We consider in this case whether the Child Pornography Prevention Act of 1996 (CPPA), 18 U.S.C. § 2251 et seq., abridges the freedom of speech. The CPPA extends the federal prohibition against child pornography to sexually explicit images that appear to depict minors but were produced without using any real children. The statute prohibits, in specific circumstances, possessing or distributing these images, which may be created by using adults who look like minors or by using computer imaging. The new technology, according to Congress, makes it possible to create realistic images of children who do not exist.

By prohibiting child pornography that does not depict an actual child, the statute goes beyond *New York v. Ferber*, 458 U.S. 747, 73 L.Ed.2d 1113, 102 S. Ct. 3348 (1982), which distinguished child pornography from other sexually explicit speech because of the State's interest in protecting the children exploited by the production process. As a general rule, pornography can be banned only if obscene, but under *Ferber*, pornography showing minors can be proscribed whether or not the images are obscene under the definition set forth in *Miller v. California*, 413 U.S. 15, 37 L. Ed. 2d 419, 93 S. Ct. 2607 (1973). *Ferber* recognized that "the *Miller* standard, like all general definitions of what may be banned as obscene, does not reflect the State's particular and more compelling interest in prosecuting those who promote the sexual exploitation of children." 458 U.S. at 761.

While we have not had occasion to consider the question, we may assume that the apparent age of persons engaged in sexual conduct is relevant to whether a depiction offends community standards. Pictures of young children engaged in certain acts might be obscene where similar depictions of adults, or perhaps even older adolescents, would not. The CPPA, however, is not directed at speech that is obscene; Congress has proscribed those materials through a separate statute. 18 U.S.C. §§ 1460–1466. Like the law in *Ferber*, the CPPA seeks to reach beyond obscenity, and it makes no attempt to conform to the *Miller* standard. For instance, the statute would reach visual depictions, such as movies, even if they have redeeming social value.

The principal question to be resolved, then, is whether the CPPA is constitutional where it proscribes a significant universe of speech that is neither obscene under *Miller* nor child pornography under *Ferber*.

Before 1996, Congress defined child pornography as the type of depictions at issue in *Ferber*, images made using actual minors. The CPPA retains that prohibition at

18 U.S.C. § 2256(8)(A) and adds three other prohibited categories of speech, of which the first, § 2256(8)(B), and the third, § 2256(8)(D), are at issue in this case. Section 2256(8)(B) prohibits "any visual depiction, including any photograph, film, video, picture, or computer or computer-generated image or picture" that "is, or appears to be, of a minor engaging in sexually explicit conduct." The prohibition on "any visual depiction" does not depend at all on how the image is produced. The section captures a range of depictions, sometimes called "virtual child pornography," which include computer-generated images, as well as images produced by more traditional means. For instance, the literal terms of the statute embrace a Renaissance painting depicting a scene from classical mythology, a "picture" that "appears to be, of a minor engaging in sexually explicit conduct." The statute also prohibits Hollywood movies, filmed without any child actors, if a jury believes an actor "appears to be" a minor engaging in "actual or simulated ... sexual intercourse." § 2256(2).

These images do not involve, let alone harm, any children in the production process; but Congress decided the materials threaten children in other, less direct, ways. Pedophiles might use the materials to encourage children to participate in sexual activity. "[A] child who is reluctant to engage in sexual activity with an adult, or to pose for sexually explicit photographs, can sometimes be convinced by viewing depictions of other children 'having fun' participating in such activity." Congressional Findings, note (3) following § 2251. Furthermore, pedophiles might "whet their own sexual appetites" with the pornographic images, "thereby increasing the creation and distribution of child pornography and the sexual abuse and exploitation of actual children." Id. notes (4), (10)(B). Under these rationales, harm flows from the content of the images, not from the means of their production. In addition, Congress identified another problem created by computer-generated images: Their existence can make it harder to prosecute pornographers who do use real minors. As imaging technology improves, Congress found, it becomes more difficult to prove that a particular picture was produced using actual children. To ensure that defendants possessing child pornography using real minors cannot evade prosecution, Congress extended the ban to virtual child pornography.

Section 2256(8)(C) prohibits a more common and lower tech means of creating virtual images, known as computer morphing. Rather than creating original images, pornographers can alter innocent pictures of real children so that the children appear to be engaged in sexual activity. Although morphed images may fall within the definition of virtual child pornography, they implicate the interests of real children and are in that sense closer to the images in *Ferber*. Respondents do not challenge this provision, and we do not consider it.

Congress may pass valid laws to protect children from abuse, and it has. The prospect of crime, however, by itself does not justify laws suppressing protected speech.

As a general principle, the First Amendment bars the government from dictating what we see or read or speak or hear. The freedom of speech has its limits; it does not embrace certain categories of speech, including defamation, incitement, obscenity, and pornography produced with real children. While these categories may be prohibited without violating the First Amendment, none of them includes the speech prohibited by the CPPA.

The CPPA prohibits speech despite its serious literary, artistic, political, or scientific value. The statute proscribes the visual depiction of an idea—that of teenagers engaging in sexual activity—that is a fact of modern society and has been a theme in art and literature throughout the ages. Under the CPPA, images are prohibited so long as the persons appear to be under 18 years of age. 18 U.S.C. § 2256(1). This is higher than the legal age for marriage in many States, as well as the age at which persons may consent to sexual relations. It is, of course, undeniable that some youths engage in sexual activity before the legal age, either on their own inclination or because they are victims of sexual abuse.

Our society, like other cultures, has empathy and enduring fascination with the lives and destinies of the young. Art and literature express the vital interest we all have in the formative years we ourselves once knew, when wounds can be so grievous, disappointment so profound, and mistaken choices so tragic, but when moral acts and self-fulfillment are still in reach. Whether or not the films we mention violate the CPPA, they explore themes within the wide sweep of the statute's prohibitions. If these films, or hundreds of others of lesser note that explore those subjects, contain a single graphic depiction of sexual activity within the statutory definition, the possessor of the film would be subject to severe punishment without inquiry into the work's redeeming value. This is inconsistent with an essential First Amendment rule: The artistic merit of a work does not depend on the presence of a single explicit scene. Under *Miller*, the First Amendment requires that redeeming value be judged by considering the work as a whole. Where the scene is part of the narrative, the work itself does not for this reason become obscene, even though the scene in isolation might be offensive. For this reason, and the others we have noted, the CPPA cannot be read to prohibit obscenity, because it lacks the required link between its prohibitions and the affront to community standards prohibited by the definition of obscenity.

The Government seeks to address this deficiency by arguing that speech prohibited by the CPPA is virtually indistinguishable from child pornography, which may be banned without regard to whether it depicts works of value. Where the images are themselves the product of child sexual abuse, *Ferber* recognized that the State had an interest in stamping it out without regard to any judgment about its content. The production of the work, not its content, was the target of the statute. The fact that a work contained serious literary, artistic, or other value did not excuse the harm it caused to its child participants. It was simply "unrealistic to equate a community's toleration for sexually oriented materials with the permissible scope of legislation aimed at protecting children from sexual exploitation."

In contrast to the speech in *Ferber*, speech that itself is the record of sexual abuse, the CPPA prohibits speech that records no crime and creates no victims by its production. Virtual child pornography is not "intrinsically related" to the sexual abuse of children, as were the materials in *Ferber*. 458 U.S. at 759. While the Government asserts that the images can lead to actual instances of child abuse, see *infra*, at 13–16, the causal link is contingent and indirect. The harm does not necessarily follow from the speech, but depends upon some unquantified potential for subsequent criminal acts.

The second flaw in the Government's position is that *Ferber* did not hold that child pornography is by definition without value. On the contrary, the Court recognized some works in this category might have significant value, see id. at 761, but relied on virtual images—the very images prohibited by the CPPA—as an alternative and permissible means of expression: "If it were necessary for literary or artistic value, a person over the statutory age who perhaps looked younger could be utilized. Simulation outside of the prohibition of the statute could provide another alternative." Id. at 763. *Ferber*, then, not only referred to the distinction between actual and virtual child pornography, it relied on it as a reason supporting its holding. *Ferber* provides no support for a statute that eliminates the distinction and makes the alternative mode criminal as well.

Here, the Government wants to keep speech from children not to protect them from its content but to protect them from those who would commit other crimes. The principle, however, remains the same: The Government cannot ban speech fit for adults simply because it may fall into the hands of children. The evil in question depends upon the actor's unlawful conduct, conduct defined as criminal quite apart from any link to the speech in question. This establishes that the speech ban is not narrowly drawn. The objective is to prohibit illegal conduct, but this restriction goes well beyond that interest by restricting the speech available to law-abiding adults.

In sum, § 2256(8)(B) covers materials beyond the categories recognized in *Ferber* and *Miller*, and the reasons the Government offers in support of limiting the freedom of speech have no justification in our precedents or in the law of the First Amendment. The provision abridges the freedom to engage in a substantial amount of lawful speech. For this reason, it is overbroad and unconstitutional.

Respondents challenge § 2256(8)(D) as well. This provision bans depictions of sexually explicit conduct that are "advertised, promoted, presented, described, or distributed in such a manner that conveys the impression that the material is or contains a visual depiction of a minor engaging in sexually explicit conduct." The parties treat the section as nearly identical to the provision prohibiting materials that appear to be child pornography.

The CPPA prohibits sexually explicit materials that "convey the impression" they depict minors. While that phrase may sound like the "appears to be" prohibition in § 2256(8)(B), it requires little judgment about the content of the image. Under § 2256(8)(D), the work must be sexually explicit, but otherwise the content is irrelevant. Even if a film contains no sexually explicit scenes involving minors, it could be treated as child pornography if the title and trailers convey the impression that the scenes would be found in the movie. The determination turns on how the speech is presented, not on what is depicted. While the legislative findings address at length the problems posed by materials that look like child pornography, they are silent on the evils posed by images simply pandered that way.

The Court has recognized that pandering may be relevant, as an evidentiary matter, to the question whether particular materials are obscene. See *Ginzburg v. United States*, 383 U.S. 463, 474, 16 L. Ed. 2d 31, 86 S. Ct. 942 (1966). Where a defendant engages in the "commercial exploitation of erotica solely for the sake of their prurient appeal," id. at 466, the context he or she creates may itself be relevant to the evaluation of the materials.

Section 2256(8)(D), however, prohibits a substantial amount of speech that falls outside *Ginzburg's* rationale. Materials falling within the proscription are tainted and unlawful in the hands of all who receive it, though they bear no responsibility for how it was marketed, sold, or described. The statute, furthermore, does not require that the context be part of an effort at "commercial exploitation." Ibid. As a consequence, the CPPA does more than prohibit pandering. It prohibits possession of material described, or pandered, as child pornography by someone earlier in the distribution chain. The provision prohibits a sexually explicit film containing no youthful actors, just because it is placed in a box suggesting a prohibited movie. Possession is a crime even when the possessor knows the movie was mislabeled. The First Amendment requires a more precise restriction. For this reason, § 2256(8)(D) is substantially over-broad and in violation of the First Amendment.

The term *identifiable minor* was added to this section as subdivision (9) via the Protect Act of 2003 in an effort to cure the constitutional infirmity involving virtual images that was resolved in *Ashcroft v. Free Speech Coalition* (535 U.S. 234 (2002)). An *identifiable minor*

- (A) means a person—
  - (i) (I) who was a minor at the time the visual depiction was created, adapted, or modified; or
    - (II) whose image as a minor was used in creating, adapting, or modifying the visual depiction; and
  - (ii) who is recognizable as an actual person by the person's face, likeness, or other distinguishing characteristic, such as a unique birthmark or other recognizable feature; and
- (B) shall not be construed to require proof of the actual identity of the identifiable minor.

This amendment seeks to distinguish the concept of virtual images from that of morphed images. A virtual image is an image of an individual (most likely an adult) that has been graphically altered through the use of computer image software to look like a child. A morphed image, on the other hand, is the image of an actual child that has been graphically altered.

18 USC § 2251: Sexual Exploitation of Children

Subdivision (a) of this section imposes criminal penalties upon any person who

1. employs, uses, persuades, induces, entices, or coerces;
2. any minor, or who has a minor assist another person to engage in, or who transports a minor in interstate or foreign commerce with intent to engage in
3. any sexually explicit conduct
4. for the purpose of producing any visual depiction of that conduct
5. knowing or having reason to know that:
   a. the visual depiction will be transported in interstate or foreign commerce, or mailed; or
   b. the visual depiction was produced using materials that were shipped or transported in interstate or foreign commerce by any means, including computer; or
   c. the visual depiction has actually been transported in interstate or foreign commerce, or mailed.

Subdivision (b) imposes criminal liability upon any parent, legal guardian, or other person having legal custody or control of a minor who

1. knowingly
2. permits their minor to engage in, or to assist another person to engage in
3. sexually explicit conduct
4. for the purpose of producing a visual depiction of that conduct

5. knowing, or with reason to know that
   a. the visual depiction will be transported in interstate or foreign commerce, or mailed; or
   b. the visual depiction was produced using materials that were mailed, shipped, or transported in interstate or foreign commerce by any means, including computer; or
   c. the visual depiction actually was transported in interstate or foreign commerce, or mailed.

18 USC § 2252: Certain Activities Relating to Material Involving the Sexual Exploitation of Minors

This section imposes criminal penalties upon the following:

(a) Any person who—
   (1) knowingly *transports or ships* in interstate or foreign commerce by any means including by computer or mails, any visual depiction, if—
      (A) the producing of such visual depiction involves the use of a minor engaging in sexually explicit conduct; and
      (B) such visual depiction is of such conduct;
   (2) knowingly *receives, or distributes* any visual depiction that has been mailed, or has been shipped or transported in interstate or foreign commerce, or which contains materials which have been mailed or so shipped or transported, by any means including by computer, or knowingly reproduces any visual depiction for distribution in interstate or foreign commerce by any means including by computer or through the mails, if—
      (A) the producing of such visual depiction involves the use of a minor engaging in sexually explicit conduct; and
      (B) such visual depiction is of such conduct;
   (3) either—
      (A) in the special maritime and territorial jurisdiction of the United States, or on any land or building owned by, leased to, or otherwise used by or under the control of the Government of the United States, or in the Indian country as defined in section 1151 of this title knowingly *sells or possesses* with intent to sell any visual depiction; or
      (B) knowingly *sells or possesses* with intent to sell any visual depiction that has been mailed, or has been shipped or transported in interstate or foreign commerce, or which was produced using materials which have been mailed or so shipped or transported, by any means, including by computer, if—
         (i) the producing of such visual depiction involves the use of a minor engaging in sexually explicit conduct; and
         (ii) such visual depiction is of such conduct; or
   (4) either—
      (A) in the special maritime and territorial jurisdiction of the United States, or on any land or building owned by, leased to, or otherwise used by or under the control of the Government of the United States, or in the Indian country as defined in section 1151 of this title, knowingly possesses 1 or more books, magazines, periodicals, films, videotapes, or other matter which contain any visual depiction; or

(B) knowingly possesses 1 or more books, magazines, periodicals, films, video-tapes, or other matter which contain any visual depiction that has been mailed, or has been shipped or transported in interstate or foreign commerce, or which was produced using materials which have been mailed or so shipped or trans-ported, by any means including by computer, if—

  (i) the producing of such visual depiction involves the use of a minor engaging in sexually explicit conduct; and
  (ii) such visual depiction is of such conduct [Emphases added].

18 USC § 2252A: Certain Activities Relating to Material Constituting or Containing Child Pornography

Subdivision (a) of this section describes the conduct constituting a criminal violation:

(a) Any person who—
  (1) knowingly mails, or transports or ships in interstate or foreign commerce by any means, including by computer, any child pornography;
  (2) knowingly receives or distributes—
    (A) any child pornography that has been mailed, or shipped or transported in interstate or foreign commerce by any means, including by computer; or
    (B) any material that contains child pornography that has been mailed, or shipped or transported in interstate or foreign commerce by any means, including by computer;
  (3) knowingly—
    (A) reproduces any child pornography for distribution through the mails, or in interstate or foreign commerce by any means, including by computer; or
    (B) advertises, promotes, presents, distributes, or solicits through the mails, or in interstate or foreign commerce by any means, including by computer, any material or purported material in a manner that reflects the belief, or that is intended to cause another to believe, that the material or purported material is, or contains—
      (i) an obscene visual depiction of a minor engaging in sexually explicit con-duct; or
      (ii) a visual depiction of an actual minor engaging in sexually explicit conduct;
  (4) either—
    (A) in the special maritime and territorial jurisdiction of the United States, or on any land or building owned by, leased to, or otherwise used by or under the control of the United States Government, or in the Indian country (as defined in section 1151 [18 USCS § 1151]), knowingly sells or possesses with the intent to sell any child pornography; or
    (B) knowingly sells or possesses with the intent to sell any child pornography that has been mailed, or shipped or transported in interstate or foreign commerce by any means, including by computer, or that was produced using materials that have been mailed, or shipped or transported in interstate or foreign com-merce by any means, including by computer;
  (5) either—
    (A) in the special maritime and territorial jurisdiction of the United States, or on any land or building owned by, leased to, or otherwise used by or under the control of the United States Government, or in the Indian country (as defined

in section 1151 [18 USCS § 1151]), knowingly possesses any book, magazine, periodical, film, videotape, computer disk, or any other material that contains an image of child pornography; or

(B) knowingly possesses any book, magazine, periodical, film, videotape, computer disk, or any other material that contains an image of child pornography that has been mailed, or shipped or transported in interstate or foreign commerce by any means, including by computer, or that was produced using materials that have been mailed, or shipped or transported in interstate or foreign commerce by any means, including by computer; or

(6) knowingly distributes, offers, sends, or provides to a minor any visual depiction, including any photograph, film, video, picture, or computer generated image or picture, whether made or produced by electronic, mechanical, or other means, where such visual depiction is, or appears to be, of a minor engaging in sexually explicit conduct—

(A) that has been mailed, shipped, or transported in interstate or foreign commerce by any means, including by computer;

(B) that was produced using materials that have been mailed, shipped, or transported in interstate or foreign commerce by any means, including by computer; or

(C) which distribution, offer, sending, or provision is accomplished using the mails or by transmitting or causing to be transmitted any wire communication in interstate or foreign commerce, including by computer, for purposes of inducing or persuading a minor to participate in any activity that is illegal.

(7) knowingly produces with intent to distribute child pornography that is an adapted or modified depiction of an identifiable minor.

Subdivisions (c) and (d) provide for two affirmative defenses. Subdivision (c) authorizes a defendant to assert that the images alleged to be visual depictions of child pornography are actually those of adults.

Subdivision (d) authorizes a defendant to assert, with respect to subparagraph (c)(5), that he or she possessed less than three images and that he or she promptly disposed of the images or turned them over to law enforcement without enabling distribution to any other person.

18 USC § 2425: Use of Interstate Facilities to Transmit Information about a Minor

Whoever, using the mail or any facility or means of interstate or foreign commerce, or within the special maritime and territorial jurisdiction of the United States, knowingly initiates the transmission of the name, address, telephone number, social security number, or electronic mail address of another individual, knowing that such other individual has not attained the age of 16 years, with the intent to entice, encourage, offer, or solicit any person to engage in any sexual activity for which any person can be charged with a criminal offense, or attempts to do so, shall be fined under this title, imprisoned not more than 5 years, or both.

Case Law Pertaining to Online Child Pornography

We will consider several child pornography cases, most of them in later chapters on search and seizure, wiretapping, and access to stored communications. The following case, however, illustrates the difficulty of applying statutory language to the use of technology. In this case, the defendant appealed two of four counts of an indictment, specifically counts of an indictment that charged him with "transporting" visual depictions of minors. The defendant, who downloaded the images from an online bulletin board, argued that his conduct in downloading the images did not constitute transporting those images. Here is how the court resolved the issue:

United States v. Mohrbacher

182 F.3D 1041 (1999)

U.S. Ct. of Appeals, Ninth Circuit

REINHARDT, Circuit Judge:

Mohrbacher's illegal conduct consisted of downloading images of child pornography from a foreign-based electronic bulletin board. As to the challenged counts, he argues that he was charged and convicted under the wrong section of the statute because while he may have received these images in violation of § 2252(a)(2) he did not transport or ship them in violation of § 2252(a)(1). We agree with his reading of the statute, and accordingly reverse these two counts of conviction.

BACKGROUND

In March 1992, Danish police seized the business records of BAMSE, a computer bulletin board system based in Denmark that sold child pornography over the Internet. The records included information that Mohrbacher, who lived in Paradise, California, had downloaded two graphic interface format (GIF) images from BAMSE in January 1992.

In March 1993, police executed a search warrant at Mohrbacher's workplace and found, among other images, two files that had been downloaded from BAMSE, one of a nude girl and one of a girl engaged in a sex act with an adult; both girls were under twelve. During the execution of the warrant, Mohrbacher was cooperative, confessing that he had downloaded the two images from BAMSE, showing police where they could find the images that they were looking for on his computer, and providing telephone records that confirmed the dates of his Internet activity. Mohrbacher subsequently cooperated with the government's investigation of child pornography. He made monitored telephone calls to a number of electronic bulletin boards, provided the name of one bulletin board operator, and testified at a grand jury hearing. At that hearing, Mohrbacher again admitted that he had downloaded at least one of the two images.

At the trial, in addition to the witnesses who linked Mohrbacher directly to the images that were the subject of the criminal charges, the prosecution presented expert testimony about the operation of the bulletin board. The expert witness testified that "[a] computer bulletin board system is kind of like a store of sorts. There's the capability of sending and receiving files and sending and receiving messages." Having studied BAMSE for two years, he provided the following description of it:

BAMSE was a computerized bulletin board system. The bulletin board system is an automated system that runs 24 hours a day, seven days a week. That's a computer system that allows people to connect to it via computer and telephone modem. Once users connect to the BBS, they log in as a user name, they provide a password, and the BBS has a list of images available for download. Individuals would select pictures, then download them to their computer.... The image files on the BAMSE BBS were GIF files, which stands for graphic interchange files. It's just a binary string of information. It's the computer's way of representing a visual image.

The expert described the process of downloading GIF image files, explaining that the bulletin board user selects an image and uses his own computer modem to download the image file through telephone lines. Once downloading has been completed, the image is contained in the user's own computer system. No human conduct is required at the bulletin board site in order to facilitate this file transfer. When asked whether a "store" analogy was appropriate, the expert agreed but then described one difference: when a customer purchases an item on the bulletin board, the supply is not depleted—rather, a copy of the original product is generated and sent.

MOTION FOR ACQUITTAL

The facts relevant to Mohrbacher's motion for acquittal are not disputed. We therefore confront directly the legal question whether downloading images from a computer bulletin board constitutes shipping or transporting within the meaning of the terms as used in 18 U.S.C. § 2252(a)(1), a question of first impression. Mohrbacher argues that downloading is properly characterized as receiving images by computer, which is proscribed by § 2252(a)(2), rather than transporting or shipping images by computer as prohibited by § 2252(a)(1). If Mohrbacher is right, then with respect to the two challenged counts he was charged and convicted under the wrong statutory provision, and those convictions must be reversed.

Mohrbacher reasons that downloading is essentially an electronic request by one computer owner to another computer owner to deliver files or data electronically to the requesting owner's computer. He presents a definition of downloading in support: "To copy data ... from a main source to a peripheral device ... the process of copying a file from an online service or bulletin board service (BBS) to one's own computer." PHILIP E. MARGOLIS, RANDOM HOUSE PERSONAL COMPUTER DICTIONARY at 156 (2d ed. 1996). This definition is in accord with the expert testimony that was presented by the prosecution at trial. As was discussed in greater detail earlier in this opinion, that expert testified that downloading is analogous to placing an order through a mail order catalogue except that a computer fills the order automatically and the inventory is not depleted because a new copy of the image is generated.

The question that we must resolve is whether, given what appears to be a noncontroversial definition of the term, Mohrbacher's "downloading" of two images constitutes a violation of § 2252(a)(1). Mohrbacher suggests an analogy for our consideration, an analogy that is consistent with that testified to by the government expert. Mohrbacher argues that his conduct was comparable to that of a customer who places a phone order requesting delivery of an item, the only difference being that the entity that was filling the order—the bulletin board—had a completely automated response and did not require any action by an individual at the time the order was filled. The government argues that the automated nature of the bulletin board's response makes Mohrbacher the one responsible for causing the visual images to move from one location to another and that an individual who causes transporting or shipping is guilty as a principal. At oral argument, when asked to clarify whether a computer bulletin board service opera-tor could be liable for transporting or shipping images under its interpretation of the statute, the government answered in the negative. In the government's view, it is only the individual who downloads the image who has caused that image to be transported. Mohrbacher responds by pointing out that a request will not be filled unless the opera-tor of the bulletin board has configured it to accept orders. Thus, he argues, it is the bul-letin board operator who has transported or shipped the images, and the downloader has only received them. The disagreement is in essence over whether the government is correct that the automated nature of the process requires the conclusion that down-loading is equivalent to transporting.

The first definition of "receive" in the *Oxford English Dictionary* is "to take into one's hand, or into one's possession (something held out or offered by another); to take delivery of (a thing) from another, either for oneself or for a third party." OXFORD'S ENGLISH DICTIONARY 2D 314 (1989). An individual who downloads material takes possession or accepts delivery of the visual image; he has therefore certainly received it. In fact, guides to computer terminology often analogize downloading to receiving information and uploading to transmitting or sending. "To transmit a file from one computer to another. When conducting the session, down-load means receive, upload means transmit." ALAN FREEDMAN, COMPUTER WORDS YOU GOTTA KNOW! ESSENTIAL DEFINITIONS FOR SURVIVAL IN A HIGH-TECH WORLD 49 (1993). "To down-load means to receive information, typically a file, from another computer to yours via your modem…. The opposite term is upload, which means to send a file to another computer." ROBIN WILLIAMS, JARGON, AN INFORMAL DICTIONARY OF COMPUTER TERMS 170–71 (1993). Even the prosecution's expert, when asked what happens when an individual downloads an image, responded, "When you down-load the pictures, you receive an exact copy of the picture that existed in Denmark." See also Peter Wayner, Plugging In to the Internet: Many Paths, Many Speeds, N.Y. TIMES (Jan. 30, 1999) ("You might be able to download, or receive, large volumes of data quickly, but the time to upload, or send, information could be much slower.").

We next look to other principles of statutory interpretation. In determining the meaning of a statutory provision, a court may consider the purpose of the statute "in its entirety," see *Alarcon v. Keller Industries, Inc.*, 27 F.3d 386, 389 (9th Cir. 1994), and whether the proposed interpretation would frustrate or advance that purpose. See *Tierney v. Kupers*, 128 F.3d 1310, 1311–12 (9th Cir. 1997). In this case, the statutory pur-pose provides no guidance as to which of its sections addresses the act of downloading child pornography. The statutory provisions therefore must be interpreted in accord with the statute's broad and general purpose of facilitating the prosecution of individu-als who are involved with child pornography. However, the decision whether down-loading is properly charged under (a)(1) or (a)(2) of the statute, or both, will neither hinder nor facilitate such prosecutions. Because the penalties and sentencing guidelines ranges for both provisions are identical, this court's decision will determine how down-loading should be prosecuted but not affect the difficulty or nature of such prosecutions. Whichever statutory provisions may be deemed applicable, the statutory purpose will be equally served.

For further interpretive guidance, a court may examine the particular statu-tory language to be construed in relation to the other parts of the statute. Here, an examination of the structure of § 2252 tends to support Mohrbacher's position. The fact that Congress chose to separate the provision that makes transporting or shipping unlawful from the subsection that criminalizes receiving or distributing suggests that the provisions are meant to regulate different types of behavior. "[A] statute must be interpreted to give significance to all of its parts.... We have long followed the principle that statutes should not be construed to make surplusage of any provision." Northwest Forest Resource Council, 82 F.3d at 833–34.

On the basis of our analysis of the nature of the process of downloading, the dictionary definitions of the terms included in the statute, the statute's purpose, and the structure of the statutory provisions, we conclude that Mohrbacher's interpretation of the statute is correct. An individual who downloads images from a computer bulletin board takes an action that is more analogous to ordering materials over the phone and receiving materials through the mail than to sending or shipping such materials. Those who are responsible for providing the images to a customer, by making them available on a computer bulletin board or by sending them via electronic mail, are properly charged with and convicted of shipping or transporting images under § 2252(a)(1). A customer who is simply on the receiving end—who downloads an image that has been made available through an automated, preconfigured process or that has been sent by another computer user—is guilty of receiving or possessing such materials under § 2252(a)(2) but not of shipping or transporting them.

We reject the argument that even if downloading itself is more analogous to receiving, Mohrbacher, by ordering the pornographic images, caused them to be transported and is therefore nonetheless criminally liable under § 2252(a)(1). Acceptance of this reasoning would allow any act of ordering, requesting, or indicating an interest in contraband to provide a basis for conviction of transporting or shipping such material, and would eliminate the distinction between purchasers and sellers or shippers and receivers. Because a request for drugs could be viewed as causing a drug sale to occur, any purchaser or receiver could be charged as a buyer or distributor at the prosecutor's discretion. For the reasons explained above, the distinctions between downloading an image and ordering an item from a human supplier—i.e., the facts that the response is automatic (because an individual has programmed it to be so) and that filling the order does not deplete the supply—provide no logical reason to limit the principle that would be established: any customer who requests or orders a product could be held liable for causing that product to be sent or sold.

The government's reliance upon 18 U.S.C. § 2(b) does not change our analysis. That provision does not eliminate the distinction between buyers and sellers, or between shippers and receivers. It serves a different purpose: it insures that an offender who utilizes an innocent agent to carry out a criminal act but may not be charged as a principal under § 2(a), the aiding and abetting provision, is not insulated from criminal liability.

Mohrbacher stands for the principle that downloading child pornography images from an automated bulletin board does not constitute transporting of those images. What if an individual has peer-to-peer file-sharing software and has numerous images on his hard drive that are available for sharing with others? If other people utilizing the same program access the individual's files and obtain the images, is the individual liable for the distribution of child pornography? That issue was resolved in the following case:

United States v. Shaffer

472 F.3D 1219 (2007)

U.S. Court of Appeals, Tenth Circuit

GORSUCH, Circuit Judge.

Aaron Shaffer challenges his conviction for distribution and possession of child por-nography on four grounds. Primary among these, Mr. Shaffer claims that he did not, as a matter of law or fact, "distribute" child pornography when he downloaded images and videos from a peer-to-peer computer network and stored them in a shared folder on his computer accessible by other users of the network.

Kazaa is a peer-to-peer computer application that allows users to trade computer files through the Internet. It is hardly a unique service; at any one time today, there are apparently in excess of four to five million people online sharing over 100 million files. Users begin at Kazaa's website. There, they obtain the software necessary for file trading by clicking an installation "wizard" that walks them through a step-by-step setup process. Before installation, the wizard requires users to acknowledge and accede to Kazaa's licensing agreement. Users then identify a destination on their computers where they want the Kazaa file sharing software located, and Kazaa creates a "shortcut" icon on the user's desktop. Upon installation, Kazaa's software walks users through certain steps to create a folder called "My Shared Folder" (hereinafter, "shared folder") on their computer's hard drive. Here, Kazaa users store the files they download from the shared folders of other Kazaa users. At the same time, anything one has in one's own Kazaa shared folder may be accessed and downloaded by other Kazaa users. The only requisites are that both users—the one whose files are being transferred as well as the one who is receiving the files—must be on the Internet and have the Kazaa software application open at the same time. Kazaa's software also shows the user in real time exactly how many of his or her files are being accessed and copied by other Kazaa users. A user can, however, select an option that precludes other users from downloading materials from his or her computer.

To download an item from another computer's shared folder, a Kazaa user simply double clicks on that file, and it is then transferred to the shared folder on the recipient user's computer. There are only two ways for items to be placed in a user's shared folder. First, one must go online, search for an item, and download the material into the shared folder. Second, one may take files already existing on his or her computer and move them into the shared folder. Either way, the placement of items in one's shared folder involves a conscious effort. A user can of course move items out of the shared folder to other folders on his or her computer, and doing so precludes other Kazaa users from accessing and downloading such material.

This case arose when Ken Rochford, an Arizona-based special agent from the United States Department of Homeland Security's Bureau of Immigration and Customs Enforcement ("ICE"), noticed that a certain Kazaa account user with the screen name shaf@Kazaa had in his shared folder accessible to other Kazaa users a large number of files containing images and videos of child pornography. Special Agent Rochford sought to download some of those images from shaf@Kazaa's computer onto his own and had no difficulty doing so.

Authorities later learned that the user associated with shaf@Kazaa was Mr. Shaffer, then a 27-year-old college student living with his mother and stepfather in Topeka, Kansas. David Zimmer, a Kansas-based ICE special agent, obtained and executed a search warrant on Mr. Shaffer's residence and computer. ICE special agents ultimately found within Mr. Shaffer's Kazaa shared folder approximately 19 image files and 25 videos containing child pornography, along with text documents describing stories of adults engaging in sex with children.

During the course of the search of his home and computer, Mr. Shaffer consented to an interview with Special Agent Zimmer. During that interview, according to Special Agent Zimmer's testimony at trial, Mr. Shaffer admitted to being the sole user of the computer in his home; employing the screen name shaf@Kazaa; and knowingly downloading through Kazaa 100 movies and 20 still photos involving child pornography, which he estimated occupied a total of approximately 10 gigabytes. Mr. Shaffer defined child pornography for Special Agent Zimmer as involving prepubescent children as young as six or seven years old. Mr. Shaffer further admitted that he stored images of child pornography in his Kazaa shared folder. He explained that he did so because, among other things, Kazaa gave him "user points" and various incentive rewards corresponding to how many images other users downloaded from his computer. Mr. Shaffer indicated he knew that other people had downloaded child pornography from him. And he stated that it takes up to 100 hours to download certain files using Kazaa, so sometimes when he went to work he would leave his computer on in order to make his images and videos available for download by other users.

Mr. Shaffer also testified at trial. He did not dispute that he gave an interview to Special Agent Zimmer or much of Special Agent Zimmer's description of that interview. Mr. Shaffer did testify, however, that he could not recall telling Special Agent Zimmer that he knew other Kazaa users had downloaded child pornography from his computer. After a four-day trial, a jury returned guilty verdicts against Mr. Shaffer for both possession and distribution of child pornography. The District Court subsequently sentenced him to 60 months of incarceration.

Mr. Shaffer contends there was insufficient evidence presented at trial to sustain his conviction for distribution of child pornography. Under Section 2252A(a)(2), it is unlawful for a person knowingly to distribute child pornography by any means, including by computer. Mr. Shaffer frankly concedes that "[h]e allowed, or caused, distribution by leaving files on his computer that other Kazaa users could access." He also now concedes that a rational jury could infer that he did so knowingly (and even intentionally): "[A] reasonable jury could conclude from this evidence that Mr. Shaffer intended to allow others to take the material from his computer." But, Mr. Shaffer argues, to "distribute" something, a person must actively transfer possession to another, "such as by mail, e-mail, or handing it to another person." Id. And here, Mr. Shaffer contends, he was only a passive participant in the process; there is no evidence that he "personally complete[d] any [such] transaction."

The relevant statute does not itself define the term "distribute," so we look to how the term is understood as a matter of plain meaning. Black's offers this definition: "1. To apportion; to divide among several. 2. To arrange by class or order. 3. To deliver. 4. To spread out; to disperse." Black's Law Dictionary 508 (8th ed. 2005). Webster's adds this understanding: "to divide among several or many … deal out … apportion esp. to members of a group or over a period of time … [allot] … [dispense] … to give out or deliver." Webster's Third New Int'l Dictionary Unabridged 660 (2002). The instruction offered by the District Court to the jury captured much the same sentiment: "To distribute something simply means to deliver or transfer possession of it to someone else."

We have little difficulty in concluding that Mr. Shaffer distributed child pornography in the sense of having "delivered," "transferred," "dispersed," or "dispensed" it to others. He may not have actively pushed pornography on Kazaa users, but he freely allowed them access to his computerized stash of images and videos and openly invited them to take, or download, those items. It is something akin to the owner of a self-serve gas station. The owner may not be present at the station, and there may be no attendant present at all. And neither the owner nor his or her agents may ever pump gas. But the owner has a roadside sign letting all passersby know that, if they choose, they can stop and fill their cars for themselves, paying at the pump by credit card. Just because the operation is self-serve, or in Mr. Shaffer's parlance, passive, we do not doubt for a moment that the gas station owner is in the business of "distributing," "delivering," "transferring" or "dispersing" gasoline; the raison d'etre of owning a gas station is to do just that. So, too, a reasonable jury could find that Mr. Shaffer welcomed people to his computer and was quite happy to let them take child pornography from it.

Indeed, Mr. Shaffer admitted that he had downloaded child pornography from other users' Kazaa shared folders and understood that file sharing was the very purpose of Kazaa. He admitted that he had child pornography stored in his computer's Kazaa shared folder. Mr. Shaffer could have, but did not, save the illicit images and videos in a computer folder not susceptible to file sharing. Likewise, he could have, but did not, activate the feature on Kazaa that would have precluded others from taking materials from his shared folder. Quite the opposite. According to Special Agent Zimmer, Mr. Shaffer acknowledged that he knew other people had downloaded child pornography from his shared folder. Mr. Shaffer cannot recall making this particular admission, but we are obliged to view the facts in the light most favorable to the government, and the jury was free to credit Special Agent Zimmer's testimony and discredit Mr. Shaffer's. According to Special Agent Zimmer, moreover, Mr. Shaffer confessed that he kept child pornography in his shared folder in order to win special concessions from Kazaa, concessions made only when others downloaded from his shared folder. And Special Agent Rochford had no trouble whatsoever picking and choosing for download images and videos from Mr. Shaffer's child pornography collection.

Though the question how Section 2252A applies to peer-to-peer file sharing programs may be relatively novel, at least one other court has faced the question we do today and reached precisely the same conclusion. In *United States v. Abraham*, the court held that "the defendant distributed a visual depiction when as a result of the defendant's installation of an Internet peer-to-peer video file sharing program on his computer, a Pennsylvania state trooper was able to download the child pornography from the defendant's computer to the trooper's computer." No. 05-344, 2006 WL 3052702, at 8, 2006 U.S. Dist. LEXIS 81006 at 22 (W.D.Pa. Oct. 24, 2006). Courts faced with related issues have, in a variety of other contexts, issued rulings similarly harmonious with our own.

Can a defendant be convicted of receiving *and* possessing child pornography? Doesn't that violate double jeopardy because they are the same act? The following decision resolves these issues:

United States v. Bobb

---

577 F.3D 1366 (2009)

U.S. COURT OF APPEALS, ELEVENTH CIRCUIT

TJOFLAT, Circuit Judge:

In this appeal, we consider whether convictions for both "receiving" and "possessing" child pornography violate the Double Jeopardy Clause of the Fifth Amendment to the Constitution. Because the indictment charged and the Government proved at trial that Edward Curtis Bobb had committed two distinct offenses, occurring on two different dates, in breach of two different statutes, we find no Double Jeopardy Clause violation and, accordingly, affirm.

In September 2004, the Federal Bureau of Investigation ("FBI") opened an investigation to find the person or persons responsible for posting numerous images of child pornography on a website operated by the Great Plains Child Care Resource and Referral Center in Oklahoma (the "Center"). As part of its investigation, the FBI extracted data from the Center's host computers that identified the IP (Internet provider) addresses of computers that had recently been used to visit the Center's website.

With this information in hand, the FBI issued subpoenas to numerous Internet Service Providers ("ISPs") to require that they reveal the subscriber information for customers who had visited the Center's website during the time frame when the images appeared on the site. After acquiring this information, the FBI identified the account holders who had visited the site and, more importantly, the account holders who had accessed the specific section of the website containing the child pornography. Focusing attention on these individuals, the FBI discovered that, on November 12, 2004, an individual located somewhere in Miami, Florida, accessed the section of the Center's website containing the child pornography and had downloaded seven videos and numerous other picture files. The FBI soon traced the person to Bobb's residence.

On August 10, 2005, FBI agents executed a search warrant at Bobb's apartment. The agents explained to Bobb that they were looking for images of child pornography that someone, on November 12, 2004, had downloaded to a computer traced to his home. Bobb told the agents that he was the only person living in the residence who used a computer to access the Internet.

Bobb's apartment consisted of three rooms: a main living room, a kitchen, and a bedroom. While searching the bedroom, the agents discovered two Apple laptop computers: one silver and the other black. In the living room, the agents found a beige desktop computer and two LaCie external hard drives. The agents removed the computers, the hard drives, and miscellaneous paperwork and correspondence related to Bobb.

After seizing Bobb's computer equipment, the agents returned to the FBI office where Special Agent Mary Katherine Koontz inventoried and reviewed the electronic contents in the computers. During this process, Koontz discovered that the silver Apple laptop contained 6,124 images of child pornography. She also discovered seven "zip files"—two of the zip files contained movies of child pornography that had been viewed on the computer. In addition, Koontz found approximately 2,000 images consisting of several images of child pornography "layered on top of one another." That is, instead of one distinct image of child pornography, each image consisted of at least two images of child pornography merged together to create a single unique image. On the other computers and hard drives, Koontz found another 1,500 images of child pornography.

Koontz submitted fifty of the images found on the silver laptop to Walter Lambert, M.D., a pediatrician at the University of Miami Hospital, and asked that he determine the ages of the children depicted in the images. After examining the images, Dr. Lambert was unable to determine the age of the person in one of the images, but he was able to discern that forty-four images depicted children, mainly girls, under the age of twelve, and that five images depicted children older than twelve, but under the age of eighteen.

Over a year later, on August 24, 2006, a federal grand jury returned an indictment charging Bobb with one count of "receiving" child pornography on November 12, 2004, in violation of 18 U.S.C. § 2252A(a)(2)(B) ("Count I"), and one count of knowingly "possessing" child pornography on August 4, 2005, in violation of 18 U.S.C. § 2252A(a)(5)(B) ("Count II"). Bobb pled not guilty to both counts.

Before trial, Bobb filed a "Motion for Relief from Joinder," arguing that, since "[t]he alleged offenses occurred on two different dates" and because "[t]he same witnesses will be used to prove both counts," there was a substantial risk that the jury would conflate the evidence used to prove Count I with the evidence used to prove Count II. Specifically, Bobb pointed out that the evidence the Government planned to use to prove Count I, the "receiving" count, was the seven zip files that Bobb had allegedly downloaded from the Center's website on November 12, 2004, and the rest of the images would be used to prove Count II, the "possessing" count. According to Bobb, he would be unduly prejudiced because the jury would likely consider the images regarding Count II when considering Count I. The district court denied the motion, and the case proceeded to trial.

After a three-day trial, a jury found Bobb guilty on both counts.

Bobb now argues, for the first time on appeal, that his sentences for both "receiving" and "possessing" child pornography are impermissible because both counts of the indictment charged him with the same offense in violation of the Fifth Amendment's Double Jeopardy Clause.

The Fifth Amendment's Double Jeopardy Clause guarantees that no person shall "be subject for the same offence to be twice put in jeopardy of life or limb." U.S. Const. amend. V. This guarantees against a second prosecution for the same offense after acquittal, a second prosecution for the same offense after conviction, and multiple punishments for the same offense. Relevant to this case is the Double Jeopardy Clause's prohibition against multiple punishments for the same offense.

As a general proposition, when a defendant has violated two different criminal statutes, the Double Jeopardy Clause is implicated when both statutes prohibit the same act or transaction or when one act is a lesser included offense of the other. See *Rutledge v. United States*, 517 U.S. 292, 297, 116 S. Ct. 1241, 1245, 134 L. Ed. 2d 419 (1996). Congress, of course, has the power to authorize multiple punishments arising out of a single act or transaction. The constitutional guarantee against double jeopardy merely assures that the court does not "exceed its legislative authorization by imposing multiple punishments for the same offense." *Brown v. Ohio*, 432 U.S. 161, 165, 97 S. Ct. 2221, 53 L. Ed. 2d 187 (1977); *accord Missouri v. Hunter*, 459 U.S. 359, 366, 103 S. Ct. 673, 678, 74 L. Ed. 2d 535 (1983) ("[T]he Double Jeopardy Clause does no more than prevent the sentencing court from prescribing greater punishment than the legislature intended."). If it is not clear, though, that the legislature intended multiple punishments for the same conduct, a presumption arises that a conviction under multiple statutes for the same offense is contrary to legislative intent. See *Hunter*, 459 U.S. at 366–67, 103 S. Ct. at 678–79; *Whalen v. United States*, 445 U.S. 684, 691–92, 100 S. Ct. 1432, 1437–1438, 63 L. Ed. 2d 715 (1980). To sum up, where two statutory provisions proscribe the same offense and there is no clear indication that the legislature intended multiple punishments for the offense, the Double Jeopardy Clause's prohibition against multiple punishments protects a defendant from being convicted under both provisions.

The Supreme Court has penned a black-letter rule for use in determining when dual statutory provisions prohibit the same offense: "Where the same act or transaction constitutes a violation of two distinct statutory provisions, the test to be applied to determine whether there are two offenses or only one, is whether each provision requires proof of a fact which the other does not." *Blockburger v. United States*, 284 U.S. 299, 304, 52 S. Ct. 180, 182, 76 L. Ed. 306 (1932). Our analysis focuses on the proof necessary to establish the statutory elements of each offense, not the actual evidence presented at trial.

We pause to acknowledge that, even in cases such as this, where the imposed sentences run concurrently, unlawfully multiplicitous convictions carry serious collateral consequences that cannot be ignored. "For example, the presence of two convictions on the record may delay the defendant's eligibility for parole or result in an increased sentence under a recidivist statute for a future offense. Moreover, the second conviction may be used to impeach the defendant's credibility and certainly carries the societal stigma accompanying any criminal conviction." *Rutledge*, 517 U.S. at 302, 116 S. Ct. at 1248 (quoting *Ball v. United States*, 470 U.S. 856, 865, 105 S. Ct. 1668, 1673, 84 L. Ed. 2d 740 (1985)). Where we conclude that a defendant has suffered a double jeopardy violation because he was improperly convicted for the same offense under two separate counts, "the only remedy consistent with the congressional intent is for the [d]istrict [c]ourt, where the sentencing responsibility resides, to exercise its discretion to vacate one of the underlying convictions." *Ball*, 470 U.S. at 864, 105 S. Ct. at 1673.

Bobb's opening argument is based on a simple proposition: it is impossible to "receive" a thing without, at least at the very instant of "receipt," also "possessing" it. This argument has merit, as courts have recognized that "[g]enerally federal statutes criminalizing the receipt of contraband [generally] require a knowing acceptance or taking of possession of the prohibited item." *United States v. Romm*, 455 F.3d 990, 1001 (9th Cir. 2006) (internal quotation omitted); see *United States v. Ladd*, 877 F.2d 1083, 1088 (1st Cir. 1989) (stating that a person must have possession of contraband to show receipt); *United States v. Griffin*, 705 F.2d 434, 437 (11th Cir. 1983) (*per curiam*) (finding that receipt, in the context of a firearms statute, "includes any knowing acceptance or taking of possession"); see also *United States v. Strauss*, 678 F.2d 886, 894 (11th Cir. 1982) ("We believe that accepting a good and having either physical control of or apparent legal power over a good is sufficient to show that an individual received it.").

Building upon this foundation, Bobb argues that the offenses described in 18 U.S.C. § 2252A(a)(2) (prohibiting receipt) comprise a subset of the offenses described in 18 U.S.C. § 2252A(a)(5)(B) (prohibiting possession), such that possession is a lesser included offense of receipt (possession being the lesser offense as demonstrated by the lower statutory penalty range). The Supreme Court has observed that comparing criminal statutes to determine whether one set of elements is a subset of another requires a strictly textual comparison. This requires that we look to the statutory elements, not the way the offenses are charged in the indictment.

18 U.S.C. § 2252A(a)(2)(B) authorizes punishment for "[a]ny person who … knowingly receives or distributes … any material that contains child pornography that has been mailed, or using any means or facility of interstate or foreign commerce shipped or transported in or affecting interstate or foreign commerce by any means, including by computer." 18 U.S.C. § 2252A(a)(5)(B) criminalizes the "knowing[ ] possess[ion] … [of] any book, magazine, periodical, film, videotape, computer disk, or any other material that contains an image of child pornography that has been mailed, or shipped or transported using any means or facility of interstate or foreign commerce or in affecting interstate or foreign commerce by any means, including by computer, or that was produced using materials that have been mailed, or shipped or transported in or affecting interstate or foreign commerce by any means, including by computer."

Accepting the proposition that, if a person takes "receipt" of a thing, they necessarily must "possess" the thing, we find that these provisions, indeed, proscribe the same conduct; by proving that a person "knowingly receives" child pornography, the Government necessarily proves that the person "knowingly possesses" child pornography. See *Blockburger*, 284 U.S. at 304, 52 S. Ct. at 182 (stating that the test for determining whether there have been multiplicitous convictions for the same offense focuses on the statutory elements of the offenses to determine if each requires proof of a fact that the other does not).

Next, we must consider whether Congress clearly intended to punish a defendant for both "receipt" and "possession" when it enacted the two provisions. See *Albernaz v. United States*, 450 U.S. 333, 340, 101 S. Ct. 1137, 1143, 67 L. Ed. 2d 275 (1981) ("The *Blockburger* test is a 'rule of statutory construction,' and because it serves as a means of discerning congressional purpose the rule should not be controlling where, for example, there is a clear indication of contrary legislative intent.") "In resolving … [a] contention that Congress did not intend to authorize multiple punishment for violations of [two distinct statutes], our starting point must be the language of the statutes. Absent a 'clearly expressed legislative intention to the contrary, that language must ordinarily be regarded as conclusive.'" Id. at 336, 101 S. Ct. at 1141 (quoting *Consumer Prod. Safety Comm'n v. GTE Sylvania, Inc.*, 447 U.S. 102, 108, 100 S. Ct. 2051, 2056, 64 L. Ed. 2d 766 (1980)). After considering the plain text of the statute and the relevant legislative history, we find no "clear indication of [] legislative intent" to impose multiplicitous punishment for "receipt" and "possession" of child pornography.

We acknowledge that this is a question of first impression for this circuit, and, while the text of the statute provides a sufficient basis for our conclusion, we note that our reasoning is consonant with the Supreme Court's decision in *Ball v. United States*, 470 U.S. 856, 105 S. Ct. 1668, 84 L. Ed. 2d 740 (1985). In *Ball*, a felon convicted of receiving a firearm in violation of 18 U.S.C. § 922(h) was also convicted of possessing that firearm in violation of 18 U.S.C. App. § 1202(a). Id. at 857–58, 105 S. Ct. at 1669–70. After applying the same-elements test advanced by *Blockburger*, the Court concluded that "proof of illegal receipt of a firearm *necessarily* includes proof of illegal possession of that weapon. When received, a firearm is necessarily possessed. In other words, Congress seems clearly to have recognized that a felon who receives a firearm must also possess it, and thus had no intention of subjecting that person to two convictions for the same criminal act." *Ball*, 470 U.S. at 862, 105 S. Ct. at 1672 (citation and internal quotation omitted; emphasis in original).

We also find support for our reasoning in the decisions rendered by two of our sister circuits on the very issue we consider today. The Third Circuit, in *United States v. Miller*, 527 F.3d 54 (3d Cir. 2008), found that *Ball* was controlling and concluded that "possession of child pornography in violation of § 2252A(a)(5)(B) is a lesser-included offense of receipt of child pornography in violation of § 2252A(a)(2)." *Miller*, 527 F.3d at 72. Since the defendant had been convicted and sentenced under both provisions for the same conduct in violation of the Double Jeopardy Clause, the court remanded the case to the district court with instructions to vacate one of the underlying convictions. Id. at 74. The Ninth Circuit reached the same conclusion in *United States v. Davenport*, 519 F.3d 940, 947–48 (9th Cir. 2008), *United States v. Giberson*, 527 F.3d 882, 891 (9th Cir. 2008), and *United States v. Brobst*, 558 F.3d 982, 1000 (9th Cir. 2009). See also *United States v. Morgan*, 435 F.3d 660, 662–63 (6th Cir. 2006) (noting that a defendant charged under § 2252A(a)(2), who pled guilty to violating § 2252A(a)(5)(B), had pled to "a lesser-included offense of the charged violation").

While we agree with Bobb's opening argument, that "possession" is a lesser included offense of "receipt," his appeal ultimately fails. Unlike the facts in *Ball, Miller, Davenport, Giberson*, and *Brobst*, where the defendants were convicted and sentenced under two different statutes for the same offense, Bobb's convictions and sentences were based on two distinct offenses, occurring on two different dates, and proscribed by two different statutes. Count I of the indictment charged Bobb with taking "receipt" of child pornography on November 12, 2004, while Count II charged Bobb with having "possession" of child pornography in August 2005. The evidence at trial proved that Bobb received child pornography on November 12, 2004, by downloading the seven zip files from the Center's website, and, in August 2005, he possessed over 6,000 additional images. Accordingly, the record shows that the indictment charged Bobb with two separate offenses, and the Government introduced evidence sufficient to convict him of those distinct offenses.

For the reasons stated above, defendant Bobb's convictions are AFFIRMED.

Online Gambling

Federal law and the laws of most states prohibit online gambling. The Internet presents interesting issues concerning the transmission of wagering information and the use of interactive websites for the placement of bets, especially in those instances where the gambling sites are located in a foreign country. For example, if a resident of New York (where online gambling is illegal) places a bet at a website hosted in Nevada (where online gambling is legal), has the Nevada site violated New York law and can the owners be prosecuted in New York for the crime? Likewise, if a resident of the United States places a bet with a website hosted in Antigua, can the owners of the Antigua site be held criminally liable for a violation of federal law?

This chapter considers the various federal laws that purport to prohibit online gambling as well as selected state statutes on the subject. Notably, no state expressly authorizes online gambling. One state, Nevada, has enacted law to the effect that if online gambling is considered to be legal by the federal government, then it is legal in that state.[3] We begin the inquiry by examining federal statutes that prohibit online gambling, as well as the online gambling statutes of New York and Nevada. Then we consider cases that attempt to resolve some of the issues raised in the previous paragraph.

Federal Law

The Unlawful Internet Gambling Act—31 USC §§ 5361–5367

In October 2006 Congress enacted the Unlawful Internet Gambling Enforcement Act of 2006 (UIGEA) (Pub. L. 109-347; 31 USC §§ 5361–5367). UIGEA makes it a crime punishable by fine or imprisonment (up to five years) to engage in the business of betting or wagering by

- knowingly accepting
  - credit, or the proceeds of credit, including the use of a credit card
  - an electronic fund transfer (EFT) or funds transmitted through a money transmitting business
  - any check, draft, or similar instrument drawn upon or payable at or through a financial institution, or
  - the proceeds of any other form of financial transaction involving a financial institution as payor or intermediary
- in connection with the participation of another person in unlawful Internet gambling

Unlawful Internet gambling means

to place, receive, or otherwise knowingly transmit a bet or wager by any means which involves the use, at least in part, of the Internet where such bet or wager is unlawful under any applicable Federal or State law in the State or Tribal lands in which the bet or wager is initiated, received, or otherwise made.

A bet or wager includes what we commonly understand to constitute gambling, but it does not include fantasy or simulated sports games not based on a single event, or what are considered to be legitimate businesses that involve risk, such as insurance or securities (31 USC § 5362 (1)). A business engaged in betting or wagering does not include a financial transaction provider, interactive computing service, or communications service (31 USC § 5362 (2)). A financial transaction provider is the party providing the gambling customer with the financial resources (credit, electronic fund transfer, check) to submit to the gambling business. The interactive computing service or communications service is the Internet or communications carrier serving as the conduit for the bet or wager.

The Wire Act—18 USC § 1084

Commonly known as the Wire Act, Section 1084 was enacted in 1961, well before the advent of the Internet. By its terms, the act is limited to gambling on sporting events and contests, and thus it has no application to other forms of gambling such as casino gambling.[4] Though initially intended to combat the unlawful gambling activities of organized crime,[5] the act applies to communications made by a "wire, cable, or any other like connection," and thus to Internet transactions. Section 1084 provides:

Transmission of Wagering Information; Penalties

(a) Whoever being engaged in the business of betting or wagering knowingly uses a wire communication facility for the transmission in interstate or foreign commerce of bets or wagers or information assisting in the placing of bets or wagers on any sporting event or contest, or for the transmission of a wire communication which entitles the recipient to receive money or credit as a result of bets or wagers, or for information assisting in the placing of bets or wagers, shall be fined under this title or imprisoned not more than two years, or both.

(b) Nothing in this section shall be construed to prevent the transmission in interstate or foreign commerce of information for use in news reporting of sporting events or contests, or for the transmission of information assisting in the placing of bets or wagers on a sporting event or contest from a State or foreign country where betting on that sporting event or contest is legal into a State or foreign country in which such betting is legal.

(c) Nothing contained in this section shall create immunity from criminal prosecution under any laws of any State.

(d) When any common carrier, subject to the jurisdiction of the Federal Communications Commission, is notified in writing by a Federal, State, or local law enforcement agency, acting within its jurisdiction, that any facility furnished by it is being used or will be used for the purpose of transmitting or receiving gambling information in interstate or foreign commerce in violation of Federal, State or local law, it shall discontinue or refuse, the leasing, furnishing, or maintaining of such facility, after reasonable notice to the subscriber, but no damages, penalty or forfeiture, civil or criminal, shall be found against any common carrier for any act done in compliance with any notice received from a law enforcement agency. Nothing in this section shall be deemed to prejudice the right of any person affected thereby to secure an appropriate determination, as otherwise provided by law, in a Federal court or in a State or local tribunal or agency, that such facility should not be discontinued or removed, or should be restored.

(e) As used in this section, the term 'State' means a State of the United States, the District of Columbia, the Commonwealth of Puerto Rico, or a commonwealth, territory or possession of the United States.

Can the Wire Act be applied to a gambling business conducted from a foreign country? In the following case, Jay Cohen and his partners established a business known as the World Sports Exchange (WSE) on the Caribbean island of Antigua. The sole business of WSE was bookmaking on American sporting events. WSE targeted U.S. customers, advertising throughout the country via radio, television, and newspapers, and enticing customers to bet with WSE, by either toll-free telephone or the Internet. Following an FBI investigation, defendant Cohen was charged with violating the Wire Act and with conspiracy to violate the act. The defendant raised three arguments: (1) that the government failed to negate application of the statute's safe harbor provisions, (2) that the conduct of his business did not constitute betting, and (3) that the *mens rea* element that he act "knowingly" required the government to establish that he knew that he was transmitting bets and that he knew the wagers were coming from a state where such wagering was illegal.

United States v. Cohen

260 F.3D 68 (2001)

U.S. Ct. of Appeals, Second Circuit

KEENAN, District Judge:

BACKGROUND

WSE operated an "account-wagering" system. It required that its new customers first open an account with WSE and wire at least $300 into that account in Antigua. A customer seeking to bet would then contact WSE either by telephone or Internet to request a particular bet. WSE would issue an immediate, automatic acceptance and confirmation of that bet, and would maintain the bet from that customer's account.

In one fifteen-month period, WSE collected approximately $5.3 million in funds wired from customers in the United States. In addition, WSE would typically retain a "vig" or commission of 10% on each bet. Cohen boasted that in its first year of operation, WSE had already attracted nearly 1,600 customers. By November 1998, WSE had received 60,000 phone calls from customers in the United States, including over 6,100 from New York.

In the course of an FBI investigation of offshore bookmakers, FBI agents in New York contacted WSE by telephone and Internet numerous times between October 1997 and March 1998 to open accounts and place bets. Cohen was arrested in March 1998 under an eight-count indictment charging him with conspiracy and substantive offenses in violation of 18 U.S.C. § 1084 ("§ 1084").

Cohen was convicted on all eight counts on February 28, 2000 after a ten-day jury trial before Judge Thomas P. Griesa.

DISCUSSION

The Safe Harbor Provision

Cohen appeals the district court for instructing the jury to disregard the safe-harbor provision contained in § 1084(b). That subsection provides a safe harbor for transmissions that occur under both of the following two conditions: (1) betting is legal in both the place of origin and the destination of the transmission; and (2) the transmission is limited to mere information that assists in the placing of bets, as opposed to including the bets themselves.

The district court ruled as a matter of law that the safe-harbor provision did not apply because neither of the two conditions existed in the case of WSE's transmissions. Cohen disputes that ruling and argues that both conditions did, in fact, exist. He argues that betting is not only legal in Antigua, it is also "legal" in New York for the purposes of §1084. He also argues that all of WSE's transmissions were limited to mere information assisting in the placing of bets. We agree with the district court's rulings on both issues.

A. "Legal" Betting

There can be no dispute that betting is illegal in New York. New York has expressly prohibited betting in both its Constitution … and its General Obligations Law.

Nevertheless, Cohen argues that Congress intended for the safe-harbor provision in § 1084(b) to exclude only those transmissions sent to or from jurisdictions in which betting was a crime. Cohen concludes that because the placing of bets is not a crime in New York, it is "legal" for the purposes of § 1084(b).

By its plain terms, the safe-harbor provision requires that betting be "legal," i.e., permitted by law, in both jurisdictions.

Betting is illegal in New York, and thus the safe-harbor provision in § 1084(b) cannot not apply in Cohen's case as a matter of law. As a result, the district court was not in error when it instructed the jury to disregard that provision.

B. Transmission of a Bet, Per Se

Cohen appeals the district court's instructions to the jury regarding what constitutes a bet per se. Cohen argues that under WSE's account-wagering system, the transmissions between WSE and its customers contained only information that enabled WSE itself to place bets entirely from customer accounts located in Antigua. He argues that this fact was precluded by the district court's instructions. We find no error in those instructions.

Judge Griesa repeatedly charged the jury as follows:

> If there was a telephone call or an Internet transmission between New York and [WSE] in Antigua, and if a person in New York said or signaled that he or she wanted to place a specified bet, and if a person on an Internet device or a telephone said or signaled that the bet was accepted, this was the transmission of a bet within the meaning of Section 1084. Congress clearly did not intend to have this statute be made inapplicable because the party in a foreign gambling business deemed or construed the transmission as only starting with an employee in an Internet mechanism located on the premises in the foreign country.

Jury instructions are not improper simply because they resemble the conduct alleged to have occurred in a given case; nor were they improper in this case. It was the Government's burden in this case to prove that someone in New York signaled an offer to place a particular bet and that someone at WSE signaled an acceptance of that offer. The jury concluded that the Government had carried that burden.

Cohen's *Mens Rea*

Cohen appeals the district court's instruction to the jury regarding the requisite *mens rea* under §1084. Section 1084 prohibits the "knowing" transmission of bets or information assisting in the placing of bets. The district court instructed the jurors that to convict, they needed only to find that Cohen "knew that the deeds described in the statute as being prohibited were being done," and that a misinterpretation of the law, like ignorance of the law, was no excuse.

Cohen argues that he lacked the requisite *mens rea* because (1) he did not "knowingly" transmit bets, and (2) he did not transmit information assisting in the placing of bets or wagers to or from a jurisdiction in which he "knew" betting was illegal. He contends that in giving its jury charge, the district court improperly instructed the jury to disregard that argument.

The district court was correct; it mattered only that Cohen knowingly committed the deeds forbidden by § 1084, not that he intended to violate the statute. Cohen's own interpretation regarding what constituted a bet was irrelevant to the issue of his *mens rea* under §1084.

In any event, Cohen is culpable under § 1084(a) by admitting that he knowingly transmitted information assisting in the placing of bets. His beliefs regarding the legality of betting in New York are immaterial. The legality of betting in a relevant jurisdiction pertains only to § 1084(b)'s safe-harbor provision. As we have already discussed, that safe-harbor provision, as a matter of law, does not apply in this case.

There are two important aspects of the *Cohen* decision. First, under the statute, the mere transmission of a signal or information by the customer is deemed to be a bet. The defendant attempted to argue that only information was transmitted from New York; that once the information was received in Antigua, the website in Antigua placed the bet on behalf of the customer. The court rejected that argument, noting that the signal or transmission of information itself was an indication that the person in New York wanted to bet.

Second, the court determined that "knowingly" means only that the defendant was aware of the conduct he was committing (the transmission of bets), not that he knew that the bets being transmitted were illegal. A core principle of criminal law is that a crime has two elements: an *actus reus*, the guilty act, and a *mens rea*, the state of mind that renders the act criminal. Stated another way, the *mens rea* is the mentality with which the act was committed. In this case, the court rejected Cohen's effort to relate "knowingly" to something other than the guilty conduct. The court observed that because Cohen's issue of illegality of the bet related to the safe-harbor provision and did not pertain to the conduct constituting the crime, the government was not required to establish that Cohen knew that the bets being transmitted were illegal.

The Travel Act—18 USC § 1952

Commonly known as the Travel Act, this law also was enacted in 1961, the same year as the Wire Act. Subdivision (a) imposes criminal sanctions upon anyone who uses "any facility in interstate or foreign commerce" with intent to:

(1) distribute the proceeds of any unlawful activity; or
(2) commit any crime of violence to further any unlawful activity; or
(3) otherwise promote, manage, establish, carry on, or facilitate the promotion, management, establishment, or carrying on, of any unlawful activity.

"Unlawful activity" is defined in subdivision (b) of this section to include "any business enterprise involving gambling." As we have seen in other contexts, the Internet is a "facility in interstate or foreign commerce." Thus, the statute also applies to those engaged in the business of unlawful gambling.

The Paraphernalia Act—18 USC § 1953

Commonly known as the Paraphernalia Act, this statute provides for the imposition of criminal penalties upon

> Whoever, except a common carrier in the usual course of its business, knowingly carries or sends in interstate or foreign commerce any record, paraphernalia, ticket, certificate, bills, slip, token, paper, writing, or other device used, or to be used, or adapted, devised, or designed for use in (a) bookmaking; or (b) wagering pools with respect to a sporting event; or (c) in the numbers, policy, bolita, or similar game …

Though also enacted in 1961, well before the Internet, an Internet service provider (ISP) would be considered a common carrier within the meaning of this law.

18 USC § 1955

This law, enacted in 1970, imposes criminal liability upon those who conduct, finance, manage, or own all or part of an illegal gambling business. Although this law contains no language suggesting that it could be applied to Internet wagering businesses, there likewise is no language indicating that the statute does not apply to illegal gambling businesses conducted on the Internet.

State Gambling Laws

Indiana

Most states do not have criminal laws that expressly prohibit Internet gambling. The laws of those states simply prohibit gambling unless specifically authorized. Indiana, however, is an example of one state that expressly prohibits Internet gambling, and further, imposes greater criminal liability (felony vs. misdemeanor) for Internet gambling. Section 35-45-5-2 of the Indiana Code provides:

> (a) A person who knowingly or intentionally engages in gambling commits unlawful gambling.
> (b) Except as provided in subsection (c), unlawful gambling is a Class B misdemeanor.
> (c) An operator who knowingly or intentionally uses the Internet to engage in unlawful gambling:
>   (1) in Indiana; or
>   (2) with a person located in Indiana;
>   commits a Class D felony.

New York

The more common legislative scenario is illustrated by New York law. New York prohibits the promotion of gambling in the first and second degrees. Promoting gambling involves conduct that "knowingly advances or profits from unlawful gambling activity" (N.Y. Penal Law §§ 225.05, 225.10). A person advances gambling activity

> when, acting other than as a player, he engages in conduct which materially aids any form of gambling activity. Such conduct includes but is not limited to conduct directed toward the

creation or establishment of the particular game, contest, scheme, device or activity involved, toward the acquisition or maintenance of premises, paraphernalia, equipment or apparatus therefore, toward the solicitation or inducement of persons to participate therein, toward the actual conduct of the playing phases thereof, toward the arrangement of any of its financial or recording phases, or toward any other phase of its operation. One advances gambling activity when, having substantial proprietary or other authoritative control over premises being used with his knowledge for purposes of gambling activity, he permits such to occur or continue or makes no effort to prevent its occurrence or continuation.

N.Y. Penal Law § 225.00 (4)   A person profits from gambling

when, other than as a player, he accepts or receives money or other property pursuant to an agreement or understanding with any person whereby he participates or is to participate in the proceeds of gambling activity.

N.Y. Penal Law § 225.00 (5)   In the following case, the New York Attorney General sought to enjoin (prohibit) a corporation from conducting gambling activity via its Web servers on the island of Antigua. The court was asked to decide whether the New York crime of promoting gambling activity could be applied to gambling conduct even though the server that hosted the gambling activity was located in a foreign country.

People v. World Interactive Gaming Corporation

185 MISC. 2D 852, 714 N.Y.S.2D 844 (1999)
SUPREME COURT OF NEW YORK, NEW YORK COUNTY

OPINION: Charles Edward Ramos, J.

This proceeding is brought by the Attorney General of the State of New York, pursuant to Executive Law § 63 (12) and General Business Law article 23-A, to enjoin the respondents, World Interactive Gaming Corporation (WIGC), Golden Chips Casino, Inc. (GCC), and their principals, officers, and directors from operating within or offering to residents of New York State gambling over the Internet.

The central issue here is whether the State of New York can enjoin a foreign corporation legally licensed to operate a casino offshore from offering gambling to Internet users in New York. At issue is section 9 (1) of article I of the New York Constitution which contains an express prohibition against any kind of gambling not authorized by the State Legislature. The prohibition represents a deep-rooted policy of the State against unauthorized gambling.

WIGC is a Delaware corporation that maintains corporate offices in New York. WIGC wholly owns GCC, an Antiguan subsidiary corporation which acquired a license from the government of Antigua to operate a land-based casino. Through contracts executed by WIGC, GCC developed interactive software, and purchased computer servers which were installed in Antigua, to allow users around the world to gamble from their home computers. GCC promoted its casino at its web site, and advertised on the Internet and in a national gambling magazine. The promotion was targeted nationally and was viewed by New York residents.

In February 1998, the Attorney General commenced an investigation into the practices of WIGC.

In June 1998, the Attorney General furthered its investigation by logging onto respondents' web site, downloading the gambling software, and in July 1998, placed the first of several bets. Users who wished to gamble in the GCC Internet casino were directed to wire money to open a bank account in Antigua and download additional software from GCC's web site. In opening an account, users were asked to enter their permanent address. A user which submitted a permanent address in a State that permitted land-based gambling, such as Nevada, was granted permission to gamble. Although a user which entered a State such as New York, which does not permit land-based gambling, was denied permission to gamble, because the software does not verify the user's actual location, a user initially denied access could easily circumvent the denial by changing the State entered to that of Nevada, while remaining physically in New York State. The user could then log onto the GCC casino and play virtual slots, blackjack or roulette. This raises the question if this constitutes a good-faith effort not to engage in gambling in New York.

Respondents contend that the transactions occurred offshore and that no State or Federal law regulates Internet gambling. They claim that they were operating a duly licensed legitimate business fully authorized by the government of Antigua and in compliance with that country's rules and regulations of a land-based casino. They further argue that the Federal and State laws upon which the State relies either do not apply to the activities of WIGC or are too vague and ambiguous to criminalize the activity of Internet gambling, when such activity is offshore in Antigua.

Personal Jurisdiction Over WIGC and GCC

Whether the exercise of personal jurisdiction comports with due process requirements depends, as in any case, upon a finding that respondent has purposefully engaged in significant activities such that he has "availed himself of the privilege of conducting business [in the forum State]." (*Burger King Corp. v Rudzewicz*, 471 US 462, 476 [1985].)

Respondents in this case are clearly doing business in New York for purposes of acquiring personal jurisdiction. Although WIGC was incorporated in Delaware, WIGC operated its entire business from its corporate headquarters in Bohemia, New York. All administrative and executive decisions as well as the computer research and development of the Internet gambling web site were made in New York. The cold-calls to investors to buy WIGC stock were made by WIGC agents employed and operating from this location. Thereafter, respondents sent the prospectus and other solicitation materials about Internet gambling from the Bohemia, New York location. WIGC's continuous and systematic contacts with New York established their physical presence in New York.

Moreover, even without physical presence in New York, WIGC's activities are sufficient to meet the minimum contacts requirement of *International Shoe Co. v Washington* (326 US 310, 316 [1945]). The nature and quality of the defendant's activity must be such that "the defendant purposefully avails itself of the privilege of conducting activities within the forum State, thus invoking the benefits and protections of its laws" (*Agrashell, Inc. v Sirotta Co.*, 344 F2d 583, 587 [2d Cir 1965]). The use of the Internet is more than the mere transmission of communications between an out-of-State defendant and a plaintiff within the jurisdiction.

WIGC and the other respondents are doing business in New York. They worked from New York in conjunction with another New York-based company, Imajix Studios, to design the graphics for their Internet gambling casino. From their New York corporate headquarters, they downloaded, viewed, and edited their Internet casino web site. Furthermore, respondents engaged in an advertising campaign all over the country to induce people to visit their web site and gamble. Knowing that these ads were reaching thousands of New Yorkers, respondents made no attempt to exclude identifiable New Yorkers from the propaganda. Phone logs from respondents' toll-free number (available to casino visitors on the GCC web site) indicate that respondents had received phone calls from New Yorkers. Respondents cannot dispute that they do business in New York and that the acts complained of are subject to this court's jurisdiction.

To establish *in personam* jurisdiction over GCC, the petitioner must show that GCC functioned merely as the alter ego of WIGC. The corporate form will be pierced only if one corporation is so controlled by the other as to be a mere agent, department or alter ego of the other. There must be some proof that the parent company dominates or controls the daily activities of the subsidiary.

The evidence indicates that GCC is a corporation completely dominated by WIGC. Aside from it being a wholly owned subsidiary of WIGC, GCC's primary asset, the web site, was purchased by WIGC pursuant to a corporate decision by WIGC's chief executive officer (CEO), respondent Mr. Burton. The use of the GCC casino web site was handled from WIGC's corporate headquarters. From WIGC's New York office, respondents also actively solicited investors to buy WIGC shares.

Subject Matter Jurisdiction and Application of New York Law

Respondents argue that the court lacks subject matter jurisdiction, and that Internet gambling falls outside the scope of New York State gambling prohibitions, because the gambling occurs outside of New York State. However, under New York Penal Law, if the person engaged in gambling is located in New York, then New York is the location where the gambling occurred (see, Penal Law § 225.00 [2]). Here, some or all of those funds in an Antiguan bank account are staked every time the New York user enters betting information into the computer. It is irrelevant that Internet gambling is legal in Antigua. The act of entering the bet and transmitting the information from New York via the Internet is adequate to constitute gambling activity within New York State.

Wide range implications would arise if this court adopted respondents' argument that activities or transactions which may be targeted at New York residents are beyond the State's jurisdiction. Not only would such an approach severely undermine this State's deep-rooted policy against unauthorized gambling, it also would immunize from liability anyone who engages in any activity over the Internet which is otherwise illegal in this State. A computer server cannot be permitted to function as a shield against liability, particularly in this case where respondents actively targeted New York as the location where they conducted many of their allegedly illegal activities. Even though gambling is legal where the bet was accepted, the activity was transmitted from New York. Contrary to respondents' unsupported allegation of an Antiguan management company managing GCC, the evidence also indicates that the individuals who gave the computer commands operated from WIGC's New York office. The respondents enticed Internet users, including New York residents, to play in their casino.

The evidence demonstrates that respondents have violated New York Penal Law which states that "[a] person is guilty of promoting gambling ... when he knowingly advances or profits from unlawful gambling activity" (Penal Law § 225.05). By having established the gambling enterprise, and advertised and solicited investors to buy its stock and to gamble through its on-line casino, respondents have "engage[d] in conduct which materially aids … gambling activity," in violation of New York law (Penal Law § 225.00 [4] [which states "conduct includes but is not limited to conduct directed toward the creation or establishment of the particular game, contest, scheme, device … (or) toward the solicitation or inducement of persons to participate therein"]).

Moreover, this court rejects respondents' argument that it unknowingly accepted bets from New York residents. New York users can easily circumvent the casino software in order to play by the simple expedient of entering an out-of-State address. Respondents' violation of the Penal Law is that they persisted in continuous illegal conduct directed toward the creation, establishment, and advancement of unauthorized gambling. The violation had occurred long before a New York resident ever staked a bet. Because all of respondents' activities illegally advanced gambling, this court finds that they have knowingly violated Penal Law § 225.05.

Key Words and Phrases

Bet
Child pornography
Distribution
Gambling business
Jurisdiction
Morphed images
Obscenity
Paraphernalia Act

Receipt or possession
Transmission of wager
Transportation
Travel Act
Virtual images
Wager
Wire Act

Review Problems

1. Describe the differences between the concept of obscenity and the concept of child pornography. Why do those differences exist?
2. What is the distinction between virtual images and morphed images? Why does the law criminalize the distribution and possession of one type but not the other?
3. Publication of material on the World Wide Web is much different than publication and distribution of a newspaper and magazine. Is the "contemporary community standards" portion of the obscenity test appropriate for Web publication?
4. Each year bills are introduced in Congress in an effort to more effectively combat online gambling. Each year those efforts fail. Why? Are current criminal laws adequate? How could they be made better?
5. Would the *World Interactive Gaming Corporation* case have been decided differently if corporate headquarters were not located in New York and if there was no control by WIGC over the casino in Antigua?

Weblinks

www.fbi.gov/innocent.htm
> This page on the Federal Bureau of Investigation website contains information on the FBI's Innocent Images Initiative child pornography program.

www.cops.usdoj.gov/mime/open.pdf?Item=1729
> This page contains a detailed report entitled "Child Pornography on the Internet." It is provided by the Office of Community Oriented Policing Services (COPS) of the U.S. Department of Justice.

www.ncpgambling.org/
> This is the website of the National Council on Problem Gambling. This site has general information on gambling, and on Internet gambling in particular.

www.jolt.unc.edu/Vol5_I1/web/Crisco%20v5i1.htm
> This page contains an excellent law review article focusing on efforts to regulate Internet gambling.

Endnotes

1. The indictment, which includes all of the factual allegations, can be found at http://news.findlaw.com/hdocs/docs/chldprn/usjhnsn62805ind.pdf.
2. See testimony of Laura Parsky, Esq., Deputy Assistant Attorney General, Criminal Division, Department of Justice, presented on January 19, 2006, before the Senate Committee on Commerce, Science and Transportation, available at www.usdoj.gov/criminal/ceos/DAAG%20Testimony%201192006.pdf.
3. See Gottfried, Jonathan. (2004). "The Federal Framework for Internet Gambling." 10 *Rich. J.L. & Tech.* 26, n. 7.
4. See *In re Mastercard Int'l. Inc.*, 132 F.Supp.2d 468 (ED La. 2001), *aff'd* 313 F.3d 257 (5th Cir. 2002).
5. See Comment. (2005). "Losing the Battle but Winning the War: The Federal Government's Attempts to Regulate Internet Gaming through Utilization of the Wire Act and Other Means." 74 *Miss. L.J.* 903, 906.

Crimes Threatening or Resulting in Physical or Mental Harm

4

Introduction

It is perhaps difficult to visualize the commission of a cybercrime that results in physical harm. However, there are many stories of individuals using the Internet to acquire chemicals that are subsequently used to commit a homicide. More directly, the incidences of cyberbullying and cyberharassment have increased significantly, particularly given the popularity of social networking sites.

In this chapter, the focus is on cyber activity that results in sexual conduct or the threat of such conduct toward a child, as well as cyberstalking and cyberharassment.

Sexual Predator Crimes

The following federal statute imposes criminal penalties upon those who solicit information regarding minors for the purpose of enticing or soliciting the minor to engage in sexual activity.

18 USC § 2425: Use of Interstate Facilities to Transmit Information about a Minor

Whoever, using the mail or any facility or means of interstate or foreign commerce, or within the special maritime and territorial jurisdiction of the United States, knowingly initiates the transmission of the name, address, telephone number, social security number, or electronic mail address of another individual, knowing that such other individual has not attained the age of 16 years, with the intent to entice, encourage, offer, or solicit any person to engage in any sexual activity for which any person can be charged with a criminal offense, or attempts to do so, shall be fined under this title, imprisoned not more than 5 years, or both.

What if the communication occurs completely within one state? Is that a "facility or means of interstate or foreign commerce"? The following case considered that issue:

United States v. Giordano

442 F.3D 30 (2006)

U.S. COURT OF APPEALS, SECOND CIRCUIT

SOTOMAYOR, Circuit Judge.

Philip A. Giordano appeals from a June 13, 2003 judgment of conviction and sentence entered after a jury trial before the United States District Court for the District of

Connecticut. Giordano, formerly the mayor of Waterbury, Connecticut, was convicted of two counts of civil rights violations under color of law in violation of 18 U.S.C. § 242, one count of conspiracy to use a facility of interstate commerce for the purpose of enticing a person under the age of sixteen years to engage in sexual activity in violation of 18 U.S.C. §§ 371 and 2425, and fourteen substantive counts of such use of a facility of interstate commerce in violation of § 2425. All of the convictions stem from Giordano's repeated sexual abuse of the minor daughter and niece of a prostitute.

BACKGROUND

Giordano's prosecution on the charges that led to this appeal grew out of an unrelated investigation by the FBI and IRS into political corruption in the city of Waterbury. Giordano, then mayor of Waterbury, was a target of this investigation. On February 18, 2001, the government obtained an order authorizing it to intercept phone communications of Giordano and other targets of the investigation. Between February and July of 2001, the government continued to monitor calls made to and from Giordano's city-issued cell phones, among others.

In the course of this surveillance, the government intercepted 151 calls on Giordano's cell phones to or from Guitana Jones, a prostitute with whom Giordano had a long-term sex-for-money relationship. On July 12, 2001, the government reviewed the contents of a brief July 9 call between Jones and Giordano that suggested that Jones was bringing a nine-year-old girl to Giordano for sex. In another, equally brief July 12 call, Giordano asked if Jones would have with her the nine-year-old or another female whose age was not discussed.

The government advised the district court, in filings on July 13 and 18, that it believed that Jones might be procuring for Giordano the sexual services of Jones' daughter and another minor female relative. On July 20, 2001, the government filed a criminal complaint against Jones charging her with violations of 18 U.S.C. §§ 371 and 2425 and obtained a warrant for her arrest. In the early hours of July 21, 2001, state authorities removed Jones' nine-year-old daughter (whom we refer to as "V1") and her eleven-year-old niece ("V2"), from the Jones household.

Giordano was tried before a jury from March 12 to March 24, 2003. In all, some fifty-three witnesses testified. The heart of the government's case was the testimony of Jones, V1 and V2, and the intercepted phone calls. Jones testified that she met Giordano well before his 1995 election to the mayor's office, when Giordano was a lawyer in private practice. From the time she first met him until the time of her arrest in 2001, she frequently had sex with Giordano in exchange for money, which she used to support her addiction to crack cocaine. She met him as often as two or three times a week, usually at his law office, and sometimes arranged for other women to come with her. Jones testified that in the summer of 2000, while he was mayor of Waterbury, Giordano asked her to bring "young girls" to perform sexual services. In response to this request, Jones brought several girls between the ages of fourteen and sixteen, including a niece, to perform oral sex on Giordano.

Jones claimed that similar episodes of oral sex for money began to occur with regularity, usually at Giordano's law office but occasionally at Jones' or Giordano's home or an apartment belonging to a friend of Giordano's. In almost every case, the appointments were arranged by telephone. On a school holiday in the winter of 2000–2001, the date of which Jones could not recall, she brought V1 and V2 to the mayor's office at

City Hall, entering through the back door. On that occasion, she directed both V1 and V2 to perform oral sex on Giordano. Jones testified that Giordano told her in a "calm voice" at the conclusion of this visit to "make sure the kids don't tell anyone [or] I'll get in trouble, I'll go to jail.... So I made sure they never said anything to anybody."

V1 and V2 testified at trial via closed-circuit television from another room in which the government attorney and defense counsel were present. Their testimony substantially corroborated Jones' as to the nature of the acts they performed, the places they performed the acts, and the warnings they received in each instance from Jones and Giordano.

The government also introduced 133 of the 151 wiretapped phone conversations between Giordano and Jones, including recordings corresponding to the particular phone conversations alleged in the indictment. Some of these calls corroborated Jones' testimony that Giordano sometimes explicitly requested that the girls be present and that he vehemently rejected offers to have Jones' 16-year-old niece come instead. The government adduced expert evidence that all of the calls were made on phones that were connected to the Public Switching Telephone Network, which is capable of transmitting phone signals between states. The evidence showed that the actual calls described in counts four through nine of the indictment, which were placed from and to Giordano's Nextel cellular phone, would necessarily have been routed through a switching center in White Plains, New York. The signals that constituted the calls described in counts eleven through eighteen of the indictment originated from or were received on a Cingular cellular phone and would not have left the State of Connecticut.

DISCUSSION

As noted above, counts four through nine and eleven through eighteen of the indictment alleged that on fourteen specified dates between February 23 and July 12, 2001, Giordano and Jones used a cellular telephone and a landline telephone, respectively, to initiate the knowing transmission of the name of either V1 or V2 or both with the intent to solicit, entice, encourage, and offer them to engage in sexual activity. The third count of the indictment alleged that Giordano conspired to violate the statute. The evidence adduced at trial showed that all of these calls were made while both Giordano and Jones were within the State of Connecticut. Giordano argues that § 2425 must be understood not to reach phone calls from one person in a given state to another person in the same state—what he terms "intrastate calls"—and that if the statute is understood to reach such calls, it exceeds Congress's power under the Commerce Clause, U.S. Const. Art. I, § 8, cl. 3, as that power has been defined by the Supreme Court in *Jones v. United States*, 529 U.S. 848, 120 S.Ct. 1904, 146 L.Ed.2d 902 (2000), *United States v. Morrison*, 529 U.S. 598, 120 S.Ct. 1740, 146 L.Ed.2d 658 (2000), and *United States v. Lopez*, 514 U.S. 549, 115 S.Ct. 1624, 131 L.Ed.2d 626 (1995). He therefore argues that the district court erred in denying his repeated motions to dismiss the indictment and in instructing the jury that they could convict Giordano of the phone counts if they found that the cellular phones were capable of transmitting communications from one state to another.

We address the issue of statutory interpretation first. The phrase "any facility or means of interstate ... commerce" is not defined for purposes of § 2425 or the chapter of which it is a part. See generally 18 U.S.C. §§ 2421–2426. Recently, however, in *United States v. Perez*, 414 F.3d 302, 304 (2d Cir.2005), we reached the unremarkable conclusion that the national telephone network is a "facility of interstate ... commerce" for purposes of the federal murder-for-hire statute, 18 U.S.C. § 1958(b)(2). We see no reason why the result should be different here. We also conclude that § 2425's prohibition on the transmission of the name of a minor "using … any facility or means of interstate … commerce" for the specified purposes includes the intrastate use of such a facility or means. In *Perez*, we addressed a related question that has divided the circuit courts: whether an intrastate phone call was sufficient to satisfy the jurisdictional element of a prior version of the murder-for-hire statute, 18 U.S.C. § 1958(a), which prohibited "use[ ]" of a "facility in interstate … commerce" for specified purposes. Joining the circuits that had held that the term "facility in interstate … commerce" was synonymous with the term "facility of interstate … commerce" in the definition section of the same statute, 18 U.S.C. § 1958(b)(2), we concluded that intrastate use of the telephone constituted use of a facility of interstate commerce within the meaning of the statute. *Perez*, 414 F.3d at 304 and *United States v. Marek*, 238 F.3d 310, 315-23 (5th Cir.2001). Likewise, § 2425, which unambiguously requires only that a "facility or means of interstate … commerce" be used in the proscribed manner, is satisfied by purely intrastate use of that facility.

We turn now to Giordano's challenge to the constitutionality of § 2425 as we have interpreted it. In *United States v. Lopez*, 514 U.S. 549, 115 S.Ct. 1624, 131 L.Ed.2d 626 (1995), the Supreme Court identified three categories of activity that Congress may regulate under the Commerce Clause: First, Congress may regulate the use of the channels of interstate commerce. Second, Congress is empowered to regulate and protect the instrumentalities of interstate commerce, or persons or things in interstate commerce, even though the threat may come only from intrastate activities. Finally, Congress' commerce authority includes the power to regulate those activities having a substantial relation to interstate commerce, i.e., those activities that substantially affect interstate commerce. Id. at 558–59, 115 S.Ct. 1624. The statute at issue in *Lopez* fell into the third category. The Court there held that the Gun-Free School Zones Act, 18 U.S.C. § 922(q), exceeded Congress's authority because it criminalized non-economic activity that did not "substantially affect" interstate commerce. Similarly, in *Morrison*, which concerned a provision of the Violence Against Women Act that provided civil remedies for gender-motivated violence, 42 U.S.C. § 13981, the Court held that Congress could not, under the third *Lopez* category, "regulate noneconomic, violent criminal conduct based solely on that conduct's aggregate effect on interstate commerce." 529 U.S. at 617, 120 S.Ct. 1740. In *Jones*, the Court considered whether the term "property used in … any activity affecting interstate or foreign commerce" as employed in the federal arson statute, 18 U.S.C. § 844(i), reached a private dwelling. 529 U.S. at 858, 120 S.Ct. 1904. In reliance on *Lopez* and the principle that an ambiguous statute should be read to avoid doubtful constitutional questions, the Court held that it did not. Id. As the language of the statute and the Court's reliance on *Lopez* make clear, *Jones* too was a *Lopez* "category three" case, concerned with Congress's power to regulate activities having a substantial effect on interstate commerce.

It is certainly true, as Giordano argues, that these cases impose limits on Congress's power to create federal criminal prohibitions on traditionally state-regulated spheres of noneconomic activity. But his attempt to bring this line of cases to bear on § 2425 overlooks the fact that § 2425, which explicitly proscribes "us[e of] the mail or any facility or means of interstate … commerce" to specified ends, is clearly founded on the second type of Commerce Clause power categorized in *Lopez*, that is, the power to regulate and protect the instrumentalities of interstate commerce "even though the threat may only come from intrastate activities." *Lopez*, 514 U.S. at 558, 115 S.Ct. 1624. It is well-established that when Congress legislates pursuant to this branch of its Commerce Clause power, it may regulate even purely intrastate use of those instrumentalities. Application of § 2425 to the conduct involved in this case therefore presents no constitutional difficulties.

Congress continues the effort to deter and prosecute the conduct of sexual predators of children. In August 2006, the House of Representatives overwhelmingly (410–15) passed the Delete Online Predators Act (DOPA). The proposed act would expand the Child Internet Protection Act (CIPA), which requires libraries that receive federal funding to install filters on computer terminals to prevent access to child pornography. DOPA would require libraries and public schools (K–12) to prohibit access to minors to social networking sites such as MySpace.com or chat rooms unless the minor's access is supervised by an adult and is conducted for educational purposes.

Cyberstalking and Cyberharassment Legislation

Federal Statutes

18 USC § 2261A: Stalking
This statute criminalizes conduct by a person who

(1) travels in interstate or foreign commerce or within the special maritime and territorial jurisdiction of the United States, or enters or leaves Indian country, with the intent to kill, injure, harass, or intimidate another person, and in the course of, or as a result of, such travel places that person in reasonable fear of the death of, or serious bodily injury to, that person, a member of the immediate family (as defined in section 115) of that person, or the spouse or intimate partner of that person; or
(2) with the intent—
   (A) to kill or injure a person in another State or tribal jurisdiction or within the special maritime and territorial jurisdiction of the United States; or
   (B) to place a person in another State or tribal jurisdiction, or within the special maritime and territorial jurisdiction of the United States, in reasonable fear of the death of, or serious bodily injury to—
      (i) that person;
      (ii) a member of the immediate family (as defined in section 115) of that person; or
      (iii) a spouse or intimate partner of that person;
(3) uses the mail or any facility of interstate or foreign commerce to engage in a course of conduct that places that person in reasonable fear of the death of, or serious bodily injury to, any of the persons described in clauses (i) through (iii).

18 USC § 875: Interstate Communications

This federal statute makes it a crime for a person who

(b) Whoever, with intent to extort from any person, firm, association, or corporation, any money or other thing of value, transmits in interstate or foreign commerce any communication containing any threat to kidnap any person or any threat to injure the person of another, shall be fined under this title or imprisoned not more than twenty years, or both.

(c) Whoever transmits in interstate or foreign commerce any communication containing any threat to kidnap any person or any threat to injure the person of another, shall be fined under this title or imprisoned not more than five years, or both.

(d) Whoever, with intent to extort from any person, firm, association, or corporation, any money or other thing of value, transmits in interstate or foreign commerce any communication containing any threat to injure the property or reputation of the addressee or of another or the reputation of a deceased person or any threat to accuse the addressee or any other person of a crime.

47 USC § 223: Obscene or Harassing Telephone Calls in the District of Columbia or in Interstate or Foreign Communications

Subsection (a)(1), which is part of the Communication Decency Act, makes it a crime commonly known as cyberharassment for a person who

(C) makes a telephone call or utilizes a telecommunications device, whether or not conversation or communication ensues, without disclosing his identity and with intent to annoy, abuse, threaten, or harass any person at the called number or who receives the communications;

(D) makes or causes the telephone of another repeatedly or continuously to ring, with intent to harass any person at the called number; or

(E) makes repeated telephone calls or repeatedly initiates communication with a telecommunications device, during which conversation or communication ensues, solely to harass any person at the called number or who receives the communication; or

(2) knowingly permits any telecommunications facility under his control to be used for any activity prohibited by paragraph (1) with the intent that it be used for such activity.

Cases on Cyberstalking and Cyberharassment

Judicial Interpretations of Federal Law

United States v. Bowker

372 F.3D 365 (2004)

U.S. COURT OF APPEALS, SIXTH CIRCUIT

OPINION: CLAY, Circuit Judge.

Defendant-Appellant Erik S. Bowker appeals his convictions and sentence for one count of interstate stalking, in violation of 18 U.S.C. § 2261A(1); one count of cyberstalking, in violation of 18 U.S.C. § 2261A(2); one count of theft of mail, in violation of 18 U.S.C. § 1708; and one count of telephone harassment, in violation of 47 U.S.C. § 223(a)(1)(C).

Facts

In March 2000, Tina Knight began working as a part-time general assignment reporter at WKBN Television in Youngstown, Ohio. WKBN has a general email account for most employees, and in June, 2000, WKBN received a number of emails relating to Knight. The emails were sent from several different email addresses and purported to be from an individual variously identified as "User x," Eric Neubauer, Karen Walters, and "BB." Several of the emails attached photographs with verbal captions. One caption referred to Knight being shot with a pellet gun, and another email said, "Thanks for my daily Tina Knight fix. Thanks for helping me get my nuts off," and another said "More Tina Knight, that is what I want and need." After receiving approximately nine of these types of email, WKBN's news director took them to the station's general manager. They then contacted Special Agent Deane Hassman of the FBI. Soon thereafter, Knight was shown the emails, and she was stunned and frightened.

FBI Agent Hassman began investigating the Tina Knight emails in July 2000. Hassman was concerned about Knight's personal safety based on the content of the emails. One of the emails that concerned Hassman stated, "I'm not the type of obsessed viewer that hides in the bushes near your home to watch you come home from work, but we shall see. That may actually be fun." Another disturbing email stated, in part, "Dear Ms. Knight. Now I'm really pissed that you were looking even cuter than normally. You fucked up a little bit and here I am watching on this black and white thrift store TV. Cute, cute, cute. I bet you were a Ho at Ohio University in Athens, doing chicks and everything. Wow."

On July 25, 2000, Hassman sent emails to the various email addresses on the correspondence pertaining to Knight. Hassman asked the sender of the emails to contact him so that he could determine the sender's intent. Within 24 to 48 hours, Hassman received a telephone call from an individual who identified himself as Erik Bowker. Hassman wanted to set up a meeting with Bowker so Hassman could positively identify the sender of the emails and also ask him to cease and desist from contacting Knight. They arranged to meet at the public library in Youngstown, but Bowker never showed.

A few weeks later, Knight began receiving hand-written notes at WKBN, the majority of which were signed by "Doug Wagner." By September, the letters were arriving at the station almost every couple of days. One of the letters included the phrase, "All this week I will be playing the role of Doug Wagner." A letter dated August 9, 2000 was signed "Chad Felton"; stated, "I think you are a super babe"; and included a necklace. The return addresses on the letters were one of two P.O. Boxes registered to Erik Bowker or his mother.

Knight left her employment at WKBN in November 2000 to take a position at WOWK CBS13 in Charleston, West Virginia. WKBN did not inform the general public of Knight's new location.

In late December 2000, Knight's parents, who reside in Medina, Ohio, received a card and a handwritten note at their home. The card purported to be from "Kathryn Harris." The letter read, "Dear Tina Knight: I am Kathryn Harris today. I didn't want your parents asking you a lot of questions, nor did I want to attract a lot of attention to you. My letters to you are all online at yahoo.com in a standard mail account. It is all explained there so please check in and read what I have written… The E-mail address is tinahatesme@yahoo.com." Agent Hassman visited the email address to check if any letters had been sent to the email address mentioned in the letter. Hassman discovered that an email had been sent December 25, 2000. At the end of the email, the name "Doug Wagner" was typed. The email read, in part, "I told you I would not contact you by mail anymore but I am sorry, I am in agony. I'm thinking about you all the time. You really are my dream girl… I am blinded with affection for you. I did not ask for this. Nope, it's all your fault… Please don't cat dance on my emotions by failing to respond to me at all."

In February 2001, Bowker filed a lawsuit against Knight in the Mahoning County Common Pleas Court. Knight's social security number was stated in the complaint, which was served at Knight's home address in West Virginia. Bowker's lawsuit accused Knight of stalking him. Agent Hassman attended a status conference for the lawsuit on March 16, 2001, so that he could make face-to-face contact with Bowker. After meeting Bowker at the hearing and confirming that Bowker had been sending the unsolicited correspondence to Knight, Hassman told Bowker that the correspondence was unwelcome and might be a violation of federal law. Hassman advised Bowker that if the conduct continued, it might result in his arrest. Bowker responded that he had a First Amendment right to engage in that type of conduct. Nevertheless, during the meeting, Bowker wrote and signed a note stating, "I understand that Tina M. Knight wishes all further contact with her or any family member to stop and I agree to do so, pursuant to conversation with Deane Hassman, special agent, Federal Bureau of Investigation …." Bowker also agreed to voluntarily dismiss his lawsuit against Knight.

Despite Bowker's March 16, 2001 agreement to cease and desist from any further contact with Knight, on that very same day, Bowker mailed a letter to Knight. Bowker also continued to attempt telephone contact with Knight. Between January 26 and August 29, 2001, Bowker made 146 telephone calls from his cell phone to WOWK CBS 13, where Knight worked. Bowker also made 16 calls to Knight's personal residential telephone in West Virginia between August 11 and 28, 2001. Knight's number was unlisted and unpublished. According to telephone records, each of the 16 calls placed to Knight's home were preceded by *67, which enables a caller to block identification of his telephone number on the recipient's caller identification display. Bowker also called Knight's co-worker and a neighbor.

As the telephone calls to Knight's television station persisted through the summer of 2001, Agent Hassman believed it was important to capture Bowker's voice on tape, so Hassman provided Knight with a recording device at the television station. On June 12, 2001, Knight recorded a 45-minute telephone call from Bowker who, at one point, identified himself as "Mike." During the conversation, Bowker referred to Knight's neighbors, her family members and her social security number. He also indicated he might be watching Knight with his binoculars. Knight provided the tape to the FBI and never spoke to Bowker again on the telephone.

On July 16, 2001, Knight received a letter at the television station. In the letter, Bowker referred to Knight's parents and stated several times, "You do not hang up on me." The letter also crassly referred to Knight's car, threatened to file a mechanic's lien on her car and her co-worker's car, accused Knight and her colleague of being "fuck-ups, assholes and seriously emotional and mentally unbalanced," and contained numerous sexual references. The letter stated that Bowker would be contacting Knight's neigh-bors, pointed out that Knight had not registered her car in West Virginia, and con-cluded with the words, "So bye-by, fuck you, you are an asshole and a sociopath and an embarrassment to mothers everywhere sir… Adios, Eric… Smooch, Smooch."

On August 10, 2001, Knight received a certified letter mailed to her residence in West Virginia. Accompanying the letter were numerous photographs of Bowker at various locations in West Virginia, Knight's home state. The letter stated, in part, "Send me an E-Mail address. It keeps me long distance, you know what I mean." Knight forwarded the letter and the photographs to the FBI. Bowker's credit card statement later revealed purchases from a Kmart and a Kroger near Knight's place of employment and resi-dence in West Virginia between June 12 and July 30, 2001.

In August 2001, Bowker left a series of messages on Knight's answering machine asking that Knight or Knight's friend call him back, which did not occur. Among other things, Bowker stated:

I don't even know why I'm nice to you ever at all, you and your fucked-up friend should not even be working in the media. You know you gotta mother-fucking realize there's like 50 per-cent men in this country and you better mother-fucking learn that you're going to have to deal with us sometime…

Well, it looks like nobody is going to answer me if Tina Knight is okay, so I'm gonna take the 1:00 a.m. bus out of Columbus, Ohio and come down there and see for myself. Okay, I'll be there about 6:00 a.m. Bye.

Knight testified that these messages made her afraid to leave the house every day, and she feared that Bowker might try to rape her. She gave the answering machine record-ings to the FBI.

Bowker was arrested on August 29, 2001 at a self-storage facility in Youngstown where he kept some of his possessions. Among other things recovered from the storage facility, Bowker's car and other locations, were a police scanner set to the frequency of the Youngstown Police Department, a paper with scanner frequencies from the Dunbar, West Virginia Police Department, letters bearing the name "Chad Felton," a credit report for Tina Knight, Knight's birth certificate, a map of Dunbar, West Virginia, Greyhound bus schedules with West Virginia routes, and photos taken by Bowker during a West Virginia trip on July 11, 2001, which included pictures of Knight's place of work, her car and CBS news trucks. The FBI also discovered that Bowker had in his possession a Discover Card credit card bill addressed to Tina Knight in West Virginia. Knight never received that statement in the mail.

[The Court first considered and concluded that probable cause existed for Bowker's Arrest.]

Motion to Dismiss Counts 1, 2 and 4 of the Indictment

Bowker argues that the district court erred in failing to dismiss Counts 1 (interstate stalking), 2 (cyberstalking) and 4 (telephone harassment) of the indictment on the ground that the indictment inadequately alleged the elements of the offenses charged, and on the ground that the statutes that the indictment alleged he violated are uncon-stitutionally vague and overbroad.

A. Sufficiency of the Indictment

Count1 (interstate stalking), Count 2 (cyberstalking) and Count 4 (telephone harassment) track the language of the relevant statutes. Count 1 alleges that, between July 10 and July 30, 2001, Bowker knowingly and intentionally traveled across the Ohio state line with the intent to injure, harass, and intimidate Tina Knight, and as a result of such travel placed Knight in reasonable fear of death or serious bodily injury, in violation of 18 U.S.C. § 2261A(1). Count 2 alleges that between December 25, 2000 and August 18, 2001 Bowker, located in Ohio, knowingly and repeatedly used the Internet to engage in a course of conduct that intentionally placed Knight, then located in West Virginia, in reasonable fear of death or serious bodily injury, in violation of 18 U.S.C. § 2261A(2). Count 4 alleges that between June 12, 2001, and August 27, 2001, Bowker, located in Ohio, knowingly made telephone calls, whether or not conversation or communication ensued, without disclosing his identity and with the intent to annoy, abuse, threaten and harass Knight, in violation of 47 U.S.C. § 223(a)(1)(C). Because the indictment stated all of the statutory elements of the offenses, and because the relevant statutes state the elements unambiguously, the district court properly denied Bowker's motion to dismiss Counts 1, 2 and 4 of the indictment. The indictment's reference to the specific dates and locations of the offenses, as well as the means used to carry them out (travel, Internet, telephone), provided Bowker fair notice of the conduct with which he was being charged.

Bowker argues that the indictment was defective because it does not charge him with making direct threats against Knight and therefore should have contained a statement of facts and circumstances surrounding the alleged indirect threats he made against her, such as an explanation of the parties' relationship. See *Landham*, 251 F.3d at 1080 (holding "because the alleged threatening statement must be viewed from the objective perspective of the recipient, which frequently involves the context of the parties' relationship…, it is incumbent on the Government to make that context clear in such an indictment, unless the alleged threat is direct").

All of the statutory elements of the prohibited conduct were properly alleged, including the intent to cause a reasonable fear of death or serious bodily harm. Bowker's relationship with Knight had no relevant bearing on the alleged illegality of his conduct. We therefore reject Bowker's challenge to the sufficiency of the indictment.

B. Overbreadth Challenge

Bowker has provided absolutely no argument as to how 18 U.S.C. § 2261A, which prohibits interstate stalking and cyberstalking, is facially overbroad, merely asserting that the statute "reaches large amounts of protected speech and conduct" and "potentially targets political or religious speech." We fail to see how a law that prohibits interstate travel with the intent to kill, injure, harass or intimidate has a substantial sweep of constitutionally protected conduct. 18 U.S.C. § 2261A(1). The same is true with respect to the prohibition of intentionally using the Internet in a course of conduct that places a person in reasonable fear of death or serious bodily injury. 18 U.S.C. § 2261A(2). It is difficult to imagine what constitutionally-protected political or religious speech would fall under these statutory prohibitions. Most, if not all, of these laws' legal applications are to conduct that is not protected by the First Amendment. Thus, Bowker has failed to demonstrate how 18 U.S.C. § 2261A is substantially overbroad.

C. Vagueness Challenge

"Even if an enactment does not reach a substantial amount of constitutionally protected conduct, it may be impermissibly vague because it fails to establish standards for the police and public that are sufficient to guard against the arbitrary deprivation of liberty interests." *Morales*, 527 U.S. at 52 (citing *Kolender v. Lawson*, 461 U.S. 352, 358, 75 L. Ed. 2d 903, 103 S. Ct. 1855 (1983)). Vagueness may invalidate a criminal statute if it either (1) fails "to provide the kind of notice that will enable ordinary people to understand what conduct it prohibits" or (2) authorizes or encourages "arbitrary and discriminatory enforcement." Id. at 56 (citing *Kolender*, 461 U.S. at 357). "It is established that a law fails to meet the requirements of the Due Process Clause if it is so vague and standardless that it leaves the public uncertain as to the conduct it prohibits...." *Giaccio v. Pennsylvania*, 382 U.S. 399, 402–03, 15 L. Ed. 2d 447, 86 S. Ct. 518 (1966).

The stalking and telephone harassment statutes charged in Bowker's indictment provide sufficient notice of their respective prohibitions because citizens need not guess what terms such as "harass" and "intimidate" mean.

Motion for a Judgment of Acquittal as to Counts 1, 2 and 4

Bowker challenges the district court's failure to grant his motion for a judgment of acquittal on Counts 1, 2 and 4 of the indictment, pursuant to Rule 29 of the Federal Rules of Criminal Procedure. For the reasons that follow, we affirm the judgment of the district court.

B. Interstate Stalking Count

Count 1 of the indictment charges Bowker with interstate stalking, in violation of 18 U.S.C. § 2261A(1). The government was required to prove:

(1) that the defendant traveled in interstate or foreign commerce;
(2) with the intent to kill, injure, harass, or intimidate another person; and
(3) in the course of, or as a result of, such travel places that person in reasonable fear of the death of, or serious bodily injury to, that person, a member of the immediate family of that person, or the spouse or intimate partner of that person.

Bowker argues that the government did not prove, pursuant to the interstate stalking count, that the "result of" Bowker's travel from Ohio to West Virginia in July 2001, was to put Knight in reasonable fear of her life or bodily injury, because Knight did not learn of Bowker's travels until August 2001, after he had completed his travel. This argument is specious. Knight learned of Bowker's travel to West Virginia because he sent her numerous photographs informing her that he had been in the state the preceding month. Accompanying the photographs was the statement, "Take the photos out to read the backs of them. Send me an E-mail address. It keeps me long distance, you know what I mean." The clear implication of this statement was that Bowker would continue to communicate with Knight, unless she provided him with her email address. The jury was entitled to infer that this statement, combined with the photographs of Bowker at various locations in West Virginia, was intended to intimidate Knight by showing her that Bowker had traveled to her state and would do so in the future. The statute did not require the government to show that Bowker actually intended to harass or intimidate Knight during his travels, only that the result of the travel was a reasonable apprehension of fear in the victim. Since Knight testified that she was afraid that Bowker might rape her, and her fear seemed reasonable, the government proved all of the elements of the interstate stalking count.

C. Cyberstalking Count

Count 2 of the indictment charges Bowker with cyberstalking, in violation of 18 U.S.C. § 2261A(2). The government was required to prove:

(1) Bowker intentionally used the mail or any facility of interstate or foreign commerce;
(2) Bowker engaged in a course of conduct with the intent to place Knight in reasonable fear of death of, or serious bodily injury to, herself, her spouse or intimate partner, or a member of her immediate family; and
(3) Bowker's course of conduct actually placed Knight in reasonable fear of death of, or serious bodily injury to, herself.

The evidence shows that Bowker intended to instill in Knight a fear of death or serious bodily harm through use of the mails and other facilities of interstate commerce, required elements of the cyberstalking count. During a June 12, 2001 telephone conversation with Knight, Bowker told her:

You don't know where I'm at. I might be in your house in Dunbar[, West Virginia]; you don't know that... I know all of your neighbors... And I have access to all that information, just like anybody else does who knows where to find it. I have an enormous amount of things about you that I'm not going to disclose unless I have to. I'm not going to tell anybody about it except if you lie to me. I might not say anything to you at the time, but that might come back, you know... I know the names of all your relatives and where they live... I know your brothers' wives['] names, their ages, their Social Security numbers and their birth dates ... and their property values... Maybe I live on 20th street in Dunbar... Maybe I watch you with binoculars all the time and maybe I don't.

A July 16, 2001 letter that Bowker sent to Knight at the television station had both sexual and threatening connotations. It read, in part:

No. 1. You do not hang up on me.
No. 2. You do not hang up on me, ever.
No. 3. If and when I call CBS 13 asking about a news story that you reported on, you do not hang up on me. You must at least do the bare minimum and answer my news related questions.

I know what you value most in life, your bullshit fake ass 1997 Pontiac Grand Am, which is about top on your list as well as two other things. As far as the Grand Am is concerned, say good-bye to it. I am going to file a mechanics lien on it immediately and later seek civil forfeiture.

All that you ... would have to do is be polite, be nice, and answer my news-related questions, just like the rest of the reporters, except your buddy April Kaull. I'm going to file a lien on her vehicle too. You are both fuck-ups, assholes and seriously emotionally and mentally unbalanced...

Also, WOWK will hire just about anyone. Or at least a pretty girl reporter, as long as she does her hair and makeup well...

That vehicle is exemplary of you, pretty on the outside and very worthless inside. You have female genitals and that is about it. You are a very slander to the word woman. Oh, yeah, you dress like one but so do transvestites. I think I would rather spend the evening with a pretty transvestite than with you...

Anyhow, I also think that it is time for your neighbors to get to know you better and I will be making attempts to inform them about how the prima donna from Ohio things [sic] she can eat from the top and throw her garbage on the sidewalk of West Virginia and Dunbar...

I also noticed that you already had the job and residence in West Virginia when you had your Ohio License plates renewed, for one year anyhow...

So bye-bye, fuck you, you are an asshole and a sociopath and an embarrassment to mothers everywhere, sir. In parenthesis: (I wasn't bringing up the mental case thing again since it is genetic.)

Yes, sir. Adios, Eric [sic]. Smooch. Smooch.

In August 2001, Bowker left a series of messages on Knight's answering machine asking that Knight or Knight's friend call him back, which did not occur. These messages contained statements that Knight reasonably could perceive to be threats to her personal safety. Excerpts include the following statements:

I don't even know why I'm nice to you ever at all, you and your fucked-up friend should not even be working in the media. You know you gotta mother-fucking realize there's like 50 percent men in this country and you better mother-fucking learn that you're going to have to deal with us sometime...

Well, it looks like nobody is going to answer me if Tina Knight is okay, so I'm gonna take the 1:00 a.m. bus out of Columbus, Ohio and come down there and see for myself. Okay, I'll be there about 6:00 a.m. Bye.

Since Knight testified that these intentionally intimidating, threatening and harassing interstate communications made her afraid to leave the house every day and that Bowker might try to rape her, the government proved all of the elements of the cyberstalking count.

United States v. Alkhabaz

104 F.3D 1492 (1997)

U.S. Ct. of Appeals, Sixth Circuit

OPINION BY BOYCE F. MARTIN, JR., Chief Judge.

Claiming that the district court erred in determining that certain electronic mail messages between Abraham Jacob Alkhabaz, a.k.a. Jake Baker, and Arthur Gonda did not constitute "true threats," the government appeals the dismissal of the indictment charging Baker with violations of 18 U.S.C. § 875(c).

From November 1994 until approximately January 1995, Baker and Gonda exchanged e-mail messages over the Internet, the content of which expressed a sexual interest in violence against women and girls. Baker sent and received messages through a computer in Ann Arbor, Michigan, while Gonda—whose true identity and where-abouts are still unknown—used a computer in Ontario, Canada.

Prior to this time, Baker had posted a number of fictional stories to "alt.sex. stories," a popular interactive Usenet news group. Using such shorthand references as "B&D," "snuff," "pedo," "mf," and "nc," Baker's fictional stories generally involved the abduction, rape, torture, mutilation, and murder of women and young girls. On January 9, Baker posted a story describing the torture, rape, and murder of a young woman who shared the name of one of Baker's classmates at the University of Michigan.

On February 9, Baker was arrested and appeared before a United States Magistrate Judge on a criminal complaint alleging violations of 18 U.S.C. § 875 (c), which prohibits interstate communications containing threats to kidnap or injure another person. The government made the complaint based on an FBI agent's affidavit, which cited language from the story involving Baker's classmate.

On February 14, a federal grand jury returned a one-count indictment charging Baker with a violation of 18 U.S.C. § 875(c). On March 15, 1995, citing several e-mail messages between Gonda and Baker, a federal grand jury returned a superseding indictment, charging Baker and Gonda with five counts of violations of 18 U.S.C. § 875(c). The e-mail messages supporting the superseding indictment were not available in any publicly accessible portion of the Internet.

On April 15, Baker filed a Motion to Quash Indictment with the district court. In *United States v. Baker*, 890 F. Supp. 1375, 1381 (E.D. Mich. 1995), the district court dismissed the indictment against Baker, reasoning that the e-mail messages sent and received by Baker and Gonda did not constitute "true threats" under the First Amendment and, as such, were protected speech. The government argues that the district court erred in dismissing the indictment because the communications between Gonda and Baker do constitute "true threats" and, as such, do not implicate First Amendment free speech protections. In response, Baker urges this Court to adopt the reasoning of the district court and affirm the dismissal of the indictment against him.

Neither the district court's opinion, nor the parties' briefs contain any discussion regarding whether Baker's e-mail messages initially satisfy the requirements of Section 875(c). For the reasons stated below, we conclude that the indictment failed, as a matter of law, to allege violations of Section 875(c). Accordingly, we decline to address the First Amendment issues raised by the parties.

Title 18, United States Code, Section 875(c) states:

> Whoever transmits in interstate or foreign commerce any communication containing any threat to kidnap any person or any threat to injure the person of another, shall be fined under this title or imprisoned not more than five years, or both.

The government must allege and prove three elements to support a conviction under Section 875(c): "(1) a transmission in interstate [or foreign] commerce; (2) a communication containing a threat; and (3) the threat must be a threat to injure [or kidnap] the person of another." *DeAndino*, 958 F.2d at 148. In this case, the first and third elements cannot be seriously challenged by the defendant. However, the second element raises several issues that this Court must address.

Although its language does not specifically contain a *mens rea* element, this Court has interpreted Section 875(c) as requiring only general intent. *DeAndino*, 958 F.2d at

148-50. Accordingly, Section 875(c) requires proof that a reasonable person would have taken the defendant's statement as "a serious expression of an intention to inflict bodily harm." Id. at 148.

Additionally, Section 875(c) does not clearly define an *actus reus*. The language of Section 875(c) prohibits the transmission of "any communication containing any threat to kidnap any person or any threat to injure the person of another."

Accordingly, to achieve the intent of Congress, we hold that, to constitute "a communication containing a threat" under Section 875(c), a communication must be such that a reasonable person (1) would take the statement as a serious expression of an intention to inflict bodily harm (the *mens rea*), and (2) would perceive such expression as being communicated to effect some change or achieve some goal through intimidation (the *actus reus*).

The dissent argues that Congress did not intend to include as an element of the crime the furthering of some goal through the use of intimidation. Emphasizing the term "any" in the language of the statute, the dissent maintains that Congress did not limit the scope of communications that constitutes criminal threats. While we agree that Congress chose inclusive language to identify the types of threats that it intended to prohibit, we cannot ignore the fact that Congress intended to forbid only those communications that in fact constitute a "threat." The conclusion that we reach here is one that the term "threat" necessarily implies.

It is important to note that we are not expressing a subjective standard. This Court has held that the *mens rea* element of a Section 875(c) violation must be determined objectively. The rationale for applying an objective standard to establish the *mens rea* element of a Section 875(c) violation is equally as compelling with regard to establishing the *actus reus* element. Accordingly, for reasons expressed in *DeAndino*, the *actus reus* element of a Section 875(c) violation must be determined objectively, from the perspective of the receiver.

Applying our interpretation of the statute to the facts before us, we conclude that the communications between Baker and Gonda do not constitute "communications containing a threat" under Section 875(c). Even if a reasonable person would take the communications between Baker and Gonda as serious expressions of an intention to inflict bodily harm, no reasonable person would perceive such communications as being conveyed to effect some change or achieve some goal through intimidation. Quite the opposite, Baker and Gonda apparently sent e-mail messages to each other in an attempt to foster a friendship based on shared sexual fantasies.

For the foregoing reasons, the judgment of the district court is affirmed.

KRUPANSKY, Circuit Judge, dissenting.

The panel majority has ruled that an interstate or international "communication containing any threat" to kidnap or injure another person is criminalized by 18 U.S.C. § 875(c) only when the subject communication was conveyed with the general intent "to effect some change or achieve some goal through intimidation." The majority concludes that because the instant indictment alleges only communications purportedly intended to foster a perverse camaraderie between the correspondents, rather than "to effect some change or realize some goal through intimidation," the indictment must be dismissed because each count fails to allege an essential element of a section 875(c) charge. Because the majority has intruded upon Congressional prerogatives by judicially legislating an exogenous element into section 875(c) that materially alters the plain language and purpose of that section and ignores the prevailing precedents of the Supreme Court and this circuit, I respectfully dissent from the majority's decision.

The words in section 875(c) are simple, clear, concise, and unambiguous. The plain, expressed statutory language commands only that the alleged communication must contain any threat to kidnap or physically injure any person, made for any reason or no reason. Section 875(c) by its terms does not confine the scope of criminalized communications to those directed to identified individuals and intended to effect some particular change or goal. This circuit has already considered and decided the meaning of section 875(c) in *United States v. DeAndino*, 958 F.2d 146, 148 (6th Cir.), cert. denied, 505 U.S. 1206, 120 L. Ed. 2d 874, 112 S. Ct. 2997 (1992), a decision in which a member of this panel concurred, wherein it defined, to the exclusion of "intimidation," the three essential elements under 18 U.S.C. § 875(c):

(1) a transmission in interstate [or foreign] commerce;
(2) a communication containing a threat; and
(3) the threat must be a threat to injure the person of another[.]

By contrast to section 875(c), a companion statutory provision, 18 U.S.C. § 875(b), criminalizes similar communications made with the intent to extort money or other value, coupled with more severe penalties than those appertaining to a threat illegalized by section 875(c):

Whoever, with intent to extort from any person, firm, association, or corporation, any money or other thing of value, transmits in interstate or foreign commerce any communication containing any threat to kidnap any person or any threat to injure the person of another, shall be fined under this title or imprisoned not more than twenty years, or both.

18 U.S.C. § 875(b)

Patently, Congress sought to punish all interstate or international communications containing a threat to kidnap or injure any person; such communications accompanied by an intent to extort value (section 875(b)) could be punished more severely than those which are not coupled with the intent to extort (section 875(c)). If Congress, by enacting section 875(c), had desired to proscribe only those threats intended by the maker to intimidate someone, it could have clearly accomplished that result as it did under section 875(b) wherein it directed that threats under that subsection must be issued with the intent to extort value. See also 18 U.S.C. § 875(d) (outlawing interstate or transnational communications, made with intent to extort money or other value, which threaten to injure the property or reputation of another or threaten to accuse another of a crime); cf. 18 U.S.C. §§ 248(a), 876, and 877.

Although some reported threat convictions have embraced a form or degree of intimidation, this circuit has not previously adopted that element as an essential component of a prosecution under 18 U.S.C. § 875(c). To the contrary, controlling precedents clearly reflect the principle that a message is a "threat" if a reasonable recipient would tend to believe that the originator of the message was serious about his words and intended to effect the violence or other harm forewarned, regardless of the speaker's actual motive for issuing the communication. In *United States v. DeAndino*, 958 F.2d 146, 148 (6th Cir.), cert. denied, 505 U.S. 1206, 120 L. Ed. 2d 874, 112 S. Ct. 2997 (1992), this court reversed the trial court's dismissal of a section 875(c) indictment, commanding that the government need prove only the author's objective (or general) intent, as opposed to a subjective (or specific) intent, to threaten a person. A "general intent" to threaten exists where a reasonable person would objectively take the defendant's statement to be a "serious expression of an intention to inflict bodily harm[,]" whereas a "specific intent" to threaten exists only where the speaker subjectively intended, in fact, to threaten a person. Because under *DeAndino* the prosecution need prove only that the speaker objectively intended to threaten a person by his statement(s), no proof that the publisher of the threat subjectively intended to threaten anyone by his communication is necessary. Similarly, no proof that the speaker had intended to intimidate anyone to attain some change or goal was required in *DeAndino*; the opinion does not suggest that the burden placed upon the government to prove a threat under section 875(c) included proof of motivation for conveying the threat.

Thus, the plain language of 18 U.S.C. § 875(c), together with its interpretive precedents, compels the conclusion that "threats" within the scope of the statute in controversy include all reasonably credible communications which express the speaker's objective intent to kidnap or physically injure another person. Whether the originator of the message intended to intimidate or coerce anyone thereby is irrelevant. Rather, the pertinent inquiry is whether a jury could find that a reasonable recipient of the communication would objectively tend to believe that the speaker was serious about his stated intention. There can be no doubt that a rational jury could find that some or all of the minacious communications charged in the superseding indictment against Baker constituted threats by the defendant to harm a female human being, which a reasonable objective recipient of the transmissions could find credible.

Accordingly, I would reverse the district court's judgment which dismissed the superseding indictment as purportedly not alleging "true threats," and remand the cause to the lower court. I DISSENT.

United States v. Morales

272 F.3D 284 (2001)

U.S. COURT OF APPEALS, FIFTH CIRCUIT

OPINION: E. GRADY JOLLY, Circuit Judge:

Eduardo Morales was an 18-year-old student at Milby High School in Houston, Texas at the time of the Internet communications at issue. He entered an Internet chatroom and, in a conversation with a stranger in the state of Washington, threatened to shoot and kill students at Milby High. The stranger alerted the police, who ultimately traced the communications to Morales. He was indicted for knowingly and intentionally transmitting in interstate commerce a threat to injure another in violation of 18 U.S.C. § 875(c). He was convicted by a jury and sentenced to twenty-four months probation. Based on this court's earlier decision in *United States v. Myers*, 104 F.3d 76, 79 (5th Cir. 1997), we affirm the conviction of Morales and the district court's holdings.

I

Morales's conviction stemmed from an Internet conversation Morales had with Crystal Lees, a 26-year-old mother of two living in Puyallup, Washington, whom Morales did not know at the time. Both Morales and Lees were in a "Young Latinos" chat room when Morales, using the screen name "Fusion_2," sent an instant message directed to Lees, who was using the screen name "Crystalita." The following exchange via instant messages ensued:

Morales	*I will kill*
Lees	*huh?—me*
	You will kill what—me
Morales	*TEACHERS AND STUDENTS AT MILBY*
Lees	*Why do you want to do that*
	Where is Milby?
Morales	*CAUSE AM TIRED ......HOUSTON*
Lees	*are you really going to go and kill people*
	Who has made you mad r u ok do you want to talk to me
Morales	*YES F NE ONE STANDS N MY WAY WILL SHOT*
Lees	*r u ok*
Morales	*I HATE LIVE*
Lees	*I am here*
Morales	*YES MY NAME S ED HARRIS*
	SEE U N A COUPLE OF MONTHS

Lees alerted the police because she was concerned about the well-being of Milby High School students. Milby High School's principal was informed, and he increased security measures at the school.

That same day, police traced the screen name "Fusion_2" to a friend of Morales, who informed the police that Morales had been using his WebTV Internet terminal device. Morales was arrested after admitting that he was the individual who had parlayed with Lees in the chat room. However, Morales insisted that he was only joking. He told police he was trying to joke that he was the ghost of Ed Harris, whom he mistakenly thought was the assailant at Columbine High School, who in fact was Eric Harris.

Morales filed a pretrial motion to dismiss the indictment on First Amendment grounds, arguing that his statements to a distant third party did not constitute a true threat under Supreme Court jurisprudence. That motion was denied. During the jury trial, Morales moved for a judgment of acquittal, asserting again that no true threat was made because the statements were made to a third party. He also argued that no evidence established that he made the statements with the intent to intimidate. Again, the motions were denied.

Morales then objected to the court's proposed jury instruction that the government was not required to prove that Morales subjectively intended to communicate a threat. The court rejected his proposed instructions that 1) the government must prove that the defendant has communicated the threat to the target or someone he intended would communicate the threat to the target, and 2) that the government must prove that the defendant intended to make a threat. The jury convicted Morales of the single § 875(c) count, charging him with knowingly and intentionally transmitting a threat to injure another. The court thereafter denied Morales's post-verdict motions for judgment of acquittal and a new trial.

On appeal, Morales challenges his conviction on three grounds. First, Morales argues that his communication was not a "true threat" given the context in which it was delivered. Second, Morales asserts that his statements were not actionable under § 875(c) because they were communicated to a third party. Third, Morales argues that the district court erred by not instructing the jury that the government must establish that Morales intended to communicate a threat.

II

We first address whether Morales's statements constituted a "true threat." In this circuit, a communication is a threat under § 875(c) if "in its context [it] would have a reasonable tendency to create apprehension that its originator will act according to its tenor." *United States v. Myers*, 104 F.3d 76, 79 (5th Cir. 1997), citing *United States v. Bozeman*, 495 F.2d 508, 510 (5th Cir. 1974) (citations and internal quotations omitted). Prosecution under § 875(c) "requires proof that the threat was made knowingly and intentionally." *Myers*, 104 F.3d at 79. An act is performed "knowingly" when it is done voluntarily and intentionally, and not because of mistake or accident. See id. "A threat is knowingly made if the maker of it comprehends the meaning of the words uttered by him, and a threat is willfully made if in addition to comprehending his words, the maker voluntarily and intelligently utters the words as a declaration of an apparent determination to carry out the threat." *United States v. Pilkington*, 583 F.2d 746, 747 (5th Cir. 1978).

However, "because § 875(c) contains nothing suggesting a specific intent requirement, it defines only a general intent offense." *Myers*, 104 F.3d at 81. The Supreme Court has held that "a statute such as this one, which makes criminal a form of pure speech, must be interpreted with the commands of the First Amendment clearly in mind. What is a threat must be distinguished from what is constitutionally protected speech." *Watts v. United States*, 394 U.S. 705, 707, 22 L. Ed. 2d 664, 89 S. Ct. 1399 (1969).

Before analyzing a defendant's willfulness or intention, the Supreme Court has noted that federal statutes prohibiting threats "initially require[] the Government to prove a true threat." Id. at 708. The Court distinguished "political hyperbole" from a "true threat," and recognized the importance of examining statements "in context" to determine whether they are true threats punishable by law. Id. Thus, in *Myers* we determined that "in order to convict, a fact finder must determine that the recipient of the in-context threat reasonably feared it would be carried out." 104 F.3d at 80, citing *Bozeman*, 495 F.2d at 510.

Morales admitted making the statements. He admitted more, however: that he did it to see how Lees would react. Morales further testified that he could see why Lees "would get scared or why she reacted the way she did." Morales admitted that he was aware of a prior incident in which a student at Milby had made threats over the Internet, and that he knew it was wrong to do so. Under *Myers* all that is required is general intent. 104 F.3d at 81. It is up to the jury to decide whether Morales made the statements knowingly and intentionally. Id. at 78. There was sufficient evidence to support the jury's finding that Morales acted with knowledge and intent.

Additionally, however, the trier of fact must have found that the communication "in its context would have a reasonable tendency to create apprehension that its originator will act according to its tenor." Id. at 79.

The jury was presented with evidence that Lees felt apprehension that "Fusion_2" would act on his threat to kill. Morales repeated his threats to kill several times, and gave no indication that he was joking. Morales admitted that he attempted to refer to Eric Harris, one of the perpetrators of the Columbine High School killings. Thus, his statement in context cannot be divorced from the reality of that tragedy. We should also observe that the context of Morales's statement is different from that in *Watts*. Unlike *Watts*, Morales was not engaged in political speech as part of a public debate, in which the listeners laughed in response to Watts's comments. See *Watts*, 394 U.S. at 708. Given these factors and the length of the communication between Morales and Lees, a reasonable juror could find all the facts necessary to make Morales's communication a "true threat."

Morales contends, however, that his statements cannot, as a matter of law, constitute a true threat because they were made to a random third party who had no connection with Milby High School.

Our precedent does not allow for this distinction. For example, in *Myers*, the defendant was a Vietnam veteran with a history of mental illness. In two telephone conversations he directly threatened a member of his congressman's staff. In a third telephone conversation, Myers communicated a threat against the Veterans Administration and Congress to an employee of the Paralyzed Veterans of America ("PVA"). Myers was convicted on three separate counts of violations of § 875(c) for each individual phone call. This court affirmed Myers's conviction, drawing no distinction between the threat made to the PVA and two other threats communicated directly to their targets. Again, the focus was on whether the threat "in its context would have a reasonable tendency to create apprehension that its originator will act according to its tenor." *Myers*, 104 F.3d at 78, quoting *Bozeman*, 495 F.2d at 510. It is this character and context of the threat that is the relevant test. As discussed in the previous section, the jury found a reasonable tendency to create such apprehension in this case, and there is no basis for us to disturb the jury's findings.

The government notes that it has never been required to show an intent to communicate the threat to the intended victim under § 875(c). The language of § 875(c) does not require that the threat be made directly to the intended target; it simply prohibits "any threat to injure the person of another" made in interstate commerce. Moreover, as we have pointed out, our precedent in *Myers* does not require that the threat be made directly to the victim. Based on *Myers* and the text of § 875(c), we hold that Morales's statements are actionable under the federal statute.

City of Dayton v. Davis

136 OHIO APP. 3D 26; 735 N.E.2D 939 (1999)

COURT OF APPEALS OF OHIO, SECOND APPELLATE DISTRICT

FREDERICK N. YOUNG, J.

Defendant-Appellant Gilbert A. Davis appeals his convictions on one count of menacing by stalking in violation of R.C. § 2903.211, and one count of aggravated menacing in violation of R.C.G.O. § 135.05(A).

According to the evidence presented by the prosecution, the defense having presented none, the events culminating in Davis' convictions have their genesis in 1996, when he was a second-year law student at the University of Dayton School of Law (hereinafter "UDSL"). In October of that year, he began dating a first-year law student, Johanna Barba, in spite of the fact that he was married and living with his wife and son at the time. According to the evidence produced at trial, Barba and Davis' relationship continued until the beginning of December 1997, at which time Davis demanded that Barba either cease studying with her classmate, Dan Perrico, or end her relationship with Davis. Barba chose to do the latter, then left the Dayton area over the winter break from school. While away, she was able to access her e-mail account provided to all students at UDSL. She received an unknown number of e-mails from Davis in which he stated he was starving himself to death and described the pain he would suffer in the process of doing so.

Upon her return to UDSL, Davis apologized profusely amid tears, and begged Barba to give him another chance, promising that he would be less controlling and more supportive of her academic endeavors. The relationship resumed, but after approximately one month, Barba determined that its quality was no different than before, and she told Davis it was over. Shortly thereafter, on the night of February 22 or the early morning hours of February 23, 1998, Davis attempted suicide by ingesting a combination of alcohol and drugs.

In the days, weeks, and months following his suicide attempt, Davis sent Barba numerous e-mails telling her he had been researching her home town in New Jersey and regularly spending time in a park near Barba's apartment. Near the end of April 1998, Davis also sent e-mails to Barba's parents in New Jersey, and a friend of Barba's at UDSL, Susan Branstetter. No explicit threats of harm to Barba were made in any of the e-mails, but Davis' tone in them fluctuated between despair over the break-up, anger, threats to commit suicide, a desire to see Barba in pain, and blaming Barba for ruining Davis' life. Davis also included in his e-mails to Barba details of her television viewing and social activities, which he could only have known by watching her, and a link to a website he had created. Davis stated he was willing to make the details of his relationship with Barba public at UDSL in order to, as he put it, get his side of the story out.

The e-mail messages Davis sent to Barba put her in such fear for her safety that she changed her phone number and gave her new number only to her closest friends with a plea that they not give it to anyone else. She took to pushing her dresser across her door when she went to sleep and kept pepper spray by her bed. Barba also had motion detectors installed in her apartment and developed the habit of calling her friend, Branstetter, to let her know when she was coming and going from her apartment, in case anything should happen to her. In addition, she contacted either the University of Dayton Police Department (hereinafter "UD police") or the Kettering Police Department numerous times concerning Davis' e-mails and an incident where he apparently came to Barba's apartment to leave a ring on her door. In March 1998, the police warned Davis to stay away from Barba's apartment, and on April 8, 1998, Barba filed a complaint with the UD police.

Davis' web page, which he created under the name "Gadbuddhaa," portrayed, among other things, the image of Barba's head transforming into a skull amidst flames, dripping blood, and charging horses ridden by robed skeletons. Interspersed with these images were quotations from the Bible and other sources in which the common theme was love, death, and destruction. On another web page, Davis had posted pictures of Barba's home town in New Jersey, although when questioned by UD police officer Harry Sweigart, Davis denied ever having been to the town.

Barba accessed Davis' web site on April 10, 1998, after having heard about its contents from her friends at UDSL. Recalling instances where Davis had described violent acts he had been involved in, his penchant for pointing out where television criminals had gone wrong in the commission of their crimes, and the timbre of his e-mails, Barba was convinced after viewing the web site that Davis was going to kill her. To her, the web site was a manifestation of a violent ideation against her rather than the suicidal thoughts Davis had previously exhibited. Branstetter and UDSL Professor Thomas Hagel noticed that Barba was frightened, unnerved, and appeared to be a terrorized person during the spring of 1998.

Soon after viewing Davis' web site, Barba moved into a hotel because of her fear of Davis. She remained there until she had completed her final examinations at UDSL in May, then immediately departed for New Jersey to complete her law school education there.

As a result of the complaint filed by Barba with the UD police, Davis was charged with three counts of aggravated menacing in violation of R.C.G.O. § 135.05(A), three counts of menacing by stalking in violation of R.C. § 2903.211, and eight counts of telephone harassment in violation of R.C.G.O. § 137.03(B). The prosecutor subsequently dismissed all but one count of aggravated menacing, one count of menacing by stalking, and three counts of telephone harassment. At the close of the prosecution's case in chief, the trial court granted Davis' Crim.R. 29 motion on the telephone harassment counts, but denied it as to the other counts. Thus, only one count of aggravated menacing and one count of menacing by stalking went to the jury, which returned guilty verdicts on both counts. On October 20, 1998, the trial court sentenced Davis to a term of 180 days on each count, to be served consecutively at the Dayton Human Rehabilitation Center. The same day, Davis filed his timely notice of appeal and requested that he be permitted to post bond pending appeal, and the trial court granted his request.

Davis contends the trial court erred by overruling his Crim.R. 29 motion for acquittal as to the aggravated menacing and menacing by stalking convictions because they were unsupported by sufficient evidence.

R.C.G.O. § 135.05(A) states that "no person shall knowingly cause another to believe that the offender will cause serious physical harm to the person or property of such other person or member of his immediate family." Davis claims that the evidence produced at trial was insufficient to support his conviction under that provision because the e-mails sent to Barba by Davis contained no explicit or direct threats of harm, and because Davis was neither armed nor in close proximity to Barba when she read the e-mails and viewed his web site. None of these circumstances are required for a conviction under R.C.G.O. § 135.05(A), however.

The record before us leaves little doubt that Barba genuinely believed Davis was going to kill her or cause serious physical harm to her. She took extreme measures to protect herself as a result, ultimately leaving UDSL and the state to get away from him. His statement in his e-mail of March 19, 1998, to the effect that he was glad to see her in pain, while falling short of constituting an explicit threat, evidenced his desire to see her suffer. Davis' increasingly angry tone in the later e-mails, his blaming Barba for ruining his life, in combination with the horrifying web site images of Barba's head metamorphosing into a skull provide fertile ground for the germination and growth of Barba's fear of serious physical harm at the hands of Davis. Consequently, we find Davis' conviction under R.C.G.O. § 135.05(A) to be supported by sufficient evidence.

Davis also claims his conviction on the menacing by stalking count is insufficiently supported by the evidence. The relevant statute, R.C. § 2903.211, provides as follows:

(A) No person by engaging in a pattern of conduct shall knowingly cause another to believe that the offender will cause physical harm to the other person or cause mental distress to the other person.

(C) As used in this section:

(1) "Pattern of conduct" means two or more actions or incidents closely related in time, whether or not there has been a prior conviction based on any of those actions or incidents.

(2) "Mental distress" means any mental illness or condition that involves some temporary substantial incapacity or mental illness or condition that would normally require psychiatric treatment.

Davis argues that the evidence produced at trial was insufficient to support a finding that he engaged in a pattern of conduct or made explicit threats to Barba, that Barba suffered mental distress, or that Barba was aware of any threatening thoughts Davis may have harbored toward her. We disagree.

Davis presumes in his argument that his posting of the gruesome web page, constituting one act, is insufficient evidence of a pattern of conduct. What he overlooks, however, is the evidence that he surreptitiously watched Barba then communicated to her via e-mail his knowledge of what television programs she watched and her social activities, that he visited her apartment and left a ring on her door on one occasion, and that he let her know he spent a considerable amount of time at the park near her house. Thus, while we agree with Davis' statement of the law respecting the requirement that a pattern of conduct be composed of more than one act, we find it to be inconclusive on the issue he raises. The evidence produced at trial was sufficient to support the jury's finding that Davis engaged in a pattern of conduct as that term is defined in R.C. § 2903.211(C)(2).

Next, Davis contends that the evidence insufficiently supported a finding that Barba suffered mental distress as a result of his conduct. A showing of actual mental distress is not an element of menacing by stalking, however. Instead, the prosecution need only show that Davis knowingly caused Barba to believe he would cause her mental distress or physical harm, which, in our view, was sufficiently accomplished at trial to support Davis' conviction for menacing by stalking.

In his last argument relating to the sufficiency of the evidence, Davis claims his conviction for menacing by stalking was insufficiently supported by the evidence because he never directly communicated an explicit threat to Barba. He also contends that any thoughts he had of threatening or harming her, having never been communicated, cannot support his conviction.

We note again, however, that explicit threats are not an element of menacing by stalking. Furthermore, Davis' frequent communication expressing his desire to see Barba in pain, his increasingly vituperative tone in his e-mails to Barba, and the grotesque web site allow an easy conclusion that Davis knowingly caused Barba to believe he would cause her mental distress or physical harm. Thus, we find Davis' conviction for menacing by stalking sufficiently supported by the evidence.

Key Words and Phrases

Cyberbullying	Implied threat
Cyberharassment	Sexual predator
Cyberstalking	Threat

Review Problems

1. If criminal liability for cyberstalking can be based on the victim's apprehension of the threat, how does a defendant know when he or she commits the act that the victim will have that fear? Does it matter?
2. In *Morales*, no threat, implied or otherwise, was communicated to an intended victim. Does this mean that any communication, like a tweet on Twitter, could result in cyberharassment even though the intended victim of the harassment doesn't twitter and is not told of the harassment?

Weblinks

www.usdoj.gov/criminal/cybercrime/cyberstalking.htm
    This page at the U.S. Department of Justice website contains a detailed report on cyberstalking. Although the data are somewhat outdated, the legal discussion is not.
www.cyberbullying.us/
    A web page devoted to a discussion of cyberbullying, including information from victims, and useful links concerning the topic.

Internet Frauds

5

Introduction

The availability and use of computers and other digital media have provided criminals with the means of committing crime in a different manner. It is not necessary to use a weapon in order to take money from a bank; a computer can do it. Also, the Internet has provided a new location for the occurrence of crime. It should be no surprise, therefore, that many fraudulent schemes perpetrated in the face-to-face world are now committed with the use of technology. Further, evidence of many face-to-face crimes can be stored on computers and other digital storage devices.

As is the case with many face-to-face fraudulent schemes, there is no criminal statute addressing the specific crime. For example, there is no federal law that makes auction fraud, per se, a crime. The same applies to Ponzi and pyramid schemes, and mail order bride frauds. Instead, as is illustrated below, more generic criminal statutes such as wire fraud and computer fraud are used by prosecutors to punish the perpetrators of those frauds.

This chapter discusses several fraudulent schemes for which there is no specific criminal statute—auction fraud, Ponzi and pyramid schemes, and mail order bride schemes, as well as other frauds that are encompassed within specific statutes—access device fraud and identity theft.

Auction Fraud

According to the Internet Crime Complaint Center, nearly 63% of all fraud on the Internet reported during 2005 involved auction fraud.[1] Even the Federal Trade Commission, which accepts complaints mainly of identity theft, reported that auction fraud, with 12%, was the leading category of non-identity theft consumer fraud reports in 2005.[2] In the legal environment, however, there is no federal law that deals specifically with auction fraud. Typically, online auction frauds are prosecuted under the wire fraud statute because use of the Internet satisfies the requirement of an interstate communication. The following case illustrates that point.

United States v. Gajdik

292 F.3D 555 (2002)

U.S. CT. OF APPEALS, 7TH CIRCUIT

Rovner, Circuit Judge.

Between January and July 2000, Gajdik operated a fraud scheme over the Internet site eBay, an electronic venue for private parties to buy and sell goods at auction. After a stint of legitimate transactions, Gajdik began selling designer sunglasses that he misrepresented as new and under manufacturer's warranty. The sunglasses were in fact broken and discarded glasses that Gajdik retrieved from a dumpster outside of a Peoria distribution warehouse and reassembled. Gajdik quickly graduated to auctioning expensive merchandise such as Rolex, Auderman Piquet, and Patek Phillipe watches, diamonds, collectable coins, and computers. Gajdik neither possessed nor intended to obtain or deliver any of these items. Still, Gajdik's fraudulent auctions attracted many bidders, and eBay users from around the world believing they were purchasing high-end goods sent him nearly $700,000. Gajdik deposited most of this money in a savings account opened for the purpose of accepting wire transfers and depositing checks from his eBay customers. Gajdik's fraudulent activities soon came to the attention of the FBI, which obtained and executed a search warrant for his Peoria home. By that time Gajdik had fled Illinois with $44,000 from the savings account. Federal agents caught up with him later in Florida. As a result of these misdeeds, he was charged in an indictment with ten counts of mail fraud, 18 U.S.C. § 1341, eight counts of wire fraud, 18 U.S.C. § 1343, two counts of money laundering, 18 U.S.C. § 1957(a), and one count of interstate transportation of stolen currency, 18 U.S.C. § 2314.

Gajdik promptly entered a plea agreement with the government and pleaded guilty to seventeen of the twenty-one charges. [*The remaining part of the court's decision involved sentencing issues.*]

Ponzi and Pyramid Schemes

That deal is just too good to be true! If that's what you've been saying, you are probably right; it's probably a Ponzi scheme. Ponzi schemes, named after the classic schemer, Charles Ponzi,[3] are schemes that typically promise to produce a high rate of return for someone who invests money with the perpetrator. The following case in which the defendant was prosecuted for mail fraud and wire fraud is an illustration of a Ponzi scheme involving a fraudulent scheme for investments in oil and gas wells.

United States v. Iannone

184 F.3D 214 (1999)

U.S. CT. OF APPEALS, 3RD CIRCUIT

HARRIS, District Judge:
Defendant-appellant John Michael Iannone ("Iannone") appeals from the sentence imposed after his guilty plea to six counts of interstate transportation of property taken by fraud, one count of mail fraud, and one count of wire fraud. In determining Iannone's sentence pursuant to the United States Sentencing Guidelines ("U.S.S.G."), the district court applied several enhancements to the offense level. Iannone challenges two actual and one de facto enhancements: (1) a two-level increase pursuant to § 3A1.1 for a vulnerable victim; (2) a two-level increase pursuant to § 3B1.3 for abuse of a position of private trust; and (3) an upward departure, achieved via a two-level increase,

pursuant to § 5K2.0 for conduct outside the "heartland" of the fraud guideline. We affirm the sentence.

I. FACTUAL BACKGROUND

Essentially, Iannone defrauded people by encouraging them to invest in oil and gas drilling ventures, but then using the investors' money for his personal expenses rather than for the promised purposes. Iannone committed these frauds against several victims, living in different states, over the course of several years. The total of the funds Iannone fraudulently obtained amounted to more than $600,000.

A. The Pennsylvania Frauds

In 1991 or 1992, Iannone started his own company, Horizon Natural Resources ("HNR"), after leaving his job as an executive at Consolidated Natural Gas. HNR was an oil exploration and natural gas tract leasing company, with an office in Wexford, Pennsylvania. At least initially, HNR was a legitimate business. Iannone was HNR's sole owner and operator, giving himself the title of Chief Executive Officer ("CEO").

In early 1992, Iannone secured several leaseholds and two contractual farm-out arrangements with Exxon Corporation to drill and operate oil wells. Pursuant to the Exxon arrangement, Iannone contracted to drill a test well, Horizon No. 1, by a stated deadline. Despite two or three extensions of the deadline, Iannone never drilled the test well. By November 1992, Iannone's business appeared to be failing. He had not drilled any wells, all but one of his leaseholds had expired, and Exxon had terminated one of the two farm-out arrangements.

In December 1992, Iannone began to solicit investment monies from his neighbors, ostensibly for the purpose of drilling and operating two wells, Horizon Nos. 1 and 2. Unaware of the precarious state of Iannone's business, his neighbors invested approximately $320,000 with him. Included among those investors were several members of one family, the Stringerts. Iannone had been a friend and neighbor of the Stringerts for several years. Iannone sold the Stringerts what he labeled "interests" or "shares" in Horizon Nos. 1 and 2 and entered into contracts with the Stringerts on behalf of HNR. However, rather than investing the money in the drilling project, Iannone used it for his own personal expenses.

Having spent all of that money by the end of October 1993, Iannone began to solicit further investments in the Horizon drilling project. Iannone told his victims various lies in order to encourage their investment. For example, he told one investor that the wells already were drilled and producing and told others that the wells were going to be drilled in December 1993 and that he had acquired Exxon's overriding royalty interest in the wells. As a result of these solicitations, Iannone received another $170,000 in investment monies from neighbors and acquaintances in October, November, and December 1993. As with the prior investments, Iannone used this money for personal expenses.

From the time Iannone received the first investment monies in December 1992 until he absconded in January 1994, Iannone continually lied to the Stringerts and the other investors in order to conceal his conversion of their money to his personal use. He told some investors that he had used their money to hire a drilling company and that he was in contact with Exxon about a process that would increase their yield from the wells. When one investor—Howard Stringert—became suspicious, Iannone agreed to buy back his $100,000 investment in the oil well project once he received a settlement from a pending suit against Consolidated Natural Gas. However, those representations were false. Iannone had not hired a drilling company, was not in contact with Exxon about a process to increase the wells' yield, and had already settled the litigation with Consolidated Natural Gas over a year-and-a-half earlier for only $17,000. Iannone did not use any of the investment monies for the drilling project; he took it all for his personal use.

Throughout the period in which Iannone was soliciting his neighbors to invest in the Horizon project, he was falsely posing as a decorated Vietnam veteran. This adopted military hero persona helped Iannone gain the trust of the Stringert family. He provided some members of the Stringert family with a resume falsely indicating that he had spent three years in Vietnam as a Captain in the U.S. Army Special Forces and that he had been awarded several medals, including the Purple Heart and the Silver Star, and he represented that he had received a recommendation for the Congressional Medal of Honor. He provided the Stringerts with a false citation recounting the heroic acts for which he supposedly received the Silver Star. Howard Stringert described the story recounted in the citation as "Ramboesque." One member of the family, Janice Stringert-Streich, visited Iannone's home where he had a Silver Star medal prominently displayed. Janice and her brother Howard Stringert both testified at the sentencing hearing that their family had great respect for military veterans and that this influenced their decisions to invest with Iannone.

By October 1993, some investors had become suspicious of Iannone, and he prepared for his disappearance, buying a truck under a false name with some of the investment money. On January 11, 1994, Iannone disappeared, leaving his wife and three children behind. Approximately $70,000 to $110,000 in investment funds were unaccounted for at the time of his abscondance. In order to avoid being pursued, Iannone faked his own death. He left behind a letter claiming that he had left on a secret mission for a government "alphabet agency" and that he feared it might result in his death. He then left his van, splattered with blood and littered with shell casings from a weapon, parked at the Greater Pittsburgh International Airport. Local police quickly realized both that the scene had been fabricated and that Iannone had not been the victim of a crime.

B. The Colorado Frauds

After his disappearance from Pennsylvania, Iannone settled in Colorado where he adopted the alias Wayne D. Hamilton, the name of a deceased Vietnam veteran. He continued to masquerade as a Vietnam War hero and told acquaintances that his family had been killed by a drunk driver. Posing as a Vietnam veteran, he befriended several people, including Clancy O'Dowd and Diana Hegler, through an America Online chat room for veterans. He developed a close friendship with O'Dowd, based on their supposed shared combat experiences in Vietnam.

Apparently, Iannone lived off the Pennsylvania fraud proceeds for about three years. When he ran low on money, Iannone essentially repeated his Pennsylvania scheme. As head of W. D. H. Associates, a sham oil and gas company, Iannone offered his new friends and neighbors the opportunity to invest in oil and/or gas wells in Texas and Nebraska. Several of his friends and neighbors acquiesced, buying percentage shares of oil and/or gas well leases from Iannone. As with the Pennsylvania frauds, Iannone did not invest this money for the purpose that it was entrusted to him, but used it for personal expenses. He received approximately $115,500 from the Colorado frauds.

Again, Iannone lied to the investors in order to conceal his fraud. Iannone told investors that the wells were producing and that they should expect their first royalty checks to arrive in March or April of 1997. When the checks did not materialize, Iannone again disappeared. On or around June 3, 1997, Iannone left Colorado, falsely informing most investors that he was going to Texas to check on the wells. He told one investor, O'Dowd, a different lie: that he was going to confront the drunk driver who had killed his family. When some of the investors began to communicate with each other and became suspicious, Iannone sent them an electronic message claiming to be an employee of an "alphabet agency" in the witness protection program. Iannone was arrested by the Federal Bureau of Investigation in July 1997.

C. The District Court's Sentence

Iannone pled guilty to six counts of interstate transportation of property taken by fraud, one count of mail fraud, and one count of wire fraud. [*The court's discussion of the sentence has been omitted.*]

A pyramid scheme also is a form of investment scheme. Though often linked with a Ponzi scheme, each has different characteristics. Although the following case did not involve cybercrime charges (although, if representations had been made electronically or digitally, cybercrime charges could have been made), the decision is instructive on the essence of a pyramid scheme.

United States v. Gold Unlimited, Inc.

---

177 F.3D 472 (1999)

U.S. Court of Appeals, 6th Circuit

BOGGS, Circuit Judge.

This appeal involves the conviction of a corporate defendant that advertised a "Get Rich Quick" program. Eager participants flocked in search of galactic profits, but only the corporation quickly got rich, so authorities intervened. We affirm.

David Crowe founded the corporation Gold Unlimited, Inc. The government pressed charges, contending that Gold Unlimited, Inc. ("Gold") operated an illegal pyramid scheme. A jury convicted David, his wife Martha, and Gold of seven counts of mail fraud, one count of money laundering conspiracy, and seven counts of money laundering.

The Crowes contend that they have always operated legal multilevel marketing (referred to as "MLM" in some documents) programs akin to Amway. MLM programs survive by making money off product sales, not new recruits. In contrast, "pyramid schemes" reward participants for inducing other people to join the program; over time, the hierarchy of participants resembles a pyramid as newer, larger layers of participants join the established structure. Ponzi schemes operate strictly by paying earlier investors with money tendered by later investors. No clear line separates illegal pyramid schemes from legitimate multilevel marketing programs; to differentiate the two, regulators evaluate the marketing strategy (e.g., emphasis on recruitment versus sales) and the percent of product sold compared with the percent of commissions granted. In this case, the jury found that Gold and the Crowes knowingly operated an illegal pyramid scheme with the intent to defraud.

American Gold Eagle

From Fall 1989 to Fall 1991, the Crowes operated American Gold Eagle ("AGE") in North Carolina. David served as CEO for this North Carolina corporation, while Martha acted as Secretary and Treasurer. AGE offered a "Gold Matching Program" to the public: participants placed a $200 down payment on $800 worth of gold and paid the balance by receiving commissions after recruiting new participants. The original participant would pay the $200 and then recruit two separate investment groups into the Gold Matching Program (much like cells in hierarchical organizations, with the original participant at the top and with two branches diverging from the center, each branch containing three recruits). For every group of three that joined the matching program, the original participant received a $300 commission toward the purchase of the laid-away gold. After recruiting two groups (six individuals), the original participant could take the gold or roll over the $600 credit into a new recruitment arrangement that offered a higher ceiling on commissions (conditioned on enrolling more participants, of course).

North Carolina suspected that AGE operated an illegal pyramid scheme, and the state Attorney General suggested that the company prove its validity by paying off existing obligations before soliciting more recruits. The corporation failed before the state took official action; while the cause of the failure remains unclear, one of the Crowes' daughters testified that problems with vendors resulted in a cessation of gold deliveries to AGE and a concomitant swelling of anger by representatives seeking to realize the fruits of their recruiting efforts. An AGE employee testified that AGE received "literally hundreds" of complaints each day. Before and after AGE's collapse, complaints flooded the office of the North Carolina Attorney General. The Crowes moved to Madisonville, Kentucky and did not act to reimburse the victims of AGE's collapse. Five hundred complaints remain unresolved, alleging losses of $370,000.

Gold Unlimited, Inc. & "Gold I"

January 22, 1992, saw the incorporation of Gold Unlimited, Inc. ("Gold") as a Delaware corporation based in Madisonville. David Crowe served as the sole officer and director of the closely-held corporation. Martha Crowe acted as office manager for the corporation, which employed a total of 89 individuals over four years. Undaunted by past troubles, the Crowes offered the public the opportunity to participate in Gold's "Gold Earning Program" ("Gold I"). Participants paid $200 toward a $400 gold coin; by recruiting new investors, the original participant earned commissions toward the cost of the coin and could earn cash commissions. At trial, Gold's corporate attorney, William Whitledge, admitted that this plan was "pretty much identical" to AGE's plan, and the South Dakota Division of Securities Enforcement agreed, calling it "almost identical" and enforcing against Gold the cease and desist order obtained against AGE. In April 1992, the Kentucky Attorney General sued Gold, and the Hopkins Circuit Court enjoined the Crowes from operating Gold. In the opinion, Judge Charles W. Boteler found that Gold I emphasized recruitment of clients, not sales of products, and thus constituted an illegal pyramid scheme. In October 1993, the Crowes and Gold signed a settlement agreement with the state, agreeing to pay restitution to Gold I's participants and submitting to a permanent injunction against operating pyramid schemes and making unrealistic earnings claims.

"Gold II"

Back in business after agreeing to the injunction, the Crowes used Gold Unlimited, Inc. to launch a new marketing plan, referred to at trial as "Gold II." Under Gold II, participants could purchase gold and jewelry from Gold and resell it, or they could join the "Binary Compensation Program." Under the Binary Compensation Program, participants made a $200 down payment towards the purchase of $400 in gold; by recruiting new participants, the original participant earned commissions to pay off the balance and to receive cash payments. Whitledge, Gold's corporate attorney, worked with the Crowes to distinguish Gold II from Gold I. For example, Gold II added more product lines (supplementing Gold I's gold coins with silver coins and gold jewelry), changed manuals, strengthened refund policies, and allegedly attempted to emphasize product sales over recruitment. To ensure compliance with the injunction, Whitledge discussed Gold II with Wendy Delaplane of the state Attorney General's office; Delaplane reiterated her concern that "a company which put emphasis upon strictly recruiting people rather than moving a product was a pyramid." Whitledge, a solo practitioner, hired an outside legal expert, and the two men concluded that Gold II constituted an illegal pyramid. When Whitledge attempted to discuss his concerns with David Crowe, Crowe told Whitledge that "it was none of [Whitledge's] business and to leave it alone," although Whitledge believes that Crowe eventually "followed my advice."

In February 1995, North Dakota issued a cease and desist order against Gold and assessed a $40,000 civil penalty for, *inter alia*, violating the outstanding cease and desist order binding AGE. South Dakota also enforced its AGE cease and desist order against Gold. Montana filed a cease and desist order. Minnesota alleged that Gold operated an illegal pyramid scheme, and it induced Gold to stipulate that Gold would stop operating in Minnesota and would reimburse residents. On March 14, 1995, a team of federal agents obtained a warrant and searched Gold's offices in Madisonville, seizing records. The United States Attorney obtained a temporary restraining order against Gold, and the company closed. As of March 1995, 96,000 participants had paid $43,000,000 to Gold II, which had disbursed $25,000,000 in commissions. Gold II resulted in sales of 12,628 coins, with a gross profit from the coins of only $552,620. Based on this and other data, the government's expert witnesses agreed that Gold II's financial success depended on the "recruitment of an increasing number of new investors into the Binary Compensation Program," and not on product sales.

The jury convicted the defendants of mail fraud (counts one through seven), money laundering conspiracy (count fifteen), and money laundering (counts sixteen through twenty two), and it acquitted the defendants of the securities violations (counts eight through fourteen).

The district court sentenced Martha Crowe to 121 months in prison, David Crowe to 135 months, and fined the corporation $3000, although Gold forfeited its assets after trial and could not pay the fine. The court deferred the forfeiture until after the court-appointed receiver paid restitution to Gold's victims and after the conclusion of a pending civil case.

A. Background

18 U.S.C. § 1341 requires the government to prove three elements: (1) that the defendant knowingly devised a scheme to defraud; (2) that the defendant did so with the intent to defraud; and (3) that the defendant mailed something or caused another to mail something to implement the scheme. The district court permitted the parties to submit proposed jury instructions, and it crafted a final set of instructions. Gold, for the first time on appeal, takes issue with the following instructions:

> A pyramid scheme is any plan, program, device, scheme, or other process characterized by the payment by participants of money to the company in return for which they receive the right to sell a product and the right to receive in return for recruiting other participants into the program rewards which are unrelated to the sale of the product to ultimate users. A pyramid scheme constitutes a scheme or artifice to defraud for purposes of this count in the indictment.

B. The Definition of "Pyramid Scheme"

Some structures pose less risk of harm to investors and the public, however, and authorities permit these programs to operate even though the programs contain some elements of a pyramid scheme. Courts and legislatures recognize a distinction between legitimate programs (known as multi-level marketing systems) and illegal schemes.

Gold contends that the jury instructions lumped acceptable MLM programs with illegal pyramid schemes; as a corollary, Gold argues that its program contained safeguards to protect against the risks that accompany illegal schemes.

The district court's instructions do not appear misleading or incorrect, however. The district court's definition of "pyramid scheme" (by which we and it mean "illegal pyramid scheme") mirrored that used in several other cases. The district court derived the instructions from the FTC's opinion in *In re Koscot Interplanetary, Inc.*, 86 F.T.C. 1106 (1975), which enjoined the defendants from, *inter alia*:

> 2. Offering, operating, or participating in, any marketing or sales plan or program wherein a participant is given or promised compensation (1) for inducing other persons to become participants in the plan or program, or (2) when a person induced by the participant induces another person to become a participant in the plan or program, Provided, That the term "compensation," as used in this paragraph only, does not mean any payment based on actually consummated sales of goods or services to persons who are not participants in the plan or program and who do not purchase such goods or services in order to resell them.

Id. at 1187. In a recent civil case, the Ninth Circuit adopted Koscot's explication as its test for the existence of pyramid schemes:

> The Federal Trade Commission has established a test for determining what constitutes a pyramid scheme. Such contrivances "are characterized by the payment by participants of money to the company in return for which they receive (1) the right to sell a product and (2) the right to receive in return for recruiting other participants into the program rewards which are unrelated to sale of the product to ultimate users" [quoting Koscot]. The satisfaction of the second element of the Koscot test is the sine qua non of a pyramid scheme.... We adopt the Koscot standard here and hold that the operation of a pyramid scheme constitutes fraud for purposes of several federal antifraud statutes.

Omnitrition, 79 F.3d at 781–82 (describing the two Koscot factors as "the essential features of an illegal pyramid scheme"). The Koscot test, reprinted above, does not materially differ from the district court's instruction.

Gold observes that the jury instructions did not inform the jury that a corporation can enact safeguards to ensure that it operates a legitimate MLM program. Gold attacks the definition because it omits the refinement that, "A pyramid is improper only if it presents a danger of market saturation—that is, only if at some point, persons on the lowest tier of the structure will not be able to find new recruits." Gold cites two civil cases that discuss anti-saturation policies, see *Ger-Ro-Mar, Inc. v. FTC*, 518 F.2d 33, 36–38 (2d Cir. 1975); *Amway*, 93 F.T.C. at 716–17, and Gold bolsters its position by alleging that the record contains evidence to support a jury finding that the program did not present a "realistic danger of market saturation" and that Gold "implemented anti-saturation policies."

One can view Gold's complaint in two ways: perhaps the government bears the burden of proving the risk of saturation as an element of its case, or perhaps Gold should have the ability to prove an affirmative defense that it established anti-saturation policies. If the government has the burden, it appears to have met it. Koscot's second factor—that an illegal pyramid rewards participants for recruitment, not for sales—implies that saturation must occur. Given the district court's instruction that a pyramid exists when a program's rewards relate to recruitment, not product sales, the jury necessarily found the possibility of saturation when it found that the defendants ran a pyramid scheme: "'The presence of this second element, recruitment with rewards unrelated to product sales, is nothing more than an elaborate chain letter device in which individuals who pay a valuable consideration with the expectation of recouping it to some degree via recruitment are bound to be disappointed.'" *Omnitrition*, 79 F.3d at 781 (quoting Koscot).

The government's proof at trial established that Gold ran an illegal pyramid scheme masked with cosmetic anti-saturation policies. Expert witnesses testified that Gold's marketing materials, organizational structure, and recruiting policies marked a program destined for collapse (with concomitant harm to investors). For example, Gold's program, ostensibly predicated on the marketing of gold and jewelry, resulted in a gross profit of only $552,620 from sales of gold coin, yet resulted in the intake of $43 million and the disbursement of but $25 million in "commissions." The government's evidence, focusing on the actual effect of the plan, deserves far more weight than Gold's trial presentation, which relied on the existence of alleged anti-saturation policies shown by the government already to have failed.

We find it more appropriate, however, that a defendant carry the burden of establishing that it has effective anti-saturation programs. Given the grave risks imposed on investors in illegal schemes, the government should have to do no more than prove that the program satisfies the definition of Koscot. The alternative—placing the burden on the government—forces the government to wait until after the collapse, as that alternative permits operators to maintain that the absence of collapse proves the success of the anti-saturation policies.

Gold failed to request an instruction on this affirmative defense, and also, as a matter of law, failed to prove that it merited one. As the *Omnitrition* court observed, "The key to any anti-pyramiding rule ... is that the rule must serve to tie recruitment bonuses to actual retail sales in some way. Only in this way can the second Koscot factor be defeated." *Omnitrition*, 79 F.3d at 783. Gold's position conflates saturation of the market for products with saturation of the market for investors and participants, and Gold's plan risked saturation of the latter market. Gold did not prove at trial that it appropriately tied recruitment bonuses to actual retail sales; as a matter of law, it did not show that its tinkering with its policies de-linked recruitment and commissions.

Having determined that the district court correctly defined "pyramid scheme," we turn to the second question implicitly raised by Gold—namely, whether a pyramid scheme without adequate anti-saturation policies constitutes a "scheme to defraud" prohibited by the mail fraud statute. Unquestionably, an illegal pyramid scheme constitutes a scheme to defraud. In *Omnitrition*, the Ninth Circuit noted that, "An inherently fraudulent pyramid scheme that meets the Koscot factors would fall within the[] broad definitions of fraud [contained in the mail fraud statute, 18 U.S.C. § 1341, and thus constitute a predicate racketeering act sufficient for the *Omnitrition* plaintiffs to invoke civil RICO]." *Omnitrition*, 79 F.3d at 786 & n.7.

For the above reasons, Gold's conviction is AFFIRMED.

KAREN NELSON MOORE, Circuit Judge, concurring in part and concurring in the judgment.

Unlike the majority, I conclude that the district court erred in instructing the jury that a pyramid scheme, as the court defined the term, necessarily constitutes a scheme to defraud for purposes of the federal mail fraud statute. I do not believe that this mistake rises to the level of reversible error in this case, however, and thus I concur in the judgment.

The district court properly instructed the jury that conviction under the mail fraud statute, 18 U.S.C. § 1341, requires proof that the defendant knowingly devised a scheme to defraud, that the defendant did so with intent to defraud, and, of course, that the defendant used the mails in carrying out the scheme. As to the first element, the court instructed the jury as follows:

> A pyramid scheme is any plan, program, device, scheme, or other process characterized by the payment by participants of money to the company in return for which they receive the right to sell a product and the right to receive in return for recruiting other participants into the program rewards which are unrelated to the sale of the product to ultimate users. A pyramid scheme constitutes a scheme or artifice to defraud for purposes of this count in the indictment.

The problem with this instruction is that a pyramid scheme, as the court defined it, does not necessarily constitute a scheme to defraud. A legitimate program similar to that operated by Amway could fall within the district court's definition, but could contain sufficient safeguards against saturation to satisfy the FTC and the courts. The majority apparently recognizes that a defendant in Gold's position could show the existence of effective anti-saturation policies, but inexplicably the majority concludes as a matter of law that a pyramid scheme, as defined, constitutes a scheme to defraud.

It is well settled that a jury instruction that relieves the prosecution of the burden of proving each element of the offense violates the defendant's due process rights. I conclude that the contested instruction here largely eliminated the government's burden of establishing the existence of a scheme to defraud. Having found certain elements that often constitute a fraudulent pyramid scheme, the jury was instructed to infer that a scheme to defraud existed. The jury should have been required to find from the evidence that this program in fact constituted a scheme to defraud.

Access Device Fraud

What Is an Access Device?

The federal crime of access device fraud was created by Congress in 1984. The federal statute, 18 USC § 1029 (e), defines an access device as

> any card, plate, code, account number, electronic serial number, mobile identification number, personal identification number, or other telecommunications service, equipment, or instrument identifier, or other means of account access that can be used, alone or in conjunction with another access device, to obtain money, goods, services, or any other thing of value, or that can be used to initiate a transfer of funds (other than a transfer originated solely by paper instrument).

Under this definition, an access device can include a credit or debit card, an account number for a local gas and electric utility company, a bank checking account number, a computer utilized to program a mobile identification number into a cellular phone, and an embosser used to emboss an account number and just an account number used on a credit or debit card.

Although it is rare for a credit card itself to be used for an online purchase, card account numbers and expiration dates frequently are used for such purchases.

How Is an Access Device Fraud Committed?

Section 1029 lists 10 different methods of committing an access device fraud:

1. producing, using or trafficking in one or more counterfeit cards or account numbers
2. trafficking or using one or more unauthorized credit card or account numbers and obtaining anything having a value of $1000 during any one-year period
3. possessing 15 or more counterfeit or unauthorized credit cards or account numbers
4. producing, trafficking in, or having custody, possession or control over equipment that produces credit cards or account numbers
5. using one or more credit cards or account numbers issued to another person to effect a transaction, or to receive payment or any other thing having a value greater than $1,000
6. soliciting another person to offer that person a credit card or account number or selling information or an application for a credit card or account number without the authorization of the issuer of the card or account number
7. causing or arranging for another person to seek payment from a credit card system member, without the authority of that member or its agent, by presenting for payment a record of a transaction made by a credit card or account number that affects interstate or foreign commerce
8. uses, produces, traffics in, or has possession, custody or control of a telecommunications instrument modified or altered to obtain the unauthorized use of telecommunication services

9. uses, produces, traffics in, or has possession, custody or control of a scanning receiver
10. uses, produces, traffics in, or has possession, custody or control of hardware or software used for altering or modifying telecommunication instruments to obtain unauthorized access to telecommunication services

Electronic Fund Transfer Fraud

The access device fraud statute is a much broader-based tool for the criminal prosecution of the fraudulent use of account numbers relating to online credit and debit card fraud. The electronic fund transfer fraud statute, however, only applies to the prosecution of online *debit* card fraud.

The electronic fund transfer (EFT) fraud statute, 15 USC § 1693n, prohibits two types of conduct: (1) providing false information, unlawfully withholding information, or otherwise failing to perform any requirement of EFT law set forth in 15 USC §§ 1693, et seq., and (2) engaging in some transaction or activity involving a counterfeit, fictitious, altered, forged, lost, stolen, or fraudulently obtained debit instrument. Subdivision (c) of Section 1693n defines a *debit instrument* as

> a card, code, or other device, other than a check, draft, or similar paper instrument, by the use of which a person may initiate an electronic fund transfer.

Clearly, this definition includes what we commonly refer to as our ATM card or our debit card. Although prosecutors have not made frequent use of this criminal provision in the past, that will likely change as the Check 21 program, which involves the electronification of the check payment and processing system, becomes fully operational.

There are six means of using a counterfeit, fictitious, stolen, lost, or fraudulently obtained debit instrument to commit a criminal violation of this statute:

1. Knowingly using, or attempting or conspiring to use, such a debit instrument in a transaction affecting interstate or foreign commerce to obtain money, merchandise, or anything else of value in an amount exceeding $1,000 within a 12-month period
2. With intent to defraud, transporting, attempting, or conspiring to transport such a debit instrument in interstate or foreign commerce, knowing it to be counterfeit, forged, stolen, etc.
3. With intent to defraud, using any instrumentality of interstate or foreign commerce (e.g., the Internet) to sell or transport such a debit instrument, knowing that it is counterfeit, forged, stolen, etc.
4. Knowingly receiving, concealing, using, or transporting money, merchandise, or anything else of value in an amount aggregating $1,000 or more within any one-year period that has moved in or is part of interstate or foreign commerce and was obtained with a counterfeit, fictitious, stolen, etc., debit instrument
5. Knowingly receiving, concealing, using, selling, or transporting in interstate or foreign commerce one or more tickets for interstate or foreign transportation

aggregating $500 or more in value within a one-year period purchased or obtained with a counterfeit, fictitious, stolen, etc., debit instrument.

6. Furnishing money, property, services, or anything else of value aggregating $1,000 or more within any one-year period in a transaction affecting interstate or foreign commerce through the use of a counterfeit, stolen, fraudulently obtained, etc., debit instrument.

Identity Theft and Fraud

Identity theft has been described as the crime of the new millennium.[4] That description was written before the incidences of phishing and pharming took identity theft as a cybercrime to a much higher level.

Identity Theft

The crime of identify theft encompasses two types of conduct: the theft of an existing person's or entity's identity, which is identity theft, and the manufacture and use of a fictitious person's or entity's identity, which is referred to as identity fraud. The occurrence of identity theft or fraud is difficult to measure because that conduct frequently also appears as an essential ingredient of other crimes, such as credit card fraud, access device fraud, computer fraud, wire fraud, bank fraud, etc.

The following events are illustrations of the crime of identity theft:

In January 2003, two individuals were charged with stealing the identity of celebrity performers. Patrick Peter Ward allegedly obtained a Nevada driver's license and a credit card in the name of Jonathan Rashleigh Knight, a member of the former group New Kids on the Block. Michael Veskovic allegedly obtained a Nevada driver's license and a credit card by posing as Backstreet Boy Kevin Scott Richardson and Daniel William Wood, a member of the former New Kids on the Block. The men have been charged with identity theft, access device fraud, and social security number fraud in connection with these events, which occurred in November and December 2002.

On January 3, 2003, the *New York Times* reported that Ivy Johnson, a former manager at an H&R Block office in White Plains, New York, and three of her friends had been charged with conspiracy to commit mail fraud and credit card fraud involving an elaborate identity theft. Johnson and her friends allegedly used the names and other personal identifying information of at least 27 H&R Block customers to obtain credit cards that were then delivered to post office boxes or diverted to specific addresses by filing change-of-address notices with the post office. The four accused individuals then used the false credit cards to obtain thousands of dollars in cash and merchandise.

In perhaps the biggest identity theft scheme in U.S. history, several individuals in Brooklyn and Bronx, New York, have been charged with wire fraud. According to charges filed in federal court, Philip Cummings, a help desk worker at Teledata Communications, a software company that provides banks with access to credit information databases, sold passwords and codes to several other people for downloading credit reports containing personal information. It appears that at least 30,000 people were victimized to the tune of at least $2.7 million.

The Federal Identity Theft Crimes

18 USC § 1028

This statute initially was enacted in 1982. At that time, the statute was designed to punish the manufacture and trafficking in false identification cards, such as alien registration cards, driver's licenses, social security cards, etc. Congress substantially revised the statute in 1998 by enacting the Identity Fraud Assumption and Deterrence Act. The statute was revised more recently in 2000, 2005, and 2006. In its current form this statute proscribes those who engage in the following conduct:

(1) knowingly and without lawful authority produces an identification document or a false identification document;

(2) knowingly transfers an identification document or a false identification document knowing that such document was stolen or produced without lawful authority;

(3) knowingly possesses with intent to use unlawfully or transfer unlawfully five or more identification documents (other than those issued lawfully for the use of the possessor) or false identification documents;

(4) knowingly possesses an identification document (other than one issued lawfully for the use of the possessor) or a false identification document, with the intent such document be used to defraud the United States;

(5) knowingly produces, transfers, or possesses a document-making implement with the intent such document-making implement will be used in the production of a false identification document or another document-making implement which will be so used;

(6) knowingly possesses an identification document that is or appears to be an identification document of the United States, or a sponsoring entity of an event designated as a special event of national significance, which is stolen or produced without lawful authority knowing that such document was stolen or produced without such authority; or

(7) knowingly transfers, possesses, or uses, without lawful authority, a means of identification of another person with the intent to commit, or to aid or abet, any unlawful activity that constitutes a violation of Federal law, or that constitutes a felony under any applicable State or local law;

(8) knowingly traffics in false or actual authentication features for use in false identification documents, document-making implements, or means of identification.

The statute contains the following definitions:

- the term "document-making implement" means any implement, impression, template, computer file, computer disc, electronic device, or computer hardware or software, that is specifically configured or primarily used for making an identification document, a false identification document, or another document-making implement;

- the term "authentication feature" means any hologram, watermark, certification, symbol, code, image, sequence of numbers or letters, or other feature that either individually or in combination with another feature is used by the issuing authority on an identification document, document-making implement, or a means of identification to determine if the document is counterfeit, altered, or otherwise falsified;

- the term "identification document" means a document made or issued by or under the authority of the United States Government, a State, political subdivision of a State, a sponsoring entity of an event designated as a special event of national significance, a foreign government, political subdivision of a foreign government, an international governmental organization which, when completed with information concerning a particular individual, is of a type intended or commonly accepted for the purpose of identification of individual;

- the terms "means of identification" means any name or number that may be used, alone or in conjunction with any other information, to identify a specific individual, including any—
  - name, social security number, date of birth, official State or government issued driver's license or identification number, alien registration number, government passport number, employer or taxpayer identification number;
  - unique biometric data, such as fingerprint, voice print, retina or iris image, or other unique physical representation;
  - unique electronic identification number, address, or routing code; or
  - telecommunication identifying information or access device (as defined in section 1029(e));
- the term "personal identification card" means an identification document issued by a State or local government solely for the purpose of identification;
- the term "produce" includes alter, authenticate, or assemble; and
- the term "State" includes any State of the United States, the District of Columbia, the Commonwealth of Puerto Rico, and any other commonwealth, possession, or territory of the United States;
- the term "transfer" includes selecting an identification document, false identification document, or document-making implement and placing or directing the placement of such identification document, false identification document, or document-making implement on an online location where it is available to others.

18 USC § 1028A

In 2004, Congress increased the penalties in those instances of identity theft involved in the perpetration of specified felonies, including terrorism felonies set forth in 18 USC § 2332b (g)(5)(B), by creating the crime of aggravated identity theft, which applies to those who:

(a) … during and in relation to any felony violation enumerated in subsection (c), [or during and in relation to any felony violation enumerated in Section 2332b(g)(5)(B)], knowingly transfers, possesses, or uses, without lawful authority, a means of identification of another person [or in the case of terrorism, a false identification document] shall, in addition to the punishment provided for such felony, be sentenced to a term of imprisonment of 2 years [or in the case of terrorism, five years].

The specified felonies include theft or embezzlement by a bank officer or employee, theft from employee benefit plans, false personation of citizenship, false statements relating to the acquisition of a firearm, any other provision of the same chapter relating to fraud and false statements, mail and wire fraud, violations of the federal criminal code relating to nationality and citizenship, passports and visas, immigration, false statements in violation of the Social Security Act, and violations of 15 USC § 6823 (the Gramm-Leach-Bliley Act), relating to the acquisition of customer information by false pretenses. With respect to sentencing, this statute mandates that persons convicted of aggravated identity theft not be placed on probation and requires that the sentence for aggravated identity theft run consecutively to any sentence imposed for the underlying felony.

Although Section 1028 is the federal statute criminalizing identity theft and fraud, it is not the sole legislative effort to combat identity theft and fraud. In 2003, Congress enacted the Fair and Accurate Credit Transaction Act (FACTA). This amendment to the Fair Credit Reporting Act (FCRA) enables consumers to place fraud alerts on credit records maintained by credit reporting agencies such as Experian, Trans Union, and Equifax; directs the Federal Trade Commission to develop guidelines for credit card issuers to follow to identify patterns and practices that lead to identity theft and requiring those issuers to verify changes of address under certain circumstances; requires credit card machines at the point of sale to truncate credit card numbers on card receipts by 2007; and prohibits anyone providing credit information to report inaccurate information if the furnisher "knows or has reasonable cause to believe that the information is inaccurate."

State Identity Theft Laws

Prior to the terrorist attacks of September 11, 2001, most states did not have criminal statutes designed specifically to address identity theft or fraud. Since then, however, there has been increased state legislative activity concerning identity theft, including a new statutory scheme in New York that appears below.

Penal Law § 190.78. Identity theft in the third degree

A person is guilty of identity theft in the third degree when he or she knowingly and with intent to defraud assumes the identity of another person by presenting himself or herself as that other person, or by acting as that other person or by using personal identifying information of that other person, and thereby:

1. obtains goods, money, property or services or uses credit in the name of such other person or causes financial loss to such person or to another person or persons; or
2. commits a class A misdemeanor or higher level crime.

Identity theft in the third degree is a class A misdemeanor.

Penal Law § 190.79. Identity theft in the second degree

A person is guilty of identity theft in the second degree when he or she knowingly and with intent to defraud assumes the identity of another person by presenting himself or herself as that other person, or by acting as that other person or by using personal identifying information of that other person, and thereby:

1. obtains goods, money, property or services or uses credit in the name of such other person in an aggregate amount that exceeds five hundred dollars; or
2. causes financial loss to such person or to another person or persons in an aggregate amount that exceeds five hundred dollars; or
3. commits or attempts to commit a felony or acts as an accessory to the commission of a felony; or
4. commits the crime of identity theft in the third degree as defined in section 190.78 of this article and has been previously convicted within the last five years of identity theft in the third degree as defined in section 190.78, identity theft in the second degree as defined in this section, identity theft in the first degree as defined in section 190.80, unlawful possession of personal identification information in the third degree as defined in section 190.81, unlawful possession of personal identification information in the second degree as defined in section 190.82, unlawful possession of personal

identification information in the first degree as defined in section 190.83, grand larceny in the fourth degree as defined in section 155.30, grand larceny in the third degree as defined in section 155.35, grand larceny in the second degree as defined in section 155.40 or grand larceny in the first degree as defined in section 155.42 of this chapter.

Identity theft in the second degree is a class E felony.

Penal Law § 190.80. Identity theft in the first degree

A person is guilty of identity theft in the first degree when he or she knowingly and with intent to defraud assumes the identity of another person by presenting himself or herself as that other person, or by acting as that other person or by using personal identifying information of that other person, and thereby:

1. obtains goods, money, property or services or uses credit in the name of such other person in an aggregate amount that exceeds two thousand dollars; or
2. causes financial loss to such person or to another person or persons in an aggregate amount that exceeds two thousand dollars; or
3. commits or attempts to commit a class D felony or higher level crime or acts as an accessory in the commission of a class D or higher level felony; or
4. commits the crime of identity theft in the second degree as defined in section 190.79 of this article and has been previously convicted within the last five years of identity theft in the third degree as defined in section 190.78, identity theft in the second degree as defined in section 190.79, identity theft in the first degree as defined in this section, unlawful possession of personal identification information in the third degree as defined in section 190.81, unlawful possession of personal identification information in the second degree as defined in section 190.82, unlawful possession of personal identification information in the first degree as defined in section 190.83, grand larceny in the fourth degree as defined in section 155.30, grand larceny in the third degree as defined in section 155.35, grand larceny in the second degree as defined in section 155.40 or grand larceny in the first degree as defined in section 155.42 of this chapter.

Identity theft in the first degree is a class D felony.

One of the issues presented by the New York statutory scheme is whether the stolen or fraudulent identity must be the identity of an actual person. In other words, can one commit identity theft under the New York criminal provisions by merely creating and using a fictitious identity? The problem is with the term *another person*. If that term is read in its ordinary meaning, the perpetrator would be one living person and the victim would be "another [living] person." We have no published decision yet. What do you think?

New York law also prohibits the possession of personal identification information:

Penal Law § 190.81. Unlawful possession of personal identification information in the third degree

A person is guilty of unlawful possession of personal identification information in the third degree when he or she knowingly possesses a person's financial services account number or code, savings account number or code, checking account number or code, brokerage account number or code, credit card account number or code, debit card number or code, automated teller machine number or code, personal identification number, mother's maiden name, computer system password, electronic signature or unique biometric data that is a fingerprint, voice print, retinal image or iris image of another person knowing such information is intended to be used in furtherance of the commission of a crime defined in this chapter.

Unlawful possession of personal identification information in the third degree is a class A misdemeanor.

A person is guilty of unlawful possession of personal identification information in the second degree, a class E felony, if that person has 150 or more items of such information and intends to use those items in the furtherance of a crime (Penal Law § 190.82). A person is guilty of unlawful possession of personal identification information in the first degree, a class D felony, if the person commits the second degree offense and, with intent to commit identity theft in the second degree, supervises three or more persons, or if the person has prior convictions for identity theft, unlawful possession of personal identification information, or grand larceny.

Cyberlaundering

Technically speaking, cyberlaundering is not the typical conduct we describe as fraud because there is no false statement. Also, cyberlaundering can be committed without an Internet transmission. Nevertheless, because it involves the electronic movement of money that in many cases is obtained through fraudulent conduct, cyberlaundering is discussed here rather than in its own separate chapter.

Although an oversimplification, cyberlaundering is the illegal movement of funds in cyberspace. Cyberlaundering is money laundering that involves the movement of monetary instruments or cash digitally, or electronically. In a general sense, money laundering is committed when a criminal deposits the proceeds from his or her criminal activity into the financial stream (placement stage), moves that money from institution to institution, often from country to country (layering stage), and then removes that money from the same or a different financial institution for either legitimate or illegitimate purposes (integration stage).

The federal government and nearly every state have a money laundering statute. The federal money laundering crimes are set forth in 18 USC §§ 1956 and 1957. Section 1956 essentially prohibits three forms of conduct:

1. conducting, or attempting to conduct, a financial transaction that involves the proceeds of specified unlawful activity with knowledge that the property used in the transaction represents the proceeds of some form of unlawful activity
   (a) with the intent to promote specified unlawful activity; or
   (b) with the intent to violate income tax laws, either 26 U.S.C. § 7201 or § 7206; or
   (c) knowing that the transaction is designed in whole or in part to (i) conceal or disguise the nature, location, source, ownership, or the control of the illicit proceeds, or (ii) to avoid a currency reporting requirement.
2. transporting, transferring, or transmitting, or attempting to transport, transfer, or transmit, a monetary instrument or funds into or outside the United States with the intent to
   (a) promote specified unlawful activity; or
   (b) knowing that such transportation, etc., is designed in whole or in part (i) to conceal or disguise the nature, location, source, ownership, or control of the proceeds of unlawful activity, or (ii) to avoid a currency transaction reporting requirement; or

3. conducting, or attempting to conduct, a financial transaction involving illicit proceeds or property used to conduct or facilitate such illegal activity, with the intent either to promote the carrying on of such illegal activity or to conceal or disguise the nature, location, source, ownership, or control of such property.

Section 1957 prohibits the engaging in a monetary transaction in "criminally derived property" having a value greater than $10,000 and derived from specified unlawful activity, provided that the offense takes place within the territorial jurisdiction of the United States or, if not, that the perpetrator is a U.S. person.

Although neither Section 1956 nor Section 1957 specifically states that it is applicable to digital or electronic transmissions, the following case resolves the point.

United States v. Prince

214 F.3D 740 (2000)

U.S. Court of Appeals, Sixth Circuit

OPINION BY: Sandra S. Beckwith, District Judge.

Beginning on or around January 2, 1991, Defendant White devised and engaged in a scheme to "defraud and obtain money by means of false and fraudulent pretenses, representations and promises." Defendant White represented to certain individuals that he was "bonded with" the U.S. Bankruptcy Court and that this enabled him to buy assets involved in bankruptcies which he could then sell for a sizeable profit. Defendants Prince and White solicited individuals to invest in their alleged plan to purchase and then sell these assets. Investors contributed money for purchasing property and for covering alleged costs associated with purchasing property involved in bankruptcies, e.g., taxes, accountant fees, closing costs, etc. The government established at trial that individuals could not purchase property from the bankruptcy court as was represented by Defendants.

According to the evidence presented at trial, Defendants physically obtained investors' money through one of three types of arrangements. Under one arrangement, Defendants directed investors to wire transfer the money into the bank accounts of third parties. Per a pre-arranged agreement with either or both Defendants, the third party wrote a check in the amount of the transfer, cashed that check, and then transferred the money in cash to Defendant Prince. On at least a couple of occasions, Prince received a personal check, rather than cash, from the third party. On at least one occasion the third party transferred the cash to another third party who then transferred the cash to Prince. On all occasions Prince eventually transferred the money to White. Prince explained to some investors that money needed to be wired to a third party's account because Prince did not have a bank account and/or that he was in bankruptcy and a monetary transfer would cause the bankruptcy court to attach his account.

Under a second arrangement, Defendants directed investors to wire transfer money via Western Union to third parties. Per a pre-arranged agreement with either or both Defendants, the third party signed for and received the money and then transferred it in cash to Defendant Prince. Prince then transferred to Defendant White the money received from the third parties.

Under a third arrangement, Defendants directed investors to wire transfer money via Western Union to Prince. Prince signed for and received the money from a Western Union representative. Prince then transferred the money to White.

It was not established at trial how Defendants disposed of the money fraudulently obtained. Victims testified that they had not received any of the money they had invested.

Defendant Prince challenges his convictions for money laundering under 18 U.S.C. section 1956(a)(1)(B)(i). The elements of the charged money laundering offenses are:

(1) use of funds that are proceeds of unlawful activity; (2) knowledge that the funds are proceeds of unlawful activity; and (3) conduct or attempt to conduct a financial transaction, knowing that the transaction is designed in whole or in part to disguise the nature, location, source, ownership or control of the proceeds.

United States v. Moss, 9 F.3d 543, 551 (6th Cir. 1993).

On appeal, Defendant Prince first asserts that the money obtained through the offense of wire fraud did not become proceeds of unlawful activity as defined in the money laundering statute until he physically obtained the funds of the wire transfer. He concludes that once he obtained these funds, he did not conduct or attempt to conduct a transaction and therefore he did not violate the statute. Second, Prince argues that if a transaction occurred, the proof does not establish that it was conducted in an attempt to conceal the nature and source of the money. Third, Prince contends that there was "no substantial evidence" to support a conviction of aiding and abetting.

Prince has failed to establish that insufficient evidence supports the three elements of money laundering.

1. Use of funds that are proceeds of an unlawful activity

Under the first element of money laundering, the funds allegedly laundered by Defendant Prince must be the proceeds of an unlawful activity. Specifically, the funds must represent proceeds from some form of activity that constitutes a felony. 18 U.S.C. § 1956 (c)(1). "Proceeds" include "'what is produced by or derived from something (as a sale, investment, levy, business) by way of total revenue.'" *Haun*, 90 F.3d at 1101 (quoting Webster's Third New International Dictionary 1807 (1971)).

In this case, the indictment identifies wire fraud as the underlying felony from which the proceeds were derived. The elements of wire fraud, as prescribed under 18 U.S.C. section 1343, are as follows: (1) a scheme or artifice to defraud; (2) use of interstate wire communications in furtherance of the scheme; and (3) intent to deprive a victim of money or property. Defendants must have used the proceeds of the acts of wire fraud to commit money laundering.

We conclude that the money, once wired by the victims, constituted proceeds of wire fraud. *United States v. Savage*, 67 F.3d 1435 (9th Cir. 1995), cert. denied, 516 U.S. 1136, 116 S. Ct. 964, 133 L. Ed. 2d 885 (1996), supports the proposition that Prince did not need to have physical possession of the money before it could be considered proceeds. In *Savage*, the defendant was convicted of various offenses including wire fraud and money laundering. The defendant defrauded individuals by promising that if they sent him $5,000, he would obtain foreign loans and earn each investor a return of $10 million. The defendant recruited assistants to help him raise money, transfer it, and launder it. The assistant would direct investors to send money to the assistant's bank account. In some of these transactions, the assistant transferred that money to a foreign bank account; at that point, the money either was sent back to the defendant's personal accounts in the United States or was used directly to pay the defendant's expenses. On appeal, the defendant in *Savage* contended that the international monetary transfers did not involve proceeds of unlawful activity as defined in section 1956. However, the Ninth Circuit concluded that the international monetary transfers did involve the proceeds of the previous acts of wire fraud. In appealing his convictions on 18 U.S.C. section 1957 offenses, the defendant argued that he did not have possession of the money when the wire transfers were sent because the money was not transferred out of his personal account. The court held that the funds transferred were criminally derived property at the time they were deposited in accounts under the defendant's control. The court found that the funds were at the defendant's disposal because the record indicated that the parties named on the accounts transferred the money at the defendant's request. The court stated that it was irrelevant that the accounts were not in the defendant's name.

In the present case, Defendants had sufficient control over the funds wired to Prince as well as the funds wired to third parties. In the instances in which victims transferred money to Prince directly, once the victims wired the money, it constituted proceeds. The same is true when victims transferred money to a third party because Prince had sufficient control over that money. In every case in which money was transferred to a third party, the third party was someone with whom Prince had a relationship. Prince solicited the help of his sister, his brother, a niece, two sister-in-laws, his accountant, two of his employees, and an individual who Prince had known his whole life. Prince had reached a prior agreement with each of them in which the third party had agreed to transfer the money to Prince. On all occasions, the third party complied. On all occasions, whether the victim transferred the money to a third party or Prince, Prince transferred the money to White. The Defendants devised, participated in, and were in constructive control of this elaborate scheme.

Even if, *arguendo*, the money did not constitute proceeds until the money was in Prince's hands, Prince fails to satisfy his burden on his claim of insufficient evidence. As is addressed below, Defendants conducted transactions after Prince had physical possession of the proceeds. Evidence established that Prince transferred each payment or contribution to White. Sufficient evidence supports the first element of money laundering.

2. Knowledge that the funds are proceeds of unlawful activity
   Prince does not argue that this element was not supported by sufficient evidence.
3. Conduct or attempt to conduct a financial transaction knowing that the transaction is designed in whole or in part to disguise the nature, location, source, ownership, or control of the proceeds
   On appeal, Defendant Prince argues that the government failed to present any proof of a subsequent financial transaction designed to conceal the nature of the funds. The term "financial transaction" means
   (A) a transaction which in any way or degree affects interstate or foreign commerce
       (i) involving the movement of funds by wire or other means or
       (ii) involving one or more monetary instruments, or
       (iii) involving the transfer of title to any real property, vehicle, vessel, or aircraft, or
   (B) a transaction involving the use of a financial institution which is engaged in, or the activities of which affect, interstate or foreign commerce in any way or degree;

18 U.S.C. § 1956 (c)(4).

The term "transaction"

includes a purchase, sale, loan, pledge, gift, transfer, delivery, or other disposition, and with respect to a financial institution includes a deposit, withdrawal, transfer between accounts, exchange of currency, loan, extension of credit, purchase or sale of any stock, bond, certificate of deposit, or other monetary instrument, use of a safe deposit box, or any other payment, transfer, or delivery by, through, or to a financial institution, by whatever means effected;

18 U.S.C. § 1956 (c)(3).

The term "monetary instruments" means

(i) coin or currency of the United States or of any other country, travelers' checks, personal checks, bank checks, and money orders, or

(ii) investment securities or negotiable instruments, in bearer form or otherwise in such form that title thereto passes upon delivery;

18 U.S.C. § 1956 (c)(5).

In the present case, Defendant Prince, in violation of the wire fraud statute, induced victims to wire money. The subsequent transactions involving the proceeds of wire fraud constitute financial transactions as defined in section 1956. In the first of the three types of arrangements, Prince directed the victims to wire money to the bank accounts of third parties. He typically directed the third party to either withdraw money from the bank account or write a check on that account and cash that check. Then, the third party would transfer the cash to Prince. The act of withdrawing the money from the bank account constitutes a transaction, specifically a withdrawal, involving the use of a financial institution. The act of transferring cash from the third party to Prince is a transaction as defined in section (c)(3) in that it is a transfer or disposition of a monetary instrument, i.e., cash. Likewise, on those few occasions when the third party wrote Prince a check, that constituted a transfer or disposition of a monetary instrument, i.e., a personal check. Prince caused two transactions to be conducted— one between the third party and the bank and one between the third party and Prince. Upon completion of the transactions or dispositions, Prince then transferred the funds to White. This constitutes yet another disposition of the proceeds of wire fraud.

Under the second type of arrangement, Defendant Prince instructed victims to wire money to third parties via Western Union. Prince effected a disposition or transfer by directing the third party, who had been instructed to retrieve the money from Western Union, to transfer the cash to him. Through such conduct, Prince has effected a disposition of the proceeds of the wire fraud.

Upon completion of the transaction or disposition from the third party to Prince, Prince then transferred the funds to White. This constitutes a second disposition of the proceeds of wire fraud.

Under the third type of arrangement, Defendant Prince instructed victims to transfer money to him via Western Union. Prince testified that all of the money that victims transferred to him he transferred to Defendant White. This delivery of the wire fraud proceeds to White constitutes a financial transaction.

Defendant Prince contends that no evidence supports the allegation that he conducted the transactions in an attempt to conceal the funds. The evidence presented suggests that Prince, at the very least, aided in a scheme in which there was an attempt to conceal the true owner and controller of funds.

On some occasions, Prince directed victims to contribute money to the scheme through a third party. This arrangement involved explaining the use of a third party to the potential investor, soliciting the assistance of a trusted third party, requiring the third party to go to their bank or to a Western Union office to obtain the money, effecting the transfer to Prince, and then arranging the transfer from Prince to White. This elaborate arrangement protected Defendants from a potential paper trail. Prince usually instructed the third parties to whom money had been transferred, to give him cash. Mrs. Bell, Prince's sister, testified that Prince requested that he receive the money in cash. At times, these instructions required the third parties to go to their bank and withdraw the money rather than simply writing a check payable to Prince, White, or the bankruptcy court for which the money was allegedly collected. Again, this prevented a paper trail.

The government presented testimony which suggested that Prince structured transactions so that a third party would never withdraw more than $10,000 from their bank account in one transaction. Chris Mathis, one of these third parties as well as Prince's accountant, testified that a transaction in excess of $10,000 would require the bank to send a cash transaction report to the Internal Revenue Service. Mrs. Bell, one of the third parties and Prince's sister, testified that on one occasion where she gave Prince $19,000, she wrote two separate checks, each for $9,500, so that the transaction would not be reported. On one occasion, $10,700 was wire transferred to Chris Mathis' account, but to withdraw the money, Mr. Mathis wrote two checks, one for $700 and one for $10,000.

The few Western Union transfers sent by victims who identified Prince as the recipient still helped conceal, as they did not identify White who, as Prince testified, was the final recipient of the proceeds of all of the transfers. By directing the transfers to himself, Prince aided White by concealing the fact that White was the true controller of the proceeds of this scheme.

The government elicited testimony that Prince, on at least two occasions, stated that due to the structure of the transactions it could not be proven that he received money. One witness, who on two occasions had received money in her account and transferred it to Prince, testified that Prince called her and told her the IRS was auditing the bank and instructed her not to mention his name. The structuring of the transactions combined with Prince's statements adequately support the theory that Prince, at the very least, aided in a scheme involving transactions conducted in an attempt to conceal the proceeds of wire fraud.

On the issue of sufficiency of the evidence on the money laundering counts, we hold that Prince has failed to satisfy his very heavy burden.

Other Fraudulent Schemes

There is no limit to the types and permutations of schemes and swindles that can be perpetrated in cyberspace. Space does not permit a complete discussion of all of the various types, but some of the additional fraudulent schemes not already discussed include:

Mail order bride schemes
Lottery and sweepstakes schemes
Social networking schemes
Disaster frauds

Key Words and Phrases

Access device

Aggravated identity theft

Auction fraud

Cyberlaundering

Debit instrument

Electronic fund transfer fraud

Identity fraud

Identity theft

Mail order bride schemes

Ponzi scheme

Pyramid scheme

Wireless fraud

Review Problems

1. Describe what conduct constitutes a Ponzi scheme and a pyramid scheme. What is the major difference between them and which one is easier to prosecute?
2. For purposes of electronic fund transfer fraud, what is a debit instrument? What are the essential elements of electronic fund transfer fraud and how does this crime differ from access device fraud?
3. Can a means of identification as defined in the identity theft statute be considered an access device under Section 1029?
4. One of the major methods of stealing one's identity is to persuade that person to part with their personal information by engaging in phishing. How does phishing work and can that conduct be prosecuted under Section 1028?

Weblinks

www.antiphishing.org/

This is the website of the Anti-Phishing Working Group, a public-private collaborative effort to combat phishing and pharming. This is an excellent site for information on phishing and the methods that are employed to commit identity theft.

www.consumer.gov/idtheft/

This website focused on identity theft is maintained by the Federal Trade Commission.

www.privacyrights.org/identity.htm

This website of the Privacy Rights Clearinghouse provides many links to information concerning identity theft and fraud.

www.aic.gov.au/conferences/2002-ml/part1.html

This website of the Australian Institute of Criminology provides information presented at a symposium on the development of cyberlaundering as a means of laundering money after 9/11.

Endnotes

1. IC3 2005 Internet Crime Report. http://www.ic3.gov/media/annualreport/2005_IC3Report.pdf (retrieved June 8, 2006).
2. Federal Trade Commission. Consumer Fraud and Identity Theft Complaint Data. January–December 2005. http://www.consumer.gov/sentinel/pubs/Top10Fraud2005.pdf (retrieved June 8, 2006).
3. Details on the coupon scheme employed by Charles Ponzi can be found at www.crimes-of-persuasion.com/Crimes/InPerson/MajorPerson/ponzi.htm.
4. See John Q. Newman. (1999). *Identity Theft: The Cybercrime of the Millennium*. Seattle, WA: Loompanics.

Crimes against Information Assets, and Data Privacy

Data Privacy Crimes

6

Introduction

The theft of personal information such as social security numbers and credit card account numbers from a corporate database or employee laptop seems to be occurring on nearly a daily basis. Corporations and institutions like ChoicePoint, LexisNexis, Card Services, University of Texas, and many others have been victimized by those intrusions.

Because the storage or transmission of sensitive personal information creates a significant risk that stolen information will be used in the commission of identity theft or fraud, access device fraud, and other crimes, Congress and the legislatures of some states have enacted laws imposing criminal penalties against those who violate data protection regulations or standards.

The Fair Credit Reporting Act (FCRA)

The Fair Credit Reporting Act was enacted in 1970 for the purpose of regulating the manner in which credit reporting agencies handle and protect the credit information of consumers. The FCRA, which appears at 15 USC §§ 1681a–x, authorizes the credit reporting agencies to provide credit reports to their customers for five purposes: credit review, insurance underwriting, licensing, employment, and the "legitimate business need" involving a "business transaction involving the consumer" (15 USC § 1681b (3)). In some instances, for example, a credit report for employment purposes, the consumer must authorize the employer to obtain that credit history.

The FCRA imposes criminal liability upon "any person who knowingly and willfully obtains information on a consumer from a consumer reporting agency under false pretenses" (15 USC § 1681q) and upon "any officer or employee of a consumer reporting agency who knowingly and willfully provides information concerning an individual from the agency's files to a person not authorized to receive that information" (15 USC § 2681r).

As illustrated by the following case, the FCRA authorizes consumers to bring civil lawsuits for violations of the act.

Phillips v. Grendahl

312 F.3D 357 (2002)

U.S. COURT OF APPEALS, EIGHTH CIRCUIT

OPINION: JOHN R. GIBSON, Circuit Judge.

Mary Grendahl's daughter Sarah became engaged to marry Phillips and moved in with him. Mary Grendahl became suspicious that Phillips was not telling the truth about his past, particularly about whether he was an attorney and whether he had done legal work in Washington, D.C. She also was confused about who his ex-wives and girl-friends were and where they lived. She did some preliminary investigation herself, but she felt that she was hampered by not being able to use a computer, so she contacted Kevin Fitzgerald, a family friend who worked for McDowell, a private investigation agency. She asked Fitzgerald to do a "background check" on Phillips, and she also gave him the name of the woman Phillips had lived with before Sarah Grendahl.

Fitzgerald began his search by obtaining Phillips's social security number from a computer database. He also searched public records in Minnesota and Alabama, where Phillips had lived earlier. He discovered one suit against Phillips for delinquent child support in Alabama, a suit to establish child support for two children in Minnesota, and one misdemeanor conviction for writing dishonored checks.

Fitzgerald then supplied the social security information to Econ Control and asked for "Finder's Reports" on Phillips and the former girlfriend. Fitzgerald testified that he believed that Finder's Reports were not consumer reports and therefore that they were not subject to the Fair Credit Reporting Act.

Econ Control was in the business of furnishing credit reports, Finder's Reports, and credit scoring for credit grantors and for private investigators. William Porter, president of Econ Control, testified in his deposition in this case that he had been advised by a representative of Computer Science Corporation that one of their products, called a "Finder's Report," could be obtained without authorization of the person who was the subject of the report because the Finder's Report contained no information on credit history or creditworthiness. Porter testified that a Credit Report, on the other hand, requires authorization from the subject. Fitzgerald learned of Econ Control from a presentation by Porter at a meeting of the Minnesota Private Investigators Association. Porter told the investigators at the seminar that no authorization was necessary to obtain a Finder's Report and that it would be useful in trying to locate people. Porter handed out sample Finder's Reports which showed information on a fictional consumer, including address, aliases, birthdate, employer addresses, and the identity of firms with which the consumer had credit accounts and firms that had made inquiries about the consumer.

Robert McDowell, on behalf of McDowell Agency, had signed an Econ Control registration agreement, titled "Agreement for Consumer Credit Services." One clause of the registration agreement stated:

3. I certify that I will order consumer reports, as defined by the Fair Credit Reporting Act, only when they are intended to be used as a factor in establishing a consumer's eligibility for new or continued credit, collections of an account, insurance, licensing, employment purposes, or otherwise in connection with a legitimate business transaction involving the consumer. Such reports will be used for no other purpose. Each time I request a report I intend to use for employment purposes, I will specifically identify it to [Econ Control] at the time I request the report.

Kevin Fitzgerald was listed in the registration agreement as an individual who was authorized "to request credit worthiness scores" for McDowell. To obtain the Finder's Report on Phillips, Fitzgerald simply faxed Econ Control a request listing Phillips's name, date of birth, address and social security number. Econ Control did not ask why McDowell wanted the report, and McDowell did not tell. Econ Control obtained a report from Computer Science Corporation on Phillips and passed it onto McDowell.

Fitzgerald met with Mary Grendahl and gave her the results of his investigation, including the Finder's Report. Someone wrote on the copy of the Finder's Report on Phillips: "Credit inquiry report and Employment Trace."

Phillips learned that Sarah Grendahl's family had investigated his past when Laura Grendahl, Sarah's sister, telephoned Sarah about nine months after the investigation. Phillips's complaint alleges that he also spoke to Laura and that she asked him in this telephone conversation whether he had ever written a bad check and how much back child support he owed. After further unpleasantness between Sarah and her family, Mary Grendahl telephoned and left the following voicemail for Sarah:

> Sarah, this is mom. I didn't directly do a credit report. I hired a PI and they have every right to do that.

The record contains evidence that each defendant has some familiarity with the fact that the law limits access to consumer credit reports. Mary Grendahl owns the Park Apartments in Minneapolis. The apartment business office obtains credit information on prospective tenants as part of its business. The office always obtains the tenant's written permission to obtain a credit report, "because it's necessary to have their signature to get a credit report," according to Mary Grendahl. Porter, the president of Econ Control, testified that he had read the section of the Fair Credit Reporting Act governing resale of credit information. Fitzgerald testified that sometime during his employment with McDowell, he had heard of the Fair Credit Reporting Act.

Phillips brought this suit against Mary Grendahl, McDowell Agency, and Econ Control, alleging, "Defendants willfully and maliciously obtained Plaintiff's credit report for impermissible and illegal purposes in violation of the Fair Credit Reporting Act § 1681q." Phillips also alleged that the defendants had invaded his privacy by disclosing "private and confidential facts to third parties," which was "highly offensive" to Phillips and of no legitimate concern to the public. He also alleged that the defendants had unreasonably intruded upon his seclusion. Phillips appended to his complaint a "Credit History" on himself, complete with lists of charged-off credit card accounts, delinquent child support obligation, government tax lien, and three judgments against him, and also showing that Sherlock Information (the trade name of Econ Control) had requested a credit history on him.

The Fair Credit Reporting Act prohibits the disclosure of consumer credit reports by consumer credit reporting agencies, except in response to the following kinds of requests: (1) court order or subpoena, § 1681b(a)(1); (2) request by governmental agencies involved in setting or enforcing child support awards, § 1681b(a)(4) and (5); (3) request authorized in writing by the consumer about whom the report is made, § 1681b(a)(2); or (4) request by a person whom the reporting agency has reason to believe intends to use the consumer report for one of a number of specific, permissible business reasons, § 1681b(a)(3).

The defendants argue that Phillips has not adduced evidence of each of the elements of his Fair Credit Reporting Act claim and therefore cannot withstand their summary judgment motion.

The first step in establishing liability under section 1681n(a) or section 1681o for obtaining a consumer report without a permissible purpose is to show that the document at issue was a "consumer report." The statutory definition is complex. Section 1681a(d) defines a consumer report as (1) any written, oral, or other communication of information (2) by a consumer reporting agency (3) bearing on a consumer's credit worthiness, credit standing, credit capacity, character, general reputation, personal characteristics, or mode of living (4) which is used or expected to be used or collected in whole or in part for the purpose of serving as a factor in establishing the consumer's eligibility for (A) credit or insurance to be used primarily for personal, family, or household purposes; (B) employment purposes; or (C) any other purposes authorized under section 1681b. Section 1681b in turn lists five major purposes, two of which have many subparts.

In this case, there is no dispute that the Finder's Report was (1) a written communication (2) by a consumer reporting agency, Computer Science Corporation. The two issues in dispute pertaining to whether the Finder's Report is a consumer report are (3) whether it contained the sort of personal information that would bring it within the definition and (4) whether anyone "expected" the Finder's Report or the information in it to be used for one of the purposes listed in the definition or "collected" the information in it for that purpose.

A consumer report must contain information "bearing on a consumer's credit worthiness, credit standing, credit capacity, character, general reputation, personal characteristics, or mode of living." 15 U.S.C. § 1681a(d). The Finder's Report listed "Trade line Information," consisting of the names of several creditors with whom Phillips had credit accounts and the existence of a child support obligation, with dates for "last activity," but no other details such as amount of obligation or payment history. The District of Columbia Circuit has held that information showing the existence of trade lines, even without any details of credit history, satisfies the minimal requirement that information "bear" on the subject's "mode of living," since it shows that he has bothered to establish credit accounts. The Finder's Report also lists Phillips's former employers, which also would bear on his mode of living by showing that he has been employed. We conclude that the Finder's Report contains the kind of personal information required by the definition of consumer report.

The second question, whether the putative consumer report or the information in it was "used or expected to be used" or "collected for" one of the listed purposes, such as use in a credit or employment decision, § 1681a(d), is more difficult. Three statutory ambiguities in this clause could affect what communications are covered by the clause: the statutory language does not specify who must do the using, collecting or expecting; whether those verbs describe a specific or habitual action; or whether those actions must be done with regard to "information" or with regard to the consumer report itself. McDowell Agency essentially argues the clause requires that either the credit agency prepared the Finder's Report in the expectation that it would be used for a statutory purpose or that the requestors did so use it. McDowell Agency contends that the Finder's Report was too incomplete to enable anyone to base a credit decision on it, so neither the requestors nor the credit agency could have expected the report to be used in a credit decision. Phillips, on the other hand, focuses on the information in the report, rather than the report itself. He argues that some of the information was of a type habitually "used" by people within the credit industry for the purposes covered by the statute and that therefore no showing about anyone's actual intent with regard to the Finder's Report was necessary to make it a consumer report.

We need not choose among the competing interpretations of the clause urged by the parties, because we conclude that the Finder's Report fell within the "used, expected to be used, or collected" clause even under the interpretation urged by McDowell Agency. The record demonstrates that the Finder's Report, not just the information in it, was actually intended by the credit reporting agency that prepared it to be used for a statutory purpose. The sample Finder's Report supplied by Econ Control to McDowell Agency states: "FINDERS delivers skip-locate power in a cost effective, easy-to-use format. This remarkable product was designed by and for collections professionals who need timely debt-recovery support at an economical price." In addition to the statutory purposes listed in section 1681a(d), such as extension of credit or offer of employment, the statute incorporates by reference the statutory purposes listed in 15 U.S.C. § 1681b. One purpose in that list is use "in connection with a credit transaction … involving … collection of an account of, the consumer," in other words, debt collection. § 1681b(a)(3)(A); *Duncan v. Handmaker*, 149 F.3d 424, 427-28 (6th Cir. 1998). It therefore appears that the Finder's Report was prepared by Computer Services Corporation with the expectation that it would be used for a statutory purpose. That being the case, the Finder's Report is a consumer report even though the requestor never used or intended to use it for a statutory purpose.

We next determine whether each of the defendants "obtained or used" the consumer report. There is no dispute that McDowell Agency and Econ Control obtained a consumer report, for each of them requested a Finder's Report.

Mary Grendahl, on the other hand, testified that she did not request the release of any credit information on Phillips. Mere passive receipt of the report would not be enough to satisfy the statutory element that she "use or obtain" a consumer report. See 15 U.S.C. § 1681b(f) ("use or obtain") and § 1681n(a)(1)(B) ("obtaining"). However, Phillips argues that the phone machine message Grendahl left for Sarah is evidence that she asked Fitzgerald to obtain credit information: "Sarah, this is mom. I didn't directly do a credit report. I hired a PI and they have every right to do that." This evidence is ambiguous. On the one hand, it could mean that Grendahl hired a private investigator because she thought he was entitled to do a credit report. On the other hand, it could mean that she simply hired a private investigator who ordered a credit report on his own initiative, which she now understood he was entitled to do. Because this case was disposed of on summary judgment, we must resolve any ambiguities in the evidence in favor of Phillips. In this procedural posture, the ambiguous telephone message is sufficient to create a genuine issue of fact as to whether Mary Grendahl asked Fitzgerald to obtain a consumer report on Phillips.

Phillips also argues that Laura Grendahl's comments about him being delinquent in child support and having written bad checks is evidence that Mary Grendahl used the Finder's Report. To the contrary, the Finder's Report does not reveal that Phillips was behind in child support or had written bad checks, so Laura could not have learned these facts from the Finder's Report. Therefore, Laura Grendahl's comments do not help to prove Mary Grendahl used the Finder's Report.

The next inquiry is whether any of the defendants had a permissible statutory purpose for obtaining the consumer report. The only purpose for obtaining the report was to obtain information on Mary Grendahl's prospective son-in-law. Investigating a person because he wants to marry one's daughter is not a statutory consumer purpose under section 1681b(a). Even if getting married can be characterized as a consumer transaction under section 1681b(a)(3), it was not Mary Grendahl, but her daughter, whom Phillips was engaged to marry. He had no business transaction pending with Mary Grendahl. There was no permissible purpose for obtaining or using a consumer report.

The element of culpability varies according to whether the cause arises under section 1681n generally, section 1681n(a), or section 1681o.

Section 1681n(a) provides civil liability for willful noncompliance with any requirement of the Fair Credit Reporting Act.

We must initially determine first, what state of mind amounts to willfulness and second, whether the defendant must willfully request the report or willfully violate a requirement of the Fair Credit Reporting Act.

The statute's use of the word "willfully" imports the requirement that the defendant know his or her conduct is unlawful.

Here, there is evidence that none of the three defendants believed their conduct to be covered by the Fair Credit Reporting Act. William Porter of Econ Control testified that a representative of Computer Science Corporation told him that a Finder's Report was not a "credit report." Kevin Fitzgerald of McDowell Agency knew of Econ Control from the Minnesota Private Investigators Association meeting, where Porter had told the attendees that they could obtain Finder's Reports without the authorization of the subject. Fitzgerald testified, "To the best of my knowledge, a finder's report is not considered a credit history." He also testified: "I did not do anything that I know to be illegal, unethical, or outside the standard practice of private investigators." Mary Grendahl testified that she only asked Fitzgerald to look into Phillips's background and that she gave him no instructions on how to do the investigation. She stated: "At no time did I ask Mr. Fitzgerald to try to obtain credit information or a 'credit report,' and it is my understanding that he did not do so."

On the other hand, there is also evidence that each defendant had some experience in dealing with credit reports and either knew of the Fair Credit Reporting Act or at least knew that such reports can only be obtained legally under certain circumstances. This kind of experience can support an inference that the defendants knew that their actions were impermissible. There is also the telephone message that could be interpreted to mean that Mary Grendahl directed Fitzgerald to obtain a credit report. Additionally, someone wrote on the Phillips Finder's Report: "Credit Inquiry Report & Employment Trace." These facts are sufficient to create a genuine issue of material fact as to whether defendants acted knowingly and with conscious disregard for Phillips's legal rights.

Section 1681o provides a private cause of action for negligent failure to comply with the Fair Credit Reporting Act. Since Phillips has raised factual issues sufficient to require trial on whether defendants willfully violated his rights under the Act, it follows that he has also made a submissible case as to negligent violation of those same rights.

The Fair and Accurate Credit Transactions Act (FACTA)

The Fair and Accurate Credit Transactions Act (FACTA), which was enacted in 2003, amended portions of the Fair Credit Reporting Act. The three most significant changes are that FACTA (1) enables consumers to obtain a free copy of their credit report, (2) enables consumers to place fraud alerts on their credit records, and (3) requires the truncation of account information on charge card receipts.

The Gramm-Leach-Bliley Act (GLBA)

The Gramm-Leach-Bliley Act (GLBA), also known as the Financial Services Modernization Act, was enacted in 1999, repealing the Glass-Steagall Act of 1933. The Glass-Steagall Act prevented certain businesses from selling products or business lines that other financial institutions were authorized to market. For example, banks could not sell securities, insurance companies could not engage in banking transactions, and securities firms could not sell insurance. With the repeal of the Glass-Steagall Act, the nature of financial institutions is redefined[1] and financial institutions are authorized to share information with business units that are affiliated with each other, as well as companies with whom they are not affiliated. Because nonpublic customer information can be shared electronically, as well as by courier or mail, the GLBA requires the Federal Trade Commission and other regulators to adopt privacy and security standards designed to protect that information while in storage or transmission. The privacy statute is set forth below.

15 U.S.C. § 6821. Privacy protection for customer information of financial institutions

(a) Prohibition on obtaining customer information by false pretenses. It shall be a violation of this subtitle [15 USCS §§ 6821 et seq.] for any person to obtain or attempt to obtain, or cause to be disclosed or attempt to cause to be disclosed to any person, customer information of a financial institution relating to another person—

    (1) by making a false, fictitious, or fraudulent statement or representation to an officer, employee, or agent of a financial institution;

    (2) by making a false, fictitious, or fraudulent statement or representation to a customer of a financial institution; or

    (3) by providing any document to an officer, employee, or agent of a financial institution, knowing that the document is forged, counterfeit, lost, or stolen, was fraudulently obtained, or contains a false, fictitious, or fraudulent statement or representation.

(b) Prohibition on solicitation of a person to obtain customer information from financial institution under false pretenses. It shall be a violation of this subtitle [15 USCS §§ 6821 et seq.] to request a person to obtain customer information of a financial institution, knowing that the person will obtain, or attempt to obtain, the information from the institution in any manner described in subsection (a).

(c) Nonapplicability to law enforcement agencies. No provision of this section shall be construed so as to prevent any action by a law enforcement agency, or any officer, employee, or agent of such agency, to obtain customer information of a financial institution in connection with the performance of the official duties of the agency.

(d) Nonapplicability to financial institutions in certain cases. No provision of this section shall be construed so as to prevent any financial institution, or any officer, employee, or agent of a financial institution, from obtaining customer information of such financial institution in the course of—

  (1) testing the security procedures or systems of such institution for maintaining the confidentiality of customer information;

  (2) investigating allegations of misconduct or negligence on the part of any officer, employee, or agent of the financial institution; or

  (3) recovering customer information of the financial institution which was obtained or received by another person in any manner described in subsection (a) or (b).

(e) Nonapplicability to insurance institutions for investigation of insurance fraud. No provision of this section shall be construed so as to prevent any insurance institution, or any officer, employee, or agency of an insurance institution, from obtaining information as part of an insurance investigation into criminal activity, fraud, material misrepresentation, or material nondisclosure that is authorized for such institution under State law, regulation, interpretation, or order.

(f) Nonapplicability to certain types of customer information of financial institutions. No provision of this section shall be construed so as to prevent any person from obtaining customer information of a financial institution that otherwise is available as a public record filed pursuant to the securities laws (as defined in section 3(a)(47) of the Securities Exchange Act of 1934 [15 USCS § 78c(a)(47)]).

(g) Nonapplicability to collection of child support judgments. No provision of this section shall be construed to prevent any State-licensed private investigator, or any officer, employee, or agent of such private investigator, from obtaining customer information of a financial institution, to the extent reasonably necessary to collect child support from a person adjudged to have been delinquent in his or her obligations by a Federal or State court, and to the extent that such action by a State-licensed private investigator is not unlawful under any other Federal or State law or regulation, and has been authorized by an order or judgment of a court of competent jurisdiction.

Parties who violate the privacy statute and rules are subject to criminal sanctions. The criminal statute is set forth below:

15 U.S.C. § 6823. Criminal penalty

(a) In general. Whoever knowingly and intentionally violates, or knowingly and intentionally attempts to violate, section 521 [15 USCS § 6821] shall be fined in accordance with title 18, United States Code, or imprisoned for not more than 5 years, or both.

(b) Enhanced penalty for aggravated cases. Whoever violates, or attempts to violate, section 521 [15 USCS § 6821] while violating another law of the United States or as part of a pattern of any illegal activity involving more than $100,000 in a 12-month period shall be fined twice the amount provided in subsection (b)(3) or (c)(3) (as the case may be) of section 3571 of title 18, United States Code, imprisoned for not more than 10 years, or both.

There currently are no published decisions that involve a criminal violation of Section 6823. The following civil action instituted by a bank to enjoin (prevent) the disclosure of the personal financial information of a consumer aptly illustrates the strength of the privacy protection contemplated by this law:

Union Planters Bank, N.A. v. Gavel

2003 U.S. DIST. LEXIS 3820 (2003)

U.S. DISTRICT COURT, EASTERN DISTRICT OF LOUISIANA

OPINION BY: G. THOMAS PORTEOUS, JR., District Judge.

I. BACKGROUND:

Union Planters Bank, N.A. ("Union Planters") seeks to prevent the release of private consumer financial information without the consent of the relevant consumers in accordance with the Gramm-Leach-Bliley Act ("GLBA"), 15 U.S.C. § 6801 et seq.

Specifically, the subpoena originally requested (1) "any and all records" wherein Union Planters requested the placement or purchase of flood insurance and the amounts of any such insurance policies; (2) the names, addresses, and telephone numbers of any party currently or formerly indebted to Union Planters by virtue of a residential mortgage/deed of trust loan, the current balance of said loan, the original loan amount, the loan balance on the effective date of any flood insurance policy where flood insurance was provided by Union Planters; and, (3) any records showing the mortgage balance and the original amount of the loan where flood insurance was placed by Union Planters.

John A. Gavel, Jr. and his employer, WNC Insurance Services, Inc. ("WNC"), filed a Motion to Quash/Motion for Protective Order with regard to the subpoena in the state court to the extent it sought information barred from disclosure by Louisiana privacy laws and the GLBA. The motion was denied; however, the state court limited the subpoena as follows:

All records regarding forced placement of insurance in the State of Louisiana from Union Planters Bank, by and through John A. Gavel, Jr., a Louisiana broker, as requested by WNC from January 1, 1991, through December 31, 2001.

II. ARGUMENTS OF THE RESPECTIVE PARTIES:

A. Arguments of Union Planters in Support of a Preliminary Injunction:

Union Planters contends that it will succeed on the merits of its claim. The GLBA clearly prohibits the disclosure of non-public information to third parties unless the consumer is given the opportunity, before the time that the information is disclosed, to direct that the information not be disclosed to said third party. See, 15 U.S.C. § 6802(b)(1). Unless Gavel is enjoined from producing the information requested, non-public personal information covered by the GLBA will be disclosed to third parties without any individual customer's advance knowledge or consent, in clear violation of the statute. Once disclosed, there is no monetary relief which could possibly provide compensation to injured victims.

Secondly, it is submitted that, as this Court found in the May 9, 2002 order granting preliminary injunction, Union Planters faces irreparable injury. The disclosure of this information by Gavel would result in an invasion of privacy of Union Planters' customers. Union Planters will surely suffer injury to its business reputation when its customers learn that their private financial information was divulged to third parties without their consent.

Next, Union Planters argues that privacy and commercial interests favor issuance of a permanent injunction. Union Planters can be issued regulatory sanctions in the event that disclosure of nonpublic personal information is made known in violation of the GLBA. Moreover, Union Planters will face the wrath of at least some of its customers. While an injunction would protect Union Planters and the rights of its customers, it would not impinge upon Mr. Gavel or, to the extent relevant, the *Salih* plaintiff's attorneys. Gavel has no particular interest in disclosing the information sought in the subpoena, which he possesses solely in his capacity as agent for Union Planters. As for the plaintiff's attorneys, there is no reason this information would be required other than for client development.

Finally, Union Planters asserts that the injunctive relief will not undermine or disserve the public interest, and will serve the public interest in vindicating congressionally mandated privacy interests. A federal statute designed to protect the privacy interests of American consumers could only serve to promote the public interest in this case. There is no countervailing public interest in allowing Gavel to violate the statute.

III. LAW AND ANALYSIS:

It is clear to this Court that federal law, the GLBA, specifically prohibits Mr. Gavel from disclosing the information sought by the subpoena issued, as modified by the state court, without the consent of the customers. 15 U.S.C. § 6802(b)(1). Mr. Gavel received the information sought by the subpoena from WNC which provides insurance services to Union Planters. Gavel, in turn, performs services for WNC with respect to Union Planters' Louisiana customers by preparing and filing surplus lines tax statements and paying the associated tax to the Louisiana Department of Insurance. As such, Mr. Gavel is included in the prohibitions of the GLBA, as said provisions apply to "financial institutions," for which Union Planters is without a doubt; but which also include any person or organization significantly engaged in an activity which is "financial in nature." The activities of Mr. Gavel in providing insurance brokerage and administrative services for loans and acting as agent or broker for purposes of insuring against loss, are "financial in nature." GLBA's non-disclosure rules, therefore, apply to the risk of Gavel's disclosure of the information requested by the Intervenors [state-court plaintiffs], since those rules apply to activities that are 'financial in nature.' 12 U.S.C. § 1843(k)(3)(B) and 12 C.F.R. § 225.28(b)(1).

Moreover, the information which Gavel has been asked to produce is clearly "nonpublic personal information" which falls within the provisions of the GLBA prohibiting disclosure. Records regarding the forced placement of flood insurance for Union Planters' customers constitutes a "grouping" of non-public personally identifiable financial information which is precluded by the GLBA. See, 15 U.S.C. § 6809 (4)(A)(ii), (C); 12 C.F.R. § 40.3(n). Furthermore, it is clear that the document sought by the Intervenors submitted to the Louisiana Department of Insurance, on its face, provides that the document is exempt from Louisiana's Public Records Law.

Finally, this Court finds that the "fraud" exception of the GLBA is not applicable in the current circumstances. See, 15 U.S.C. § 6802(e)(3). To apply this exception, to the circumstances presented in this case, would render the protections provided by the GLBA meaningless. This Court is in agreement with Union Planters that said exception is intended for situations in which the customer is using the privacy associated with his financial account to perpetrate a fraud. Under those circumstances, a financial institution would be free to disclose the information about that customer and said account.

Accordingly, as discussed above, this Court finds that Union Planters has succeeded on the merits of its claim. Secondly, this Court believes that irreparable injury would result if Gavel were allowed to disclose the private financial information provided to him from Union Planters with respect to its customers, resulting in an invasion of privacy of Union Planters' customers, as well as injury to Union Planters' business reputation when its customers learn that their private financial information was divulged to third parties without their consent. Once this information has been provided, in contradiction to the dictates of the GLBA, there is no monetary relief which could compensate such a loss. Gavel would not be injured in any way should the injunction be entered, as he is merely the possessor of information with no real interest in the proceedings, and as he has admitted in his answer, but for an injunction by this Court, he would disclose without notice to Union Planters' customers those customers' personal information in response to an order of the Civil District Court for the Parish of Orleans. In the issuance of the preliminary injunction, this Court found that Union Planters could suffer grave consequences should the information sought in the subpoena be disclosed. Mr. Gavel has no interest in the disclosure of the information that would yield harm to him if he were to be enjoined from releasing the information. Since he has no personal stake in the outcome of the state court proceedings and no harm would come to him, the harm that would befall Union Planters significantly outweighs the harm that would come to Mr. Gavel if the nonpublic customer information were to be revealed. Additionally, Mr. Gavel did not object to the granting of the preliminary injunction, and he does not object to the granting of the immediate motion either. Finally, the injunction in no way would disserve the public interest as the injunction would merely uphold and enforce a federal statute. A federal statute designed to protect the privacy interests of American consumers could only serve to promote the public interest in this case. There is no countervailing public interest in allowing Gavel to violate this statue. While it may have been the legislative intent of Congress to avoid 'handing a private action bonanza' to the plaintiff bar, as the Intervenor so aptly stated in his opposition brief, it was distinctly the legislative intent that:

> It is the policy of the Congress that each financial institution has an affirmative and continuing obligation to respect the privacy of its customers and to protect the security and confidentiality of those customers' nonpublic personal information. 15 U.S.C. § 6801(a).

The GLBA is written with the protection of the customers of the financial institutions in mind. This protection continues in all aspects of the GLBA. Such protection can be seen when financial institutions are allowed to provide nonpublic personal information to nonaffiliated third parties, whereupon the nonaffiliated third party must maintain confidentiality. 15 U.S.C. § 6802 (b)(2). The subpoena issued in the state court proceeding seeks full disclosure of the very nonpublic consumer information which GLBA seeks to protect. Union Planters was the proprietor of the information, and in compliance with the GLBA, it disclosed the information to WNC, who, in turn, disclosed the information to its agent solely for business purposes. Since the subpoena seeks disclosure of information which otherwise would, by law, remain confidential, the action by Plaintiff to seek injunctive relief as to the specific nonpublic consumer information is correct. While Intervenor correctly states that a breach of the confidentiality agreement would engage WNC with federal regulators, the information that would be released pursuant to the subpoena would already have been released. The purpose of the injunction action is to stop the release of that information before it is made public. The Plaintiff has a definite right of action in that this injunction seeks to protect the Plaintiff's information. Although the state court subpoena was directed at Mr. Gavel and WNC, the Plaintiff would otherwise rely on the security agreement between the financial institutions and be secure that the nonpublic consumer information would remain nonpublic consumer information. The subpoena asks that this information be yanked out from the cloak of the protection not only of the security agreement, but also the GLBA. This Court has twice ruled that the Intervenor should be enjoined from gaining access to the nonpublic consumer information, and today, the Court maintains its previous reasoning.

The Health Insurance Portability and Accountability Act (HIPAA)

The Health Insurance Portability and Accountability Act was enacted in 1996. Among the purposes of the act was the effort to make the provision of health care services and the processing of health care insurance claims more efficient by substituting electronic records for the stacks of paper documentation. Because patient confidential medical information would be stored and transmitted electronically, HIPAA, like the GLBA, imposes privacy and security standards. HIPAA also makes it a crime to wrongfully disclose patient medical information, which the statute refers to as "individually identifiable health information." The act also makes it a crime to wrongfully disclose a "unique health identifier," which is the unique ID number assigned to each patient.

42 U.S.C. § 1320d-6. Wrongful disclosure of individually identifiable health information

(a) Offense. A person who knowingly and in violation of this part [42 USCS §§ 1320d et seq.]—
   (1) uses or causes to be used a unique health identifier;
   (2) obtains individually identifiable health information relating to an individual; or
   (3) discloses individually identifiable health information to another person,
   shall be punished as provided in subsection (b).
(b) Penalties. A person described in subsection (a) shall—
   (1) be fined not more than $50,000, imprisoned not more than 1 year, or both;
   (2) if the offense is committed under false pretenses, be fined not more than $100,000, imprisoned not more than 5 years, or both; and
   (3) if the offense is committed with intent to sell, transfer, or use individually identifiable health information for commercial advantage, personal gain, or malicious harm, be fined not more than $250,000, imprisoned not more than 10 years, or both.

After the Breach: Is There a Duty to Notify the Consumer That the Security of Their Data Has Been Compromised?

Previous portions of this chapter have explored the criminal sanctions that can be imposed when nonpublic credit, financial, or medical information is wrongfully disclosed. What happens, though, when the party who stored the information is the victim of an external intrusion and the nonpublic information is stolen from the database, or when an employee's laptop holding such information is stolen? Is there an obligation on the part of the holder of that information to notify the consumer of the breach? There is no federal law that directly applies. California, however, is the national leader in that respect. The California statute appears below:

California Civil Code § 1798.82. Disclosure of breach insecurity by business maintaining computerized data that includes personal information

(a) Any person or business that conducts business in California, and that owns or licenses computerized data that includes personal information, shall disclose any breach of the security of the system following discovery or notification of the breach in the security of the data to any resident of California whose unencrypted personal information was, or is reasonably believed to have been, acquired by an unauthorized person. The disclosure shall be made in the most expedient time possible and without unreasonable delay, consistent with the legitimate needs of law enforcement, as provided in subdivision (c), or any measures necessary to determine the scope of the breach and restore the reasonable integrity of the data system.

(b) Any person or business that maintains computerized data that includes personal information that the person or business does not own shall notify the owner or licensee of the information of any breach of the security of the data immediately following discovery, if the personal information was, or is reasonably believed to have been, acquired by an unauthorized person.

(c) The notification required by this section may be delayed if a law enforcement agency determines that the notification will impede a criminal investigation. The notification required by this section shall be made after the law enforcement agency determines that it will not compromise the investigation.

(d) For purposes of this section, "breach of the security of the system" means unauthorized acquisition of computerized data that compromises the security, confidentiality, or integrity of personal information maintained by the person or business. Good faith acquisition of personal information by an employee or agent of the person or business for the purposes of the person or business is not a breach of the security of the system, provided that the personal information is not used or subject to further unauthorized disclosure.

(e) For purposes of this section, "personal information" means an individual's first name or first initial and last name in combination with any one or more of the following data elements, when either the name or the data elements are not encrypted:
  (1) Social security number.
  (2) Driver's license number or California Identification Card number.
  (3) Account number, credit or debit card number, in combination with any required security code, access code, or password that would permit access to an individual's financial account.

(f) For purposes of this section, "personal information" does not include publicly available information that is lawfully made available to the general public from federal, state, or local government records.

(g) For purposes of this section, "notice" may be provided by one of the following methods:
   (1) Written notice.
   (2) Electronic notice, if the notice provided is consistent with the provisions regarding electronic records and signatures set forth in Section 7001 of Title 15 of the United States Code.
   (3) Substitute notice, if the person or business demonstrates that the cost of providing notice would exceed two hundred fifty thousand dollars ($250,000), or that the affected class of subject persons to be notified exceeds 500,000, or the person or business does not have sufficient contact information. Substitute notice shall consist of all of the following:
       (A) E-mail notice when the person or business has an e-mail address for the subject persons.
       (B) Conspicuous posting of the notice on the Web site page of the person or business, if the person or business maintains one.
       (C) Notification to major statewide media.

(h) Notwithstanding subdivision (g), a person or business that maintains its own notification procedures as part of an information security policy for the treatment of personal information and is otherwise consistent with the timing requirements of this part, shall be deemed to be in compliance with the notification requirements of this section if the person or business notifies subject persons in accordance with its policies in the event of a breach of security of the system.

California does not impose a criminal penalty for the failure to provide notice pursuant to this statute. Instead, the following civil remedies are available:

California Civil Code § 1798.84. Violations and remedies

(a) Any waiver of a provision of this title is contrary to public policy and is void and unenforceable.

(b) Any customer injured by a violation of this title may institute a civil action to recover damages.

(c) In addition, for a willful, intentional, or reckless violation of Section 1798.83, a customer may recover a civil penalty not to exceed three thousand dollars ($3,000) per violation; otherwise, the customer may recover a civil penalty of up to five hundred dollars ($500) per violation for a violation of Section 1798.83.

(d) Unless the violation is willful, intentional, or reckless, a business that is alleged to have not provided all the information required by subdivision (a) of Section 1798.83, to have provided inaccurate information, failed to provide any of the information required by subdivision (a) of Section 1798.83, or failed to provide information in the time period required by subdivision (b) of Section 1798.83, may assert as a complete defense in any action in law or equity that it thereafter provided regarding the information that was alleged to be untimely, all the information, or accurate information, to all customers who were provided incomplete or inaccurate information, respectively, within 90 days of the date the business knew that it had failed to provide the information, timely information, all the information, or the accurate information, respectively.

(e) Any business that violates, proposes to violate, or has violated this title may be enjoined.

(f) A prevailing plaintiff in any action commenced under Section 1798.83 shall also be entitled to recover his or her reasonable attorney's fees and costs.

(g) The rights and remedies available under this section are cumulative to each other and to any other rights and remedies available under law.

Several states and the federal government currently are considering legislation that follows in whole or in part the California breach law.

Key Words and Phrases

Credit report
Customer information
Data security
Data security breach
Financial institution
Health care insurer
Health care provider
Individually identifiable health information

Information sharing
Opt in
Opt out
Privacy standards
Security standards
Truncation
Unique health identifier

Review Problems

1. Did Mrs. Grendahl intend to obtain a credit report? Although this was a civil case, what would the government have to establish in order to bring a criminal proceeding against Grendahl?
2. Can criminal liability under the Fair Credit Reporting Act be imposed on both the credit bureau and the customer who fraudulently obtains information from the credit bureau?
3. What remedies exist under Gramm-Leach-Bliley for unlawful information sharing of individually identifiable financial information?
4. HIPAA imposes both privacy and security safeguards. Why does the statutory scheme require both types of requirements?

Weblinks

www.privacyinternational.com/
This is the home page of the website of Privacy International. The site provides links to articles and papers on privacy and data security.
www.ftc.gov/privacy/index.html
This page at the website of the Federal Trade Commission has links and information relating to financial privacy and credit reporting.
www.epic.org/
This is the home page of the Electronic Privacy Information Center. The site has numerous links to useful information on financial privacy, health information privacy, and the full range of issues pertaining to privacy and security of information.

www.keytlaw.com/Links/glbact.htm
> This lawyer's site provides links to useful information specific to financial privacy under the Gramm-Leach-Bliley Act.

www.usdoj.gov/dag/pubdoc/health98.htm
> This page at the U.S. Department of Justice website is a detailed report on health care fraud, including HIPAA efforts to control and combat fraud.

www.hhs.gov/ocr/hipaa/
> This is the HIPAA area of the U.S. Department of Health and Human Services website. This page has numerous links to information on HIPAA requirements for data privacy and security.

www.hipaa.org/
> This website devoted exclusively to HIPAA has links to every topic, document, regulation, and article imaginable relevant to HIPAA privacy and security.

Endnotes

1. For purposes of privacy and security protections, the GLBA (15 USC § 6827 (a)) defines a *financial institution* as "any institution engaged in the business of providing financial services to customers who maintain a credit, deposit, trust, or other financial account or relationship with the institution." Subdivision (b) provides that the term *financial institution* specifically includes "any depository institution ..., any broker or dealer, any investment advisor, any insurance company, any loan or finance company, any credit card issuer or operator of a credit card system, and any consumer reporting agency that compiles and maintains files on consumers on a nationwide basis."

Intellectual Property Fraud

7

Introduction

Intellectual property crimes continue to be one of the most damaging in dollars of all types of cybercrimes. For our purposes, there are four types of intellectual property: patents, copyrights, trademarks, and service marks. In this chapter, we focus on copyrights, trademarks, and service marks, the most common types of intellectual property that are victimized by cybercrime.

Property rights that are entitled to copyright protection are described in 17 USC § 102 to include:

> original works of authorship fixed in any tangible medium of expression, now known or later developed, from which they can be perceived, reproduced, or otherwise communicated, either directly or with the aid of a machine or device. Works of authorship include the following categories:

> (1) literary works;
> (2) musical works, including any accompanying words;
> (3) dramatic works, including any accompanying music;
> (4) pantomimes and choreographic works;
> (5) pictorial, graphic, and sculptural works;
> (6) motion pictures and other audiovisual works;
> (7) sound recordings; and
> (8) architectural works.

The owner of a mark also is entitled to intellectual property protection. There are four types of marks: trade, service, collective, and certification. A trademark is a mark that is applied to some type of goods or merchandise, for example, the corporate logo that is applied to a Coach handbag. A service mark is a type of mark that protects a product that constitutes an intangible service, rather than a tangible item of goods. For example, LexisNexis provides Academic Universe, which is a service, not an item of merchandise. A collective mark is a mark that applies to a collective body, such as MLB (Major League Baseball) or PGA (Professional Golfers' Association of America). Finally, a certification mark is a mark that applies to attest to the certification standard of a product or service, for example, UL (Underwriters Laboratories), which is applied to electrical products.

Fortunately, the legal protections for the different types of marks are the same; all marks are protected in the same manner as trademarks.

Criminal Copyright Infringement

The general crime of copyright infringement appears at 17 USC § 506(a), which provides that it is a crime punishable as set forth in 18 USC § 2319 to willfully infringe a copyright

if the infringement was committed—

(A) for purposes of commercial advantage or private financial gain;

(B) by the reproduction or distribution, including by electronic means, during any 180-day period, of 1 or more copies or phonorecords of 1 or more copyrighted works, which have a total retail value of more than $1,000; or

(C) by the distribution of a work being prepared for commercial distribution, by making it available on a computer network accessible to members of the public, if such person knew or should have known that the work was intended for commercial distribution.

Infringement of a copyright is defined as the violation of the exclusive rights of the copyright owner or author, or the importation of copies or phonorecords into the United States in violation of 17 USC § 602. The exclusive rights of the copyright owner or author are set forth in several sections of the copyright law, specifically 17 USC §§ 106 through 122. Section 106 (quoted above) describes generally those exclusive rights that cannot be violated. There are a number of limitations upon those rights, the most important being fair use, which is the right all of us have to make fair use of material entitled to copyright protection. Fair use is defined in 17 USC § 107. Though a complex subject, fair use encompasses the use of a copyrighted work

for purposes such as criticism, comment, news reporting, teaching (including multiple copies for classroom use), scholarship, or research.

That section further provides:

In determining whether the use made of a work in any particular case is a fair use the factors to be considered shall include—

(1) the purpose and character of the use, including whether such use is of a commercial nature or is for nonprofit educational purposes;

(2) the nature of the copyrighted work;

(3) the amount and substantiality of the portion used in relation to the copyrighted work as a whole; and

(4) the effect of the use upon the potential market for or value of the copyrighted work.

The application of those four factors has created a significant amount of jurisprudence well beyond the scope of this text. It is enough to remember that there is a fair use exception. Also, remember that the victim of infringement can sue to recover damages for infringement in a civil action.

There are three legal forms of infringement: direct, contributory, and vicarious. A person or entity commits a direct infringement by violating the exclusive copyright of the owner or author. Contributory infringement is committed by those who knowingly contribute in a material (significant) way to the direct infringement of others. Vicarious infringement involves the conduct of persons or entities that have some relationship with the direct, or primary, infringer, and that have the right to supervise the conduct of the infringer. Thus, in order to establish either contributory or vicarious infringement, the prosecution in a criminal case or the civil plaintiff must establish that there was a direct infringement.

The following case is an example of direct infringement:

United States v. Manzer

69 F.3D 222 (1995)

U.S. COURT OF APPEALS, EIGHTH CIRCUIT

OPINION: FLOYD R. GIBSON, Circuit Judge.

Jan Manzer appeals his convictions for two counts of mail fraud in violation of 18 U.S.C. §§ 1341 and 1342, two counts of wire fraud in violation of 18 U.S.C. §§ 1343 and 1342, and one count of copyright infringement in violation of 17 U.S.C. § 506(a).

BACKGROUND

This appeal deals with the business of unauthorized decryption of premium channel broadcasts. Premium channel broadcasters such as HBO transmit programming to subscribing individuals and cable affiliates across the United States via satellite. In order to prevent nonsubscribers from accessing their programming, they encrypt or "scramble" their electromagnetic broadcast signals. A descrambling device such as the Videocipher II unit (VCII unit), manufactured and sold by General Instrument Corporation (General Instrument), is necessary to decrypt the scrambled signals. When a viewer subscribes to a premium channel, the premium channel broadcaster programs that viewer's electronic "unit address" into its satellite transmissions. Each VCII unit has its own unique coded "unit address" contained within the copyrighted "Controlled Microprocessor Software" stored in an integrated circuit identified as the "U-30 Chip" which ensures that only authorized addresses are able to decrypt the broadcast transmissions.

In 1988, General Instrument hired a private investigator, Robert Bottorff, to investigate persons involved in the illegal modification of VCII units. Bottorff obtained a copy of *The Blank Box Newsletter*, an underground newsletter devoted to the unauthorized decryption of cable satellite transmissions, containing an advertisement by "V.C. Hacker." Bottorff called the number listed in the advertisement and spoke to an individual who called himself Don Davis. That individual was later identified as Jan Manzer. During the course of a subsequent phone conversation on April 18, Manzer agreed to modify five VCII units to enable them to receive encrypted broadcasts in exchange for $525.00 per unit. Bottorff shipped the units along with the proper payment to an address in Little Rock, Arkansas provided by Manzer. Manzer shipped the five VCII units back to Bottorff a few days later, modified as agreed.

On April 27, Manzer and Bottorff made plans over the phone for Bottorff to deliver an additional 270 VCII units to Manzer's place of business for modification. In exchange, Manzer was to receive three Videocipher units for each one modified. On May 4, Bottorff delivered seventy VCII units to Manzer in Hot Springs, Arkansas. Manzer modified the units as agreed and returned them to Bottorff the next day. Later that day the FBI executed a search warrant on Manzer's place of business, seizing computer equipment, computer chips, computer discs, modified and unmodified VCII modules, advertisements, and business records.

It was established at trial that Manzer had been operating a business out of Hot Springs, Arkansas since August of 1987 under the alias "V.C. Hacker." As part of his business, Manzer sold cloned chips containing the unit addresses from authorized VCII units to both individual customers and satellite dealers. By replacing the existing U-30 chip with a "cloned" chip containing an authorized unit address, unauthorized viewers were able to receive premium channel broadcasts without having to pay the required subscription fee. Manzer's business also sold "cloning packages" or discs containing the information and unit addresses needed to clone additional counterfeit chips. Dealers who did not wish to modify their own VCII units were able to send their VCII circuitboards directly to Manzer, whose technicians would then modify them and return them to the dealer.

DISCUSSION

Copyright Infringement

Manzer challenges the sufficiency of the evidence supporting his conviction for knowing infringement of a copyright in violation of 17 U.S.C. § 506(a). In order to convict Manzer under 17 U.S.C. § 506(a), the government had to prove: (1) that the computer program in the satellite descrambler modules had a valid copyright; (2) that Manzer infringed on the copyright by preparing one or more derivative works or computer programs, or by reproducing or selling unauthorized copies of the computer program; (3) that Manzer willfully infringed on the copyright; and (4) that the act of infringement was for commercial advantage or private financial gain. Manzer asserts that the government failed to prove the second and third elements of the offense.

In regard to the second element, Manzer argues that the government failed to produce sufficient evidence that the computer programs he sold were derivative of the copyrighted "Controlled Microprocessor Software" contained in the U-30 chip. This argument fails to take into account the testimony of Brant Candelore, an electrical engineer employed by General Instrument, who testified that the computer files sold by Manzer were more than seventy-percent similar to the copyrighted software. As such, the jury's determination that the computer programs sold by Manzer were derivative of copyrighted material is supported by sufficient evidence.

Manzer also challenges the sufficiency of the evidence supporting the third element of the statute. Manzer claims that he is a businessman, not a technician, and had no notice that the contents of the U-30 chip were copyrighted. As such, he argues that the government produced no evidence that he willfully infringed on the copyrighted software. It was established at trial, however, that the sealed plastic module containing the copyrighted operating software utilized in the U-30 chip bore a legible copyright notice. In addition, the software program itself contained a copyright notice capable of being read through the use of either a common "debug" program or "DUMP" file. Were this a civil suit seeking actual or statutory damages for copyright infringement, either one of these methods would be sufficient to place Manzer on notice that the contents of the U-30 chip were copyrighted material for purposes of refuting a defense based on innocent infringement. We believe that a reasonable jury could also find this type of notice sufficient to alert Manzer to the fact that the contents of the U-30 chip were copyrighted for purposes of proving willful infringement under 17 U.S.C. § 506(a).

The record also supports the reasonable inference that Manzer had actual notice that the software contained in the U-30 chip was copyrighted material. Specifically, it was established at trial that Manzer, under his alias "V.C. Hacker" in a purported interview published in the *Blank Box Newsletter*, acknowledged the illegality of selling, leasing, or giving away a copy of copyrighted material such as that contained in the U-30 Chip. Consequently, we find the evidence of Manzer's willful infringement to be sufficient.

In the following case, the Supreme Court considered whether two companies that provided peer-to-peer software programs could be criminally liable for contributory infringement:

Metro-Goldwyn-Mayer Studios Inc. v. Grokster, Ltd.

545 U.S. 913 (2005)

U.S. SUPREME COURT

JUSTICE SOUTER delivered the opinion of the Court:

The question is under what circumstances the distributor of a product capable of both lawful and unlawful use is liable for acts of copyright infringement by third parties using the product. We hold that one who distributes a device with the object of promoting its use to infringe copyright, as shown by clear expression or other affirmative steps taken to foster infringement, is liable for the resulting acts of infringement by third parties.

I

Respondents, Grokster, Ltd., and StreamCast Networks, Inc., defendants in the trial court, distribute free software products that allow computer users to share electronic files through peer-to-peer networks, so called because users' computers communicate directly with each other, not through central servers. The advantage of peer-to-peer networks over information networks of other types shows up in their substantial and growing popularity. Because they need no central computer server to mediate the exchange of information or files among users, the high-bandwidth communications capacity for a server may be dispensed with, and the need for costly server storage space is eliminated. Since copies of a file (particularly a popular one) are available on many users' computers, file requests and retrievals may be faster than on other types of networks, and since file exchanges do not travel through a server, communications can take place between any computers that remain connected to the network without risk that a glitch in the server will disable the network in its entirety. Given these benefits in security, cost, and efficiency, peer-to-peer networks are employed to store and distribute electronic files by universities, government agencies, corporations, and libraries, among others.[*]

---

[*] Peer-to-peer networks have disadvantages as well. Searches on peer-to-peer networks may not reach and uncover all available files because search requests may not be transmitted to every computer on the network. There may be redundant copies of popular files. The creator of the software has no incentive to minimize storage or bandwidth consumption, the costs of which are borne by every user of the network. Most relevant here, it is more difficult to control the content of files available for retrieval and the behavior of users.

Other users of peer-to-peer networks include individual recipients of Grokster's and StreamCast's software, and although the networks that they enjoy through using the software can be used to share any type of digital file, they have prominently employed those networks in sharing copyrighted music and video files without authorization. A group of copyright holders (MGM for short, but including motion picture studios, recording companies, songwriters, and music publishers) sued Grokster and StreamCast for their users' copyright infringements, alleging that they knowingly and intentionally distributed their software to enable users to reproduce and distribute the copyrighted works in violation of the Copyright Act, 17 U.S.C. § 101 *et seq.* MGM sought damages and an injunction.

Discovery during the litigation revealed the way the software worked, the business aims of each defendant company, and the predilections of the users. Grokster's eponymous software employs what is known as FastTrack technology, a protocol developed by others and licensed to Grokster. StreamCast distributes a very similar product except that its software, called Morpheus, relies on what is known as Gnutella technology. A user who downloads and installs either software possesses the protocol to send requests for files directly to the computers of others using software compatible with FastTrack or Gnutella. On the FastTrack network opened by the Grokster software, the user's request goes to a computer given an indexing capacity by the software and designated a supernode, or to some other computer with comparable power and capacity to collect temporary indexes of the files available on the computers of users connected to it. The supernode (or indexing computer) searches its own index and may communicate the search request to other supernodes. If the file is found, the supernode discloses its location to the computer requesting it, and the requesting user can download the file directly from the computer located. The copied file is placed in a designated sharing folder on the requesting user's computer, where it is available for other users to download in turn, along with any other file in that folder.

In the Gnutella network made available by Morpheus, the process is mostly the same, except that in some versions of the Gnutella protocol there are no supernodes. In these versions, peer computers using the protocol communicate directly with each other. When a user enters a search request into the Morpheus software, it sends the request to computers connected with it, which in turn pass the request along to other connected peers. The search results are communicated to the requesting computer, and the user can download desired files directly from peers' computers. As this description indicates, Grokster and StreamCast use no servers to intercept the content of the search requests or to mediate the file transfers conducted by users of the software, there being no central point through which the substance of the communications passes in either direction.

Although Grokster and StreamCast do not therefore know when particular files are copied, a few searches using their software would show what is available on the networks the software reaches. MGM commissioned a statistician to conduct a systematic search, and his study showed that nearly 90% of the files available for download on the FastTrack system were copyrighted works. Grokster and StreamCast dispute this figure, raising methodological problems and arguing that free copying even of copyrighted works may be authorized by the rightholders. They also argue that potential noninfringing uses of their software are significant in kind, even if infrequent in practice.

Some musical performers, for example, have gained new audiences by distributing their copyrighted works for free across peer-to-peer networks, and some distributors of unprotected content have used peer-to-peer networks to disseminate files, Shakespeare being an example. Indeed, StreamCast has given Morpheus users the opportunity to download the briefs in this very case, though their popularity has not been quantified.

As for quantification, the parties' anecdotal and statistical evidence entered thus far to show the content available on the FastTrack and Gnutella networks does not say much about which files are actually downloaded by users, and no one can say how often the software is used to obtain copies of unprotected material. But MGM's evidence gives reason to think that the vast majority of users' downloads are acts of infringement, and because well over 100 million copies of the software in question are known to have been downloaded, and billions of files are shared across the FastTrack and Gnutella networks each month, the probable scope of copyright infringement is staggering.

Grokster and StreamCast concede the infringement in most downloads, and it is uncontested that they are aware that users employ their software primarily to download copyrighted files, even if the decentralized FastTrack and Gnutella networks fail to reveal which files are being copied, and when. From time to time, moreover, the companies have learned about their users' infringement directly, as from users who have sent e-mail to each company with questions about playing copyrighted movies they had downloaded, to whom the companies have responded with guidance. And MGM notified the companies of 8 million copyrighted files that could be obtained using their software.

Grokster and StreamCast are not, however, merely passive recipients of information about infringing use. The record is replete with evidence that from the moment Grokster and StreamCast began to distribute their free software, each one clearly voiced the objective that recipients use it to download copyrighted works, and each took active steps to encourage infringement.

After the notorious file-sharing service, Napster, was sued by copyright holders for facilitation of copyright infringement, StreamCast gave away a software program of a kind known as OpenNap, designed as compatible with the Napster program and open to Napster users for downloading files from other Napster and OpenNap users' computers. Evidence indicates that "it was always [StreamCast's] intent to use [its OpenNap network] to be able to capture email addresses of [its] initial target market so that [it] could promote [its] StreamCast Morpheus interface to them"; indeed, the OpenNap program was engineered "to leverage Napster's 50 million user base."

StreamCast monitored both the number of users downloading its OpenNap program and the number of music files they downloaded. It also used the resulting OpenNap network to distribute copies of the Morpheus software and to encourage users to adopt it. Internal company documents indicate that StreamCast hoped to attract large numbers of former Napster users if that company was shut down by court order or otherwise, and that StreamCast planned to be the next Napster. A kit developed by StreamCast to be delivered to advertisers, for example, contained press articles about StreamCast's potential to capture former Napster users, and it introduced itself to some potential advertisers as a company "which is similar to what Napster was." It broadcast banner advertisements to users of other Napster-compatible software, urging them to adopt its OpenNap. An internal e-mail from a company executive stated: "'We have put this network in place so that when Napster pulls the plug on their free service ... or if the Court orders them shut down prior to that ... we will be positioned to capture the flood of their 32 million users that will be actively looking for an alternative.'"

Thus, StreamCast developed promotional materials to market its service as the best Napster alternative. One proposed advertisement read: "Napster Inc. has announced that it will soon begin charging you a fee. That's if the courts don't order it shut down first. What will you do to get around it?" Another proposed ad touted StreamCast's software as the "# 1 alternative to Napster" and asked "when the lights went off at Napster ... where did the users go?" StreamCast even planned to flaunt the illegal uses of its software; when it launched the OpenNap network, the chief technology officer of the company averred that "the goal is to get in trouble with the law and get sued. It's the best way to get in the news."

The evidence that Grokster sought to capture the market of former Napster users is sparser but revealing, for Grokster launched its own OpenNap system called Swaptor and inserted digital codes into its Web site so that computer users using Web search engines to look for "Napster" or "free filesharing" would be directed to the Grokster Web site, where they could download the Grokster software. And Grokster's name is an apparent derivative of Napster.

StreamCast's executives monitored the number of songs by certain commercial artists available on their networks, and an internal communication indicates they aimed to have a larger number of copyrighted songs available on their networks than other file-sharing networks. The point, of course, would be to attract users of a mind to infringe, just as it would be with their promotional materials developed showing copyrighted songs as examples of the kinds of files available through Morpheus. Morpheus in fact allowed users to search specifically for "Top 40" songs, which were inevitably copyrighted. Similarly, Grokster sent users a newsletter promoting its ability to provide particular, popular copyrighted materials.

In addition to this evidence of express promotion, marketing, and intent to promote further, the business models employed by Grokster and StreamCast confirm that their principal object was use of their software to download copyrighted works. Grokster and StreamCast receive no revenue from users, who obtain the software itself for nothing. Instead, both companies generate income by selling advertising space, and they stream the advertising to Grokster and Morpheus users while they are employing the programs. As the number of users of each program increases, advertising opportunities become worth more. While there is doubtless some demand for free Shakespeare, the evidence shows that substantive volume is a function of free access to copyrighted work. Users seeking Top 40 songs, for example, or the latest release by Modest Mouse, are certain to be far more numerous than those seeking a free Decameron, and Grokster and StreamCast translated that demand into dollars.

Finally, there is no evidence that either company made an effort to filter copyrighted material from users' downloads or otherwise impede the sharing of copyrighted files. Although Grokster appears to have sent e-mails warning users about infringing content when it received threatening notice from the copyright holders, it never blocked anyone from continuing to use its software to share copyrighted files. StreamCast not only rejected another company's offer of help to monitor infringement, but blocked the Internet Protocol addresses of entities it believed were trying to engage in such monitoring on its networks.

After discovery, the parties on each side of the case cross-moved for summary judgment. The District Court limited its consideration to the asserted liability of Grokster and StreamCast for distributing the current versions of their software, leaving aside whether either was liable "for damages arising from *past* versions of their software, or from other past activities." The District Court held that those who used the Grokster and Morpheus software to download copyrighted media files directly infringed MGM's copyrights, a conclusion not contested on appeal, but the court nonetheless granted summary judgment in favor of Grokster and StreamCast as to any liability arising from distribution of the then current versions of their software. Distributing that software gave rise to no liability in the court's view, because its use did not provide the distributors with actual knowledge of specific acts of infringement.

The Court of Appeals affirmed. In the court's analysis, a defendant was liable as a contributory infringer when it had knowledge of direct infringement and materially contributed to the infringement. But the court read *Sony Corp. of America v. Universal City Studios, Inc.*, 464 U.S. 417 (1984), as holding that distribution of a commercial product capable of substantial noninfringing uses could not give rise to contributory liability for infringement unless the distributor had actual knowledge of specific instances of infringement and failed to act on that knowledge. The fact that the software was capable of substantial noninfringing uses in the Ninth Circuit's view meant that Grokster and StreamCast were not liable, because they had no such actual knowledge, owing to the decentralized architecture of their software. The court also held that Grokster and StreamCast did not materially contribute to their users' infringement because it was the users themselves who searched for, retrieved, and stored the infringing files, with no involvement by the defendants beyond providing the software in the first place.

The Ninth Circuit also considered whether Grokster and StreamCast could be liable under a theory of vicarious infringement. The court held against liability because the defendants did not monitor or control the use of the software, had no agreed-upon right or current ability to supervise its use, and had no independent duty to police infringement. We granted *certiorari*.

II

One infringes contributorily by intentionally inducing or encouraging direct infringement, and infringes vicariously by profiting from direct infringement while declining to exercise a right to stop or limit it. Although "the Copyright Act does not expressly render anyone liable for infringement committed by another," *Sony Corp. v. Universal City Studios*, 464 U.S., at 434, these doctrines of secondary liability emerged from common law principles and are well established in the law.

Despite the currency of these principles of secondary liability, this Court has dealt with secondary copyright infringement in only one recent case, and because MGM has tailored its principal claim to our opinion there, a look at our earlier holding is in order. In *Sony Corp. v. Universal City Studios, supra*, this Court addressed a claim that secondary liability for infringement can arise from the very distribution of a commercial product. There, the product, novel at the time, was what we know today as the videocassette recorder or VCR. Copyright holders sued Sony as the manufacturer, claiming it was contributorily liable for infringement that occurred when VCR owners taped copyrighted programs because it supplied the means used to infringe, and it had constructive knowledge that infringement would occur. At the trial on the merits, the evidence showed that the principal use of the VCR was for "'time-shifting,'" or taping a program for later viewing at a more convenient time, which the Court found to be a fair, not an infringing, use. There was no evidence that Sony had expressed an object of bringing about taping in violation of copyright or had taken active steps to increase its profits from unlawful taping. Although Sony's advertisements urged consumers to buy the VCR to "'record favorite shows'" or "'build a library'" of recorded programs, neither of these uses was necessarily infringing.

On those facts, with no evidence of stated or indicated intent to promote infringing uses, the only conceivable basis for imposing liability was on a theory of contributory infringement arising from its sale of VCRs to consumers with knowledge that some would use them to infringe. But because the VCR was "capable of commercially signifi-cant noninfringing uses," we held the manufacturer could not be faulted solely on the basis of its distribution.

This analysis reflected patent law's traditional staple article of commerce doctrine, now codified, that distribution of a component of a patented device will not violate the patent if it is suitable for use in other ways. The doctrine was devised to identify instances in which it may be presumed from distribution of an article in commerce that the distributor intended the article to be used to infringe another's patent, and so may justly be held liable for that infringement.

We agree with MGM that the Court of Appeals misapplied *Sony*, which it read as lim-iting secondary liability quite beyond the circumstances to which the case applied. *Sony* barred secondary liability based on presuming or imputing intent to cause infringe-ment solely from the design or distribution of a product capable of substantial lawful use, which the distributor knows is in fact used for infringement. The Ninth Circuit has read *Sony*'s limitation to mean that whenever a product is capable of substantial lawful use, the producer can never be held contributorily liable for third parties' infringing use of it; it read the rule as being this broad, even when an actual purpose to cause infring-ing use is shown by evidence independent of design and distribution of the product, unless the distributors had "specific knowledge of infringement at a time at which they contributed to the infringement, and failed to act upon that information." Because the Circuit found the StreamCast and Grokster software capable of substantial lawful use, it concluded on the basis of its reading of *Sony* that neither company could be held liable, since there was no showing that their software, being without any central server, afforded them knowledge of specific unlawful uses.

Sony's rule limits imputing culpable intent as a matter of law from the characteristics or uses of a distributed product. But nothing in *Sony* requires courts to ignore evidence of intent if there is such evidence, and the case was never meant to foreclose rules of fault-based liability derived from the common law. Thus, where evidence goes beyond a product's characteristics or the knowledge that it may be put to infringing uses, and shows statements or actions directed to promoting infringement, *Sony*'s staple-article rule will not preclude liability.

The classic case of direct evidence of unlawful purpose occurs when one induces commission of infringement by another, or "entices or persuades another" to infringe, as by advertising. Thus at common law a copyright or patent defendant who "not only expected but invoked [infringing use] by advertisement" was liable for infringement "on principles recognized in every part of the law." *Kalem Co. v. Harper Brothers*, 222 U.S., at 62-63 (copyright infringement).

The rule on inducement of infringement as developed in the early cases is no different today. Evidence of "active steps … taken to encourage direct infringement," *Oak Industries, Inc. v. Zenith Electronics Corp.*, 697 F. Supp. 988, 992 (ND Ill. 1988), such as advertising an infringing use or instructing how to engage in an infringing use, show an affirmative intent that the product be used to infringe, and a showing that infringement was encouraged overcomes the law's reluctance to find liability when a defendant merely sells a commercial product suitable for some lawful use.

III

The only apparent question about treating MGM's evidence as sufficient to withstand summary judgment under the theory of inducement goes to the need on MGM's part to adduce evidence that StreamCast and Grokster communicated an inducing message to their software users. The classic instance of inducement is by advertisement or solicitation that broadcasts a message designed to stimulate others to commit violations. MGM claims that such a message is shown here. It is undisputed that StreamCast beamed onto the computer screens of users of Napster-compatible programs ads urging the adoption of its OpenNap program, which was designed, as its name implied, to invite the custom of patrons of Napster, then under attack in the courts for facilitating massive infringement. Those who accepted StreamCast's OpenNap program were offered software to perform the same services, which a factfinder could conclude would readily have been understood in the Napster market as the ability to download copyrighted music files. Grokster distributed an electronic newsletter containing links to articles promoting its software's ability to access popular copyrighted music. And anyone whose Napster or free file-sharing searches turned up a link to Grokster would have understood Grokster to be offering the same file-sharing ability as Napster, and to the same people who probably used Napster for infringing downloads; that would also have been the understanding of anyone offered Grokster's suggestively named Swaptor software, its version of OpenNap. And both companies communicated a clear message by responding affirmatively to requests for help in locating and playing copyrighted materials.

Three features of this evidence of intent are particularly notable. First, each company showed itself to be aiming to satisfy a known source of demand for copyright infringement, the market comprising former Napster users. StreamCast's internal documents made constant reference to Napster, it initially distributed its Morpheus software through an OpenNap program compatible with Napster, it advertised its OpenNap program to Napster users, and its Morpheus software functions as Napster did except that it could be used to distribute more kinds of files, including copyrighted movies and software programs. Grokster's name is apparently derived from Napster, it too initially offered an OpenNap program, its software's function is likewise comparable to Napster's, and it attempted to divert queries for Napster onto its own Web site. Grokster and StreamCast's efforts to supply services to former Napster users, deprived of a mechanism to copy and distribute what were overwhelmingly infringing files, indicate a principal, if not exclusive, intent on the part of each to bring about infringement.

Second, this evidence of unlawful objective is given added significance by MGM's showing that neither company attempted to develop filtering tools or other mechanisms to diminish the infringing activity using their software. While the Ninth Circuit treated the defendants' failure to develop such tools as irrelevant because they lacked an independent duty to monitor their users' activity, we think this evidence underscores Grokster's and StreamCast's intentional facilitation of their users' infringement.

Third, there is a further complement to the direct evidence of unlawful objective. It is useful to recall that StreamCast and Grokster make money by selling advertising space, by directing ads to the screens of computers employing their software. As the record shows, the more the software is used, the more ads are sent out and the greater the advertising revenue becomes. Since the extent of the software's use determines the gain to the distributors, the commercial sense of their enterprise turns on high-volume use, which the record shows is infringing. This evidence alone would not justify an inference of unlawful intent, but viewed in the context of the entire record its import is clear.

The unlawful objective is unmistakable.

In addition to intent to bring about infringement and distribution of a device suitable for infringing use, the inducement theory of course requires evidence of actual infringement by recipients of the device, the software in this case. As the account of the facts indicates, there is evidence of infringement on a gigantic scale, and there is no serious issue of the adequacy of MGM's showing on this point in order to survive the companies' summary judgment requests. Although an exact calculation of infringing use, as a basis for a claim of damages, is subject to dispute, there is no question that the summary judgment evidence is at least adequate to entitle MGM to go forward with claims for damages and equitable relief.

There is substantial evidence in MGM's favor on all elements of inducement, and summary judgment in favor of Grokster and StreamCast was error. On remand, reconsideration of MGM's motion for summary judgment will be in order.

The judgment of the Court of Appeals is vacated, and the case is remanded for further proceedings consistent with this opinion.

Software Piracy

In 1998, Congress enacted the Digital Millennium Copyright Act, 17 USC §§ 1201–1204. The Act contains three criminal provisions. The first, unlawful circumvention of a technological measure is set forth in § 1201:

> (a) Violations regarding circumvention of technological measures.—
>> (1) (A) No person shall circumvent a technological measure that effectively controls access to a work protected under this title. The prohibition contained in the preceding sentence shall take effect at the end of the 2-year period beginning on the date of the enactment of this chapter.
>> (2) No person shall manufacture, import, offer to the public, provide, or otherwise traffic in any technology, product, service, device, component, or part thereof, that—
>>> (A) is primarily designed or produced for the purpose of circumventing a technological measure that effectively controls access to a work protected under this title;

(B) has only limited commercially significant purpose or use other than to circumvent a technological measure that effectively controls access to a work protected under this title; or

(C) is marketed by that person or another acting in concert with that person with that person's knowledge for use in circumventing a technological measure that effectively controls access to a work protected under this title.

(3) As used in this subsection—

(A) to "circumvent a technological measure" means to descramble a scrambled work, to decrypt an encrypted work, or otherwise to avoid, bypass, remove, deactivate, or impair a technological measure, without the authority of the copyright owner; and

(B) a technological measure "effectively controls access to a work" if the measure, in the ordinary course of its operation, requires the application of information, or a process or a treatment, with the authority of the copyright owner, to gain access to the work.

(b) Additional violations.—

(1) No person shall manufacture, import, offer to the public, provide, or otherwise traffic in any technology, product, service, device, component, or part thereof, that—

(A) is primarily designed or produced for the purpose of circumventing protection afforded by a technological measure that effectively protects a right of a copyright owner under this title in a work or a portion thereof;

(B) has only limited commercially significant purpose or use other than to circumvent protection afforded by a technological measure that effectively protects a right of a copyright owner under this title in a work or a portion thereof; or

(C) is marketed by that person or another acting in concert with that person with that person's knowledge for use in circumventing protection afforded by a technological measure that effectively protects a right of a copyright owner under this title in a work or a portion thereof.

(2) As used in this subsection—

(A) to "circumvent protection afforded by a technological measure" means avoiding, bypassing, removing, deactivating, or otherwise impairing a technological measure; and

(B) a technological measure "effectively protects a right of a copyright owner under this title" if the measure, in the ordinary course of its operation, prevents, restricts, or otherwise limits the exercise of a right of a copyright owner under this title.

This provision does not apply to users of copyright-protected property, nonprofit libraries, archives, educational institutions, law enforcement, intelligence gathering and other governmental activities, security testing, the protection of personal private information, and those who perform reverse engineering or encryption research.

Reverse engineering and encryption research activities are permitted by § 1201 as follows:

(f) Reverse engineering.—

(1) Notwithstanding the provisions of subsection (a)(1)(A), a person who has lawfully obtained the right to use a copy of a computer program may circumvent a technological measure that effectively controls access to a particular portion of that program for the sole purpose of identifying and analyzing those elements of the program that are necessary to achieve interoperability of an independently created

computer program with other programs, and that have not previously been readily available to the person engaging in the circumvention, to the extent any such acts of identification and analysis do not constitute infringement under this title.

(2) Notwithstanding the provisions of subsections (a)(2) and (b), a person may develop and employ technological means to circumvent a technological measure, or to circumvent protection afforded by a technological measure, in order to enable the identification and analysis under paragraph (1), or for the purpose of enabling interoperability of an independently created computer program with other programs, if such means are necessary to achieve such interoperability, to the extent that doing so does not constitute infringement under this title.

(3) The information acquired through the acts permitted under paragraph (1), and the means permitted under paragraph (2), may be made available to others if the person referred to in paragraph (1) or (2), as the case may be, provides such information or means solely for the purpose of enabling interoperability of an independently created computer program with other programs, and to the extent that doing so does not constitute infringement under this title or violate applicable law other than this section.

(4) For purposes of this subsection, the term "interoperability" means the ability of computer programs to exchange information, and of such programs mutually to use the information which has been exchanged.

(g) Encryption research.—

(1) Definitions.—For purposes of this subsection—

(A) the term "encryption research" means activities necessary to identify and analyze flaws and vulnerabilities of encryption technologies applied to copyrighted works, if these activities are conducted to advance the state of knowledge in the field of encryption technology or to assist in the development of encryption products; and

(B) the term "encryption technology" means the scrambling and descrambling of information using mathematical formulas or algorithms.

(2) Permissible acts of encryption research.—Notwithstanding the provisions of subsection (a)(1)(A), it is not a violation of that subsection for a person to circumvent a technological measure as applied to a copy, phonorecord, performance, or display of a published work in the course of an act of good faith encryption research if—

(A) the person lawfully obtained the encrypted copy, phonorecord, performance, or display of the published work;

(B) such act is necessary to conduct such encryption research;

(C) the person made a good faith effort to obtain authorization before the circumvention; and

(D) such act does not constitute infringement under this title or a violation of applicable law other than this section, including section 1030 of title 18 and those provisions of title 18 amended by the Computer Fraud and Abuse Act of 1986.

(3) Factors in determining exemption.—In determining whether a person qualifies for the exemption under paragraph (2), the factors to be considered shall include—

(A) whether the information derived from the encryption research was disseminated, and if so, whether it was disseminated in a manner reasonably calculated to advance the state of knowledge or development of encryption technology, versus whether it was disseminated in a manner that facilitates infringement under this title or a violation of applicable law other than this section, including a violation of privacy or breach of security;

(B) whether the person is engaged in a legitimate course of study, is employed, or is appropriately trained or experienced, in the field of encryption technology; and

(C) whether the person provides the copyright owner of the work to which the technological measure is applied with notice of the findings and documentation of the research, and the time when such notice is provided.

(4) Use of technological means for research activities.—Notwithstanding the provisions of subsection (a)(2), it is not a violation of that subsection for a person to—

(A) develop and employ technological means to circumvent a technological measure for the sole purpose of that person performing the acts of good faith encryption research described in paragraph (2); and

(B) provide the technological means to another person with whom he or she is working collaboratively for the purpose of conducting the acts of good faith encryption research described in paragraph (2) or for the purpose of having that other person verify his or her acts of good faith encryption research described in paragraph (2).

In the following case, the defendants challenged the constitutionality of § 1201:

United States v. Elcom Ltd.

203 F.SUPP.2D 1111 (2002)

U.S. DISTRICT COURT, N.D. OF CALIFORNIA

WHYTE, District Judge.

Adobe Systems is a software company headquartered in San Jose, California. Adobe's Acrobat eBook Reader product provides the technology for the reading of books in digital form (i.e., electronic books, or "ebooks") on personal computers. Use of the Adobe eBook format allows publishers or distributors of electronic books to control the subsequent distribution of the ebook, typically by limiting the distribution to those who pay for a copy. These restrictions are imposed by the publisher's use of the Adobe Content Server, which allows the publisher to grant or withhold a range of privileges from the consumer. For example, the ebook publisher may choose whether the consumer will be able to copy the ebook, whether the ebook can be printed to paper (in whole, in part, or not at all), whether the "lending function" is enabled to allow the user to lend the ebook to another computer on the same network of computers, and whether to permit the ebook to be read audibly by a speech synthesizer program. When a consumer purchases an ebook formatted for Adobe Acrobat eBook Reader from an Internet website, the ebook is downloaded directly to the consumer's computer from the ebook distributor's Adobe Content Server. The ebook is accompanied by an electronic "voucher" which is recognized and read by the Adobe Acrobat eBook Reader, which then "knows" that the copy of the ebook can only be read on the computer onto which it has been downloaded. Thus, typically, the purchaser of an ebook may only read the ebook on the computer onto which the ebook was downloaded but may not e-mail or copy the ebook to another computer. The user may or may not be able to print the ebook in paper form or have it audibly read by the computer.

Defendant Elcomsoft Company Ltd. ("Elcomsoft") developed and sold a product known as the Advanced eBook Processor ("AEBPR"). AEBPR is a Windows-based software program that allows a user to remove use restrictions from Adobe Acrobat PDF files and files formatted for the Adobe eBook Reader. The program allows a purchaser of an eBook Reader formatted electronic book to convert the format to one that is readable in any PDF viewer without the use restrictions imposed by the publisher. Thus, the restrictions imposed by the publisher are stripped away, leaving the ebook in a "naked PDF" format that is readily copyable, printable, and easily distributed electronically. The conversion accomplished by the AEBPR program enables a purchaser of an ebook to engage in "fair use" of an ebook without infringing the copyright laws, for example, by allowing the lawful owner of an ebook to read it on another computer, to make a back-up copy, or to print the ebook in paper form. The same technology, however, also allows a user to engage in copyright infringement by making and distributing unlawful copies of the ebook. Defendant was indicted for alleged violations of Section 1201(b)(1)(A) and (C) of the Digital Millennium Copyright Act ("DMCA"), 17 U.S.C. §§ 1201(b)(1)(A) and (C), for allegedly trafficking in and marketing of the AEBPR.

Congress enacted the DMCA following the adoption of the World Intellectual Property Organization Copyright Treaty as an expansion of traditional copyright law in recognition of the fact that in the digital age, authors must employ protective technologies in order to prevent their works from being unlawfully copied or exploited.

Through the DMCA, Congress sought to prohibit certain efforts to unlawfully circumvent protective technologies, while at the same time preserving users' rights of fair use. Some understanding of the interplay between copyright and fair use is essential to understanding the issues confronting Congress and the issues presented here. [C]opyright grants authors the exclusive right to make and distribute copies of their original works of authorship but the doctrine of fair use permits a certain amount of copying for limited purposes without infringing the copyright, notwithstanding the exclusive rights of the copyright owner.

As part of the balance Congress sought to strike in protecting the rights of copyright owners while preserving fair use, Congress enacted three new anti-circumvention prohibitions, Section 1201(a)(1), Section 1201(a)(2) and Section 1201(b). The first two provisions target circumvention of technological measures that effectively control access to a copyrighted work; the third targets circumvention of technological measures that impose limitations on the use of protected works.

[C]ircumventing use restrictions is not unlawful, but in order to protect the rights of copyright owners while maintaining fair use, Congress banned trafficking in devices that are primarily designed for the purpose of circumventing any technological measure that "effectively protects a right of a copyright owner," or that have limited commercially significant purposes other than circumventing use restrictions, or that are marketed for use in circumventing the use restrictions.

The difficulty is created by Section 1201(b)'s use of the phrase "effectively protects a right of a copyright owner" to define the prohibited device because the rights of a copyright owner are intertwined with the rights of others. The rights of a copyright owner include the exclusive rights to reproduce the copyrighted work, to prepare derivative works based upon the copyrighted work, to distribute copies by sale or otherwise, to perform the copyrighted work publicly, and to display the copyrighted work publicly. Exceptions to the copyright owner's exclusive rights are set forth in 17 U.S.C.

§§ 107–120. One of those exceptions is that the copyright owner loses control over the disposition of a copy of a work upon the sale or transfer of the copy. Thus, once a published copy is sold, the copyright owner has no right to restrict the further sale or transfer of that copy. In addition, one of the most significant exceptions to the rights of a copyright owner is the doctrine of fair use.

Fair use is a defense to copyright infringement, allowing a certain amount of direct copying for certain uses, without the permission of the copyright owner and notwithstanding the copyright owner's exclusive rights. Section 107 provides that the fair use of a copyrighted work for purposes such as criticism, comment, news reporting, teaching, scholarship or research is not an infringement of a copyright. Section 107 also sets forth a series of factors for determining whether any particular use is a "fair use," including: "(1) the purpose and character of the use, including whether such use is of a commercial nature or is for nonprofit educational purposes; (2) the nature of the copyrighted work; (3) the amount and substantiality of the portion used in relation to the copyrighted work as a whole; and (4) the effect of the use upon the potential market for or value of the copyrighted work." There is no bright line test for determining whether any particular use is a "fair use" or is instead an act of copyright infringement, and each use requires a case-by-case determination.

The interplay between fair use and copyright weaves throughout defendant's motions to dismiss. The parties dispute whether Congress banned, or intended to ban, all circumvention tools or instead banned only those circumvention devices that would facilitate copyright infringement, and if, as a result, the DMCA is unconstitutionally vague. The parties also dispute whether, because of its effect on the fair use doctrine, the DMCA is an unconstitutional infringement upon the First Amendment and whether Congress had the power to enact the legislation. It is to these issues the court will next turn.

Defendant first contends that Section 1201(b) is unconstitutionally vague as applied to Elcomsoft because it does not clearly delineate the conduct which it prohibits. A criminal statute is not vague if it provides adequate notice of the prohibited conduct in terms that a reasonable person of ordinary intelligence would understand.

Thus, the court's initial task is to determine whether the DMCA bans trafficking in all circumvention tools, regardless of whether they are designed to enable fair use or to facilitate infringement, or whether instead the statute bans only those tools that circumvent use restrictions for the purpose of facilitating copyright infringement. If all circumvention tools are banned, defendant's void-for-vagueness challenge necessarily fails.

The first element targets "any technology, product, service, device, component, or part thereof." This language is not difficult to decipher and is all-encompassing: it includes any tool, no matter its form, that is primarily designed or produced to circumvent technological protection. Section 1201(b) prohibits trafficking in any tool that avoids, bypasses, removes, deactivates, or otherwise impairs any technological measure that prevents, restricts or otherwise limits the exercise of the right to reproduce the work, prepare derivative works, distribute copies of the work, perform the work publicly or by digital audio transmission, or display the work publicly. In short, the statute bans trafficking in any device that bypasses or circumvents a restriction on copying or performing a work. Nothing within the express language would permit trafficking in devices designed to bypass use restrictions in order to enable a fair use, as opposed to an infringing use. The statute does not distinguish between devices based on the uses to which the device will be put. Instead, all tools that enable circumvention of use restrictions are banned, not merely those use restrictions that prohibit infringement.

The inescapable conclusion from the statutory language adopted by Congress and the legislative history discussed above is that Congress sought to ban all circumvention tools because most of the time those tools would be used to infringe a copyright. Thus, while it is not unlawful to circumvent for the purpose of engaging in fair use, it is unlawful to traffic in tools that allow fair use circumvention. That is part of the sacrifice Congress was willing to make in order to protect against unlawful piracy and promote the development of electronic commerce and the availability of copyrighted material on the Internet.

Accordingly, there is no ambiguity in what tools are allowed and what tools are prohibited because the statute bans trafficking in or the marketing of all circumvention devices. The law, as written, allows a person to conform his or her conduct to a comprehensible standard and is thus not unconstitutionally vague. Therefore, defendant's motion to dismiss the indictment on due process grounds is denied.

Defendant asserts several First Amendment challenges, arguing that the DMCA violates the First Amendment as applied to the sale of the AEBPR, that the DMCA violates the First Amendment because it infringes the First Amendment rights of third parties, and that the DMCA violates the First Amendment because it is impermissibly vague, thus chilling otherwise protected speech.

First, the government erroneously contends that the DMCA does not implicate the First Amendment because defendant's sale of circumvention technology is not speech. While selling is the act giving rise to potential criminal liability under Section 1201(b), the DMCA bans trafficking in the AEBPR, software which at some level contains expression, thus implicating the First Amendment. As noted by defendant in reply, the government could not ban the sale of newspapers without implicating the First Amendment, even if newspapers themselves were not banned. First Amendment scrutiny is triggered because the statute bans the sale of something that at some level contains protected expression.

Second, the government contends that computer code is not speech and hence is not subject to First Amendment protections. The court disagrees. Computer software is expression that is protected by the copyright laws and is therefore "speech" at some level, speech that is protected at some level by the First Amendment. As computer code—whether source or object—is a means of expressing ideas, the First Amendment must be considered before dissemination may be prohibited or regulated. In that sense, computer code is covered, or as sometimes said, "protected" by the First Amendment. Accordingly, it is appropriate to consider defendant's First Amendment challenges.

Defendant first argues that the DMCA, as applied to the sale of defendant's AEBPR, violates the First Amendment. Defendant's argument is structured as follows: computer code is speech protected by the First Amendment; the DMCA regulates that speech based upon its content because it bans the code that conveys a certain message (i.e., circumventing use restrictions); content-based regulations must be narrowly tailored; the DMCA is not narrowly tailored; ergo, the DMCA is unconstitutional.

[T]he court concludes that intermediate scrutiny, rather than strict scrutiny, is the appropriate standard to apply. Under this test, the regulation will be upheld if it furthers an important or substantial government interest unrelated to the suppression of free expression, and if the incidental restrictions on First Amendment freedoms are no greater than essential to the furtherance of that interest.

In this case, there are two asserted governmental interests: preventing the unauthorized copying of copyrighted works and promoting electronic commerce. Congress recognized that a primary threat to electronic commerce and to the rights of copyright holders was the plague of digital piracy. The Senate Report notes:

> Due to the ease with which digital works can be copied and distributed worldwide virtually instantaneously, copyright owners will hesitate to make their works readily available on the Internet without reasonable assurance that they will be protected against massive piracy.
>
> Legislation implementing the treaties provides this protection and creates the legal platform for launching the global digital on-line marketplace for copyrighted works. It will facilitate making available quickly and conveniently via the Internet the movies, music, software, and literary works that are the fruit of American creative genius. It will also encourage the continued growth of the existing off-line global marketplace for copyrighted works in digital format by setting strong international copyright standards.

S.Rep. No. 105-190, at 8 (1998).

Congress has elsewhere expressed its concern over the state of intellectual property piracy:

> Notwithstanding [penalties for copyright infringement] copyright piracy of intellectual property flourishes, assisted in large part by today's world of advanced technologies. For example, industry groups estimate that counterfeiting and piracy of computer software cost the affected copyright holders more than $11 billion last year (others believe the figure is closer to $20 billion). In some countries, software piracy rates are as high as 97% of all sales. The U.S. rate is far lower (25%) but the dollar losses ($2.9 billion) are the highest worldwide.
>
> The effect of this volume of theft is substantial: lost U.S. jobs, lost wages, lower tax revenue, and higher prices for honest purchasers of copyrighted software. Unfortunately, the potential for this problem to worsen is great.

Reimerdes, 111 F.Supp.2d at 335 n. 230 (citing H.R.Rep. No. 106-216 (1999)).

These governmental interests are both legitimate and substantial.

The next step is to determine whether these governmental interests would be promoted less effectively absent the regulation and whether the means chosen burden substantially more speech than is necessary to further the government's interests. Without the ban on trafficking in circumvention tools, the government's interest in promoting electronic commerce, preserving the rights of copyright holders, and preventing piracy would be undermined. The absence of effective technological restrictions to prevent copyright infringement would inevitably result in even more rampant piracy, with a corresponding likely decrease in the willingness of authors and owners of copyrighted works to produce them in digital form or make the works available on-line. Thus, there is little question that the governmental interests would be promoted less effectively in the absence of the regulation. Nevertheless, there is substantial disagreement between the parties with regard to whether or not the regulation "substantially burdens more speech than is necessary" to achieve the government's interests.

Under intermediate scrutiny, it is not necessary that the government select the least restrictive means of achieving its legitimate governmental interest. By its very nature, the intermediate scrutiny test allows some impingement on protected speech in order to achieve the legitimate governmental objective. A sufficiently important government interest in regulating the targeted conduct can justify incidental limitations on First Amendment freedoms. Having considered the arguments asserted by the parties, the court finds that the DMCA does not burden substantially more speech than is necessary to achieve the government's asserted goals of promoting electronic commerce, protecting copyrights, and preventing electronic piracy.

In a facial challenge on overbreadth grounds, the challenger contends that the statute at issue is invalid because it is so broadly written that it infringes unacceptably on the First Amendment rights of third parties. Defendant contends that the DMCA is unconstitutionally overbroad on two grounds: first, the statute impairs the First Amendment right to access non-copyrighted works; and second, the statute precludes third parties from exercising their rights of fair use.

The fatal flaw in defendant's argument, however, is that facial attacks on overbreadth grounds are limited to situations in which the statute or regulation by its terms regulates spoken words or expressive conduct. By its terms, the statute is directed to trafficking in or the marketing of "any technology, product, service, device, component, or part thereof," that circumvents usage control restrictions. The statute is not directed "narrowly and specifically at expression or conduct commonly associated with expression." Software as well as hardware falls within the scope of the Act, as does any other technology or device. Accordingly, an overbreadth facial challenge is not available.

Defendant's final First Amendment challenge is that the DMCA is unconstitutionally vague under the First Amendment because it "provokes uncertainty among speakers" about precisely what speech is prohibited. Defendant's premise is that the DMCA regulates expression based at least in part upon the motive of the speaker, specifically, the purpose for which the program was primarily designed and the extent to which there was a commercially significant purpose in doing so other than the circumvention of copyrighted works. In order to determine if the code violates the DMCA, the seller must assess all possible uses of the technology and determine which are the "significant purpose[s]" and what it is "primarily" designed to do.

Once again, defendant's arguments are not persuasive. The primary flaw in defendant's argument is that the court rejects the contention that the DMCA is a content-based restriction on speech. [T]he DMCA is not a content-based restriction on speech and its restrictions do not "provoke uncertainty among speakers" about what speech is permitted and what speech is prohibited. The statute is not unconstitutionally vague in violation of the First Amendment.

Defendant's final challenge is that Congress exceeded its authority in enacting the DMCA and that, as a result, the statute is unconstitutional. The federal government is one of enumerated powers and Congress may exercise only those powers granted to it. The Constitution contains several express grants of power to Congress, among them the Intellectual Property Clause and the Commerce Clause.

Under the Intellectual Property Clause, Congress is empowered "to promote the Progress of Science and the useful Arts, by securing for limited Times to Authors and Inventors the exclusive Right to their respective Writings and Discoveries." U.S. Const., art. I, § 8 cl. 8. This power, while broad, is not unlimited. More than a century ago, the Supreme Court held that Congress could not exercise its Intellectual Property power to grant exclusive rights in matters other than "writings" or "discoveries" such that the Trademark Act of 1876 was not a proper exercise of Congress' Intellectual Property power. Congress may not, for example, grant exclusive rights to writings that do not constitute original works of authorship. Similarly, the Intellectual Property Clause limits Congress' powers so that patents may only be granted in new inventions that are not obvious in view of the existing art and Congress may not authorize the issuance of a patent whose effects are to remove existing knowledge from the public domain.

Under the Commerce Clause, Congress' power is quite broad. Congress may regulate the use of the channels of interstate commerce; may regulate and protect the instrumentalities of interstate commerce, including persons or things in interstate commerce; and may regulate those activities having a substantial relation to, or which substantially affect, interstate commerce. Once again, however, the power is not unlimited and Congress does not have the authority to legislate matters that are of such a local character that there is too remote a connection to interstate commerce. Both parties also agree that, as broad as Congress' Commerce Power is, Congress may not use that power in such a way as to override or circumvent another constitutional restraint.

Defendant argues that Congress exceeded its powers under the Intellectual Property Clause in enacting the DMCA. The government responds that Congress used its Commerce Power to regulate trafficking in devices for gain. Thus, the issue presented is whether the DMCA was within Congress' Commerce Power, generally, and if so, whether Congress was nevertheless prohibited from enacting the DMCA because of other restraints on Congress' power imposed by the Intellectual Property Clause.

With regard to the first issue, Congress plainly has the power to enact the DMCA under the Commerce Clause. "The commerce power 'is the power to regulate; that is, to prescribe the rule by which commerce is to be governed. This power, like all others vested in Congress, is complete in itself, may be exercised to its utmost extent, and acknowledges no limitations, other than are prescribed by the Constitution.'" *Lopez*, 514 U.S. at 553, 115 S.Ct. 1624 (citing *Gibbons v. Ogden*, 22 U.S. 1, 9 Wheat. 1, 196, 6 L.Ed. 23 (1824)). The DMCA prohibits conduct that has a substantial effect on commerce between the states and commerce with foreign nations. Trafficking in or the marketing of circumvention devices "for gain," as proscribed by Sections 1201(b) and 1204, has a direct effect on interstate commerce. To the extent that circumvention devices enable wrongdoers to engage in on-line piracy by unlawfully copying and distributing copyrighted works of authorship, the sale of such devices has a direct effect on suppressing the market for legitimate copies of the works. Accordingly, there is a rational basis for concluding that the regulated activity sufficiently affects interstate commerce to establish that Congress had authority under the Commerce Clause to enact the legislation.

The more difficult question, however, is whether Congress was nevertheless precluded from enacting the DMCA by restraints imposed by the Intellectual Property Clause.

The first issue is to determine whether the DMCA is "not fundamentally inconsistent" with the purpose of the Intellectual Property Clause. The purpose of the Intellectual Property Clause is to promote the useful arts and sciences. Thus, the government is empowered to grant exclusive rights to inventors and authors in their respective inventions and original works of authorship, for limited times. This allows the inventor/author a reasonable time in which to reap the economic fruits of his or her inventive or creative labor. As a result of this economic incentive, people are encouraged to engage in inventive and originally expressive endeavors, thereby promoting the arts and sciences. In addition, because the grant of property rights is to be of limited duration, the public will generally benefit, once the exclusive rights expire and the invention or expression becomes dedicated to the public.

Protecting the exclusive rights granted to copyright owners against unlawful piracy by preventing trafficking in tools that would enable widespread piracy and unlawful infringement is consistent with the purpose of the Intellectual Property Clause's grant to Congress of the power to "promote the useful arts and sciences" by granting exclusive rights to authors in their writings. In addition, Congress did not ban the use of circumvention tools out of a concern that enacting such a ban would unduly restrict the fair use doctrine and expressly sought to preserve fair use. Therefore, on the whole, the DMCA's anti-device provisions are not fundamentally inconsistent with the Intellectual Property Clause.

Finally, the DMCA does not allow a copyright owner to effectively prevent an ebook from ever entering the public domain, despite the expiration of the copyright. Upon the expiration of the copyright, there is no longer any protectable intellectual property right in the work's expression. The expression may be copied, quoted, republished in new format and sold, without any legally enforceable restriction on the use of the expression. The publisher/copyright owner has no right to prevent any user from using the work any way the user prefers. At best, the publisher has a technological measure embedded within the digital product precluding certain uses of that particular copy of the work and, in many cases, the user/purchaser has acquiesced in this restriction when purchasing/licensing the work. The essence of a copyright is the legally enforceable exclusive rights to reproduce and distribute copies of an original work of authorship, to make derivative works, and to perform the work publicly, for a limited period of time. None of those rights is extended beyond the statutory term merely by prohibiting the trafficking in or marketing of devices primarily designed to circumvent use restrictions on works in electronic form.

Accordingly, the DMCA does not run afoul of any restraint on Congress' power imposed by the Intellectual Property Clause. Section 1201(b) of the DMCA was within Congress' Commerce Power to enact, and because it is not irreconcilably inconsistent with any provision of the Intellectual Property Clause, Congress did not exceed its constitutional authority in enacting the law.

Section 1202 creates a separate criminal violation involving the integrity of copyright management information. That section provides:

  (a) False copyright management information.— No person shall knowingly and with the intent to induce, enable, facilitate, or conceal infringement—
    (1) provide copyright management information that is false, or
    (2) distribute or import for distribution copyright management information that is false.
  (b) Removal or alteration of copyright management information.— No person shall, without the authority of the copyright owner or the law—
    (1) intentionally remove or alter any copyright management information,

(2) distribute or import for distribution copyright management information knowing that the copyright management information has been removed or altered without authority of the copyright owner or the law, or

(3) distribute, import for distribution, or publicly perform works, copies of works, or phonorecords, knowing that copyright management information has been removed or altered without authority of the copyright owner or the law, knowing, or, with respect to civil remedies under section 1203, having reasonable grounds to know, that it will induce, enable, facilitate, or conceal an infringement of any right under this title.

(c) Definition.— As used in this section, the term "copyright management information" means any of the following information conveyed in connection with copies or phonorecords of a work or performances or displays of a work, including in digital form, except that such term does not include any personally identifying information about a user of a work or of a copy, phonorecord, performance, or display of a work:

(1) The title and other information identifying the work, including the information set forth on a notice of copyright.

(2) The name of, and other identifying information about, the author of a work.

(3) The name of, and other identifying information about, the copyright owner of the work, including the information set forth in a notice of copyright.

(4) With the exception of public performances of works by radio and television broadcast stations, the name of, and other identifying information about, a performer whose performance is fixed in a work other than an audiovisual work.

(5) With the exception of public performances of works by radio and television broadcast stations, in the case of an audiovisual work, the name of, and other identifying information about, a writer, performer, or director who is credited in the audiovisual work.

(6) Terms and conditions for use of the work.

(7) Identifying numbers or symbols referring to such information or links to such information.

(8) Such other information as the Register of Copyrights may prescribe by regulation, except that the Register of Copyrights may not require the provision of any information concerning the user of a copyrighted work.

Section 1204 provides for the imposition of criminal liability if the defendant "willfully and for purposes of commercial advantage or private financial gain" violates either § 1201 or § 1202. That section further provides that such criminal liability will not be imposed upon nonprofit libraries, archives, educational institutions, and public broadcasting entities.

Section 1203 authorizes intellectual property owners or users to commence civil actions to recover damages for a violation of either § 1201 or § 1202.

Key Words and Phrases

Circumvention

Contributory infringement

Copyright

Encryption

Fair use

False copyright management info

Infringement

Peer-to-peer networks

Reverse engineering

Service mark

Software piracy

Trademark

Vicarious infringement

Review Problems

1. What does it mean to infringe a copyright? How does the concept of fair use apply to copyright infringement?
2. What is the difference between direct, contributory, and vicarious infringement?
3. Describe reverse engineering and encryption research and how those activities affect copyright management technologies.
4. Describe the difference between a trademark, service mark, certification mark, and collective mark. Are these marks governed by the same principles that apply to copyright infringement?
5. Based upon your reading of the *Grokster* decision, why did the Supreme Court conclude that Grokster and Streamcast committed contributory infringement?

Weblinks

www.cybercrime.gov/ipcases.html
> This page at the Department of Justice Computer Crime and Intellectual Property website provides numerous links to documents and information on intellectual property fraud cases.

www.law.arizona.edu/Library/Research/LegalLinks/Topical/intellectualproperty. cfm?page=research
> This page at the University of Arizona Law School website has numerous links to documents and information specific to intellectual property fraud.

www.wipo.int/about-ip/en/
> This page at the website of the World Intellectual Property Organization has links to information concerning intellectual property at the international level.

www.siia.net/govt/issue.asp?issue=ip
> This page at the website of the Software and Information Industry Association focuses on information pertaining to intellectual property.

Investigation and Enforcement of Cybercrimes

IV

Search and Seizure
Beginning Principles

8

Introduction

At some point in every cybercrime investigation the investigator will need to obtain evidence of the crime. Unless the evidence is dropped on the investigator's lap, the investigator will need to obtain the evidence by searching a workplace, home, or other physical location (for example, cyber café or public library) for digital evidence and seize a computer or other device, removing it to a forensic lab and analyzing the device in a search for the evidence. Thus, investigators, whether members of law enforcement or private sector employees, should not undertake that investigation without a basic understanding of the law that applies to searches and seizures and the potential liability that might result from a violation of statutory or case law in this area.

One case clearly illustrates the point. A plastic surgeon in Kirkland, Washington, was suspected of sexually molesting patients. The police obtained a warrant to search the physician's home for pictures he allegedly had taken of the victims while under anesthesia. During execution of the warrant, the police searched a computer that was situated near a digital camera. That search revealed pictures of child pornography. The police stopped the search and asked a prosecutor whether they should seek a new warrant to search for child pornography. The prosecutor, concerned that a warrant based on the child pornography already viewed would be suppressed, asked whether the police had found other evidence of child pornography at the scene. When advised that computer printouts of child pornography had been found, the prosecutor advised the police to apply for a warrant based solely on the pornography that was not found on the computer. The police were successful in obtaining a new warrant. They searched the computer for child pornography and found digital images of child porn. The prosecution charged defendant with sexual exploitation of a minor, in addition to sexual assault charges. The trial court, however, upon learning that the police had not informed the warrant judge about the initial search of the computer, suppressed the evidence of child pornography and dismissed the sexual exploitation charges.[1] In that case, even a prosecutor schooled in the law of search and seizure provided advice that led ultimately to the suppression of evidence found during a search.

Constitutional Principles

The Fourth Amendment

The Fourth Amendment of the U.S. Constitution provides:

> The right of the people to be secure in their persons, houses, papers, and effects, against unreasonable searches and seizures, shall not be violated, and no Warrants shall issue, but

upon probable cause, supported by Oath or affirmation, and particularly describing the place to be searched, and the persons or things to be seized.

Each state has its own constitution, and most states have a search and seizure provision similar to the Fourth Amendment to the U.S. Constitution. However, because states may provide greater protection than the federal constitution provides, several state courts have concluded that their own state constitution provides greater protection from unreasonable searches and seizures than the Fourth Amendment (see, for example, *People v. Johnson*, 66 NY2d 398 (1985), which declined to apply the "totality of circumstances" test adopted by the U.S. Supreme Court in *Illinois v. Gates* (462 U.S. 213 (1983)) in determining whether police had probable cause for a search).

Several countries also provide protection from unreasonable searches and seizures (see, for example, Canadian Charter of Rights and Freedoms, § 8). Section 8 of the Canadian Charter contains language similar to the text of the Fourth Amendment, and Canadian courts frequently cite decisions of the U.S. Supreme Court in resolving search and seizure issues.

A detailed consideration of search and seizure law is not possible within the context of these materials. It is important, however, to discuss briefly those principles that apply to the preliminary issue: whether certain conduct violates the Fourth Amendment. Following that discussion, Chapter 11 considers the application of search and seizure law to computers, digital media, and digital evidence.

Reasonable Expectation of Privacy

The Fourth Amendment prohibits only *unreasonable* searches and seizures. A search or seizure can be unreasonable because it fails to satisfy a legal requirement (for example, the search was conducted without probable cause) or because law enforcement personnel acted unreasonably while executing the search (for example, ransacking through the dresser drawers of an apartment while looking for a stolen television). In studying the reasonableness of conducting a search for digital media or evidence, we will focus on the legal requirement issue.

Subsequent to adoption of the Fourth Amendment, the U.S. Supreme Court, in deciding whether a search or seizure violated the privacy of an individual or business, considered whether law enforcement personnel had intruded upon the property interests of the occupant (see *Olmstead v. United States,* 277 U.S. 438 (1928)). That analytical framework changed, however, when the Court decided *Katz v. United States* (389 U.S. 347 (1967)). In *Katz*, FBI agents had attached a listening device to the outside of a public telephone booth, enabling them to listen to telephone conversations made by Katz while inside the booth. The court held that although the FBI agents intercepted the communications without intruding physically into the booth, the Fourth Amendment "protects people—and not simply 'areas,'" and the fact that the device did not penetrate the walls of the booth was of "no constitutional significance" (*Katz v. United States, supra* at 353). The issue was whether Katz, once inside the booth, had a reasonable expectation of privacy with respect to his telephone conversations. To resolve that issue, the court established a two-prong test. The first prong is subjective: whether Katz personally believed that his conversations would be private. The second prong is objective: whether the subjective expectation of privacy one has is an expectation society is prepared to recognize as reasonable. The court in *Katz v. United States* resolved both prongs of the test in favor of Katz.

More recently, the U.S. Supreme Court had the opportunity to consider the property vs. reasonable expectation theories in the context of a technology-enhanced search. Although the following case did not involve a cybercrime, it clearly may have implications for the use of technology in cybercrime investigations.

Kyllo v. United States

533 U.S. 27 (2001)

U.S. SUPREME COURT

JUSTICE SCALIA delivered the opinion of the Court.

This case presents the question whether the use of a thermal-imaging device aimed at a private home from a public street to detect relative amounts of heat within the home constitutes a "search" within the meaning of the Fourth Amendment.

I

In 1991 Agent William Elliott of the United States Department of the Interior came to suspect that marijuana was being grown in the home belonging to petitioner Danny Kyllo, part of a triplex on Rhododendron Drive in Florence, Oregon. Indoor marijuana growth typically requires high-intensity lamps. In order to determine whether an amount of heat was emanating from petitioner's home consistent with the use of such lamps, at 3:20 a.m. on January 16, 1992, Agent Elliott and Dan Haas used an Agema Thermovision 210 thermal imager to scan the triplex. Thermal imagers detect infrared radiation, which virtually all objects emit but which is not visible to the naked eye. The imager converts radiation into images based on relative warmth—black is cool, white is hot, shades of gray connote relative differences; in that respect, it operates somewhat like a video camera showing heat images. The scan of Kyllo's home took only a few minutes and was performed from the passenger seat of Agent Elliott's vehicle across the street from the front of the house and also from the street in back of the house. The scan showed that the roof over the garage and a side wall of petitioner's home were relatively hot compared to the rest of the home and substantially warmer than neighboring homes in the triplex. Agent Elliott concluded that petitioner was using halide lights to grow marijuana in his house, which indeed he was. Based on tips from informants, utility bills, and the thermal imaging, a Federal Magistrate Judge issued a warrant authorizing a search of petitioner's home, and the agents found an indoor growing operation involving more than 100 plants. Petitioner was indicted on one count of manufacturing marijuana, in violation of 21 U.S.C. § 841(a)(1). He unsuccessfully moved to suppress the evidence seized from his home and then entered a conditional guilty plea.

II

The Fourth Amendment provides that "the right of the people to be secure in their persons, houses, papers, and effects, against unreasonable searches and seizures, shall not be violated." "At the very core" of the Fourth Amendment "stands the right of a man to retreat into his own home and there be free from unreasonable governmental intrusion." *Silverman v. United States*, 365 U.S. 505, 511, 5 L. Ed. 2d 734, 81 S. Ct. 679 (1961). With few exceptions, the question whether a warrantless search of a home is reasonable and hence constitutional must be answered no.

On the other hand, the antecedent question of whether or not a Fourth Amendment "search" has occurred is not so simple under our precedent. The permissibility of ordinary visual surveillance of a home used to be clear because, well into the 20th century, our Fourth Amendment jurisprudence was tied to common-law trespass. We have since decoupled violation of a person's Fourth Amendment rights from trespassory violation of his property, but the lawfulness of warrantless visual surveillance of a home has still been preserved. As we observed in *California v. Ciraolo*, 476 U.S. 207, 213, 90 L. Ed. 2d 210, 106 S. Ct. 1809 (1986), "the Fourth Amendment protection of the home has never been extended to require law enforcement officers to shield their eyes when passing by a home on public thoroughfares."

One might think that the new validating rationale would be that examining the portion of a house that is in plain public view, while it is a "search" despite the absence of trespass, is not an "unreasonable" one under the Fourth Amendment. But in fact we have held that visual observation is no "search" at all—perhaps in order to preserve somewhat more intact our doctrine that warrantless searches are presumptively unconstitutional. In assessing when a search is not a search, we have applied somewhat in reverse the principle first enunciated in *Katz v. United States*, 389 U.S. 347, 19 L. Ed. 2d 576, 88 S. Ct. 507 (1967). *Katz* involved eavesdropping by means of an electronic listening device placed on the outside of a telephone booth—a location not within the catalog ("persons, houses, papers, and effects") that the Fourth Amendment protects against unreasonable searches. We held that the Fourth Amendment nonetheless protected Katz from the warrantless eavesdropping because he "justifiably relied" upon the privacy of the telephone booth. As Justice Harlan's oft-quoted concurrence described it, a Fourth Amendment search occurs when the government violates a subjective expectation of privacy that society recognizes as reasonable. We have subsequently applied this principle to hold that a Fourth Amendment search does not occur—even when the explicitly protected location of a house is concerned—unless "the individual manifested a subjective expectation of privacy in the object of the challenged search," and "society [is] willing to recognize that expectation as reasonable."

The present case involves officers on a public street engaged in more than naked-eye surveillance of a home. We have previously reserved judgment as to how much technological enhancement of ordinary perception from such a vantage point, if any, is too much. While we upheld enhanced aerial photography of an industrial complex in *Dow Chemical*, we noted that we found "it important that this is not an area immediately adjacent to a private home, where privacy expectations are most heightened."

III

It would be foolish to contend that the degree of privacy secured to citizens by the Fourth Amendment has been entirely unaffected by the advance of technology. For example, as the cases discussed above make clear, the technology enabling human flight has exposed to public view (and hence, we have said, to official observation) uncovered portions of the house and its curtilage that once were private. The question we confront today is what limits there are upon this power of technology to shrink the realm of guaranteed privacy.

The *Katz* test—whether the individual has an expectation of privacy that society is prepared to recognize as reasonable—has often been criticized as circular, and hence subjective and unpredictable. While it may be difficult to refine *Katz* when the search of areas such as telephone booths, automobiles, or even the curtilage and uncovered portions of residences are at issue, in the case of the search of the interior of homes—the prototypical and hence most commonly litigated area of protected privacy—there is a ready criterion, with roots deep in the common law, of the minimal expectation of privacy that exists, and that is acknowledged to be reasonable. To withdraw protection of this minimum expectation would be to permit police technology to erode the privacy guaranteed by the Fourth Amendment. We think that obtaining by sense-enhancing technology any information regarding the interior of the home that could not otherwise have been obtained without physical "intrusion into a constitutionally protected area," *Silverman*, 365 U.S. at 512, constitutes a search—at least where (as here) the technology in question is not in general public use. This assures preservation of that degree of privacy against government that existed when the Fourth Amendment was adopted. On the basis of this criterion, the information obtained by the thermal imager in this case was the product of a search.

The Government maintains, however, that the thermal imaging must be upheld because it detected "only heat radiating from the external surface of the house." The dissent makes this its leading point, contending that there is a fundamental difference between what it calls "off-the-wall" observations and "through-the-wall surveillance." But just as a thermal imager captures only heat emanating from a house, so also a powerful directional microphone picks up only sound emanating from a house—and a satellite capable of scanning from many miles away would pick up only visible light emanating from a house. We rejected such a mechanical interpretation of the Fourth Amendment in *Katz*, where the eavesdropping device picked up only sound waves that reached the exterior of the phone booth. Reversing that approach would leave the homeowner at the mercy of advancing technology—including imaging technology that could discern all human activity in the home. While the technology used in the present case was relatively crude, the rule we adopt must take account of more sophisticated systems that are already in use or in development.

The Government also contends that the thermal imaging was constitutional because it did not "detect private activities occurring in private areas." It points out that in *Dow Chemical* we observed that the enhanced aerial photography did not reveal any "intimate details." *Dow Chemical*, however, involved enhanced aerial photography of an industrial complex, which does not share the Fourth Amendment sanctity of the home. The Fourth Amendment's protection of the home has never been tied to measurement of the quality or quantity of information obtained. In *Silverman*, for example, we made clear that any physical invasion of the structure of the home, "by even a fraction of an inch," was too much, and there is certainly no exception to the warrant requirement for the officer who barely cracks open the front door and sees nothing but the nonintimate rug on the vestibule floor. In the home, our cases show, all details are intimate details, because the entire area is held safe from prying government eyes.

Limiting the prohibition of thermal imaging to "intimate details" would not only be wrong in principle; it would be impractical in application, failing to provide "a workable accommodation between the needs of law enforcement and the interests protected by the Fourth Amendment," *Oliver v. United States*, 466 U.S. 170, 181, 80 L. Ed. 2d 214, 104 S. Ct. 1735 (1984). To begin with, there is no necessary connection between the sophistication of the surveillance equipment and the "intimacy" of the details that it observes—which means that one cannot say (and the police cannot be assured) that use of the relatively crude equipment at issue here will always be lawful. The Agema Thermovision 210 might disclose, for example, at what hour each night the lady of the house takes her daily sauna and bath—a detail that many would consider "intimate"; and a much more sophisticated system might detect nothing more intimate than the fact that someone left a closet light on. We could not, in other words, develop a rule approving only that through-the-wall surveillance which identifies objects no smaller than 36 by 36 inches, but would have to develop a jurisprudence specifying which home activities are "intimate" and which are not. And even when (if ever) that jurisprudence were fully developed, no police officer would be able to know in advance whether his through-the-wall surveillance picks up "intimate" details—and thus would be unable to know in advance whether it is constitutional.

We have said that the Fourth Amendment draws "a firm line at the entrance to the house," *Payton*, 445 U.S. at 590. That line, we think, must be not only firm but also bright—which requires clear specification of those methods of surveillance that require a warrant. While it is certainly possible to conclude from the videotape of the thermal imaging that occurred in this case that no "significant" compromise of the homeowner's privacy has occurred, we must take the long view, from the original meaning of the Fourth Amendment forward.

Where, as here, the Government uses a device that is not in general public use, to explore details of the home that would previously have been unknowable without physical intrusion, the surveillance is a "search" and is presumptively unreasonable without a warrant.

Since we hold the Thermovision imaging to have been an unlawful search, it will remain for the District Court to determine whether, without the evidence it provided, the search warrant issued in this case was supported by probable cause—and if not, whether there is any other basis for supporting admission of the evidence that the search pursuant to the warrant produced.

The judgment of the Court of Appeals is reversed; the case is remanded for further proceedings consistent with this opinion.

Justice STEVENS, with whom THE CHIEF JUSTICE, JUSTICE O'CONNOR, and JUSTICE KENNEDY join, dissenting.

There is, in my judgment, a distinction of constitutional magnitude between "through-the-wall surveillance" that gives the observer or listener direct access to information in a private area, on the one hand, and the thought processes used to draw inferences from information in the public domain, on the other hand. The Court has crafted a rule that purports to deal with direct observations of the inside of the home, but the case before us merely involves indirect deductions from "off-the-wall" surveillance, that is, observations of the exterior of the home. Those observations were made with a fairly primitive thermal imager that gathered data exposed on the outside of petitioner's home but did not invade any constitutionally protected interest in privacy. Moreover, I believe that the supposedly "bright-line" rule the Court has created in response to its concerns about future technological developments is unnecessary, unwise, and inconsistent with the Fourth Amendment.

Indeed, the ordinary use of the senses might enable a neighbor or passerby to notice the heat emanating from a building, particularly if it is vented, as was the case here. Additionally, any member of the public might notice that one part of a house is warmer than another part or a nearby building if, for example, rainwater evaporates or snow melts at different rates across its surfaces. Such use of the senses would not convert into an unreasonable search if, instead, an adjoining neighbor allowed an officer onto her property to verify her perceptions with a sensitive thermometer. Nor, in my view, does such observation become an unreasonable search if made from a distance with the aid of a device that merely discloses that the exterior of one house, or one area of the house, is much warmer than another. Nothing more occurred in this case.

Thus, the notion that heat emissions from the outside of a dwelling is a private matter implicating the protections of the Fourth Amendment (the text of which guarantees the right of people "to be secure in their ... houses" against unreasonable searches and seizures is not only unprecedented but also quite difficult to take seriously. Heat waves, like aromas that are generated in a kitchen, or in a laboratory or opium den, enter the public domain if and when they leave a building. A subjective expectation that they would remain private is not only implausible but also surely not "one that society is prepared to recognize as 'reasonable.'" *Katz*, 389 U.S. at 361 (Harlan, J., concurring).

To be sure, the homeowner has a reasonable expectation of privacy concerning what takes place within the home, and the Fourth Amendment's protection against physical invasions of the home should apply to their functional equivalent. But the equipment in this case did not penetrate the walls of petitioner's home, and while it did pick up "details of the home" that were exposed to the public, it did not obtain "any information regarding the interior of the home." In the Court's own words, based on what the thermal imager "showed" regarding the outside of petitioner's home, the officers "concluded" that petitioner was engaging in illegal activity inside the home. It would be quite absurd to characterize their thought processes as "searches," regardless of whether they inferred (rightly) that petitioner was growing marijuana in his house, or (wrongly) that "the lady of the house [was taking] her daily sauna and bath." In either case, the only conclusions the officers reached concerning the interior of the home were at least as indirect as those that might have been inferred from the contents of discarded garbage, or pen register data, or, as in this case, subpoenaed utility records. For the first time in its history, the Court assumes that an inference can amount to a Fourth Amendment violation.

Therefore, to establish that a search or seizure was unreasonable and thus violated the Fourth Amendment, it must be shown that the defendant subjectively believed that the item or communication would be private and that the defendant's subjective expectation of privacy is one that society is prepared to accept as reasonable. Is there a reasonable expectation of privacy when a student uses a computer provided by a college in a computer lab? Consider the following case:

United States v. Butler

151 F. SUPP. 2D 82 (2001)

U.S. DISTRICT COURT, DISTRICT OF MAINE

D. BROCK HORNBY, District Judge.

The Indictment asserts that the defendant has previously been convicted of a crime relating to sexual abuse and abusive sexual conduct involving a minor or ward. It charges that four times thereafter, he knowingly and illegally received child pornography over the Internet, contrary to 18 U.S.C. § 2252A(a)(2)(A). The defendant's motions to suppress, dismiss and continue are DENIED.

1. Students' Fourth Amendment Rights in University Computers

The Indictment charges that the images in question came over the Internet to computers at the Lewiston-Auburn College of the University of Maine. The defendant moves to suppress the University logs identifying when he used the University computers, as well as the contents of the hard drives from two University computers he used. I accept as true, for purposes of the motion, the assertions in the defendant's motion to suppress.

At the time, the defendant was a student enrolled in the University of Maine system. Because he was an enrolled student, he had access to a computer lab on the Lewiston-Auburn campus. On one Occasion, he left on a University computer screen a frozen image that a University employee considered pedophilia. That incident led to an investigation by University authorities, which revealed more such images on hard drives, and ultimately the police were involved. As a result, the prosecution now has the hard drives of two University computers, as well as session logs showing when the defendant used the computers. The defendant wants all of these suppressed as the product of searches in violation of the Fourth Amendment.

To assert a right under the Fourth Amendment, a defendant must demonstrate both a subjective expectation of privacy and an expectation that society judges as objectively reasonable. *Kyllo v. United States*, 530 U.S. 1305, 121 S. Ct. 29, 147 L. Ed. 2d 1052, (2001). What that objectively reasonable expectation is for computers, under circumstances of shared usage, presents questions of some difficulty in today's environment of rapidly changing technology and provisions of service. I do not have to confront these difficult issues because the defendant has made not even a minimal showing that he had a reasonable expectation of privacy in either his session logs or the hard drives of these University-owned computers. Session logs are obviously maintained for the benefit of the University and therefore not suppressible on the defendant/student's motion. See *United States v. Simons*, 206 F.3d 392, 398-99 (4th Cir. 2000) (finding no reasonable expectation of privacy in files downloaded from the Internet to hard drives of employee's office computer where employer had express policy of monitoring Internet activities of employees).

The defendant relies upon "a legitimate and reasonable expectation of privacy recognized by society in any work performed on, or documents and files produced on, computers he used while a student at the University of Maine." Unlike the Supreme Court's treatment of generic payphone booths in 1967 in *Katz*, I conclude that in 2001 there is no generic expectation of privacy for shared usage on computers at large. Conditions of computer use and access still vary tremendously. The burden remains on the defendant to show that his expectations were reasonable under the circumstances of the particular case. Without meeting that burden, he cannot challenge the University's decision to examine the computers he used, nor the warrant the police obtained later to search the hard drives of the University's computers.

SO ORDERED.

In Chapter 12, we discuss how the courts have considered an individual's reasonable expectation of privacy in light of *Kyllo v. United States* in the context of emerging technologies.

Workplace Searches

One of the more problematic areas has been the extent of an employee's expectation of privacy in the workplace, and particularly with respect to the public workplace. The authority on this issue is *O'Connor v. Ortega,* which follows:

O'Connor v. Ortega

480 U.S. 709 (1987)

U.S. SUPREME COURT

Justice O'CONNOR delivered the Opinion of the Court:

This suit under 42 U.S.C. § 1983 presents two issues concerning the Fourth Amendment rights of public employees. First, we must determine whether the respondent, a public employee, had a reasonable expectation of privacy in his office, desk, and file cabinets at his place of work. Second, we must address the appropriate Fourth Amendment standard for a search conducted by a public employer in areas in which a public employee is found to have a reasonable expectation of privacy.

I

Dr. Magno Ortega, a physician and psychiatrist, held the position of Chief of Professional Education at Napa State Hospital (Hospital) for 17 years, until his dismissal from that position in 1981. As Chief of Professional Education, Dr. Ortega had primary responsibility for training young physicians in psychiatric residency programs.

In July 1981, Hospital officials, including Dr. Dennis O'Connor, the Executive Director of the Hospital, became concerned about possible improprieties in Dr. Ortega's management of the residency program. In particular, the Hospital officials were concerned with Dr. Ortega's acquisition of an Apple II computer for use in the residency program. The officials thought that Dr. Ortega may have misled Dr. O'Connor into believing that the computer had been donated, when in fact the computer had been financed by the possibly coerced contributions of residents. Additionally, the Hospital officials were concerned with charges that Dr. Ortega had sexually harassed two female Hospital employees, and had taken inappropriate disciplinary action against a resident.

On July 30, 1981, Dr. O'Connor requested that Dr. Ortega take paid administrative leave during an investigation of these charges. At Dr. Ortega's request, Dr. O'Connor agreed to allow Dr. Ortega to take two weeks' vacation instead of administrative leave. Dr. Ortega, however, was requested to stay off Hospital grounds for the duration of the investigation. On August 14, 1981, Dr. O'Connor informed Dr. Ortega that the investigation had not yet been completed, and that he was being placed on paid administrative leave. Dr. Ortega remained on administrative leave until the Hospital terminated his employment on September 22, 1981.

Dr. O'Connor selected several Hospital personnel to conduct the investigation, including an accountant, a physician, and a Hospital security officer. Richard Friday, the Hospital Administrator, led this "investigative team." At some point during the investigation, Mr. Friday made the decision to enter Dr. Ortega's office. The specific reason for the entry into Dr. Ortega's office is unclear from the record. The petitioners claim that the search was conducted to secure state property. Initially, petitioners contended that such a search was pursuant to a Hospital policy of conducting a routine inventory of state property in the office of a terminated employee. At the time of the search, however, the Hospital had not yet terminated Dr. Ortega's employment; Dr. Ortega was still on administrative leave. Apparently, there was no policy of inventorying the offices of those on administrative leave. Before the search had been initiated, however, petitioners had become aware that Dr. Ortega had taken the computer to his home. Dr. Ortega contends that the purpose of the search was to secure evidence for use against him in administrative disciplinary proceedings.

The resulting search of Dr. Ortega's office was quite thorough. The investigators entered the office a number of times and seized several items from Dr. Ortega's desk and file cabinets, including a Valentine's Day card, a photograph, and a book of poetry all sent to Dr. Ortega by a former resident physician. These items were later used in a proceeding before a hearing officer of the California State Personnel Board to impeach the credibility of the former resident, who testified on Dr. Ortega's behalf. The investigators also seized billing documentation of one of Dr. Ortega's private patients under the California Medicaid program. The investigators did not otherwise separate Dr. Ortega's property from state property because, as one investigator testified, "[trying] to sort State from non-State, it was too much to do, so I gave it up and boxed it up." Thus, no formal inventory of the property in the office was ever made. Instead, all the papers in Dr. Ortega's office were merely placed in boxes, and put in storage for Dr. Ortega to retrieve.

Dr. Ortega commenced this action against petitioners in Federal District Court under 42 U.S.C. § 1983, alleging that the search of his office violated the Fourth Amendment.

II

The strictures of the Fourth Amendment, applied to the States through the Fourteenth Amendment, have been applied to the conduct of governmental officials in various civil activities. Searches and seizures by government employers or supervisors of the private property of their employees, therefore, are subject to the restraints of the Fourth Amendment.

The Fourth Amendment protects the "right of the people to be secure in their persons, houses, papers, and effects, against unreasonable searches and seizures...." Our cases establish that Dr. Ortega's Fourth Amendment rights are implicated only if the conduct of the Hospital officials at issue in this case infringed "an expectation of privacy that society is prepared to consider reasonable." *United States v. Jacobsen*, 466 U.S. 109, 113 (1984).

Because the reasonableness of an expectation of privacy, as well as the appropriate standard for a search, is understood to differ according to context, it is essential first to delineate the boundaries of the workplace context. The workplace includes those areas and items that are related to work and are generally within the employer's control. At a hospital, for example, the hallways, cafeteria, offices, desks, and file cabinets, among other areas, are all part of the workplace. These areas remain part of the workplace context even if the employee has placed personal items in them, such as a photograph placed in a desk or a letter posted on an employee bulletin board.

Within the workplace context, this Court has recognized that employees may have a reasonable expectation of privacy against intrusions by police.

Individuals do not lose Fourth Amendment rights merely because they work for the government instead of a private employer. The operational realities of the workplace, however, may make some employees' expectations of privacy unreasonable when an intrusion is by a supervisor rather than a law enforcement official. Public employees' expectations of privacy in their offices, desks, and file cabinets, like similar expectations of employees in the private sector, may be reduced by virtue of actual office practices and procedures, or by legitimate regulation. The employee's expectation of privacy must be assessed in the context of the employment relation. An office is seldom a private enclave free from entry by supervisors, other employees, and business and personal invitees. Instead, in many cases offices are continually entered by fellow employees and other visitors during the workday for conferences, consultations, and other work-related visits. Simply put, it is the nature of government offices that others—such as fellow employees, supervisors, consensual visitors, and the general public—may have frequent access to an individual's office.

The Court of Appeals concluded that Dr. Ortega had a reasonable expectation of privacy in his office, and five Members of this Court agree with that determination. Because the record does not reveal the extent to which Hospital officials may have had work-related reasons to enter Dr. Ortega's office, we think the Court of Appeals should have remanded the matter to the District Court for its further determination. But regardless of any legitimate right of access the Hospital staff may have had to the office as such, we recognize that the undisputed evidence suggests that Dr. Ortega had a reasonable expectation of privacy in his desk and file cabinets. The undisputed evidence discloses that Dr. Ortega did not share his desk or file cabinets with any other employees. Dr. Ortega had occupied the office for 17 years and he kept materials in his office, which included personal correspondence, medical files, correspondence from private patients unconnected to the Hospital, personal financial records, teaching aids and notes, and personal gifts and mementos. The files on physicians in residency training were kept outside Dr. Ortega's office. Indeed, the only items found by the investigators were apparently personal items because, with the exception of the items seized for use in the administrative hearings, all the papers and effects found in the office were simply placed in boxes and made available to Dr. Ortega. Finally, we note that there was no evidence that the Hospital had established any reasonable regulation or policy discouraging employees such as Dr. Ortega from storing personal papers and effects in their desks or file cabinets, although the absence of such a policy does not create an expectation of privacy where it would not otherwise exist.

On the basis of this undisputed evidence, we accept the conclusion of the Court of Appeals that Dr. Ortega had a reasonable expectation of privacy at least in his desk and file cabinets.

The following case is another government workplace search. This case is unique in that it involves both warrantless searches and a search pursuant to a warrant.

United States v. Simons

---

206 F.3D 392 (2000)

U.S. COURT OF APPEALS, FOURTH CIRCUIT

OPINION: WILKINS, Circuit Judge:

Mark L. Simons appeals his convictions for receiving and possessing materials constituting or containing child pornography, see 18 U.S.C.A. § 2252A(a)(2)(A), (a)(5)(B). Simons, who received the unlawful materials at his government workplace via the Internet, argues that the district court erred in denying his motion to suppress. We affirm in part and remand in part.

Simons was employed as an electronic engineer at the Foreign Bureau of Information Services (FBIS), a division of the Central Intelligence Agency (CIA). FBIS provided Simons with an office, which he did not share with anyone, and a computer with Internet access.

In June 1998, FBIS instituted a policy regarding Internet usage by employees. The policy stated that employees were to use the Internet for official government business only. Accessing unlawful material was specifically prohibited. The policy explained that FBIS would conduct electronic audits to ensure compliance. The policy also stated that "users shall … understand FBIS will periodically audit, inspect, and/or monitor the user's Internet access as deemed appropriate."

FBIS contracted with Science Applications International Corporation (SAIC) for the management of FBIS' computer network, including monitoring for any inappropriate use of computer resources. On July 17, 1998, Clifford Mauck, a manager at SAIC, began exploring the capabilities of a firewall recently acquired by SAIC, because Mauck believed that SAIC needed to become more familiar with the firewall to service the FBIS contract properly. Mauck entered the keyword "sex" into the firewall database for July 14 and 17, 1998, and found a large number of Internet "hits" originating from Simons' computer. It was obvious to Mauck from the names of the sites that they were not visited for official FBIS purposes.

Mauck reported this discovery to his contact at FBIS, Katherine Camer. Camer then worked with another SAIC employee, Robert Harper, to further investigate the apparently unauthorized activity. Camer instructed Harper to view one of the websites that Simons had visited. Harper complied and found that the site contained pictures of nude women.

At Camer's direction and from his own workstation, Harper examined Simons' computer to determine whether Simons had downloaded any picture files from the Internet; Harper found over 1,000 such files. Again from his own workstation, Harper viewed several of the pictures and observed that they were pornographic in nature. Also at Camer's request and from his own workstation, Harper printed a list of the titles of the downloaded picture files. Harper was then asked to copy all of the files on the hard drive of Simons' computer; Harper accomplished this task, again, from his own workstation.

On or about July 31, 1998, two representatives from the CIA Office of the Inspector General (OIG), one of whom was a criminal investigator, viewed selected files from the copy of Simons' hard drive; the pictures were of minors. Later that day, Harper physically entered Simons' office, removed the original hard drive, replaced it with a copy, and gave the original to the FBIS Area Security Officer. The Security Officer turned it over to the OIG criminal investigator the same day. This last assignment was the only one that required Harper to physically enter Simons' office.

On August 5, 1998, FBI Special Agent John Mesisca viewed over 50 of the images on the hard drive that had been removed from Simons' office; many of the images contained child pornography. Mesisca, Harper, the two OIG representatives, and Assistant United States Attorney Tom Connolly worked together to prepare an application for a warrant to search Simons' office and computer. An affidavit from Mesisca supported the warrant application. The affidavit stated, *inter alia*, that Simons had connected a zip drive to his computer. The affidavit also expressed a "need" to conduct the search in secret.

The warrant was issued on August 6, 1998. It stated that the executing officers were to leave at Simons' office a copy of the warrant and a receipt for any property taken. The warrant mentioned neither permission for, nor prohibition of, secret execution.

Mesisca and others executed the search during the evening of August 6, 1998, when Simons was not present. The search team copied the contents of Simons' computer; computer diskettes found in Simons' desk drawer; computer files stored on the zip drive or on zip drive diskettes; videotapes; and various documents, including personal correspondence. No original evidence was removed from the office. Neither a copy of the warrant nor a receipt for the property seized was left in the office or otherwise given to Simons at that time, and Simons did not learn of the search for approximately 45 days. When Mesisca reviewed the computer materials copied during the search, he found over 50 pornographic images of minors.

In September 1998, Mesisca applied for a second search warrant. The supporting affidavit, like the affidavit that supported the August application, stated that Simons had connected a zip drive to his computer. The September affidavit described the August application as an application for a surreptitious search warrant.

A second search warrant was obtained on September 17, 1998 and executed on September 23, 1998, with Simons present. Original evidence was seized and removed from the office. The executors left Simons with a copy of the warrant and an inventory of the items seized.

Simons subsequently was indicted on one count of knowingly receiving child pornography that had been transported in interstate commerce, see 18 U.S.C.A. § 2252A(a)(2)(A), and one count of knowingly possessing material containing images of child pornography that had been transported in interstate commerce, see 18 U.S.C.A. § 2252A(a)(5)(B). Simons moved to suppress the evidence, arguing that the searches of his office and computer violated his Fourth Amendment rights. Following a hearing, the district court denied the motion. With regard to the warrantless searches, the district court first concluded that Simons lacked a legitimate expectation of privacy in his Internet use. The court nevertheless determined that, even if Simons did have a legitimate expectation of privacy, all of the warrantless searches satisfied the reasonableness requirement of the Fourth Amendment. The district court also upheld the warrant searches.

At a bench trial on stipulated facts, four computer picture files depicting child pornography were introduced as evidence of Simons' guilt. The district court found Simons guilty on both counts and sentenced him to 18 months imprisonment. Simons now appeals, maintaining that the district court erred in denying his motion to suppress.

Inexplicably, the record does not indicate which search or searches yielded the four computer picture files used against Simons at trial. Consequently, we are called upon to review the constitutionality of all of the searches. We consider first the warrantless searches, then turn to Simons' challenges to the searches conducted pursuant to the August search warrant.

The Fourth Amendment prohibits "unreasonable searches and seizures" by government agents, including government employers or supervisors. To establish a violation of his rights under the Fourth Amendment, Simons must first prove that he had a legitimate expectation of privacy in the place searched or the item seized. And in order to prove a legitimate expectation of privacy, Simons must show that his subjective expectation of privacy is one that society is prepared to accept as objectively reasonable.

Government employees may have a legitimate expectation of privacy in their offices or in parts of their offices such as their desks or file cabinets.

We first consider Simons' challenge to the warrantless searches of his computer and office by FBIS.[*] We conclude that the remote searches of Simons' computer did not violate his Fourth Amendment rights because, in light of the Internet policy, Simons lacked a legitimate expectation of privacy in the files downloaded from the Internet. Additionally, we conclude that Simons' Fourth Amendment rights were not violated by FBIS' retrieval of Simons' hard drive from his office.

Simons did not have a legitimate expectation of privacy with regard to the record or fruits of his Internet use in light of the FBIS Internet policy. The policy clearly stated that FBIS would "audit, inspect, and/or monitor" employees' use of the Internet, including all file transfers, all websites visited, and all e-mail messages, "as deemed appropriate." This policy placed employees on notice that they could not reasonably expect that their Internet activity would be private. Therefore, regardless of whether Simons subjectively believed that the files he transferred from the Internet were private, such a belief was not objectively reasonable after FBIS notified him that it would be overseeing his Internet use. Accordingly, FBIS' actions in remotely searching and seizing the computer files Simons downloaded from the Internet did not violate the Fourth Amendment.

We next consider whether Harper's warrantless entry into Simons' office to retrieve his hard drive violated the Fourth Amendment. The district court did not separately

[*] Although an SAIC employee conducted the searches, for ease of reference and in light of the fact that SAIC was an FBIS contractor, we refer to the searches as having been carried out by FBIS

address this search; rather, it evaluated all of the warrantless searches together. Although we agree with the district court that Simons lacked a legitimate expectation of privacy in his Internet use, and thus in the hard drive itself, Harper's entry into Simons' office to retrieve the hard drive presents a distinct question.

The burden is on Simons to prove that he had a legitimate expectation of privacy in his office. Here, Simons has shown that he had an office that he did not share. As noted above, the operational realities of Simons' workplace may have diminished his legitimate privacy expectations. However, there is no evidence in the record of any workplace practices, procedures, or regulations that had such an effect. We therefore conclude that, on this record, Simons possessed a legitimate expectation of privacy in his office.

We will reconsider the *O'Connor* and *Simons* cases in the next chapter in connection with the reasonableness of the search procedures in each case.

Protection from Government Activity

The Fourth Amendment protects "people" from unreasonable searches and seizures by *government* personnel or their agents. The amendment does not apply to searches or seizures conducted by private parties.

At what point is a private individual or entity considered to be a government agent? Consider the following case:

United States v. Jarrett

338 F.3D 339 (2003)

U.S. Ct. of Appeals, Fourth Circuit

DIANA GRIBBON MOTZ, Circuit Judge:

In this case, the Government used information provided by an anonymous computer hacker to initiate a search which produced evidence that William Jarrett violated federal statutes prohibiting the manufacture and receipt of child pornography. The district court suppressed this evidence on the ground that the hacker acted as a Government agent, and so violated the Fourth Amendment, when he procured pornographic files from Jarrett's computer. The Government appeals.

I.

The parties do not dispute the underlying facts. Prior to his involvement in the case at hand, the hacker, referred to as Unknownuser, provided information through emails during July 2000 to the FBI and law enforcement agents in Alabama regarding a child pornographer, Dr. Bradley Steiger. In an early email, Unknownuser identified himself only as someone "from Istanbul, Turkey," who could not "afford an overseas phone call and cannot speak English fluently."

Employing the same method that he would later use to hack into Jarrett's computer, Unknownuser obtained access to Steiger's computer via a so-called Trojan Horse program that Unknownuser had attached to a picture he posted to a news group frequented by pornography enthusiasts. When Steiger downloaded the picture to his own computer, he inadvertently downloaded the Trojan Horse program, which then permitted Unknownuser to enter Steiger's computer undetected via the Internet. After searching Steiger's hard drive and finding evidence of child pornography, Unknownuser copied certain files and then emailed the information to the law enforcement officials who used it to identify and apprehend Steiger. A jury convicted Steiger of violating various federal statutes prohibiting the sexual exploitation of minors. He was sentenced to 210 months in prison.

Shortly after Steiger was indicted, in late November 2000, FBI Special Agent James Duffy, who served as Legal Attache for the FBI in Turkey, contacted Unknownuser via email and phone. In addition to informing Unknownuser that he would not be prosecuted for his assistance in apprehending Steiger, Duffy requested a meeting and posed a series of questions to Unknownuser, with the hope that Unknownuser would reveal his identity and perhaps agree to testify at Steiger's trial. Although Unknownuser was quite forthcoming in his responses, he refused to meet with Agent Duffy, stating emphatically that he would never allow himself to be identified. Agent Duffy closed this exchange (in an email dated December 4, 2000) by thanking Unknownuser for his assistance and stating that "If you want to bring other information forward, I am available."

Five months later, Agent Duffy contacted Unknownuser via email, informing him of a postponement in the *Steiger* trial, thanking him again for his assistance, and assuring him that he would not be prosecuted for his actions should he decide to serve as a witness in the *Steiger* trial. Unknownuser responded, repeating that he had no intention of revealing his identity.

The next contact between Unknownuser and law enforcement did not occur until December 3, 2001, almost seven months later, when Unknownuser sent an unsolicited email to his contact at the Montgomery, Alabama Police Department, Kevin Murphy, informing Murphy that he had "found another child molester ... from Richmond, VA" and requesting contact information for someone at the FBI dealing with these sorts of crimes. The alleged child molester referred to in the email was William Jarrett.

After contacting the FBI, Murphy informed Unknownuser that the FBI preferred that Unknownuser send the new information to Murphy's email address. On December 4, 2001, Unknownuser sent thirteen email messages to Murphy, including a ten-part series of emails with some forty-five attached files containing the "evidence" that Unknownuser had collected on Jarrett. Murphy forwarded the information to agents at the FBI, who initiated an investigation.

Based on the information provided by Unknownuser, the Government filed a criminal complaint and application for a search warrant against Jarrett on December 13, 2001. After receiving authorization from the district court, the FBI promptly executed the search warrant and arrested Jarrett.

Several days after Jarrett's arrest, on December 16, 2001, Agent Duffy sent Unknownuser an email informing him of Steiger's sentence and thanking Unknownuser for his assistance in the case. At the time, Duffy was unaware of the Jarrett investigation. The next day, Unknownuser replied, informing Duffy of his efforts to identify Jarrett and inquiring why he had heard nothing since he sent the Jarrett files to Murphy on December 4. Unknownuser sent a similar message the following day (December 18) indicating that he had read about Jarrett's arrest in the newspaper and asking Agent Duffy to have Agent Margaret Faulkner—a special agent based in Alabama who had been involved in the *Steiger* investigation—contact him. On December 19, 2001, Agent Duffy sent an email to Unknownuser thanking him again for his assistance, providing information on the Jarrett investigation and prosecution, and requesting that Unknownuser maintain email contact with Agent Faulkner via her personal email address.

Three weeks later, on January 9, 2002, a grand jury indicted Jarrett on one count of manufacturing child pornography in violation of 18 U.S.C.A. § 2251(a) (West 2000) and seven counts of receiving child pornography in violation of 18 U.S.C.A. § 2252A (a) (2)(A) (West 2000). Jarrett moved to suppress the evidence obtained through the execution of the search warrant on the ground that the Government violated his Fourth Amendment rights in using the information provided by Unknownuser to secure the search warrant. The district court denied the motion. Jarrett then entered a conditional guilty plea to a one-count criminal information charging him with manufacturing child pornography.

Prior to sentencing, however, Jarrett moved to reconsider his earlier motion to suppress on the basis of new evidence—a series of emails exchanged between Unknownuser and FBI agent Faulkner, beginning shortly after Jarrett's arrest and extending for almost two months. The Government did not disclose these emails until after Jarrett had entered his guilty plea.

In the initial email in this series, dated December 19, 2001, Agent Faulkner explicitly thanked Unknownuser for providing the information to law enforcement officials. She then engaged in what can only be characterized as the proverbial "wink and a nod":

> I can not ask you to search out cases such as the ones you have sent to us. That would make you an agent of the Federal Government and make how you obtain your information illegal and we could not use it against the men in the pictures you send. But if you should happen across such pictures as the ones you have sent to us and wish us to look into the matter, please feel free to send them to us. We may have lots of questions and have to email you with the questions. But as long as you are not 'hacking' at our request, we can take the pictures and identify the men and take them to court. We also have no desire to charge you with hacking. You are not a US citizen and are not bound by our laws.

Over the course of the next two months, Agent Faulkner sent at least four additional email messages, which constituted, in the words of the district court, a "'pen-pal' type correspondence" with Unknownuser. In addition to expressing gratitude and admiration for Unknownuser, Faulkner repeatedly sought to reassure Unknownuser that he was not a target of law enforcement for his hacking activities. For example, in an email dated January 29, 2002, she stated that

> the FACT still stands that you are not a citizen of the United States and are not bound by our laws. Our Federal attorneys have expressed NO desire to charge you with any CRIMINAL offense. You have not hacked into any computer at the request of the FBI or other law enforcement agency. You have not acted as an agent for the FBI or other law enforcement agency. Therefore, the information you have collected can be used in our criminal trials.

In his responses to Agent Faulkner, Unknownuser spoke freely of his "hacking adventures" and suggested in no uncertain terms that he would continue to search for child pornographers using the same methods employed to identify Steiger and Jarrett. As found by the district court, Agent Faulkner, despite her knowledge of Unknownuser's illegal hacking, "never instructed Unknownuser that he should cease hacking."

Upon consideration of this series of emails, the district court reversed its earlier decision and suppressed the evidence obtained during the search of Jarrett's residence. At the same time, the court deemed Jarrett's motion to reconsider as a motion to withdraw his guilty plea, which it promptly granted. The court reasoned that the "totality of all the contact between law enforcement and Unknownuser encouraged Unknownuser to continue his behavior and to remain in contact with the FBI." The district court thus concluded that the Government and Unknownuser had "expressed their consent to an agency relationship," thereby rendering any evidence obtained on the basis of Unknownuser's hacking activities inadmissible on the ground that it was procured in violation of Jarrett's Fourth Amendment rights.

II.

The Fourth Amendment protects against unreasonable searches and seizures by Government officials and those private individuals acting as "instruments or agents" of the Government. It does not provide protection against searches by private individuals acting in a private capacity. Thus, "'evidence secured by private searches, even if illegal, need not be excluded from a criminal trial.'" *Ellyson*, 326 F.3d at 527 (quoting *United States v. Kinney*, 953 F.2d 863, 865 (4th Cir. 1992)).

Determining whether the requisite agency relationship exists "necessarily turns on the degree of the Government's participation in the private party's activities, ... a question that can only be resolved 'in light of all the circumstances.'" *Skinner v. Railway Labor Executives' Ass'n*, 489 U.S. 602, 614-15, 103 L. Ed. 2d 639, 109 S. Ct. 1402 (1989) (quoting *Coolidge*, 403 U.S. 487). This is a "fact-intensive inquiry that is guided by common law agency principles." *Ellyson*, 326 F.3d at 527. The defendant bears the burden of proving that an agency relationship exists.

In order to run afoul of the Fourth Amendment, therefore, the Government must do more than passively accept or acquiesce in a private party's search efforts. Rather, there must be some degree of Government participation in the private search. In *Skinner*, for example, the Supreme Court found that private railroads, in performing drug tests on their employees in a manner expressly encouraged and authorized under Government regulations, acted as Government agents sufficient to implicate the Fourth Amendment. As the Court concluded, "specific features of the regulations combine to convince us that the Government did more than adopt a passive position toward the underlying private conduct."

Following the Supreme Court's pronouncements on the matter, the Courts of Appeals have identified two primary factors that should be considered in determining whether a search conducted by a private person constitutes a Government search triggering Fourth Amendment protections. These are: (1) whether the Government knew of and acquiesced in the private search; and (2) whether the private individual intended to assist law enforcement or had some other independent motivation. Although we have never articulated a specific "test," we too have embraced this two-factor approach, which we have compressed into "one highly pertinent consideration."

In this case, the Government concedes the existence of the second factor—that Unknownuser's motivation for conducting the illicit searches stemmed solely from his interest in assisting law enforcement authorities. Thus, the only question before us concerns the first factor—did the Government know of and acquiesce in Unknownuser's search in a manner sufficient to transform Unknownuser into an agent of the Government, and so render the search unconstitutional.

In seeking to give content to this factor, we have required evidence of more than mere knowledge and passive acquiescence by the Government before finding an agency relationship.

Viewed in the aggregate, then, three major lessons emerge from the case law. First, courts should look to the facts and circumstances of each case in determining when a private search is in fact a Government search. Second, before a court will deem a private search a Government search, a defendant must demonstrate that the Government knew of and acquiesced in the private search and that the private individual intended to assist law enforcement authorities. Finally, simple acquiescence by the Government does not suffice to transform a private search into a Government search. Rather, there must be some evidence of Government participation in or affirmative encouragement of the private search before a court will hold it unconstitutional. Passive acceptance by the Government is not enough.

With these principles in mind, we turn to the case at hand.

III.

Although, as the Government conceded at oral argument, the Faulkner email exchange probably does constitute the sort of active Government participation sufficient to create an agency relationship going forward (absent other countervailing facts), the district court erred in relying on this exchange to find that the Government knew of and acquiesced in the Jarrett search. This is so because Unknownuser's email exchange with Faulkner took place after Unknownuser had hacked into Jarrett's computer, after the fruits of Unknownuser's hacking had been made available to the FBI, after Jarrett's home and computer had been searched, and after Jarrett himself had been arrested. Thus, Faulkner's knowledge and acquiescence was entirely post-search. Such after-the-fact conduct cannot serve to transform the prior relationship between Unknownuser and the Government into an agency relationship with respect to the search of Jarrett's computer.

As for the November–December 2000 and May 2001 exchanges between Unknownuser and Agent Duffy, although they did occur prior to the Jarrett search, all of these exchanges were brief and took place seven to twelve months before the Jarrett search. Moreover, these exchanges consisted of nothing more than perfunctory expressions of gratitude for Unknownuser's assistance in the *Steiger* investigation, assurances that Unknownuser would not be prosecuted should he decide to testify as a witness in the *Steiger* trial, and a vague offer of availability to receive more information in the future. Without more, these exchanges do not suffice to create an agency relationship that would embrace the Jarrett search. Were we to allow the Duffy communications to effect such an agency relationship, virtually any Government expression of gratitude for assistance well prior to an investigation would effectively transform any subsequent private search by the party into a Government search. We find no support for such a position in the existing case law, and we decline to extend the protections of the Fourth Amendment to embrace it.

Although the Government operated close to the line in this case, it did not (at least on the evidence before the district court) demonstrate the requisite level of knowledge and acquiescence sufficient to make Unknownuser a Government agent when he hacked into Jarrett's computer. When Unknownuser came forward with the Jarrett information, he had not been in contact with the Government for almost seven months, and nothing indicates that the Government had any intention of re-establishing contact with him. The only communications that could possibly be construed as signaling an agency relationship prior to the search of Jarrett's computer (the Duffy communications from November–December 2000 and May 2001) were simply too remote in time and too tenuous in substance to bring the Jarrett search within the scope of an agency relationship.

IV.

For the reasons set forth within, we reverse the judgment of the district court suppressing the evidence obtained from William Jarrett's residence and remand for further proceedings consistent with this opinion.

With specific reference to computers and other devices that store data in digital form, what happens when evidence of a crime is discovered by a third party (nongovernmental person or entity)? Consider the following case where a computer was delivered to a technician for repair:

Rogers v. State of Texas

---

113 S.W.3D 452 (2003)
COURT OF APPEALS OF TEXAS, 4TH DISTRICT

OPINION BY Marion, Justice.

This appeal raises novel issues regarding privacy rights with regard to computers. Charles L. Rogers ("Rogers") was convicted of possession of child pornography pursuant to a plea bargain agreement and was placed on ten years community supervision. Rogers filed written motions to suppress and a motion to dismiss, which the trial court ruled on prior to trial. On appeal, Rogers contends that the trial court erred in denying his motions. We overrule Rogers's contentions and affirm the trial court's judgment.

BACKGROUND

On August 7, 2000, Rogers brought his computer into Help Me Computers, because he could not get his computer system to function properly. The computer repair technician "booted" up the computer system and determined that the computer system had a virus. This virus was determined to be an ICQ Trojan virus, which infects all executable files. Executable files are needed by the computer to make a program open or close.

A standard virus eradication program was run. As a result of the virus, damage occurred to the system registry which also required repair. The technician discovered that many areas had been corrupted, including the backup in the computer system. Rogers was contacted by the computer repair technician and advised of what had been found (damage and corruption of the backup in the system) and what needed to be done. Rogers was advised that his only option to fix the problem on his computer was to wipe the hard drive and reload it.

At this point, Rogers requested that some files be backed up. According to the technician, Rogers was adamant about having two main things backed up: (1) all of the documents on the system; and (2) all of the photos on the system. Rogers specifically asked that all his photos be backed up on his computer. He told the technician "I have a lot of pictures on my hard drive. I want all my photos backed up." On the same day, Rogers went by the computer repair shop and brought in the programs to reload and a list of items he wanted backed up on his computer system. Fox Rover (a news downloading program) was included on the list of items/programs to be backed up. Additionally, Rogers called the technician later the same day and specifically instructed the technician to back up Image Expert and all jpeg files.

According to the computer repair technician, proper procedure in the computer repair industry requires "verification of data that has been backed up so that when you return the data to the customer, you don't overcharge him for some that was not properly done." In backing up files, the technician was required to double check the information being backed up. In verifying that the programs opened after the repairs, the technician opened the Fox Rover program. This program was pointing to a Lolita site which is site terminology for child pornography on the Internet. As the technician was going through the verification process in backing up the jpeg files in the Agent folder (the directory for the Fox Rover program, which Rogers had specifically requested be backed up on his computer), the technician detected some photographs that he thought might be child pornography. The technician then came across a photo of a child that he was certain was child pornography. The technician later found "well over a hundred picture files that were child pornography in the Agent folder."

During the initial investigation by Detective Lowry, a determination was made that the images on Rogers's computer contained child pornography. At this time, the computer was shut down, seized, and taken directly to the property room of the SAPD. A forensic search of the computer was later undertaken after a search warrant was obtained.

MOTIONS TO SUPPRESS

Rogers filed two motions to suppress. The first motion sought to suppress all physical evidence, including all evidence seized from Rogers's computer hard drive, that was obtained prior to the issuance of a search warrant. The second motion sought to suppress all evidence seized as a result of a search of Rogers's computer because the search warrant relied on in conducting the search was not lawful.

3. Reasonable Expectation of Privacy

The trial court entered written conclusions of law, stating, "In this case, defendant lost [his] expectation of privacy not only when he voluntarily turned over his computer to the repair shop for analysis, but more specifically when he made the specific request (which is acknowledged by the defendant in his own statement) that all the jpeg files (photos) be backed up. This action seems to indicate the defendant did not seek to preserve the pictures as private. Secondly, it can be said that upon delivering the computer to the repair shop for analysis/repair, society would not recognize as reasonable the expectation of privacy when the defendant voluntarily conveyed the computer to a third party for unknown malfunction which required accessing the hard drive and in turn, requiring further work and access which was ultimately given by the defendant, thus extinguishing any reasonable expectation of privacy in the jpeg files (photos) found within the defendant's computer." Rogers contends that the trial court erred in concluding that he had lost his reasonable expectation of privacy in his computer and in his jpeg files. Rogers asserts that the owner of the computer repair shop testified that computer owners who bring their computers into his shop have a right to privacy. Rogers also emphasizes that he did not sign any written authorization permitting the computer repair technician to view his files during the repair or back up process.

The purpose of both the Fourth Amendment and Article I, section 9 of the Texas Constitution is to safeguard an individual's legitimate expectation of privacy from unreasonable governmental intrusions. An accused has standing to challenge the admission of evidence obtained by an intrusion by the government or a private individual only if he had a legitimate expectation of privacy in the place invaded, and the accused has the burden of proving facts to establish this expectation. To carry this burden, the accused must normally prove: (a) that by his conduct, he exhibited an actual subjective expectation of privacy, i.e., a genuine intention to preserve something as private; and (b) that circumstances existed under which society was prepared to recognize his subjective expectation as objectively reasonable. Id.

In *United States v. Barth*, the defendant called a computer technician after experiencing problems with his office computer. 26 F. Supp. 2d 929, 932 (W.D. Tex. 1998). As the computer technician began opening individual files in search of potential viruses, he came across a file containing child pornography. The court concluded that protection of closed computer files and hard drives is similar to the protection afforded a person's closed containers and closed personal effects. The court then reasoned, "outside of automobile searches, a warrant is usually required to search the contents of a closed container, because the owner's expectation of privacy relates to the contents of that container rather than to the container itself." The court held that the defendant did not lose his reasonable expectation of privacy in his closed individual computer files when he gave the hard drive to a third party to repair because he gave the hard drive to the technician "for the limited purpose of repairing a problem unrelated to specific files and also expected that he would have the unit back the following morning to continue his business."

In its conclusions of law in this case, the trial court expressly distinguished *Barth*, because Rogers specifically requested that his jpeg files be backed up which were the specific files containing the child pornography. We agree with the trial court that our case is factually distinguishable from *Barth* because Rogers expressly directed the computer technician to back up the jpeg files.

The evidence established that Rogers had a subjective expectation of privacy in his jpeg files; therefore, the question is whether society is prepared to recognize that expectation as objectively reasonable. The Texas Court of Criminal Appeals has held that the following factors are relevant to the court's determination of whether the accused's subjective expectation was one that society was prepared to recognize as objectively reasonable: (1) whether the accused had a property or possessory interest in the place invaded; (2) whether he was legitimately in the place invaded; (3) whether he had complete dominion or control and the right to exclude others; (4) whether, before the intrusion, he took normal precautions customarily taken by those seeking privacy; (5) whether he put the place to some private use; and (6) whether his claim of privacy is consistent with historical notions of privacy. These factors are more applicable when discussing the expectation of privacy in a place than in discussing the expectation of privacy in a computer hard drive or even a closed container. However, applying the more relevant factors would weigh against a finding of objective reasonableness.

For example, although Rogers had an interest in the computer hard drive, he did not have complete dominion or control because he had voluntarily relinquished control to the computer repair store. In addition, Rogers did not take normal precautions to protect his privacy because he expressly directed the computer repair technician to back up the jpeg files. Finally, his claim of privacy is not consistent with historical notions of privacy. The courts have generally held that a person has no legitimate expectation of privacy in information that is voluntarily turned over to third parties. In requesting that the computer repair technician back up the jpeg files, Rogers voluntarily turned those files over to the technician for backing up, and standard operating procedure required the files to be viewed during that process. Therefore, after Rogers directed the computer technician to back up his jpeg files, he no longer had a legitimate expectation of privacy in those files, and the trial court did not err in denying Rogers's motions to suppress.

The Mere Evidence Rule

What kind of evidence can be the object of a search or seizure?

Historically, the search for, or seizure of, contraband, the instrumentalities used to commit a crime (for example, the computer used to commit an identity theft), and the fruits of a crime (for example, the stolen identity information) was deemed reasonable under the Fourth Amendment. In *Warden v. Hayden* (387 U.S. 294 (1967)), the court considered whether officers could search for "mere evidence," i.e., items that were relevant to an investigation but not contraband, fruits, or instrumentalities. The court approved the search for, or seizure of, mere evidence, provided that the evidence had some nexus to the crime under investigation.

The mere evidence rule is important in relation to cybercrime investigations. Computers are frequently used as the repository of evidence of a crime. A spreadsheet utilized by a drug dealer for the maintenance of transaction records is mere evidence of drug trafficking.

Searches with and without a Warrant

Although the procedures for conducting searches are considered in the next chapter, it is important to provide some background on constitutional principles at this point.

The language of the Fourth Amendment provides that a search or seizure is reasonable when conducted pursuant to a warrant issued "upon probable cause, supported by Oath or affirmation, and particularly describing the place to be searched, and the persons or things to be seized." The U.S. Supreme Court, in its interpretation of the Fourth Amendment, has concluded that searches conducted without a warrant may also be reasonable in certain defined circumstances. It is frequently stated that a search or seizure conducted pursuant to a warrant is presumptively reasonable and that a search or seizure conducted *without* a warrant is presumptively unreasonable, and therefore unlawful, unless an exception applies. Each of those exceptions to the warrant requirement is briefly considered below.

Consent

Government personnel may search computers and other digital devices or evidence without a warrant if authorized to do so by a person having the authority to consent to such a search. The consent must be given knowingly and voluntarily. It may be given orally or in writing, or even though no consent is expressed verbally, it may be implied from the circumstances. For example, consent might be implied from silence or acquiescence during a search under circumstances calling for the owner to express a refusal to consent.

Persons other than the owner can consent to a search or seizure. A third party (meaning a person other than the owner and law enforcement) who is of suitable age and discretion *and* who has joint access to or control of the place or thing that law enforcement seeks to search may give consent. Thus, a spouse, parent, or child who shares use of the computer with its owner may consent to a search of that computer. The same applies to a co-occupant of premises or even to an overnight guest, provided that the individual has been provided access to the computer or other digital device. What happens when the owner and third party are both present, and the third party grants consent but the owner refuses to consent? Does the law enforcement officer have consent for a warrantless search? The U.S. Supreme Court recently rejected the government's claim that it had consent to search under those circumstances (see *Georgia v. Randolph*, 547 U.S. 103 (2006)).

Can an employer, as the third party, consent? Further, what if the employer is the government? In private sector situations the employer usually owns the computer or other digital media or at least has joint access or control of the equipment or workplace and thus would have the authority to consent to a search or seizure of the computer used by the employee (see, for example, *United States v. Gargiso*, 456 F.2d 584 (2nd Cir. 1972)). Although courts are not unanimous on the point, the better position seems to be that the employer has the authority to consent even though the employee has exclusive use of the computer and the employer's permission to use it for personal as well as business purposes.

The situation becomes muddier when the government is the employer. The general rule is that the government employer cannot consent to a search by a law enforcement officer of the employee's workspace. In effect, the courts conclude that because the employer and law enforcement represent the government, there is no third party to give consent (see *United States v. Blok*, 188 F.2d 1019 (D.C. Cir. 1951)).

When sufficient consent is given, the government is not required to establish probable cause for the search.

Plain View

Law enforcement personnel may, without a warrant, seize evidence found in plain view. Two conditions must exist: (1) the law enforcement personnel must be in a place where they have a legal right to be and engaging in authorized conduct, i.e., acting lawfully; and (2) the criminal nature of the evidence must be "readily apparent."

There are an unlimited variety of scenarios that could give rise to a plain view search of digital devices. In the following case, law enforcement personnel obtained consent for the search of the defendant's residence. While lawfully on the defendant's premises and conducting a search pursuant to that consent, the officers seized a computer and removed it to the police computer lab.

United States v. Carey

172 F.3D 1268 (1999)

U.S. COURT OF APPEALS, TENTH CIRCUIT

PORFILIO, Circuit Judge.

Patrick J. Carey was charged with one count of possessing a computer hard drive that contained three or more images of child pornography produced with materials shipped in interstate commerce. See 18 U.S.C. § 2252A(a)(5)(B) (1996). Following a conditional plea of guilty, he appeals an order of the district court denying his motion to suppress the material seized from his computer on grounds it was taken as the result of a general, warrantless search. We conclude the motion to suppress should have been granted and reverse.

Mr. Carey had been under investigation for some time for possible sale and possession of cocaine. Controlled buys had been made from him at his residence, and six weeks after the last purchase, police obtained a warrant to arrest him. During the course of the arrest, officers observed in plain view a "bong," a device for smoking marijuana, and what appeared to be marijuana in defendant's apartment.

Alerted by these items, a police officer asked Mr. Carey to consent to a search of his apartment. The officer said he would get a search warrant if Mr. Carey refused permission. After considerable discussion with the officer, Mr. Carey verbally consented to the search and later signed a formal written consent at the police station. Because he was concerned that officers would "trash" his apartment during the search, Mr. Carey gave them instructions on how to find drug related items.

The written consent to search authorized Sergeant William Reece "to have conducted a complete search of the premises and property located at 3225 Canterbury # 10, Manhattan, KS 66503." It further provided, "I do freely and voluntarily consent and agree that any property under my control … may be removed by the officers … if said property shall be essential in the proof of the commission of any crime in violation of the Laws of the United States…." Armed with this consent, the officers returned to the apartment that night and discovered quantities of cocaine, marijuana, and hallucinogenic mushrooms. They also discovered and took two computers, which they believed would either be subject to forfeiture or evidence of drug dealing.

The computers were taken to the police station and a warrant was obtained by the officers allowing them to search the files on the computers for "names, telephone numbers, ledger receipts, addresses, and other documentary evidence pertaining to the sale and distribution of controlled substances." Detective Lewis and a computer technician searched the contents of the computers, first viewing the directories of both computers' hard drives. They then downloaded onto floppy disks and printed the directories. Included in the directories were numerous files with sexually suggestive titles and the label "JPG."[*2] Lewis then inserted the disks into another computer and began searching the files copied from Mr. Carey's computers. His method was to enter key words

---

[*] Detective Lewis later testified at the time he discovered the first JPG or image file, he did not know what it was nor had he ever experienced an occasion in which the label "JPG" was used by drug dealers to disguise text files. He stated, however, image files could contain evidence pertinent to a drug investigation such as pictures of "a hydroponic growth system and how it's set up to operate."

such as, "money, accounts, people, so forth" into the computer's explorer to find "text-based" files containing those words. This search produced no files "related to drugs."

Undaunted, Detective Lewis continued to explore the directories and encountered some files he "was not familiar with." Unable to view these files on the computer he was using, he downloaded them to a disk which he placed into another computer. He then was "immediately" able to view what he later described as a "JPG file." Upon opening this file, he discovered it contained child pornography.

Detective Lewis downloaded approximately two hundred forty-four JPG or image files. These files were transferred to nineteen disks, only portions of which were viewed to determine that they contained child pornography. Although none of the disks was viewed in its entirety, Detective Lewis looked at "about five to seven" files on each disk. Then, after viewing the contents of the nineteen disks in that fashion, he returned to the computers to pursue his original task of looking for evidence of drug transactions.

Mr. Carey moved to suppress the computer files containing child pornography. During the hearing on the motion, Detective Lewis stated although the discovery of the JPG files was completely inadvertent, when he saw the first picture containing child pornography, he developed probable cause to believe the same kind of material was present on the other image files. When asked why, therefore, he did not obtain a warrant to search the remaining image files for child pornography, he stated, "that question did arise, and my captain took care of that through the county attorney's office." No warrant was obtained, but the officer nonetheless continued his search because he believed he "had to search these files as well as any other files contained [in the computer]."

Upon further questioning by the government, Detective Lewis retrenched and stated until he opened each file, he really did not know its contents. Thus, he said, he did not believe he was restricted by the search warrant from opening each JPG file. Yet, after viewing a copy of the hard disk directory, the detective admitted there was a "phalanx" of JPG files listed on the directory of the hard drive.[*3] He downloaded and viewed these files knowing each of them contained pictures. He claimed, however, "I wasn't conducting a search for child pornography, that happened to be what these turned out to be."

At the close of the hearing, the district court ruled from the bench. Without any findings, the court denied the motion, saying: "at this point, the Court feels that the … Defendant's Motion to Suppress … would be—should be denied. And that will be the order of the Court, realizing that they are close questions." No subsequent written order containing findings of fact or conclusions of law was filed.

Mr. Carey argues the search of the computers transformed the warrant into a "general warrant" and resulted in a general and illegal search of the computers and their files. The Fourth Amendment requires that a search warrant describe the things to be seized with sufficient particularity to prevent a general exploratory rummaging in a person's belongings. As we have instructed:

> The essential inquiry when faced with challenges under the Fourth Amendment is whether the search or seizure was reasonable—reasonableness is analyzed in light of what was reasonable

---

[*] We note the JPG files shown on Detective Lewis' directory printout featured sexually suggestive or obscene names, many including the word "teen" or "young." The detective testified drug dealers often obscure or disguise evidence of their drug activity.

at the time of the Fourth Amendment's adoption…. It is axiomatic that the 4th Amendment was adopted as a directed response to the evils of the general warrants in England and the writs of assistance in the Colonies.

Mr. Carey argues that examined against history and case law, the search constituted general rummaging in "flagrant disregard" for the terms of the warrant and in violation of the Fourth Amendment. Despite the specificity of the search warrant, files not pertaining to the sale or distribution of controlled substances were opened and searched, and according to Mr. Carey, these files should have been suppressed.

The government responds that the plain view doctrine authorized the police search. A police officer may properly seize evidence of a crime without a warrant if:

(1) the officer was lawfully in a position from which to view the object seized in plain view; (2) the object's incriminating character was immediately apparent—i.e., the officer had probable cause to believe the object was contraband or evidence of a crime; and (3) the officer had a lawful right of access to the object itself.

According to the government, "a computer search such as the one undertaken in this case is tantamount to looking for documents in a file cabinet, pursuant to a valid search warrant, and instead finding child pornography." Just as if officers has [sic] seized pornographic photographs from a file cabinet, seizure of the pornographic computer images was permissible because officers had a valid warrant, the pornographic images were in plain view, and the incriminating nature was readily apparent as the photographs depicted children under the age of twelve engaged in sexual acts. The warrant authorized the officer to search any file because "any file might well have contained information relating to drug crimes and the fact that some files might have appeared to have been graphics files would not necessarily preclude them from containing such information." Further, the government states the defendant's consent to search of the apartment overrides all of these questions because it extended to the search of every file on both computers.

The Supreme Court has instructed, "the plain view doctrine may not be used to extend a general exploratory search from one object to another until something incriminating at last emerges." The warrant obtained for the specific purpose of searching defendant's computers permitted only the search of the computer files for "names, telephone numbers, ledgers, receipts, addresses, and other documentary evidence pertaining to the sale and distribution of controlled substances." The scope of the search was thus circumscribed to evidence pertaining to drug trafficking. The government's argument the files were in plain view is unavailing because it is the contents of the files and not the files themselves which were seized. Detective Lewis could not at first distinguish between the text files and the JPG files upon which he did an unsuccessful word search. Indeed, he had to open the first JPG file and examine its contents to determine what the file contained. Thus, until he opened the first JPG file, he stated he did not suspect he would find child pornography. At best, he says he suspected the files might contain pictures of some activity relating to drug dealing.

In his own words, however, his suspicions changed immediately upon opening the first JPG file. After viewing the contents of the first file, he then had "probable cause" to believe the remaining JPG files contained similar erotic material. Thus, because of the officer's own admission, it is plainly evident each time he opened a subsequent JPG file, he expected to find child pornography and not material related to drugs. Armed with this knowledge, he still continued to open every JPG file to confirm his expectations. Under these circumstances, we cannot say the contents of each of those files were inadvertently discovered. Moreover, Detective Lewis made clear as he opened each of the JPG files he was not looking for evidence of drug trafficking. He had temporarily abandoned that search to look for more child pornography, and only "went back" to searching for drug-related documents after conducting a five hour search of the child pornography files.

We infer from his testimony Detective Lewis knew he was expanding the scope of his search when he sought to open the JPG files. Moreover, at that point, he was in the same position as the officers had been when they first wanted to search the contents of the computers for drug related evidence. They were aware they had to obtain a search warrant and did so. These circumstances suggest Detective Lewis knew clearly he was acting without judicial authority when he abandoned his search for evidence of drug dealing.

Although the question of what constitutes "plain view" in the context of computer files is intriguing and appears to be an issue of first impression for this court, and many others, we do not need to reach it here. Judging this case only by its own facts, we conclude the items seized were not authorized by the warrant. Further, they were in closed files and thus not in plain view.

We do note the recent decision in *United States v. Turner*, 169 F.3d 84 (1st Cir. 1999) affirming the district court's suppression of several images of child pornography found on the defendant's computer. In *Turner*, the defendant's neighbor was the victim of a nighttime assault in her apartment, and police officers obtained the defendant's consent to search his apartment for signs of the intruder and for evidence of the assault itself. While searching the apartment, an officer noticed the defendant's computer screen suddenly illuminate with a photograph of a nude woman resembling the assault victim. He then sat at the computer and itemized the files most recently accessed. Several of the files had the "suffix '.jpg,' denoting a file containing a photograph." The officer opened these files and found photographs of nude blonde women in bondage. After calling the district attorney's office for guidance, the officer copied these adult pornography files onto a floppy disk and then searched the computer hard drive for other incriminating files. He opened a folder labeled "G-Images" and "noted several files with names such as 'young' and 'young with breasts.'" After opening one of these files and observing child pornography, the officer shut down and seized the computer, and the defendant was charged in a single count of possessing child pornography. The government contended the "consent was so broad—authorizing search of all [the defendant's] 'personal property' that it necessarily encompassed a comprehensive search of his computer files." But the First Circuit affirmed the suppression of the computer files on grounds "the consent did not authorize the search of the computer" because "an objectively reasonable person assessing in context the exchange between [the defendant] and these detectives would have understood that the police intended to search only in places where an intruder hastily might have disposed of any physical evidence of the … assault…." The court also held:

We cannot accept the government's contention that the sexually suggestive image which suddenly came into "plain view" on the computer screen rendered [the defendant]'s computer files "fair game" under a consensual search simply because the [neighbor's] assault had a sexual component…. The critical consideration in this regard is that the detectives never announced, before [the defendant] gave his consent, that they were investigating a sexual assault or attempted rape.

As in *Turner*, the government argues here the consent Mr. Carey gave to the search of his apartment carried over to the contents of his computer files. We disagree. The arresting officer sought permission to search only the "premises and property located at 3225 Canterbury # 10." Thus, the scope of the consensual search was confined to the apartment itself. The seizure of the computer was permitted by Mr. Carey's consent "that any property under my control … may be removed by the officers … if said property shall be essential in the proof of the commission of any crime…." This agreement, by its own terms, did not permit the officer to open the files contained in the computer, a fact he obviously recognized because he obtained a proper warrant to search for drug related evidence before he began opening files.

The warrant constrained the officer to search for items it listed. In our judgment, the case turns upon the fact that each of the files containing pornographic material was labeled "JPG" and most featured a sexually suggestive title. Certainly after opening the first file and seeing an image of child pornography, the searching officer was aware—in advance of opening the remaining files—what the label meant. When he opened the subsequent files, he knew he was not going to find items related to drug activity as specified in the warrant, just like the officer in *Turner* knew he was not going to find evidence of an assault as authorized by the consent.

At oral argument the government suggested this situation is similar to an officer having a warrant to search a file cabinet containing many drawers. Although each drawer is labeled, he had to open a drawer to find out whether the label was misleading and the drawer contained the objects of the search. While the scenario is likely, it is not representative of the facts of this case. This is not a case in which ambiguously labeled files were contained in the hard drive directory. It is not a case in which the officers had to open each file drawer before discovering its contents. Even if we employ the file cabinet theory, the testimony of Detective Lewis makes the analogy inapposite because he stated he knew, or at least had probable cause to know, each drawer was properly labeled and its contents were clearly described in the label.

Further, because this case involves images stored in a computer, the file cabinet analogy may be inadequate. "Since electronic storage is likely to contain a greater quantity and variety of information than any previous storage method, computers make tempting targets in searches for incriminating information." Raphael Winick, Searches and Seizures of Computers and Computer Data, 8 *Harv. J. L. & Tech.* 75, 104 (1994). Relying on analogies to closed containers or file cabinets may lead courts to "oversimplify a complex area of Fourth Amendment doctrines and ignore the realities of massive modern computer storage." Alternatively, courts can acknowledge computers often contain "intermingled documents." Under this approach, law enforcement must engage in the intermediate step of sorting various types of documents and then only search the ones specified in a warrant. Where officers come across relevant documents so intermingled with irrelevant documents that they cannot feasibly be sorted at the site, the officers may seal or hold the documents pending approval by a magistrate of the conditions and limitations on a further search through the documents. The magistrate should then require officers to specify in a warrant which type of files are sought. *United States v. Tamura*, 694 F.2d 591, 595-96 (9th Cir. 1982), held seizure of all of a corporation's documents during a relevant time period, rather than limiting seizure to categories of documents described in a search warrant, was unreasonable despite the government's contention irrelevant documents were intermingled with described documents. Although this case did not arise in the context of a computer search, we find the concept of "intermingled documents" helpful here.

Because in Mr. Carey's case, officers had removed the computers from his control, there was no "exigent circumstance or practical reason to permit officers to rummage through all of the stored data regardless of its relevance or its relation to the information specified in the warrant." With the computers and data in their custody, law enforcement officers can generally employ several methods to avoid searching files of the type not identified in the warrant: observing files types and titles listed on the directory, doing a key word search for relevant terms, or reading portions of each file stored in the memory. In this case, Detective Lewis and the computer technician did list files on the directory and also performed a key word search, but they did not use the information gained to limit their search to items specified in the warrant, nor did they obtain a new warrant authorizing a search for child pornography.

We must conclude Detective Lewis exceeded the scope of the warrant in this case. His seizure of the evidence upon which the charge of conviction was based was a consequence of an unconstitutional general search, and the district court erred by refusing to suppress it. Having reached that conclusion, however, we are quick to note these results are predicated only upon the particular facts of this case, and a search of computer files based on different facts might produce a different result.*[10]

REVERSED and REMANDED for further proceedings in accordance with this opinion.

BALDOCK, J., concurring.

I join in the court's opinion, but write separately to emphasize that the questions presented in this case are extremely close calls and, in my opinion, are totally fact driven.

First, absent Detective Lewis' testimony, I would not suppress the evidence. "The plain view doctrine may not be used to extend a general exploratory search from one object to another until something incriminating at last emerges." In light of Detective Lewis' testimony, just this sort of impermissible general rummaging occurred in this case. The detective's testimony makes clear that from the time he found the first image of child pornography, he switched from his authorized search for drug-related evidence to another subject—child pornography. At this point, the detective should have ceased his search and obtained a warrant to search the computer files for evidence of child pornography. As Detective Lewis testified, it was clear to him that after he discovered

---

˙ *United States v. Hall*, 142 F.3d 988, 993–94 (7th Cir. 1998) (Viewing images of child pornography on the defendant's computer by a repair company employee was a private search. Although a police officer then improperly copied the files to a floppy disk without a warrant, a subsequent search of the computer files by the police officer did not require suppression because the employee's statements provided an independent basis for the warrant.).

the first image, he had probable cause to believe the computer contained additional images of child pornography, and no exigent circumstances existed because the computer had been removed to the police station.

In contrast, if the record showed that Detective Lewis had merely continued his search for drug-related evidence and, in doing so, continued to come across evidence of child pornography, I think a different result would be required. That is not what happened here, however.

Second, while agreeing with the majority that Defendant's consent to the search of his apartment did not carry over to his computer hard drive, I write separately to explain why I think the scope of Defendant's consent is limited to evidence of drug-related activity. The scope of a consensual search is "generally defined by its expressed object."

The waiver signed by Defendant granted the officers permission to search the "premises and property located at 3255 Canterbury # 10" and authorized the officers to remove any property "if said property shall be essential in the proof of the commission of any crime...." The officer testified that after he arrested Defendant, he told him that "based on what I had just observed in his apartment that I was going to apply for a search warrant." The officer had just found, in plain view, a bong typically used for smoking marijuana and a small quantity of what appeared to be marijuana. The officer then explained to Defendant that he could consent to a search instead of the officer obtaining a warrant. Defendant told the officer he was unsure. En route to the police station, Defendant asked several questions about the search. Upon arrival at the station, Defendant indicated that he wished to consent. He also told the officer where he would find additional drugs, a scale, a firearm and cash. In addition, Defendant told him where he would find a pornographic videotape. The officer responded that he "couldn't care less about his pornographic videotapes" and "that wasn't of concern to me."

In light of the officer's conversations with Defendant, a reasonable person would conclude that the statements by the officer limited the scope of the request to drugs and drug-related items in the apartment.

In *Carey*, Detective Lewis was in a place where he was lawfully entitled to be (the police computer lab) and his viewing of the first file he believed to be child pornography was inadvertent: he was looking for evidence of drug transactions and did not know what a JPEG file was. Thus, the first file was in plain view. However, Detective Lewis then continued a search for additional JPEG files, believing that they would contain further depictions of child pornography. At that point, Detective Lewis's search was no longer inadvertent and he had exceeded the scope of the initial consent. Thus, as the court found, Detective Lewis should have applied for a warrant to conduct a further search for child pornography.

Exigent Circumstances

When law enforcement officers are confronted with exigent circumstances and probable cause exists to believe that relevant evidence exists, they may search or seize without a warrant. Exigent circumstances exist if a reasonable person would believe that an immediate search or seizure is necessary to prevent any of the following: (1) physical harm to the officers or other persons, (2) the destruction of relevant evidence, (3) the escape of the suspect, including the hot pursuit of a suspect, or (4) other conduct that might improperly frustrate legitimate law enforcement efforts. Whether or not such circumstances exist vary with the factual circumstances of each case.

In the following case, the issue is whether the probable existence of evidence on the computer and storage capacity of the computer constituted exigent circumstances justifying the seizure of a personal computer found in a hotel room during a search pursuant to a warrant. The court resolved the issue as follows:

United States v. Walser

---

275 F.3D 981 (2001)

U.S. Court of Appeals, Tenth Circuit

OPINION: SEYMOUR, Circuit Judge.

Russell Lane Walser appeals the district court's denial of his motion to suppress evidence garnered in two searches of his personal computer.

On June 1, 2000, the manager of the Radisson Hotel in Casper, Wyoming, went to Room 617 to check on a smoke alarm sounding there. The room was unoccupied. In the course of shutting off the alarm, the manager noticed two small plastic bags containing what he believed to be cocaine and marijuana. He contacted the local police, who arrived on the scene and secured the room without entering it. The police ascertained that Mr. Walser, who was accompanied by Debbie Wilcox, had rented the room earlier that day. The police found Mr. Walser and Ms. Wilcox in the hotel parking lot, sitting in Mr. Walser's car. They spoke with Mr. Walser who, during that conversation, told them he had brought a computer with him and set it up in the room.

Based on the information gleaned from the hotel manager, the police investigation, and the conversation with Mr. Walser, police sought and obtained a search warrant covering Room 617 and Mr. Walser's car. The warrant granted permission to search for:

> Controlled substances, evidence of the possession of controlled substances, which may include, but not be limited to, cash or proceeds from the sales of controlled substances, items, substances, and other paraphernalia designed or used in the weighing, cutting, and packaging of controlled substances, firearms, records, and/or receipts, written or electronically stored, income tax records, checking and savings records, records that show or tend to show ownership or control of the premises and other property used to facilitate the distribution and delivery [of] controlled substances.

Armed with the warrant, Special Agent Steve McFarland of the Wyoming Division of Criminal Investigation (DCI) and local police entered Mr. Walser's room to conduct the search. While there they found, among other things, plastic bags containing what was believed to be marijuana, drug paraphernalia (including a glass tube, a butane torch, a roach clip, and syringes), a digital scale, a computer, and a digital camera attached to the computer. The computer was on when the police first entered the room and the computer's "wallpaper" showed an image of Ms. Wilcox that appeared to have been taken in Room 617.

Special Agent McFarland sat down at the computer and did a cursory search of the hard drive. Based on his experience and a 40-hour "Cybercop" course he had completed, he had reason to believe there might be ledgers of drug transactions or images of drug use (taken with the digital camera attached to the computer) saved on the computer's hard drive. He began his search in the "My Documents" folder and opened approximately ten JPEG files. These files contained images of adult pornography. Agent McFarland shut down the computer and seized it in anticipation of conducting a more thorough search at the DCI office.

Five days later, on June 6, Agent McFarland resumed his search of the computer at the Casper DCI office. In conducting the search, Agent McFarland followed a specific methodology. He first checked the "Recycle Bin" and found no relevant files. He next used the "Windows Explorer" search mechanism to search the computer's hard drive. Through this technique, he opened the "Program Files" folder. Agent McFarland testified that based on his training and personal experience, most of the files containing evidence of drug transactions (i.e. address books, spreadsheets, databases) would be found there. He looked for and located a sub-folder containing Microsoft Works, a spreadsheet program. That folder contained approximately ninety files and four sub-folders. Agent McFarland opened the second file from the top, named "bstfit.avi." When he did so, the "Compupic" program started-up and a "thumbnail" image of the file appeared on the left side of the Explorer window. Looking at the thumbnail, Agent McFarland saw images of girls engaged in sexual acts with men. Believing this to be child pornography, he enlarged the thumbnail and confirmed his belief.

Agent McFarland immediately ceased his search of the computer hard drive and contacted another agent in the DCI who had greater experience in computer forensics and child pornography. That agent told Agent McFarland to shut down the computer and submit an affidavit for a new search warrant specifically authorizing a search for evidence of possession of child pornography. Agent McFarland did so and obtained the warrant under which he conducted the search that produced the evidence in the present case.

Following a hearing at which the district court denied Mr. Walser's motion to suppress the evidence discovered in the searches of his computer, Mr. Walser pled guilty to one count of possession of child pornography and the court sentenced him to twenty-seven months imprisonment and three years supervised release.

Mr. Walser first maintains that DCI Special Agent McFarland lacked probable cause to seize the computer from the hotel room at the time of the original search.

This court and other circuits have approved the seizure and storage of property when the facts of the case supported a finding that exigent circumstances existed. In *United States v. Hargus*, 128 F.3d 1358, 1363 (10th Cir. 1997), we held that the seizure of an entire file cabinet was acceptable when such seizure was motivated by the impracticability of on-site sorting, among other factors. The other concern relative to conducting such computer searches lies in the fact that computer evidence is vulnerable to tampering or destruction.

In the case before us, the size of the computer's hard drive—over 22 Gigabytes—combined with the importance that the search take place in a controlled laboratory setting, where proper forensic expertise and equipment would be available, provided sufficient exigency to support the district court's decision. We therefore hold that the district court's failure to grant Mr. Walser's motion to suppress on grounds that the seizure of his computer lacked probable cause does not rise to the level of plain error.

Mr. Walser also argues that in opening an AVI file while conducting a search for records of drug transactions, Agent McFarland exceeded the scope of the warrant. For that reason, Mr. Walser contends the district court erred when it denied his motion to suppress evidence of the June 6 search of his computer.

In *United States v. Carey*, 172 F.3d 1268, 1275 n.7 (10th Cir. 1999), this court recognized the particular Fourth Amendment issues surrounding the search and seizure of computer equipment. The advent of the electronic age and, as we see in this case, the development of desktop computers that are able to hold the equivalent of a library's worth of information, go beyond the established categories of constitutional doctrine. Analogies to other physical objects, such as dressers or file cabinets, do not often inform the situations we now face as judges when applying search and seizure law. This does not, of course, mean that the Fourth Amendment does not apply to computers and cyberspace. Rather, we must acknowledge the key differences and proceed accordingly.

The underlying premise in *Carey* is that officers conducting searches (and the magistrates issuing warrants for those searches) cannot simply conduct a sweeping, comprehensive search of a computer's hard drive. Because computers can hold so much information touching on many different areas of a person's life, there is a greater potential for the "intermingling" of documents and a consequent invasion of privacy when police execute a search for evidence on a computer. Thus, when officers come across relevant computer files intermingled with irrelevant computer files, they "may seal or hold" the computer pending "approval by a magistrate of the conditions and limitations on a further search" of the computer. *Carey*, 172 F.3d at 1275. Officers must be clear as to what it is they are seeking on the computer and conduct the search in a way that avoids searching files of types not identified in the warrant.

Agent McFarland met the requirements of *Carey* in this case. Armed with a search warrant authorizing a search for electronic records of drug trafficking, Agent McFarland searched Mr. Walser's computer. Using a clear search methodology, Agent McFarland searched for relevant records in places where such records might logically be found. He began with the "My Documents" file, proceeded to the "Recycle Bin," and then, using the Windows Explorer search program, opened the "Program Files" folder. Rather than searching each sub-folder in the "Program Files" folder, Agent McFarland selectively proceeded to the "Microsoft Works" sub-folder on the premise that because Works is a spreadsheet program, that folder would be most likely to contain records relating to the business of drug trafficking.

It was while searching the contents of the Works folder that Agent McFarland came across the file labeled "bstfit.avi" and opened it to see what it was. When he viewed the contents in thumbnail format he believed the file consisted of child pornography images. He enlarged the images to confirm that fact and, once he had, immediately suspended his search and went to a magistrate for a new warrant.

Mr. Walser contends Agent McFarland exceeded the scope of the search warrant when the Agent opened the AVI file. Because an AVI file is an audiovisual or video file, he argues, it could not possibly have contained the type of evidence the Agent was authorized to search for, namely, records of drug transactions or still images of drug use. The government counters that because computer files can be re-labeled to disguise their contents, an agent is free to open any file in order to determine its contents and that therefore, opening the AVI file did not exceed the scope of the warrant.

We leave the government's argument regarding "disguised" files for another day. We agree with the district court's determination that opening the "bstfit.avi" file did not constitute an impermissible broadening of the warrant. In *Carey*, the officer was engaged in a similar search for electronic records of drug dealing. As in this case, the officer in *Carey* inadvertently discovered the first image of child pornography while searching for documents relating to drug activity. In *Carey*, however, after opening the first file, the officer's conduct was the opposite of that which occurred in the present case. Specifically, he proceeded to rummage through the hard drive for more images of child pornography despite the fact that he did not possess a warrant to conduct such a search. Had Agent McFarland conducted a more extensive search than he did here by rummaging in folders and files beyond those he searched, he might well have exceeded the bounds of the warrant and the requirements of *Carey*. The fact of the matter, however, is that no such wholesale searching occurred here. Agent McFarland showed restraint by returning to the magistrate for a new warrant before commencing a new search for evidence of child pornography.

Based on the facts found by the district court, we are persuaded the search was reasonable and within the parameters of the search warrant. Consequently, the denial of the motion to suppress does not constitute clear error.

If you are thinking at this point that the analysis in the *Walser* case is inconsistent with the analysis in *Carey*, you are correct. The existence of exigent circumstances in *Walser* and the absence of that exception in *Carey* explains away most, if not all, of the apparent inconsistency. In each case, the court concluded that the officer's viewing of the first image file (in *Walser*, the thumbnail file; in *Carey*, the JPEG file) was inadvertent and consistent with a plain view search. What occurred thereafter distinguishes the result in each case. In *Walser*, Agent McFarland stopped the search and applied for a warrant. In *Carey*, however, Detective Lewis continued his search for child pornography without obtaining a second warrant and thereby changed the scope of the warrant. Because the subsequent image files were viewed intentionally and not inadvertently, the search could not be justified as a plain view search. Further, because the computer was in the laboratory, no exigent circumstances or other exception to the warrant requirement justified further search.

Incident to a Lawful Arrest

When officers make a lawful arrest, they may search the person arrested as well as the area within the immediate reach or control of the arrestee (*Chimel v. California*, 395 U.S. 752 (1969)). Persons frequently carry laptops, PDAs, pagers, MP3 devices, cell phones, and smartphones on their person. Can officers search the contents of those devices incidental to a lawful arrest? Courts have consistently permitted the search of electronic pagers, frequently justifying seizure of the pager under the incidental-to-lawful-arrest exception and justifying a search of the pager under the exigent circumstances exception. The search of a cell phone has been justified for the same reasons (see *United States v. Young*, 2006 U.S. Dist. LEXIS 28141 (N.D. W.Va. 2006); *United States v. Zamora*, 2005 U.S. Dist. LEXIS 40775 (N.D. Ga. 2005); *United States v. Brookes*, 2005 U.S. Dist. LEXIS 16844 (D.V.I. 2005)).

Inventory Search

Law enforcement officers may, without a warrant, search an item in their custody for the purpose of completing an inventory of the contents. This exception to the warrant initially arose in the context of arrests made during vehicle stops and the need to impound the vehicle and its contents (see *South Dakota v. Opperman*, 428 U.S. 364 (1976)). A vehicle could, however, contain a desktop computer, a laptop computer, a pager, a PDA, a smartphone, an iPod, and other digital media. Does the inventory search exception permit a search of the files on the laptop? What if, while performing the inventory and looking for the serial number on the pager, a number is observed? Or, what if the PDA is powered on and a file is on the screen? Or better yet, a person is arrested while carrying an attaché. Inside is a laptop, MP3 player, and Blackberry smartphone. Each of those items needs to be inventoried during the booking process. The Blackberry is powered and a file is on the screen. An officer looks at the screen and records names and numbers on the screen. Does that search come within the inventory search exception?

The inventory search exception may justify seizure of digital devices, but it is unlikely that the exception, by itself, will justify a *search* of those devices. As suggested by the above scenarios, a warrantless search might be justified by the plain view or exigent circumstances exception. Prudence would dictate, if something was observed in plain view, that the officer would apply for a warrant.

Border Search

The general rule is that officers or agents may conduct a warrantless search or seizure at or near the border of the United States. Does this mean that border agents can detain a traveler at the border and search the contents of a computer in a briefcase sitting on the back seat of the car? The following case is helpful in resolving that question:

United States v. Ickes

393 F.3D 501

U.S. COURT OF APPEALS, FOURTH CIRCUIT (2005)

OPINION BY: WILKINSON, Circuit Judge:

John Woodward Ickes, Jr., was attempting to enter the United States from Canada when U.S. Customs agents searched his van. The agents found several illegal items, most notably images of child pornography stored in photo albums and on Ickes's computer. Ickes was charged and convicted of transporting child pornography in violation of federal law. Prior to trial, the district court denied Ickes's motion to suppress the evidence obtained at the border.

Ickes first claims that Congress has not authorized the search of his computer and disks. We cannot agree. Congress has been emphatic in its empowerment of U.S. Customs officials. The statutory language is sweeping:

> Any officer of the customs may at any time go on board of any vessel or vehicle at any place in the United States or within the customs waters, ... or at any other authorized place ... and examine the manifest and other documents and papers and examine, inspect, and search the vessel or vehicle and every part thereof and any person, trunk, package, or cargo on board.

> 19 U.S.C. § 1581(a).

Ickes claims that this statutory language is insufficient to cover the search of his computer and disks. He bases this argument on the fact that the statute does not explicitly mention electronic equipment. He concludes from this omission that it is "obvious" that Congress did not intend its statute to cover those items. He invokes the maxim of statutory construction that the inclusion of several items in a list—here, "trunk, package, or cargo"—implies the exclusion of others.

Despite Ickes's contentions to the contrary, the plain language of the statute authorizes expansive border searches.

First, the statutory language. Congress chose to use the embracive term "cargo" in § 1581(a). A "fundamental canon of statutory construction requires that unless otherwise defined, words will be interpreted as taking their ordinary, contemporary, common meaning." *United States v. Maxwell*, 285 F.3d 336, 340 (4th Cir. 2002). *Black's Law Dictionary* defines "cargo" to mean "goods transported by a vessel, airplane, or vehicle."

In this case, it is undisputed that Ickes's computer and disks were being transported by his vehicle. We are unpersuaded that these particular transported goods are somehow exempt from the ordinary definition of "cargo." To hold otherwise would undermine the longstanding practice of seizing goods at the border even when the type of good is not specified in the statute.

Second, Ickes's narrow interpretation of the word "cargo" is inconsistent with the specific context in which the word is used. In drafting §1581(a), Congress chose to use the word "any" no less than five times. The statute reads:

> Any officer ... may at any time go on board of any vessel or vehicle at any place in the United States ... [and search the vehicle] ... and any person, trunk, package or cargo on board.

§1581(a).

As we have explained before, "the word 'any' is a term of great breadth. Read naturally, [it] has an expansive meaning...." *Mapoy v. Carroll*, 185 F.3d 224, 229 (4th Cir. 1999). Given Congress's repeated use of the word "any" immediately preceding its list of what may be searched, we find it unreasonable to construe the list restrictively.

Finally, we are convinced that Ickes's argument must fail after analyzing the "broader context of the statute as a whole." *Robinson*, 519 U.S. at 341. We construe § 1581(a) against the back-drop of an "impressive historical pedigree of the Government's power and interest" at the border. *Flores-Montano*, 124 S. Ct. at 1586. As detailed below, since the founding of our country Congress has "granted the Executive plenary authority to conduct routine searches and seizures at the border." Id. at 1585, citing *United States v. Montoya de Hernandez*, 473 U.S. 531, 537, 87 L. Ed. 2d 381, 105 S. Ct. 3304 (1985).

We hold that the government was authorized by 19 U.S.C. §1581(a) to search Ickes's computer and disks.

Ickes further argues that even if Congress purports to permit the search of his computer and disks, such a search would be unconstitutional. We disagree.

Last term, the Supreme Court instructed that:

> The Government's interest in preventing the entry of unwanted persons and effects is at its zenith at the international border. Time and again, we have stated that searches made at the border ... are reasonable simply by virtue of the fact that they occur at the border.

> *Flores-Montano*, 124 S. Ct. at 1585 (holding that the government's authority to conduct border searches is broad enough to permit the removal, disassembly, and reassembly of a vehicle's fuel tank).

The border search doctrine is not a recent development in the law. The "longstanding recognition that searches at our borders without probable cause and without a warrant are nonetheless 'reasonable' has a history as old as the Fourth Amendment itself." *United States v. Ramsey*, 431 U.S. 606, 619, 52 L. Ed.2d 617, 97 S. Ct. 1972 (1977). In fact, the same Congress which proposed the Fourth Amendment to state legislatures also enacted the first far-reaching customs statute in 1790. Thus, since the birth of our country, customs officials have wielded broad authority to search the belongings of would-be entrants without obtaining a warrant and without establishing probable cause.

This well-recognized exception to the safeguards of the Fourth Amendment comes with an equally well-established rationale. For it is "axiomatic that the United States, as sovereign, has the inherent authority to protect, and a paramount interest in protecting, its territorial integrity." *Flores-Montano*, 124 S. Ct. at 1586. The government has an overriding interest in securing the safety of its citizens and to do this it must seek to prevent "the introduction of contraband into this country." *Montoya de Hernandez*, 473 U.S. at 537.

A greater interest on the side of the government at the border is coupled with a lesser interest on the side of the potential entrant. Since "a port of entry is not a traveler's home," his expectation of privacy there is substantially lessened. *United States v. Thirty-Seven Photographs*, 402 U.S. 363, 376, 28 L. Ed. 2d 822, 91 S. Ct. 1400 (1971). When someone approaches a border, he should not be surprised that "customs officers characteristically inspect luggage ...; it is an old practice and is intimately associated with excluding illegal articles from the country." Id.

Despite the Supreme Court's insistence that U.S. officials be given broad authority to conduct border searches, Ickes argues that the search of his computer was nonetheless invalid since it involved the search of expressive material. In essence, Ickes asks us to carve out a First Amendment exception to the border search doctrine.

However, the ramifications of accepting Ickes's First Amendment argument would be quite staggering. Ickes suggests that the border search doctrine does not apply when the item being searched is something "expressive." But this cannot be the case. The border search doctrine is justified by the "longstanding right of the sovereign to protect itself." *Flores-Montano*, 124 S. Ct. at 1585, quoting *Ramsey*, 431 U.S. at 616. Particularly in today's world, national security interests may require uncovering terrorist communications, which are inherently "expressive." Following Ickes's logic would create a sanctuary at the border for all expressive material—even for terrorist plans. This would undermine the compelling reasons that lie at the very heart of the border search doctrine. Ickes's argument, at bottom, proves too much.

Furthermore, recognizing a First Amendment exception to the border search doctrine would ensure significant headaches for those forced to determine its scope. Disputes about whether material is obscene, for example, are not always easily resolved. Were we to carve out this First Amendment exception, government agents at the border (and subsequently courts) would be faced with drawing difficult lines. First, agents would have to decide—on their feet—which expressive material is covered by the First Amendment. And then, in cases where they conclude that the exception applies, they would still have to determine if probable cause existed. These sorts of legal wrangles at the border are exactly what the Supreme Court wished to avoid by sanctioning expansive border searches. See *Flores-Montano*, 124 S. Ct. at 1585–86. We refuse to put these issues into play and thereby divert customs officials from their charge of policing our borders and protecting our country.

Ickes claims that our ruling is sweeping. He warns that "any person carrying a laptop computer … on an international flight would be subject to a search of the files on the computer hard drive." This prediction seems far-fetched. Customs agents have neither the time nor the resources to search the contents of every computer.

Indeed, the fallacy of Ickes's argument is no better illustrated than by the facts of his own case. The agents did not inspect the contents of Ickes's computer until they had already discovered marijuana paraphernalia, photo albums of child pornography, a disturbing video focused on a young ball boy, and an outstanding warrant for Ickes's arrest. As a practical matter, computer searches are most likely to occur where—as here—the traveler's conduct or the presence of other items in his possession suggest the need to search further. However, to state the probability that reasonable suspicions will give rise to more intrusive searches is a far cry from enthroning this notion as a matter of constitutional law. The essence of border search doctrine is a reliance upon the trained observations and judgments of customs officials, rather than upon constitutional requirements applied to the inapposite context of this sort of search.

We therefore reject Ickes's constitutional argument, and hold that the border search doctrine is not subject to a First Amendment exception.

Administrative Searches

Government officials may conduct administrative, or regulatory, inspections of business premises without a warrant and without probable cause as a basis for the inspection. Many businesses and professions increasingly rely upon electronic data instead of paper records. It will be interesting to see how the courts deal with a regulatory inspection scheme that permits the viewing of business records in electronic format.

Automobile Exception

Where officers stop a vehicle on the highway or approach a parked vehicle on a city street, they may conduct a warrantless search of the vehicle if they have probable cause to believe that the vehicle contains evidence of a crime and if they lack the time to obtain a warrant. Because most every type of digital storage device can be transported in a vehicle, it could be the subject of a search or seizure. In most instances, a detailed search of a hard drive would not be allowed because the officer could, if the vehicle is being impounded, inventory the item and seek a warrant. Other exceptions, such as plain view and exigent circumstances, might allow further search.

Special Needs Exception

The special needs exception authorizes government officials to conduct a warrantless search on less than probable cause. For example, in *New Jersey v. T.L.O.* (469 U.S. 325 (1985)), the U.S. Supreme Court determined that "in those exceptional circumstances in which special needs, beyond the normal need for law enforcement, make the warrant and probable cause requirement impracticable," government officials may conduct a warrantless search based upon reasonable suspicion. In *T.L.O.*, a high school vice principal searched the contents of the purse belonging to a student suspected of smoking in the school building. The court concluded that the "heightened obligation to safeguard students" and the impracticality of obtaining a warrant in every student disciplinary proceeding justified a finding of special need. Of course, with the increased use of smaller digital devices such as cell phones with digital cameras, smartphones, pagers, and laptops, the search of a student's digital device could also be justified as a "special need."

Other issues that pertain to search and seizure, such as the good faith exception to the exclusionary rule, are discussed in the following chapter.

Key Words and Phrases

Administrative search
Automobile exception
Border search
Consent
Exigent circumstances
Hot pursuit

Incidental to a lawful arrest
Inventory search
Mere evidence
Plain view
Reasonable expectation of privacy
Special needs exception

Review Problems

1. In *United States v. Moran*, the court determined that the defendant did not have a subjective expectation of privacy while driving on public highways. However, when law enforcement personnel install the device, how do they know that the vehicle will be driven solely on public highways? Or, does the court only consider what evidence derived from the GPS device is being used during the trial? For example, if the defendant drove on public highways and private driveways, and parked in a private garage, would the court suppress any evidence derived from the GPS device while the vehicle was parked in the private garage (where defendant had a reasonable expectation of privacy) but admit GPS locator evidence obtained while the vehicle was on a public highway (where defendant has no reasonable expectation of privacy)?
2. When conducting a search, does the role that the computer played in the crime under investigation (i.e., whether it was the instrumentality, the target, or merely the repository of evidence) have any impact on whether the computer will be seized and removed from the scene or examined at the scene?
3. Are computer files not yet accessed in plain view? If not, can they come into plain view once accessed? Explain.

Weblinks

www.cybercrime.gov/ssmanual/index.html
   This site contains the 2009 version of the search and seizure manual published by the Computer Crime and Intellectual Property Section (CCIPS) of the U.S. Department of Justice. This is an invaluable (priceless) resource on the law pertaining to the search for digital evidence and seizure of computer-related devices and material. Chapter 1 of the manual discusses many of the principles presented in this chapter.

www.secretservice.gov/electronic_evidence.shtml

This site contains the *Best Practices for Seizing Electronic Evidence* manual. The manual is intended as a guide for first responders who do not handle computer evidence or forensics on a daily basis.

www.fjc.gov/public/home.nsf/autoframe?openform&url_l=/public/home.nsf/inavgeneral?openpage&url_r=/public/home.nsf/pages/334

This page is from the website of the Federal Judicial Center. It contains numerous links pertaining to the search and seizure of computers and data in criminal cases.

Endnotes

1. The facts of this case are based on *Washington v. Johnson*, No. 97-1-02564-9 (Wash. Super. Ct. 1997), as reported by Ivan Orton. "The Investigation and Prosecution of a Cybercrime." In Clifford, Ralph D. (2001). *Cybercrime: The Investigation, Prosecution and Defense of a Computer-Related Crime*. Durham, NC: Carolina Academic Press.

Search and Seizure
Electronic Evidence

9

Introduction

This chapter covers the process of applying for and executing a search and seizure pursuant to a warrant, and the application of those concepts to computers and digital storage devices. The discussion will barely scratch the surface of search and seizure law, and the diligent investigator should always consult with legal counsel whenever possible *before* conducting a search.

As previously stated, when a search or seizure is conducted with a warrant, the Fourth Amendment requires that the warrant be issued by a judge only after the judge is persuaded that the applicant for the warrant has shown probable cause, supported by oath or affirmation, that evidence of a crime will be found in a particular place. Further, the warrant must particularly describe the "place to be searched and the persons or things to be seized."

Probable cause: In order to obtain a warrant for a search or seizure, the law enforcement officer must submit to the judge a sworn application and any other supporting evidentiary material the officer decides to include that is sufficient to establish probable cause to believe that the evidence sought will be found in the place to be searched or thing to be seized.

Specificity requirement: The Fourth Amendment protects against the general rummaging through a person's home or business by requiring that a warrant describe the "place to be searched and the persons or things to be seized." The specificity requirement will be addressed in cases presented later in this chapter.

Scope of the warrant: The Fourth Amendment can be violated at the application stage, i.e., when the officer applies for a warrant, or at the execution stage, when officers physically enter the designated premises and commence the search. In executing a search warrant, officers are limited to the search or seizure of items that are within the scope of the warrant.

Exclusionary rule and the good faith exception: What is the penalty if a government official, federal or state, violates the Fourth Amendment (or in the case of a state official, the Fourteenth Amendment)? The Supreme Court has concluded that the appropriate penalty is to exclude the unconstitutionally obtained evidence from use at trial as part of the government's case, the so-called exclusionary rule (*Mapp v. Ohio*, 367 U.S. 643 (1961); *Weeks v. United States*, 232 U.S. 383 (1914)). Does that mean evidence must be excluded when officers act in good faith? The good faith exception is discussed below in the *Hunter* case.

The following case, *United States v. Adjani*, is illustrative of several concepts discussed above. That case discusses the issues of probable cause, specificity, and scope of the warrant. *United States v. Hunter* (below) also discusses specificity and the good faith exception to the exclusionary rule. *United States v. Campos* (below) also discusses an issue relating to scope of the warrant. You should refer back at this point to *United States v. Carey*, which was discussed in Chapter 8. *Carey* is an important case that illustrates when a search exceeds the scope of a warrant.

United States v. Adjani

452 F.3D 1140 (2006)

U.S. COURT OF APPEALS, NINTH CIRCUIT

OPINION: FISHER, Circuit Judge:

While executing a search warrant at the home of defendant Christopher Adjani to obtain evidence of his alleged extortion, agents from the Federal Bureau of Investigation seized Adjani's computer and external storage devices, which were later searched at an FBI computer lab. They also seized and subsequently searched a computer belonging to defendant Jana Reinhold, who lived with Adjani, even though she had not at that point been identified as a suspect and was not named as a target in the warrant. Some of the emails found on Reinhold's computer chronicled conversations between her and Adjani that implicated her in the extortion plot. Relying in part on the incriminating emails, the government charged both Adjani and Reinhold with conspiring to commit extortion in violation of 18 U.S.C. § 371 and transmitting a threatening communication with intent to extort in violation of 18 U.S.C. § 875(d).

The defendants brought motions to suppress the emails, arguing that the warrant did not authorize the seizure and search of Reinhold's computer and its contents; but if it did, the warrant was unconstitutionally overbroad or, alternatively, the emails fell outside the scope of the warrant. The district court granted the defendants' motion to suppress the email communications between Reinhold and Adjani, finding that the agents did not have sufficient probable cause to search Reinhold's computer, and that once they discovered information incriminating her, the agents should have obtained an additional search warrant. The government appeals this evidentiary ruling, but only with respect to three emails dated January 12, 2004.

We hold that the government had probable cause to search Reinhold's computer, the warrant satisfied our test for specificity and the seized e-mail communications fell within the scope of the properly issued warrant. Accordingly, we reverse the district court's order suppressing the January 12, 2004 e-mail communications between Reinhold and Adjani.

I. Background

A. The Extortion Scheme

Adjani was once employed by Paycom Billing Services Inc. (formerly Epoch), which facilitates payments from Internet users to its client websites. As a payment facilitator, Paycom receives and stores vast amounts of data containing credit card information. On January 8, 2004, a woman (later identified as Reinhold) delivered envelopes to three Paycom partners, Christopher Mallick, Clay Andrews and Joel Hall. Each envelope contained a letter from Adjani advising that he had purchased a copy of Paycom's database containing its clients' sensitive financial information. The letter threatened that Adjani would sell the Paycom database and master client control list if he did not receive $3 million. To prove his threats were real, Adjani included samples of the classified data. He directed the Paycom partners to sign an enclosed agreement attesting to the proposed quid pro quo and fax it back to him by January 12. The letter included Adjani's email address, cadjani@mac.com, and a fax number. Agents later learned that Adjani's email address was billed to Reinhold's account.

Evidence suggested that Adjani left Los Angeles on January 9, 2004, and ultimately ended up in Zurich, Switzerland. From Switzerland, Adjani sent an email on January 12 to Joel Hall to confirm that Hall and the others had received the envelopes. Adjani followed up on this email on January 13 by instructing Hall to contact him through AOL/Mac iChat instant messaging if he wanted to discuss the settlement agreement. With the FBI monitoring, Hall conversed several times with Adjani on the Internet and over the telephone. In spite of Adjani's insistence that he remain overseas, Hall convinced him to come to Los Angeles on January 26 to pick up $2.5 million in exchange for the database.

Adjani returned to Los Angeles on January 22, under FBI surveillance.

Reinhold, driving in a car that the FBI had earlier identified as Adjani's, was observed leaving Adjani's residence in Venice, California, picking him up from the airport and returning to his residence. The FBI also observed Reinhold using an Apple computer, the same brand of computer Adjani used to email and chat with Paycom.

B. Obtaining and Executing the Search Warrant

On January 23, 2004, based on the facts recited above and attested to in FBI Agent Cloney's affidavit (which was affixed to the warrant), a federal magistrate judge granted the government an arrest warrant for Adjani and a search warrant covering Adjani's Venice residence, his vehicle, his person and the residence of the individual who had stolen the confidential information from Paycom. The warrant specifically sought "evidence of violations of [18 U.S.C. § 875(d)]: Transmitting Threatening Communications With Intent to Commit Extortion." Further, the warrant expressly authorized seizure of:

5g. Records, documents and materials containing Paycom's or Epoch's master client control documents, Paycom's or Epoch's email database, or other company information relating to Paycom or Epoch.

5h. Records, documents and materials which reflect communications with Christopher Mallick, Clay Andrews, Joel Hall or other employees or officers of Paycom or Epoch.

5i. Any and all evidence of travel, including hotel bills and receipts, gasoline receipts, plane tickets, bus tickets, train tickets, or any other documents related to travel from January 8, 2004 to the present.

5k. Computer, hard drives, computer disks, CD's, and other computer storage devices.

With respect to the computer search, the warrant prescribed the process to be followed: "In searching the data, the computer personnel will examine all of the data contained in the computer equipment and storage devices to view their precise contents and determine whether the data falls within the items to be seized as set forth herein." Additionally, it noted that "[i]n order to search for data that is capable of being read or intercepted by a computer, law enforcement personnel will need to seize and search … [a]ny computer equipment and storage device capable of being used to commit, further, or store evidence of the offense listed above."

On January 26, 2004, agents observed Reinhold driving Adjani, in a car registered to him, to his meeting with Paycom. While Adjani went into a hotel, Reinhold slipped into the backseat of his car, placing curtains over the windows. At this point, agents proceeded to search Adjani's car. That same day, agents executed the search warrant for Adjani's Venice residence. There they found and seized various computers and hard drives, including Reinhold's computer, which were later sent to an FBI computer lab to be searched. During that search process, the hard drive from Reinhold's computer revealed certain email correspondence between Reinhold and Adjani, implicating Reinhold in the extortion plot and supporting a charge of conspiracy against both of them.

The defendants successfully sought suppression of these seized email communications in the district court. This appeal requires us to determine whether the agents permissibly searched Reinhold's computer; whether the warrant satisfied our specificity standards; and whether the emails seized fell within the scope of the otherwise properly issued warrant.

II. Analysis

A. Probable Cause

The government principally argues that contrary to the district court's finding and the defendants' assertions, the search warrant affidavit established probable cause to search all instrumentalities that might contain "evidence of violations of" 18 U.S.C. § 875(d), including Reinhold's computer and emails. Reinhold counters that the affidavit may have generally established probable cause, but did not do so with respect to her computer, because "[i]n the affidavit, Reinhold was not labeled as a target, suspect, or co-conspirator."

1. Probable cause to issue the warrant

"A search warrant … is issued upon a showing of probable cause to believe that the legitimate object of a search is located in a particular place, and therefore safeguards an individual's interest in the privacy of his home and possessions against the unjustified intrusion of the police." *Steagald v. United States*, 451 U.S. 204, 213, 101 S. Ct. 1642, 68 L. Ed. 2d 38 (1981). As the Supreme Court has explained, the "probable cause standard … is a practical, nontechnical conception." *Illinois v. Gates*, 462 U.S. 213, 231, 103 S. Ct. 2317, 76 L. Ed. 2d 527 (1983) (quoting *Brinegar v. United States*, 338 U.S. 160, 176, 69 S. Ct. 1302, 93 L. Ed. 1879 (1949)). Furthermore, "probable cause is a fluid concept—turning on the assessment of probabilities in particular factual contexts—not readily, or even usefully, reduced to a neat set of legal rules." Id. at 232.

The warrant here was supported by probable cause, because the affidavit submitted to the magistrate judge established that "there [was] a fair probability that contraband or evidence of a crime [would] be found in" computers at Adjani's residence. The extensive 24-page supporting affidavit described the extortion scheme in detail, including that Adjani possessed a computer-generated database and communicated with Paycom over email, requiring the use of a computer. Furthermore, the agent's affidavit explained the need to search computers, in particular, for evidence of the extortion scheme: "I know that considerable planning is typically performed to construct and consummate an extortion. The plan can be documented in the form of a simple written note or more elaborate information stored on computer equipment."

The crime contemplated by the warrant was transmitting a threatening communication with intent to extort. See 18 U.S.C. § 875(d). To find evidence of extortion, the government would have probable cause to search for and seize instrumentalities likely to have been used to facilitate the transmission. The magistrate judge could rightfully assume that there was a "fair probability" that such evidence could be contained on computers or storage devices found in Adjani's residence.

2. Probable cause to search "Reinhold's computer"

Having held that the affidavit supporting the warrant established probable cause to search for and seize instrumentalities of the extortion (including records, files and computers) in Adjani's residence, we turn to Reinhold's contention that the probable cause for the Adjani warrant did not extend so far as to permit a search of her property. We disagree. The agents, acting pursuant to a valid warrant to look for evidence of a computer-based crime, searched computers found in Adjani's residence and to which he had apparent access. That one of the computers actually belonged to Reinhold did not exempt it from being searched, especially given her association with Adjani and participation (however potentially innocuous) in some of his activities as documented in the agent's supporting affidavit. The officers therefore did not act unreasonably in searching Reinhold's computer as a source of the evidence targeted by the warrant.

Reinhold's argument that there was no probable cause to search her computer, a private and personal piece of property, because the warrant failed to list her as a "target, suspect, or co-conspirator" misunderstands Fourth Amendment jurisprudence. Although individuals undoubtedly have a high expectation of privacy in the files stored on their personal computers, we have never held that agents may establish probable cause to search only those items owned or possessed by the criminal suspect. The law is to the contrary. "The critical element in a reasonable search is not that the owner of the property is suspected of crime but that there is reasonable cause to believe that the specific 'things' to be searched for and seized are located on the property to which entry is sought." *Zurcher v. Stanford Daily*, 436 U.S. 547, 556, 98 S. Ct. 1970, 56 L. Ed. 2d 525 (1978).

In *United States v. Hay*, 231 F.3d 630 (9th Cir. 2000), the defendant made an argument similar to Reinhold's, challenging the district court's ruling allowing evidence of child pornography found on his computer to be used against him at trial. Hay claimed that the affidavit submitted by officers to obtain a warrant did not establish probable cause to engage in a search of Hay's computer because "there was no evidence that he fell within a class of persons likely to collect and traffic in child pornography because the affidavit does not indicate that he was a child molester, pedophile, or collector of child pornography and sets forth no evidence that he solicited, sold or transmitted child pornography." Id. at 635. We rejected Hay's challenge, holding that "[i]t is well established that a location can be searched for evidence of a crime even if there is no probable cause to arrest the person at the location." Id. (citing *Zurcher*, 436 U.S. at 556).

Likewise, there was no need here for the agents expressly to claim in the affidavit that they wanted to arrest Reinhold, or even that Reinhold was suspected of any criminal activity. The government needed only to satisfy the magistrate judge that there was probable cause to believe that evidence of the crime in question—here extortion—could be found on computers accessible to Adjani in his home, including—as it developed—Reinhold's computer. By setting forth the details of the extortion scheme and the instrumentalities of the crime, augmented by descriptions of Reinhold's involvement with Adjani, the government satisfied its burden. The magistrate judge therefore properly approved the warrant, which in turn encompassed all the computers found at Adjani's residence.

B. Specificity Requirement

The Fourth Amendment's specificity requirement prevents officers from engaging in general, exploratory searches by limiting their discretion and providing specific guidance as to what can and cannot be searched and seized. However, the level of detail necessary in a warrant is related to the particular circumstances and the nature of the evidence sought. See *United States v. Spilotro*, 800 F.2d 959, 963 (9th Cir. 1986). "Warrants which describe generic categories of items are not necessarily invalid if a more precise description of the items subject to seizure is not possible." Id.

In determining whether a warrant is sufficiently particular, we consider one or more of the following factors:

> (1) whether probable cause exists to seize all items of a particular type described in the warrant; (2) whether the warrant sets out objective standards by which executing officers can differentiate items subject to seizure from those which are not; and (3) whether the government was able to describe the items more particularly in light of the information available to it at the time the warrant was issued.

> Id. at 963.

Spilotro involved a warrant issued against individuals suspected of loan sharking and gambling activities. The warrant authorized "the seizure of address books, notebooks, notes, documents, records, assets, photographs, and other items and paraphernalia evidencing violations of the multiple criminal statutes listed." It failed, however, to state the "precise identity, type, or contents of the records sought." Partly because of this reason, we held that the warrant was not sufficiently specific to pass muster under the Fourth Amendment. More could have been done to tie the documents sought to the crimes alleged by, for example, stating that the police were searching for "records relating to loan sharking and gambling, including pay and collection sheets, lists of loan customers, loan accounts and telephone numbers….".

In contrast to *Spilotro*, the warrant to search Adjani's residence satisfied our specificity criteria. First, we have already held that there was probable cause to search the computers. As to the second factor, the warrant objectively described the items to be searched and seized with adequate specificity and sufficiently restricted the discretion of agents executing the search. The warrant affidavit began by limiting the search for evidence of a specific crime—transmitting threatening communications with intent to commit extortion. Further, unlike in *Spilotro*, the Adjani warrant provided the "precise identity" and nature of the items to be seized. For example, paragraph 5h of the warrant instructed agents to search for documents reflecting communications with three individuals or other employees of a specific company. Also, paragraph 5i authorized seizure of "any" evidence of travel but provided a specific, though not exhaustive, list of possible documents that fell within this category and temporally restricted the breadth of the search. Moreover, the extensive statement of probable cause in the affidavit detailed the alleged crime and Adjani's unlawful scheme.

With respect to the final *Spilotro* factor, we conclude that the government described the items to be searched and seized as particularly as could be reasonably expected given the nature of the crime and the evidence it then possessed. The Adjani warrant "describe[d] in great[]detail the items one commonly expects to find on premises used for the criminal activities in question...." *Spilotro*, 800 F.2d at 964; see also *United States v. Mann*, 389 F.3d 869, 877 (9th Cir. 2004) ("While a search warrant must describe items to be seized with particularity sufficient to prevent a general, exploratory rummaging in a person's belongings, it need only be reasonably specific, rather than elaborately detailed.").

Center Art Galleries-Hawaii, Inc. v. United States, 875 F.2d 747 (9th Cir. 1989), the principal case defendants rely upon in making their overbreadth argument, is distinguishable. In that case, we held that a warrant providing for "the almost unrestricted seizure of items which are 'evidence of violations of federal criminal law' without describing the specific crimes suspected is constitutionally inadequate." Id. at 750 (quoting *Spilotro*, 800 F.2d at 964). In contrast, the government here did describe at some length both the nature of and the means of committing the crime. Further, unlike in *Center Art Galleries*, the affidavit was expressly incorporated into the warrant. Id. ("An affidavit can cure the overbreadth of a warrant if the affidavit is 'attached to and incorporated by reference in' the warrant.") (quoting *Spilotro*, 800 F.2d at 967, and citing *United States v. Leary*, 846 F.2d 592, 603 (10th Cir. 1988)).

We understand the heightened specificity concerns in the computer context, given the vast amount of data they can store. As the defendants urge, the warrant arguably might have provided for a "less invasive search of Adjani's [email] 'inbox' and 'outbox' for the addressees specifically cited in the warrant, as opposed to the wholesale search of the contents of all emails purportedly looking for evidence 'reflecting' communications with those individuals." Avoiding that kind of specificity and limitation was not unreasonable under the circumstances here, however. To require such a pin-pointed computer search, restricting the search to an email program or to specific search terms, would likely have failed to cast a sufficiently wide net to capture the evidence sought. Cf. *Ross*, 456 U.S. at 821 ("When a legitimate search is under way, and when its purpose and its limits have been precisely defined, nice distinctions between closets, drawers, and containers, in the case of a home, or between glove compartments, upholstered seats, trunks, and wrapped packages, in the case of a vehicle, must give way to the interest in the prompt and efficient completion of the task at hand.").

Computer files are easy to disguise or rename, and were we to limit the warrant to such a specific search protocol, much evidence could escape discovery simply because of Adjani's (or Reinhold's) labeling of the files documenting Adjani's criminal activity. The government should not be required to trust the suspect's self-labeling when executing a warrant.

C. Scope of the Warrant

Even assuming that the warrant was supported by probable cause and was adequately specific such that a search of Reinhold's computer and emails were permissible, Reinhold argues that the actual emails sought to be introduced into evidence were outside the scope of the warrant. Again, we disagree.

The three seized emails the government seeks to admit clearly fall within the scope of paragraph 5h of the warrant affidavit, authorizing seizure of "[r]ecords, documents and materials which reflect communications with Christopher Mallick, Clay Andrews, Joel Hall or other employees or officers of Paycom or Epoch," which are relevant evidence of violations of 18 U.S.C. § 875(d). Each email specifically refers to communication with Joel Hall or one of the stated companies (identifying them by name). Reinhold's argument that the term "reflect communications with" should be read narrowly to cover only those emails sent between one of the named Paycom employees and Adjani is nonsensical. The government already had the emails sent between the victims of the extortion and Adjani—obtained from the victims themselves. The purpose of the warrant was to obtain further and corroborating evidence of the extortion scheme and Adjani's criminal intent in communicating with the victims, and the three emails plainly "reflect" the relevant communications specified in paragraph 5h.

To the extent Reinhold argues that the emails were outside the scope of the warrant because they implicated her in the crime and supported a charge of conspiracy to commit extortion (a crime not specifically mentioned in the warrant), we reject the argument. There is no rule, and Reinhold points to no case law suggesting otherwise, that evidence turned up while officers are rightfully searching a location under a properly issued warrant must be excluded simply because the evidence found may support charges for a related crime (or against a suspect) not expressly contemplated in the warrant.

The agents were rightfully searching Reinhold's computer for evidence of Adjani's crime of extortion. They were looking in Reinhold's email program when they came across information that was both related to the purposes of their search and implicated Reinhold in the crime. That the evidence could now support a new charge against a new (but already identified) person does not compel its suppression. On these facts, we disagree with the district court's conclusion that the officers should have obtained a new search warrant when they came across the incriminating emails. In so concluding, we are careful to note that in this case the evidence discovered was clearly related to the crime referred to in the warrant. We need not decide to what extent the government would be able to introduce evidence discovered that the police knew, at the time of discovery, was not related to the crime cited in the warrant. Cf. *United States v. Carey*, 172 F.3d 1268, 1272–73 (10th Cir. 1999) (excluding certain evidence of child pornography where the warrant authorized only seizure of drug evidence and the detective knew he was expanding the scope of the warrant, and holding that the officer should have stopped the search and obtained a new warrant.).

Conducting the Search or Seizure

Various federal statutes designate those law enforcement agencies that can apply for a warrant and the statutory authority to conduct searches and seizures (18 USC §§ 2231–2236, 3101–3116). The procedure for obtaining and executing search warrants is set forth in Rule 41 of the Federal Rules of Criminal Procedure, which, to the extent relevant here, provides:

Rule 41. Search and Seizure

(a) Scope and Definitions.
   (1) Scope. This rule does not modify any statute regulating search or seizure, or the issuance and execution of a search warrant in special circumstances.

(2) Definitions. The following definitions apply under this rule:

  (A) "Property" includes documents, books, papers, any other tangible objects, and information.

  (B) "Daytime" means the hours between 6:00 a.m. and 10:00 p.m. according to local time.

  (C) "Federal law enforcement officer" means a government agent (other than an attorney for the government) who is engaged in enforcing the criminal laws and is within any category of officers authorized by the Attorney General to request a search warrant.

  (D) "Domestic terrorism" and "international terrorism" have the meanings set out in 18 U.S.C. § 2331.

  (E) "Tracking device" has the meaning set out in 18 U.S.C. § 3117(b).

(b) Authority to Issue a Warrant. At the request of a federal law enforcement officer or an attorney for the government:

  (1) a magistrate judge with authority in the district—or if none is reasonably available, a judge of a state court of record in the district—has authority to issue a warrant to search for and seize a person or property located within the district;

  (2) a magistrate judge with authority in the district has authority to issue a warrant for a person or property outside the district if the person or property is located within the district when the warrant is issued but might move or be moved outside the district before the warrant is executed; and

  (3) a magistrate judge—in an investigation of domestic terrorism or international terrorism (as defined in 18 U.S.C. § 2331)—having authority in any district in which activities related to the terrorism may have occurred, may issue a warrant for a person or property within or outside that district.

  (4) a magistrate judge with authority in the district has authority to issue a warrant to install within the district a tracking device; the warrant may authorize use of the device to track the movement of a person or property located within the district, outside the district, or both; and

  (5) a magistrate judge having authority in any district where activities related to the crime may have occurred, or in the District of Columbia, may issue a warrant for property that is located outside the jurisdiction of any state or district, but within any of the following:

    (A) a United States territory, possession, or commonwealth;

    (B) the premises—no matter who owns them—of a United States, diplomatic or consular mission in a foreign state, including any appurtenant building, part of building, or land used for the mission's purposes; or

    (C) a residence and any appurtenant land owned or leased by the United States and used by United States personnel assigned to a United States diplomatic or consular mission in a foreign state.

(c) Persons or Property Subject to Search or Seizure. A warrant may be issued for any of the following:

  (1) evidence of a crime;

  (2) contraband, fruits of crime, or other items illegally possessed;

  (3) property designed for use, intended for use, or used in committing a crime; or

  (4) a person to be arrested or a person who is unlawfully restrained.

(d) Obtaining a Warrant.

  (1) In General. After receiving an affidavit or other information, a magistrate judge— or if authorized by Rule 41(b), a judge of a state court of record—must issue the

warrant if there is probable cause to search for and seize a person or property or to install and use a tracking device.

(2) Requesting a Warrant in the Presence of a Judge.

    (A) Warrant on an Affidavit. When a federal law enforcement officer or an attorney for the government presents an affidavit in support of a warrant, the judge may require the affiant to appear personally and may examine under oath the affiant and any witness the affiant produces.

    (B) Warrant on Sworn Testimony. The judge may wholly or partially dispense with a written affidavit and base a warrant on sworn testimony if doing so is reasonable under the circumstances.

    (C) Recording Testimony. Testimony taken in support of a warrant must be recorded by a court reporter or by a suitable recording device, and the judge must file the transcript or recording with the clerk, along with any affidavit.

(3) Requesting a Warrant by Telephonic or Other Means.

    (A) In General. A magistrate judge may issue a warrant based on information communicated by telephone or other reliable electronic means.

    (B) Recording Testimony. Upon learning that an applicant is requesting a warrant, a magistrate judge must:

        (i) place under oath the applicant and any person on whose testimony the application is based; and

        (ii) make a verbatim record of the conversation with a suitable recording device, if available, or by a court reporter, or in writing.

    (C) Certifying Testimony. The magistrate judge must have any recording or court reporter's notes transcribed, certify the transcription's accuracy, and file a copy of the record and the transcription with the clerk. Any written verbatim record must be signed by the magistrate judge and filed with the clerk.

    (D) Suppression Limited. Absent a finding of bad faith, evidence obtained from a warrant issued under Rule 41(d)(3)(A) is not subject to suppression on the ground that issuing the warrant in that manner was unreasonable under the circumstances.

(e) Issuing the Warrant.

  (1) In General. The magistrate judge or a judge of a state court of record must issue the warrant to an officer authorized to execute it.

  (2) Contents of the Warrant.

    (A) Warrant to Search for and Seize a Person or Property. Except for a tracking-device warrant, the warrant must identify the person or property to be searched, identify any person or property to be seized, and designate the magistrate judge to whom it must be returned. The warrant must command the officer to:

        (i) execute the warrant within a specified time no longer than 14 days;

        (ii) execute the warrant during the daytime, unless the judge for good cause expressly authorizes execution at another time; and

        (iii) return the warrant to the magistrate judge designated in the warrant.

    (B) Warrant Seeking Electronically Stored Information. A warrant under Rule 41(e)(2)(A) may authorize the seizure of electronic storage media or the seizure or copying of electronically stored information. Unless otherwise specified, the warrant authorizes a later review of the media or information consistent with the warrant. The time for executing the warrant in Rule 41(e)(2)(A) and (f)(1)(A) refers to the seizure or on-site copying of the media or information, and not to any later off-site copying or review.

(C) Warrant for a Tracking Device. A tracking-device warrant must identify the person or property to be tracked, designate the magistrate judge to whom it must be returned, and specify a reasonable length of time that the device may be used. The time must not exceed 45 days from the date the warrant was issued. The court may, for good cause, grant one or more extensions for a reasonable period not to exceed 45 days each. The warrant must command the officer to:

  (i) complete any installation authorized by the warrant within a specific time no longer than 10 calendar days;

  (ii) perform any installation authorized by the warrant during the daytime, unless the judge for good cause expressly authorizes installation at another time; and

  (iii) return the warrant to the judge designated in the warrant.

(3) Warrant by Telephonic or Other Means. If a magistrate judge decides to proceed under Rule 41(d)(3)(A), the following additional procedures apply:

  (A) Preparing a Proposed Duplicate Original Warrant. The applicant must prepare a "proposed duplicate original warrant" and must read or otherwise transmit the contents of that document verbatim to the magistrate judge.

  (B) Preparing an Original Warrant. If the applicant reads the contents of the proposed duplicate original warrant, the magistrate judge must enter those contents into an original warrant. If the applicant transmits the contents by reliable electronic means, that transmission may serve as the original warrant.

  (C) Modifications. The magistrate judge may modify the original warrant. The judge must transmit any modified warrant to the applicant by reliable electronic means under Rule 41(e)(3)(D) or direct the applicant to modify the proposed duplicate original warrant accordingly.

  (D) Signing the Warrant. Upon determining to issue the warrant, the magistrate judge must immediately sign the original warrant, enter on its face the exact time it is issued, and transmit it by reliable electronic means to the applicant or direct the applicant to sign the judge's name on the duplicate original warrant.

(f) Executing and Returning the Warrant.

  (1) Warrant to Search for and Seize a Person or Property.

  (A) Noting the Time. The officer executing the warrant must enter on its face the exact date and time it is executed.

  (B) Inventory. An officer present during the execution of the warrant must prepare and verify an inventory of any property seized. The officer must do so in the presence of another officer and the person from whom, or from whose premises, the property was taken. If either one is not present, the officer must prepare and verify the inventory in the presence of at least one other credible person. In a case involving the seizure of electronically stored information, the inventory may be limited to describing the physical storage media that were seized or copied. The officer may retain a copy of the electronically stored information that was seized or copied.

  (C) Receipt. The officer executing the warrant must give a copy of the warrant and a receipt for the property taken to the person from whom, or from whose premises, the property was taken or leave a copy of the warrant and receipt at the place where the officer took the property.

  (D) Return. The officer executing the warrant must promptly return it—together with a copy of the inventory—to the magistrate judge designated on the warrant. The judge must, on request, give a copy of the inventory to the person from whom, or from whose premises, the property was taken and to the applicant for the warrant.

(2) Warrant for a Tracking Device.

(A) Noting the Time. The officer executing a tracking-device warrant must enter on it the exact date and time the device was installed and the period during which it was used.

(B) Return. Within 10 calendar days after the use of the tracking device has ended, the officer executing the warrant must return it to the judge designated in the warrant.

(C) Service. Within 10 calendar days after the use of the tracking device has ended, the officer executing a tracking-device warrant must serve a copy of the warrant on the person who was tracked or whose property was tracked. Service may be accomplished by delivering a copy to the person who, or whose property, was tracked; or by leaving a copy at the person's residence or usual place of abode with an individual of suitable age and discretion who resides at that location and by mailing a copy to the person's last known address. Upon request of the government, the judge may delay notice as provided in Rule 41(f)(3).

(3) Delayed Notice. Upon the government's request, a magistrate judge—or if authorized by Rule 41(b), a judge of a state court of record—may delay any notice required by this rule if the delay is authorized by statute.

[paragraphs g, h, and i have not been included here]

The laws of each state similarly designate those law enforcement agencies within the state that may exercise the powers of arrest and search and seizure and set forth the manner in which that power may be exercised.

Consider the following cases, which involve applications for search warrants in circumstances where the evidence is on the computer:

People v. Ulloa

101 CAL. APP. 4TH 1000 (2002)

COURT OF APPEAL OF CALIFORNIA, 4TH APPELLATE DISTRICT

OPINION BY HOLLENHORST, Acting P.J.

Defendant's primary contention on appeal is that the trial court erred in admitting into evidence America Online (AOL) instant messages seized from his home computer.

2. THE ADMISSION OF THE AOL INSTANT MESSAGES INTO EVIDENCE

Defendant contends the trial court erred in admitting the AOL instant messages into evidence because the messages were taken from a computer seized from his home. He argues the evidence should have been suppressed because the search warrant was unconstitutionally broad and because the warrant was not supported by an affidavit which established the requisite probable cause.

Defendant argues that the warrant was constitutionally overbroad. He specifically objects to portions of the warrant which authorized the seizure of "Photographs which depict actual or simulated sexual acts between human beings" (item 2), "Video Tapes and or [*sic*] movies which depict actual or simulated sexual acts between human beings" (item 3) and "computers [etc.] containing any of the items noted above" (item 11).

Defendant argues that the Fourth Amendment's particularity requirement was not met because these categories authorized a general search for incriminating materials rather than a specific limited search. "General warrants of course, are prohibited by the Fourth Amendment. 'The problem [posed by the general warrant] is not that of intrusion per se, but of a general, exploratory rummaging in a person's belongings.... [The Fourth Amendment addresses the problem] by requiring a "particular description" of the things to be seized.' This requirement "'makes general searches ... impossible and prevents the seizure of one thing under a warrant describing another. As to what is to be taken, nothing is left to the discretion of the officer executing the warrant."' [Citations.]" (*Andresen v. Maryland* (1976) 427 U.S. 463, 480 [96 S.Ct. 2737, 49 L. Ed. 2d 627].)

After independent review (*People v. Kraft* (2000) 23 Cal. 4th 978, 1036 [99 Cal. Rptr. 2d 1, 5 P.3d 68]), we conclude that the particularity requirement was met, i.e., the warrant sufficiently describes the items to be seized. The descriptions in items 2 and 3, *ante*, are sufficiently detailed to instruct the officers what to search for, and what to seize, i.e., depiction of actual or simulated sexual acts between human beings. The return to the warrant states that miscellaneous photographs were seized but the record does not indicate whether they fell within the item 2 description or not. No videotapes or movies are listed as seized on the return to the warrant.

A more serious issue is presented by the breadth requirement. As noted above, that requirement ties the probable cause stated in the affidavit to the items seized. Since the crimes under investigation were oral copulation and sodomy with a minor, defendant argues that the warrant sought evidence which had nothing to do with those crimes, and was therefore overbroad.

We first observe that there is no requirement that each item seized be supported by probable cause. Indeed, "searching officers may seize items not listed in the warrant, provided such items are in plain view while the officers are lawfully in the location where they are searching and the incriminating character of the items is immediately apparent." (*People v. Kraft, supra*, 23 Cal. 4th 978, 1049.)

Kraft points out another deficiency in defendant's argument: None of the photographs seized were introduced against him at trial. Thus, even if the descriptions of items 2 and 3 were overbroad, the photographs seized pursuant to those descriptions were not used, and there was no resulting trial error.

The only records derived from the search that were admitted at trial were transcripts of the AOL instant messages taken from defendant's home computer. The affidavit for the search warrant states that the officers had been told that defendant had been communicating with the minor through AOL's instant messaging service. The officers and the trial court could reasonably conclude that examination of defendant's computer would either confirm or dispel the allegations of a relationship between defendant and the minor. The seizure of all computers at defendant's home was thus likely to produce relevant information.

The warrant authorizes seizure of any computers, and subsequent search of those computers to discover "any of the items noted above." (Items 11 & 12.) The items noted above include "Correspondence which appears to relate to the exploitation of children."

(Item 9.) Thus, the officers were specifically authorized to seize any computers found in the home, and to search the seized computers to obtain such evidence.[*] Since the AOL instant messages fall within the correspondence category, we find no merit to defendant's argument that the AOL instant messages should have been suppressed, and should not have been introduced into evidence.

We therefore conclude that the particularity and overbreadth objections were directed at categories of potential evidence which were not used at trial. The only evidence used at trial was the AOL instant messages, and that evidence was properly authorized to be seized by the search warrant.

In a closely related argument, defendant contends that there is no information in the search warrant affidavit to support the conclusion that incriminating evidence would be found at defendant's home. Specifically, the argument boils down to the contention that the officers did not actually know that defendant had a home computer containing incriminating evidence.

But home computers are now common, and the officers had specific information that defendant had been communicating with the minor by computer. It was reasonable to assume that the computer would contain relevant incriminating information, and that the computer would be located in defendant's home. If defendant did not have a computer, there would be nothing to seize. The situation is the same as the designation of a diary (item 7). The officers did not know if defendant had a diary or not, but they were authorized to seize a diary if one was found during the search. In other words, the statute does not differentiate between things to be searched and things to be searched for.

As noted above, our Supreme Court has rejected the contention that there must be a precise correlation between the items in the warrant and the probable cause declarations in the affidavit. Instead, it is well settled that "the task of the issuing magistrate is simply to make a practical, commonsense decision whether, given all the circumstances set forth in the affidavit before him, including the 'veracity' and 'basis of knowledge' of persons supplying hearsay information, there is a fair probability that contraband or evidence of a crime will be found in a particular place. And the duty of a reviewing court is simply to ensure that the magistrate had a 'substantial basis for … concluding' that probable cause existed." (*Illinois v. Gates* (1983) 462 U.S. 213, 238–239) That test is satisfied here because the officers were informed that defendant and the minor communicated by using AOL's instant messaging service. Accordingly, there was a fair probability that evidence of a crime would be found in defendant's computer. The evidence, which was found to be intensely personal communications with the minor on AOL's instant messaging service, tended to confirm the existence of a sexual relationship between defendant and the minor, thus directly casting doubt on defendant's assertion that no such relationship existed. We therefore conclude that the trial court correctly denied defendant's motion to suppress AOL instant messages seized from

---

[*] Defendant does not argue that a warrant for the seizure of the entire computer system is overbroad. Federal courts have rejected such an argument because the only physical way to search a computer system for evidence is to seize the whole system. (*U.S. v. Hay* (9th Cir. 2000) 231 F.3d 630, 637. See also *Guest v. Leis* (6th Cir. 2001) 255 F.3d 325, 337 ["[A] seizure of the whole computer system was not unreasonable, so long as there was probable cause to conclude that evidence of a crime would be found on the computer"]; *Mahlberg v. Mentzer* (8th Cir. 1992) 968 F.2d 772 [seizure of computer equipment, programs, and disks not listed in warrant].)

defendant's home computer. There is no merit in defendant's argument that the evidence should have been suppressed because the officers did not know if defendant actually had a home computer or not.

United States v. Hill

459 F.3D 996 (2006)

U.S. COURT OF APPEALS, NINTH CIRCUIT

OPINION: FISHER, Circuit Judge.

Justin Hill conditionally pled guilty to possession of child pornography subject to his challenge to the admission of evidence that he contends was seized in violation of the Fourth Amendment. His appeal involves the validity of a warrant to search his computer and storage media for evidence that he possessed pornographic (i.e., lascivious) images of children. We must also decide whether it was reasonable under the Fourth Amendment for the police to take all of Hill's computer storage media from his home (they did not find his computer) so they could conduct their search offsite in a police laboratory, rather than carrying out the search onsite and taking only whatever evidence of child pornography they might find. As we recently discussed in *United States v. Adjani*, 452 F.3d 1140, 2006 WL 1889946 (9th Cir. July 11, 2006), because computers typically contain so much information beyond the scope of the criminal investigation, computer-related searches can raise difficult Fourth Amendment issues different from those encountered when searching paper files. [W]e affirm the district court's denial of the defendant's motion to suppress evidence.

Background

As the district court explained:

A computer technician was repairing defendant's computer when she discovered what she believed to be child pornography. She called Long Beach police, and the detective who took the call obtained a search warrant from a judge of the Long Beach Superior Court. The warrant authorized a search of the computer repair store and seizure of the computer, any work orders relating to the computer, "all storage media belonging to either the computer or the individual identifying himself as defendant at the location," and "all sexually explicit images depicting minors contained in the storage media." By the time the detective arrived at the store to execute the warrant, defendant had picked up his computer.... [T]he detective [submitted an affidavit, which included the computer technician's sworn statement describing the images. On the basis of this affidavit, the officer obtained] a second warrant, this one directed at defendant's home, authorizing seizure of the same items.

The affidavit on which the warrants were based described "two images of child pornography":

Image 1

Is a color picture of a female, white, approximately 15 years old, with long dark brown hair. The female is in a room standing between a couch and a coffee table. There is a framed picture on the wall above the couch. She is wearing only a long blouse and pair of socks. The blouse is open and she is exposing her breast and pubic area to the camera, which she is facing while leaning to her left.

Image 2

Is a color picture of a [*sic* in affidavit] two females, white, approximately 7–9 years of age, both with dirty blond hair. These females are standing on a beach during the daytime. The shorter of the two females is standing to the right of the picture while the other female is standing behind her. Both females are facing the camera askew and wearing only a robe, which is open exposing the undeveloped breast and pubic area of both girls. They both are turning their faces away from the camera preventing the viewer from seeing their faces.

Officers executed the search warrant but did not find the computer in defendant's apartment. In what appeared to be defendant's bedroom, they found and seized computer storage media[, specifically: 22 5.25-inch floppy disks, two CD-ROMs, 124 3.5-inch floppy disks and six zip disks.] [Two of the zip disks] were eventually determined to contain images of child pornography; [officers] also seized other evidence consistent with the warrant. Defendant was subsequently charged with one count of possession of child pornography, in violation of 18 U.S.C. § 2252A(a)(5)(B).

Hill, 322 F.Supp.2d at 1083–84 (alterations in original).

Discussion

A. Probable Cause

The defendant argues first that the affidavit submitted in support of the search warrant was insufficient to establish probable cause to believe the defendant was guilty of criminal activity. We do not agree.

Child pornography is a particularly repulsive crime, but not all images of nude children are pornographic. For example, "a family snapshot of a nude child bathing presumably would not" be criminal. *Hill*, 322 F.Supp.2d at 1086. Moreover, the law recognizes that some images of nudity may merit First Amendment protection because they serve artistic or other purposes, and possessing those images cannot be criminal. Images depicting "minor[s] engag[ed] in sexually explicit conduct" are, however, prohibited. 18 U.S.C. § 2256(8)(A). "[S]exually explicit conduct," in turn, is defined to include "graphic or simulated lascivious exhibition of the genitals or pubic area of any person." 18 U.S.C. § 2256(2)(A)(v).

Based on our independent review of the affidavit describing the two images, we are satisfied that the state judge's finding of probable cause was well within his discretion. There was a fair probability that the images were "so presented by the photographer as to arouse or satisfy the sexual cravings of a voyeur." *Wiegand*, 812 F.3d at 1244. The affidavit described in some detail the images of three partially nude children, who were provocatively and unnaturally dressed in light of the photographs' settings. The girls' clothing was opened so as to reveal their breasts and pubic areas, with the girls appearing in sexually suggestive poses. Moreover the descriptions themselves did not raise doubts that the images served some purpose other than that proscribed in *Wiegand*. The affidavit was sufficient to create "a substantial basis for concluding that probable cause existed" to believe that evidence of a violation of 18 U.S.C. § 2252A(a)(5)(B) could be found on the defendant's computer.

B. Overbreadth

1. Seizure of All Computer Media

The defendant argues that the search warrant was overbroad because it authorized the officers to seize and remove from his home his computer and storage media without first determining whether they actually contained child pornography. Given the nature of computers and storage media, this argument sweeps too broadly, as the district court explained in addressing the defendant's suggested limitations on the nature and scope of the search:

Search warrants must be specific. "Specificity has two aspects: particularity and breadth. Particularity is the requirement that the warrant must clearly state what is sought. Breadth deals with the requirement that the scope of the warrant be limited by the probable cause on which the warrant is based." *United States v. Towne*, 997 F.2d 537, 544 (9th Cir. 1993). A warrant describing a category of items is not invalid if a more specific description is impossible. The level of specificity required "varies depending on the circumstances of the case and the type of items involved."

The warrant here commanded the officers to search for and seize: "1) An IBM 'clone' medium tower personal computer … 3) All storage media belonging to either item # 1 or the individual identifying himself as defendant at the location. 4) All sexually explicit images depicting minors contained in item # 3."

Defendant argues the warrant was overbroad because it authorized seizure of storage media whether or not they contained child pornography. He suggests it should have authorized seizure only of media containing child pornography. But it is impossible to tell what a computer storage medium contains just by looking at it. Rather, one has to examine it electronically, using a computer that is running the appropriate operating system, hardware and software. The police had no assurance they would find such a computer at the scene—nor did they, for that matter—or that, if they found one, they could bypass any security measures and operate it.

Defendant suggests that the police could have brought their own laptop computer: Having probable cause to seize only computer storage media that contained certain types of files, the police should have been required to bring with them the equipment necessary to separate the sheep from the goats. Defendant's argument raises an important question about how police must execute seizures pursuant to a warrant. Because seizable materials are seldom found neatly separated from their non-seizable counterparts, how much separating must police do at the scene to avoid taking items that are neither contraband nor evidence of criminal activity?

As always under the Fourth Amendment, the standard is reasonableness. To take an extreme example, if police have probable cause to seize business records, the warrant could not authorize seizure of every piece of paper on the premises on the theory that the police conducting the search might not know how to read….

[T]he court concludes that the police were not required to bring with them equipment capable of reading computer storage media and an officer competent to operate it. Doing so would have posed significant technical problems and made the search more intrusive. To ensure that they could access any electronic storage medium they might find at the scene, police would have needed far more than an ordinary laptop computer. Because computers in common use run a variety of operating systems—various versions or flavors of Windows, Mac OS and Linux, to name only the most common—police would have had to bring with them a computer (or computers) equipped to read not only all of the major media types, but also files encoded by all major operating systems. Because operating systems, media types, file systems and file types are continually evolving, police departments would frequently have to modify their computers to keep them up-to-date. This would not be an insuperable obstacle for larger police departments and federal law enforcement agencies, but it would pose a significant burden on smaller agencies.

Even if the police were to bring with them a properly equipped computer, and someone competent to operate it, using it would pose two significant problems. First, there is a serious risk that the police might damage the storage medium or compromise the integrity of the evidence by attempting to access the data at the scene. As everyone who has accidentally erased a computer file knows, it is fairly easy to make mistakes when operating computer equipment, especially equipment one is not intimately familiar with. The risk that the officer trying to read the suspect's storage medium on the police laptop will make a wrong move and erase what is on the disk is not trivial. Even if the officer executes his task flawlessly, there might be a power failure or equipment malfunction that could affect the contents of the medium being searched. For that reason, experts will make a back-up copy of the medium before they start manipulating its contents. Various other technical problems might arise; without the necessary tools and expertise to deal with them, any effort to read computer files at the scene is fraught with difficulty and risk.

Second, the process of searching the files at the scene can take a long time. To be certain that the medium in question does not contain any seizable material, the officers would have to examine every one of what may be thousands of files on a disk—a process that could take many hours and perhaps days. Taking that much time to conduct the search would not only impose a significant and unjustified burden on police resources, it would also make the search more intrusive. Police would have to be present on the suspect's premises while the search was in progress, and this would necessarily interfere with the suspect's access to his home or business. If the search took hours or days, the intrusion would continue for that entire period, compromising the Fourth Amendment value of making police searches as brief and non-intrusive as possible.

Hill, 322 F.Supp.2d at 1087–89.

We agree with the district court that under the circumstances here, the warrant was not fatally defective in failing to require an onsite search and isolation of child pornography before removing storage media wholesale. That does not mean, however, that the government has an automatic blank check when seeking or executing warrants in computer-related searches. Although computer technology may in theory justify blanket seizures for the reasons discussed above, the government must still demonstrate to the magistrate factually why such a broad search and seizure authority is reasonable in the case at hand. There may well be situations where the government has no basis for believing that a computer search would involve the kind of technological problems that would make an immediate onsite search and selective removal of relevant evidence impracticable. Thus, there must be some threshold showing before the government may "seize the haystack to look for the needle."

Our cases illustrate this principle. In *United States v. Hay*, for example, we held permissible a "generic classification" authorizing seizure of an "entire computer system and virtually every document in [the defendant's] possession without referencing child pornography or any particular offense conduct" because, although officers "knew that [a party] had sent 19 images [of child pornography] directly to [the defendant's] computer, [they] had no way of knowing where the images were stored." 231 F.3d 630, 637 (9th Cir. 2000). Similarly *United States v. Lacy* allowed "blanket seizure" of the defendant's "entire computer system." 119 F.3d 742, 746 (9th Cir. 1997). We reasoned that "no more specific description of the computer equipment sought was possible," because the agents "did not know whether the images were stored on the hard drive or on one or more of [the defendant's] many computer disks." Id. Significantly, in both *Hay* and *Lacy* we carefully noted the critical role played by the officers' affidavits supporting the warrants. See *Hay*, 231 F.3d at 637 ("[T]he affidavit explained why it was necessary to seize the entire computer system in order to examine the electronic data for contraband. It also justified taking the entire system off site because of the time, expertise, and controlled environment required for a proper analysis."); *Lacy*, 119 F.3d at 746–47 ("In the affidavit supporting the search warrant application, a Customs agent explained there was no way to specify what hardware and software had to be seized to retrieve the images accurately."). By contrast, although the warrant in this case authorized a wholesale seizure, the supporting affidavit did not explain why such a seizure was necessary. See *United States v. Adjani*, 452 F.3d at 1149, n7 (noting favorably an affidavit's computer search and seizure protocol explaining when a computer had to be searched offsite, because "[s]uch specificity increases our confidence that the magistrate judge was well aware of what he was authorizing and that the agents knew the bounds of their authority in executing the search"); U.S. Dep't of Justice, *Searching and Seizing Computers and Obtaining Electronic Evidence in Criminal Investigations* 43, 69 (July 2002) (recommending that "if agents expect that they may need to seize a personal computer and search it off-site to recover the relevant evidence, the affidavit should explain this expectation and its basis to the magistrate judge. The affidavit should inform the court of the practical limitations of conducting an on-site search, and should articulate the plan to remove the entire computer from the site if it becomes necessary."); cf. *United States v. Tamura*, 694 F.2d 591, 596 (9th Cir. 1982) ("If the need for transporting the documents is known to the officers prior to the search, they may apply for specific authorization for large-scale removal of material, which should be granted by the magistrate issuing the warrant only where on site sorting is infeasible and no other practical alternative exists.").

We do not approve of issuing warrants authorizing blanket removal of all computer storage media for later examination when there is no affidavit giving a reasonable explanation, such as that provided in *Hay* and *Lacy*, as to why a wholesale seizure is necessary. See *Tamura*, 694 F.2d at 595 ("[T]he wholesale seizure for later detailed examination of records not described in a warrant is significantly more intrusive, and has been characterized as 'the kind of investigatory dragnet that the fourth amendment was designed to prevent'" (quoting *United States v. Abrams*, 615 F.2d 541, 543 (1st Cir. 1980))). Without such individualized justification being presented to the magistrate, we cannot be sure that the judge was aware of the officers' intent and the technological limitations meriting the indiscriminate seizure—and thus was intelligently able to exercise the court's oversight function. An explanatory statement in the affidavit also assures us that the officers could not reasonably describe the objects of their search with more specificity. Accordingly, we hold that the warrant here was overbroad in authorizing a blanket seizure in the absence of an explanatory supporting affidavit, which would have documented the informed endorsement of the neutral magistrate.

Nonetheless, as in *Tamura*, we conclude that suppression of the evidence of child pornography found on the defendant's seized zip disks is not an appropriate remedy. *Tamura* involved an indiscriminate seizure of all files found in an office even though the warrant authorized the officers to search for only three categories of records for evidence of various alleged crimes. Although we refused to sanction the "wholesale seizure for later detailed examination of records not described in a warrant," id. at 595, we held that "the exclusionary rule does not require the suppression of evidence within the scope of a warrant simply because other items outside the scope of the warrant were unlawfully taken as well," id. at 597.

Similarly, the pornographic images from the defendant's zip disks that he sought to exclude as evidence at trial was "seized and retained lawfully because described in and therefore taken pursuant to the valid search warrant." Id. As we have discussed above, the officers' wholesale seizure was flawed here because they failed to justify it to the magistrate, not because they acted unreasonably or improperly in executing the warrant. Because the officers were "motivated by considerations of practicality rather than by a desire to engage in indiscriminate 'fishing,' we cannot say ... that the officers so abused the warrant's authority that the otherwise valid warrant was transformed into a general one, thereby requiring all fruits to be suppressed." Id.

Therefore, we hold that the district court properly admitted the evidence of child pornography found on the defendant's computer storage media notwithstanding the lack of a sufficiently detailed supporting affidavit describing the need for wholesale seizure of such media.

2. Absence of Search Protocol

The defendant also argues that the search warrant was overbroad because it did not include a search protocol to limit the officers' discretion as to what they could examine when searching the defendant's computer media, nor did the affidavit explain why such a protocol was unnecessary. We, like the district court, find no error in the search warrant on this ground and adopt the district court's analysis:

Defendant also argues that the warrant was overbroad because it did not define a "search methodology." He claims that the search should have been limited to certain files that are more likely to be associated with child pornography, such as those with a ".jpg" suffix (which usually identifies files containing images) or those containing the word "sex" or other key words.

Defendant's proposed search methodology is unreasonable.

"Computer records are extremely susceptible to tampering, hiding, or destruction, whether deliberate or inadvertent." *United States v. Hunter*, 13 F.Supp.2d 574, 583 (D.Vt. 1998). Images can be hidden in all manner of files, even word processing documents and spreadsheets. Criminals will do all they can to conceal contraband, including the simple expedient of changing the names and extensions of files to disguise their content from the casual observer.

Forcing police to limit their searches to files that the suspect has labeled in a particular way would be much like saying police may not seize a plastic bag containing a powdery white substance if it is labeled "flour" or "talcum powder." There is no way to know what is in a file without examining its contents, just as there is no sure way of separating talcum from cocaine except by testing it. The ease with which child pornography images can be disguised—whether by renaming sexyteenyboppersxxx.jpg as sundayschoollesson.doc, or something more sophisticated—forecloses defendant's proposed search methodology.

Hill, 322 F.Supp.2d at 1090–1091; see also Adjani, 452 F.3d at 1149.

Moreover, in contrast to our discussion of the overbroad seizure claim above, there is no case law holding that an officer must justify the lack of a search protocol in order to support issuance of the warrant. As we have noted, we look favorably upon the inclusion of a search protocol; but its absence is not fatal. We have also held that even though a warrant authorizing a computer search might not contain a search protocol restricting the search to certain programs or file names, the officer is always "limited by the longstanding principle that a duly issued warrant, even one with a thorough affidavit, may not be used to engage in a general, exploratory search." Id. The reasonableness of the officer's acts both in executing the warrant and in performing a subsequent search of seized materials remains subject to judicial review.

The following cases consider issues that arise during the execution of computer searches:

United States v. Hunter

---

13 F.SUPP.2D 574 (1998)

U.S. DISTRICT COURT, VERMONT DISTRICT

WILLIAM K. SESSIONS III, District Court Judge.

Defendant William A. Hunter ("Hunter") has filed a motion to suppress the evidence and the fruits thereof obtained from a search of his house at approximately 4 a.m. on June 9, 1995. Hunter challenges the constitutionality of the warrant and its execution on several grounds: (1) the warrant was not supported by probable cause; (2) a nighttime search was unreasonable; (3) the warrant was impermissibly overbroad; and (4) the warrant was executed improperly. For the reasons that follow, Hunter's motion is denied.

In early 1995, agents of the Drug Enforcement Administration ("DEA") conducted an investigation into the illegal drug activities of Frank Sargent. During the course of their investigation, agents spoke with a confidential source who stated that she was aware of a meeting among Sargent, Gloria Radcliffe, and Sargent's lawyer, William A. Hunter. The source told the investigators that Hunter laundered money for Sargent, and that the purpose of the meeting was to collect a drug debt from Radcliffe.

On June 8, 1995, DEA agents arrested Sargent and his sister Lazzell Merrill on drug charges. Both Sargent and Merrill agreed to cooperate with the government. On the evening of June 8, Sargent told the agents that Hunter was aware of Sargent's drug activities and that Connecticut Realty Trust ("CRT"), a corporation managed by Hunter, was used to launder proceeds of drug transactions. He said that Hunter invested money with him and that Hunter knew Sargent used the funds to buy drugs. He stated that in fact Hunter had given him $15,000.00 that day, for which Sargent provided a receipt. Sargent also stated that Hunter kept CRT's records at his law office located at his residence.

The agents applied for a warrant to search Hunter's residence and law office that same evening. They requested authorization to search for documents and records pertaining to specific individuals, business entities and real estate, and to seize all computers, computer storage devices and software for search at a later date by FBI computer experts. They also requested authorization for an immediate search, based on concern that evidence might be destroyed once it was learned that Sargent and Merrill had been arrested.

To minimize invasion of materials protected by attorney-client privilege, lawyers within the United States Attorney's Office designed a protocol for execution of the warrant. Two agents from the United States Customs Service were to handle the search in the presence of an Assistant United States Attorney ("AUSA"). None of these individuals were to have had any previous involvement in the investigation. The AUSA was to be present to resolve any questions about whether an item was subject to seizure. No law enforcement personnel other than the search team and the AUSA were to be inside the premises during the search.

Magistrate Judge Jerome J. Niedermeier signed the warrant at 12:59 a.m. The search team, accompanied by three DEA agents, arrived at the Hunter residence at approximately 4:00 a.m. They knocked, identified themselves to Hunter and presented the warrant. One Customs agent and one DEA agent conducted a security sweep of the house, checking each room of the house by flashlight. Following the security sweep Hunter assisted the agents in searching his basement law office. The dining room area also was searched. Hunter collected the specific files sought and handed them over to one of the Customs agents. The search team also seized checks and check registers, three computers and numerous computer disks.

Although the protocol specified that no DEA agents would be present during the search, it is undisputed that in fact DEA agents were inside the house during the search. Two DEA agents questioned Hunter about his knowledge of the matter under investigation. The search term and the AUSA were not shown a copy of the protocol and were unaware of the restriction on DEA's presence. Government witnesses testified that the DEA agents were on the premises to provide security only, and that they did not participate in the search. They admitted that DEA agent Thomas Doud activated one of Hunter's computers, at the direction of AUSA Gregory Waples, in order to download some files unrelated to the investigation that Hunter needed for his work.

According to the defense, the DEA agents were much more actively involved in the search. Hunter testified that a DEA agent questioned him about the location of an item he wanted to seize; that a DEA agent decided whether a particular computer was going to be seized; and that a DEA agent seized a quantity of computer disks in the course of the search.

[The court concluded that probable cause existed for the search of the home, as evidence established that Hunter's law office was in the home, and for a nighttime search. The court then considered Hunter's contention that the affidavits failed to provide probable cause to search his computers, disks, and similar property—that there is no indication in the affidavits that computers were present or that records sought were maintained on computers.]

Today, computers and computer disks store most of the records and data belonging to businesses and attorneys. Probable cause existed to search for and seize the computer-related property because probable cause existed to search for the records concerning the individuals and entities listed in the other sections of the attachment. See *United States v Gawrysiak*, 972 F.Supp. 853, 861 (DNJ 1997) (approving warrant to search business office; government need not know the exact "form that records may take"). A finding of probable cause is not predicated on the government's knowing precisely how certain records are stored.

Hunter contends that the warrant's authorization to seize all computer hardware and software and documentation violated the Fourth Amendment's particularity requirement. The seizure of computer equipment is vulnerable to a particularity challenge. Computers store vast numbers of records, and access [to] them cannot be obtained with the same ease as examining file folders in an office. Computer records are extremely susceptible to tampering, hiding, or destruction, whether deliberate or inadvertent. Often it is impractical to search a computer at the search site because of time and expertise required to unlock all sources of information.

The wholesale removal of computer equipment can undoubtedly disable a business or professional practice and disrupt personal lives, and should be avoided when possible. Still, until technology and law enforcement expertise render on-site computer records searching both possible and practical, the government should copy and return the equipment as soon as possible. See *Steve Jackson Games, Inc. v United States Secret Serv.*, 816 F.Supp. 432, 437 (W.D. Tex. 1993) (owner of electronic bulletin board had computers and disks seized; court found no valid reason why information sought could not be copied and equipment returned within hours), aff'd 36 F.3d 457 (5th Cir. 1994).

[T]he warrant itself was defectively composed. Attachment C described the property to be searched. Computer disks were included in the illustrative list for Sections II and III; those disks were appropriately particularized. All other computers and related equipment, however, were listed in Section IV, without limitation and without reference to the limitations in other sections. Section IV did not indicate the specific crimes for which the equipment was sought, nor were supporting affidavits or the limits contained in the searching instructions incorporated by reference.

To withstand an overbreadth challenge, the search warrant itself, or materials incorporated by reference, must have specified the purpose for which the computers were seized and delineated the limits of their subsequent search. Section IV was insufficiently particularized, and all computer equipment and disks seized under that paragraph were taken in violation of the Fourth Amendment's particularity requirement.

[The court concluded, however, that the computers were seized in good faith—that the government agents and attorneys devised a comprehensive plan for the search and seizure, drafting instructions for those officers who would conduct the search and for the FBI analysts.] The instructions and the evidence before the Court are convincing proof of the government's intention to search computers and storage devices only for the records as particularized in the first three sections of Attachment C. There is no indication that the government in fact sought the wholesale seizure of computer equipment so that every file could be scrutinized for evidence of any violation of the law. [Although Section IV was impermissibly broad, [s]uppression of any evidence obtained pursuant to Section IV of Attachment C is not warranted.]

For the foregoing reasons, Hunter's Motion to Suppress Evidence Seized June 9, 1995 and Any Fruits Thereof (Paper 47) is DENIED.

United States v. Carey, which is discussed in Chapter 8, and the following case consider whether officers conducting a search pursuant to a warrant exceeded the scope of the warrant:

United States v. Campos

221 F.3D 1143 (2000)

U.S. Court of Appeals, Tenth Circuit

HENRY, Circuit Judge.

Terry Joe Lee Campos appeals his conviction following a jury trial for transporting child pornography through interstate commerce via computer, a violation of 18 U.S.C. § 2252(a)(1).

I. BACKGROUND

The government alleged that Mr. Campos transmitted two photographs constituting child pornography from his home in Broken Arrow, Oklahoma, to a resident of Aurora, Illinois (hereafter "the complainant"). The complainant testified at trial that, on the evening of April 16–17, 1997, he participated in a gay and lesbian chat room on America Online (AOL). While in the chat room, he exchanged messages and photographs with several people, including another AOL subscriber who used the screen name "IAMZEUS." After spending two hours in the chat room, the complainant signed off AOL and went to bed.

When he awoke at approximately 4:00 a.m. on April 17, the complainant signed onto AOL again. He discovered that IAMZEUS had sent him electronic mail, including several images of adult male men, and two images of children engaged in sexually explicit conduct. The complainant copied the images of the child pornography to a floppy disk, notified the Federal Bureau of Investigation (FBI), and gave the disk to the special agent who interviewed him.

Law enforcement agents determined that the AOL subscriber who used the name "IAMZEUS" was Mr. Campos, a resident of Broken Arrow, Oklahoma. Based on this information, the FBI obtained a warrant to search Mr. Campos's home and computer. On October 1, 1997, the agents conducted a search of the Broken Arrow residence occupied by Mr. Campos and Lester Hibbs. They discovered a computer in a back room of the house and seized it. In examining the hard drive of the computer, the agents found the two images that had been transmitted to the complainant, six similar images of children engaging in sexually explicit conduct, and a copy of a newspaper article describing the conviction and sentencing of a defendant in Wisconsin federal court for possessing and transporting child pornography.

During the trial, the government presented several witnesses to bolster its contention that it was Mr. Campos who had sent the pornographic images to the complainant. After hearing all the evidence, the jury convicted Mr. Campos. The district court sentenced him to thirty-seven months' imprisonment.

II. DISCUSSION

A. Computer Search

Mr. Campos first argues that the district court erred in denying his motion to suppress the evidence obtained from the search of his residence. According to Mr. Campos, the law enforcement agents who sought the warrant had grounds to search only for the two images that had been sent to the complainant by IAMZEUS. He, therefore, maintains that the warrant authorizing agents to search for other evidence of child pornography was overly broad and that therefore violated the Fourth Amendment.

"The Fourth Amendment requires that a search warrant describe the things to be seized with sufficient particularity to prevent a general exploratory rummaging in a person's belongings." *United States v. Carey*, 172 F.3d 1268, 1271 (10th Cir. 1999). It was adopted in response to the evils of general warrants—those that allow such exploratory rummaging.

Upon review of the record, we are not convinced that the warrant was overly broad. Rather than authorizing an unfocused inspection of all of Mr. Campos's property, the warrant was directed at items relating to child pornography. It authorized the agents to seize computer equipment "which may be, or [is] used to visually depict child pornography, child erotica, information pertaining to the sexual activity with children or the distribution, possession, or receipt of child pornography, child erotica or information pertaining to an interest in child pornography or child erotica." It also authorized the seizure of books, magazines, films, and videos containing images of minors engaged in sexually explicit conduct.

Additionally, the affidavit presented by an FBI agent in support of the warrant provided an explanation of the ways in which computers facilitate the production, communication, distribution, and storage of child pornography. Moreover, the FBI agent provided an explanation as to why it was not usually feasible to search for particular computer files in a person's home:

Computer storage devices … can store the equivalent of thousands of pages of information. Especially when the user wants to conceal criminal evidence, he often stores it in random order with deceptive file names. This requires searching authorities to examine all the stored data to determine whether it is included in the warrant. This sorting process can take weeks or months, depending on the volume of data stored, and it would be impractical to attempt this kind of data search on site; and searching computer systems for criminal evidence is a highly technical process requiring expert skill and a properly controlled environment. The wide variety of computer hardware and software available requires even computer experts to specialize in some systems and applications, so it is difficult to know before a search which expert should analyze the system and its data.… Since computer evidence is extremely vulnerable to tampering or destruction (both from external sources or from destructive code embedded into the system as "booby trap"), the controlled environment of a laboratory is essential to its complete analysis.

We disagree with Mr. Campos that our decision in *United States v. Carey*, 172 F.3d 1268, 1271 (10th Cir. 1999), provides grounds for overturning the search of his computer files. In that case, we did conclude that a police officer violated the Fourth Amendment in conducting a computer search. However, the officer had obtained a warrant to search for computer records pertaining to the distribution of illegal drugs. When the officer inadvertently discovered a pornographic file, he began looking for similar files, thereby expanding the scope of the search without obtaining a second warrant. We characterized this conduct as "an unconstitutional general search." Unlike the officer in *Carey*, the officers here did not expand the scope of their search in a manner not authorized by the warrant.

Nevertheless, our opinion in *Carey* notes several important limitations on the scope of computer searches of which the parties should be aware. In particular, we observed that the storage capacity of computers may require law enforcement officers to take a special approach. Computers often contain "intermingled documents" (i.e., documents containing both relevant and irrelevant information). When law enforcement officers confront such documents a more particularized inquiry may be required:

> Law enforcement must engage in the intermediate step of sorting various types of documents and then only search the ones specified in a warrant. Where officers come across relevant documents so intermingled with irrelevant documents that they cannot feasibly be sorted at the site, the officers may seal or hold the documents pending approval by a magistrate of the conditions and limitations on a further search through the documents. The magistrate should then require officers to specify in a warrant which type of files are sought.

Here, Mr. Campos offered no evidence as to the methods used by the officers in searching through his computer files. As a result, we need not consider whether they followed the approach we outlined in *Carey*. We, therefore, conclude that the district court did not err in denying Mr. Campos's motion to suppress.

Searches and Seizures without a Warrant

Whether or not a combined government employer–law enforcement search is reasonable under the Fourth Amendment is determined under the principles set forth in *O'Connor v. Ortega*, which follows. (We considered the *O'Connor* decision in the previous chapter when discussing the concept of reasonable expectation of privacy. Here we consider only that portion of the decision dealing with the reasonableness of the search. You should refer back to Chapter 8 for the factual background in the case.)

O'Connor v. Ortega

480 U.S. 709 (1987)

U.S. SUPREME COURT

Justice O'CONNOR delivered the Opinion of the Court:

III

Having determined that Dr. Ortega had a reasonable expectation of privacy in his office, we must determine the appropriate standard of reasonableness applicable to the search. A determination of the standard of reasonableness applicable to a particular class of searches requires "[balancing] the nature and quality of the intrusion on the individual's Fourth Amendment interests against the importance of the governmental interests alleged to justify the intrusion." *United States v. Place*, 462 U.S. 696, 703 (1983); *Camara v. Municipal Court*, 387 U.S., at 536–537. In the case of searches conducted by a public employer, we must balance the invasion of the employees' legitimate expectations of privacy against the government's need for supervision, control, and the efficient operation of the workplace.

There is surprisingly little case law on the appropriate Fourth Amendment standard of reasonableness for a public employer's work-related search of its employee's offices, desks, or file cabinets. Generally, however, the lower courts have held that any "work-related" search by an employer satisfies the Fourth Amendment reasonableness requirement.

The legitimate privacy interests of public employees in the private objects they bring to the workplace may be substantial. Against these privacy interests, however, must be balanced the realities of the workplace, which strongly suggest that a warrant requirement would be unworkable. While police, and even administrative enforcement personnel, conduct searches for the primary purpose of obtaining evidence for use in criminal or other enforcement proceedings, employers most frequently need to enter the offices and desks of their employees for legitimate work-related reasons wholly unrelated to illegal conduct. Employers and supervisors are focused primarily on the need to complete the government agency's work in a prompt and efficient manner. An employer may have need for correspondence, or a file or report available only in an employee's office while the employee is away from the office. Or, as is alleged to have been the case here, employers may need to safeguard or identify state property or records in an office in connection with a pending investigation into suspected employee misfeasance.

In our view, requiring an employer to obtain a warrant whenever the employer wished to enter an employee's office, desk, or file cabinets for a work-related purpose would seriously disrupt the routine conduct of business and would be unduly burdensome. Imposing unwieldy warrant procedures in such cases upon supervisors, who would otherwise have no reason to be familiar with such procedures, is simply unreasonable. In contrast to other circumstances in which we have required warrants, supervisors in offices such as at the Hospital are hardly in the business of investigating the violation of criminal laws. Rather, work-related searches are merely incident to the primary business of the agency. Under these circumstances, the imposition of a warrant requirement would conflict with "the common-sense realization that government offices could not function if every employment decision became a constitutional matter." *Connick v. Myers*, 461 U.S. 138, 143 (1983).

Whether probable cause is an inappropriate standard for public employer searches of their employees' offices presents a more difficult issue.

As an initial matter, it is important to recognize the plethora of contexts in which employers will have an occasion to intrude to some extent on an employee's expectation of privacy. Because the parties in this case have alleged that the search was either a noninvestigatory work-related intrusion or an investigatory search for evidence of suspected work-related employee misfeasance, we undertake to determine the appropriate Fourth Amendment standard of reasonableness only for these two types of employer intrusions and leave for another day inquiry into other circumstances.

The governmental interest justifying work-related intrusions by public employers is the efficient and proper operation of the workplace. Government agencies provide myriad services to the public, and the work of these agencies would suffer if employers were required to have probable cause before they entered an employee's desk for the purpose of finding a file or piece of office correspondence. Indeed, it is difficult to give the concept of probable cause, rooted as it is in the criminal investigatory context, much meaning when the purpose of a search is to retrieve a file for work-related reasons. Similarly, the concept of probable cause has little meaning for a routine inventory conducted by public employers for the purpose of securing state property. To ensure the efficient and proper operation of the agency, therefore, public employers must be given wide latitude to enter employee offices for work-related, noninvestigatory reasons.

We come to a similar conclusion for searches conducted pursuant to an investigation of work-related employee misconduct. Even when employers conduct an investigation, they have an interest substantially different from "the normal need for law enforcement." Public employers have an interest in ensuring that their agencies operate in an effective and efficient manner, and the work of these agencies inevitably suffers from the inefficiency, incompetence, mismanagement, or other work-related misfeasance of its employees. Indeed, in many cases, public employees are entrusted with tremendous responsibility, and the consequences of their misconduct or incompetence to both the agency and the public interest can be severe. In contrast to law enforcement officials, therefore, public employers are not enforcers of the criminal law; instead, public employers have a direct and overriding interest in ensuring that the work of the agency is conducted in a proper and efficient manner. In our view, therefore, a probable cause requirement for searches of the type at issue here would impose intolerable burdens on public employers. The delay in correcting the employee misconduct caused by the need for probable cause rather than reasonable suspicion will be translated into tangible and often irreparable damage to the agency's work, and ultimately to the public interest. Additionally, while law enforcement officials are expected to "[school] themselves in the niceties of probable cause," no such expectation is generally applicable to public employers, at least when the search is not used to gather evidence of a criminal offense. It is simply unrealistic to expect supervisors in most government agencies to learn the subtleties of the probable cause standard.

Balanced against the substantial government interests in the efficient and proper operation of the workplace are the privacy interests of government employees in their place of work which, while not insubstantial, are far less than those found at home or in some other contexts. The employee may avoid exposing personal belongings at work by simply leaving them at home.

In sum, we conclude that the "special needs, beyond the normal need for law enforcement make the … probable-cause requirement impracticable," for legitimate work-related, noninvestigatory intrusions as well as investigations of work-related misconduct. A standard of reasonableness will neither unduly burden the efforts of government employers to ensure the efficient and proper operation of the workplace, nor authorize arbitrary intrusions upon the privacy of public employees. We hold, therefore, that public employer intrusions on the constitutionally protected privacy interests of government employees for noninvestigatory, work-related purposes, as well as for investigations of work-related misconduct, should be judged by the standard of reasonableness under all the circumstances. Under this reasonableness standard, both the inception and the scope of the intrusion must be reasonable.

Ordinarily, a search of an employee's office by a supervisor will be "justified at its inception" when there are reasonable grounds for suspecting that the search will turn up evidence that the employee is guilty of work-related misconduct, or that the search is necessary for a noninvestigatory work-related purpose such as to retrieve a needed file. Because petitioners had an "individualized suspicion" of misconduct by Dr. Ortega, we need not decide whether individualized suspicion is an essential element of the standard of reasonableness that we adopt today. The search will be permissible in its scope when "the measures adopted are reasonably related to the objectives of the search and not excessively intrusive in light of ... the nature of the [misconduct]."

Accordingly, the judgment of the Court of Appeals is reversed, and the case is remanded to that court for further proceedings consistent with this opinion.

JUSTICE SCALIA, concurring in the judgment.

Although I share the judgment that this case must be reversed and remanded, I disagree with the reason for the reversal given by the plurality opinion, and with the standard it prescribes for the Fourth Amendment inquiry.

To address the latter point first: The plurality opinion instructs the lower courts that existence of Fourth Amendment protection for a public employee's business office is to be assessed "on a case-by-case basis," in light of whether the office is "so open to fellow employees or the public that no expectation of privacy is reasonable." No clue is provided as to how open "so open" must be; much less is it suggested how police officers are to gather the facts necessary for this refined inquiry.

Whatever the plurality's standard means, however, it must be wrong if it leads to the conclusion on the present facts that if Hospital officials had extensive "work-related reasons to enter Dr. Ortega's office" no Fourth Amendment protection existed. It is privacy that is protected by the Fourth Amendment, not solitude. A man enjoys Fourth Amendment protection in his home, for example, even though his wife and children have the run of the place—and indeed, even though his landlord has the right to conduct unannounced inspections at any time. Similarly, in my view, one's personal office is constitutionally protected against warrantless intrusions by the police, even though employer and co-workers are not excluded. Just as the secretary working for a corporation in an office frequently entered by the corporation's other employees is protected against unreasonable searches of that office by the government, so also is the government secretary working in an office frequently entered by other government employees. There is no reason why this determination that a legitimate expectation of privacy exists should be affected by the fact that the government, rather than a private entity, is the employer. Constitutional protection against unreasonable searches by the government does not disappear merely because the government has the right to make reasonable intrusions in its capacity as employer.

I cannot agree, moreover, with the plurality's view that the reasonableness of the expectation of privacy (and thus the existence of Fourth Amendment protection) changes "when an intrusion is by a supervisor rather than a law enforcement official." The identity of the searcher (police v. employer) is relevant not to whether Fourth Amendment protections apply, but only to whether the search of a protected area is reasonable. Pursuant to traditional analysis the former question must be answered on a more "global" basis. Where, for example, a fireman enters a private dwelling in response to an alarm, we do not ask whether the occupant has a reasonable expectation of privacy (and hence Fourth Amendment protection) vis-à-vis firemen, but rather whether—given the fact that the Fourth Amendment covers private dwellings—intrusion for the purpose of extinguishing a fire is reasonable. A similar analysis is appropriate here.

I would hold, therefore, that the offices of government employees, and *a fortiori* the drawers and files within those offices, are covered by Fourth Amendment protections as a general matter. Since it is unquestioned that the office here was assigned to Dr. Ortega, and since no special circumstances are suggested that would call for an exception to the ordinary rule, I would agree with the District Court and the Court of Appeals that Fourth Amendment protections applied.

The case turns, therefore, on whether the Fourth Amendment was violated—i.e., whether the governmental intrusion was reasonable. It is here that the government's status as employer, and the employment-related character of the search, become relevant. While as a general rule warrantless searches are per se unreasonable, we have recognized exceptions when "special needs, beyond the normal need for law enforcement, make the warrant and probable-cause requirement impracticable...." *New Jersey v. T. L. O.*, 469 U.S. 325, 351 (BLACKMUN, J., concurring in judgment). Such "special needs" are present in the context of government employment. The government, like any other employer, needs frequent and convenient access to its desks, offices, and file cabinets for work-related purposes. I would hold that government searches to retrieve work-related materials or to investigate violations of workplace rules—searches of the sort that are regarded as reasonable and normal in the private-employer context—do not violate the Fourth Amendment.

Because the conflicting and incomplete evidence in the present case could not conceivably support summary judgment that the search did not have such a validating purpose, I agree with the plurality that the decision must be reversed and remanded.

The following case is another government workplace search. This case is unique in that it involves both warrantless searches and a search pursuant to a warrant. (We also considered the *Simons* case in Chapter 8. We discuss here only the portion of the decision dealing with the search itself.)

United States v. Simons

---

206 F.3D 392 (2000)

U.S. Court of Appeals, Fourth Circuit

OPINION: WILKINS, Circuit Judge:

Consequently, we must determine whether FBIS' warrantless entry into Simons' office to retrieve the hard drive was reasonable under the Fourth Amendment. A search conducted without a warrant issued by a judge or magistrate upon a showing of probable cause is "per se unreasonable" unless it falls within one of the "specifically established and well-delineated exceptions" to the warrant requirement. One exception to the warrant requirement arises when the requirement is rendered impracticable by a "special needs, beyond the normal need for law enforcement." *Vernonia Sch. Dist. 47J v. Acton*, 515 U.S. 646, 653, 132 L. Ed. 2d 564, 115 S. Ct. 2386 (1995). In *O'Connor*, the Supreme Court held that a government employer's interest in "the efficient and proper operation of the workplace" may justify warrantless work-related searches. *O'Connor*, 480 U.S. at 723. In particular, the *O'Connor* Court held that when a government employer conducts a search pursuant to an investigation of work-related misconduct, the Fourth Amendment will be satisfied if the search is reasonable in its inception and its scope. See id. at 725–26. A search normally will be reasonable at its inception "when there are reasonable grounds for suspecting that the search will turn up evidence that the employee is guilty of work-related misconduct." Id. at 726. "The search will be permissible in its scope when 'the measures adopted are reasonably related to the objectives of the search and not excessively intrusive in light of ... the nature of the misconduct.'" Id. (quoting *New Jersey v. T.L.O.*, 469 U.S. 325, 342, 83 L. Ed. 2d 720, 105 S. Ct. 733 (1985)).

The question thus becomes whether the search of Simons' office falls within the ambit of the *O'Connor* exception to the warrant requirement, i.e., whether the search was carried out for the purpose of obtaining "evidence of suspected work-related employee misfeasance." 480 U.S. at 723. The district court found that all of the warrantless searches, and thus the office search, were work-related. The court reasoned that FBIS had an interest in fully investigating Simons' misconduct, even if the misconduct was criminal. We agree.

As it does not appear from the record that FBIS utilized the hard drive for internal investigatory purposes before turning it over to the criminal investigator at OIG, we will assume that the dominant purposes of the warrantless search of Simons' office was to acquire evidence of criminal activity, which had been committed at FBIS using FBIS equipment. Nevertheless, the search remains within the *O'Connor* exception to the warrant requirement; FBIS did not lose its special need for "the efficient and proper operation of the workplace," id., merely because the evidence obtained was evidence of a crime. Simons' violation of FBIS' Internet policy happened also to be a violation of criminal law; this does not mean that FBIS lost the capacity and interests of an employer.

We have little trouble concluding that the warrantless entry of Simons' office was reasonable under the Fourth Amendment standard announced in *O'Connor*. At the inception of the search FBIS had "reasonable grounds for suspecting" that the hard drive would yield evidence of misconduct because FBIS was already aware that Simons had misused his Internet access to download over a thousand pornographic images, some of which involved minors. *O'Connor*, 480 U.S. at 726. The search was also permissible in scope. The measure adopted, entering Simons' office, was reasonably related to the objective of the search, retrieval of the hard drive. And, the search was not excessively intrusive. Indeed, there has been no suggestion that Harper searched Simons' desk or any other items in the office; rather, Harper simply crossed the floor of Simons' office, switched hard drives, and exited.

In the final analysis, this case involves an employee's supervisor entering the employee's government office and retrieving a piece of government equipment in which the employee had absolutely no expectation of privacy—equipment that the employer knew contained evidence of crimes committed by the employee in the employee's office. This situation may be contrasted with one in which the criminal acts of a government employee were unrelated to his employment. Here, there was a conjunction of the conduct that violated the employer's policy and the conduct that violated the criminal law. We consider that FBIS' intrusion into Simons' office to retrieve the hard drive is one in which a reasonable employer might engage.

For the foregoing reasons, we agree with the district court that Simons' Fourth Amendment rights were not violated by any of FBIS' activities in searching his computer and office.

Simons also challenges the search conducted pursuant to the August search warrant. We reject Simons' arguments that the search violated his constitutional rights.

However, we remand for further proceedings concerning Simons' claim that the search team violated Federal Rule of Criminal Procedure 41(d) when it failed to leave, at the time of the search, a copy of the warrant or a receipt for the property taken.

Simons first alleges that the warrant was invalid as to the zip drive and zip drive diskettes because the affidavit supporting the warrant application contained a deliberately misleading statement—that Simons had attached a zip drive to his computer. At the suppression hearing, Mauck stated that he did not know whether a zip drive was connected to Simons' computer, and Harper essentially testified that he did not believe there was a zip drive connected to Simons' computer. Because at least Harper participated in preparing the warrant application, Simons attributes the knowledge of these SAIC employees to Mesisca, the author of the affidavit. Simons argues that the affidavit therefore contained a knowingly false statement and that the statement impermissibly expanded the scope of the search because without the statement there was no probable cause to search the zip drive or zip drive diskettes.

Simons has introduced no evidence showing that Mesisca made the statement regarding the zip drive deliberately or with reckless disregard for the truth, nor has he shown that the statement was critical to the finding of probable cause. At most, the scope of the misstatement was that the zip drive was connected to the computer. As the magistrate judge found probable cause to search other items in the office not connected to the computer, whether the zip drive was actually connected to the computer was obviously not essential to the probable cause determination. We therefore conclude that the statement in the affidavit regarding the zip drive being connected to the computer did not render the seizure of the zip drive and zip drive diskettes unlawful.

Next, Simons argues that the August search violated the Fourth Amendment and Federal Rule of Criminal Procedure 41(d) because the search team executing the warrant left neither a copy of the warrant nor a receipt for the property taken. We conclude that these failings did not violate Simons' constitutional rights, but we remand for the district court to determine whether the executors of the warrant deliberately violated Rule 41(d).

Federal Rule of Criminal Procedure 41(d) provides, in pertinent part, that

> the officer taking property under the warrant shall give to the person from whom or from whose premises the property was taken a copy of the warrant and a receipt for the property taken or shall leave the copy and receipt at the place from which the property was taken.
>
> Fed. R. Crim. P. 41(d).

The August search warrant stated substantially the same requirements. However, the search team that executed the warrant left neither a copy of the warrant nor a receipt for the property taken. Therefore, it is clear that the executors of the warrant violated Rule 41(d). Simons argues that the failure to leave notice of the search violated his Fourth Amendment rights and was a deliberate violation of Rule 41(d); he maintains that suppression is an appropriate remedy.

There are two categories of Rule 41 violations: those involving constitutional violations, and all others. Nonconstitutional violations of Rule 41 warrant suppression only when the defendant is prejudiced by the violation, or when "there is evidence of intentional and deliberate disregard of a provision in the Rule," Burke, 517 F.2d at 387.

First, we conclude that the failure of the team executing the warrant to leave either a copy of the warrant or a receipt for the items taken did not render the search unreasonable under the Fourth Amendment. The Fourth Amendment does not mention notice, and the Supreme Court has stated that the Constitution does not categorically proscribe covert entries, which necessarily involve a delay in notice. And, insofar as the August search satisfied the requirements of the Fourth Amendment, i.e., it was conducted pursuant to a warrant based on probable cause issued by a neutral and detached magistrate, we perceive no basis for concluding that the 45-day delay in notice rendered the search unconstitutional.

Having concluded that the Rule 41(d) violation at issue here did not infringe on Simons' constitutional rights, we must now evaluate his argument that the violation was deliberate. As described above, the affidavit supporting the August warrant application stated a "need" to conduct the search in secret. However, the warrant required its executors to leave a copy of the warrant and a receipt for the property taken. Based on these facts, Simons argues that the search team applied for, but the magistrate judge denied, a warrant to conduct a secret search. Simons further maintains that the team deliberately circumvented the denial of its request when it failed to leave notice of the search. The Government responds that the search team applied for and believed that it had received a warrant that authorized a secret search.

We conclude that FBIS' searches of Simons' computer and office did not violate Simons' Fourth Amendment rights. We also determine that the August search warrant was valid and that the violation of Rule 41(d) did not render the search constitutionally unreasonable. However, we remand for the district court to consider whether Rule 41(d) was intentionally and deliberately disregarded.

Key Words and Phrases

Exclusionary rule
Good faith exception
Knock and announce
No-knock warrant
Probable cause

Reasonable suspicion
Scope of the warrant
Sneak and peek warrant
Specificity requirement
Taint team

Review Problems

1. Why did the court in *Hunter* specify who should participate in execution of the search warrant and how the search should be conducted?
2. If an assistant U.S. attorney was a member of the search team, why did the court in *Hunter* conclude that members of the search team acted in good faith? Shouldn't good faith in the execution of a warrant be considered under a different standard when attorneys participate in the process?
3. In the *Hill* decision, the court seems to adopt as a constitutional requirement that the applicant for a search warrant specify why seizure of computers and peripherals for subsequent examination in the forensic lab is necessary. Why did the court take that position?

Weblinks

www.cybercrime.gov/ssmanual/index.html

Chapter 2 of the 2009 manual discusses the topic of conducting searches and seizures with a warrant.

www.fjc.gov/public/home.nsf/autoframe?openform&url_l=/public/home.nsf/inavgeneral?openpage&url_r=/public/home.nsf/pages/334

This page from the website of the Federal Judicial Center provides numerous links to excellent material on the search and seizure of electronic evidence.

www.securityfocus.com/infocus/1244

This page at the website of Security Focus contains the first part of the three-part *Field Guide for Investigating Computer Crime*, authored by Timothy Wright, a cybercrime investigator employed by a financial institution. This page has a link to Part 2 of the field guide, and the Part 2 page has a link to Part 3.

Wiretapping and Eavesdropping

10

Introduction

Various government intelligence agencies, law enforcement, and private sector companies engage in the surveillance of electronic and digital communications. Some agencies conduct surveillance on an international scale, for example, the reputed use of Echelon, a satellite-operated technology utilized to listen to oral communications around the globe. Other agencies, such as the FBI, have monitored domestic digital communications through the use of a technology commonly known as Carnivore, subsequently officially known as DCS-1000. Also, private businesses monitor network traffic under a variety of circumstances and for a variety of reasons. Federal and state laws apply to the conduct of each of these efforts in a different way.

Because wiretapping and eavesdropping invade the privacy of communications, the Fourth Amendment to the U.S. Constitution applies to the conduct of government officials that constitutes wiretapping and eavesdropping. Pen registers, which are devices that record the numbers called by a suspect phone, and trap and trace devices, which record the number that is calling the suspect phone, do not implicate the Fourth Amendment because they do not invade the privacy of the home or of a communication. Congress, however, has enacted laws that govern the ability of officials to utilize pen registers and trap and trace devices (see Chapter 12). Moreover, because Congress views the interception of communications to be the greatest form of invasion of privacy, it has enacted the Wiretap Act, which provides greater protection from governmental invasion than the Fourth Amendment.

Statutes and Regulations

Congress enacted the Wiretap Act (18 USC §§ 2510–2522) in 1968. It has been amended on two notable occasions: in 1986 by enactment of the Electronic Communications Privacy Act (ECPA), and in 2001 by enactment of the USA PATRIOT Act. The ECPA distinguishes between the interception of communications (which we discuss in this chapter) and access to stored communications (which is discussed in the next chapter).

A working knowledge of ECPA is critical; this federal law governs federal, state, and local governmental conduct. Although states may enact laws that provide greater protections to their citizens than provided by the ECPA, they cannot enact laws that provide less protection.

The crime of wiretapping is set forth in 18 USC § 2511. That section makes it a crime as follows:

18 U.S.C. § 2511. Interception and disclosure of wire, oral, or electronic communications prohibited.

(1) Except as otherwise specifically provided in this chapter any person who—

  (a) intentionally intercepts, endeavors to intercept, or procures any other person to intercept or endeavor to intercept, any wire, oral, or electronic communication;

  (b) intentionally uses, endeavors to use, or procures any other person to use or endeavor to use any electronic, mechanical, or other device to intercept any oral communication when—

    (i) such device is affixed to, or otherwise transmits a signal through, a wire, cable, or other like connection used in wire communication; or

    (ii) such device transmits communications by radio, or interferes with the transmission of such communication; or

    (iii) such person knows, or has reason to know, that such device or any component thereof has been sent through the mail or transported in interstate or foreign commerce; or

    (iv) such use or endeavor to use (A) takes place on the premises of any business or other commercial establishment the operations of which affect interstate or foreign commerce; or (B) obtains or is for the purpose of obtaining information relating to the operations of any business or other commercial establishment the operations of which affect interstate or foreign commerce; or

    (v) such person acts in the District of Columbia, the Commonwealth of Puerto Rico, or any territory or possession of the United States;

  (c) intentionally discloses, or endeavors to disclose, to any other person the contents of any wire, oral, or electronic communication, knowing or having reason to know that the information was obtained through the interception of a wire, oral, or electronic communication in violation of this subsection;

  (d) intentionally uses, or endeavors to use, the contents of any wire, oral, or electronic communication, knowing or having reason to know that the information was obtained through the interception of a wire, oral, or electronic communication in violation of this subsection; or

  (e) (i) intentionally discloses, or endeavors to disclose, to any other person the contents of any wire, oral, or electronic communication, intercepted by means authorized by sections 2511(2)(a)(ii), 2511(2)(b)–(c), 2511(2)(e), 2516, and 2518 of this chapter [18 USCS §§ 2511(2)(a)(ii), 2511(2)(b)–(c), 2511(2)(e), 2516, and 2518], (ii) knowing or having reason to know that the information was obtained through the interception of such a communication in connection with a criminal investigation, (iii) having obtained or received the information in connection with a criminal investigation, and (iv) with intent to improperly obstruct, impede, or interfere with a duly authorized criminal investigation,

shall be punished as provided in subsection (4) or shall be subject to suit as provided in subsection (5).

Subsection (4) authorizes the imposition of a fine or imprisonment for not more than five years for any violation of the above subsection. Subsection (5) provides that civil liability may be imposed upon the person who violates Subsection (1).

There are exceptions, or course. Subsection (2) lists those occasions in which it is not a crime to commit conduct set forth in subsection (1) of Section 2511. Essentially, it is not a crime:

- for an operator of a switchboard, or an officer, employee, or agent of a provider of wire or electronic communication service, whose facilities are used in the transmission of a wire or electronic communication, to intercept, disclose, or use that communication in the normal course of his employment while engaged in any activity which is a necessary incident to the rendition of his service or to the protection of the rights or property of the provider of that service, except that a provider of wire communication service to the public shall not utilize service observing or random monitoring except for mechanical or service quality control checks.

- for providers of wire or electronic communication service, their officers, employees, and agents, landlords, custodians, or other persons, to provide information, facilities, or technical assistance to persons authorized by law to intercept wire, oral, or electronic communications or to conduct electronic surveillance, as defined in section 101 of the Foreign Intelligence Surveillance Act of 1978 [50 USCS § 1801] if such provider, its officers, employees, or agents, landlord, custodian, or other specified person, has been provided with

    (A) a court order directing such assistance signed by the authorizing judge, or

    (B) a certification in writing by a person specified in section 2518(7) of this title or the Attorney General of the United States that no warrant or court order is required by law, that all statutory requirements have been met, and that the specified assistance is required, setting forth the period of time during which the provision of the information, facilities, or technical assistance is authorized and specifying the information, facilities, or technical assistance required. No provider of wire or electronic communication service, officer, employee, or agent thereof, or landlord, custodian, or other specified person shall disclose the existence of any interception or surveillance or the device used to accomplish the interception or surveillance with respect to which the person has been furnished an order or certification under this subparagraph, except as may otherwise be required by legal process and then only after prior notification to the Attorney General or to the principal prosecuting attorney of a State or any political subdivision of a State, as may be appropriate. Any such disclosure, shall render such person liable for the civil damages provided for in section 2520 [18 USCS § 2520]. No cause of action shall lie in any court against any provider of wire or electronic communication service, its officers, employees, or agents, landlord, custodian, or other specified person for providing information, facilities, or assistance in accordance with the terms of a court order, statutory authorization, or certification under this chapter.

- for an officer, employee, or agent of the Federal Communications Commission, in the normal course of his employment and in discharge of the monitoring responsibilities exercised by the Commission in the enforcement of chapter 5 of title 47 [47 USCS §§ 151 et seq.] of the United States Code, to intercept a wire or electronic communication, or oral communication transmitted by radio, or to disclose or use the information thereby obtained.

- for a person acting under color of law to intercept a wire, oral, or electronic communication, where such person is a party to the communication or one of the parties to the communication has given prior consent to such interception.

- for a person not acting under color of law to intercept a wire, oral, or electronic communication where such person is a party to the communication or where one of the parties to the communication has given prior consent to such interception unless such communication is intercepted for the purpose of committing any criminal or tortious act in violation of the Constitution or laws of the United States or of any State.

- for an officer, employee, or agent of the United States in the normal course of his official duty to conduct electronic surveillance, as defined in section 101 of the Foreign Intelligence Surveillance Act of 1978 [50 USCS § 1801], as authorized by that Act [50 USCS §§ 1801 et seq.].

- for any person—
    (i) to intercept or access an electronic communication made through an electronic communication system that is configured so that such electronic communication is readily accessible to the general public;
    (ii) to intercept any radio communication which is transmitted—
        (I) by any station for the use of the general public, or that relates to ships, aircraft, vehicles, or persons in distress;
        (II) by any governmental, law enforcement, civil defense, private land mobile, or public safety communications system, including police and fire, readily accessible to the general public;
        (III) by a station operating on an authorized frequency within the bands allocated to the amateur, citizens band, or general mobile radio services; or
        (IV) by any marine or aeronautical communications system;
    (iii) to engage in any conduct which—
        (I) is prohibited by section 633 of the Communications Act of 1934 [47 USCS § 553]; or
        (II) is excepted from the application of section 705(a) of the Communications Act of 1934 [47 USCS § 605(a)] by section 705(b) of that Act [47 USCS § 605(b)];
    (iv) to intercept any wire or electronic communication the transmission of which is causing harmful interference to any lawfully operating station or consumer electronic equipment, to the extent necessary to identify the source of such interference; or
    (v) for other users of the same frequency to intercept any radio communication made through a system that utilizes frequencies monitored by individuals engaged in the provision or the use of such system, if such communication is not scrambled or encrypted.
- for a person acting under color of law to intercept the wire or electronic communications of a computer trespasser transmitted to, through, or from the protected computer, if—
        (I) the owner or operator of the protected computer authorizes the interception of the computer trespasser's communications on the protected computer;
        (II) the person acting under color of law is lawfully engaged in an investigation;
        (III) the person acting under color of law has reasonable grounds to believe that the contents of the computer trespasser's communications will be relevant to the investigation; and
        (IV) such interception does not acquire communications other than those transmitted to or from the computer trespasser.
    (f) Nothing contained in this chapter or chapter 121 or 206 of this title, or section 705 of the Communications Act of 1934 [47 USCS § 605], shall be deemed to affect the acquisition by the United States Government of foreign intelligence information from international or foreign communications, or foreign intelligence activities conducted in accordance with otherwise applicable Federal law involving a foreign electronic communications system, utilizing a means other than electronic surveillance as defined in section 101 of the Foreign Intelligence Surveillance Act of 1978 [50 USCS § 1801], and procedures in this chapter or chapter 121 or 206 of this title and the Foreign Intelligence Surveillance Act of 1978 [50 USCS §§ 1801 et seq.] shall be the exclusive means by which electronic surveillance, as defined in section 101 of such Act [50 USCS § 1801], and the interception of domestic wire, oral, and electronic communications may be conducted.

(h) It shall not be unlawful under this chapter—
   (i) to use a pen register or a trap and trace device (as those terms are defined for the purposes of chapter 206 (relating to pen registers and trap and trace devices) of this title) [18 USCS §§ 3121 et seq.]; or
   (ii) for a provider of electronic communication service to record the fact that a wire or electronic communication was initiated or completed in order to protect such provider, another provider furnishing service toward the completion of the wire or electronic communication, or a user of that service, from fraudulent, unlawful or abusive use of such service.

Section 2511 prohibits the *interception* of oral, wire, or electronic communications. Section 2510 (4) provides that

"intercept" means the aural or other acquisition of the contents of any wire, electronic, or oral communication through the use of any electronic, mechanical, or other device.

Further, Section 2510, Subsections 1, 2, and 12 define oral, wire, and electronic communications as follows:

(1) "wire communication" means any aural transfer made in whole or in part through the use of facilities for the transmission of communications by the aid of wire, cable, or other like connection between the point of origin and the point of reception (including the use of such connection in a switching station) furnished or operated by any person engaged in providing or operating such facilities for the transmission of interstate or foreign communications or communications affecting interstate or foreign commerce
(2) "oral communication" means any oral communication uttered by a person exhibiting an expectation that such communication is not subject to interception under circumstances justifying such expectation, but such term does not include any electronic communication

(12) "electronic communication" means any transfer of signs, signals, writing, images, sounds, data, or intelligence of any nature transmitted in whole or in part by a wire, radio, electromagnetic, photoelectronic or photooptical system that affects interstate or foreign commerce, but does not include—
   (A) any wire or oral communication;
   (B) any communication made through a tone-only paging device;
   (C) any communication from a tracking device (as defined in section 3117 of this title); or
   (D) electronic funds transfer information stored by a financial institution in a communications system used for the electronic storage and transfer of funds.

Federal law also prohibits the manufacture, distribution, possession, and advertising of devices that can intercept oral, wire, or electronic communications (18 USC § 2512) and authorizes the recovery of damages for violations of the Wiretap Act (18 USC § 2520).

Section 2516 delineates the situations in which law enforcement officials may seek a wiretap order and lists the offenses for which a wiretap order may be obtained to assist in the investigation. Section 2518 sets forth the information that a law enforcement official must submit to the court in the application for a wiretap order:

(a) the identity of the investigative or law enforcement officer making the application, and the officer authorizing the application;
(b) a full and complete statement of the facts and circumstances relied upon by the applicant, to justify his belief that an order should be issued, including (i) details as to the

particular offense that has been, is being, or is about to be committed, (ii) except as provided in subsection (11), a particular description of the nature and location of the facilities from which or the place where the communication is to be intercepted, (iii) a particular description of the type of communications sought to be intercepted, (iv) the identity of the person, if known, committing the offense and whose communications are to be intercepted;

(c) a full and complete statement as to whether or not other investigative procedures have been tried and failed or why they reasonably appear to be unlikely to succeed if tried or to be too dangerous;

(d) a statement of the period of time for which the interception is required to be maintained. If the nature of the investigation is such that the authorization for interception should not automatically terminate when the described type of communication has been first obtained, a particular description of facts establishing probable cause to believe that additional communications of the same type will occur thereafter;

(e) a full and complete statement of the facts concerning all previous applications known to the individual authorizing and making the application, made to any judge for authorization to intercept, or for approval of interceptions of, wire, oral, or electronic communications involving any of the same persons, facilities or places specified in the application, and the action taken by the judge on each such application; and

(f) where the application is for the extension of an order, a statement setting forth the results thus far obtained from the interception, or a reasonable explanation of the failure to obtain such results.

It is important to note that those requirements exceed the constitutional mandate that probable cause be shown in order to obtain a search warrant.

Case Law

Congress has distinguished between wiretapping, which it defines as the interception of a wire or electronic communication, and access to stored communications. As discussed previously, unless an exception applies, only law enforcement officials can conduct a wiretap pursuant to a court order. However, access to certain stored information can be obtained by documents that require less evidence. Thus, the critical question is whether the conduct of law enforcement officials involved the interception of a wire or electronic communication. The following cases illustrate problems the courts have encountered in deciding whether an interception has occurred.

Steve Jackson Games v. United States Secret Service

36 F.3D 457 (1994)

U.S. COURT OF APPEALS, FIFTH CIRCUIT

Steve Jackson Games, Inc. (SJG) publishes books, magazines, and computer games. It operated an electronic bulletin board system (BBS) from one of its computers to post information to the public about its business, games, publications, and to communicate with its customers by e-mail. SJG customers also could utilize that e-mail service to send and receive private e-mail. Such private e-mail was stored on the BBS computer's hard drive temporarily until SJG customers accessed the computer and read their e-mail. At that point, the customer could choose to store the read e-mail on the BBS computer or delete it. In February 1990, 365 customers used the e-mail service.

Network Security Technology, an affiliate Bell Telephone Company, undertook an investigation of the unauthorized duplication and distribution of a text file containing information about Bell's emergency call system. Company investigators informed the U.S. Secret Service that the suspect document was available on a computer bulletin board operated by Loyd Blankenship in Austin, Texas, and that Blankenship was an SJG employee and cosystems operator of the SJG BBS. The Secret Service was aware that as system operator, Blankenship had the ability to review and perhaps delete any data on the SJG bulletin board. Secret Service Agent Foley applied for a warrant to search SGJ's premises and Blankenship's residence for evidence of violations of 18 USC § 1030 (interstate transportation of computer access information) and § 2314 (interstate transportation of stolen property). The search warrant authorized the seizure of:

computer hardware ... and computer software ... and ... documents relating to the use of the computer system ..., and financial documents and licensing documentation relative to the computer programs and equipment at ... [SJG] ... which constitute evidence ... of federal crimes.... This warrant is for the seizure of the above described computer and computer data and for the authorization to read information stored and contained on the above described computer and computer data.

The Secret Service executed the warrant on May 1, 1990. The Secret Service seized the computer that operated the SJG BBS. At the time, the computer stored 162 items of unread private e-mail. The trial court found that Secret Service personnel or delegates read and deleted the private e-mail. Appellants, users of the BBS and private e-mail service, commenced a civil action against the Secret Service and U.S. government, claiming violations of the Privacy Protection Act (42 USC § 2000aa), Federal Wiretap Act (18 USC §§ 2510–2521), and the Stored Communications Act (18 USC §§ 2701–2712).

The District Court held that the Secret Service violated the Privacy Protection Act and the Stored Communications Act. The court awarded actual damages of $51,040 to SJG for the Privacy Protection Act violation, and statutory damages of $1,000 to each appellant, attorneys' fees of $195,000, and approximately $57,000 in costs. The court held that the seizure and reading of stored e-mails did not constitute a violation of the Wiretap Act. Appellants then appealed, claiming that the district court erred in concluding that there was no Wiretap Act violation.

BARKSDALE, Circuit Judge:

The narrow issue before us is whether the seizure of a computer, used to operate an electronic bulletin board system, and containing private electronic mail which had been sent to (stored on) the bulletin board, but not read (retrieved) by the intended recipients, constitutes an unlawful intercept under the Federal Wiretap Act, 18 U.S.C. § 2510, et seq., as amended by Title I of the Electronic Communications Privacy Act of 1986, Pub. L. No. 99-508, Title I, 100 Stat. 1848 (1986). We hold that it is not, and therefore AFFIRM.

Section 2511 was enacted in 1968 as part of Title III of the Omnibus Crime Control and Safe Streets Act of 1968, often referred to as the Federal Wiretap Act. Prior to the 1986 amendment by Title I of the ECPA, it covered only wire and oral communications.

Title I of the ECPA extended that coverage to electronic communications. In relevant part, § 2511(1)(a) proscribes "intentionally intercepting … any wire, oral, or electronic communication," unless the intercept is authorized by court order or by other exceptions not relevant here. Section 2520 authorizes, *inter alia*, persons whose electronic communications are intercepted in violation of § 2511 to bring a civil action against the interceptor for actual damages, or for statutory damages of $10,000 per violation or $100 per day of the violation, whichever is greater.

The Act defines "intercept" as "the aural or other acquisition of the contents of any wire, electronic, or oral communication through the use of any electronic, mechanical, or other device." 18 U.S.C. § 2510(4).

Prior to the 1986 amendment by the ECPA, the Wiretap Act defined "intercept" as the "aural acquisition" of the contents of wire or oral communications through the use of a device. 18 U.S.C. § 2510 (4) (1968). The ECPA amended this definition to include the "aural or other acquisition of the contents of … wire, electronic, or oral communications…." 18 U.S.C. § 2510 (4) (1986). The significance of the addition of the words "or other" in the 1986 amendment to the definition of "intercept" becomes clear when the definitions of "aural" and "electronic communication" are examined; electronic communications (which include the non-voice portions of wire communications), as defined by the Act, cannot be acquired aurally.

Webster's Third New International Dictionary (1986) defines "aural" as "of or relating to the ear" or "of or relating to the sense of hearing." And, the Act defines "aural transfer" as "a transfer containing the human voice at any point between and including the point of origin and the point of reception." 18 U.S.C. § 2510(18). This definition is extremely important for purposes of understanding the definition of a "wire communication," which is defined by the Act as

any aural transfer made in whole or in part through the use of facilities for the transmission of communications by the aid of wire, cable, or other like connection between the point of origin and the point of reception (including the use of such connection in a switching station) … and such term includes any electronic storage of such communication.

18 U.S.C. § 2510 (1).

In contrast, as noted, an "electronic communication" is defined as "any transfer of signs, signals, writing, images, sounds, data, or intelligence of any nature transmitted in whole or in part by a wire, radio, electromagnetic, photoelectronic or photooptical system … but does not include … any wire or oral communication…."

18 U.S.C. § 2510(12).

Critical to the issue before us is the fact that, unlike the definition of "wire communication," the definition of "electronic communication" does not include electronic storage of such communications. See 18 U.S.C. § 2510(12). "Electronic storage" is defined as

(A) any temporary, intermediate storage of a wire or electronic communication incidental to the electronic transmission thereof; and
(B) any storage of such communication by an electronic communication service for purposes of backup protection of such communication …

18 U.S.C. § 2510 (17).

The E-mail in issue was in "electronic storage." Congress' use of the word "transfer" in the definition of "electronic communication," and its omission in that definition of the phrase "any electronic storage of such communication" (part of the definition of "wire communication") reflects that Congress did not intend for "intercept" to apply to "electronic communications" when those communications are in "electronic storage."

As the district court noted, the ECPA's legislative history makes it crystal clear that Congress did not intend to change the definition of "intercept" as it existed at the time of the amendment. The Senate Report explains:

Section 101(a)(3) of the [ECPA] amends the definition of the term "intercept" in current section 2510 (4) of title 18 to cover electronic communications. The definition of "intercept" under current law is retained with respect to wire and oral communications except that the term "or other" is inserted after "aural." This amendment clarifies that it is illegal to intercept the nonvoice portion of a wire communication. For example, it is illegal to intercept the data or digitized portion of a voice communication.

1986 U.S.C.C.A.N. at 3567.

Our conclusion is reinforced further by consideration of the fact that Title II of the ECPA clearly applies to the conduct of the Secret Service in this case. Needless to say, when construing a statute, we do not confine our interpretation to the one portion at issue but, instead, consider the statute as a whole.

Title II generally proscribes unauthorized access to stored wire or electronic communications. Section 2701(a) provides:

Except as provided in subsection (c) of this section whoever—

(1) intentionally accesses without authorization a facility through which an electronic communication service is provided; or
(2) intentionally exceeds an authorization to access that facility;

and thereby obtains, alters, or prevents authorized access to a wire or electronic communication while it is in electronic storage in such system shall be punished.

18 U.S.C. § 2701(a).

As stated, the district court found that the Secret Service violated § 2701 when it

intentionally accessed without authorization a facility [the computer] through which an electronic communication service is provided … and thereby obtained [and] prevented authorized access [by appellants] to an … electronic communication while it is in electronic storage in such system.

18 U.S.C. § 2701(a).

The Secret Service does not challenge this ruling. We find no indication in either the Act or its legislative history that Congress intended for conduct that is clearly prohibited by Title II to furnish the basis for a civil remedy under Title I as well. Indeed, there are persuasive indications that it had no such intention.

First, the substantive and procedural requirements for authorization to intercept electronic communications are quite different from those for accessing stored electronic communications. For example, a governmental entity may gain access to the contents of electronic communications that have been in electronic storage for less than 180 days by obtaining a warrant. See 18 U.S.C. § 2703(a). But there are more stringent, complicated requirements for the interception of electronic communications; a court order is required. See 18 U.S.C. § 2518.

Second, other requirements applicable to the interception of electronic communications, such as those governing minimization, duration, and the types of crimes that may be investigated, are not imposed when the communications at issue are not in the process of being transmitted at the moment of seizure, but instead are in electronic storage. For example, a court order authorizing interception of electronic communications is required to include a directive that the order shall be executed "in such a way as to minimize the interception of communications not otherwise subject to interception." 18 U.S.C. § 2518 (5). Title II of the ECPA does not contain this requirement for warrants authorizing access to stored electronic communications.

Obviously, when intercepting electronic communications, law enforcement officers cannot know in advance which, if any, of the intercepted communications will be relevant to the crime under investigation, and often will have to obtain access to the contents of the communications in order to make such a determination. Interception thus poses a significant risk that officers will obtain access to communications which have no relevance to the investigation they are conducting. That risk is present to a lesser degree, and can be controlled more easily, in the context of stored electronic communications, because, as the Secret Service advised the district court, technology exists by which relevant communications can be located without the necessity of reviewing the entire contents of all of the stored communications. For example, the Secret Service claimed (although the district court found otherwise) that it reviewed the private E-mail on the BBS by use of key word searches.

Next, as noted, court orders authorizing an intercept of electronic communications are subject to strict requirements as to duration. An intercept may not be authorized "for any period longer than is necessary to achieve the objective of the authorization, nor in any event longer than thirty days." 18 U.S.C. § 2518 (5). There is no such requirement for access to stored communications.

Finally, as also noted, the limitations as to the types of crimes that may be investigated through an intercept, see 18 U.S.C. § 2516, have no counterpart in Title II of the ECPA.

United States v. Councilman

---

418 F.3D 67 (2005)

U.S. COURT OF APPEALS, FIRST CIRCUIT

LIPEZ, Circuit Judge.

This case presents an important question of statutory construction. We must decide whether interception of an e-mail message in temporary, transient electronic storage states an offense under the Wiretap Act, as amended by the Electronic Communications Privacy Act of 1986, 18 U.S.C. §§ 2510–2522. The government believes it does, and indicted Councilman under that theory. The district court disagreed and dismissed the indictment. A divided panel of this court affirmed. We granted review *en banc* and now reverse.

I.

A. An Introduction to Internet E-mail

The Internet is a network of interconnected computers. Data transmitted across the Internet are broken down into small "packets" that are forwarded from one computer to another until they reach their destination, where they are reconstituted. Each service on the Internet—e.g., e-mail, the World Wide Web, or instant messaging—has its own protocol for using packets of data to transmit information from one place to another. The e-mail protocol is known as Simple Mail Transfer Protocol ("SMTP").

After a user composes a message in an e-mail client program, a program called a mail transfer agent ("MTA") formats that message and sends it to another program that "packetizes" it and sends the packets out to the Internet. Computers on the network then pass the packets from one to another; each computer along the route stores the packets in memory, retrieves the addresses of their final destinations, and then determines where to send them next. At various points the packets are reassembled to form the original e-mail message, copied, and then repacketized for the next leg of the journey. Sometimes messages cannot be transferred immediately and must be saved for later delivery. Even when delivery is immediate, intermediate computers often retain backup copies, which they delete later. This method of transmission is commonly called "store and forward" delivery.

Once all the packets reach the recipient's mail server, they are reassembled to form the e-mail message. A mail delivery agent ("MDA") accepts the message from the MTA, determines which user should receive the message, and performs the actual delivery by placing the message in that user's mailbox. One popular MDA is "procmail," which is controlled by short programs or scripts called "recipe files." These recipe files can be used in various ways. For example, a procmail recipe can instruct the MDA to deposit mail addressed to one address into another user's mailbox (e.g., to send mail addressed to "help" to the tech support department), to reject mail from certain addresses, or to make copies of certain messages.

Once the MDA has deposited a message into the recipient's mailbox, the recipient simply needs to use an e-mail client program to retrieve and read the message. While the journey from sender to recipient may seem rather involved, it usually takes just a few seconds, with each intermediate step taking well under a second.

B. Facts Alleged in the Indictment

Defendant-appellee Bradford C. Councilman was Vice President of Interloc, Inc., which ran an online rare and out-of-print book listing service. As part of its service, Interloc gave book dealer customers an e-mail address at the domain "interloc.com" and acted as the e-mail provider. Councilman managed the e-mail service and the dealer subscription list.

According to the indictment, in January 1998, Councilman directed Interloc employees to intercept and copy all incoming communications to subscriber dealers from Amazon.com, an Internet retailer that sells books and other products. Interloc's systems administrator modified the server's procmail recipe so that, before delivering any message from Amazon.com to the recipient's mailbox, procmail would copy the message and place the copy in a separate mailbox that Councilman could access. Thus, procmail would intercept and copy all incoming messages from Amazon.com before they were delivered to the recipient's mailbox, and therefore, before the intended recipient could read the message. This diversion intercepted thousands of messages, and Councilman and other Interloc employees routinely read the e-mail messages sent to Interloc subscribers in the hope of gaining a commercial advantage.

C. Procedural History

On July 11, 2001, a grand jury returned a two-count indictment against Councilman. Count One charged him under 18 U.S.C. § 371, the general federal criminal conspiracy statute, for conspiracy to violate the Wiretap Act, 18 U.S.C. § 2511, by intercepting electronic communications, disclosing their contents, using their contents, and causing a person providing an electronic communications service to divulge the communications' contents to persons other than the addressees. The object of the conspiracy was to exploit the content of e-mail from Amazon.com to dealers in order to develop a list of books, learn about competitors, and attain a commercial advantage for Interloc and its parent company.

The parties stipulated to certain undisputed facts: the procmail recipe worked only within the confines of Interloc's computer; at all times at which procmail performed operations affecting the e-mail system, the messages existed "in the random access memory (RAM) or in hard disks, or both, within Interloc's computer system"; and each e-mail message, while traveling through wires, was an "electronic communication" under 18 U.S.C. § 2510(12).

Councilman moved to dismiss the indictment for failure to state an offense under the Wiretap Act, arguing that the intercepted e-mail messages were in "electronic storage," as defined in 18 U.S.C. § 2510(17), and therefore were not, as a matter of law, subject to the prohibition on "intercept[ing] ... electronic communication[s]," 18 U.S.C. § 2511(1)(a). The district court initially denied the motion to dismiss. As trial preparation began, however, the district court *sua sponte* reconsidered its decision in light of the then-recently decided case of *Konop v. Hawaiian Airlines, Inc.*, 302 F.3d 868 (9th Cir. 2002). After further briefing, the district court granted Councilman's motion to dismiss Count One, ruling that the messages were not, at the moment of interception, "electronic communications" under the Wiretap Act.

A divided panel of this court affirmed. The full court granted the government's petition for rehearing *en banc*.

II.

The Wiretap Act of 1968 specified, *inter alia*, the conditions under which law enforcement officers could intercept wire communications, and the penalties for unauthorized private interceptions of wire communications. As amended by the Electronic Communications Privacy Act of 1986, the Act makes it an offense to "intentionally intercept[], endeavor[] to intercept, or procure[] any other person to intercept or endeavor to intercept, any wire, oral, or electronic communication." 18 U.S.C. § 2511(1). Two terms are at issue here: "electronic communication" and "intercept."

Councilman contends that the e-mail messages he obtained were not, when procmail copied them, "electronic communication[s]," and moreover the method by which they were copied was not "intercept[ion]" under the Act. Because these contentions raise important questions of statutory construction with broad ramifications, we discuss in some detail the Act's text, structure, and legislative history. We conclude that Councilman's interpretation of the Wiretap Act is inconsistent with Congress's intent. We then turn to whether Councilman had fair warning that the Act would be construed to cover his alleged conduct in a criminal case, and whether the rule of lenity or other principles require us to construe the Act in his favor. We find no basis to apply any of the fair warning doctrines.

A. "Electronic Communication"

The government contends that "electronic communication" means what it says, and no less: "any transfer of signs, signals, writing, images, sounds, data, or intelligence of any nature transmitted in whole or in part by a wire, radio, electromagnetic, photoelectronic or photooptical system that affects interstate or foreign commerce," with four specific exceptions not relevant here. 18 U.S.C. § 2510(12). Councilman argues, however, that Congress intended to exclude any communication that is in (even momentary) electronic storage. In his view, "electronic communication[s]" under the Wiretap Act are limited to communications traveling through wires between computers. Once a message enters a computer, he says, the message ceases (at least temporarily) to be an electronic communication protected by the Wiretap Act. He claims that Congress considered communications in computers to be worthy of less protection than communications in wires because users have a lower expectation of privacy for electronic communications that are in electronic storage even fleetingly, and that the Act embodies this understanding.

1. Text

We begin, as we must, with the statute's text. As noted above, the statutory definition of "electronic communication" is broad and, taken alone, would appear to cover incoming e-mail messages while the messages are being processed by the MTA.

Councilman argues, however, that the plain text of the statute exempts electronic communications that are in storage from the purview of the Wiretap Act. He contends that the definition of "electronic communication" must be read alongside the definition of "wire communication" and limited by what the latter includes but the former does not. The ECPA amended the 1968 definition of "wire communication" to specify that "such term includes any electronic storage of such communication." 18 U.S.C. § 2510(1); ECPA § 101(a)(1)(D). By contrast, the definition of "electronic communication" does not mention electronic storage. See 18 U.S.C. § 2510(12). Therefore, Councilman infers, Congress intended wire communications, but not electronic communications, to include electronic storage. Moreover, Congress defined "electronic storage" expansively to include "any temporary, intermediate storage of a wire or electronic communication incidental to the electronic transmission thereof." 18 U.S.C. § 2510(17). Since the parties stipulated that the messages in this case were "in the random access memory (RAM) or in the hard disks, or both, within Interloc's computer system" at the time of the interception, those messages fall under the statutory definition of "storage."

As often happens under close scrutiny, the plain text is not so plain. The statute contains no explicit indication that Congress intended to exclude communications in transient storage from the definition of "electronic communication," and, hence, from the scope of the Wiretap Act. Councilman, without acknowledging it, looks beyond the face of the statute and makes an inferential leap. He infers that Congress intended to exclude communications in transient storage from the definition of "electronic communication," regardless of whether they are in the process of being delivered, simply because it did not include the term "electronic storage" in that definition. This inferential leap is not a plain text reading of the statute.

The definitions of "wire communication" and "electronic communication" in the Wiretap Act are not parallel. The former is defined in a single lengthy clause that specifies multiple independent criteria, with the electronic storage clause tacked onto the end. The revised definition hews closely to its original definition in the 1968 Wiretap Act; the ECPA simply amended that definition by replacing the phrase "communication" with "aural transfer," making certain modifications not relevant here, and, of course, adding the clause "and such term includes any electronic storage of such communication." By contrast, "electronic communication" is first defined in broad terms which are narrowed by four specific exclusions enumerated in separate subparagraphs.

Congress knew how to, and in fact did, explicitly exclude four specific categories of communications from the broad definition of "electronic communication." Congress never added the exclusion urged by Councilman: "any electronic communication in electronic storage." This interpretative principle then applies: "Where Congress explicitly enumerates certain exceptions to a general prohibition, additional exceptions are not to be implied, in the absence of evidence of a contrary legislative intent." *TRW v. Andrews*, 534 U.S. 19, 28 (2001).

In short, the ECPA's plain text does not clearly state whether a communication is still an "electronic communication" within the scope of the Wiretap Act when it is in electronic storage during transmission. Applying canons of construction does not resolve the question. Given this continuing ambiguity, we turn to the legislative history.

2. Legislative History

As we explain below, the purpose of the broad definition of electronic storage was to enlarge privacy protections for stored data under the Wiretap Act, not to exclude e-mail messages stored during transmission from those strong protections. Moreover, Congress's sole purpose in adding electronic storage to the definition of "wire communication" was to protect voice mail, and not to affect e-mail at all.

a. Background of the ECPA

By the early 1980s, the advent of electronic communications, principally e-mail, suggested to many that the Wiretap Act needed revision. To update the Act, Senator Patrick Leahy introduced the Electronic Communications Privacy Act of 1985. That bill would have amended the Act by striking out the existing definition of "wire communication," substituting the phrase "electronic communication" for "wire communication" throughout the Act, and subsuming wire communications within the newly-defined term "electronic communication."

Shortly after the bill was introduced, the Congressional Office of Technology Assessment released a long-awaited study of the privacy implications of electronic surveillance. The report identified the different points at which an e-mail message could be intercepted:

There are at least five discrete stages at which an electronic mail message could be intercepted and its contents divulged to an unintended receiver: at the terminal or in the electronic files of the sender, while being communicated, in the electronic mailbox of the receiver, when printed into hardcopy, and when retained in the files of the electronic mail company for administrative purposes. Existing law offers little protection.

It emphasized that "interception of electronic mail at any stage involves a high level of intrusiveness and a significant threat to civil liberties."

The Department of Justice (DOJ) was the principal opponent of the original bill. DOJ conceded that "the level of intrusion during [an e-mail message's] transmission is higher than when it is stored," but urged that "the interception of electronic mail should include some but not all of the procedural requirements of [the Wiretap Act]." Electronic Communications Privacy Act: Hearings on H.R. 3378 Before the Subcomm. on Courts, Civil Liberties, and the Admin. of Justice, House Comm. on the Judiciary, 99th Cong. 214, 230 (1986) ("House Hearings") (statement of James Knapp, Deputy Assistant Attorney General, Criminal Division, U.S. Dep't of Justice). DOJ asked Congress to treat prospective surveillance of electronic communications differently from surveillance of wire communications in three specific respects that are related solely to law enforcement and are not relevant here. DOJ's willingness to extend some of the Wiretap Act's protections to e-mail did not, however, extend to "the time after a specific communication has been sent and while it is in the electronic mail firm's computers but has not been delivered, or has been delivered to the electronic mailbox but has not been received by the recipient." Id. at 234. In such cases, DOJ suggested, the message should be treated like first-class mail, and law enforcement should be able to seize it with an ordinary search warrant.

A new version of the bill was introduced to meet some, but not all, of DOJ's concerns. The new bill rejected DOJ's preferred solution and instead added electronic communications to the Wiretap Act's existing prohibitions on interception of wire communications. As the House report made clear, Congress intended to give the term "electronic communication" a broad definition:

The term 'electronic communication' is intended to cover a broad range of communication activities.... As a rule, a communication is an electronic communication if it is neither carried by sound waves nor can fairly be characterized as one containing the human voice (carried in part by wire). Communications consisting solely of data, for example ... would be electronic communications.

H.R. Rep. No. 99-647 (1986), at 35.

By incorporating electronic communications into the Wiretap Act, the bill largely rejected DOJ's view that e-mail should receive no (or little) more protection than first class mail. Nevertheless, because some of DOJ's specific concerns were addressed, DOJ acknowledged that "the bill has been substantially modified to accommodate our concerns" and supported it. Id. at 30-31.

b. The broad definition of electronic storage

Responding to concerns raised in the OTA Report, Congress sought to ensure that the messages and by-product files that are left behind after transmission, as well as messages stored in a user's mailbox, are protected from unauthorized access. E-mail messages in the sender's and recipient's computers could be accessed by electronically "breaking into" those computers and retrieving the files. OTA Report at 48–49. Before the ECPA, the victim of such an attack had few legal remedies for such an invasion. Furthermore, the e-mail messages retained on the service provider's computers after transmission—which, the report noted, are primarily retained for "billing purposes and as a convenience in case the customer loses the message"—could be accessed and possibly disclosed by the provider. Id. at 50. Before the ECPA, it was not clear whether the user had the right to challenge such a disclosure. Similar concerns applied to temporary financial records and personal data retained after transmission.

Given this background and the evidence in the legislative history that Congress responded to the OTA Report in refining the legislation, see, e.g., House Hearings at 42–73, it appears that Congress had in mind these types of pre- and post-transmission "temporary, intermediate storage of a wire or electronic communication incidental to the electronic transmission thereof," see 18 U.S.C. § 2510(17), when it established the definition of "electronic storage." Its aim was simply to protect such data. There is no indication that it meant to exclude the type of storage used during transmission from the scope of the Wiretap Act.

c. The electronic storage clause in the definition of "wire communication"
The original version of the ECPA of 1986 included the definition of "electronic storage" as it reads today, but did not include electronic storage in the definition of "wire communication." Neither Senator Leahy's floor statement upon introducing the bill nor the staff bill summary mentioned voice mail in the context of the Wiretap Act amendments. Voice mail had not, apparently, been a major subject of discussion in the context of the ECPA.

Similarly, when Representative Kastenmeier introduced his identical bill in the House, he did not mention voice mail in his remarks. The electronic storage clause in the wire communications definition first appeared in Senate committee markup after the House had already passed the bill without the clause. Senator Leahy, in his statement in support of the amended bill, specifically mentioned voice mail, which he had not done in his remarks earlier that year, and the staff summary explained that one effect of the amended bill was that "[w]ire communications in storage, like voice mail, remain wire communications."

If the addition of the electronic storage clause to the definition of "wire communication" was intended to remove electronic communications from the scope of the Wiretap Act for the brief instants during which they are in temporary storage en route to their destinations—which, as it turns out, are often the points where it is technologically easiest to intercept those communications—neither of the Senate co-sponsors saw fit to mention this to their colleagues, and no one, evidently, remarked upon it. No document or legislator ever suggested that the addition of the electronic storage clause to the definition of "wire communication" would take messages in electronic storage out of the definition of "electronic communication." Indeed, we doubt that Congress contemplated the existential oddity that Councilman's interpretation creates: messages—conceded by stipulation to be electronic communications—briefly cease to be electronic communications for very short intervals, and then suddenly become electronic communications again.

In sum, the legislative history indicates that Congress included the electronic storage clause in the definition of "wire communication" provision for the sole reason that, without it, access to voicemail would have been regulated solely by the Stored Communications Act. Indeed, that is exactly what happened when Congress later removed the explicit reference to "electronic storage" from the definition of "wire communication" in the Uniting and Strengthening America by Providing Appropriate Tools Required to Intercept and Obstruct Terrorism (USA PATRIOT) Act, Pub. L. No. 107-56, tit. II, § 209(1)(A)(2001).

3. Conclusion

We conclude that the term "electronic communication" includes transient electronic storage that is intrinsic to the communication process for such communications.

B. "Intercept"

Even though we conclude that the temporarily stored e-mail messages at issue here constitute electronic communications within the scope of the Wiretap Act, the statute also requires the conduct alleged in the indictment to be an "intercept[ion]." 18 U.S.C. § 2511(1) (making it an offense to "intentionally intercept[], endeavor[] to intercept, or procure[] any other person to intercept or endeavor to intercept, any … electronic communication"). The term "intercept" is defined broadly as "the aural or other acquisition of the contents of any wire, electronic, or oral communication through the use of any electronic, mechanical, or other device." Id. § 2510(4).

Councilman's core argument on appeal is that because the messages at issue, when acquired, were in transient electronic storage, they were not "electronic communication[s]" and, therefore, section 2511(1)'s prohibition on "intercept[ion]" of any "electronic communication" did not apply. That is the argument that we have now rejected in holding that an e-mail message does not cease to be an "electronic communication" during the momentary intervals, intrinsic to the communication process, at which the message resides in transient electronic storage. See *supra* Part II.A.

Consequently, this appeal does not implicate the question of whether the term "intercept" applies only to acquisitions that occur contemporaneously with the transmission of a message from sender to recipient or, instead, extends to an event that occurs after a message has crossed the finish line of transmission (whatever that point may be). We therefore need not decide that question.

C. Intersection of the Wiretap Act and the Stored Communications Act

Thus far we have considered only the Wiretap Act, not the Stored Communications Act, 18 U.S.C. §§ 2701–2712, because the indictment only alleged a violation of the former. Councilman argues that acquisition of electronic communications in temporary electronic storage is regulated by the Stored Communications Act. From this he infers that such acquisition is not regulated by the Wiretap Act, or that, at minimum, the potential overlap implicates the rule of lenity or other doctrines of "fair warning."

1. The Stored Communications Act's Coverage

While drafting the ECPA's amendments to the Wiretap Act, Congress also recognized that, with the rise of remote computing operations and large databanks of stored electronic communications, threats to individual privacy extended well beyond the bounds of the Wiretap Act's prohibition against the "interception" of communications. These types of stored communications—including stored e-mail messages—were not protected by the Wiretap Act. Therefore, Congress concluded that "the information [in these communications] may be open to possible wrongful use and public disclosure by law enforcement authorities as well as unauthorized private parties." S. Rep. No. 99-541, at 3 (1986), reprinted in 1986 U.S.C.C.A.N. 3555, 3557.

Congress added Title II to the ECPA to halt these potential intrusions on individual privacy. This title, commonly referred to as the Stored Communications Act, established new punishments for accessing, without (or in excess of) authorization, an electronic communications service facility and thereby obtaining access to a wire or electronic communication in electronic storage. 18 U.S.C. § 2701(a). Another provision bars electronic communications service providers from "divulg[ing] to any person or entity the contents of a communication while in electronic storage by that service." Id. § 2702(a)(1).

The privacy protections established by the Stored Communications Act were intended to apply to two categories of communications defined by the statutory term "electronic storage":

(A) any temporary, intermediate storage of a wire or electronic communication incidental to the electronic transmission thereof; and
(B) any storage of such communication by an electronic communication service for purposes of backup protection of such communication.

> 18 U.S.C. § 2510(17); id. § 2711(a) (incorporating Wiretap Act
> definitions into Stored Communications Act).

The first category, which is relevant here, refers to temporary storage, such as when a message sits in an e-mail user's mailbox after transmission but before the user has retrieved the message from the mail server.

Councilman's conduct may appear to fall under the Stored Communications Act's main criminal provision:

(a) Offense. Except as provided in subsection (c) of this section whoever—
    (1) intentionally accesses without authorization a facility through which an electronic communication service is provided; or
    (2) intentionally exceeds an authorization to access that facility;
and thereby obtains, alters, or prevents authorized access to a wire or electronic communication while it is in electronic storage in such system shall be punished....

> 18 U.S.C. § 2701(a).

At the same time, Councilman would arguably be exempted by the Stored Communications Act's provider exception: "Subsection (a) of this section does not apply with respect to conduct authorized (1) by the person or entity providing a wire or electronic communications service." Id. § 2701(c). Under this theory, § 2701(c)(1) establishes virtually complete immunity for a service provider that "obtains, alters, or prevents authorized access to" e-mail that is "in electronic storage" in its system. The district court surmised that § 2701(a) would have covered Councilman's conduct but that § 2701(c)(1) exempted him.

A second provision of the Stored Communications Act prohibits "a person or entity providing an electronic communication service to the public [from] knowingly divulg[ing] to any person or entity the contents of a communication while in electronic storage by that service." 18 U.S.C. § 2702(a)(1). Yet this provision, too, has service provider exceptions, permitting a provider to divulge an electronic communication "to a person employed or authorized or whose facilities are used to forward such communication to its destination," id. § 2702(b)(4), or "as may be necessarily incident to the rendition of the service or to the protection of the rights or property of the provider of that service," id. § 2702(b)(5). We assume, *dubitante*, that one or both of these provisions would exempt Councilman under § 2702.

On this premise, he argues that if he is not liable under the Stored Communications Act, then he cannot be liable under the Wiretap Act either. Since Congress enacted the ECPA as a package, he says, it did not intend to lay traps in the overlap between the two titles. If conduct that potentially falls under both titles is exempt from one of them, then that exemption provides a "safe harbor" and the conduct does not violate the other title either.

We find this argument unpersuasive. In general, if two statutes cover the same conduct, the government may charge a violation of either. Moreover, the exceptions in the Stored Communications Act do not, by their terms, apply to the Wiretap Act.

2. Fair Warning

Councilman argues in the alternative that the two titles are sufficiently confusing that principles of fair warning require dismissal of the indictment. Those principles are expressed in the law through three related doctrines: the rule of lenity, the vagueness doctrine, and the prohibition against unforeseeably expansive judicial constructions. We address each in turn.

a. Lenity

Under the rule of lenity, grievous ambiguity in a penal statute is resolved in the defendant's favor. "The simple existence of some statutory ambiguity, however, is not sufficient to warrant application of that rule, for most statutes are ambiguous to some degree." *Muscarello v. United States*, 524 U.S. 125, 138–39 (1998). Rather, the rule only applies if "there is a grievous ambiguity or uncertainty in the statute." Id. at 139.

Here, while the statute contains some textual ambiguity, it is not "grievous." We have construed it using traditional tools of construction, particularly legislative history, and lenity is therefore inapplicable.

Furthermore, Congress specifically anticipated that communication service providers might, in good faith, misapprehend their lawful ability to intercept or disclose communications in certain circumstances. Congress addressed that problem with a broad, affirmative good faith defense:

> A good faith reliance on ... (3) a good faith determination that [§ 2511(3)] permitted the conduct complained of[] is a complete defense against any civil or criminal action brought under [the Wiretap Act] or any other law.

> 18 U.S.C. § 2520(d)(3).

Section 2511(3), in turn, authorizes a communication service provider to divulge a communication to one other than the recipient in four specified circumstances. Thus,

Congress contemplated that service providers might, in good faith, misunderstand the limits of their authority on a particular set of facts, and provided a statutory mechanism to solve this problem. We may neither expand the good faith defense's scope, nor convert it from a fact-based affirmative defense to a basis for dismissing an indictment on legal grounds.

b. Vagueness

The vagueness doctrine bars enforcement of a statute whose terms are "so vague that men of common intelligence must necessarily guess at its meaning and differ as to its application." *Lanier*, 520 U.S. at 266. But vagueness is more than just "garden-variety, textual ambiguity." *Sabetti v. Dipaolo*, 16 F.3d 16, 18 (1st Cir. 1994).

The Wiretap Act is not unconstitutionally vague in its application here. From its text, a person of average intelligence would, at the very least, be on notice that "[e]xcept as otherwise specifically provided in" the Act, "electronic communication[s]," which are defined expansively, may not be "intercepted." 18 U.S.C. § 2511(1)(a). An exception is provided for electronic communication service providers, but it only applies to "activity which is a necessary incident to the rendition of [the] service or to the protection of the rights or property of the provider of that service." 18 U.S.C. § 2511(2)(a)(i). The Act puts the service provider on notice of both the prohibited conduct and the narrow provider exception. That is adequate notice.

We therefore conclude that the term "electronic communication" includes transient electronic storage that is intrinsic to the communication process, and hence that interception of an e-mail message in such storage is an offense under the Wiretap Act. Moreover, the various doctrines of fair warning do not bar prosecution for that offense. Consequently, the district court erred in dismissing the indictment.

TORRUELLA, Circuit Judge, with whom CYR, Senior Circuit Judge, joins (Dissenting).

Although I commend Judge Lipez on his erudite and articulate majority opinion, I am impeded from joining the same for two reasons. First, the indictment is legally insufficient to establish a criminal violation of 18 U.S.C. § 371 for conspiracy to violate the Wiretap Act, 18 U.S.C. § 2511, insofar as the e-mails Councilman is alleged to have retrieved were in "electronic storage," 18 U.S.C. § 2510(17), when that action took place, and therefore, the Wiretap Act's requisite element of "interception," 18 U.S.C. § 2511, is lacking. Second, and in the alternative, the result reached by the *en banc* majority deprives Councilman of due process of law, because he had no "fair warning" of the potential criminal consequences of his actions.

I.

The facts of this case as stipulated by the parties state that "[a]t all times that sendmail and procmail performed operations affecting the email messages at issue, the messages existed in the random access memory (RAM) or in hard disks, or both, within Interloc's computer system."

Stripped of all technical jargon, the sole legal issue presented by this appeal is whether the information contained in this computer system is data that can be "intercepted" within the meaning of the Wiretap Act.

The statute that Councilman is charged with conspiring to violate provides for criminal sanctions against "any person who—(a) intentionally intercepts, endeavors to intercept, or procures any other person to intercept or endeavor to intercept, any wire, oral, or electronic communication." 18 U.S.C. § 2511(1). The term "electronic communication" is defined as "any transfer of signs, signals, writing, images, sounds, data, or intelligence of any nature transmitted in whole or in part by wire, radio, electromagnetic, photoelectronic or photooptical system." 18 U.S.C. § 2510(12). In contrast, the term "wire communication" is defined as "any aural transfer made in whole or in part through the use of facilities for the transmission of communications by the aid of wire, cable, or other like connection between the point of origin and the point of reception ... furnished or operated by any person engaged in providing or operating such facilities ... and such term includes any electronic storage Footnote of such communication." 18 U.S.C. § 2510(1).

It is not by coincidence that every court that has passed upon the issue before us has reached a conclusion opposite to that of the *en banc* majority: that the Wiretap Act's prohibition on intercepting electronic communications does not apply when they are contained in electronic storage, whether such storage occurs pre- or post-delivery, and even if the storage lasts only a few mili-seconds [*sic*]. See *Theofel v. Farey-Jones*, 359 F.3d 1066, 1077–78 (9th Cir. 2004) (post-delivery); *Fraser v. Nationwide Mut. Ins. Co.*, 352 F.3d 107, 113–14 (3d Cir. 2003) (post-delivery); *United States v. Steiger*, 318 F.3d 1039, 1048–49 (11th Cir. 2003) (on hard drive), cert. denied, 538 U.S. 1051 (2003); *Konop v. Hawaiian Airlines*, 302 F.3d 868, 878–79 (9th Cir. 2002) (on website server), cert. denied, 537 U.S. 1193 (2003); *Steve Jackson Games, Inc. v. United States Secret Serv.*, 36 F.3d 457, 461–62 (5th Cir. 1994) (pre-retrieval); see also *United States v. Reyes*, 922 F. Supp. 818, 836 (S.D.N.Y. 1996) (finding no interception where messages were retrieved from pagers' memories prior to their retrieval by intended recipients because the messages were in "electronic storage").

Contrary to the *en banc* majority's view, our interpretation of the statute does not require that we assume that Congress contemplated the complete evisceration of the privacy protections for e-mail. When considering the intra-computer "interceptions" at issue here, Congress rationally may well have concluded that the public's privacy rights, or more specifically those between an e-mail service provider and its own customers, could be adequately controlled by normal contract principles rather than by federal statute. Councilman's "interception" of Interloc customers' e-mail was not akin to an interception engaged in by an outside party who was unrelated or unknown to the contracting parties. When a customer signs up with an e-mail provider like Interloc, he routinely is asked to read and expressly sign off on a privacy agreement which defines his expectations of privacy vis-à-vis the provider. If the protections are inadequate, he may decline the e-mail service and seek an alternative service contract which will afford him the protections he requires. Neither the Wiretap Act nor its legislative history forecloses the inference that Congress, in its exclusion of "electronic storage" from the definition of "electronic communication," intended to leave such matters to the exigencies of the contracting parties. If Interloc did intercept its customers' messages in breach of a privacy agreement, the remedy lies in contract, not in the Wiretap Act.

I see no point in rummaging through the legislative history of a statute whose language, or more accurately, absence thereof, speaks for itself.

II.

Unfortunately, the matter does not end here. As demonstrated by the results of previous efforts by this and other courts to grapple with the statute in question, any lingering ambiguity that makes room for the majority's interpretation certainly qualifies as "grievous." Due process, therefore, requires that the statute be construed against criminal liability, in accordance with the rule of lenity. Even if the ambiguity is not so serious, and "clarity at the requisite level may be supplied by [the majority's] judicial gloss on an otherwise uncertain statute, due process bars courts from applying a novel construction of a criminal statute to conduct that neither the statute nor any prior judicial decision has fairly disclosed to be within its scope." *Lanier*, 520 U.S. at 266. Whichever doctrine of "fair warning" one might apply, the bottom line is that the statute and the cases construing it did not make it "reasonably clear at the relevant time that the defendant's conduct was criminal." *Id.* at 267.

At the time that Councilman allegedly violated the Wiretap Act in 1998, he would have had available the following to guide his conduct: (1) the statute in question, and (2) the *Jackson Games* case (1994) and, tangentially, the *Reyes* case (1996). There is little in any of these that would have given Councilman fair notice of the *en banc* majority's interpretation, which itself requires reliance on legislative "history" that resembles a Byzantine maze.

Thus, I am at a loss to conceive how Councilman would have had fair notice of the majority's interpretation at the time of his actions.

Finally, Congress's provision of a good faith exception for those who divulge intercepted communications because they misconstrued the Wiretap Act's narrow exceptions to criminal liability as an affirmative defense, is irrelevant. Councilman should not have to show he relied on those exceptions to divulge the e-mails he obtained, because he had no "reasonably clear" indication that to do so would otherwise violate the Wiretap Act.

Councilman is being held to a level of knowledge which would not be expected of any of the judges who have dealt with this problem, to say nothing of "men [and women] of common intelligence." *Lanier*, 520 U.S. at 266 (quoting *Connally v. Gen. Constr. Co.*, 269 U.S. 385, 391 (1926)). If the issue presented be "garden-variety," maj. op. at 37 (quoting *Sabetti v. Diapaolo*, 16 F.3d 16, 18 (1st Cir. 1994)), this is a garden in need of a weed killer.

For the reasons stated, I respectfully dissent.

The following case considers whether the recording of alphanumeric page messages from one police officer to another constitutes a wiretap:

Bohach v. City of Reno

---

932 F. SUPP. 1232 (1996)

U.S. DISTRICT COURT, DISTRICT OF NEVADA

Bohach and Catalano, officers with the Reno Police Department, sent messages to each other and another member of the Department over the Department's "Alphapage" message system. The Alphapage system is a software program installed on the department's local area network (LAN). The system allows for the transmission of brief alphanumeric messages to visual display pagers. At the time the system was installed, between 40 and 70 pages were issued to members of the press in addition to the officers. According to the department's chief of police, the purpose was to allow the broadcast of "mini news releases" and distribution of other information to the media, thereby freeing up the department's phone lines. The chief's order warned all users that "every Alphapage message is logged on the network" and prohibited certain types of messages (for example, messages critical of department policy or those that violate the department's anti-discrimination policy).

All of the messages at issue were initiated from a computer terminal. To utilize the system, the computer user would log on to the Department's computer terminal, select "Alphapage" from a menu of available functions, select from another menu the intended recipient of the message, type the message, and hit the send key. The message would go to the "Inforad Message Directory" on the network server, where it would be stored. The user would receive a message on the computer screen indicating that the message was being processed. The computer then would dial the commercial paging company, send the message by modem, then disconnect. A "page sent" message would appear on the computer screen. At that point the paging company would send the message to the recipient by radio broadcast.

EDWARD C. REED, District Judge:

Faced with an internal affairs investigation based on the contents of those messages, they filed this lawsuit, claiming that both the storage of the messages by the Department's computer network, and their subsequent retrieval from the computer's files, were violations of the federal wiretapping statutes and of their constitutional right to privacy. They sought to stop the investigation and to bar any disclosure of the contents of the messages.

Officers Bohach and Catalano can succeed on their § 1983 Fourth Amendment claim only if, at a minimum, they demonstrate that they had a reasonable expectation of privacy in their use of the Alphapage system. We assume that they did indeed have a subjective expectation of privacy, if only because we cannot believe that, had they thought otherwise, they would ever have sent over the system the sorts of messages they did send. The question is whether their expectation was objectively reasonable. Based on the evidence now available, we think that is most unlikely.

To begin with, all messages are recorded and stored not because anyone is "tapping" the system, but simply because that's how the system works. It is an integral part of the technology, and in this respect Alphapage is like most pager systems, which store messages in a central computer until they are retrieved by, or sent to, the intended recipient. Moreover, while one phase of an Alphapage transmission (from the pager company to the recipient pager) may involve a radio broadcast, the earlier phase at issue here (from the user's keyboard to the computer) is essentially electronic mail—and e-mail messages are, by definition, stored in a routing computer.

That only a diminished expectation of privacy would be reasonable in this case is also suggested by then-Chief of Police Kirkland's order, issued when Alphapage was first installed and long before the messages in this case were sent, notifying all users that their messages would be "logged on the network" and that certain types of messages (e.g., those violating the Department's antidiscrimination policy) were banned from the system. Now, that is not the same thing as saying that the contents of all messages will be recorded and retained, but it suggests that one should expect less privacy on Alphapage than on, say, a private telephone line. We note, also, that Alphapage is accessible to anyone with access to, and a working knowledge of, the Department's computer system. No special password or clearance is needed. The current Chief of the Reno Police Department, James Weston, testified that the Department's janitor, if he had general access to the computer system, could roam at will through Alphapage.

Finally, and more generally, we note that police stations often record all outgoing and incoming phone calls, "for a variety of reasons: to make sure that their dispatches are accurate, to verify information, and to keep a log of emergency and nonemergency calls." *Fishman, supra*, § 2:38 & n.28. This may or may not violate the wiretapping statutes, depending upon how it is done. For fourth amendment purposes, however, the point is that the practice is part of the "ordinary course of business" for police departments, and it is all the more reasonable in this case in light of Alphapage's purpose and limitations. Unlike a telephone, the system is not designed to communicate with the public generally. It was installed to allow communications among police personnel, and between police personnel and the press, about police matters; that it can be used to send private communications between police personnel is incidental to its primary function. Further, unlike a telephone line, Alphapage can be used to communicate only with a recipient who has an Alphapage pager, i.e., a member of the Department or the press. So, while officers Bohach and Catalano attempt liken their communications to private telephone calls, we think that some aspects of the system (its primary though not exclusive purpose, the restrictions placed on the contents of messages, the limited number of persons with whom one can communicate using it, and the fact that police departments routinely and properly record their communications with the public) suggest that one should expect, when using it, less privacy than one might expect when, say, making a private telephone call, even from a police station.

The federal wiretapping statutes cover "wire," "oral" and "electronic" communications. The messages at issue here were "electronic" communications within the meaning of 18 U.S.C. § 2510(12). (They did not involve a human voice and thus were not "wire" or "oral" communications. See § 2510(1), (2), (18).) An "electronic communication" consists of the "transfer" of the signals, data, and other items listed at § 2510(12), but does not include their "electronic storage." An electronic communication may be put into electronic storage, but the storage is not itself a part of the communication. *Steve Jackson Games, Inc. v. United States Secret Service*, 36 F.3d 457, 461–62 (5th Cir. 1994); compare § 2510(1) (a "wire communication" is both a transfer and electronic storage of the communication). The statutes therefore distinguish the "interception" of an electronic communication at the time of transmission from the retrieval of such a communication after it has been put into "electronic storage." Interceptions are covered by §§ 2510–22, and access to information in electronic storage by §§ 2701–11.

Section 2511(1)(a) forbids, among other things, the interception of electronic communications. An "interception" is the "acquisition of the contents of any … electronic … communication through the use of any electronic, mechanical or other device." § 2510(4). One might ask how any "interception," as the word is usually understood, could be thought to have occurred here. After all, no computer or phone lines have been tapped, no conversations picked up by hidden microphones, no duplicate pager "cloned" to tap into messages intended for another recipient. Compare *Brown v. Waddell*, 50 F.3d 285 (4th Cir. 1995) (clone pagers); *Jackson v. State*, 636 So. 2d 1372 (Fla. Dist. Ct. App. 1994), aff'd 650 So. 2d 24 (Fla. 1995) (same).

This view is supported by both the statute and the nature of the pager system's operation. To begin with, we think no one would object if the computer were just a passive conduit for a communication, on its way from the sender's keyboard to the pager company and on to recipient's pager. After all, if the computer received an electronic communication from a terminal and passed it on to the pager company, but did not store or otherwise record its contents, it would not have acquired "information concerning the [communication's] substance, purport, or meaning," and therefore no "intercept" would have taken place. (And if there were an intercept, consent would likely be implied under § 2511(2)(c), for one who sends a message using a computer surely must understand that the message will pass through the computer.)

Indeed, we do not understand the plaintiffs to object to the mere passage of their messages through the computer. Their complaint, as we understand it, is that the computer stored (or recorded, or downloaded) the contents of those messages. And that, we think, is where their argument breaks down. The computer's storage of an electronic communication, whether that storage was "temporary" and "intermediate" and "incidental to" its impending "electronic transmission," or more permanent storage for backup purposes, was "electronic storage." An "electronic communication," by definition, cannot be "intercepted" when it is in "electronic storage," because only "communications" can be "intercepted," and, as the Fifth Circuit held in Steve Jackson Games, the "electronic storage" of an "electronic communication" is by definition not part of the communication. The treatment of messages in "electronic storage" is governed by §§ 2701–11, not by the restrictions on "interception" set out at §§ 2501–22.

This leads us to the plaintiffs' claim that the City acted unlawfully when, months after the messages were sent, it accessed and retrieved them from storage in the computer. The problem with the claim is simple. The City is the "provider" of the "electronic communications service" at issue here: the Reno Police Department's terminals, computer and software, and the pagers it issues to its personnel, are, after all, what provide those users with "the ability to send or receive" electronic communications. But § 2701(c)(1) allows service providers to do as they wish when it comes to accessing communications in electronic storage. Because the City is the provider of the "service," neither it nor its employees can be liable under § 2701.

IV. Conclusion

The plaintiffs have not established that they had an objectively reasonable expectation of privacy in the messages at issue. To the extent that the computer acted as a mere conduit of their messages to one another, we do not understand the plaintiffs to complain, and in any event we that think no "interception" occurred; even if there had been an interception, we would likely find implied consent in light of the plaintiffs' decision to send those messages via the computer. We understand the plaintiffs' real complaint to be that their messages were recorded and stored in, and later retrieved from, the computer. But the initial act of storage was "electronic storage," and the applicable statutes are therefore §§ 2701–11 rather than §§ 2501–22. Under those statutes, the City, as the system provider, was free to access the stored messages as it pleased.

What about the use of systems such as "On Star" installed in vehicles? If law enforcement utilized the system to listen to conversations within a vehicle, would that constitute an interception?

349 F.3D 1132 (2003)

U.S. Ct. of Appeals, 9th Circuit

BERZON, Circuit Judge:

Giving new meaning to the automotive advertising slogans "The Ultimate Driving Machine" and "We've Got You Covered," some luxury cars are now equipped with telecommunication devices that provide a set of innovative services to car owners. These on-board systems assist drivers in activities from the mundane—such as navigating an unfamiliar neighborhood or finding a nearby Chinese restaurant—to the more vital—such as responding to emergencies or obtaining road-side assistance. Such systems operate via a combination of GPS (global positioning system, using satellite technology) and cellular technology. The appellant ("the Company") runs one such service ("the System").

One feature of the System allows the Company to open a cellular connection to a vehicle and listen to oral communications within the car. This feature is part of a stolen vehicle recovery mode that provides assistance to car owners and law enforcement authorities in locating and retrieving stolen cars. The same technology that permits the interception of the conversations of thieves absconding with the car also permits eavesdropping on conversations within the vehicle.

The Federal Bureau of Investigation ("FBI"), realizing that the System can be used as a roving "bug" and following the procedures mandated for "bugging" private individuals suspected of criminal activity, sought and obtained a series of court orders requiring the Company to assist in intercepting conversations taking place in a car equipped with the System. The Company challenges the court's authority to order the use of the Company's equipment, facilities, system, and employees. The question for decision is whether the statute governing private parties' obligations to assist the federal government in intercepting communications permits such an order.

I

A. The System

The physical components that permit the System to operate are manufactured by an independent company but installed by the car maker. The car maker then subcontracts with the Company for the provision of the service aspects of the System. When a new car is purchased, owners have the option to subscribe, for a fee, to the System. The System is serviced by two different call centers, one of which is operated by the Company.

A national cellular telephone company provides the cellular airtime for the System and sends bills in batches to the Company. The Company then "forwards" these bills to its customers. It is our understanding from oral argument that the Company includes the cellular phone charges on its own bill sent out to its customers rather than sending on the cellular phone company's bill, but the record is not clear on this matter. Customers write only a single check, payable to the Company, for all System-related fees, including cellular airtime. The System does not allow users to make traditional cellular telephone calls; it only permits a user to communicate with one of the two designated call centers.

Each System console has three buttons: (1) an emergency button, which routes customers' calls to the Company; (2) an information button, which routes customers' calls to the other company that assists the customer with navigation; and (3) the roadside assistance button, which routes customers' calls to the other company for assistance in getting on-site service for vehicles. The System automatically contacts the Company if an airbag deploys or the vehicle's supplemental restraint system activates.

If a customer's car is stolen and the customer verifies the theft, the customer can ask the Company to put the car into stolen vehicle recovery mode. Once the car is in this mode, the Company sends a signal to the car's System. The signal is sent continuously until the car responds or until the Company deactivates the mode. If the System has cellular reception and the engine is running, the System will automatically call the Company. The call will be directed to the next available operator. The Company maintains that it cannot determine when such a call will be made from the car or direct the call to a specific operator.

Once the call from the System is answered, the operator and anyone else listening in can hear sound from inside the vehicle. Occupants of the vehicle will not know of the cellular phone connection and will be unaware of the eavesdropping. The connection remains active until the driver turns off the ignition or loses cellular reception, or the Company disconnects the call. The System returns to normal when the Company deactivates vehicle recovery mode. At this point, one of two things happens: (1) if the radio in the vehicle is on, it will be muted and its screen will display a message saying "[System] Active;" or (2) if the radio is not on, the System will emit a beeping tone, regardless of whether the vehicle is on at the time. There is no way to prevent such signals that the car has been in recovery mode from reaching the customer.

When the System is in stolen vehicle recovery mode, the customer cannot use any of the other System services. If a customer presses any of the non-emergency buttons—for example, the roadside assistance or information buttons—nothing will happen. If the customer presses the emergency button or the airbags deploy while the recovery mode is enabled, it appears to the user that the system is attempting to open up a cellular phone connection to the response center but it is not. Instead, an audio tone is sent over the already open connection. The Company is concerned that if no operator is on the line and only the FBI is listening in, there will be no response to the subscriber's emergency signaled by the transmitted tone.

B. This Case

Upon request by the FBI, the district court issued several *ex parte* orders pursuant to 18 U.S.C. § 2518(4), requiring the Company to assist in intercepting oral communications occurring in a certain vehicle equipped with the System. The Company complied with the first thirty-day order but not the next. After the government filed a Motion to Compel and for Contempt, the Company responded and filed motions for reconsideration and to quash or modify the court's order. The district court held an evidentiary hearing, denied the government's contempt motion, and ordered the Company to comply with the contested order. The Company has since complied with all subsequent court orders. In explaining its order, the district court found that "[The Company] is a 'telecommunications carrier' and 'provider of wire or electronic communication service' within the scope of 18 U.S.C. § 2518(4) and § 2522;" that the FBI request and the court order were not "unreasonably burdensome," that the Company's due process rights had not been violated; and that no "taking" had occurred.

The district court ordered two further, similar *ex parte* interception orders, and the Company both contested and complied with each order. The district court then held a hearing on the Company's pending motions and denied them all. The Company now appeals from this denial.

II

B. Overview of 18 U.S.C. § 2518

Section 2518 was first enacted as part of the Omnibus Crime Control and Safe Streets Act of 1968, Pub. L. No. 90-351(1968). Title III of the Act, Wiretapping and Electronic Surveillance, has the dual goals of: "(1) protecting the privacy of wire and oral communications, and (2) delineating on a uniform basis the circumstances and conditions under which the interception of wire and oral communications may be authorized." S. Rep. No. 90-1097, at 66 (1968), reprinted in 1968 U.S.C.C.A.N. 2112, 2153. Title III therefore attempts to balance protecting the privacy interests of individuals with facilitating the investigation of crime, especially organized crime. Pub. L. No. 90-351, § 801 (1968); S. Rep. No. 90-1097, at 66-73, reprinted in 1968 U.S.C.C.A.N. at 2153-63.

"To assure the privacy of oral and wire communications, title III prohibits all wiretapping and electronic surveillance by persons other than duly authorized law enforcement officers."

S. Rep. No. 90-1097, at 66, reprinted in 1968 U.S.C.C.A.N. at 2153. Law enforcement officers may only intercept communications after receiving "the authorization of a court order obtained after a showing and finding of probable cause." Id. Any person who illegally intercepts oral, wire, or electronic communications is subject to civil and criminal penalties. §§ 2511 & 2520. The statute prohibits the admission of most evidence obtained in violation of title III. § 2518(10)(a).

The statute also has provided, since 1970, that certain enumerated entities and individuals must assist law enforcement in wiretapping or eavesdropping when directed by a court order to do so. Presently, § 2518(4) requires:

> that a provider of wire or electronic communication service, landlord, custodian or other person shall furnish the [law enforcement] applicant forthwith all information, facilities, and technical assistance necessary to accomplish the interception unobtrusively and with a minimum of interference with the services that such service provider, landlord, custodian, or person is according the person whose communications are to be intercepted.

18 U.S.C. § 2518(4).

The question before us is: When may a company, not a common carrier but possessing a unique ability to facilitate the interception of oral communications, be required to assist law enforcement in intercepting such communications?

C. Application of § 2518(4) to the Company

The district court held that the Company was a "provider of wire or electronic communication service" and therefore obligated to assist the FBI under § 2518(4). Determining whether the Company is so obligated under the statute is difficult, as the statutory language is complex.

1. Type of Communications Intercepted

Court orders in this case required the Company to assist the FBI in eavesdropping on conversations occurring inside a vehicle equipped with the System. An "oral communication" is defined in the Act, solipsistically, as "any oral communication uttered by a person exhibiting an expectation that such communication is not subject to interception under circumstances justifying such expectation." § 2510(2); see also *Price v. Turner*, 260 F.3d 1144, 1147–48 (9th Cir. 2001) (cordless telephone calls are not oral communications because the communication is made via radio waves). "In essence, an oral communication is one carried by sound waves, not by an electronic medium." S. Rep. No. 99-541, at 29 (1986), reprinted in 1986 U.S.C.C.A.N. 3555, 3567. The communications intercepted here were in-person voice communications, involving no means of transmission except for natural sound waves. Neither party disputes that the occupants of the vehicle reasonably expected that words spoken between them would be private, not subject to interception or transmission. The communications at issue therefore were "oral communications" within the ambit of the statute.

True, the FBI used wire communications via the System's cellular phone technology to intercept the oral communications made within the vehicle. The FBI, however, sought to intercept the oral communications between the occupants of the vehicle, not the wire communications between the vehicle's occupants and the Company. The manner in which the communication was intercepted does not change the fact that the FBI intercepted oral communications.

The Company contends that title III does not cover the interception of oral communications via a wire transmission. The statute, however, does include such interceptions within its purview. "Both wiretapping and bugging are regulated under Title III." (*Dalia*, 441 U.S. at 241 n.1). Bugging "includes the interception of all oral communication in a given location.... This interception typically is accomplished by installation of a small microphone in the room to be bugged and transmission to some nearby receiver." Id. No reason appears why transmission through wire technology rather than in some other fashion does not fall under the ambit of title III.

2. "Provider of Wire or Electronic Communication Service"

The question next becomes whether the Company had an obligation pursuant to § 2518(4) to assist law enforcement in intercepting the oral communications in the car. If the Company is "a provider of wire or electronic communication service, landlord, custodian or other person," then it is so obligated. See § 2518(4).

The Company contends that it is not a "provider of wire or electronic communication service" because it does not operate the cellular service used as part of the System. This contention lacks force.

Under our reading of the statute, the Company is the "provider" and the System is the "electronic communication service" that it offers, even though the Company neither "furnishes" nor "operates" the cellular facilities that actually perform the "aural transfer" referred to in § 2510(1).

The Company's customers are billed by the Company for the airtime and have no direct dealings with the cellular telephone company. Using the term "provides" as one would in ordinary discourse, it is the Company, not the cellular telephone company, that "provides" the communication service to its customers.

That the "provider of wire or electronic communication service" mentioned in § 2518(4) may be distinct from the "person" in § 2510(1) who "furnishes or operates" "facilities for the transmission of communications" is confirmed by a separate provision of the wiretapping statute—§ 2511(2)(a)(i). Section 2511(2)(a)(i), which exempts designated persons from the wiretapping laws when "intercepting" communications is a "necessary incident" to their business, specifies that the exemption only extends to "an officer, employee, or agent of a provider of wire or electronic communication service, whose facilities are used in the transmission of a wire or electronic communication." Id. Thus, the statute distinguishes between those service providers that furnish their own facilities, and those service providers like the Company that do not. Section 2518(4), in contrast, makes no such distinction. So the Company is covered by that section and required to provide such assistance as that section requires.

3. "Other Person"

There is a second, distinct reason for concluding that the Company is covered by § 2518(4). That provision obligates not only a "provider of wire or electronic communication service" but also a "landlord, custodian or other person" to assist law enforcement in intercepting communications. The government maintains that the Company is an "other person" within the meaning of the statute. We agree.

[W]e read the term "other person" in § 2518(4) to mean an individual or entity who both provides some sort of service to the target of the surveillance and is uniquely situated to assist in intercepting communications through its facilities or technical abilities.

The Company regularly supplies to the car owner the services provided by the System. The Company is also uniquely situated to facilitate the interception of the oral communications within the vehicle; only it can contact the car and place it into stolen vehicle recovery mode by opening a phone line to the car. Even though it might be possible for the cellular phone company to assist law enforcement in monitoring the oral communications within the vehicle once the phone line is open, the Company can do so much more simply, as the System is programmed to place a call to the Company's operators.

The Company therefore fits our understanding of "other person." Thus, for this reason as well, if the orders are otherwise proper under the statute, the Company can be obligated pursuant to § 2518(4) to assist the FBI by "furnishing ... information, facilities and technical assistance...." § 2518(4).

D. Requirement of a Minimum of Interference

That the Company is both a "provider of wire or electronic communication service" and an "other person" within the meaning of § 2518(4), and may therefore be required to furnish facilities and technical assistance is not, however, the end of the story. The question remains whether the order goes too far in interfering with the service provided by the Company, by preventing the Company from supplying the System's services to its customers when a vehicle is under surveillance. We conclude that it does.

Court orders granted pursuant to the authority of § 2518 must specify that assistance be provided "unobtrusively and with a minimum of interference with the services that such service provider, landlord ... or person is according the person whose communications are to be intercepted." § 2518(4). The "a minimum of interference" language was added in 1970 as part of the amendment that added the explicit assistance requirement to title III. Pub. L. No. 91-358, § 211(b) (1970).

Looking at the language of the statute, the "a minimum of interference" requirement certainly allows for some level of interference with customers' service in the conducting of surveillance. We need not decide precisely how much intereference [*sic*] is permitted. "A minimum of interference" at least precludes total incapacitation of a service while interception is in progress. Put another way, eavesdropping is not performed with "a minimum of interference" if a service is completely shut down as a result of the surveillance.

In this case, FBI surveillance completely disabled the monitored car's System. The only function that worked in some form was the emergency button or automatic emergency response signal. These emergency features, however, were severely hampered by the surveillance: Pressing the emergency button and activation of the car's airbags, instead of automatically contacting the Company, would simply emit a tone over the already open phone line. No one at the Company was likely to be monitoring the call at such a time, as the call was transferred to the FBI once received. There is no assurance that the FBI would be monitoring the call at the time the tone was transmitted; indeed, the minimization requirements, preclude the FBI from listening in to conversations unrelated to the purpose of the surveillance. Also, the FBI, however well-intentioned, is not in the business of providing emergency road services, and might well have better things to do when listening in than respond with such services to the electronic signal sent over the line. The result was that the Company could no longer supply any of the various services it had promised its customer, including assurance of response in an emergency.

We hold that whatever the precise limits Congress intended with its "a minimum of interference" limitation, the level of interference with the System worked by the FBI's surveillance is not "a minimum of interference with the services" that the Company "accords the person whose communications are to be intercepted." § 2518(4). Because, given the setup of the System, the surveillance could not be completed with "a minimum of interference," the district court erred in ordering the Company's assistance.

Conclusion

The Company can properly be considered an "other person" for purposes of § 2518(4), and therefore the district court could have ordered the Company to assist the FBI in intercepting oral communications if the other requirements of § 2518(4) had been met. In this instance, however, the Company could not assist the FBI without disabling the System in the monitored car. Therefore, under the "a minimum of interference" requirement of § 2518(4), the order should not have issued. We therefore REVERSE the order of the district court.

TALLMAN, Circuit Judge, dissenting:

I respectfully dissent. I agree that 18 U.S.C. § 2518(4) applies to the Company as a "provider" or "other person" and therefore the district court had the authority to order it to assist the FBI in intercepting conspiratorial conversations held in the car and transmitted electronically via the Company's System. I disagree, however, with the majority's conclusion that the order cannot be carried out in conformance with § 2518(4). The FBI established to the district court's satisfaction the existence of probable cause to believe that individuals engaged in a continuing criminal enterprise were using the car as a venue for planning illegal activities. Pursuant to § 2518(4), the district court found the necessity for this type of intercept and authorized federal agents to surreptitiously monitor the individuals' conversations.

The majority opinion nonetheless invalidates the district court's order, despite express statutory language commanding the Company to assist the government in such eavesdropping. The court reaches this result by erroneously concluding that the district court's order cannot be carried out "with 'a minimum of interference.'" This holding cannot be reconciled with the plain text of the statute.

I

Section 2518(4) sets out the requirements for the execution of a judicially authorized intercept order where the assistance of a communication service provider is necessary. Specifically, the provider

> shall furnish the [government] forthwith all information, facilities, and technical assistance necessary to accomplish the interception unobtrusively and with a minimum of interference with the services that such service provider, landlord, custodian, or person is according the person whose communications are to be intercepted.

> 18 U.S.C. § 2518(4).

The plain meaning of the phrase "minimum of interference" is clear: an order must be executed in the manner that causes the least amount of disruption necessary to intercept the targeted communication. Significantly, § 2518(4) does not require the method of interception to allow the monitored communication service to continue without any interruption. Here, the record leaves no doubt that the Company complied with the challenged order in the way least likely to interfere with its subscriber's services and that, in fact, no actual service disruption occurred. The majority opinion ignores the record on how the intercept was implemented and contorts the meaning of "a minimum of interference."

As a threshold matter, there is no evidence that any service disruption actually occurred. The record does not indicate that the subjects of the surveillance tried to use the System while the FBI was listening. One cannot disrupt a service unless and until it is being utilized. Moreover, even accepting *arguendo* the majority's characterization of the emergency call function as "severely hampered" by the surveillance, this characterization by its own terms belies the claim that the Service was "completely shut down." The record reflects that the emergency call function was still operational, albeit monitored by the FBI rather than a Company operator. In any event, as there is no record that an emergency signal or a call for service was ever transmitted on the System during government surveillance, the majority can only speculate that federal agents would have done nothing had the occupants sought help by pushing a button or if the emergency call function had been automatically activated by the deployment of an airbag.

The majority opinion also makes the fundamental mistake of treating "a minimum of interference" as an absolute threshold instead of a relative standard. As revealed by a brief review of dictionary definitions, a "minimum" is a concept that depends upon there being no lesser amount. See, e.g., *American Heritage Dictionary of the English Language*, New College Edition 835 (1976) (defining "minimum" in its noun form as "the least possible quantity or degree ... or the lowest quantity, degree, or number reached or recorded; the lower limit of variation").

These definitions confirm that "a minimum of interference" must mean the lowest, least, and smallest amount of interference possible, whatever that amount might be. The record indicates that the only method of executing the intercept order in this case involved activating the car's microphone and transferring the car's cellular telephone link to the FBI. This conduct might have amounted to a service disruption had the subjects of the surveillance attempted to use the System, but there is no evidence that they did. The majority concludes that "eavesdropping is not performed with 'a minimum of interference' if a service is completely shut down as a result of the surveillance." However, even the complete shutdown of a service can represent the minimum interference, so long as no lesser amount of interference could satisfy the intercept order. It is not an ineluctable conclusion that no compliance is required if nothing less will do the job.

The majority creates—under the guise of limiting the assistance a provider or other person may be required to render—a wide-ranging form of protection for the legitimate targets of government surveillance. But Congress legislated only very limited restrictions on the effect of intercept orders once authorized by Article III judges under § 2518. As it fails to identify any real service disruption, much less explain how the Company could have administered the intercept in a way that would cause less interference, the majority's statutory argument is unsupportable.

III

It is undisputed in this case that the intercept order was administered in the manner that caused the least possible interference with the subscriber's service and that the district court determined that the order was not unduly burdensome. This should end the analysis and lead to the conclusion that the district court properly ordered the provider to comply. Because the court's holding that the order violated § 2518(4) is based on a flawed reading of the statute, disregards the factual findings of the district court, and undermines an important investigative tool in a manner that defies common sense, I respectfully dissent.

What is the result when spyware is installed on the computer? The following case illustrates the legal problems that arise when a suspicious spouse installs spyware on the family computer:

O'Brien v. O'Brien

---

899 SO. 2D 1133 (2005)

COURT OF APPEAL OF FLORIDA, FIFTH DISTRICT

SAWAYA, Chief Judge

Emanating from a rather contentious divorce proceeding is an issue we must resolve regarding application of certain provisions of the Security of Communications Act (the Act) found in Chapter 934, Florida Statutes (2003). Specifically, we must determine whether the trial court properly concluded that pursuant to section 934.03(1), Florida

Statutes (2003), certain communications were inadmissible because they were illegally intercepted by the Wife who, unbeknownst to the Husband, had installed a spyware program on a computer used by the Husband that copied and stored electronic communications between the Husband and another woman.

When marital discord erupted between the Husband and the Wife, the Wife secretly installed a spyware program called Spector on the Husband's computer. It is undisputed that the Husband engaged in private on-line chats with another woman while playing Yahoo Dominoes on his computer. The Spector spyware secretly took snapshots of what appeared on the computer screen, and the frequency of these snapshots allowed Spector to capture and record all chat conversations, instant messages, e-mails sent and received, and the websites visited by the user of the computer. When the Husband discovered the Wife's clandestine attempt to monitor and record his conversations with his Dominoes partner, the Husband uninstalled the Spector software and filed a Motion for Temporary Injunction, which was subsequently granted, to prevent the Wife from disclosing the communications. Thereafter, the Husband requested and received a permanent injunction to prevent the Wife's disclosure of the communications and to prevent her from engaging in this activity in the future. The latter motion also requested that the trial court preclude introduction of the communications into evidence in the divorce proceeding. This request was also granted. The trial court, without considering the communications, entered a final judgment of dissolution of marriage. The Wife moved for rehearing, which was subsequently denied.

The Wife appeals the order granting the permanent injunction, the final judgment, and the order denying the Wife's motion for rehearing on the narrow issue of whether the trial court erred in refusing to admit evidence of the Husband's computer activities obtained through the spyware the Wife secretly installed on the computer. The Wife argues that the electronic communications do not fall under the umbra of the Act because these communications were retrieved from storage and, therefore, are not "intercepted communications" as defined by the Act. In opposition, the Husband contends that the Spector spyware installed on the computer acquired his electronic communications real-time as they were in transmission and, therefore, are intercepts illegally obtained under the Act.

The trial court found that the electronic communications were illegally obtained in violation of section 934.03(1)(a)–(e), and so we begin our analysis with the pertinent provisions of that statute, which subjects any person to criminal penalties who engages in the following activities:

(a) Intentionally intercepts, endeavors to intercept, or procures any other person to intercept or endeavor to intercept any wire, oral, or electronic communication;
(b) Intentionally uses, endeavors to use, or procures any other person to use or endeavor to use any electronic, mechanical, or other device to intercept any oral communication when:
    1. Such device is affixed to, or otherwise transmits a signal through, a wire, cable, or other like connection used in wire communication; or
    2. Such device transmits communications by radio or interferes with the transmission of such communication;
(c) Intentionally discloses, or endeavors to disclose, to any other person the contents of any wire, oral, or electronic communication, knowing or having reason to know that the

information was obtained through the interception of a wire, oral, or electronic communication in violation of this subsection;

(d) Intentionally uses, or endeavors to use, the contents of any wire, oral, or electronic communication, knowing or having reason to know that the information was obtained through the interception of a wire, oral, or electronic communication in violation of this subsection; or

(e) Intentionally discloses, or endeavors to disclose, to any other person the contents of any wire, oral, or electronic communication intercepted by means authorized by subparagraph (2)(a)2., paragraph (2)(b), paragraph (2)(c), s.934.07, or s.934.09 when that person knows or has reason to know that the information was obtained through the interception of such a communication in connection with a criminal investigation, has obtained or received the information in connection with a criminal investigation, and intends to improperly obstruct, impede, or interfere with a duly authorized criminal investigation;

shall be punished as provided in subsection (4).

§ 934.03(1)(a)–(e), Fla. Stat. (2003).

Enactment of these prohibitions connotes "a policy decision by the Florida legislature to allow each party to a conversation to have an expectation of privacy from interception by another party to the conversation." *Shevin v. Sunbeam Television Corp.*, 351 So. 2d 723, 726–27 (Fla. 1977). The purpose of the Act is to protect every person's right to privacy and to prevent the pernicious effect on all citizens who would otherwise feel insecure from intrusion into their private conversations and communications.

The clear intent of the Legislature in enacting section 934.03 was to make it illegal for a person to intercept wire, oral, or electronic communications. It is beyond doubt that what the trial court excluded from evidence are "electronic communications."*

The core of the issue lies in whether the electronic communications were intercepted. The term "intercept" is defined by the Act as "the aural or other acquisition of the contents of any wire, electronic, or oral communication through the use of any electronic, mechanical, or other device." § 934.02(3), Fla. Stat. (2003). We discern that there is a rather fine distinction between what is transmitted as an electronic communication subject to interception and the storage of what has been previously communicated. It is here that we tread upon new ground. Because we have found no precedent rendered by the Florida courts that considers this distinction, and in light of the fact that the Act was modeled after the Federal Wiretap Act, we advert to decisions by the federal courts that have addressed this issue for guidance.

The federal courts have consistently held that electronic communications, in order to be intercepted, must be acquired contemporaneously with transmission and that electronic communications are not intercepted within the meaning of the Federal Wiretap Act if they are retrieved from storage. See *Fraser v. Nationwide Mut. Ins. Co.*, 352 F.3d 107 (3d Cir. 2003); *Theofel v. Farey-Jones*, 359 F.3d 1066 (9th Cir.), cert. denied,

---

* The term "electronic communications" is defined in section 934.02(12), Florida Statutes (2003), as "any transfer of signs, signals, writing, images, sounds, data, or intelligence of any nature transmitted in whole or in part by a wire, radio, electromagnetic, photoelectronic, or photooptical system that affects intrastate, inter-state, or foreign commerce...."

160 L. Ed. 2d 17, 125 S. Ct. 48 (2004); *United States v. Steiger*, 318 F.3d 1039 (11th Cir.), cert. denied, 538 U.S. 1051, 155 L. Ed. 2d 1095 (2003); *Konop v. Hawaiian Airlines, Inc.*, 302 F.3d 868 (9th Cir. 2002), cert. denied, 537 U.S. 1193, 154 L. Ed. 2d 1028 (2003). These courts arrived at this conclusion based on the federal law definitions of (1) the term "intercept," which is very similar to the definition in the Florida Act, (2) the term "wire communication," which provides for electronic storage, and (3) the term "electronic communication," which does not provide for electronic storage. The fact that the definition of "wire communication" provides for electronic storage while the definition of "electronic communication" does not, suggests to the federal courts that Congress intended "intercept" to include retrieval from storage of wire communications, but exclude retrieval from storage of electronic communications. The definition of "wire communication" in the Florida Act, unlike the Federal Wiretap Act, does not include a provision for retrieval from storage and, therefore, it is not clear whether the same rationale would be applied by the federal courts to provisions identical to the Florida Act. However, we need not decide whether electronic communications may never be intercepted from storage under the Florida Act because the particular facts and circumstances of the instant case reveal that the electronic communications were intercepted contemporaneously with transmission.

The Spector spyware program that the Wife surreptitiously installed on the computer used by the Husband intercepted and copied the electronic communications as they were transmitted. We believe that particular method constitutes interception within the meaning of the Florida Act, and the decision in *Steiger* supports this conclusion. In *Steiger*, an individual was able to hack into the defendant's computer via a Trojan horse virus that allowed the hacker access to pornographic materials stored on the hard drive. The hacker was successful in transferring the pornographic material from that computer to the hacker's computer. The court held that because the Trojan horse virus simply copied information that had previously been stored on the computer's hard drive, the capture of the electronic communication was not an interception within the meaning of the Federal Wiretap Act. The court did indicate, however, that interception could occur if the virus or software intercepted the communication as it was being transmitted and copied it. The court stated:

> There is only a narrow window during which an E-mail interception may occur—the seconds or mili-seconds before which a newly composed message is saved to any temporary location following a send command. Therefore, unless some type of automatic routing software is used (for example, a duplicate of all of an employee's messages are automatically sent to the employee's boss), interception of E-mail within the prohibition of [the Wiretap Act] is virtually impossible.

> *Steiger*, 318 F.3d at 1050 (quoting Jarrod J. White, *E-Mail at Work.com: Employer Monitoring of Employee E-Mail*, 48 Ala. L. Rev. 1079, 1083 (1997)).

Hence, a valid distinction exists between a spyware program similar to that in *Steiger*, which simply breaks into a computer and retrieves information already stored on the hard drive, and a spyware program similar to the one installed by the Wife in the instant case, which copies the communication as it is transmitted and routes the copy to a storage file in the computer.

The Wife argues that the communications were in fact stored before acquisition because once the text image became visible on the screen, the communication was no longer in transit and, therefore, not subject to intercept. We disagree. We do not believe that this evanescent time period is sufficient to transform acquisition of the communications from a contemporaneous interception to retrieval from electronic storage. We conclude that because the spyware installed by the Wife intercepted the electronic communication contemporaneously with transmission, copied it, and routed the copy to a file in the computer's hard drive, the electronic communications were intercepted in violation of the Florida Act.

We must next determine whether the improperly intercepted electronic communications may be excluded from evidence under the Act. The exclusionary provisions of the Act are found in section 934.06, Florida Statutes (2003), which provides that "whenever any wire or oral communication has been intercepted, no part of the contents of such communication and no evidence derived therefrom may be received in evidence...." Conspicuously absent from the provisions of this statute is any reference to electronic communications. The federal courts, which interpreted an identical statute contained in the Federal Wiretap Act, have held that because provision is not made for exclusion of intercepted electronic communications, Congress intended that such communications not be excluded under the Federal Wiretap Act. We agree with this reasoning and conclude that the intercepted electronic communications in the instant case are not excludable under the Act. But this does not end the inquiry.

Although not specifically excludable under the Act, it is illegal and punishable as a crime under the Act to intercept electronic communications. § 934.03, Fla. Stat. (2003). The trial court found that the electronic communications were illegally intercepted in violation of the Act and ordered that they not be admitted in evidence. Because the evidence was illegally obtained, we conclude that the trial court did not abuse its discretion in refusing to admit it.

We affirm the orders and the final judgment under review in the instant case.

And finally, does the installation of a keylogger and the capture of keystrokes constitute an interception? Consider the following:

United States v. Scarfo

---

180 F. SUPP. 2D 572 (2001)

U.S. DISTRICT COURT, DISTRICT OF NEW JERSEY

On January 15, 1999, FBI agents entered the business office of Merchants Services of Essex County, operated by Nicodemo S. Scarfo and Paolercio, pursuant to a search warrant authorizing a search for evidence of illegal gambling and loan sharking. During the search, the FBI located a computer and attempted to access the files on its hard drive. Unable to gain entry to an encrypted file named "Factors" and suspecting that the file contained the evidence of gambling and loan sharking, the FBI returned to the business office and, pursuant to two search warrants, installed a key logger system (KLS) on either the computer or computer keyboard in order to capture the password to the encrypted file. The KLS records keystrokes made on the computer keyboard. The computer was equipped with a modem for communication over telephone lines and an America Online account. On execution of the second warrant related to the

KLS, the FBI discovered the passwords, accessed the file named "Factors," and acquired what is alleged to be incriminating evidence of gambling and loan sharking.

After the grand jury returned an indictment charging Scarfo and Paolercio with gambling and loan sharking, the defendants moved for discovery and suppression of evidence seized from the computer upon the ground that the evidence obtained by the key logger necessarily intercepted communications while it was installed on the business computer. The district court expressed concern whether the KLS may have operated when Scarfo was communicating over telephone lines with the modem and directed the United States to file a report. When the government refused, citing secrecy concerns, the court issued the following decision:

POLITAN, District Judge

This case presents an interesting issue of first impression dealing with the ever-present tension between individual privacy and liberty rights and law enforcement's use of new and advanced technology to vigorously investigate criminal activity. Of course, the matter takes on added importance in light of recent events and potential national security implications.

As a result of these concerns, on August 7, 2001, this Court ordered the United States to file with the Court a report explaining fully how the KLS device functions and describing the KLS technology and how it works vis-a-vis the computer modem, Internet communications, e-mail and all other uses of a computer. In light of the government's grave concern over the national security implications such a revelation might raise, the Court permitted the United States to submit any additional evidence which would provide particular and specific reasons how and why disclosure of the KLS would jeopardize both ongoing and future domestic criminal investigations and national security interests.

[T]he United States submitted the affidavit of Neil J. Gallagher, Assistant Director, Federal Bureau of Investigation, dated September 6, 2001. In his affidavit, Mr. Gallagher stated that the characteristics and/or functional components of the KLS were previously classified and marked "SECRET" at or around November 1997.

The Court heard oral argument on September 7, 2001, to explore whether the government may invoke CIPA and, specifically, whether the government had classified the KLS. Although the defense conceded that the KLS was classified for purposes of CIPA, the Court reserved on that question and ordered the government to provide written submissions to the Court. The government then filed an *ex parte*, in camera motion for the Court's inspection of the classified material.

On September 26, 2001, the Court held an in camera, *ex parte* hearing with several high-ranking officials from the United States Attorney General's office and the FBI Because of the sensitive nature of the material presented, all CIPA regulations were followed and only those persons with top-secret clearance were permitted to attend. Pursuant to CIPA's regulations, the United States presented the Court with detailed and top-secret, classified information regarding the KLS, including how it operates in connection with a modem. The government also demonstrated to the Court how the KLS affects national security.

After reviewing the classified material, I issued a Protective Order pursuant CIPA on October 2, 2001, wherein I found that the government could properly invoke CIPA and

that the government made a sufficient showing to warrant the issuance of an order protecting against disclosure of the classified information. The October 2, 2001, Protective
Order also directed that the government's proposed unclassified summary of information relating to the KLS under Section 4 of CIPA would be sufficient to allow the
defense to effectively argue the motion to suppress. Accordingly, the Protective Order
permitted the government to provide Scarfo with the unclassified summary statement
in lieu of the classified information regarding the KLS. Pursuant to Section 6(d) of
CIPA, the Court also sealed the transcript of the September 26th *ex parte*, in camera
hearing and the government's supporting Affidavits. The government filed with the
Court and served on Scarfo the unclassified summary on October 5, 2001, in the form
of an October 4, 2001, Affidavit of Randall S. Murch, Supervisory Special Agent of the
Federal Bureau of Investigation, Laboratory Division (the "Murch Affidavit").

Having the benefit of the September 26th *ex parte*, in camera hearing and the many
supplemental submissions of the parties, the Defendants' motion for discovery and
suppression is now ripe for resolution.

DISCUSSION

Defendants Scarfo and Paolercio advance several arguments in moving to suppress certain evidence seized by the FBI. The Defendants first contend that the KLS constituted
an unlawful general warrant in violation of the Fourth Amendment to the Constitution.
In addition, the Defendants, after reviewing the government's unclassified summary,
i.e., the Murch Affidavit, argue that the Murch Affidavit is inadequate under CIPA and
would conflict with the United States Supreme Court decision of *Jencks v. United States*,
353 U.S. 657, 77 S. Ct. 1007, 1 L. Ed. 2d 1103 (1957). Lastly, Defendants urge the Court
to suppress the evidence because the KLS effectively intercepted a wire communication
in violation of Title III, 18 U.S.C. § 2510.

I. General Warrant

Scarfo argues that since the government had the ability to capture and record only those
keystrokes relevant to the "passphrase" to the encrypted file, and because it received an
unnecessary over-collection of data, the warrants were written and executed as general
warrants. This claim is without merit.

Typically, the proponent of a motion to suppress bears the burden of establishing
that his Fourth Amendment rights were violated. The standard of proof in this regard
is a preponderance of the evidence.

The Fourth Amendment states that "no Warrants shall issue, but upon probable
cause, supported by Oath or affirmation, and particularly describing the place to be
searched, and the persons or things to be seized." U.S. Const. amend. IV. Where a search
warrant is obtained, the Fourth Amendment requires a certain modicum of particularity in the language of the warrant with respect to the area and items to be searched
and/or seized. The particularity requirement exists so that law enforcement officers are
constrained from undertaking a boundless and exploratory rummaging through one's
personal property.

From a review of the two Court Orders authorizing the searches along with the
accompanying Affidavits, it is clear that the Court Orders suffer from no constitutional
infirmity with respect to particularity. Magistrate Judge Donald Haneke's May 8, 1999,

Order permitting the search of Scarfo's computer clearly states that Judge Haneke found probable cause existed to believe that "Nicodemo S. Scarfo has committed and continues to commit offenses in violation of Title 18, U.S.C. §§ 371, 892–94, 1955 and § 1962." That Order further stated that there was "probable cause to believe that Nicodemo S. Scarfo's computer, located in the TARGET LOCATION, is being used to store business records of Scarfo's illegal gambling business and loansharking operation, and that the above mentioned records have been encrypted."

Because the encrypted file could not be accessed via traditional investigative means, Judge Haneke's Order permitted law enforcement officers to "install and leave behind software, firmware, and/or hardware equipment which will monitor the inputted data entered on Nicodemo S. Scarfo's computer in the TARGET LOCATION so that the FBI can capture the password necessary to decrypt computer files by recording the key related information as they are entered." The Order also allowed the FBI to search for and seize business records in whatever form they are kept (e.g., written, mechanically or computer maintained and any necessary computer hardware, including computers, computer hard drives, floppy disks or other storage disks or tapes as necessary to access such information, as well as, seizing the mirror hard drive to preserve configuration files, public keys, private keys, and other information that may be of assistance in interpreting the password)—including address and telephone books and electronic storage devices; ledgers and other accounting-type records; banking records and statements; travel records; correspondence; memoranda; notes; calendars; and diaries—that contain information about the identities and whereabouts of conspirators, betting customers and victim debtors, and/or that otherwise reveal the origin, receipt, concealment or distribution of criminal proceeds relating to illegal gambling, loansharking and other racketeering offenses.

On its face, the Order is very comprehensive and lists the items, including the evidence in the encrypted file, to be seized with more than sufficient specificity. One would be hard-pressed to draft a more specified or detailed search warrant than the May 8, 1999 Order. Indeed, it could not be written with more particularity. It specifically identifies each piece of evidence the FBI sought which would be linked to the particular crimes the FBI had probable cause to believe were committed. Most importantly, Judge Haneke's Order clearly specifies the key piece of the puzzle the FBI sought—Scarfo's passphrase to the encrypted file.

That the KLS certainly recorded keystrokes typed into Scarfo's keyboard other than the searched-for passphrase is of no consequence. This does not, as Scarfo argues, convert the limited search for the passphrase into a general exploratory search. During many lawful searches, police officers may not know the exact nature of the incriminating evidence sought until they stumble upon it. Just like searches for incriminating documents in a closet or filing cabinet, it is true that during a search for a passphrase "some innocuous [items] will be at least cursorily perused in order to determine whether they are among those [items] to be seized." *United States v. Conley*, 4 F.3d 1200, 1208 (3d Cir. 1993).

Hence, "no tenet of the Fourth Amendment prohibits a search merely because it cannot be performed with surgical precision." *Conley*, 4 F.3d at 1208 (quoting *United States v. Christine*, 687 F.2d 749, 760 (3d Cir. 1982)). Where proof of wrongdoing depends upon documents or computer passphrases whose precise nature cannot be known in advance, law enforcement officers must be afforded the leeway to wade through a potential morass of information in the target location to find the particular evidence which is properly specified in the warrant. * * * Accordingly, Scarfo's claim that the warrants were written and executed as general warrants is rejected.

III. CIPA

Congress enacted CIPA on October 15, 1980, to address the issues which accompany criminal prosecutions involving national security secrets. CIPA establishes certain pre-trial, trial and appellate procedures regarding the handling of classified information in criminal cases and protects against disclosure of sensitive, classified information. Section 1(a) of CIPA defines the term "classified information" as follows:

> any information or material that has been determined by the United States Government pursuant to an Executive order, statute, or regulation, to require protection against unauthorized disclosure for reasons of national security and any restricted data, as defined in paragraph r. of section 11 of the Atomic Energy Act of 1954 (42 U.S.C. 2014(y)).

The term "national security" is defined in Section 1(b) of the Act as "the national defense and foreign relations of the United States." Section 2 allows "any party [to] move for a pretrial conference to consider matters relating to classified information that may arise in connection with the prosecution."

Pursuant to CIPA, the United States requested a hearing in order to block the disclosure of supposedly classified information concerning the KLS technique. The Court held an in camera, *ex parte* hearing on September 26, 2001, to assess the classified nature of the KLS and the sufficiency of the unclassified summary proposed by the government.

[T]he Court is now satisfied that the KLS was in fact classified as defined by CIPA. The Court also concludes that under Section 4 and 6(c) of CIPA the government met its burden in showing that the information sought by the Defendants constitutes classified information touching upon national security concerns as defined in CIPA. Moreover, it is the opinion of the Court that as a result of the September 26th hearing, the government presented to the Court's satisfaction proof that disclosure of the classified KLS information would cause identifiable damage to the national security of the United States. The Court is precluded from discussing this information in detail since it remains classified.

Further, upon comparing the specific classified information sought and the government's proposed unclassified summary, the Court finds that the United States met its burden in showing that the summary in the form of the Murch Affidavit would provide Scarfo with substantially the same ability to make his defense as would disclosure of the specific classified information regarding the KLS technique. The Murch Affidavit explains, to a reasonable and sufficient degree of specificity without disclosing the highly sensitive and classified information, the operating features of the KLS. The Murch Affidavit is more than sufficient and has provided ample information for the Defendants to litigate this motion. Therefore, no further discovery with regard to the KLS technique is necessary.

IV. Whether the KLS Intercepted Wire Communications

The principal mystery surrounding this case was whether the KLS intercepted a wire communication in violation of the wiretap statute by recording keystrokes of e-mail or other communications made over a telephone or cable line while the modem operated. These are the only conceivable wire communications which might emanate from Scarfo's computer and potentially fall under the wiretap statute.

Upon a careful and thorough review of the classified information provided to the Court on September 26th and the Murch Affidavit, the Court finds that the KLS technique utilized in deciphering the passphrase to Scarfo's encrypted file did not intercept any wire communications and therefore did not violate the wiretap statute, Title III, 18 U.S.C. § 2510. I am satisfied the KLS did not operate during any period of time in which the computer's modem was activated.

Scarfo's computer contained an encryption program called PGP (Pretty Good Privacy), which is used to encrypt or scramble computer files so that decrypting or unscrambling the files requires use of the appropriate passphrase. According to the Murch Affidavit, in order to decrypt an encrypted file, the PGP software displays on the user's computer screen a "dialog box." The user then must enter, via the keyboard, the "passphrase" into the dialog box. When the proper passphrase is entered, PGP verifies that the passphrase is correct and, after several steps, leads to the decryption of the selected file.

The KLS, which is the exclusive property of the FBI, was devised by FBI engineers using previously developed techniques in order to obtain a target's key and key-related information. As part of the investigation into Scarfo's computer, the FBI "did not install and operate any component which would search for and record data entering or exiting the computer from the transmission pathway through the modem attached to the computer." Neither did the FBI "install or operate any KLS component which would search for or record any fixed data stored within the computer."

Recognizing that Scarfo's computer had a modem and thus was capable of transmitting electronic communications via the modem, the FBI configured the KLS to avoid intercepting electronic communications typed on the keyboard and simultaneously transmitted in real time via the communication ports. To do this, the FBI designed the component "so that each keystroke was evaluated individually." As Mr. Murch explained:

> The default status of the keystroke component was set so that, on entry, a keystroke was normally not recorded. Upon entry or selection of a keyboard key by a user, the KLS checked the status of each communication port installed on the computer, and, all communication ports indicated inactivity, meaning that the modem was not using any port at that time, then the keystroke in question would be recorded.
>
> Murch Aff., P 6.

Hence, when the modem was operating, the KLS did not record keystrokes. It was designed to prohibit the capture of keyboard keystrokes whenever the modem operated. Since Scarfo's computer possessed no other means of communicating with another computer save for the modem, the KLS did not intercept any wire communications. Accordingly, the Defendants' motion to suppress evidence for violation of Title III is denied.

In this day and age, it appears that on a daily basis we are overwhelmed with new and exciting, technologically-advanced gadgetry. Indeed, the amazing capabilities bestowed upon us by science are at times mind-boggling. As a result, we must be ever vigilant against the evisceration of Constitutional rights at the hands of modern technology. Yet, at the same time, it is likewise true that modern-day criminals have also embraced technological advances and used them to further their felonious purposes. Each day, advanced computer technologies and the increased accessibility to the Internet means criminal behavior is becoming more sophisticated and complex. This includes the ability to find new ways to commit old crimes, as well as new crimes beyond the comprehension of courts. As a result of this surge in so-called "cyber crime," law enforcement's ability to vigorously pursue such rogues cannot be hindered where all Constitutional limitations are scrupulously observed.

Key Words and Phrases

Electronic communication	Spyware
Interception	Wire communication
Keylogger	Wiretap
Oral communication	Wiretap order

Review Problems

1. The decisions in *Steve Jackson Games* and *Councilman* appear to be at odds. Is there any way of reconciling the two decisions? What are the critical factual distinctions between the two cases?
2. The Wiretap Act allows only law enforcement officials to obtain an order permitting the installation of a wiretap. Why is the power to tap limited to law enforcement? Are there circumstances when a private party can lawfully wiretap?

Weblinks

www.cybercrime.gov/ssmanual/index.html
   Chapter 3 of the *Search and Seizure Manual* discusses access to stored communications. Chapter 4 of the manual discusses wiretapping.
www.epic.org/privacy/wiretap/
   This page from the website of the Electronic Privacy Information Center (EPIC) provides information and case law on wiretapping.
www.eff.org/Privacy/Surveillance/
   This page from the website of the Electronic Frontier Foundation contains an archive of documents on wiretapping and surveillance.
www.findlaw.com
   This is the home page of the Findlaw website. By entering *wiretapping* or *pen registers* or *stored communications* into the search window, you will be taken to all resources in Findlaw's database on that topic. This is an excellent resource for research material.

Access to Stored Communications

11

Introduction

The important distinction between wiretapping and access to stored communications is that wiretapping involves an interception of a live communication, and accessing a stored communication involves a communication where the content is in temporary storage somewhere.

Chapter 10 focused on the concept of interception. In this chapter we focus on stored communications and consider those circumstances when law enforcement officials can obtain information that has been stored, albeit temporarily, by a communications provider.

The Stored Communications Act (18 USC §§ 2701–2712) was enacted as part of the Electronic Communications Privacy Act of 1986. The Stored Communications Act, and specifically 18 USC § 2701 (a), imposes criminal liability upon any person who

(1) intentionally accesses without authorization a facility through which an electronic communication service is provided; or
(2) intentionally exceeds an authorization to access that facility; and thereby obtains, alters, or prevents authorized access to a wire or electronic communication while it is in electronic storage in such system.

Thus, the statutory scheme applies to law enforcement, other government personnel, individuals, and private sector organizations. Subsection (c) of Section 2701, however, exempts from criminal liability conduct that is

authorized—

(1) by the person or entity providing a wire or electronic communications service;
(2) by a user of that service with respect to a communication of or intended for that user; or
(3) in section 2703, 2704 or 2518.

The criminal liability provision of the Stored Communications Act, 18 USC § 2701, does not, therefore, apply to users of the communications service, authorized conduct by communications providers, or conduct authorized by Sections 2703, 2704, and 2518. We considered in Chapter 10 conduct authorized by Section 2518, the wiretapping crime. It is now important to consider access that is authorized by Sections 2703 and 2704.

Section 2703 specifies the circumstances in which the providers of an electronic communications service (ECS) or remote computing service (RCS) can disclose information contained in stored electronic communications to federal, state, and local law enforcement officials. Section 2510 (15) defines an electronic communications service as

any service which provides to users thereof the ability to send or receive wire or electronic communications

Section 2711 (2) defines a remote computing service as

the provision to the public of computer storage or processing services by means of an electronic communications system.

Typical examples of an ECS include an Internet service provider (ISP), instant messaging provider, and e-mail service provider. Even a network e-mail service like that provided at a college would constitute an ECS. A remote computing service, however, includes only those services that provide storage or processing to all members of the public. This could include an ISP or an e-mail provider, but it clearly would not include those e-mail providers that extend their service to a limited sector of individuals or clients. For example, college networks typically provide data storage to faculty, staff, and students of the college, but not to the public at large. Thus, the college's network would not constitute a remote computing service.

The Stored Communications Act applies to three types of information concerning stored electronic communications that can be obtained from an ECS or RCS: basic subscriber information, transaction records, and the contents of those communications. Basic subscriber information, as set forth in Subsection (c)(2) of Section 2703, consists of a subscriber's:

(A) name;
(B) address;
(C) local and long distance telephone connection records, or records of session times and durations;
(D) length of service (including start date) and types of service utilized;
(E) telephone or instrument number or other subscriber number or identity, including any temporarily assigned network address; and
(F) means and source of payment for such service (including any credit card or bank account number).

The "contents" of a communication are defined in Section 2510 as

(8) "contents," when used with respect to any wire, oral, or electronic communication, includes any information concerning the substance, purport, or meaning of that communication.

Subsection 2703 (d) authorizes the court to order disclosure to law enforcement officers for basic subscriber information and other information that does not constitute the contents of communications. That "other information" includes transaction records, such as account and transaction logs.

The following chart indicates when ECS or RCS providers can disclose a specific category of information to law enforcement officers:

Type of Information	Subpoena with Prior Notice	Subpoena without Prior Notice or with Delayed Notice	Court Order under Section 2703 (d) with Notice	Section 2703 (d) Court Order without Prior Notice	Warrant
Basic subscriber information	Yes *Source: §2703 (c)(2)*	Yes *Source: §2703 (c)(2)*	Yes *Source: §2703 (d)*	Yes *Source: §2703 (d)*	Yes *Source: §2703*

Type of Information	With Prior Notice Subpoena	Subpoena without Prior Notice or with Delayed Notice	Court Order under Section 2703 (d) with Notice	Section 2703 (d) Court Order without Prior Notice	Warrant
Transaction records	No	No	Yes *Source: §2703 (c)(1)*	Yes *Source: §2703 (c)(1)*	Yes *Source: §2703 (c)(1)*
Contents held in storage 180 days or more	Yes, from ECS/RCS *Source: §2703 (b)*	No	Yes, from ECS/RCS *Source: §2703 (b)*	No	Yes, from ECS/RCS *Source: §2703 (b)*
Contents held in storage less than 180 days	No	No	No	No	Yes, from ECS/RCS *Source: §2703 (a)(b)*

Providers can also disclose all categories of information except the contents of electronic communications if the subscriber or user of the service has given consent to such disclosure.

The law enforcement officer seeking to obtain the disclosure of information must submit the following levels of proof depending upon the type of authority required:

Warrant: Probable cause (same as required for a search warrant under the Federal Rules of Criminal Procedure).

§ 2703 (d) court order: "Specific and articulable facts showing that there are reasonable grounds to believe that the contents of a wire or electronic communication, or the records or other information sought, are relevant and material to an ongoing criminal investigation."

Subpoena: Relevance to investigation.

Case Law

Fraser v. Nationwide Mutual Insurance Co.

352 F.3D 107 (2003)

U.S. Court of Appeals, Third Circuit

AMBRO, Circuit Judge:

Richard Fraser, an independent insurance agent for Nationwide Mutual Insurance Company, was terminated by Nationwide as an agent.

I. Background

This dispute stems from Nationwide's September 2, 1998 termination of Fraser's Agent's Agreement (the "Agreement"). It provided that Fraser sell insurance policies as an independent contractor for Nationwide on an exclusive basis. The relationship was terminable at will by either party.

The parties disagree on the reason for Fraser's termination. Fraser argues Nationwide terminated him because he filed complaints with the Pennsylvania Attorney General's office regarding Nationwide's allegedly illegal conduct, including its discriminatory refusal to write car insurance for unmarried and new drivers. Fraser also contends that he was terminated for criticizing Nationwide while acting as an officer of the Nationwide Insurance Independent Contractors Association and for attempting to obtain the passage of legislation in Pennsylvania to ensure that independent insurance agents could be terminated only for "just cause."

Nationwide argues, however, that it terminated Fraser because he was disloyal. It points out that Fraser drafted a letter to two competitors—Erie Insurance Company ("Erie") and Zurich American Insurance ("Zurich")—expressing Contractors Association members' dissatisfaction with Nationwide and seeking to determine whether Erie and Zurich would be interested in acquiring the policyholders of the agents in the Contractors Association. Fraser claims that the letters only were drafted to get Nationwide's attention and were not sent. (Were the letters sent, however, they would constitute a violation of the "exclusive representation" provision of Fraser's Agreement with Nationwide.)

When Nationwide learned about these letters, it claims that it became concerned that Fraser might also be revealing company secrets to its competitors. It therefore searched its main file server—on which all of Fraser's e-mail was lodged—for any e-mail to or from Fraser that showed similar improper behavior. Nationwide's general counsel testified that the e-mail search confirmed Fraser's disloyalty. Therefore, on the basis of the two letters and the e-mail search, Nationwide terminated Fraser's Agreement. It is this search of his e-mail that gives rise to Fraser's claim for damages under the Electronic Communications Privacy Act of 1986 ("ECPA"), 18 U.S.C. § 2510, et seq., and a parallel Pennsylvania statute, 18 Pa. Cons. Stat. § 5702, et seq.

II. Discussion

B. ECPA Claims and Parallel State Law Claims

1. Title I

Fraser argues that, by accessing his e-mail on its central file server without his express permission, Nationwide violated Title I of the ECPA, which prohibits "intercepts" of electronic communications such as e-mail. The statute defines an "intercept" as "the aural or other acquisition of the contents of any wire, electronic, or oral communication through the use of any electronic, mechanical, or other device." 18 U.S.C. § 2510(4). Nationwide argues that it did not "intercept" Fraser's e-mail within the meaning of Title I because an "intercept" can only occur contemporaneously with transmission and it did not access Fraser's e-mail at the initial time of transmission.

Every circuit court to have considered the matter has held that an "intercept" under the ECPA must occur contemporaneously with transmission. See *United States v. Steiger*, 318 F.3d 1039, 1048–49 (11th Cir. 2003); *Konop v. Hawaiian Airlines, Inc.*, 302 F.3d 868 (9th Cir. 2002); *Steve Jackson Games, Inc. v. U.S. Secret Serv.*, 36 F.3d 457 (5th Cir. 1994); see also *Wesley College v. Pitts*, 974 F. Supp. 375 (D. Del. 1997), summarily aff'd, 172 F.3d 861 (3d Cir. 1998).

The first case to do so, *Steve Jackson Games*, noted that "intercept" was defined as contemporaneous in the context of an aural communication under the old Wiretap Act, and that when Congress amended the Wiretap Act in 1986 (to create what is now known as the ECPA) to extend protection to electronic communications, it "did not intend to change the definition of 'intercept.'" *Steve Jackson Games*, 36 F.3d at 462. Moreover, the Fifth Circuit noted that the differences in definition between "wire communication" and "electronic communication" in the ECPA supported its conclusion that stored e-mail could not be intercepted within the meaning of Title I. A "wire communication" under the ECPA was (until recent amendment by the USA Patriot Act) "any aural transfer made in whole or in part through the use of facilities for the transmission of communications by the aid of wire, cable, or other like connection between the point of origin and the point of reception ... and such term includes any electronic storage of such communication." 18 U.S.C. § 2510(1) (superseded by USA Patriot Act).* By contrast, an "electronic communication" is defined as "any transfer of signs, signals, writing, images, sounds, data, or intelligence of any nature transmitted in whole or in part by a wire, radio, electromagnetic, photoelectronic or photooptical system ... but does not include ... any wire or oral communication." 18 U.S.C. § 2510(12). Thus, the Fifth Circuit reasoned that because "wire communication" explicitly included electronic storage but "electronic communication" did not, there can be no "intercept" of an e-mail in storage, as an e-mail in storage is by definition not an "electronic communication." *Steve Jackson Games*, 36 F.3d at 461–62.

Subsequent cases have agreed with the Fifth Circuit's result. While Congress's definition of "intercept" does not appear to fit with its intent to extend protection to electronic communications, it is for Congress to cover the bases untouched. We adopt the reasoning of our sister circuits and therefore hold that there has been no "intercept" within the meaning of Title I of ECPA.

2. Title II

Fraser also argues that Nationwide's search of his e-mail violated Title II of the ECPA. That Title creates civil liability for one who "(1) intentionally accesses without authorization a facility through which an electronic communication service is provided; or (2) intentionally exceeds an authorization to access that facility; and thereby obtains, alters, or prevents authorized access to a wire or electronic communication while it is in electronic storage in such system." 18 U.S.C. § 2701(a). The statute defines "electronic storage" as "(A) any temporary, intermediate storage of a wire or electronic communication incidental to the electronic transmission thereof; and (B) any storage of such communication by an electronic communication service for purposes of backup protection of such communication." Id. § 2510(17).

The District Court granted summary judgment in favor of Nationwide, holding that Title II does not apply to the e-mail in question because the transmissions were neither in "temporary, intermediate storage" nor in "backup" storage. Rather, according to the District Court, the e-mail was in a state it described as "post-transmission storage." We agree that Fraser's e-mail was not in temporary, intermediate storage. But to us it seems

---

* The USA Patriot Act § 209, Pub. L. No. 107-56, § 209(1)(A), 115 Stat. 272, 283 (2001), amended the definition of "wire communication" to eliminate electronic storage from the definition of wire communication.

questionable that the transmissions were not in backup storage—a term that neither the statute nor the legislative history defines. Therefore, while we affirm the District Court, we do so through a different analytical path, assuming without deciding that the e-mail in question was in backup storage.

18 U.S.C. § 2701(c)(1) excepts from Title II seizures of e-mail authorized "by the person or entity providing a wire or electronic communications service." There is no circuit court case law interpreting this exception. However, in *Bohach v. City of Reno*, 932 F. Supp. 1232 (D. Nev. 1996), a district court held that the Reno police department could, without violating Title II, retrieve pager text messages stored on the police department's computer system because the department "is the provider of the 'service'" and "service providers [may] do as they wish when it comes to accessing communications in electronic storage." Id. at 1236. Like the court in *Bohach*, we read § 2701(c) literally to except from Title II's protection all searches by communications service providers. Thus, we hold that, because Fraser's e-mail was stored on Nationwide's system (which Nationwide administered), its search of that e-mail falls within § 2701(c)'s exception to Title II.

III. Conclusion

We affirm the District Court's grant of summary judgment in favor of Nationwide on Fraser's wrongful termination claim, his ECPA and parallel state claims, and his bad-faith claim.

Sherman & Company v. Salton Maxim Housewares, Inc.

94 F. SUPP. 2D 817 (2000)

U.S. District Ct., Eastern District of Michigan

STEVEN D. PEPE, Magistrate Judge.

I. BACKGROUND

In January 1997, Salton won a multi-year contract to sell kitchen and small household appliances under the mark of "White Westinghouse" to Kmart. Sherman entered into a contract with Salton in May 1997, whereby Sherman would act as a manufacturer's representative to Kmart. Sherman was also a product representative to Kmart for other companies than Salton including Windmere. Salton alleges that Sherman's performance was deficient and that Sherman "alienated and antagonized" several Kmart buyers and contacts. In June 1998 Sherman stopped working for Salton, allegedly at Kmart's request and Salton's insistence. Sherman continued to act as a manufacturing representative for Windmere for other electric products.

In its original counterclaim for relief, defendant/counter-plaintiff Salton asserted that Sherman materially breached its contract and sought a declaratory judgment "that the contract between Sherman and Salton is canceled and Salton is relieved of any obligations or liabilities under the contract." There was no demand for money damages or injunctive relief. Salton now seeks to add claims that Sherman (1) intentionally accessed unauthorized information in violation of the ECPA, 18 U.S.C. § 2701 et seq., and (2) misappropriated a trade secret in violation of MCL § 445.1902(b)(ii)(A).

Salton alleges that after James Sherman no longer worked for it, he used a computer access code that Kmart provided him when he worked for Salton to gain access to certain Salton sales data in the Kmart computer system and thereafter provided that information to Windmere. Salton claims that it had instructed Kmart to cut off Sherman's access to Salton's data, but apparently that denial of access was not done until later. Thus, Salton's data was available to James Sherman using the computer access code Kmart provided him. Salton alleges that even though "Sherman did have authorization to log on to the Kmart computer system to access information about various venders and their products that he was representing" and that "in fact Kmart continued to provide [James Sherman] access to Salton information in addition to information about his other vendors," that "Salton certainly did not authorize him to view this information, and he knew he was not so authorized." While James Sherman disputes this and believed he had access and authorization, for purposes of this motion, which is reviewed under a similar standard as a Fed. R. Civ. P. 12(b)(6) motion, Salton's allegations are accepted as true. Salton contends that this actual access that Sherman had and used was "unauthorized" under the ECPA.

Sherman maintains that the Kmart network system allows access to information on all vendors and does not require a separate access code for each specific vendor. Sherman asserts that the counterclaim does not allege that Kmart revoked authorization before Sherman accessed the information and such access would not be a criminal violation of the anti-hacking statute, and therefore the amendment would be futile.

II. ANALYSIS

A. Salton's ECPA Claim

The general purpose of the ECPA was to create a cause of action against "computer hackers (e.g., electronic trespassers)." *State Wide Photocopy Corp. v. Tokai Financial, Inc.*, 909 F. Supp. 137, 145 (S.D.N.Y. 1995). The provisions of section 2701 of the Act apply to persons or entities in general and prohibit intentional accessing of electronic data without authorization or in excess of authorization. Section 2702 prohibits disclosure of electronic data, but this prohibition is limited to persons or entities that (1) provide an electronic communication service to the public; or (2) provide remote computing service to the public. In this case there is no indication that Sherman falls under either of the two limited categories of covered persons or entities of section 2702. Thus, if Salton has a viable claim against Sherman under the ECPA, it will have to fall under section 2701 of that Act.

Salton alleges in Count II of its proposed amended complaint that Sherman obtained Salton sales information and disclosed it to a competitor, Windmere. Yet, unlike section 2702, section 2701(a) of the ECPA does not prohibit the disclosure or use of information gained without authorization. Rather, section 2701(a) prohibits the intentional unauthorized access of an electronic communication service and the subsequent obtainment, alteration or prevention of authorized access to the service. Because the language of section 2701(a) specifically refers to "access" and not disclosure or use, "a person who does not provide an electronic communication service ... can disclose or use with impunity the contents of an electronic communication unlawfully obtained from electronic storage." While at least one district court has found this gap troubling, it is the role of Congress to address this deficiency and not the courts.

The ECPA's prohibition on intentional exceeding of authorized access anticipates that a person with authorization to a computer database or certain public portions of a database is not thereby authorized to visit "private" zones of data in the system. Yet, for "intentional" access in excess of authorization to be a crime and actionable civilly, the offender must have obtained the access to private files without authorization (e.g., using a computer he was not to use, or obtaining and using someone else's password or code without authorization). At a minimum, there must be a clearer and more explicit restriction on the authorized access than presented by Salton's proposed counterclaim. Here Sherman's access to the Salton data in the Kmart network system was in no way restricted by technical means or by any express limitation. Because section 2701 of the ECPA prohibits only unauthorized access and not the misappropriation or disclosure of information, there is no violation of section 2701 for a person with authorized access to the database no matter how malicious or larcenous his intended use of that access. Section 2701 outlaws illegal entry, not larceny.

Salton asserts that James Sherman accessed certain of its sales information located in the Kmart network after his dismissal. The question is whether Salton has alleged and proffered sufficient proofs to create a colorable claim that such access was "unauthorized." Where a party consents to another's access to its computer network, it cannot claim that such access was unauthorized. Salton admits that Kmart provided Sherman with authorization to log on to the computer network to access information about vendors and products that Sherman was representing. Further, Kmart continued to provide James Sherman access to Salton's information after his dismissal by Salton. Salton has not pled nor offered to show that Kmart instructed Sherman that he no longer had authorization to access Salton's sales information. Nor has Salton pled or offered to show that there was an agreement between the parties that limited plaintiff's access on the Kmart network.

Because section 2701 does not prohibit the disclosure or use of information obtained without authorization, and without a more specific allegation of facts that Sherman's access was "unauthorized" within the meaning of the ECPA, the undersigned finds that Salton's proposed claim under the ECPA does not state a claim and the amendment to add it would thus be futile. Accordingly, Salton's motion to amend its counterclaim is denied as to this claim.

Accordingly,

IT IS ORDERED that the motion to amend the counterclaim by defendant/counter-plaintiff Salton Maxim Housewares, Inc., is DENIED IN PART and GRANTED IN PART.

Andersen Consulting LLP v. UOP

991 F. SUPP. 1041 (1998)

U.S. DISTRICT CT., NORTHERN DISTRICT OF ILLINOIS

OPINION by Elaine E. Bucklo, District Judge:

Plaintiff, Andersen Consulting LLP ("Andersen"), brought an eight count complaint against the defendants, UOP and its counsel, the law firm of Bickel & Brewer. In Count I,

Andersen alleges that the defendants knowingly divulged, or caused to be divulged, the contents of Andersen's e-mail messages in violation of the Electronic Communications Privacy Act ("ECPA"), 18 U.S.C. § 2701 et seq. In the remaining seven counts, Andersen raises related state law claims against the defendants. The defendants move to dismiss all counts of the complaint. For the reasons set forth below, the defendants' motion to dismiss is granted.

Background

UOP hired Andersen to perform a systems integration project in 1992. During the project, Andersen employees had access to and used UOP's internal e-mail system to communicate with each other, with UOP, and with third parties.

Dissatisfied with Andersen's performance, UOP terminated the project in December 1993. Subsequently UOP hired Bickel and Brewer and brought suit in Connecticut state court charging Andersen with breach of contract, negligence, and fraud. Andersen countersued in two different suits for defamation.

While these three cases were pending, UOP and Bickel and Brewer divulged the contents of Andersen's e-mail messages on UOP's e-mail system to the *Wall Street Journal*. The *Journal* published an article on June 19, 1997 titled "E-Mail Trail Could Haunt Consultant in Court." The article excerpted some of Andersen's e-mail messages made during the course of its assignment at UOP. This disclosure of the e-mail messages and their subsequent publication is the basis of this suit.

ECPA Claim

18 U.S.C. § 2702(a)(1) states that "a person or entity providing an electronic communication service to the public shall not knowingly divulge to any person or entity the contents of a communication while in electronic storage by that service." Andersen claims that the defendants violated this section by knowingly divulging the contents of its e-mail message to the *Wall Street Journal*.

To be liable for the disclosure of Andersen's e-mail messages, UOP must fall under the purview of the Act: UOP must provide "electronic communication service to the public." 18 U.S.C. § 2702(a)(1). The statute defines "electronic communication service" as "any service which provides to users thereof the ability to send or receive wire or electronic communications." 18 U.S.C. § 2510 (15). The statute does not define "public." The word "public," however, is unambiguous. Public means the "aggregate of the citizens" or "everybody" or "the people at large" or "the community at large." Black's Law Dictionary 1227 (6th ed. 1990). Thus, the statute covers any entity that provides electronic communication service (e.g., e-mail) to the community at large.

Andersen attempts to render the phrase "to the public" superfluous by arguing that the statutory language indicates that the term "public" means something other than the community at large. It claims that if Congress wanted public to mean the community at large, it would have used the term "general public." However, the fact that Congress used both "public" and "general public" in the same statute does not lead to the conclusion that Congress intended public to have any other meaning than its commonly understood meaning.

Andersen argues that the legislative history indicates that a provider of electronic communication services is subject to Section 2702 even if that provider maintains the system primarily for its own use and does not provide services to the general public.

This legislative history argument is misguided. "A court's starting point to determine the intent of Congress is the language of the statute itself." *United States v. Hayward*, 6 F.3d 1241, 1245 (7th Cir. 1993). If the language is "clear and unambiguous," the court must give effect to the plain meaning of the statute. Since the meaning of "public" is clear, there is no need to resort to legislative history.

Even if the language was somehow ambiguous, the legislative history does not support Andersen's interpretation. The legislative history indicates that there is a distinction between public and proprietary. In describing "electronic mail," the legislative history stated that "electronic mail systems may be available for public use or may be proprietary, such as systems operated by private companies for internal correspondence." S. Rep. No. 99-541, at 8 (1986), reprinted in 1986 U.S.C.C.A.N. 3555, 3562. Thus, Andersen must show that UOP's electronic mail system was available for public use.

In its complaint, Andersen alleges that UOP "is a general partnership which licenses process technologies and supplies catalysts, specialty chemicals, and other products to the petroleum refining, petrochemical, and gas processing industries." UOP is not in the business of providing electronic communication services. It does, however, have an e-mail system for internal communication as e-mail is a necessary tool for almost any business today. See *State Wide Photocopy v. Tokai Fin. Servs., Inc.*, 909 F. Supp. 137, 145 (S.D.N.Y. 1995) (finding that defendant was in the business of financing and that the mere use of fax machines and computers, as necessary tools of business, did not make it an electronic communication service provider).

UOP hired Andersen to provide services in connection with the integration of certain computer systems. As part of the project, "UOP provided an electronic communication service for Andersen to use. That electronic communication service could be used, and was used by Andersen and UOP personnel, to electronically communicate with (i.e., send e-mail messages to, and receive e-mail messages from) other Andersen personnel, UOP personnel, third-party vendors and other third-parties both in and outside of Illinois."

Based on these allegations, Andersen claims that UOP provides an electronic communication service to the public. However, giving Andersen access to its e-mail system is not equivalent to providing e-mail to the public. Andersen was hired by UOP to do a project and as such, was given access to UOP's e-mail system similar to UOP employees. Andersen was not any member of the community at large, but a hired contractor. Further, the fact that Andersen could communicate to third-parties over the Internet and that third-parties could communicate with it did not mean that UOP provided an electronic communication service to the public. UOP's internal e-mail system is separate from the Internet. UOP must purchase Internet access from an electronic communication service provider like any other consumer; it does not independently provide Internet services.

Conclusion

Defendants' motion to dismiss all counts of Andersen's complaint is granted.

Key Words and Phrases

Basic subscriber information
Electronic communication service
Provider
Remote computing service

Subpoena
Temporary storage
Transaction records
Warrant

Review Problems

1. How long is "temporary" storage while in transmission? Suppose that in *Councilman* (discussed in Chapter 10), the software procmail was designed to afford a five-second delay between arrival on the server and processing into the intended recipient's mailbox. Would that be "temporary" enough to constitute a stored communication?
2. Why does the Stored Communications Act require a court order to obtain transaction records but only a subpoena to obtain basic subscriber information?
3. Is the warrant required by the Stored Communications Act the same as the warrant for searches and seizures?

Weblinks

www.cybercrime.gov/ssmanual/index.html
    Chapter 3 of the manual discusses access to stored communications under the Stored Communications Act.

http://ilt.eff.org/index.php/Privacy:_Stored_Communications_Act
    This is the Internet Law Treatise portion of the web page sponsored by the Electronic Frontier Foundation. This web page discusses key features of the Stored Communications Act and provides links to documents and other vital information concerning the act.

Pen Register, Trap and Trace, and GPS Devices

12

Introduction

Technology has for some time enabled law enforcement to obtain information about suspects without acquiring the content of a communication. Pen registers and trap and trace devices have been used to acquire the number of an incoming or outgoing account. Historically, those devices were used to acquire telephone account numbers, but as we shall see, they can now be utilized also to acquire the number or address of a digital device. Similarly, tracking beepers and global positioning system (GPS) devices have been used to acquire information concerning the location of a person, equipment, or device that is being tracked, and radio frequency identification (RFID) is more frequently being used for similar tracking purposes.

This chapter considers when those technologies can be employed by law enforcement personnel, either to conduct surveillance preliminary to an arrest or indictment or to obtain evidence in support of a criminal charge.

Pen Register and Trap and Trace Devices

The authority to utilize pen registers and trap and trace devices in criminal investigations is set forth in 18 USC §§ 3121–3127. Section 3127 defines a pen register and a trap and trace device as follows:

(3) the term "pen register" means a device or process which records or decodes dialing, routing, addressing, or signaling information transmitted by an instrument or facility from which a wire or electronic communication is transmitted, provided, however, that such information shall not include the contents of any communication, but such term does not include any device or process used by a provider or customer of a wire or electronic communication service for billing, or recording as an incident to billing, for communications services provided by such provider or any device or process used by a provider or customer of a wire communication service for cost accounting or other like purposes in the ordinary course of its business;

(4) the term "trap and trace device" means a device or process which captures the incoming electronic or other impulses which identify the originating number or other dialing, routing, addressing, and signaling information reasonably likely to identify the source of a wire or electronic communication, provided, however, that such information shall not include the contents of any communication.

To summarize, a pen register device is designed to capture an *outgoing* number or account address, and a trap and trace device is designed to capture an *incoming* number or account address of the suspect subscriber.

Does an individual have a reasonable expectation of privacy to the number that has been dialed on the phone? That issue was addressed in *Smith v. Maryland*, discussed below:

Smith v. Maryland

442 U.S. 735 (1979)

U.S. SUPREME COURT

MR. JUSTICE BLACKMUN delivered the Opinion of the Court:

This case presents the question whether the installation and use of a pen register constitutes a "search" within the meaning of the Fourth Amendment, made applicable to the States through the Fourteenth Amendment.

On March 5, 1976, in Baltimore, Md., Patricia McDonough was robbed. She gave the police a description of the robber and of a 1975 Monte Carlo automobile she had observed near the scene of the crime. After the robbery, McDonough began receiving threatening and obscene phone calls from a man identifying himself as the robber. On one occasion, the caller asked that she step out on her front porch; she did so, and saw the 1975 Monte Carlo she had earlier described to police moving slowly past her home. On March 16, police spotted a man who met McDonough's description driving a 1975 Monte Carlo in her neighborhood. By tracing the license plate number, police learned that the car was registered in the name of petitioner, Michael Lee Smith.

The next day, the telephone company, at police request, installed a pen register at its central offices to record the numbers dialed from the telephone at petitioner's home. The police did not get a warrant or court order before having the pen register installed. The register revealed that on March 17 a call was placed from petitioner's home to McDonough's phone. On the basis of this and other evidence, the police obtained a warrant to search petitioner's residence. The search revealed that a page in petitioner's phone book was turned down to the name and number of Patricia McDonough; the phone book was seized. Petitioner was arrested, and a six-man lineup was held on March 19. McDonough identified petitioner as the man who had robbed her.

Petitioner was indicted in the Criminal Court of Baltimore for robbery. By pretrial motion, he sought to suppress "all fruits derived from the pen register" on the ground that the police had failed to secure a warrant prior to its installation. The trial court denied the suppression motion, holding that the warrantless installation of the pen register did not violate the Fourth Amendment. Petitioner then waived a jury, and the case was submitted to the court on an agreed statement of facts. The pen register tape (evidencing the fact that a phone call had been made from petitioner's phone to McDonough's phone) and the phone book seized in the search of petitioner's residence were admitted into evidence against him. Petitioner was convicted and was sentenced to six years. He appealed to the Maryland Court of Special Appeals, but the Court of Appeals of Maryland issued a *writ of certiorari* to the intermediate court in advance of its decision in order to consider whether the pen register evidence had been properly admitted at petitioner's trial.

The Court of Appeals affirmed the judgment of conviction, holding that "there is no constitutionally protected reasonable expectation of privacy in the numbers dialed into a telephone system and hence no search within the fourth amendment is implicated by the use of a pen register installed at the central offices of the telephone company." 389 A.2d, at 867. Because there was no "search," the court concluded, no warrant was needed. Three judges dissented, expressing the view that individuals do have a legitimate expectation of privacy regarding the phone numbers they dial from their homes; that the installation of a pen register thus constitutes a "search"; and that, in the absence of exigent circumstances, the failure of police to secure a warrant mandated that the pen register evidence here be excluded. 389 A.2d, at 868, 870.

In applying the *Katz* analysis to this case, it is important to begin by specifying precisely the nature of the state activity that is challenged. The activity here took the form of installing and using a pen register. Since the pen register was installed on telephone company property at the telephone company's central offices, petitioner obviously cannot claim that his "property" was invaded or that police intruded into a "constitutionally protected area." Petitioner's claim, rather, is that, notwithstanding the absence of a trespass, the State, as did the Government in *Katz*, infringed a "legitimate expectation of privacy" that petitioner held. Yet a pen register differs significantly from the listening device employed in *Katz*, for pen registers do not acquire the contents of communications. This Court recently noted:

"Indeed, a law enforcement official could not even determine from the use of a pen register whether a communication existed. These devices do not hear sound. They disclose only the telephone numbers that have been dialed—a means of establishing communication. Neither the purport of any communication between the caller and the recipient of the call, their identities, nor whether the call was even completed is disclosed by pen registers."

United States v. New York Tel. Co., 434 U.S. 159 (1977).

Given a pen register's limited capabilities, therefore, petitioner's argument that its installation and use constituted a "search" necessarily rests upon a claim that he had a "legitimate expectation of privacy" regarding the numbers he dialed on his phone.

This claim must be rejected. First, we doubt that people in general entertain any actual expectation of privacy in the numbers they dial. All telephone users realize that they must "convey" phone numbers to the telephone company, since it is through telephone company switching equipment that their calls are completed.

All subscribers realize, moreover, that the phone company has facilities for making permanent records of the numbers they dial, for they see a list of their long-distance (toll) calls on their monthly bills. In fact, pen registers and similar devices are routinely used by telephone companies "for the purposes of checking billing operations, detecting fraud and preventing violations of law." *United States v. New York Tel. Co.*, 434 U.S., at 174–175. Electronic equipment is used not only to keep billing records of toll calls, but also "to keep a record of all calls dialed from a telephone which is subject to a special rate structure." *Hodge v. Mountain States Tel. & Tel. Co.*, 555 F.2d 254, 266 (CA9 1977) (concurring opinion). Pen registers are regularly employed "to determine whether a home phone is being used to conduct a business, to check for a defective dial, or to check for overbilling." Note, The Legal Constraints upon the Use of the Pen Register as a Law Enforcement Tool, 60 *Cornell L. Rev.* 1028, 1029 (1975) (footnotes omitted). Although most people may be oblivious to a pen register's esoteric functions, they presumably have some awareness of one common use: to aid in the identification of persons making annoying or obscene calls. Most phone books tell subscribers, on a page entitled "Consumer Information," that the company "can frequently help in identifying to the authorities the origin of unwelcome and troublesome calls." E.g., Baltimore Telephone Directory 21 (1978); District of Columbia Telephone Directory 13 (1978). Telephone users, in sum, typically know that they must convey numerical information to the phone company; that the phone company has facilities for recording this information; and that the phone company does in fact record this information for a variety of legitimate business purposes. Although subjective expectations cannot be scientifically gauged, it is too much to believe that telephone subscribers, under these circumstances, harbor any general expectation that the numbers they dial will remain secret.

Petitioner argues, however, that, whatever the expectations of telephone users in general, he demonstrated an expectation of privacy by his own conduct here, since he "us[ed] the telephone in his house to the exclusion of all others." But the site of the call is immaterial for purposes of analysis in this case. Although petitioner's conduct may have been calculated to keep the contents of his conversation private, his conduct was not and could not have been calculated to preserve the privacy of the number he dialed. Regardless of his location, petitioner had to convey that number to the telephone company in precisely the same way if he wished to complete his call. The fact that he dialed the number on his home phone rather than on some other phone could make no conceivable difference, nor could any subscriber rationally think that it would.

Second, even if petitioner did harbor some subjective expectation that the phone numbers he dialed would remain private, this expectation is not "one that society is prepared to recognize as 'reasonable.'" *Katz v. United States*, 389 U.S., at 361. This Court consistently has held that a person has no legitimate expectation of privacy in information he voluntarily turns over to third parties.

[P]etitioner can claim no legitimate expectation of privacy here. When he used his phone, petitioner voluntarily conveyed numerical information to the telephone company and "exposed" that information to its equipment in the ordinary course of business. In so doing, petitioner assumed the risk that the company would reveal to police the numbers he dialed. The switching equipment that processed those numbers is merely the modern counterpart of the operator who, in an earlier day, personally completed calls for the subscriber. Petitioner concedes that if he had placed his calls through an operator, he could claim no legitimate expectation of privacy. We are not inclined to hold that a different constitutional result is required because the telephone company has decided to automate.

Petitioner argues, however, that automatic switching equipment differs from a live operator in one pertinent respect. An operator, in theory at least, is capable of remembering every number that is conveyed to him by callers. Electronic equipment, by contrast can "remember" only those numbers it is programmed to record, and telephone companies, in view of their present billing practices, usually do not record local calls. Since petitioner, in calling McDonough, was making a local call, his expectation of privacy as to her number, on this theory, would be "legitimate."

This argument does not withstand scrutiny. The fortuity of whether or not the phone company in fact elects to make a quasi-permanent record of a particular number dialed does not in our view, make any constitutional difference.

Regardless of the phone company's election, petitioner voluntarily conveyed to it information that it had facilities for recording and that it was free to record. In these circumstances, petitioner assumed the risk that the information would be divulged to police. Under petitioner's theory, Fourth Amendment protection would exist, or not, depending on how the telephone company chose to define local-dialing zones, and depending on how it chose to bill its customers for local calls. Calls placed across town, or dialed directly, would be protected; calls placed across the river, or dialed with operator assistance, might not be. We are not inclined to make a crazy quilt of the Fourth Amendment, especially in circumstances where (as here) the pattern of protection would be dictated by billing practices of a private corporation.

We therefore conclude that petitioner in all probability entertained no actual expectation of privacy in the phone numbers he dialed, and that, even if he did, his expectation was not "legitimate." The installation and use of a pen register, consequently, was not a "search," and no warrant was required.

It is a crime for any person to "install or use a pen register or a trap and trace device without first obtaining a court order under Section 3123 of this title or under the Foreign Intelligence Surveillance Act of 1978 (50 USC 1801 et seq.) (18 USC § 3121 (a)). Section 3121 (b) contains three exceptions. It is not a crime for a provider of wire or electronic communications to install either device (1) if it has the consent of the user of the service, or (2) if it is necessary to protect the property of the provider or users of the service from abuse or unlawful use of the service, or (3) if it is necessary to record fraudulent, unlawful, or abusive use of the service.

Because pen registers and trap and trace devices do not obtain the contents of a communication, the level of privacy invasion is much less than the interception of the contents of a communication or the search of premises. Thus, the law enforcement official seeking a court order authorizing the installation of a pen register or trap and trace device need only show that "the information likely to be obtained is relevant to an ongoing criminal investigation being conducted by that agency" (18 USC § 3122 (b)(2)). It is not necessary to establish probable cause.

Global Positioning Systems (GPSs)

Global positioning systems have become popular devices for automobile operators seeking to find the location of a restaurant, shopping mall, friend's house, etc. GPSs also are an embedded technology utilized in services such as OnStar that enable others to determine the location of a vehicle. That same technology has been and will continue to be used by law enforcement to find the location of a vehicle or to track the location of a vehicle. Does the operator of a motor vehicle have a reasonable expectation of privacy regarding information imparted by a GPS tracking device? If the answer is yes, then it would seem that a warrant should be required prior to the installation of a GPS device by law enforcement. The courts are not in agreement.

The first case, *Knotts v. United States*, considered the reasonable expectation of privacy issue in connection with a beeper tracking device, which is now considered an early primitive version of GPS.

Knotts v. United States

460 U.S. 276 (1983)

U.S. SUPREME COURT

MR. JUSTICE REHNQUIST delivered the Opinion of the Court:

A beeper is a radio transmitter, usually battery operated, which emits periodic signals that can be picked up by a radio receiver. In this case, a beeper was placed in a five gallon drum containing chloroform purchased by one of respondent's codefendants. By monitoring the progress of a car carrying the chloroform Minnesota law enforcement agents were able to trace the can of chloroform from its place of purchase in Minneapolis, Minnesota to respondent's secluded cabin near Shell Lake, Wisconsin. The issue presented by the case is whether such use of a beeper violated respondent's rights secured by the Fourth Amendment to the United States Constitution.

Respondent and two codefendants were charged in the United States District Court for the District of Minnesota with conspiracy to manufacture controlled substances, including but not limited to methamphetamine, in violation of 21 U.S.C. § 846 (1976).

Suspicion attached to this trio when the 3M Company, which manufactures chemicals in St. Paul, notified a narcotics investigator for the Minnesota Bureau of Criminal Apprehension that Armstrong, a former 3M employee, had been stealing chemicals which could be used in manufacturing illicit drugs. Visual surveillance of Armstrong revealed that after leaving the employ of 3M Company, he had been purchasing similar chemicals from the Hawkins Chemical Company in Minneapolis. The Minnesota narcotics officers observed that after Armstrong had made a purchase, he would deliver the chemicals to codefendant Petschen.

With the consent of the Hawkins Chemical Company, officers installed a beeper inside a five gallon container of chloroform, one of the so-called "precursor" chemicals used to manufacture illicit drugs. Hawkins agreed that when Armstrong next purchased chloroform, the chloroform would be placed in this particular container. When Armstrong made the purchase, officers followed the car in which the chloroform had been placed, maintaining contact by using both visual surveillance and a monitor which received the signals sent from the beeper.

Armstrong proceeded to Petschen's house, where the container was transferred to Petschen's automobile. Officers then followed that vehicle eastward towards the state line, across the St. Croix River, and into Wisconsin. During the latter part of this journey, Petschen began making evasive maneuvers, and the pursuing agents ended their visual surveillance. At about the same time officers lost the signal from the beeper, but with the assistance of a monitoring device located in a helicopter the approximate location of the signal was picked up again about one hour later. The signal now was stationary and the location identified was a cabin occupied by respondent near Shell Lake, Wisconsin. The record before us does not reveal that the beeper was used after the location in the area of the cabin had been initially determined.

Relying on the location of the chloroform derived through the use of the beeper and additional information obtained during three days of intermittent visual surveillance of respondent's cabin, officers secured a search warrant. During execution of the warrant,

officers discovered a fully operable, clandestine drug laboratory in the cabin. In the laboratory area officers found formulas for amphetamine and methamphetamine, over $10,000 worth of laboratory equipment, and chemicals in quantities sufficient to produce 14 pounds of pure amphetamine.

Under a barrel outside the cabin, officers located the five gallon container of chloroform.

After his motion to suppress evidence based on the warrantless monitoring of the beeper was denied, respondent was convicted for conspiring to manufacture controlled substances in violation of 21 U.S.C. § 846 (1976). He was sentenced to five years imprisonment. A divided panel of the United States Court of Appeals for the Eighth Circuit reversed the conviction, finding that the monitoring of the beeper was prohibited by the Fourth Amendment because its use had violated respondent's reasonable expectation of privacy, and that all information derived after the location of the cabin was a fruit of the illegal beeper monitoring. We granted *certiorari*, and we now reverse the judgment of the Court of Appeals.

"Consistently with *Katz*, this Court uniformly has held that the application of the Fourth Amendment depends on whether the person invoking its protection can claim a 'justifiable,' a 'reasonable,' or a 'legitimate expectation of privacy' that has been invaded by government action." [Citations omitted].

The governmental surveillance conducted by means of the beeper in this case amounted principally to the following of an automobile on public streets and highways. We have commented more than once on the diminished expectation of privacy in an automobile:

"One has a lesser expectation of privacy in a motor vehicle because its function is transportation and it seldom serves as one's residence or as the repository of personal effects. A car has little capacity for escaping public scrutiny. It travels public thoroughfares where both its occupants and its contents are in plain view."

Cardwell v. Lewis, 417 U.S. 583, 590 (1974).

A person travelling in an automobile on public thoroughfares has no reasonable expectation of privacy in his movements from one place to another.

When Petschen travelled over the public streets he voluntarily conveyed to anyone who wanted to look the fact that he was travelling over particular roads in a particular direction, the fact of whatever stops he made, and the fact of his final destination when he exited from public roads onto private property.

Knotts, as the owner of the cabin and surrounding premises to which Petschen drove, undoubtedly had the traditional expectation of privacy within a dwelling place insofar as the cabin was concerned.

But no such expectation of privacy extended to the visual observation of Petschen's automobile arriving on his premises after leaving a public highway, nor to movements of objects such as the drum of chloroform outside the cabin in the "open fields." *Hester v. United States*, 265 U.S. 57 (1924).

Visual surveillance from public places along Petschen's route or adjoining Knotts' premises would have sufficed to reveal all of these facts to the police. The fact that the officers in this case relied not only on visual surveillance, but on the use of the beeper to signal the presence of Petschen's automobile to the police receiver, does not alter the situation. Nothing in the Fourth Amendment prohibited the police from augmenting the sensory faculties bestowed upon them at birth with such enhancement as science and technology afforded them in this case.

Respondent expresses the generalized view that the result of the holding sought by the government would be that "twenty-four hour surveillance of any citizen of this country will be possible, without judicial knowledge or supervision." But the fact is that the "reality hardly suggests abuse," *Zurcher v. Stanford Daily*, 436 U.S. 547, 566 (1978); if such dragnet type law enforcement practices as respondent envisions should eventually occur, there will be time enough then to determine whether different constitutional principles may be applicable. Insofar as respondent's complaint appears to be simply that scientific devices such as the beeper enabled the police to be more effective in detecting crime, it simply has no constitutional foundation. We have never equated police efficiency with unconstitutionality, and we decline to do so now.

Respondent specifically attacks the use of the beeper insofar as it was used to determine that the can of chloroform had come to rest on his property at Shell Lake, Wisconsin. He repeatedly challenges the "use of the beeper to determine the location of the chemical drum at Respondent's premises"; he states that "[t]he government thus overlooks the fact that this case involves the sanctity of Respondent's residence, which is accorded the greatest protection available under the Fourth Amendment."

We think that respondent's contentions to some extent lose sight of the limited use which the government made of the signals from this particular beeper. As we have noted, nothing in this record indicates that the beeper signal was received or relied upon after it had indicated that the drum containing the chloroform had ended its automotive journey at rest on respondent's premises in rural Wisconsin. Admittedly, because of the failure of the visual surveillance, the beeper enabled the law enforcement officials in this case to ascertain the ultimate resting place of the chloroform when they would not have been able to do so had they relied solely on their naked eyes. But scientific enhancement of this sort raises no constitutional issues which visual surveillance would not also raise. A police car following Petschen at a distance throughout his journey could have observed him leaving the public highway and arriving at the cabin owned by respondent, with the drum of chloroform still in the car. This fact, along with others, was used by the government in obtaining a search warrant which led to the discovery of the clandestine drug laboratory. But there is no indication that the beeper was used in any way to reveal information as to the movement of the drum within the cabin, or in any way that would not have been visible to the naked eye from outside the cabin. Just as notions of physical trespass based on the law of real property were not dispositive in *Katz, supra*, neither were they dispositive in *Hester v. United States*, 265 U.S. 57 (1924).

In the following two cases we move from the beeper to GPS devices. In *United States v. Moran*, law enforcement personnel surreptitiously installed a GPS device on the vehicle of the defendant while it was parked in the defendant's driveway without obtaining a warrant. The court, in the decision below, determined that the defendant had no reasonable expectation of privacy while on the public highways, and thus no warrant was required prior to installation of the GPS device.

United States v. Moran

349 F. SUPP. 2D 425 (2005)

U.S. DISTRICT COURT, NORTHERN DISTRICT OF N.Y.

In the course of a lengthy investigation concerning the involvement of members of a motorcycle gang and others in the distribution and sale of methamphetamine, law enforcement officers installed a global positioning system (GPS) tracking device on defendant Moran's vehicle. Moran moved to suppress evidence obtained through the use of the GPS device, contending that the Fourth Amendment requires that law enforcement officials obtain a warrant.

OPINION BY: DAVID N. HURD, District Judge

Moran separately moves for suppression of any evidence obtained from a GPS device attached to his vehicles as well as any evidence derived from information obtained from the GPS tracking device, as violative of his Fourth Amendment rights.

The Fourth Amendment protects against unreasonable searches and seizures. However, where there is no legitimate expectation of privacy, there is no search or seizure within the ambit of the Fourth Amendment. *United States v. Knotts*, 460 U.S. 276, 285, 75 L. Ed. 2d 55, 103 S. Ct. 1081, 1087 (1983). There is a diminished expectation of privacy in a vehicle because of its availability to public scrutiny. "A person travelling in an automobile on public thoroughfares has no reasonable expectation of privacy in his movements from one place to another." Id.

Here Moran complains of a GPS device attached to his vehicle by law enforcement personnel without a warrant. The GPS device tracked the whereabouts of Moran's vehicle on July 29 and 30, 2003, upon his return from a one-day trip to Arizona. Law enforcement personnel could have conducted a visual surveillance of the vehicle as it traveled on the public highways. Moran had no expectation of privacy in the whereabouts of his vehicle on a public roadway. Thus, there was no search or seizure and no Fourth Amendment implications in the use of the GPS device.

The cases Moran cites in support of his argument that the GPS information must be suppressed are inapposite. In *United States v. Berry*, 300 F. Supp. 2d 366 (D. Md. 2004), the police obtained a court order permitting placement of a GPS device on a vehicle. Thus, the court found admissible the evidence obtained when the device was authorized. With regard to evidence obtained after expiration of the court order, the court found it unnecessary to decide the question since the government did not plan to introduce the evidence. In *United States v. Mack*, 272 F. Supp. 2d 1174, 1180 (D. Colo. 2003), the court merely mentioned the use of a GPS device, pursuant to a court order, in its discussion of traditional investigative techniques used.

In *People v. Lacey*, 3 Misc. 3d 1103A, 787 N.Y.S.2d 680, (N.Y. Nassau County Ct. May 6, 2004), the court found that "in the absence of exigent circumstances … the police should have obtained a warrant prior to attaching the GPS to the "vehicle." 3 Misc. 3d 1103A, at 8. However, the court went on to determine that the defendant had no expectation of privacy in the vehicle to which the GPS device was attached because "he did not own [it] and [it] was used for the sole purpose of furthering a criminal enterprise." 3 Misc. 3d 1103A, (WL) at 9. Accordingly, the defendant's motion to suppress was denied. It is also noteworthy that despite surveying cases from other jurisdictions on this issue, the *Lacey* Court failed to reconcile its reasoning with that of the United States Supreme Court in *Knotts*. In fact, the *Lacey* Court did not even mention *Knotts*.

In *State v. Jackson*, 150 Wn.2d 251, 76 P.3d 217 (Wash. 2003) the court held that a warrant was required for the installation of a GPS device on a vehicle, pursuant to the Washington State Constitution. The court noted that there was no Fourth Amendment issue. Rather, the issue was whether the warrantless use of the GPS device ran afoul of the more restrictive state constitutional provisions. Subjective expectations of privacy played no role in the analysis.

Accordingly, there was no Fourth Amendment violation and suppression of the GPS information is not warranted.

More recently, however, in *United States v. Maynard* (discussed below), the U.S. Court of Appeals reached a contrary conclusion.

United States v. Maynard

---

615 F.3D 544 (2010)

U.S. COURT OF APPEALS, D.C. CIRCUIT

GINSBURG, Circuit Judge:

Jones owned and Maynard managed the "Levels" nightclub in the District of Columbia. In 2004 an FBI–Metropolitan Police Department Safe Streets Task Force began investigating the two for narcotics violations. The investigation culminated in searches and arrests on October 24, 2005.

A joint trial of Jones and Maynard began in November 2007 and ended in January 2008, when the jury found them both guilty.

Jones argues his conviction should be overturned because the police violated the Fourth Amendment prohibition of "unreasonable searches" by tracking his movements 24 hours a day for four weeks with a GPS device they had installed on his Jeep without a valid warrant.

Jones argues the use of the GPS device violated his "reasonable expectation of privacy," *Katz v United States*, 389 U.S. 347, 360–61 (Harlan, J., concurring), and was therefore a search subject to the reasonableness requirement of the Fourth Amendment. Of course, the Government agrees the *Katz* test applies here, but it argues we need not consider whether Jones's expectation of privacy was reasonable because that question was answered in *United States v Knotts*, 460 U.S. 276 (1983), in which the Supreme Court held the use of a beeper device to aid in tracking a suspect to his drug lab was not a search. As explained below, we hold *Knotts* does not govern this case and the police action was a search because it defeated Jones's reasonable expectation of privacy. We then turn to the Government's claim our holding necessarily implicates prolonged visual surveillance.

The Government argues this case falls squarely within the holding in *Knotts* that "[a] person traveling in an automobile on public thoroughfares has no reasonable expectation of privacy in his movements from one place to another." 460 U.S. at 281. In that case the police had planted a beeper in a five-gallon container of chemicals before it was purchased by one of Knotts's co-conspirators; monitoring the progress of the car carrying the beeper, the police followed the container as it was driven from the "place of purchase, in Minneapolis, Minnesota, to [Knotts's] secluded cabin near Shell Lake, Wisconsin," 460 U.S. at 277, a trip of about 100 miles. Because the co-conspirator, by driving on public roads, "voluntarily conveyed to anyone who wanted to look" his progress and route, he could not reasonably expect privacy in "the fact of his final destination." Id., at 281.

The Court explicitly distinguished between the limited information discovered by use of the beeper—movements during a discrete journey—and more comprehensive or sustained monitoring of the sort at issue in this case. Most important for the present case, the Court specifically reserved the question whether a warrant would be required in a case involving "twenty-four hour surveillance," stating if such dragnet-type law enforcement practices as respondent envisions should eventually occur, there will be time enough then to determine whether different constitutional principles may be applicable. Id., at 283–84.

In short, Knotts held only that "[a] person traveling in an automobile on public thoroughfares has no reasonable expectation of privacy in his movements from one place to another," id., at 281, not that such a person has no reasonable expectation of privacy in his movements whatsoever, world without end, as the Government would have it. The Fifth Circuit likewise has recognized the limited scope of the holding in Knotts, see United States v Butts, 729 F.2d 1514, 1518 n. 4 (1984) ("As did the Supreme Court in Knotts we pretermit any ruling on worst-case situations that may involve persistent, extended, or unlimited violations of a warrant's terms"), as has the New York Court of Appeals, see People v Weaver, 12 N.Y.3d 433, 440–44 (2009) (Knotts involved a "single trip" and Court "pointedly acknowledged and reserved for another day the question of whether a Fourth Amendment issue would be posed if 'twenty-four hour surveillance of any citizen of this country [were] possible'"). See also Renee McDonald Hutchins, Tied Up in Knotts? GPS Technology and the Fourth Amendment, 419 UCLA L.Rev. 409, 457 (2007).

Two considerations persuade us the information the police discovered in this case—the totality of Jones's movements over the course of a month—was not exposed to the public: First, unlike one's movements during a single journey, the whole of one's movements over the course of a month is not *actually* exposed to the public because the likelihood anyone will observe all those movements is effectively nil. Second, the whole movement is exposed, because that whole reveals more—sometimes a great deal more—than does the sum of its parts.

The holding in Knotts flowed naturally from the reasoning in Katz: "What a person knowingly exposes to the public ... is not a subject of Fourth Amendment protection," 389 U.S at 351. See Knotts, 460 U.S. at 281–82 (movements observed by police were "voluntarily conveyed to anyone who wanted to look"). The Government argues the same reasoning applies here as well. We first consider the precedent governing our analysis of whether the subject of a purported search has been exposed to the public, then hold the information the police discovered using the GPS device was not so exposed.

The Government argues Jones's movements over the course of a month were actually exposed to the public because the police lawfully could have followed Jones everywhere he went on public roads over the course of a month. The Government implicitly poses the wrong question, however.

In considering whether something is "exposed" to the public as that term was used in *Katz* we ask not what another person can physically and may lawfully do but rather what a reasonable person expects another might actually do.

The Supreme Court re-affirmed this approach in *Bond v United States*, 529 U.S. 334 (2000). There a passenger on a bus traveling to Arkansas from California had placed his soft luggage in the overhead storage area above his seat. During a routine stop at an off-border immigration checkpoint in Sierra Blanca, Texas, a Border Patrol agent squeezed the luggage in order to determine whether it contained drugs and thus detected a brick of what turned out to be methamphetamine. The defendant argued the agent had defeated his reasonable expectation of privacy, and the Government argued his expectation his bag would not be squeezed was unreasonable because he had exposed it to the public. The Court responded:

> [A] bus passenger clearly expects that his bag may be handled. He does not expect that other passengers or bus employees will, as a matter of course, feel the bag in an exploratory manner. But this is exactly what the agent did here. We therefore hold that the agent's physical manipulation of petitioner's bag violated the Fourth Amendment.

> Id. at 338–39.

The Court focused not upon what other passengers could have done or what a bus company employee might have done, but rather upon what a reasonable bus passenger expects others he may encounter, i.e., fellow passengers or bus company employees, might actually do. A similar focus can be seen in Kyllo in which the Court held use of a thermal imaging device defeats the subject's reasonable expectation of privacy, "at least where … the technology in question is not in general public use." 533 U.S. at 34.

Applying the foregoing analysis to the present facts, we hold the whole of a person's movements over the course of a month is not actually exposed to the public because the likelihood a stranger would observe all those movements is not just remote, it is essentially nil. It is one thing for a passerby to observe or even to follow someone during a single journey as he goes to the market or returns home from work. It is another thing entirely for that stranger to pick up the scent again the next day and the day after that, week in and week out, dogging his prey until he has identified all the places, people, amusements, and chores that make up that person's hitherto private routine.

The whole of one's movements over the course of a month is not constructively exposed to the public because, like a rap sheet, that whole reveals far more than the individual movements it comprises. The difference is not one of degree but of kind, for no single journey reveals the habits and patterns that mark the distinction between a day in the life and a way of life, nor the departure from a routine that, like the dog that did not bark in the Sherlock Holmes story, may reveal even more.

Application of the test in *Katz* and its sequellae to the facts of this case can lead to only one conclusion: Society recognizes Jones's expectation of privacy in his movements over the course of a month as reasonable, and the use of the GPS device to monitor those movements defeated that reasonable expectation. As we have discussed, prolonged GPS monitoring reveals an intimate picture of the subject's life that he expects no one to have—short perhaps of his spouse.

We note without surprise, therefore, that the Legislature of California, in making it unlawful for anyone but a law enforcement agency to "use an electronic tracking device to determine the location or movement of a person," specifically declared "electronic tracking of a person's location without that person's knowledge violates that person's reasonable expectation of privacy," and implicitly but necessarily thereby required a warrant for police use of a GPS, California Penal Code Section 637.7. Several other states have enacted legislation imposing civil and criminal penalties for the use of electronic tracking devices and expressly requiring exclusion of evidence produced by such a device unless obtained by the police acting pursuant to a warrant.

A search conducted without a warrant is "per se unreasonable under the Fourth Amendment—subject only to a few specifically established and well-delineated exceptions." *Katz*, 389 U.S. at 357. Here, because the police installed the GPS device on Jones's vehicle without a valid warrant, the Government argues the resulting search can be upheld as a reasonable application of the automobile exception to the warrant requirement. Under that exception, "[i]f a car is readily mobile and probable cause exists to believe it contains contraband, the Fourth Amendment ... permits police to search the vehicle without more." *Pennsylvania v Labron*, 518 U.S. 938 (1996).

As Jones points out, this argument is doubly off the mark. First, the Government did not raise it below. Second, the automobile exception permits the police to search a car without a warrant if they have reason to believe it contains contraband; the exception does not authorize them to install a tracking device on a car without the approval of a neutral magistrate.

How would a state court resolve this issue under the state's own constitution? The New York Court of Appeals (the state's highest court) considered the issue in the following case:

People v. Weaver

---

12 N.Y.3D 433 (2009)

N.Y. COURT OF APPEALS

LIPPMAN, Chief Judge.

In the early morning hours of December 21, 2005, a State Police Investigator crept underneath defendant's street-parked van and placed a global positioning system (GPS) tracking device inside the bumper. The device remained in place for 65 days, constantly monitoring the position of the van. This nonstop surveillance was conducted without a warrant.

The GPS device, known as a "Q-ball," once attached to the van, operated in conjunction with numerous satellites, from which it received tracking data, to fix the van's location. The Q-ball readings indicated the speed of the van and pinpointed its location within 30 feet. Readings were taken approximately every minute while the vehicle was in motion, but less often when it was stationary. The device's battery required replacement during the monitoring period, which resulted in yet another nocturnal visit by the investigator to the van's undercarriage. To download the location information retrieved by the Q-ball, the investigator would simply drive past the van and press a button on a corresponding receiver unit, causing the tracking history to be transmitted to and saved by a computer in the investigator's vehicle.

It is not clear from the record why defendant was placed under electronic surveillance. What is clear is that he was eventually charged with and tried in a single proceeding for crimes relating to two separate burglaries—one committed in July 2005 at the Latham Meat Market and the other on Christmas Eve of the same year at the Latham KMart.

The prosecution sought to have admitted at trial GPS readings showing that, on the evening of the Latham KMart burglary at 7:26, defendant's van traversed the store's parking lot at a speed of six miles per hour. Without a hearing, County Court denied defendant's motion to suppress the GPS data, and the electronic surveillance evidence was received. The additional evidence against defendant came primarily from Amber Roche, who was charged in connection with the Latham Meat Market burglary and was deemed an accomplice in the commission of that burglary.

Roche testified that prior to the date of the burglary, she drove through the parking lot of the Latham KMart with defendant and John Scott Chiera, while the men looked for the best place to break into the store. She stated that on the night of the burglary, defendant and Chiera left her apartment wearing dark clothing. When they returned, Chiera's hand was bleeding. Other evidence showed that, during the burglary, a jewelry case inside the KMart had been smashed and stained with blood containing DNA matching that of Chiera. Notably, Roche's initial statement to the police did not implicate defendant in the KMart burglary, but rather indicated that Chiera had committed the crime with a different individual. A few weeks later, Roche gave the police a second statement implicating defendant instead of that individual.

The jury convicted defendant of two counts relating to the KMart burglary, but acquitted him of the counts pertaining to the Meat Market burglary. The ensuing judgment of conviction was affirmed by a divided Appellate Division. The majority rejected defendant's argument that his Fourth Amendment rights had been violated by the warrantless placement and use of the GPS device, and found that he had no greater right to relief under the State Constitution. It premised its decision largely upon what it deemed to be defendant's reduced expectation of privacy in the exterior of his vehicle.

Our constitutional provision (art I, s 12), in addition to tracking the language of the Fourth Amendment, provides:

> "The right of the people to be secure against unreasonable interception of telephone and telegraph communications shall not be violated, and *ex parte* orders or warrants shall issue only upon oath or affirmation that there is reasonable ground to believe that evidence of crime may be thus obtained, and identifying the particular means of communication, and particularly describing the person or persons whose communications are to be intercepted and the purpose thereof."

Since *Katz*, the existence of a privacy interest within the Fourth Amendment's protective ambit has been understood to depend upon whether the individual asserting the interest has demonstrated a subjective expectation of privacy and whether that expectation would be accepted as reasonable by society (see *Katz*, 389 U.S. at 361 [Harlan, J., concurring]). However, while *Katz* purported to deemphasize location as a determinant in judging the reach of the Fourth Amendment, the analysis it seemed to require naturally reintroduced considerations of place back into the calculus since the social reasonableness of an individual's expectation of privacy will quite often turn upon the quality of the space inhabited or traversed, i.e., whether it is public or private space. An individual has been held to have a significantly reduced expectation of privacy when passing along a public way, particularly in a motor vehicle.

The amalgam of issues with which we here deal, arising from the use of a new and potentially doctrine-forcing surveillance technology by government law enforcers to track movements over largely public terrain, was most significantly dealt with by the Supreme Court in the post-*Katz* era in *United States v. Knotts*, 460 U.S. 276 (1983).

At first blush, it would appear that *Knotts* does not bode well for Mr. Weaver, for in his case, as in *Knotts*, the surveillance technology was utilized for the purpose of tracking the progress of a vehicle over what may be safely supposed to have been predominantly public roads and, as in *Knotts*, these movements were at least in theory exposed to "anyone who wanted to look" (id. at 281). This, however, is where the similarity ends.

Knotts involved the use of what we must now, more than a quarter of a century later, recognize to have been a very primitive tracking device. The device was, moreover, used in a focused binary police investigation for the discreet purpose of ascertaining the destination of a particular container of chloroform. And, in this application, during the single trip from the place where the chloroform was purchased to the Knotts cabin, the beeper was fairly described by the Court as having functioned merely as an enhancing adjunct to the surveilling officers' senses; the officers actively followed the vehicle and used the beeper as a means of maintaining and regaining actual visual contact with it. The technology was, in this context, not unconvincingly analogized by the Court to a searchlight, a marine glass, or a field glass (id. at 283, citing *United States v. Lee*, 274 U.S. 559, 563 [1927]).

Here, we are not presented with the use of a mere beeper to facilitate visual surveillance during a single trip. GPS is a vastly different and exponentially more sophisticated and powerful technology that is easily and cheaply deployed and has virtually unlimited and remarkably precise tracking capability. With the addition of new GPS satellites, the technology is rapidly improving so that any person or object, such as a car, may be tracked with uncanny accuracy to virtually any interior or exterior location, at any time and regardless of atmospheric conditions. Constant, relentless tracking of anything is now not merely possible but entirely practicable, indeed much more practicable than the surveillance conducted in *Knotts*. GPS is not a mere enhancement of human sensory capacity, it facilitates a new technological perception of the world in which the situation of any object may be followed and exhaustively recorded over, in most cases, a practically unlimited period. The potential for a similar capture of information or "seeing" by law enforcement would require, at a minimum, millions of additional police officers and cameras on every street lamp.

That such a surrogate technological deployment is not—particularly when placed at the unsupervised discretion of agents of the state "engaged in the often competitive enterprise of ferreting out crime" (*Johnson v. United States*, 333 U.S. 10, 14 [1948])—compatible with any reasonable notion of personal privacy or ordered liberty would appear to us obvious. One need only consider what the police may learn, practically effortlessly, from planting a single device. The whole of a person's progress through the world, into both public and private spatial spheres, can be charted and recorded over lengthy periods possibly limited only by the need to change the transmitting unit's batteries. Disclosed in the data retrieved from the transmitting unit, nearly instantaneously with the press of a button on the highly portable receiving unit, will be trips the indisputably private nature of which takes little imagination to conjure: trips to the psychiatrist, the plastic surgeon, the abortion clinic, the AIDS treatment center, the strip club, the criminal defense attorney, the by-the-hour motel, the union meeting, the mosque, synagogue or church, the gay bar and on and on. What the technology yields and records with breathtaking quality and quantity is a highly detailed profile, not simply of where we go, but by easy inference, of our associations—political, religious, amicable and amorous, to name only a few—and of the pattern of our professional and avocational pursuits. When multiple GPS devices are utilized, even more precisely resolved inferences about our activities are possible. And, with GPS becoming an increasingly routine feature in cars and cell phones, it will be possible to tell from the technology with ever increasing precision who we are and are not with, when we are and are not with them, and what we do and do not carry on our persons—to mention just a few of the highly feasible empirical configurations.

It would appear clear to us that the great popularity of GPS technology for its many useful applications may not be taken simply as a massive, undifferentiated concession of personal privacy to agents of the state. Indeed, contemporary technology projects our private activities into public space as never before. Cell technology has moved presumptively private phone conversation from the enclosure of Katz's phone booth to the open sidewalk and the car, and the advent of portable computing devices has resituated transactions of all kinds to relatively public spaces. It is fair to say, and we think consistent with prevalent social views, that this change in venue has not been accompanied by any dramatic diminution in the socially reasonable expectation that our communications and transactions will remain to a large extent private. Here, particularly, where there was no voluntary utilization of the tracking technology, and the technology was surreptitiously installed, there exists no basis to find an expectation of privacy so diminished as to render constitutional concerns *de minimis*.

It is, of course, true that the expectation of privacy has been deemed diminished in a car upon a public thoroughfare. But, it is one thing to suppose that the diminished expectation affords a police officer certain well-circumscribed options for which a warrant is not required and quite another to suppose that when we drive or ride in a vehicle our expectations of privacy are so utterly diminished that we effectively consent to the unsupervised disclosure to law enforcement authorities of all that GPS technology can and will reveal. Even before the advent of GPS, it was recognized that a ride in a motor vehicle does not so completely deprive its occupants of any reasonable expectation of privacy.

The residual privacy expectation defendant retained in his vehicle, while perhaps small, was at least adequate to support his claim of a violation of his constitutional right to be free of unreasonable searches and seizures. The massive invasion of privacy entailed by the prolonged use of the GPS device was inconsistent with even the slightest reasonable expectation of privacy.

While there may and, likely will, be exigent situations in which the requirement of a warrant issued upon probable cause authorizing the use of GPS devices for the purpose of official criminal investigation will be excused, this is not one of them. Plainly, no emergency prompted the attachment of the Q-ball to defendant's van.

In reaching this conclusion, we acknowledge that the determinative issue remains open as a matter of federal constitutional law, since the United States Supreme Court has not yet ruled upon whether the use of GPS by the state for the purpose of criminal investigation constitutes a search under the Fourth Amendment, and, indeed, the issue has not yet been addressed by the vast majority of the Federal Circuit Courts. Thus, we do not presume to decide the question as a matter of federal law. The very same principles are, however, dispositive of this matter under our State Constitution. If, as we have found, defendant had a reasonable expectation of privacy that was infringed by the State's placement and monitoring of the Q-ball on his van to track his movements over a period of more than two months, there was a search under article I, § 12 of the State Constitution. And that search was illegal because it was executed without a warrant and without justification under any exception to the warrant requirement.

In light of the unsettled state of federal law on the issue, we premise our ruling on our State Constitution alone.

Before us is a defendant whose movements have, for no apparent reason, been tracked and recorded relentlessly for 65 days. It is quite clear that this would not and, indeed, realistically could not have been done without GPS and that this dragnet use of the technology at the sole discretion of law enforcement authorities to pry into the details of people's daily lives is not consistent with the values at the core of our State Constitution's prohibition against unreasonable searches.

We find persuasive the conclusions of other state courts that have addressed this issue and have held that the warrantless use of a tracking device is inconsistent with the protections guaranteed by their state constitutions (*State v. Jackson*, 150 Wash.2d 251 [2003]; *State v. Campbell*, 306 Or. 157 [1988]). The corresponding provision of the Washington State Constitution differs from and has been held to be more protective than the Fourth Amendment. However, the court noted that the use of a GPS device was not merely an augmentation of an officer's senses (see *Jackson*, 150 Wash.2d at 261–262) and that the means of surveillance allowed the government to access an enormous amount of additional information, including a person's associations and activities (see, 150 Wash.2d at 260). The court concluded that "citizens of this State have a right to be free from the type of governmental intrusion that occurs when a GPS device is attached to a citizen's vehicle, regardless of reduced privacy expectations due to advances in technology" and that a warrant was needed before such a device could be installed (150 Wash.2d at 264).

Similarly, the Supreme Court of Oregon held that the government's use of a radio transmitter to monitor the location of defendant's car was a search under the State Constitution as it was a significant limitation on the defendant's freedom from scrutiny (*Campbell*, 306 Or. at 171), and that the warrantless use of the transmitter in the absence of exigent circumstances was "nothing short of a staggering limitation upon personal freedom" (306 Or. at 172).

Technological advances have produced many valuable tools for law enforcement and, as the years go by, the technology available to aid in the detection of criminal conduct will only become more and more sophisticated. Without judicial oversight, the use of these powerful devices presents a significant and, to our minds, unacceptable risk of abuse. Under our State Constitution, in the absence of exigent circumstances, the installation and use of a GPS device to monitor an individual's whereabouts requires a warrant supported by probable cause.

Accordingly, the order of the Appellate Division should be reversed, defendant's motion to suppress the evidence obtained from the GPS device should be granted and a new trial ordered.

RFID Technology

Radio frequency identification (RFID) technology has been implemented commercially to track the shipment and storage of goods. It can also be utilized to identify objects, such as a credit card. Because RFID technology can be utilized as a tracking and identification tool, can this technology be used by law enforcement for such purposes? The answer would seem to be yes, but there is no published decision concerning the use of RFID by law enforcement.

Key Words and Phrases

Beeper   RFID technology
Global positioning system   Trap and trace device
Pen register

Review Problems

1. Does it make sense, with today's notions of the need for privacy, to conclude, as the Supreme Court did in *Smith*, that because the telephone number dialed is known by the telephone company, the user knowingly exposed the information to the public? Does the user of a communications service have a choice? Does it make more sense to conclude that in order for one to relinquish the privacy of a number that is being dialed, the user must *voluntarily* provide the number? After all, if given a choice, would we voluntarily give up the number?
2. In *United States v. Maynard* and *People v. Weaver*, the courts in each case distinguished the result in *Knotts* because the tracking device had been installed for a lengthy period of time, as opposed to a single trip. Suppose that the operator of a vehicle takes a cross-country trip, stopping seven times along the way. Is that a single trip, or is each stop and start along the way a separate trip? How long must the installation period last? A week? A month? Does it make sense to determine whether the operator had an expectation of privacy based upon the length of the trip or the length of time that the device was installed?

Weblinks

https://ssd.eff.org/wire/govt/pen-registers
> This web page maintained by the Electronic Frontier Foundation provides a discussion of the privacy implications of pen registers and trap and trace devices, as well as links to other topics involving Internet surveillance.

www.cybertelecom.org/security/ecpatrapandtrace.htm
> This web page, sponsored by Cyber Telecom, an educational nonprofit organization that provides information on Federal Internet law and policy, contains a lengthy discussion of pen registers, trap and trace devices, and other legal issues pertaining to surveillance on the Internet.

http://itlaw.wikia.com/wiki/The_IT_Law_Wiki
> This is the main page of the IT Law Wiki, which provides numerous definitions on technology subjects, including pen registers, trap and trace devices, and global positioning systems.

Digital Evidence and Forensic Analysis
13

Introduction

The evidence has been obtained—lawfully. This chapter discusses the legal principles that apply to the determination whether that evidence is admissible in court or in an administrative proceeding.

Nature of Evidence

In a criminal case, the prosecution must establish guilt by presenting evidence of every element of the crime beyond a reasonable doubt (see *Commonwealth v. Webster*, 59 Mass. (5 Cush.) 295 (1850)). Evidence consists of any matter or thing that a party submits to prove or disprove a fact. There are three basic types of evidence: testimonial, documentary, and real. Testimonial evidence is oral evidence given by a witness. Documentary evidence refers to items that are in the form of a writing. Real evidence is an object (for example, photograph or digital image) or person presented or exhibited to the fact finder.

Evidence also may be classified as either direct or circumstantial. Direct evidence is something that can prove a fact without the need of any other evidence. For example, if the issue is whether Jones was present at a meeting, the testimony of Jones that he was present is direct evidence. Circumstantial evidence is evidence of a fact other than the fact at issue (also referred to as a collateral fact) from which, either by itself or proof of some other fact, the fact finder (usually the jury) can infer the fact at issue. For example, if the fact in issue is whether the defendant poisoned his wife, evidence that the defendant purchased the poison four days before the event would be circumstantial.

Admissibility of Evidence

Having evidence that will establish a material fact in the prosecution or defense case is important, but being able to persuade the court to admit that evidence at the trial is critical. To be admissible, the evidence must be relevant, material, and not barred by some evidentiary exclusionary rule. Rule 402 of the Federal Rules of Evidence, for example, provides that "all relevant evidence is admissible, except as otherwise provided by the Constitution of the United States, by Act of Congress, by these rules, or by other rules prescribed by the Supreme Court pursuant to statutory authority."

Relevant evidence tends to prove or disprove a fact in issue. Material evidence is relevant evidence that has some meaningful bearing on the issue. For example, if evidence would tend to prove a fact but is so remote or inconsequential, that evidence is considered immaterial. Thus, to be admissible, evidence must be both relevant and material.

The Federal Rules of Evidence also require that, as a precondition to admissibility, the party offering the evidence identify it and establish its authenticity. Rule 901 provides:

Requirement of Authentication or Identification

(a) General provision.

The requirement of authentication or identification as a condition precedent to admissibility is satisfied by evidence sufficient to support a finding that the matter in question is what its proponent claims.

(b) Illustrations.

By way of illustration only, and not by way of limitation, the following are examples of authentication or identification conforming with the requirements of this rule:

(1) Testimony of witness with knowledge. Testimony that a matter is what it is claimed to be.

(2) Nonexpert opinion on handwriting. Nonexpert opinion as to the genuineness of handwriting, based upon familiarity not acquired for purposes of the litigation.

(3) Comparison by trier or expert witness. Comparison by the trier of fact or by expert witnesses with specimens which have been authenticated.

(4) Distinctive characteristics and the like. Appearance, contents, substance, internal patterns, or other distinctive characteristics, taken in conjunction with circumstances.

(5) Voice identification. Identification of a voice, whether heard firsthand or through mechanical or electronic transmission or recording, by opinion based upon hearing the voice at any time under circumstances connecting it with the alleged speaker.

(6) Telephone conversations. Telephone conversations, by evidence that a call was made to the number assigned at the time by the telephone company to a particular person or business, if (A) in the case of a person, circumstances, including self-identification, show the person answering to be the one called, or (B) in the case of a business, the call was made to a place of business and the conversation related to business reasonably transacted over the telephone.

(7) Public records or reports. Evidence that a writing authorized by law to be recorded or filed and in fact recorded or filed in a public office, or a purported public record, report, statement, or data compilation, in any form, is from the public office where items of this nature are kept.

(8) Ancient documents or data compilation. Evidence that a document or data compilation, in any form, (A) is in such condition as to create no suspicion concerning its authenticity, (B) was in a place where it, if authentic, would likely be, and (C) has been in existence 20 years or more at the time it is offered.

(9) Process or system. Evidence describing a process or system used to produce a result and showing that the process or system produces an accurate result.

(10) Methods provided by statute or rule. Any method of authentication or identification provided by Act of Congress or by other rules prescribed by the Supreme Court pursuant to statutory authority.

In many criminal cases involving digital evidence, proof of authenticity, i.e., that the item is what it is claimed to be, requires that the prosecution establish that the item has not been tampered with or beyond the control of the party from the time it was seized. These issues are discussed below.

Preservation of Evidence

A computer crime scene is no different than the scene of a bank robbery or a murder. Evidence collected at the scene must be "bagged and tagged" and its condition at the time of discovery preserved until the time of trial. Preservation of evidence is essential to establish its authenticity.

Chain of Custody

Chain of custody refers to the listing of all persons having access to an item of evidence from the time of its collection or seizure until the time of its presentation at trial. Evidence of an unbroken chain of custody can establish that an item has not been tampered with, and thus that it is authentic.

Evidence of a chain of custody is not the only means of establishing authenticity. In *United States v. Brown,* 136 F.3d 1176 (7th Cir. 1998), the defense on appeal challenged the trial court's admission into evidence of audiotapes of undercover purchases of food stamps. The defense maintained that because the government failed to present chain of custody evidence, the trial court improperly admitted the tapes. The Seventh Circuit disagreed, stating:

Appellants argue that the district court committed reversible error by allowing the admission of six audio tapes depicting the undercover sales of food stamps for cash. Specifically, appellants argue that the tapes were admitted without proof of a chain of custody. The government concedes that it failed to establish a chain of custody for the six tapes. However, it argues, and we agree, that such a mistake does not render the tapes inadmissible. We have held that lack of proof regarding a chain of custody does not render tapes inadmissible. *United States v. Craig,* 573 F.2d 455, 478 (7th Cir. 1977). In *Craig,* the defendant argued, *inter alia,* that because the government failed to establish a chain of custody, the tape recorded conversations of he and a co-schemer should not have been admitted into evidence. We disagreed, stating that the purpose of the chain of custody requirement is to insure that the items offered into evidence are in substantially the same condition as they were at the time the proponent came into possession of the evidence. We went on to note that "the purpose of the rule is served where, as here, a proper foundation demonstrating the accuracy and trustworthiness of the evidence is laid." Id.

We believe that just as the purpose of the chain of custody rule was served in *Craig,* so is it served here. The government laid a proper foundation for the admission of the tapes at trial. Before offering each tape into evidence, the government questioned Patches, the confidential informant, about the events that occurred during the undercover sales of food stamps to the appellants on each of the six different occasions. Patches testified that he listened to the tapes, that the tapes truly and accurately recorded the conversation that occurred, that his initials were written on each tape, and that the tapes were in the same condition as when he last saw them. Patches also identified the speakers on each tape.

Additionally, Agents Manley and Lienard testified to these same conversations. Agent Manley testified that he listened to the conversations on a wire transmitter as Patches conducted each sale of food stamps to the appellants. He testified that he listened to the conversations during each of the six transactions, and that he personally saw the fourth transaction take place between Patches and Jenkins. In this circuit, the recollections of eyewitnesses to the events in question are sufficient to establish a foundation for the admission of tapes. *United States v. Carrasco*, 887 F.2d 794, 802 (7th Cir. 1989) ("In the case of an original or a duplicate tape the government may establish a foundation for accuracy and truth of the tape through 'evidence of a chain of custody and by the correspondence between the tape's version of the events … and the recollections of the eyewitnesses to those events; in this circuit, either variety of evidence can establish a tape's foundation.'"). That the tapes depicted conversations which occurred five years earlier is irrelevant; a sufficient foundation was laid for the admission of the tapes.

Appellants do not suggest that there was a break in the chain of custody; they do not try to establish any tampering or altering of the tapes, nor do they allege that the tapes did not adequately depict the conversations between themselves and Patches. They simply insinuate that "any person with a thousand dollar computer can easily alter a tape recording." Merely raising the possibility (however hypothetical) of tampering is not sufficient to render evidence inadmissible. When chain of custody is in question but there is no evidence of any tampering, there is a presumption that a system of regularity accompanied the handling of the evidence if the exhibits are at all times within official custody. Furthermore, the possibility of a break in the chain of custody of evidence goes to the weight of the evidence, not its admissibility. The district court was satisfied that the proper foundation was established for the admissibility of the tapes and so are we. On the basis of the record before us, we cannot say that the district court abused its discretion in admitting the tapes into evidence.

There are instances, however, when the failure to establish a chain of custody will be fatal. Consider the following:

United States v. Wyss

2006 WL 1722288

U.S. DISTRICT COURT, SOUTHERN DIST. OF MISSISSIPPI

DAVID BRAMLETTE, District Judge.

This matter having come on for trial without a jury and upon the presentation of evidence by the United States of America, the defendant, John Richard Wyss, made a motion to suppress the evidence and also moved for a dismissal, and the Court sustained the motion and dismissed the case against the defendant.

The Government called as its first witness, Stanley Felter, who testified that the defendant, John Richard Wyss, rented from Felter's father a house in Adams County, and that the defendant was delinquent in rental payments. Felter testified further that he entered the house, made an inspection thereof, and removed items therefrom. He testified also that the house appeared to be in order, with furnishings contained therein, although he noticed what appeared to be blood on the sheets, walls and carpet, causing him to call for an inspection and further investigation by the Sheriff's Department. He testified further that it appeared that the tenant was not living in the house at the time, although his testimony in this regard was somewhat indefinite. Moreover, this witness gave no testimony which would explain what authority, if any, he had to enter upon the property, other than the property owner is his father.

Deputy John Manley, who now is employed with the University Medical Center as a campus police officer, testified that he, at the instance of Mr. Felter, entered a storage unit on Highway 61 North, and removed property therefrom, including a computer. His removal of the computer was based upon his suspicion of child pornography, although his testimony as to what caused this suspicion is somewhat indefinite. It is clear, however, that Officer Manley had neither sought nor received a warrant to search the storage unit.

It is the Government's contention that the computer was obtained by Mr. Felter and not by a law enforcement officer and, therefore, Fourth Amendment issues are not involved. The Government did not explain, however, by what authority the Sheriff's Deputy entered the storage unit and took possession of the computer. More importantly, assuming that the computer found in the storage unit is the same computer which was found at the home, there is no evidence regarding what happened to the computer after it was removed from the home and before it came into the custody of Officer Manley, a period of approximately ten days.

Rule 29 of the Federal Rules of Criminal Procedure provides, in relevant part:

> After the government closes its evidence or after the close of all the evidence, the court on the defendant's motion must enter a judgment of acquittal of any offense for which the evidence is insufficient to sustain a conviction. The court may on its own consider whether the evidence is insufficient to sustain a conviction.

On a motion for judgment of acquittal, the district judge must determine whether the evidence is substantial enough for a reasonable fact-finder to find guilt beyond a reasonable doubt. In doing so, the Court must view the evidence in the light most favorable to the prosecution and resolve all doubts in the prosecution's favor. The purpose of testimonial tracing of evidence is, *inter alia*, to render it improbable that the evidence has been tampered with. *United States v. Abreu*, 952 F.2d 1458, 1467 (1st Cir. 1992). There is a presumption of regularity when evidence is in official custody. See *United States v. Boykins*, 9 F.3d 1278, 1285 (7th Cir. 1993). Here, however, the computer was not in official custody, and the presumption does not apply. Furthermore, the possibility of intermeddling or tampering was present for approximately ten days. FBI Agent Wayne Mitchell testified as to the possibility of someone manipulating the dates of image files to make them appear to have been created at an earlier date. The Court therefore finds that the evidence is insufficient to sustain a conviction by a reasonable fact-finder.

The Court finds it unnecessary to make an analysis of Fourth Amendment issues or the Private Search Doctrine, inasmuch as a failure to prove the chain of custody raises a reasonable doubt as to whether this defendant is responsible for the images on the hard drive, since the images could have been placed there by someone else after the computer was removed from his household and before it came into official custody. The Court's decision to grant the Rule 29 motion and dismiss the defendant is supported by a lack of evidence from which a reasonable finder of fact could determine that the images found on the computer were put there by this defendant, under circumstances where unidentified individuals possessed this equipment for at least a ten day period.

Admissibility of Digital Evidence

Establishing the chain of custody and the integrity of the evidence from the time of its seizure until its presentation at the trial is not the only requirement for authenticity. Where the evidence to be presented involves a scientific or technical process as, for example, DNA evidence or the result of the forensic analysis of a computer or other digital device, the reliability of that process must be established. The initial evidentiary standard used to ensure that such evidence is reliable was the *Frye* test. Currently, there are three tests in common use: the *Frye* test, *Frye* plus, and the *Daubert* test.

The *Frye* Test

The *Frye* test that established the standard that was then applied in federal court and in most state courts was announced in *Frye v. United States*, 293 Fed. 1013 (D.C. Cir. 1923). In that case, the court stated (at p. 1014) that the party offering evidence of a scientific or technical process, in that case the results of a lie detector test, must establish that "the thing from which the deduction is made must be sufficiently established to have gained general acceptance in the particular field in which it belongs." Essentially, the *Frye* test requires the party offering the evidence to present testimony that the scientific or technical process, let's say the use of a forensic product to recover "deleted" e-mail messages, is generally accepted by examiners or analysts in the computer forensic community.

In the following case, the issue was whether the accident was caused by excessive speed and the failure to negotiate a curve or from the loss of control of the vehicle caused by swerving to avoid striking a deer. The state's expert testified that as a result of the use of a computer software program to conduct an accident reconstruction, the accident was caused by excessive speed. On appeal, the court rejected the defendant's contention that the computer software program was inadmissible under the *Frye* test.

State v. Phillips

123 WASH. APP. 761, 98 P.3D 838 (2004)
COURT OF APPEALS OF WASHINGTON

QUINN-BRINTNALL, C.J.

A jury convicted Kevin Michael Phillips of vehicular homicide and vehicular assault. One of Phillips's passengers died at the scene and the other was critically injured when the car Phillips was driving crossed the centerline, left the road, and crashed into a telephone pole, shearing the pole in two. On appeal, Phillips challenges the trial court's ruling allowing the State's accident reconstruction expert to testify using computer assisted reconstruction calculations. We affirm.

[T]he State charged Phillips with one count of vehicular homicide and one count of vehicular assault. During trial, the State presented John Hunter as an expert witness. In analyzing the accident, Hunter used PC-Crash, a software program that performs physics calculations from input data to reconstruct and simulate traffic accidents. Based on Clithero's diagram, Hunter input data into PC-Crash to simulate Phillips's accident. Hunter adjusted the potential speeds of the vehicle, simulating the vehicle's path over the tire track marks, through the bushes, and hitting the pole. Based on his analysis, Hunter testified that Phillips's vehicle was traveling at approximately 80 mph when the accident occurred. Hunter opined that Phillips's failure to negotiate the sweeping curve was due to the vehicle's speed, rather than Phillips's asserted swerving maneuver.

Phillips also presented an expert, Kenneth Cottingham, who was a mechanical engineer. Cottingham testified that the tire marks at the scene were "yaw marks," meaning that "[t]he car [was] going sideways, point[ing] one way and sliding and going another way, [simultaneously] rotating." Cottingham testified that based on the critical speed analysis on the yaw marks, Phillips's vehicle was traveling at 60 mph at the time of the accident. Cottingham also opined that the curve did not put the vehicle "into a yaw" and that the vehicle went into a yaw when Phillips suddenly swerved, as he would have done to avoid hitting a deer. Cottingham testified that once the vehicle went into a yaw, it was "irrevocable."

The main question on appeal is whether the trial court committed reversible error by admitting Hunter's accident reconstruction testimony. Hunter used a computer software program called PC-Crash to assist in reconstructing the collision and estimating the speed Phillips's car was traveling when it sheared the telephone pole. Phillips does not challenge Hunter's qualification as an accident reconstruction expert. Instead, he claims that PC-Crash is not generally accepted in the scientific community and, thus, the trial court erred in ruling that the State carried its burden of establishing that testimony from an accident reconstruction expert who used PC-Crash to analyze data was admissible under the *Frye* test.

In Washington, evidence derived from a novel scientific theory or principle is admissible only if the theory or principle has achieved general acceptance in the relevant scientific community. *State v. Copeland*, 130 Wash.2d 244, 261, 922 P.2d 1304 (1996) (affirming Washington's adherence to *Frye v. United States*, 293 F. 1013 (D.C. Cir. 1923), despite U.S. Supreme Court's adoption of a different test in *Daubert v. Merrell Dow Pharmaceuticals, Inc.*, 509 U.S. 579, 113 S.Ct. 2786, 125 L.Ed.2d 469 (1993)). But if the evidence does not involve a novel scientific theory, a *Frye* hearing is not required.

Trial courts routinely admit testimony from qualified accident reconstruction experts. Phillips does not challenge Hunter's qualifications as an accident reconstruction expert. Instead he claims that because Hunter used PC-Crash, a computerized reconstruction software program, to calculate the speed of the vehicle and reconstruct the crash, it is PC-Crash and not Hunter that is giving evidence and that PC-Crash must meet the *Frye* standard.

Under *Frye*, novel scientific, technical, or other specialized knowledge may be admitted or relied upon only if generally accepted as reliable by the relevant scientific, technical, or specialized community. General acceptance may be found "from testimony that asserts it, from articles and publications, from widespread use in the community, or from the holdings of other courts." *Kunze*, 97 Wash. App. at 853, 988 P.2d 977. If there is a significant dispute between qualified experts as to the validity of scientific evidence, there is no general acceptance. Mere disagreement as to the conclusions or weight to be given the results, however, does not amount to a significant dispute.

Here, the State provided substantial evidence of the acceptance underlying the principles that PC-Crash uses and the general acceptance in the accident reconstruction community of similar software. Hunter, an accident reconstruction expert with 30 years experience, testified to the use of accident simulation programs such as PC-Crash in the accident reconstruction community. Hunter has used PC-Crash since 1995 or 1996 over a thousand times. And he used PC-Crash in connection with his testimony in one other vehicular homicide trial in Snohomish County and two or three civil trials. Hunter also testified that there are many two-dimensional accident simulation software programs available and that PC-Crash is one of two major three-dimensional software reconstruction programs available.

Hunter also testified about two validation articles on PC-Crash published in accident reconstruction journals, one favorable and the other critical. He testified that the critical review on which Phillips's attorney relied had been discredited and the accident reconstruction community no longer embraces this article's criticism. Specifically, Hunter testified that the article had not been properly peer reviewed; it was his understanding that the article had been withdrawn from publication by the Society of Automotive Engineers; and his review of the critical article suggested that the authors had improperly applied two-dimensional analysis to the three-dimensional PC-Crash program and that this error had created the unreliable results reported in the article.

Hunter testified that several accident reconstruction agencies have or use PC-Crash, including the Society of Automotive Engineers, the Seattle corporation MDE Engineering, and the Washington State Patrol Major Accident Investigation Team. He named other accident reconstruction experts he knew who were using the program and who had used the program results in their testimony in Washington courts.

In evaluating general acceptance in the scientific community, we also look to decisions from other jurisdictions. Our inquiry is not whether other courts have accepted the evidence, but whether the scientific community accepts the evidence and whether other jurisdictions have found evidence of widespread use. There is no published federal or state case in the United States that has specifically ruled on the validity of the PC-Crash software. But other jurisdictions have accepted accident reconstruction software and computer simulations as based on the application of long-standing scientific principles. In *State v. Clark*, 101 Ohio App.3d 389, 416, 655 N.E.2d 795 (Ohio Ct. App. 1995), aff'd, 75 Ohio St.3d 412, 662 N.E.2d 362 (Ohio 1996), the appellate court affirmed the admission of computer reconstructed models based on "the reliability of such simulations within the relevant technical community." The court in Clark noted that similar simulations have been found reliable and admissible in other jurisdictions.

Here, the State demonstrated by a preponderance of the evidence that the use of computer-assisted accident reconstruction software, such as PC-Crash, is accepted in the accident reconstruction community. Accident reconstruction software programs and computer simulations have been used in other jurisdictions. Although Phillips offered a copy of one unverified article critical of the PC-Crash reconstruction program, there was testimony that this article had been discredited and may even have been withdrawn from publication. More importantly, there was no evidence that a significant dispute among experts exists regarding the use of computer-assisted accident reconstruction programs.

Computer-assisted accident reconstruction programs, including PC-Crash, calculate from established laws of physics and are sufficiently accepted in the field of accident reconstruction to satisfy the *Frye v. United States*, 293 F. 1013 (D.C. Cir. 1923), standard for admissibility. An otherwise qualified accident reconstruction expert is not prohibited from giving expert opinion testimony on the cause of an accident merely because he uses the assistance of such a software program in making his calculations. Phillips's challenges to the proper use of the software go to the weight not the admissibility of Hunter's expert testimony and the trial court properly admitted Hunter's expert accident reconstruction testimony.

Although the *Frye* test is no longer used in federal court, the states may use their own evidentiary standard. Several states continue to apply the "general acceptance" test announced in *Frye*.

Frye Plus

Some states also utilize evidentiary standards that are neither exact versions of *Frye* nor the federal *Daubert* standard. The following decision of a Texas appellate court involves the application of its own "*Frye* plus" standard to the question whether a particular forensic software tool, EnCase by Guidance Software, is admissible.

Sanders v. State

---

191 S.W.3D 272 (2006)

COURT OF APPEALS OF TEXAS

BILL VANCE, Justice.

Appellant Roger Sanders was sentenced to life in prison after his conviction on ten counts of aggravated sexual assault of a child under the age of fourteen. We will affirm.

C., Sanders's former stepdaughter, testified that Sanders began sexually abusing her in the fall of 1999, when C. was eleven. Sometimes during the abuse, Sanders made C. look at child pornography on his computer or at pornographic movies. The abuse continued until 2002, when the marriage between C.'s mother and Sanders ended in separation and divorce. After C. reported the abuse, police obtained and executed a search warrant at Sanders's apartment, seizing a computer and various disks containing a large amount of child pornography.

Expert Testimony

Sanders complains of the trial court's admission of expert testimony from Jessie Lee, the State's forensic computer examiner who recovered the child pornography from computer media found in Sanders's apartment. Sanders asserts that the State failed to show that the testimony was sufficiently reliable.

To be reliable, evidence derived from a scientific theory must satisfy three criteria: (a) the underlying scientific theory must be valid; (b) the technique applying the principle must be valid; and (c) the technique must have been properly applied on the particular occasion. *Kelly v. State*, 824 S.W.2d 568, 573 (Tex. Crim. App. 1992). Factors affecting the trial court's proper determination of these three criteria include, but are not limited to: (1) the extent to which the underlying scientific theory and technique are accepted as valid by the relevant scientific community, if such community can be ascertained; (2) the qualifications of any expert testifying; (3) the existence of literature supporting or rejecting the underlying scientific theory and technique; (4) the potential rate of error of the technique; (5) the availability of other experts to test and evaluate the technique; (6) the clarity with which the underlying scientific theory and technique can be explained to the court; and (7) the experience and skill of any person who applied the technique on the occasion in question. Id.

Lee, a certified peace officer and criminal investigator for the district attorney for four years, said that he performs computer forensic analysis daily. He had over 600 hours of training in his field, had attended various training programs in his field, and, at the time of trial, was certified by the International Association of Computer Investigation Specialists. His training included software programs like EnCase and Forensic Toolkit. EnCase is a "field standard" for forensic computer examination; treatises about EnCase have been published. Lee explained that when he takes a hard drive from a computer, he uses a program like EnCase to automate the task of searching and finding the files on it. An image of the drive is taken; the files are copied, and EnCase validates the copy by an "MD5 hash," a 128-bit algorithm that verifies the image. The MD5 hash is essentially a "digital fingerprint" of a drive, and if the hash values match, Lee said that "basically there's no chance" that an error occurred in making an exact duplicate of the original computer file.

Lee used EnCase on computer files taken from Sanders's computer. EnCase indexed the files, and Sanders was able to retrieve deleted files containing child pornography from Sanders's computer.[*] We find that the trial court did not abuse its discretion in admitting Lee's testimony and the evidence from Sanders's computer in the punishment phase. See *Williford v. State*, 127 S.W.3d 309, 312–13 (Tex. App.-Eastland 2004, pet. ref'd) (finding similar testimony about EnCase reliable in child pornography case).[†]

Daubert Test

Section 702 of the Federal Rules of Evidence provides:

Testimony by Experts

If scientific, technical, or other specialized knowledge will assist the trier of fact to understand the evidence or to determine a fact in issue, a witness qualified as an expert by knowl-

---

[*] Sanders in original. Probably should be Lee.

[†] We find that Detective Owings's testimony satisfied the Kelly criteria for reliability. Detective Owings provided testimony on each of the seven factors identified in Kelly. Detective Owings is the computer expert for the Brownwood Police Department and is knowledgeable about EnCase. He testified that EnCase is generally accepted in the computer forensic investigation community, that EnCase is used worldwide, that he knew how to use EnCase, that he knew how EnCase worked, that he had successfully used EnCase in the past, that EnCase can be tested by anyone because it was commercially available and anyone could purchase it, that EnCase has been tested, that there have been several articles written about EnCase and other computer forensic software programs, that SC Magazine gave EnCase an overall five-star rating out of five stars, that EnCase has a low potential rate of error, that he successfully copied appellant's hard drive by using EnCase, and that EnCase verified that he had successfully copied appellant's hard drive. Detective Owings described in detail for the trial court how EnCase worked. Detective Owings's testimony established EnCase's reliability. The trial court did not abuse its discretion.... 127 S.W.3d at 312–13; see also Hernandez v. State, 116 S.W.3d 26, 28–29 (Tex. Crim. App. 2003) ("once some courts have, through a Daubert/Kelly 'gatekeeping' hearing, determined the scientific reliability and validity of a specific methodology to implement or test the particular scientific theory, other courts may take judicial notice of the reliability (or unreliability) of that particular methodology.").

edge, skill, experience, training, or education, may testify thereto in the form of an opinion or otherwise, if (1) the testimony is based upon sufficient facts or data, (2) the testimony is the product of reliable principles and methods, and (3) the witness has applied the principles and methods reliably to the facts of the case.

In *Daubert v. Merrill Dow Pharmaceuticals Co.*, 509 U.S. 579 (1993), the Supreme Court determined that the *Frye* test did not satisfy the requirements of Rule 702. The court determined:

In the 70 years since its formulation in the *Frye* case, the "general acceptance" test has been the dominant standard for determining the admissibility of novel scientific evidence at trial. Although under increasing attack of late, the rule continues to be followed by a majority of courts, including the Ninth Circuit.

The *Frye* test has its origin in a short and citation-free 1923 decision concerning the admissibility of evidence derived from a systolic blood pressure deception test, a crude precursor to the polygraph machine. In what has become a famous (perhaps infamous) passage, the then Court of Appeals for the District of Columbia described the device and its operation and declared:

"Just when a scientific principle or discovery crosses the line between the experimental and demonstrable stages is difficult to define. Somewhere in this twilight zone the evidential force of the principle must be recognized, and while courts will go a long way in admitting expert testimony deduced from a well-recognized scientific principle or discovery, the thing from which the deduction is made must be sufficiently established to have gained general acceptance in the particular field in which it belongs." 54 App. D.C. at 47, 293 F. at 1014.

Because the deception test had "not yet gained such standing and scientific recognition among physiological and psychological authorities as would justify the courts in admitting expert testimony deduced from the discovery, development, and experiments thus far made," evidence of its results was ruled inadmissible. Ibid.

Petitioners' primary attack, however, is not on the content but on the continuing authority of the rule. They contend that the *Frye* test was superseded by the adoption of the Federal Rules of Evidence. We agree.

Frye, of course, predated the Rules by half a century. In *United States v. Abel*, 469 U.S. 45, 83 L. Ed. 2d 450, 105 S. Ct. 465 (1984), we considered the pertinence of background common law in interpreting the Rules of Evidence. We noted that the Rules occupy the field, but that the common law nevertheless could serve as an aid to their application.

Here there is a specific Rule that speaks to the contested issue.

Nothing in the text of this Rule establishes "general acceptance" as an absolute prerequisite to admissibility. Nor does respondent present any clear indication that Rule 702 or the Rules as a whole were intended to incorporate a "general acceptance" standard. The drafting history makes no mention of *Frye*, and a rigid "general acceptance" requirement would be at odds with the "liberal thrust" of the Federal Rules and their "general approach of relaxing the traditional barriers to 'opinion' testimony." Given the Rules' permissive backdrop and their inclusion of a specific rule on expert testimony that does not mention "general acceptance," the assertion that the Rules somehow assimilated *Frye* is unconvincing. *Frye* made "general acceptance" the exclusive test for admitting expert scientific testimony. That austere standard, absent from, and incompatible with, the Federal Rules of Evidence, should not be applied in federal trials.

That the *Frye* test was displaced by the Rules of Evidence does not mean, however, that the Rules themselves place no limits on the admissibility of purportedly scientific evidence. To the contrary, under the Rules the trial judge must ensure that any and all scientific testimony or evidence admitted is not only relevant, but reliable.

The primary locus of this obligation is Rule 702, which clearly contemplates some degree of regulation of the subjects and theories about which an expert may testify. "If scientific, technical, or other specialized knowledge will assist the trier of fact to understand the evidence or to determine a fact in issue" an expert "may testify thereto." The subject of an expert's testimony must be "scientific ... knowledge." The adjective "scientific" implies a grounding in the methods and procedures of science. Similarly, the word "knowledge" connotes more than subjective belief or unsupported speculation. The term "applies to any body of known facts or to any body of ideas inferred from such facts or accepted as truths on good grounds." Webster's Third New International Dictionary 1252 (1986). Of course, it would be unreasonable to conclude that the subject of scientific testimony must be "known" to a certainty; arguably, there are no certainties in science. But, in order to qualify as "scientific knowledge," an inference or assertion must be derived by the scientific method. Proposed testimony must be supported by appropriate validation—i.e., "good grounds," based on what is known. In short, the requirement that an expert's testimony pertain to "scientific knowledge" establishes a standard of evidentiary reliability.

Rule 702 further requires that the evidence or testimony "assist the trier of fact to understand the evidence or to determine a fact in issue." This condition goes primarily to relevance. "Expert testimony which does not relate to any issue in the case is not relevant and, ergo, non-helpful." The study of the phases of the moon, for example, may provide valid scientific "knowledge" about whether a certain night was dark, and if darkness is a fact in issue, the knowledge will assist the trier of fact. However (absent creditable grounds supporting such a link), evidence that the moon was full on a certain night will not assist the trier of fact in determining whether an individual was unusually likely to have behaved irrationally on that night. Rule 702's "helpfulness" standard requires a valid scientific connection to the pertinent inquiry as a precondition to admissibility.

That these requirements are embodied in Rule 702 is not surprising. Unlike an ordinary witness, see Rule 701, an expert is permitted wide latitude to offer opinions, including those that are not based on firsthand knowledge or observation. Presumably, this relaxation of the usual requirement of firsthand knowledge—a rule which represents "a 'most pervasive manifestation' of the common law insistence upon 'the most reliable sources of information,'" Advisory Committee's Notes on Fed. Rule Evid. 602, 28 U.S.C. App., p. 755 (citation omitted)—is premised on an assumption that the expert's opinion will have a reliable basis in the knowledge and experience of his discipline.

Faced with a proffer of expert scientific testimony, then, the trial judge must determine at the outset, pursuant to Rule 104(a), whether the expert is proposing to testify to (1) scientific knowledge that (2) will assist the trier of fact to understand or determine a fact in issue. This entails a preliminary assessment of whether the reasoning or methodology underlying the testimony is scientifically valid and of whether that reasoning or methodology properly can be applied to the facts in issue. Many factors will bear on the inquiry, and we do not presume to set out a definitive checklist or test. But some general observations are appropriate.

Ordinarily, a key question to be answered in determining whether a theory or technique is scientific knowledge that will assist the trier of fact will be whether it can be (and has been) tested.

Another pertinent consideration is whether the theory or technique has been subjected to peer review and publication. [S]ubmission to the scrutiny of the scientific community is a component of "good science," in part because it increases the likelihood that substantive flaws in methodology will be detected. The fact of publication (or lack thereof) in a peer reviewed journal thus will be a relevant, though not dispositive, consideration in assessing the scientific validity of a particular technique or methodology on which an opinion is premised.

Additionally, in the case of a particular scientific technique, the court ordinarily should consider the known or potential rate of error, and the existence and maintenance of standards controlling the technique's operation.

Finally, "general acceptance" can yet have a bearing on the inquiry. Widespread acceptance can be an important factor in ruling particular evidence admissible, and "a known technique which has been able to attract only minimal support within the community," may properly be viewed with skepticism.

The inquiry envisioned by Rule 702 is, we emphasize, a flexible one. Its overarching subject is the scientific validity—and thus the evidentiary relevance and reliability—of the principles that underlie a proposed submission. The focus, of course, must be solely on principles and methodology, not on the conclusions that they generate.

The inquiries of the District Court and the Court of Appeals focused almost exclusively on "general acceptance," as gauged by publication and the decisions of other courts. Accordingly, the judgment of the Court of Appeals is vacated, and the case is remanded for further proceedings consistent with this opinion.

Although *Daubert* was limited in its scope to scientific matters, the test was extended to technical matters in *Kumho Tire Co. v. Carmichael*, 526 U.S. 137 (1999).

Expert Opinion Evidence

Cybercrime investigators and computer forensic examiners frequently are needed to provide expert opinion evidence. Expert opinion evidence can be presented whenever evidence of a technical nature beyond the common understanding of jurors is necessary. In that instance, an individual who qualifies as an expert can testify as to the conclusion that can be drawn from a certain set of facts.

How does one qualify as an expert? Rule 702 simply states that a witness may qualify as an expert "by knowledge, skill, experience, training, or education." Can a witness provide opinion testimony typically given by a forensic expert even though the witness does not consider himself to be such an expert? The following case, which involves a pretrial motion in a civil case, illustrates the point:

Davison v. Eldorado Resorts LLC

2006 WL 587587

U.S. District Court, District of Nevada

MCKIBBEN, Magistrate J.

Plaintiff Carol Davison filed an ERISA complaint on January 12, 2005 against Defendants Eldorado and Coresource. Plaintiff was employed at the Eldorado and received group medical insurance that was an ERISA plan. The plan was administered by Coresource, a third-party administrator. The case arises out of Plaintiff's alleged "emergency" medical stay at Washoe Medical Center in September 2002 as a result of premature labor. Plaintiff incurred many costs through a series of hospital visits, and she alleges that Defendants failed to provide her with the medical coverage in her group plan.

The series of motions presently before the court concerns the admissibility of nine letters authored by Plaintiff. These letters were allegedly written by Plaintiff at different times between November 2002 and February 2003, and according to Plaintiff, evidence her attempts to administratively appeal the denial medical benefits. Defendants deny ever receiving any of the letters. As far as Defendants are concerned, Plaintiff has not exhausted her administrative remedies.

Plaintiff produced the letters at issue during discovery as a result of her deposition testimony. They are all unsigned versions that were printed out after the fact from a CD created by Plaintiff. Because Defendants never received Plaintiff's letters, and because Plaintiff could not produce signed copies of the letters she allegedly sent, Defendants came to question the authenticity of the letters she purportedly saved to CD. The CD from which these letters were printed was examined by both parties and their experts.

Plaintiff testified that she typed the purported appeal letters on her home computer. Specifically, Plaintiff would type the letter, save it, print it out, then sign and mail them from home. When asked whether she ever saved the documents to her hard drive, she replied that she saved them all to a CD, every time she wrote a letter and on the same day she would write a letter. Plaintiff explained that she normally backed things up on a CD because her computer had crashed three times.

Mr. "Paul Mudgett is a security and technology professional with over 12 years of experience in information security, computer forensics, technology integration and project management." His analysis of Plaintiff's CD was based on the "representation" that "[t]he files in question were ... directly saved on a CD rather than saved to a computer hard drive and subsequently copied to CD."

Mr. Mudgett explained that an operating system such as Windows logs three time stamps when a file is saved. The first stamp is titled "created" and keeps track of the date and time the file was first saved. The second stamp, "modified," shows the last time the file was opened and changed. Finally, the last stamp, "accessed," displays the date and time the file was most recently opened regardless of whether any changes were made to the file. Thus, when a file is saved to a CD, the "created" date will be the same as the "modified" date, and cannot change on a finalized CD. According to Plaintiff's testimony then, that she would save directly to CD the same day she wrote each letter, the "created" dates on the CD should reflect the dates written on each of the letters. However, after examining the word files on the CD, Mr. Mudgett discovered the following:

Bates Label No.	Hard copy date	"Created" time stamp as shown on CD files
P78	December 10, 2002	September 13, 2004 at 8:13:58 pm
P85	December 1, 2002	September 15, 2004 at 1:06:21 pm
P87	November 15, 2002	September 15, 2004 at 1:08:53 pm
P65	February 2, 2003	September 15, 2004 at 1:10:48 pm
P67	February 2, 2003	September 15, 2004 at 1:11:43 pm
P61	February 15, 2003	September 15, 2004 at 1:14:47 pm
P69	January 15, 2003	September 15, 2004 at 1:15:24 pm
P74	December 10, 2002	September 15, 2004 at 1:18:53 pm
P80	December 2, 2002	September 15, 2004 at 1:20:32 pm

Mr. Ira Victor is a certified information security specialist. One of his certifications, a G17799 ISO, covers data integrity, forensics, chain of custody, incident handling, malware, and other areas of information security. His analysis of Plaintiff's CD began with some information that he obtained directly from Plaintiff during a personal interview, Plaintiff's deposition testimony, and Defendants' expert report.

Mr. Victor's opinion was that the true creation dates of the CD files could not be determined without further information. This was because, for example, the potential movement of data back and forth between CD and hard drive, inaccurate computer time settings, or malware infections could have changed the "created" or "modified" dates on the CD at issue. Indeed, Mr. Victor was informed by Plaintiff and her computer rental center that Plaintiff's computer had been reformatted or "wiped out" on several occasions due to malicious code infections. Plaintiff also told Mr. Victor that she backed-up her letters onto a CD after she saved them onto the hard drive, and that she did not save her word documents directly to CD. In fact, according to Mr. Victor, Plaintiff would not have been able to save directly to CD without saving to her hard drive first unless she had a particular kind of software, which she did not.

Plaintiff also informed Mr. Victor that after her computer would get reformatted, she would reload all the information onto the hard drive that she had previously backed-up on CD. Mr. Victor explained, however, that the process of transferring materials back to the hard drive from a CD would change the "created" date of the document saved onto the hard drive to the date of transfer—it would not share the same "created" date belonging to the document saved to the CD. In addition, by re-burning that newly transferred document onto a second CD, the "created" date would again change to the date of burning.

Mr. Mudgett's deposition testimony was essentially the same. He testified that moving a file from a CD to the hard drive "may change [the created date], but you wouldn't be able to change that create date on the CD once the CD has been created." However, if one were to reburn the file onto a new CD, it would be possible for the create date to have changed.

The proponent of any particular item of evidence bears the burden of showing that the evidence is what the proponent claims it to be. Fed. R. Evid. 901; see Fed. R. Evid. 104(b). The determination of authenticity and admissibility is within the court's discretion. Once admitted, the trier of fact determines the credibility and probative value of the evidence.

Defendants' Supplemental Motion for an Evidentiary Ruling seeks a preliminary determination regarding the admissibility of Plaintiff's purported appeal letters.

Before the court can reach the main issue of the letters' admissibility, it must deal with the preliminary issue of Mr. Victor's competence to testify as an expert. Courts have broad discretion in determining whether a person qualifies as an expert. Under Federal Rule of Evidence 702, in order to qualify as an expert one must possess the "'knowledge, skill, experience, training, or education relevant to such evidence or fact in issue." Defendants challenge Mr. Victor's qualification and argue that he is not competent to give an expert opinion because he lacks any real knowledge and experience in forensic investigations.

In the court's view, however, Mr. Victor's collective experiences sufficiently demonstrate that there is a reliable basis for his technical knowledge and opinion in this matter. Mr. Victor is a certified information security specialist who currently works for an information security consulting firm. He has two security certifications, and has experience setting up various computer systems for businesses, managing data in secure environments, and an overall thirteen years of experience in the field of information technology and e-commerce. Although forensics may not be his direct focus, his field of work necessarily involves and overlaps with the field of forensics in that there are different stages of security incident management and compliance that require one to evaluate and investigate what may have happened to certain data. In fact, "[d]ata movement, transmission, and forensics like the kind under discussion in Ms. Davison's case, are key areas of concern for specialists in the information security field." Mr. Victor's reluctance to call himself an expert in forensics is inconsequential to the court's determination. It is clear from the course of his deposition that Mr. Victor was unaware of the legal definition of an "expert," and was instead using the layman's definition. However, the law does not limit expert testimony to those who are considered the absolute best in the field. The law only requires that Mr. Victor possess "such knowledge and experience in [the] field or calling as to make it appear that his opinion or inference will probably aid the trier in his search for the truth[,]" *Fineberg*, 393 F.2d at 421, and the court finds that he does.

The substance of Defendants' Motion is that Plaintiff cannot present sufficient evidence to sustain a preliminary determination of admissibility for the appeal letters. Defendants argue that no reasonable juror could find Plaintiff's letters are authentic because it is undisputed that the "created" dates tagged onto each letter on the CD are well after the 180-day appeal time limit. Letters that were purportedly written from November 2002 to February 2003 bear tags from September 2004. According to Defendants, however, the individual documents should have "created" dates that mirror the dates they were purportedly written on, because Plaintiff testified at her deposition that she "would type [a letter] up on the computer, save it to the disk, print one out, sign it and put it in an envelope and mail it to Coresource." She testified she would do that each time she wrote another letter. The fact that the "created" dates do not match the dates on each letter therefore is contrary to Plaintiff's assertions. Defendants contend that Plaintiff authored these documents after the fact. Thus, Defendants assert that no reasonable juror could determine the letters are authentic.

Plaintiff and her expert attempt to explain the mismatching of dates and establish a *prima facie* case of authenticity in several ways. Most of their explanations are insufficient, however, and cannot be relied upon by the court in determining the admissibility of the letters because they are not sufficiently grounded in the facts. For example, Mr. Victor explains that letters which should bear a creation date of January 2003 may instead be marked as "created" in September 2004 if the computer's internal calendar and clock were incorrectly set. Yet there is no testimony or any other form of evidence showing that Plaintiff's computer calendar and clock malfunctioned. There are also no facts upon which Mr. Victor could conclude that Plaintiff's computer was incorrectly set to the same day in September 2004 for almost four months. The court cannot make a finding of admissibility based solely on conjecture and speculation.

Mr. Victor also tried to explain that computer malware may have somehow changed the creation dates of the documents before they were saved to CD. Yet again, no diagnostic reports have been presented to the court despite the fact that Plaintiff had her computer reformatted several times over. There is no showing of what kind of viruses, worms, or spyware Plaintiff's computer may have had, and there is nothing to show that Mr. Victor had any real information beyond Plaintiff's own vague descriptions to substantiate his opinions. Again, this possible explanation does not provide sufficient information for the court to conclude the letters are authentic and admissible. See Fed. R. Evid. 702.

Third, Mr. Victor explained that because a number of people in Plaintiff's household had administrative access to her computer anybody could have manually reset the computer's clock setting, moved files off and back onto the computer, or changed the "created" dates on Plaintiff's documents, and so on. This attempted form of authentication, along with the rest, have no end in sight. Plaintiff could provide any number of possibilities to explain the hard facts when their likelihood is based on further speculation. Of course, experts may give opinions that are not based on firsthand knowledge, Fed. R. Evid. 703, but this goes too far. Most of Mr. Victor's report is only based on a very superficial investigation. A reasonable jury could not make a finding of authenticity from any of these explanations because there is no underlying evidence to support them. Fed. R. Evid. 702.

The last explanation proffered by Mr. Victor is the only possibility presented to the court that has some factual basis. It involves a complicated series of transactions, which if they occurred, would have changed the "created" dates tagged onto the files saved on the CD. This explanation, however, is dependent on the use of several CDs, and would necessarily mean that the CD in question is not the original CD to which Plaintiff burned her appeal letters. Indeed, Plaintiff asserted that was the case in her opposition, and in a supplemental response to a request for production. Nevertheless, Defendants maintain that Mr. Victor's explanation is untenable because the CD that was analyzed by both experts was in fact the original.

However, given that this part of Mr. Victor's report is factually grounded in an interview with Plaintiff, the court finds Plaintiff has met the low threshold for admissibility under Federal Rule of Evidence 901. A reasonable juror could find that Plaintiff's letters are authentic considering the totality of the circumstances, including Mr. Victor's report, Mr. Victor's interview with Plaintiff, and the confusion in Plaintiff's deposition. That is, the court recognizes that portions of Plaintiff's deposition, when pieced together with her response to requests for production, create the appearance that the CD in question is the original and the letters are back-dated as Defendants contend. However, both Plaintiff and counsel evidenced a lack of understanding or familiarity with computers, electronic file storage mediums, and technical jargon throughout her deposition testimony, and apparently, in the responses to requests for production. The court recognizes these weaknesses on both sides, and that Defendants' argument gains much strength from their exploitation.

For example, there were references to "disks" in general throughout the deposition. Defendants claim that every single time Plaintiff referred to saving a document to "disk," she meant that she saved directly to CD and never to her hard drive. That, however, is an assumption on Defendants' part that the court is unwilling to embrace. The term "disk" is a general one, and it could refer to a floppy, CD, or hard drive. In fact, the parties were alluding to a floppy disk for a significant amount of time before it was finally clarified that the electronic file storage medium was actually a CD. Moreover, both experts agreed that Plaintiff could not have burned documents to a CD directly through her word program without additional software, yet there is no indication that Plaintiff possessed such software. There is no indication that Plaintiff, her counsel, and even counsel for the opposition were aware that she was testifying inaccurately.

In exercising its discretion, the court is also conscious of the circumstances surrounding the discovery of the CD and Defendants' Motion. This motion for evidentiary ruling only arose after the experts viewed the CD, and the experts analyzed the CD only after Plaintiff had already been deposed. No party, including Plaintiff's own attorneys, seemed to know or appreciate how important it was to use specific terms and ask specific questions concerning the maintenance of Plaintiff's back-up CDs. Indeed, there were no real questions on that topic during her deposition, and Mr. Mudgett's report was based solely off of Plaintiff's deposition testimony.

Thus, considering the totality of the circumstances, the court finds that Plaintiff has made a *prima facie* case of authenticity. A reasonable jury could determine Plaintiff's appeal letters are authentic, Fed. R. Evid. 901(b)(1), given that portion of Mr. Victor's report that breaks down the transfer of documents between the hard drive and CDs, has an adequate factual basis, and is not irreconcilable with Plaintiff's deposition testimony. Defendants' arguments are more appropriate before the trier of fact, whose province it is to decide the weight of the evidence at trial.

Rules Requiring the Exclusion of Evidence

There are numerous rules that operate to exclude evidence. For our purposes, we will consider only those most relevant to computer or digital evidence.

Hearsay Rule

The general rule is that hearsay testimony is not admissible at trial. Section 802 of the Federal Rules of Evidence provides: "Hearsay is not admissible except as provided by these rules or by other rules prescribed by the Supreme Court pursuant to statutory authority or by Act of Congress." Hearsay is evidence of an out-of-court statement made by someone other than the witness that is offered for the truth of the statement. The out-of-court statement may be verbal, or it may consist of written material. Hearsay is not admissible if the person who made the statement is not present and available for cross-examination. It is said that the hearsay lacks reliability because the truthfulness of it cannot be tested by the rigors of cross-examination.

Section 801 of the Federal Rules of Evidence provides the following definitions related to the hearsay rule:

Definitions

The following definitions apply under this article:

(a) Statement.
A "statement" is (1) an oral or written assertion or (2) nonverbal conduct of a person, if it is intended by the person as an assertion.

(b) Declarant.
A "declarant" is a person who makes a statement.

(c) Hearsay.
"Hearsay" is a statement, other than one made by the declarant while testifying at the trial or hearing, offered in evidence to prove the truth of the matter asserted.

(d) Statements which are not hearsay.
A statement is not hearsay if—

(1) Prior statement by witness. The declarant testifies at the trial or hearing and is subject to cross-examination concerning the statement, and the statement is (A) inconsistent with the declarant's testimony, and was given under oath subject to the penalty of perjury at a trial, hearing, or other proceeding, or in a deposition, or (B) consistent with the declarant's testimony and is offered to rebut an express or implied charge against the declarant of recent fabrication or improper influence or motive, or (C) one of identification of a person made after perceiving the person; or

(2) Admission by party-opponent. The statement is offered against a party and is
(A) the party's own statement, in either an individual or a representative capacity or
(B) a statement of which the party has manifested an adoption or belief in its truth, or
(C) a statement by a person authorized by the party to make a statement concerning the subject, or
(D) a statement by the party's agent or servant concerning a matter within the scope of the agency or employment, made during the existence of the relationship, or
(E) a statement by a coconspirator of a party during the course and in furtherance of the conspiracy.

The contents of the statement shall be considered but are not alone sufficient to establish the declarant's authority under subdivision (C), the agency or employment relationship and scope thereof under subdivision (D), or the existence of the conspiracy and the participation therein of the declarant and the party against whom the statement is offered under subdivision (E).

Exceptions to the Rule

There are, however, numerous exceptions to the hearsay rule even though the declarant (person who made the out-of-court statement) is available to testify. Section 803 of the Federal Rules of Evidence provides the following listing of exceptions:

Hearsay Exceptions; Availability of Declarant Immaterial

The following are not excluded by the hearsay rule, even though the declarant is available as a witness:

(1) **Present sense impression.** A statement describing or explaining an event or condition made while the declarant was perceiving the event or condition, or immediately thereafter.

(2) **Excited utterance.** A statement relating to a startling event or condition made while the declarant was under the stress of excitement caused by the event or condition.

(3) **Then existing mental, emotional, or physical condition.** A statement of the declarant's then existing state of mind, emotion, sensation, or physical condition (such as intent, plan, motive, design, mental feeling, pain, and bodily health), but not including a statement of memory or belief to prove the fact remembered or believed unless it relates to the execution, revocation, identification, or terms of declarant's will.

(4) **Statements for purposes of medical diagnosis or treatment.** Statements made for purposes of medical diagnosis or treatment and describing medical history, or past or present symptoms, pain, or sensations, or the inception or general character of the cause or external source thereof insofar as reasonably pertinent to diagnosis or treatment.

(5) **Recorded recollection.** A memorandum or record concerning a matter about which a witness once had knowledge but now has insufficient recollection to enable the witness to testify fully and accurately, shown to have been made or adopted by the witness when the matter was fresh in the witness' memory and to reflect that knowledge correctly. If admitted, the memorandum or record may be read into evidence but may not itself be received as an exhibit unless offered by an adverse party.

(6) **Records of regularly conducted activity.** A memorandum, report, record, or data compilation, in any form, of acts, events, conditions, opinions, or diagnoses, made at or near the time by, or from information transmitted by, a person with knowledge, if kept in the course of a regularly conducted business activity, and if it was the regular practice of that business activity to make the memorandum, report, record or data compilation, all as shown by the testimony of the custodian or other qualified witness, or by certification that complies with Rule 902(11), Rule 902(12), or a statute permitting certification, unless the source of information or the method or circumstances of preparation indicate lack of trustworthiness. The term "business" as used in this paragraph includes business, institution, association, profession, occupation, and calling of every kind, whether or not conducted for profit.

(7) **Absence of entry in records kept in accordance with the provisions of paragraph (6).** Evidence that a matter is not included in the memoranda reports, records, or data compilations, in any form, kept in accordance with the provisions of paragraph (6), to prove the nonoccurrence or nonexistence of the matter, if the matter was of a kind of which a memorandum, report, record, or data compilation was regularly made and preserved, unless the sources of information or other circumstances indicate lack of trustworthiness.

(8) **Public records and reports.** Records, reports, statements, or data compilations, in any form, of public offices or agencies, setting forth (A) the activities of the office or agency, or (B) matters observed pursuant to duty imposed by law as to which matters there was a duty to report, excluding, however, in criminal cases matters observed by police officers and other law enforcement personnel, or (C) in civil actions and proceedings and against the Government in criminal cases, factual findings resulting from an investigation made pursuant to authority granted by law, unless the sources of information or other circumstances indicate lack of trustworthiness.

(9) **Records of vital statistics.** Records or data compilations, in any form, of births, fetal deaths, deaths, or marriages, if the report thereof was made to a public office pursuant to requirements of law.

(10) **Absence of public record or entry.** To prove the absence of a record, report, statement, or data compilation, in any form, or the nonoccurrence or nonexistence of a matter of which a record, report, statement, or data compilation, in any form, was regularly made and preserved by a public office or agency, evidence in the form of a certification in accordance with rule 902, or testimony, that diligent search failed to disclose the record, report, statement, or data compilation, or entry.

(11) **Records of religious organizations.** Statements of births, marriages, divorces, deaths, legitimacy, ancestry, relationship by blood or marriage, or other similar facts of personal or family history, contained in a regularly kept record of a religious organization.

(12) **Marriage, baptismal, and similar certificates.** Statements of fact contained in a certificate that the maker performed a marriage or other ceremony or administered a sacrament, made by a clergyman, public official, or other person authorized by the rules or practices of a religious organization or by law to perform the act certified, and purporting to have been issued at the time of the act or within a reasonable time thereafter.

(13) **Family records.** Statements of fact concerning personal or family history contained in family Bibles, genealogies, charts, engravings on rings, inscriptions on family portraits, engravings on urns, crypts, or tombstones, or the like.

(14) **Records of documents affecting an interest in property.** The record of a document purporting to establish or affect an interest in property, as proof of the content of the original recorded document and its execution and delivery by each person by whom it purports to have been executed, if the record is a record of a public office and an applicable statute authorizes the recording of documents of that kind in that office.

(15) **Statements in documents affecting an interest in property.** A statement contained in a document purporting to establish or affect an interest in property if the matter stated was relevant to the purpose of the document, unless dealings with the property since the document was made have been inconsistent with the truth of the statement or the purport of the document.

(16) **Statements in ancient documents.** Statements in a document in existence twenty years or more the authenticity of which is established.

(17) **Market reports, commercial publications.** Market quotations, tabulations, lists, directories, or other published compilations, generally used and relied upon by the public or by persons in particular occupations.

(18) **Learned treatises.** To the extent called to the attention of an expert witness upon cross-examination or relied upon by the expert witness in direct examination, statements contained in published treatises, periodicals, or pamphlets on a subject of history, medicine, or other science or art, established as a reliable authority by the testimony or admission of the witness or by other expert testimony or by judicial notice. If admitted, the statements may be read into evidence but may not be received as exhibits.

(19) **Reputation concerning personal or family history.** Reputation among members of a person's family by blood, adoption, or marriage, or among a person's associates, or in the community, concerning a person's birth, adoption, marriage, divorce, death, legitimacy, relationship by blood, adoption, or marriage, ancestry, or other similar fact of personal or family history.

(20) **Reputation concerning boundaries or general history.** Reputation in a community, arising before the controversy, as to boundaries of or customs affecting lands in the community, and reputation as to events of general history important to the community or State or nation in which located.

(21) **Reputation as to character.** Reputation of a person's character among associates or in the community.

(22) **Judgment of previous conviction.** Evidence of a final judgment, entered after a trial or upon a plea of guilty (but not upon a plea of *nolo contendere*), adjudging a person guilty of a crime punishable by death or imprisonment in excess of one year, to prove any fact essential to sustain the judgment, but not including, when offered by the Government in a criminal prosecution for purposes other than impeachment, judgments against persons other than the accused. The pendency of an appeal may be shown but does not affect admissibility.

(23) **Judgment as to personal, family or general history, or boundaries.** Judgments as proof of matters of personal, family or general history, or boundaries, essential to the judgment, if the same would be provable by evidence of reputation.

Business Records Exception   One of the most frequently applied of the listed exceptions is paragraph (6), the business records exception. This exception allows the admission of various records if (1) the record was made at or about the time of the event it records, (2) it is the regular practice of that business to maintain such a record, and (3) the record was kept in the regular course of that business. Perhaps the most common example of a business record is a police accident report. The accident report is made "at or about" the time of the accident by a person who has the duty to make the report, it is the duty of the police department to maintain the reports, and the officer will testify that he prepared and filed the report in the regular course of police business. That report usually contains out-of-court statements, for example, statements by witnesses and drivers of the vehicles about the accident. Many business records are now maintained in electronic format. They will qualify as business records in the same manner as paper records.

Best Evidence Rule

The general rule is that when offering a document or other object as evidence, the original of that item must be submitted. Rule 1001 (3) of the Federal Rules of Evidence defines an original as follows:

> (3) Original. An "original" of a writing or recording is the writing or recording itself or any counterpart intended to have the same effect by a person executing or issuing it. An "original" of a photograph includes the negative or any print therefrom. If data are stored in a computer or similar device, any printout or other output readable by sight, shown to reflect the data accurately, is an "original."

Note in particular that a computer printout of data is considered to be an original of that information.

Rule 1002 of the Federal Rules of Evidence states the principle as follows:

> To prove the content of a writing, recording, or photograph, the original writing, recording, or photograph is required, except as otherwise provided in these rules or by Act of Congress.

Rule 1003 of the Federal Rules of Evidence provides that a duplicate may be submitted if no issue is raised concerning its authenticity, unless it would be unfair to substitute the copy for the original. Rule 1004 further provides:

Admissibility of Other Evidence of Contents

The original is not required, and other evidence of the contents of a writing, recording, or photograph is admissible if—

(1) Originals lost or destroyed. All originals are lost or have been destroyed, unless the proponent lost or destroyed them in bad faith; or

(2) Original not obtainable. No original can be obtained by any available judicial process or procedure; or

(3) Original in possession of opponent. At a time when an original was under the control of the party against whom offered, that party was put on notice, by the pleadings or otherwise, that the contents would be a subject of proof at the hearing, and that party does not produce the original at the hearing; or

(4) Collateral matters. The writing, recording, or photograph is not closely related to a controlling issue.

Finally, the Federal Rules of Evidence also permit the submission of summaries of data that are created by computer. Rule 1006 provides:

Summaries

The contents of voluminous writings, recordings, or photographs which cannot conveniently be examined in court may be presented in the form of a chart, summary, or calculation. The originals, or duplicates, shall be made available for examination or copying, or both, by other parties at reasonable time and place. The court may order that they be produced in court.

Key Words and Phrases

Admissible	Expert
Authenticity	*Frye* plus
Best evidence rule	*Frye* test
Business records exception	Hearsay
Chain of custody	Opinion evidence
Circumstantial evidence	Real evidence
Daubert rule	Relevant
Direct evidence	Summaries
Documentary evidence	Testimonial evidence

Review Problems

1. Compare the differing analyses concerning chain of custody evidence in *United States v. Brown* and *United States v. Wyss*. What factors account for the different results in those cases?

2. You have been certified as a forensic computer examiner by the International Association of Computer Investigative Specialists, but you have conducted only a few examinations and have never testified in court regarding your examinations. Can you qualify as a forensic expert?

3. Describe the difference between the *Frye* test, the *Frye* plus test, and the *Daubert* test.

4. Provide an example of evidence on a computer that would be considered hearsay. Are there any exceptions that would render that evidence admissible?

Weblinks

www.answers.com/topic/evidence
   This site contains an excellent summary discussion from various sources concerning basic principles of evidence.

www.law.cornell.edu/rules/fre
   This site maintained at Cornell University Law School contains the text of the Federal Rules of Evidence and the notes of the advisory committee that explain the rule.

www.ncsconline.org/WC/FAQs/StoEviFAQ.htm
   This website of the National Center for State Courts has useful information on the collection and preservation of evidence.

www.fbi.gov/hq/lab/fsc/backissu/oct2000/computer.htm
   This page contains an excellent article (although published in October 2000) on recovering and examining computer forensic evidence.

International Issues Involving the Investigation and Prosecution of Cybercrime

14

Introduction

Because cybercrimes can be committed from any state or country and victimize individuals and businesses in any other state or country, the prosecution of cybercrimes presents unique issues. This chapter focuses on two of those issues: jurisdiction and the extraterritorial application of a jurisdiction's laws.

Jurisdiction

The term *jurisdiction* refers to the power or authority of the court. The term is used in many ways, but typically is classified as follows:

- Subject matter: The authority to hear a particular type of case. For example, the U.S. Supreme Court hears only cases and controversies between litigants; it lacks subject matter jurisdiction to provide advisory opinions. Subject matter jurisdiction may also be geographic in nature. For example, the New York courts lack subject matter jurisdiction to resolve a contractual dispute between two residents of Hawaii that has no connection with New York.
- *In personam*: The authority to resolve a dispute involving the defendant, also known as personal jurisdiction. For example, the general rule is that a court cannot proceed against someone for the commission of a crime unless the court has acquired custody and control over that person.
- *In rem*: The authority to resolve a dispute involving property. In this instance, the court must have control over the thing.

The most important of these concepts in terms of international cooperation are subject matter jurisdiction and personal jurisdiction. The following case illustrates application of concepts involving subject matter jurisdiction:

United States v. Andrews

383 F.3D 374

U.S. COURT OF APPEALS, SIXTH CIRCUIT

MARTHA CRAIG DAUGHTREY, Circuit Judge.

The defendant, Lonny Andrews, was convicted on 27 counts of a 28-count indictment that charged him with the production, receipt, and possession of child pornography, in violation of 18 U.S.C. §§2251(b), 2252(a)(2), and 2252(a)(4)(B) respectively. On appeal, he challenges only his convictions on the first two counts, contending that §2251(b) is unconstitutional as applied to him because the government failed to establish a sufficient nexus between his alleged activities and interstate or foreign commerce, thereby depriving the district court of jurisdiction to try the case.

FACTUAL AND PROCEDURAL BACKGROUND

The record in this case establishes that defendant Andrews lived in a four-bedroom trailer in Nicholasville, Kentucky, with his wife, his seven-year-old step-daughter, and the couple's two-year-old daughter. In May 2002, his two nieces, aged 12 and 16, came to Andrews's home from Alabama to spend the summer. Apparently, the 16-year-old left the house with the defendant's wife at various times, leaving Andrews in the house with the other children. On one occasion, he took advantage of their absence to show the seven-year-old and the 12-year-old a "video of naked people" engaged in sexual relations. After the two children watched the video, Andrews told them that he wanted them to do similar things with him and forced his step-daughter to perform oral sex on him. At another time, Andrews showed the girls a picture of a "naked teenager" from his computer's "picture gallery," telling them that he had received the picture from a friend.

Andrews had purchased a small "pen camera" at Wal-Mart that he could use to produce photographs on his computer screen. Andrews taught his niece and step-daughter how to use the pen camera and, on two occasions, he told them to take pictures of each other's "privates" while they were naked. The first time, Andrews watched his niece take pictures of his step-daughter. After the girls took the pictures of each other, Andrews loaded the pictures into his computer's "picture gallery." These pictures could also be uploaded onto the Internet, although there was no evidence presented at trial that Andrews actually did so. Andrews frightened the two children into silence by threatening that "if [they] ever told on him that he—that he would go to jail and it would be all [their] fault and that he would beat [them]."

Nevertheless, the younger of the two nieces apparently confided in her older sister, who then told Andrews's wife, Stacy, that the 12-year-old had something to tell her. From her ensuing conversation with the 12-year-old, Stacy Andrews learned that her husband was making the two children take sexually explicit photos of each other with the pen camera. She contacted the local sheriff's office and filed a petition for an emergency protective order on behalf of the children. The order was granted and, as a result of its directive, Lonny Andrews was removed from the residence.

After the defendant's departure, the sheriff searched the trailer with Stacy's consent and seized various items, including the defendant's computer, some compact disks, hard disk drives, and the pen camera—all of which had been manufactured or acquired from out-of-state or abroad. During the search, a detective examined Andrews's computer there on the premises, opened some electronic files, and found "visual depictions," each of which was described in the indictment as involving "a minor female engaged in the lascivious exhibition of her genitals or pubic area." The hard drive on Andrews's computer also contained 107 photographs of his niece and his step-daughter, mostly of the girls' genitals and buttocks, that Andrews had directed the girls to take of each other using his pen camera.

The detective found the pen camera attached to Andrews's computer. Nearby, he also found a compact disk containing over 200 pornographic images of unidentified prepubescent girls, defined as under the age of 12. Research verified that these images were available on the Internet and could be downloaded onto a disk using the disk "burner" found among the defendant's computer equipment. They appeared to have been downloaded from the Internet in December 1999 and January 2000. Once, in the fall of 2000, almost two years before the events at issue here took place, Stacy Andrews was using the computer and happened upon an image of a young, nude child. According to her testimony at trial, she told her husband to remove the image from the computer or she would "throw the computer out in the front yard."

Lonny Andrews testified at trial, denying that he had enticed his niece or his stepdaughter to use his pen camera to take the pornographic photos. He also denied uploading their pictures onto the computer or the Internet, or downloading the pornographic images of prepubescent girls onto the compact disk. Because the file on the compact disk was labeled "Jimmy," he argued that a friend of his named Jim must have downloaded the images while he was staying at the Andrews house. The jury nevertheless convicted the defendant on all 27 counts of the indictment, presumably finding that his testimony was not credible, and the district court imposed consecutive sentences totaling 405 years, pursuant to sentencing guidelines mandated by Congress as part of the Sex Crimes Against Children Prevention Act, and enhanced by a finding that Andrews had obstructed justice by testifying falsely at trial.

DISCUSSION

At the time of Andrews's trial, § 2251(b) provided as follows:

> Any parent, legal guardian, or person having custody or control of a minor who knowingly permits such minor to engage in, or to assist any other person to engage in, sexually explicit conduct for the purpose of producing any visual depiction of such conduct shall be punished as provided under subsection (d) of this section, if such parent, legal guardian, or person knows or has reason to know that such visual depiction will be transported in interstate or foreign commerce or mailed, **if that visual depiction was produced using materials that have been mailed, shipped, or transported in interstate or foreign commerce by any means, including by computer,** or if such visual depiction has actually been transported in interstate or foreign commerce or mailed (emphasis added).

Federal jurisdiction over the offenses charged in counts one and two was based on the fact that Andrews purchased his computer from New Jersey and that the pen camera was made in China. Andrews does not argue that § 2251(b) is facially unconstitutional, instead contending that it is unconstitutional under the Commerce Clause as applied to him because his activities did not substantially relate to interstate commerce.

Andrews relies almost exclusively on our opinion in *United States v. Corp*, 236 F.3d 325 (6th Cir. 2001), to support his argument that § 2251(b) is unconstitutional as applied to the facts of this case. Corp was a 23-year-old defendant who was prosecuted under 18 U.S.C. §2252(a)(4)(B) for possessing child pornography, consisting of photographs of his 17-year-old girlfriend and his 26-year-old wife engaged in consensual sexual activity. Section 2252(a)(4)(B) provides that an offender will be punished if he or she

... knowingly possesses 1 or more books, magazines, periodicals, films, video tapes, or other matter which contain any visual depiction that has been mailed, or has been shipped or transported in interstate or foreign commerce, or which was produced using materials which have been mailed or so shipped or transported, by any means including by computer, if—

(i) the producing of such visual depiction involves the use of a minor engaging in sexually explicit conduct; and

(ii) such visual depiction is of such conduct[.]

Federal jurisdiction in *Corp* was alleged to arise from the fact that the photo-graphic paper on which the pornography was produced had been manufactured out-of-state, specifically in Germany. Corp argued that the statute was unconstitutional on its face and as applied in his case because it exceeded Congress's Commerce Clause powers. In reviewing this claim, the *Corp* court applied the framework developed by the Supreme Court in *United States v. Lopez*, 514 U.S. 549 (1995) (striking down the Gun-Free School Zones Act because Congress exceeded its power under the Commerce Clause), and in *United States v. Morrison*, 529 U.S. 598 (2000) (striking down the civil remedy provision of the Violence Against Women Act as unconstitutional under the Commerce Clause), to hold that §2252(a)(4)(B) was facially constitutional. On the other hand, the court also held that because the defendant's activity was not substantially related to interstate commerce, the statute was unconstitutional as applied to the facts in his case. But in doing so, the court emphasized that those facts were unique and that Corp's conduct was not the type of activity that Congress had intended to prohibit:

Under the undisputed circumstances here, Corp was not involved, nor intended to be involved, in the distribution or sharing with others of the pictures in question. Sauntman [the seventeen-year-old] was not an "exploited child" nor a victim in any real and practical sense in this case. In the other cases that have addressed this issue, the courts were faced with the much more threatening situation where an adult was taking advantage of a much younger child or using the imagery for abusive or semi-commercial purposes....

Corp was not alleged to be a pedophile nor was he alleged to have been illegally sexually involved with minors other than Sauntman, who was merely months away from reaching majority. Clearly, Corp was not the typical offender feared by Congress that would become addicted to pornography and perpetuate the industry via interstate connections. Under these circumstances, the government has failed to make a showing that Corp's sort of activity would substantially affect interstate commerce.

Moreover, the *Corp* opinion contains a suggestion that in future cases, courts should undertake the following examination in order to ensure that the jurisdictional reach of the statute is properly circumscribed:

Was the activity in this case related to explicit and graphic pictures of children engaged in sexual activity, particularly children about fourteen years of age or under, for commercial or exploitive purposes? Were there multiple children so pictured? Were the children otherwise sexually abused? Was there a record that defendant repeatedly engaged in such conduct or other sexually abusive conduct with children? Did defendant move from place to place, or state to state, and repeatedly engage in production of such pictures of children?

These questions are relevant to a determination on a case-by-case basis about whether the activity involved in a certain case had a substantial effect on commerce.

Although not all the *Corp* questions are pertinent here, an inquiry along the lines it suggests produces a stark distinction between the facts in *Corp* and the facts in this case. Andrews was clearly involved in exactly the type of child-exploitive and abusive behavior that Congress sought to prohibit in § 2251(b), using computer equipment that had been shipped in interstate commerce. Andrews first forced two children aged 12 and under to watch sexually explicit photographs that presumably had been transmitted over interstate lines. He then compelled them to engage in and to photograph similar sexually explicit behavior, undoubtedly for the purpose of transmitting those photographs in the same manner. The children were vulnerable not only because of their age but also because they were under his care and control at the time, and their cooperation was clearly the result of coercion and outright threats to their safety. In addition, Andrews was in possession of several hundred pornographic photographs depicting unidentified children who appeared to be under the age of 12. As early as two years before his arrest on these charges, his wife had seen the pornographic image of a child on his computer.

Given the scope of the evidence in the record, we have no doubt that the government established a sufficient nexus between the activity described in the first two counts of the indictment and interstate commerce to establish jurisdiction in this case. We therefore find no merit to the defendant's argument that § 2251(b) was unconstitutional as applied to that activity.

CONCLUSION

For the reasons set out above, we AFFIRM the judgment of the district court in all respects.

Extraterritorial Application of Criminal Laws

Another issue involving subject matter jurisdiction is the question whether the criminal laws of the United States (or of a particular state) can be applied to conduct that occurs in whole or in part outside the country (or the state). What if someone physically present in Russia hacks into a website maintained in the United States? Can the federal computer crime law be applied to that conduct? The following case considers that issue:

United States v. Ivanov

175 F.SUPP.2D 367 (2001)

U.S. DISTRICT CT., DIST. OF CONNECTICUT

OPINION by Thompson, Dist. Judge:

Defendant Aleksey Vladimirovich Ivanov ("Ivanov") has been indicted, in a superseding indictment, on charges of conspiracy, computer fraud and related activity, extortion and possession of unauthorized access devices. Ivanov has moved to dismiss the indictment on the grounds that the court lacks subject matter jurisdiction. Ivanov argues that because it is alleged that he was physically located in Russia when the offenses were committed, he can not be charged with violations of United States law. For the reasons set forth below, the defendant's motion is being denied.

I. Background

Online Information Bureau, Inc. ("OIB"), the alleged victim in this case, is a Connecticut corporation based in Vernon, Connecticut. It is an "e-commerce" business which assists retail and Internet merchants by, among other things, hosting their websites and processing their credit card data and other financial transactions. In this capacity, OIB acts as a financial transaction "clearinghouse," by aggregating and assisting in the debiting or crediting of funds against each account for thousands of retail and Internet purchasers and vendors. In doing so, OIB collects and maintains customer credit card information, merchant account numbers, and related financial data from credit card companies and other financial institutions.

The government alleges that Ivanov "hacked" into OIB's computer system and obtained the key passwords to control OIB's entire network. The government contends that in late January and early February 2000, OIB received from Ivanov a series of unsolicited e-mails indicating that the defendant had obtained the "root" passwords for certain computer systems operated by OIB. A "root" password grants its user access to and control over an entire computer system, including the ability to manipulate, extract, and delete any and all data. Such passwords are generally reserved for use by the system administrator only.

The government claims that Ivanov then threatened OIB with the destruction of its computer systems (including its merchant account database) and demanded approximately $10,000 for his assistance in making those systems secure. It claims, for example, that on February 3, 2000, after his initial solicitations had been rebuffed, Ivanov sent the following e-mail to an employee of OIB:

> [name redacted], now imagine please Somebody hack you network (and not notify you about this), he download Atomic software with more than 300 merchants, transfer money, and after this did 'rm-rf/' and after this you company be ruined. I don't want this, and because this I notify you about possible hack in you network, if you want you can hire me and im allways be check security in you network. What you think about this?

The government contends that Ivanov's extortionate communications originated from an e-mail account at Lightrealm.com, an Internet Service Provider based in Kirkland, Washington. It contends that while he was in Russia, Ivanov gained access to the Lightrealm computer network and that he used that system to communicate with OIB, also while he was in Russia. Thus, each e-mail sent by Ivanov was allegedly transmitted from a Lightrealm.com computer in Kirkland, Washington through the Internet to an OIB computer in Vernon, Connecticut, where the e-mail was opened by an OIB employee.

The parties agree that the defendant was physically located in Russia (or one of the other former Soviet Bloc countries) when, it is alleged, he committed the offenses set forth in the superseding indictment.

The superseding indictment comprises eight counts. Count One charges that beginning in or about December 1999, or earlier, the defendant and others conspired to commit the substantive offenses charged in Counts Two through Eight of the indictment, in violation of 18 U.S.C. § 371. Count Two charges that the defendant, knowingly and with intent to defraud, accessed protected computers owned by OIB and by means of this conduct furthered a fraud and obtained something of value, in violation of 18 U.S.C. §§ 2, 1030(a)(4) and 1030(c)(3)(A). Count Three charges that the defendant intentionally accessed protected computers owned by OIB and thereby obtained information, which conduct involved interstate and foreign communications and was engaged in for purposes of financial gain and in furtherance of a criminal act, in violation of 18 U.S.C. §§ 2, 1030(a)(2)(C) and 1030(c)(2)(B). Counts Four and Five do not pertain to this defendant.

Count Six charges that the defendant transmitted in interstate and foreign commerce communications containing a threat to cause damage to protected computers owned by OIB, in violation of 18 U.S.C. §§ 1030(a)(7) and 1030(c)(3)(A). Count Seven charges that the defendant obstructed, delayed and affected commerce, and attempted to obstruct, delay and affect commerce, by means of extortion by attempting to obtain property from OIB with OIB's consent, inducing such consent by means of threats to damage OIB and its business unless OIB paid the defendant money and hired the defendant as a security consultant, in violation of 18 U.S.C. § 1951(a). Count Eight charges that the defendant, knowingly and with intent to defraud, possessed unauthorized access devices, which conduct affected interstate and foreign commerce, in violation of 18 U.S.C. §§ 1029(a)(3).

II. Discussion

The defendant and the government agree that when Ivanov allegedly engaged in the conduct charged in the superseding indictment, he was physically present in Russia and using a computer there at all relevant times. Ivanov contends that for this reason, charging him under the Hobbs Act, 18 U.S.C. § 1951, under the Computer Fraud and Abuse Act, 18 U.S.C. § 1030, and under the access device statute, 18 U.S.C. § 1029, would in each case require extraterritorial application of that law and such application is impermissible. The court concludes that it has jurisdiction, first, because the intended and actual detrimental effects of Ivanov's actions in Russia occurred within the United States, and second, because each of the statutes under which Ivanov was charged with a substantive offense was intended by Congress to apply extraterritorially.

A. The Intended and Actual Detrimental Effects of the Charged Offenses Occurred Within the United States

As noted by the court in *United States v. Muench*, 694 F.2d 28 (2d Cir. 1982), "the intent to cause effects within the United States … makes it reasonable to apply to persons outside United States territory a statute which is not expressly extraterritorial in scope." "It has long been a commonplace of criminal liability that a person may be charged in the place where the evil results, though he is beyond the jurisdiction when he starts the train of events of which that evil is the fruit." *United States v. Steinberg*, 62 F.2d 77, 78 (2d Cir. 1932). "The Government may punish a defendant in the same manner as if [he] were present in the jurisdiction when the detrimental effects occurred." *Marc Rich & Co., A.G. v. United States*, 707 F.2d 663, 666 (2d Cir. 1983).

The Supreme Court has quoted with approval the following language from *Moore's International Law Digest*:

The principle that a man, who outside of a country willfully puts in motion a force to take effect in it, is answerable at the place where the evil is done, is recognized in the criminal jurisprudence of all countries. And the methods which modern invention has furnished for the performance of criminal acts in that manner has made this principle one of constantly growing importance and of increasing frequency of application.

Ford v. United States, 273 U.S. 593, 623, 71 L. Ed. 793, 47 S. Ct. 531 (1927).

Moreover, the court noted in *Rich* that:

It is certain that the courts of many countries, even of countries which have given their criminal legislation a strictly territorial character, interpret criminal law in the sense that offences, the authors of which at the moment of commission are in the territory of another State, are nevertheless to be regarded as having been committed in the national territory, if one of the constituent elements of the offence, and more especially its effects, have taken place there.

Rich, 707 F.2d at 666.

Here, all of the intended and actual detrimental effects of the substantive offenses Ivanov is charged with in the indictment occurred within the United States. In Counts Two and Three, the defendant is charged with accessing OIB's computers. Those computers were located in Vernon, Connecticut. The fact that the computers were accessed by means of a complex process initiated and controlled from a remote location does not alter the fact that the accessing of the computers, i.e. part of the detrimental effect prohibited by the statute, occurred at the place where the computers were physically located, namely OIB's place of business in Vernon, Connecticut.

Count Two charges further that Ivanov obtained something of value when he accessed OIB's computers, that "something of value" being the data obtained from OIB's computers. In order for Ivanov to violate § 1030(a)(4), it was necessary that he do more than merely access OIB's computers and view the data. See *United States v. Czubinski*, 106 F.3d 1069, 1078 (6th Cir. 1997) ("Merely viewing information cannot be deemed the same as obtaining something of value for purposes of this statute. ... This section should apply to those who steal information through unauthorized access...."). The indictment charges that Ivanov did more than merely gain unauthorized access and view the data. Ivanov allegedly obtained root access to the OIB computers located in Vernon, Connecticut. Once Ivanov had root access to the computers, he was able to control the data, e.g., credit card numbers and merchant account numbers, stored in the OIB computers; Ivanov could copy, sell, transfer, alter, or destroy that data. That data is intangible property of OIB.

At the point Ivanov gained root access to OIB's computers, he had complete control over that data, and consequently, had possession of it. That data was in OIB's computers. Since Ivanov possessed that data while it was in OIB's computers in Vernon, Connecticut, the court concludes that he obtained it, for purposes of § 1030(a)(4), in Vernon, Connecticut. The fact that Ivanov is charged with obtaining OIB's valuable data by means of a complex process initiated and controlled from a remote location, and that he subsequently moved that data to a computer located in Russia, does not alter the fact that at the point when Ivanov first possessed that data, it was on OIB's computers in Vernon, Connecticut.

Count Three charges further that when he accessed OIB's computers, Ivanov obtained information from protected computers. The analysis as to the location at which Ivanov obtained the information referenced in this count is the same as the analysis as to the location at which he obtained the "something of value" referenced in Count Two. Thus, as to both Counts Two and Three, it is charged that the balance of the detrimental effect prohibited by the pertinent statute, i.e., Ivanov's obtaining something of value or obtaining information, also occurred within the United States.

Count Six charges that Ivanov transmitted a threat to cause damage to protected computers. The detrimental effect prohibited by § 1030(a)(7), namely the receipt by an individual or entity of a threat to cause damage to a protected computer, occurred in Vernon, Connecticut because that is where OIB was located, where it received the threat, and where the protected computers were located. The analysis is the same as to Count Seven, the charge under the Hobbs Act.

Count Eight charges that Ivanov knowingly and with intent to defraud possessed over ten thousand unauthorized access devices, i.e., credit card numbers and merchant account numbers. For the reasons discussed above, although it is charged that Ivanov later transferred this intangible property to Russia, he first possessed it while it was on OIB's computers in Vernon, Connecticut. Had he not possessed it here, he would not have been able to transfer it to his computer in Russia. Thus, the detrimental effect prohibited by the statute occurred within the United States.

Finally, Count One charges that Ivanov and others conspired to commit each of the substantive offenses charged in the indictment. The Second Circuit has stated that "the jurisdictional element should be viewed for purposes of the conspiracy count exactly as we view it for purposes of the substantive offense…." *United States v. Blackmon*, 839 F.2d 900, 910 (2d Cir. 1988) (internal citations and quotation marks omitted). Here, Ivanov is charged with planning to commit substantive offenses in violation of federal statutes, and it is charged that at least one overt act was committed in furtherance of the conspiracy. As discussed above, the court has jurisdiction over the underlying substantive charges. Therefore, the court has jurisdiction over the conspiracy charge, at a minimum, to the extent it relates to Counts Two, Three, Six, Seven or Eight.

Accordingly, the court concludes that it has subject matter jurisdiction over each of the charges against Ivanov, whether or not the statutes under which the substantive offenses are charged are intended by Congress to apply extraterritorially, because the intended and actual detrimental effects of the substantive offenses Ivanov is charged with in the indictment occurred within the United States.

B. Intended Extraterritorial Application

The defendant's motion should also be denied because, as to each of the statutes under which the defendant has been indicted for a substantive offense, there is clear evidence that the statute was intended by Congress to apply extraterritorially. This fact is evidenced by both the plain language and the legislative history of each of these statutes.

[T]his court concludes that the Hobbs Act encompasses not only all extortionate interference with interstate commerce by means of conduct occurring within the United States, but also all such conduct which, although it occurs outside the United States, affects commerce within the borders of the United States. Therefore, it is immaterial whether Ivanov's alleged conduct can be said to have taken place entirely outside the United States, because that conduct clearly constituted "interference with interstate commerce by extortion," in violation of the Hobbs Act. Consequently, the court has jurisdiction over this charge against him.

2. 18 U.S.C. § 1030: The Computer Fraud and Abuse Act

The Computer Fraud and Abuse Act ("CFAA") was amended in 1996 by Pub. L. No. 104-294, 110 Stat. 3491, 3508. The 1996 amendments made several changes that are relevant to the issue of extraterritoriality, including a change in the definition of "protected computer" so that it included any computer "which is used in interstate or foreign commerce or communication." 18 U.S.C. § 1030 (e)(2)(B). The 1996 amendments also added subsections (a)(2)(C) and (a)(7), which explicitly address "interstate or foreign commerce," and subsection (e)(9), which added to the definition of "government entity" the clause "any foreign country, and any state, province, municipality or other political subdivision of a foreign country."

The plain language of the statute, as amended, is clear. Congress intended the CFAA to apply to computers used "in interstate or foreign commerce or communication." The defendant argues that this language is ambiguous. The court disagrees. * * * In order for the word "foreign" to have meaning, and not be superfluous, it must mean something other than "interstate." In other words, "foreign" in this context must mean international. Thus, Congress has clearly manifested its intent to apply § 1030 to computers used either in interstate or in foreign commerce.

The legislative history of the CFAA supports this reading of the plain language of the statute. The Senate Judiciary Committee issued a report explaining its reasons for adopting the 1996 amendments. S. Rep. No. 357, 104th Congr., 2d Sess. (1996). In that report, the Committee specifically noted its concern that the statute as it existed prior to the 1996 amendments did not cover "computers used in foreign communications or commerce, despite the fact that hackers are often foreign-based." The Committee cited two specific cases in which foreign-based hackers had infiltrated computer systems in the United States, as examples of the kind of situation the amendments were intended to address:

> For example, the 1994 intrusion into the Rome Laboratory at Griffiss Air Force Base in New York, was perpetrated by a 16-year-old hacker in the United Kingdom. More recently, in March 1996, the Justice Department tracked down a young Argentinean man who had broken into Harvard University's computers from Buenos Aires and used those computers as a staging ground to hack into many other computer sites, including the Defense Department and NASA.

Congress has the power to apply its statutes extraterritorially, and in the case of 18 U.S.C. § 1030, it has clearly manifested its intention to do so.

3. 18 U.S.C. § 1029: The Access Device Statute

Section 1029 of Title 18 of the United States Code provides for the imposition of criminal sanctions on any person who uses, possesses or traffics in a counterfeit access device "if the offense affects interstate or foreign commerce." 18 U.S.C. § 1029 (2000). * * * Therefore, based on the same reasoning applied above in the discussion of § 1030, the court concludes that the plain language of § 1029 indicates a congressional intent to apply the statute extraterritorially.

4. 18 U.S.C. § 371: The Conspiracy Statute

The Second Circuit has recently noted that where the court has jurisdiction over the underlying substantive criminal counts against a defendant, the court also has jurisdiction over the conspiracy counts. A court may "infer[] the extra-territorial reach of conspiracy statutes on the basis of a finding that the underlying substantive statute reached extra-territorial offenses, even though the conspiracy charges came under separate code sections...." *United States v. Evans*, 667 F. Supp. 974, 981 (S.D.N.Y. 1987) (internal quotation marks and citations omitted). Because the court finds that each of the underlying substantive statutes in this case was intended by Congress to apply extraterritorially, it also finds that it has jurisdiction over the conspiracy charge.

The *Ivanov* decision involves the extraterritorial application of *substantive* criminal law. The following case, which involved his coconspirator, considers a number of issues relating to search and seizure, including the question of whether Fourth Amendment search and seizure law applies to the search of a computer in Russia:

United States v. Gorshkov

2001 WL 1024026

U.S. District Court, District of Washington

COUGHENOUR, J.

Following an extensive national investigation of a series of computer hacker intrusions into the computer systems of businesses in the United States emanating from Russia, Alexey Ivanov was identified as one of the intruders. Around June, 2000, the FBI set up Invita, a "sting" computer security company in Seattle. On/about November 10, 2000 Ivanov, along with his "business partner," Vasiliy Gorshkov, flew from Russia to SeaTac.

In Seattle, the two men met with undercover FBI agents at the Invita office located in Seattle. During the meeting and at the behest of the FBI, Defendant Gorshkov used an FBI IBM Thinkpad computer ("IBM") ostensibly to demonstrate his computer hacking and computer security skills and to access his computer system, "tech.net.ru," in Russia. After the meeting and demonstration, both Gorshkov and Ivanov were arrested.

Following the Defendants' arrest, without Defendant Gorshkov's knowledge or consent, the FBI searched and seized the IBM and all key strokes made by the Defendant while he used it, by means of a "sniffer" program which allowed the FBI to track and store the information. The FBI thereby obtained the Defendant's computer user name and password that he had used to access the Russian computer.

Armed with this information the FBI logged onto the subject computer(s) located in Russia. Faced with the possibility that a confederate of the defendant could destroy the files in the Russian computer, the FBI decided to download the file contents of the subject computer(s). This was done without reading same until after a search warrant was obtained.

The FBI's downloading and copying of the downloaded data onto CD disk format took until November 21. The warrant was applied for and obtained on December 1, 2000. The delay between the downloading of the data and the procurement of the warrant was due to the slow process of obtaining approval and permission from FBI headquarters and the Department of Justice.

A. The FBI Did Not Violate the Fourth Amendment By Obtaining Defendant's Password

The first issue is whether the FBI violated the Fourth Amendment by obtaining Defendant's user name and password using a "sniffer program." The Court determines that under the circumstances of this case, the FBI did not violate the Fourth Amendment.

In *Rakas v. Illinois*, 349 U.S. 128 (1978), the Court stated that "capacity to claim the protection of the Fourth Amendment depends not upon a property right in the invaded place but upon whether the person who claims a protection of the Amendment has a legitimate expectation of privacy in the invaded Place." *Rakas*, 349 U.S at 143.

The Court finds that Defendant could not have had an actual expectation of privacy in a private computer network belonging to a U.S. company. It was not his computer. When Defendant sat down at the networked computer at the Invita undercover site, he knew that the systems administrator could and likely would monitor his activities. Indeed, the undercover agents told Defendant that they wanted to watch in order to see what he was capable of doing. With the agents present in the room and frequently standing and looking over his shoulder, Defendant sat down at the networked computer and logged on to an account at a computer named "freebsd.tech net.ru." Therefore the Defendant had no expectation of privacy in his actions on the Invita computer. Even if Defendant could assert a subjective expectation of privacy, such an expectation would be unreasonable under these circumstances.

This case is similar to that of *United States v. David*, 756 F.Supp. 1385 (D. Nev 1991). In *David*, the defendant was cooperating with law enforcement and meeting with an agent in the agent's office when he accessed his "computer memo book" in the agent's presence. The agent, looking over David's shoulder, saw the password he entered. The court found that David had no reasonable expectation of privacy because of the agent's presence and monitoring.

The circumstances in the present case even more thoroughly refute the notion that the Defendant had a reasonable expectation of privacy in his activities on the Invita computer, because it was not his computer and the entire purpose for his use of it was to demonstrate his hacking acumen for Invita personnel to review. Therefore, under the circumstances of this case, the FBI did not violate the Fourth Amendment by obtaining Defendant's password.

B. The FBI Did Not Violate the Fourth Amendment By Accessing the Russian Computers and Downloading Data

The second issue is whether the FBI violated the Fourth Amendment by using the password to access the Russian computers and downloading the data. The Court finds that the Fourth Amendment was inapplicable to the accessing of the Russian computer and the downloading of the data. Moreover, the Court determines that even if the accessing of the Russian computers and the downloading of the data was a search and seizure for purposes of the Fourth Amendment, the FBI's actions were reasonable under the exigent circumstances and therefore, no constitutional violation occurred.

1. Fourth Amendment Does Not Apply

The use of the password to access the Russian computers and download the data did not constitute a Fourth Amendment violation. The Fourth Amendment does not apply to the agents' extraterritorial access to computers in Russia and their copying of data contained thereon. First, the Russian computers are not protected by the Fourth Amendment because they are property of a non-resident and located outside the territory of the United States. Under *United States v. Verdugo-Urquidez*, 494 U.S. 259 (1990), the Fourth Amendment does not apply to a search or seizure of a non-resident alien's property outside the territory of the United States. In this case, the computers accessed by the agents were located in Russia, as was the data contained on those computers that the agents copied. Until the copied data was transmitted to the United States, it was outside the territory of this country and not subject to the protections of the Fourth Amendment.

Defendant attempts to distinguish *Verdugo* by first noting that the defendant in that case was found not to have significant contacts with the United States because he involuntarily entered the country after his arrest, while in this case Defendant Gorshkov voluntarily entered the country. The Court finds, however, that a single entry into the United States that is made for a criminal purpose is hardly the sort of voluntary association with this country that should qualify Defendant as part of our national community for purposes of the Fourth Amendment. Defendant also attempts to distinguish *Verdugo* by noting that the search in *Verdugo* was effected by a joint effort made lawfully pursuant to Mexican law, with the consent and authorization of Mexican officials, while in this case the search was done by FBI fiat. Nothing in the opinion, however, indicates that the reach of the Fourth Amendment turns on this issue. Therefore, the search of the Russian computers was not protected by the Fourth Amendment.

Second, the agents' act of copying the data on the Russian computers was not a seizure under the Fourth Amendment because it did not interfere with Defendant's or anyone else's possessory interest in the data. The data remained intact and unaltered. It remained accessible to Defendant and any co-conspirators or partners with whom he had shared access. The copying of the data had absolutely no impact on his possessory rights. Therefore it was not a seizure under the Fourth Amendment. See *Arizona v. Hicks*, 480 U.S. 321, 324 (1987) (recording of serial number on suspected stolen property was not seizure because it did not "meaningfully interfere" with respondent's possessory interest in either the serial number or the equipment"); *Bills v. Aseltine*, 958 F.2d 697, 707 (6th Cir. 1992) (officer's photographic recording of visual images of scene was not seizure because it did not "meaningfully interfere" with any possessory interest).

2. Even if the Fourth Amendment Applied, the Search and Seizure Were Reasonable

Even if the Fourth Amendment were to apply to the Government's actions, the Court finds that those actions were reasonable under all of the circumstances and therefore met Fourth Amendment requirements. The Supreme Court recently stated "We have found no case in which this Court has held unlawful a temporary seizure that was supported by probable cause and was designed to prevent the loss of evidence while the police diligently obtained a warrant in a reasonable period of time." *Illinois v. McArthur*, 121 S Ct. 946, 950–51 (2001); see *Segura v. United States*, 468 U.S. 796 (1984) (holding that it was not an unreasonable search or seizure under the Fourth Amendment when officers secured the premises to preserve the status quo until a search warrant was obtained 19 hours later).

In *McArthur*, the Court held that it was "reasonable"—and thus consistent with the Fourth Amendment—for police to prevent someone from entering his trailer home until a search warrant could be obtained, based on the risk that evidence might be destroyed otherwise. In the context of pressing or urgent law enforcement needs such as exigent circumstances, the Fourth Amendment requires courts to "balance the privacy-related and law enforcement related concerns to determine if the intrusion was reasonable." *McArthur*, 121 S.Ct. at 950. Several circumstances supported the Court's conclusion in *McArthur* that the restraint met with Fourth Amendment requirements: (1) the police had probable cause to believe that the trailer home contained evidence of a crime, (2) the police had good reason to fear that if they did not restrain the defendant, he would destroy the evidence before a warrant could be obtained, (3) the police made "reasonable efforts" to reconcile law enforcement needs with the defendant's privacy needs, leaving his home and his belongings intact until the warrant was issued; and (4) the police imposed the restraint for a limited period of time.

Analogous circumstances exist in the present case. The Government's agents had probable cause to believe that the Russian computers contained evidence of crimes. The agents had good reason to fear that if they did not copy the data, Defendant's coconspirators would destroy the evidence, or make it unavailable before any assistance could be obtained from Russian authorities. The agents made "reasonable efforts" to reconcile their needs with Defendant's privacy interest by copying the data, without altering it or examining its contents until a search warrant could be obtained. Finally, the agents imposed no "restraint" on Defendant's data, and obtained a search warrant as soon as diplomatic notification was made to Russia's government. Therefore, under the law of the Fourth Amendment, because the agents were acting under exigent circumstances, the agents' actions in accessing the Russian computers and downloading the data without a warrant were fully legal and the evidence should not be suppressed.

As to Defendant's contention that the evidence should be suppressed based on the Electronic Communications Privacy Act, 18 U.S.C. §§ 2701–2711, and the Wiretap Act or "Title III," 18 U.S.C. § 2510, et seq., the Government is correct in noting that a statutory suppression remedy is not available under either of these statutes for the FBI's alleged violations.

C. Independent Source Doctrine Applies

Even if the Court were to find that the copying and downloading of the data was somehow a violation of the Fourth Amendment, the evidence at issue is not subject to suppression because it was obtained through the independent source of a valid search warrant that did not depend upon anything observed during the copying and downloading of the files. Probable cause for the warrant was based entirely upon information that was independent of the copying and downloading. As a result, the affidavit provided an independent source for the warrant.

D. The Warrant Was Not Overbroad

The Court also finds that the warrant in this case was not overbroad. The Court notes that the magnitude of the information answerable to the warrant is a reflection of the astonishingly broad scope of the alleged criminal activity of these Defendants. The warrant in this case was not subject to the flaws of the warrant in *United States v. Kow*, 58 F.3d 423 (9th Cir. 1995). The face of the warrant specified that the search was for evidence of specified crimes, and statutory citations were included both on the face of the warrant and in Attachment A. That Attachment, in addition to limiting the search to information "that constitutes evidence, fruits or instrumentalities" of the specified crimes, particularly described the types of information to be the subject of the search. Therefore, the warrant was not overbroad.

Having carefully considered all of the testimony in this matter and all of the materials submitted, for the above mentioned reasons, the Court hereby DENIES the motion.

International Enforcement and Cooperation

What happens when our laws apply to a criminal event that occurred beyond the territorial jurisdiction of U.S. law enforcement? What investigative and legal processes can be used in the foreign country to obtain evidence and to acquire jurisdiction over the perpetrator?

There are three essential methods of international cooperation: informal, letters rogatory, and treaties. By informal, we mean direct contact and cooperation between law enforcement colleagues of different countries who know each other or trust each other. That type of cooperation is the most efficient and enabling, but unfortunately often is not available. Where informal relationships are not available, law enforcement officers must utilize legal tools.

Letters Rogatory

The term *letters rogatory* traditionally refers to a request from a court in one country to a court in another country that a witness be examined in the requested country upon interrogatories (questions) forwarded by the requesting country. Historically, letters rogatory were not available for use in criminal cases in some countries, including the United States. That position changed with the adoption of multilateral treaties and conventions, as well as bilateral MLATs. Prior to such international agreements, the use of letters rogatory was a matter of comity, i.e., the willingness of courts in each country to extend their courtesy and aid another country. The use of letters rogatory is now authorized by federal law, 18 USC § 3492.

Mutual Legal Assistance Treaty

The United States has entered into mutual legal assistance treaties (MLATs) in criminal matters with many countries. These treaties contain provisions enabling one country to request the collection of evidence or apprehension of a suspect from law enforcement officials in another country. A weblink to access the United States–Canada Mutual Legal Assistance Treaty is provided at the end of the chapter.

Typically those agreements require that a criminal action be pending in the requesting country. The following case, however, considers whether legal assistance is available under the U.S.-Canada MLAT before the case actually begins:

In re: Commissioner's Subpoenas

325 F.3D 1287 (2003)

U.S. Court of Appeals, Eleventh Circuit

OPINION BY: ANDERSON, Circuit Judge:

This case involves a request made by Canadian law enforcement authorities, pursuant to a mutual legal assistance treaty between Canada and the United States, for the legal assistance of the United States government in subpoenaing seven individuals residing in the Southern District of Florida. The Canadian authorities sought to interview these individuals in connection with an ongoing investigation into possible criminal activities. The subpoenas were initially issued, but upon a motion filed by the subpoenaed witnesses, the district judge quashed the subpoenas. The United States, on behalf of the Canadian authorities, appeals the district court's order quashing the subpoenas.

This case presents an issue of first impression for the federal appellate courts. We must ascertain whether this mutual legal assistance treaty between the two countries obligates the United States, at the request of Canada, to issue subpoenas to compel the testimony of witnesses in a criminal investigation prior to the filing of formal charges. Because we construe this Treaty to obligate both countries to execute requests for the issuance of subpoenas for purposes of compelling testimony in criminal investigations and to arrange for the taking of such testimony even prior to the actual initiation of formal charges, we hold that the Canadian request for assistance should have been granted and the subpoenas should not have been quashed by the district court.

I. BACKGROUND

A. The MLAT Between the United States and Canada

The Treaty Between the United States and Canada on Mutual Legal Assistance in Criminal Matters, Mar. 18, 1985, ("MLAT" or "Treaty"), was signed at Quebec City, Canada on March 18, 1985, the advice and consent of the United States Senate was received on October 24, 1989, and the Treaty was entered into force on January 24, 1990. The Treaty obligates the two governments to provide "mutual legal assistance in all matters relating to the investigation, prosecution and suppression of offences." MLAT, art. II, P 1.

Traditionally, evidence sought by a foreign government had to be obtained through a process whereby a written request known as a "letter rogatory" was sent from the court of one country to the court of another asking the receiving court to provide the assistance. A federal statute authorizes federal district courts in this country to entertain such requests and provides that "[t]he district court of the district in which a person resides or is found may order him to give his testimony or statement or to produce a document or other thing for use in a proceeding in a foreign or international tribunal, including criminal investigations conducted before formal accusation." 28 U.S.C. § 1782. Not only can a foreign tribunal bring a request in the form of a "letter rogatory," but section 1782 has been amended to also allow similar requests for assistance to be brought by "interested persons" including foreign governments in foreign investigations or proceedings and private litigants of a foreign proceeding. Requests for assistance initiated directly by an interested person rather than a foreign court are often referred to as "letters of request." Despite the apparent versatility of 28 U.S.C. § 1782, law enforcement authorities found the statute to be an unattractive option in practice because it provided wide discretion in the district court to refuse the request and did not obligate other nations to return the favor that it grants. MLATs, on the other hand, have the desired quality of compulsion as they contractually obligate the two countries to provide to each other evidence and other forms of assistance needed in criminal cases while streamlining and enhancing the effectiveness of the process for obtaining needed evidence. This MLAT between the United States and Canada provides for a broad range of cooperation in criminal matters.

Under this Treaty, Canada makes a request for assistance by contacting the United States' "Central Authority" under the Treaty, which is "the Attorney General or officials designated by him." If the particular type of assistance requested requires action of a federal district court, the Attorney General and his officials utilize existing statutory authority including 28 U.S.C. § 1782 to bring an action seeking the requested evidence or information. Because the Attorney General simply utilizes the preexisting statutory authority provided under 28 U.S.C. § 1782 when satisfying treaty obligations under the MLAT, the Treaty itself is self-executing obviating the need for implementing legislation. Upon its entry into force on January 24, 1990, the MLAT became a law of this land on par with a federal statute.

B. Factual Background

For the past several years, Canadian law enforcement authorities have been investigating an alleged smuggling operation. According to Canadian authorities, goods have been legally exported to the United States and then smuggled back into Canada without payment of the Canadian duty, resulting in a revenue loss for the Canadian government. The smuggling activities allegedly began in 1989. The United States began its own investigation. During the investigations, the two governments shared information and resources. Appellees in this case are seven individuals allegedly involved. After unsuccessfully attempting to conduct voluntary interviews with the seven appellees, the Canadian authorities turned to formal legal process.

In 2000, Canadian authorities asked the United States for assistance. On February 22, 2001, the United States filed a petition in the United States District Court for the Southern District of Florida seeking an order appointing an assistant United States attorney as a "commissioner" to assist the Canadian government in obtaining the requested evidence. On March 2, 2001, the district court entered an order appointing an assistant United States attorney from the Southern District of Florida, as the "commissioner" and authorizing him to "take such steps as are necessary, including issuance of commissioner's subpoenas to be served on persons within the jurisdiction of this Court, to collect the evidence requested." On April 30, 2001, he issued subpoenas to each of the appellees commanding their appearance at the federal courthouse in Miami on a given date and time, to give testimony to Canadian authorities concerning the Canadian smuggling investigation. Prior to the scheduled testimony, however, the appellees moved in the district court to quash the subpoenas and for a protective order.

On August 23, 2001, a magistrate judge ordered that the subpoenas be quashed. First, the magistrate judge held that by its own terms, the MLAT fully incorporates the existing substantive law of the United States as the "Requested State," including 28 U.S.C. § 1782. According to this Circuit, section 1782 contains an implicit foreign discoverability requirement. This rule requires that the information sought in the United States be discoverable under the laws of the foreign jurisdiction. The magistrate judge reasoned that since Canadian authorities are not allowed to compel witness testimony in domestic criminal investigations at the pre-charge stage, such testimony cannot be compelled in this case by virtue of this circuit's construction of 28 U.S.C. § 1782. Second, the magistrate judge focused on the second paragraph of section 1782(a) which explicitly states that "a person may not be compelled to give his testimony ... in violation of any legally applicable privilege." The district court entered a final order quashing the subpoenas.

II. DISCUSSION

In accordance with the terms of the Treaty, officials from the Department of Justice utilized 28 U.S.C. § 1782 to execute Canada's request for assistance under the Treaty. The officials brought a petition in federal court seeking the appointment of a commissioner to issue seven witness subpoenas. Article II, P 2(e) of the MLAT states that "[a]ssistance [under the Treaty] shall include ... taking of evidence of persons" and Article VII, P 1 states, in part, that "[t]he Courts of the Requested State shall have jurisdiction to issue subpoenas, search warrants or other orders necessary to execute the request." Stated even more directly, Article XII, P 1 provides that "[a] person requested to testify and produce documents, records or other articles in the Requested State may be compelled by subpoena or order to appear and testify and produce such documents, records and other articles, in accordance with the requirements of the law of the Requested State." Without question, this general type of assistance, the compelled testimony of witnesses, is expressly within the scope of the Treaty.

In granting the motion to quash, however, the magistrate judge determined that, according to the Treaty itself, all Canadian requests under the MLAT were subject to the entire substantive law of the United States, including 28 U.S.C. § 1782. The magistrate judge reasoned that "[u]nder the MLAT, Canada's request is to be evaluated under U.S. law." This conclusion was based upon the magistrate judge's interpretation of Article VII, P 2 of the Treaty, which states that "[a] request shall be executed in accordance with the law of the Requested State and, to the extent not prohibited by the law of the Requested State, in accordance with the directions stated in the request." The magistrate judge concluded that "[b]y its own terms therefore, the MLAT mandates that this Court apply 28 U.S.C. § 1782 as the statutory authority or law of the Requested State."

As a law of the Requested State, the magistrate judge then considered cases from this Circuit construing 28 U.S.C. § 1782. The magistrate judge recognized that the law of this Circuit requires a foreign government conducting a criminal investigation prior to filing formal charges and seeking assistance under 28 U.S.C. § 1782 by way of a letter of request to first establish that the information sought in this country would be discoverable under the domestic laws of the foreign country (the requesting state).

Reading Article VII, P 2 of the MLAT to incorporate by reference the entire substantive law of the Requested State, the magistrate judge concluded that the treaty request was subject to this circuit's interpretation of 28 U.S.C. § 1782 requiring foreign discoverability as a condition precedent to granting requests made by foreign governments through letters of request and letters rogatory. Since the parties agreed that there was no authority under Canadian law to compel this type of testimony from witnesses in a domestic criminal investigation where no charges had yet been filed, the magistrate judge held that 28 U.S.C. § 1782 and its foreign discoverability requirement precluded the assistance in this case.

We must decide whether the magistrate judge correctly interpreted the MLAT between the United States and Canada. That question turns on the intended role of 28 U.S.C. § 1782 in requests for assistance under the MLAT. The precise issue facing this court is whether the MLAT permits, at the request of Canada, the issuance of subpoenas and the taking of compelled testimony in a pre-charge Canadian criminal investigation of seven witnesses who reside in the Southern District of Florida.

A. Principles of Treaty Interpretation

To decide the question presented, we turn to fundamental principles of treaty construction and interpretation. The goal of treaty interpretation is to determine the actual intention of the parties "because it is our responsibility to give the specific words of the treaty a meaning consistent with the shared expectations of the contracting parties." *Air France v. Saks*, 470 U.S. 392, 399, 105 S. Ct. 1338, 1342, 84 L. Ed. 2d 289 (1985). The analysis of the parties' intentions "begin[s] with the text of the treaty and the context in which the written words are used." *Eastern Airlines, Inc. v. Floyd*, 499 U.S. 530, 534, 111 S. Ct. 1489, 1493, 113 L. Ed. 2d 569 (1991).

As Justice Story wrote long ago, "to alter, amend, or add to any treaty, by inserting any clause, whether small or great, important or trivial, would be on our part an usurpation of power, and not an exercise of judicial functions. It would be to make, and not to construe a treaty." *The Amiable Isabella*, 19 U.S. 1, 6 Wheat. 1, 71, 5 L. Ed. 191 (1821). But, if the treaty text is ambiguous when read in context in light of its object and purpose, then extraneous sources may be consulted to elucidate the parties' intent from the ambiguous text.

B. Ambiguity in the Text of the Treaty

Upon our reading of the text of this Treaty, we conclude that the magistrate judge erred in construing the MLAT to express a clear and unambiguous intent to make requests under the Treaty subject to the limitations of all other substantive law of the United States including 28 U.S.C. § 1782. Undeniably, the magistrate judge's interpretation finds some support in the treaty text. As the magistrate judge points out, Article VII, P 2 states that "[a] request shall be executed in accordance with the law of the Requested State and, to the extent not prohibited by the law of the Requested State." While not mentioned by the magistrate judge, Article XII, P 1 also contains a similar reference to the "law of the Requested State." Those two sentences, if read in isolation, arguably incorporate the substantive limitations of 28 U.S.C. § 1782 as a law of the United States. And as discussed above, that statute has been held to implicitly require a showing of foreign discoverability, at least in the traditional case involving a letter rogatory or letter of request. Given the fact acknowledged by all parties that Canada lacks the power to compel the taking of testimony in a pre-charge setting, the application of a foreign discoverability requirement to MLAT requests by Canada would deny the court the power to grant Canada the type of assistance sought in this case. But when the entire Treaty is read in context, we conclude that other language in its text, apparently overlooked in the lower court, suggests an alternate, reasonable, construction of the "law of the Requested State" phrases contained in Articles VII and XII of the MLAT.

Starting with the Preamble, the MLAT expresses an intent to obligate both countries to provide assistance to each other in criminal matters during both the pre-charge "investigation" and post-charge "prosecution" stages.

Article V of the MLAT is entitled "Limitations on Compliance" and explicitly limits the situations where the Requested State may deny the other parties' request for assistance. Article V limits these situations to those involving requests not in conformity with the provisions of the Treaty and requests that are "contrary to [the Requested State's] public interest." "Public Interest" is defined in Article I as "any substantial interest related to national security or other essential public policy." If Article VII, P 2 is to be construed as placing a much more restrictive limitation by allowing a request only if consistent with the entire substantive law of the Requested State, then the narrow limitations on providing assistance laid out in Article V would be rendered meaningless.

The phrase in Article VII, P 2 that guided the magistrate judge's interpretation can be reasonably interpreted to address the procedures and methods employed in executing treaty requests and not the substantive law influencing the decision to grant or deny a request. Article VII, entitled "Execution of Requests," states:

1. The Central Authority of the Requested State shall promptly execute the request, or when appropriate, transmit it to the competent authorities, who shall make best efforts to execute the request. The Courts of the Requested State shall have jurisdiction to issue subpoenas, search warrants or other orders necessary to execute the request.
2. A request shall be executed in accordance with the law of the Requested State and, to the extent not prohibited by the law of the Requested State, in accordance with the directions stated in the request.

MLAT, Art. VII.

While the magistrate judge interpreted P 2 of this article to require a district court to ensure that a MLAT request that is otherwise permitted by the Treaty to also be consistent with all other existing United States substantive law, an alternative construction can be reasonably discerned from a reading of Article VII in its entirety. The article addresses the "Execution of Requests." Paragraph 1 contains two sentences. The first sentence directs the "Central Authority of the Requested State," to make best efforts to promptly "execute" the request. The second sentence of P 1 grants the "Courts of the Requested State" jurisdiction to issue subpoenas and other forms of assistance necessary for the execution of the request. The appellees focus solely on P 2 read in isolation. But, in treaty interpretation as in statutory interpretation, particular provisions may not be divorced from the document as a whole and read in isolation. In carefully reading all of Article VII, paragraph 2 can reasonably be construed as requiring the Attorney General's office to follow existing procedures of United States law in seeking the requested assistance on behalf of Canada notwithstanding any contrary directions stated by Canada in the request that are prohibited by United States law.

The text of Article XII adds to the ambiguity of the Treaty with respect to the issue before this court. In addressing the "Taking of Evidence in the Requested State," Article XII, P 1 states that "[a] person requested to testify and produce documents, records or other articles in the Requested State may be compelled by subpoena or order to appear and testify and produce such documents, records and other articles, in accordance with the requirements of the law of the Requested State." This article explicitly embraces the very assistance sought by Canada in this case—subpoenas to compel witness testimony. But at the same time, it uses "in accordance with … the law of the Requested State" language that is similar to that found in Article VII. Again, because subpoenas are expressly embraced, the limiting phrase can reasonably be read to require the taking of the evidence in the Requested State to follow the existing procedures used in the Requested State, i.e., the law of the Requested State with respect to the issuance of subpoenas, the taking of testimony, etc.

C. Resolving the Ambiguity: "Law of the Requested State" Addresses Procedural Methods not Substantive Laws

We conclude that the most logical construction of the phrase "law of the Requested State" in the MLAT is that the Treaty partners intended to utilize the established procedures set forth in the existing laws of the Requested State to execute the treaty requests, rather than to subject each and every treaty request to any and all limitations of existing law of the Requested State. That is, the Treaty utilizes § 1782 as a procedure for executing requests, but not as a means for deciding whether or not to grant or deny a request so made. This construction is more plausible primarily because of Article V, which delineates only narrowly confined circumstances in which the Requested State "may deny assistance." Article V is entitled "Limitations on Compliance" and provides, in relevant part:

> 1. The Requested State may deny assistance to the extent that
>   a) the request is not made in conformity with the provisions of this Treaty; or
>   b) execution of the request is contrary to its public interest, as determined by its Central Authority.

1.Treaty Negotiation and Ratification History

(a) Executive Branch's Official Explanation of Article VII, P 2

The negotiators' explanation of P 2 of Article VII, provided in the Technical Analysis, does not support the appellees' reading. The Technical Analysis, included in the ratification history at S. Treaty Doc. 100–14, 100th Cong., 2d Sess. (1988), "was prepared by the United States negotiating team, [and] constitutes the formal executive branch representation as to the meaning of this treaty and the obligations to be assumed by the United States under it." The Analysis states that "Article VII(2) provides that the Requested State is to execute the request pursuant to its own laws, practices, and procedures, except that 'directions stated in the request' will be honored unless prohibited by domestic law." After carefully reading the entire explanation of Article VII, it is clear that the negotiators did not intend P 2 to incorporate and subject all treaty requests to the entire substantive law of the Requested State, but rather they intended Article VII, P 2 to address the procedures and methods to be used by the Requested State in executing the treaty requests. This official interpretation by the executive branch is entitled to great deference by this Court.

(b) Article VII is Intended to Provide "Slightly Broader Authority" than 28 U.S.C. § 1782
In its Technical Analysis, the executive branch states that one purpose of P 1 of Article VII of the MLAT, is to "provide[] slightly broader authority than 28 U.S.C. 1782 for U.S. federal courts to use their power to issue subpoenas and other process when Canada needs evidence for use before an administrative agency...." The real significance of this executive branch statement in this case is the fact that the negotiators were making clear that P 1 of Article VII allowed assistance that would not otherwise be permitted under section 1782 as it was being construed at that time. This makes clear that the negotiators read the MLAT as not being simply subject to the limits of 28 U.S.C. § 1782. If all MLAT requests were subject to the limits of section 1782, then the MLAT necessarily could not "provide slightly broader authority than 28 U.S.C. 1782 for U.S. federal courts to use their power to issue subpoenas ... when Canada needs assistance."

(c) Rejection of "Dual Criminality"
Another provision of the Treaty lends additional support to this interpretation. Article II of the MLAT, entitled "Scope of Application," contains a provision rejecting the rule of "dual criminality." "Dual criminality" is the rule that the offense for which the foreign state seeks assistance must also constitute a crime in the requested state. Article II, P 3 explicitly provides that "[a]ssistance shall be provided without regard to whether the conduct under investigation or prosecution in the Requesting State constitutes an offence or may be prosecuted by the Requested State." The negotiators state in the Technical Analysis that "[b]y avoiding a dual criminality provision in this Treaty, the United States expects to receive assistance for such important crimes as, for instance, money laundering, even though Canada has yet to enact similar legislation." This provision makes clear an intent that requests for assistance not be routinely impeded or denied by virtue of the Requested State's own laws. If Article VII, as appellees contend, subjects all requests to the limitations of existing Requested State substantive law, then many requests would be impeded by the operation of an indirect dual criminality provision that is explicitly rejected in Article II. Therefore, if Article VII, P 2 is read as the appellees contend, dual criminality provision will be brought into the Treaty through the back door.

Interpreting the MLAT to subject each and every request to the existing substantive law of the requested state runs contrary to another fundamental principle of treaty interpretation. "Treaties that lay down rules to be enforced by the parties through their internal courts or administrative agencies should be construed so as to achieve uniformity of result despite differences between national legal systems." Restatement (Third) of Foreign Relations § 325 cmt. d; *United States v. Lombera-Camorlinga*, 206 F.3d 882, 888 (9th Cir. 2000).

We find no statements anywhere in the text of the Treaty or its negotiation and ratification history to suggest that the parties did not intend the obligations to be reciprocal and uniform. In fact, a desire for uniform treatment of similar requests made by the two countries underlies the decision to enter into the MLAT in the first place. The Treaty's ratification history reveals that in conjunction with signing the Treaty, Canada enacted implementing legislation to give its courts the authority to execute requests from the United States for assistance in criminal investigations prior to the filing of formal charges. That implementing legislation is known as the Mutual Legal Assistance in Criminal Matters Act (MLACMA), R.S.C. 1985, c. 30 (4th Supp.), s. 18.

Prior to the MLAT, because Canada's domestic law prohibited compelled testimony from witnesses prior to charges being filed, assistance was denied to authorities from the United States. The MLACMA was enacted along with the MLAT "to remove the legal barrier and permit (indeed, obligate) Canada to provide assistance prior to indictment ... [and make] assistance available at the investigative stage." Technical Analysis at 2. That legislation was intended to make sure that there would be no remaining legal impediments to MLAT requests made back-and-forth between the two countries.

3. Additional Weaknesses in Appellees' Construction

(A) The Treaty Partners Did Not Contemplate a Foreign Discoverability Requirement
First, in light of the history of the Treaty and the overall context in which it was created, we conclude that the Treaty's reference to the "law of the Requested State" does not in fact indicate that the parties expected to incorporate the doctrine of foreign discoverability.

If there were any doubt about our conclusion that the parties did not intend to subject Canadian treaty requests to a foreign discoverability requirement, the Technical Analysis provides significant clarity. The "Introduction" section of the Technical Analysis discusses the reasons for the creation of the Treaty and notes the fact that, in the past, the Canadian courts would refuse many requests for assistance by law enforcement officials from the United States because the information sought was for investigative purposes prior to the initiation of formal criminal charges. In so noting, the negotiators recognized that this created "unequal treatment since the United States provided assistance [to Canada] without regard to whether the case was pre- or post-indictment." Technical Analysis at 1. In an endnote, the negotiators elaborated that "[a]ssistance is available for a foreign country under 28 U.S.C. 1782 without regard to whether the action has already been filed." Here, the negotiating team specifically discussed requests by Canada under section 1782 and understood section 1782 to allow for assistance without regard to lack of discoverability in Canada of compelled testimony prior to the actual filing of criminal charges.

Considering both textual and nontextual sources, we conclude that the MLAT allows for the issuance of subpoenas in this case pursuant to the Canadian request for assistance.

III. CONCLUSION

For the foregoing reasons, we hold that the information sought by Canada in this case, subpoena-compelled testimony pursuant to a Canadian criminal investigation occurring prior to the filing of formal charges, was within the scope of the two countries' obligations under the MLAT. Consequently, the subpoenas should not have been quashed.

Extradition Treaty

Let's assume that law enforcement officials have all the evidence they need, but they don't have their suspect. The suspect physically resides in another country. How do we obtain custody of the suspect, and thus personal jurisdiction over the defendant?

In those instances where the suspect is physically in a foreign country and does not submit voluntarily to the jurisdiction of the domestic court, the domestic authorities must utilize a legal procedure known as *extradition* in order to acquire physical custody of the defendant. Extradition is an agreement by one country to relinquish physical custody of one of its residents upon an appropriate request by the country seeking to prosecute that resident for a crime. Most bilateral agreements (agreements between two countries) follow the provisions of the Model Treaty on Extradition, adopted by the Eighth United Nations Crime Congress in 1990.

The United States has entered into extradition agreements with nearly all countries. Notable exceptions include Afghanistan, Algeria, Bahrain, Bangladesh, Belarus, Bosnia, Cambodia, China (but we do have one with Hong Kong), Croatia, Ethiopia, Indonesia, Iran, Mongolia, Morocco, Nicaragua, Russian Federation (the current government), Saudi Arabia, Syria, Taiwan, and Vietnam.

The typical extradition agreement to which the United States is a party contains a provision requiring that the accused be shown to have violated the laws of the United States and the foreign country, which is known as the principle of dual criminality; that extradition only applies to offenses named in the agreement; and that political crimes (except terrorism) are excluded from the treaty.

There are also multilateral extradition agreements, i.e., agreements between several countries. The European Convention on Extradition of 1957 (amended by the Additional Protocol of 1975) constitutes a multilateral agreement between those members of the Council of Europe who are signatories to the agreement, including France and the United Kingdom. Under the convention, requests for extradition are to be forwarded through diplomatic channels, unless countries otherwise agree. Although the convention excluded extradition for political or military offenses initially, the 1975 Additional Protocol has altered the exclusion for political offenses where the underlying conduct involves terrorism. The added protocol (Article 1) specifies that "extradition is a particularly effective measure" for ensuring that terrorists do not escape prosecution and punishment. Nevertheless, a party may still refuse extradition "if the requested State has substantial grounds for believing that the request for extradition … has been made for the purpose of prosecuting or punishing a person on account of his race, religion, nationality or political opinion, or that that person's position may be prejudiced for any of these reasons" (European Terrorism Convention, Article 5).

The Council of Europe's Convention on Cybercrime also contains a provision enabling extradition for those offenses set forth in the convention. Like the legal assistance provisions of the Convention on Cybercrime, the extradition agreement only applies if the two countries involved do not have an extradition agreement that applies to the conduct at issue.

Council of Europe Convention on Cybercrime

The Council of Europe has created, and a sufficient number of countries have ratified, the Convention on Cybercrime. *Convention* is another term for *treaty*. The United States has signed and the Senate has ratified the Convention on Cybercrime.

The Convention requires signatory nations to enact laws prohibiting five types of criminal conduct:

1. Offenses against the confidentiality, integrity, and availability of computer data and systems, including:
   a. Illegal access
   b. Illegal interception
   c. Data interference
   d. System interference
   e. Misuse of data
2. Computer-related forgery
3. Computer-related fraud
4. Offenses relating to child pornography
5. Offenses relating to infringement of copyrights and related rights

The Convention also provides procedures for international cooperation in the collection and preservation of evidence in aid of signatory nations.

The full text of the Convention on Cybercrime and explanatory notes relating to the text may be obtained by utilizing the appropriate Weblinks that appear at the end of the chapter.

Key Words and Phrases

Convention	Jurisdiction
Extradition	Letters rogatory
Extraterritorial application	Mutual extradition treaty
In personam jurisdiction	Mutual legal assistance treaty
In rem jurisdiction	Subject matter jurisdiction

Review Problems

1. What are the differences in the evidence gathering procedure between letters rogatory and mutual legal assistance treaties?
2. What is meant by the concept of dual criminality?
3. If the United States has a mutual legal assistance treaty on criminal matters with the United Kingdom, do the provisions of the Convention on Cybercrime apply?
4. What international principles apply to the extraterritorial application of criminal laws?
5. What process is applied in order to obtain personal jurisdiction of a person who physically resides in a foreign country? How is that process exercised?

Weblinks

http://conventions.coe.int/Treaty/EN/Treaties/Html/185.htm
    This is the URL to access the text of the Council of Europe Convention on Cybercrime.
http://conventions.coe.int/Treaty/EN/Reports/Html/185.htm
    This is the URL for the text of the Explanatory Report on the Convention on Cybercrime. The Explanatory Report will be a useful reference for decision making on future issues that arise under the convention.

www.usdoj.gov/criminal/cybercrime/intl.html
> This page at the website of the U.S. Department of Justice Computer Crime and Intellectual Property Sections provides numerous valuable links to information on international aspects of computer crime.

www.oas.org/Juridico/mla/en/traites/en_traites-mla-can-usa2.html
> This is the page for the United States–Canada Mutual Legal Assistance Treaty on Criminal Matters and Extradition.

www.state.gov/p/eur/rls/fs/34885.htm
> This page of the U.S. Department of State website contains the United States–United Kingdom Treaty on Extradition.

http://travel.state.gov/law/info/judicial/judicial_690.html
> This site at the U.S. Department of State website contains links to helpful information on mutual legal assistance.

References

Arquilla, John and Ronfeldt, David (eds.) (2001). *Networks and Netwars: The Future of Terror, Crime, and Militancy*. Santa Monica, CA: RAND.

Brenner, Susan W. (2010). *Cybercrime: Criminal Threats from Cyberspace*. Santa Barbara, CA: Praeger.

Britz, Marjie T. (2009). *Computer Forensics and Cyber Crime: An Introduction (2d ed.)*. Upper Saddle Brook, NJ: Pearson (Prentice Hall).

Casey, Eoghan (2010). *Handbook of Digital Forensics and Investigation*. Burlington MA: Elsevier Academic Press.

Clifford, Ralph D. (ed.) (2006). *Cybercrime: The Investigation, Prosecution and Defense of a Computer-Related Crime (2d ed.)*. Durham, NC: Carolina Academic Press.

Donovan, Felicia and Bernier, Kristyn (2008). *Cyber Crime Fighters: Tales from the Trenches*. Indianapolis, IN: Pearson Education (Que).

Ferraro, Monique M. and Casey, Eoghan (2005*). Investigating Child Exploitation and Pornography: The Internet, Law, and Forensic Science*. Burlington, MA: Elsevier, Inc. (Academic Press).

Kerr, Orin S. (2009). *Computer Crime Law (2d ed.)*. St. Paul, MN: Thomson Reuters (West).

Moore, Robert (2011). *Cybercrime: Investigating High-Technology Computer Crime (2d ed.)*. Burlington, MA: Anderson Publishing.

Schroeder, Steve (2011). *The Lure*. Boston, MA: Course Technology.

Smith, Russell G., Grabosky, Peter, and Urbas, Gregor (2004). *Cyber Criminals on Trial*. Cambridge, UK: Cambridge University Press.

United States Department of Justice (2009). *Searching and Seizing Computers and Obtaining Electronic Evidence in Criminal Investigations (3d ed.)*. Available at: http://www.cybercrime.gov/ssmanual/

Index